CHINA UNDER
MONGOL RULE

China under Mongol Rule

EDITED BY

John D. Langlois, Jr.

CONTRIBUTORS

Hok-lam Chan *Yan-shuan Lao*

David M. Farquhar *John D. Langlois, Jr.*

Herbert Franke *Chu-tsing Li*

Marilyn Wong Fu *Morris Rossabi*

David Gedalecia *K'o-k'uan Sun*

Stephen H. West

PRINCETON UNIVERSITY PRESS

Copyright © 1981 by Princeton University Press
Published by Princeton University Press, Princeton, New Jersey
In the United Kingdom:
Princeton University Press, Guildford, Surrey

All Rights Reserved
Library of Congress Cataloging in Publication Data will be
found on the last printed page of this book

Publication of this book has been aided by a grant from
the Paul Mellon Fund of Princeton University Press

This book has been composed in Monophoto Times New Roman
by Asco Trade Typesetting Ltd., Hong Kong

Clothbound editions of Princeton University Press books
are printed on acid-free paper, and binding materials are
chosen for strength and durability

Printed in the United States of America by
Princeton University Press, Princeton, New Jersey

CONTENTS

CONTENTS

LIST OF ILLUSTRATIONS

rgyal mc'an dpal bzaṅ po'i t'og draṅs / k'ams gsum pa'i sems čan t'ams čad t'og pa daṅ bral ba'i yid rab tu gus pas p'yag 'c'al lo

The monk who commissioned the painting has not been identified. (Sixteenth Century, courtesy Collection Jack Zimmerman, New York City)

NOTE ON TRANSCRIPTION OF
MONGOLIAN NAMES AND TERMS

The system adopted in this book follows that in A. Mostaert, *Dictionnaire ordos*, III, "Index des mots du mongol écrit et du mongol ancien," Peiping, 1944, and standardized by Professor Francis W. Cleaves in his articles in *Harvard Journal of Asiatic Studies*, with the following minor changes:

ǰ is replaced by j
č is replaced by ch
š is replaced by sh
γ is replaced by gh
q is replaced by kh

Thus the following common names and term are transformed as:

Činggis Qan	Chinggis Khan
Qubilai Qaγan	Khubilai Khaghan
daruγači	darughachi

The following proper noun is simply Anglicized:

ǰürčen	Jurchen/Jurchens

ABBREVIATIONS USED IN THE NOTES

1475 HCFC	Ch'en Ch'i 陳頎 and Chang Yüan 張淵, eds., *Hu-chou fu-chih* 湖州府志, 24 *chüan* 卷, 1475 ed.
1542 HCFC	Chang To 張鐸, ed., *Hu-chou fu-chih*, 16 *chüan*, 1542 ed.
1573 HCFC	T'ang Shu 唐樞 (1497–1574) and Li Ch'i 栗祁 (1531–1578), eds., *Hu-chou fu-chih*, 14 *chüan*, Wan-li 萬曆 period ed.
1874 HCFC	Chou Hsüeh-chün 周學濬, ed., *Hu-chou fu-chih*, 96 *chüan*, 1874 edition, recollated 1883; rpt.in *Chung-kuo fang-chih ts'ung-shu* 中國方志叢書 (Taipei: Ch'eng-wen Ch'u-pan-she 成文出版社, 1970).
Chan Hok-lam	*The Historiography of the Chin Dynasty: Three Studies. Münchener Ostasiatische Studien*, Band 4 (Wiesbaden, 1970).
Ch'en Fang-ming	陳芳明, "Sung Liao Chin shih ti tsuan-hsiu yü cheng-t'ung chih cheng 宋遼金史的纂修與正統之爭," *Shih-huo yüeh-k'an* 食貨月刊, 2:8 (Nov. 1972), pp. 10–23.
Ch'en/Goodrich	Ch'en Yüan, *Western and Central Asians in China Under the Mongols*, tr. Ch'ien Hsing-hai and L. Carrington Goodrich (Los Angeles, 1966).
Chin Yü-fu	金毓黻, *Chung-kuo shih-hsüeh shih* 中國史學史 (Shanghai, 1957).
CKC	*Chung-kuo ku-tien hsi-ch'ü lun-chu chi-ch'eng* 中國古典戲曲論著集成 (Peking, 1959).
CS	*Chin shih* 金史 (Peking: Chung-hua Shu-chü 中華書局, 1975)
CYYY	*Chung-yang yen-chiu yüan Li-shih yu-yen yen-chiu so chi-k'an* 中央研究院歷史語言研究所集刊.
DMB	L. C. Goodrich and Chaoying Fang, eds., *Dictionary of Ming Biography* (New York: Columbia University Press, 1976).
Feng Chia-sheng	馮家昇, *Liao-shih cheng-wu san-chung* 遼史證誤三種 (Shanghai, 1959).

FGMY   *Four Great Masters of the Yüan* (*Yüan ssu ta chia* 元四大家) (Taipei: National Palace Museum, 1975).

Fong and Fu   Wen Fong and Marilyn Fu, *Sung and Yüan Paintings* (New York, 1973).

Herbert Franke   "Chinese Historiography under Mongol Rule: The Role of History in Acculturation," *Mongolian Studies*, 1 (1974), pp. 15–19.

HC and HL   T'ang Hou 湯垕, *Hua chien* 畫鑑 and *Hua lun* 畫論, Ma Ts'ai 馬采, ed. (Peking: Jen-min Mei-shu Ch'u-pan-she 人民美術出版社, 1959).

HJAS   *Harvard Journal of Asiatic Studies.*

Hsia: THPC   Hsia Wen-yen 夏文顏, *T'u-hui pao-chien* 圖繪寶鑑 (ISTP ed.).

Hsü Hao   徐浩, *Nien-wu shih lun-kang* 廿五史論綱 (Hong Kong, 1964).

HYS   *Hsin Yüan shih* 新元史 .

ISTP   *I-shu ts'ung-pien* 藝術叢編 .

KKFS   *Ku-kung fa-shu* 故宮法書 (Taipei, 1962–).

KHCP   *Kuo-hsüeh chi-pen ts'ung-shu* 國學基本叢書.

KKSHL   *Ku-kung shu-hua lu* 故宮書畫錄 (Taipei: National Palace Museum, 1965).

K'un-tsa   Hsien-yü Shu, *K'un-hsüeh chai tsa-lu* 困學齋雜錄 (*Chih-pu-tsu chai ts'ung-shu* 知不足齋叢書 ed.).

KYTS   *Kuang-ya shu-chü ts'ung-shu* 廣雅書局叢書 (1880–1900).

Lee and Ho   Sherman Lee and Wai-kam Ho, *Chinese Art Under the Mongols* (Cleveland, 1968).

Li, *Autumn Colors* Chu-tsing Li, *The Autumn Colors on the Ch'iao and Hua Mountains: A Landscape by Chao Meng-fu* (Ascona: Artibus Asiae, 1965).

NESCC   Chao I 趙翼, *Nien-er shih cha-chi* 廿二史箚記 (TSCC ed.).

NESKI   Ch'ien Ta-hsin 錢大昕, *Nien-er shih k'ao-i* 廿二史考異 (Shanghai, 1958).

Otagi Matsuo	愛宕松男, "Ryō Kin Sō sanshi no hensan to hokuzoku ōchō no tachiba 遼金宋三史の編纂と北族王朝の立場," *Bunka* 文化, 15:4 (1951), pp. 294–322.
Pien: SKT	Pien Yung-yü 卞永譽, *Shih-ku t'ang shu-hua hui-k'ao* 式古堂書畫彙考 (rpt. Taipei, 1968).
SB	Herbert Franke, ed., *Sung Biographies*, 4 vols. (Wiesbaden: Franz Steiner, 1977).
SHCW	Chao Meng-fu 趙孟頫, *Sung-hsüeh chai wen-chi* 松雪齋文集 (SPTK ed.).
Shuo-fu 52: *K'un-tsa*	*K'un-hsüeh chai tsa-lu* (*Shuo-fu* 説郛 ed., rpt. Shanghai, 1927).
Sirén, CP	Osvald Sirén, *Chinese Painting: Leading Masters and Principles*, 7 vols. (New York, 1956–58).
SKCSCP	*Ssu-k'u ch'üan-shu chen-pen* 四庫全書珍本.
SSHY	T'ao Tsung-i 陶宗儀, *Shu-shih hui-yao* 書史會要 (1376 ed., rpt. 1929).
SKTY	Chi Yün 紀昀, ed., *Ssu-k'u ch'üan-shu tsung-mu t'i-yao* 四庫全書總目題要 (Shanghai, 1934 ed.).
SMS	*Shoseki meihin sōkan* 書跡名品叢刊 (1964).
SPPY	*Ssu-pu pei-yao* 四部備要.
SPTK	*Ssu-pu ts'ung-k'an* 四部叢刊.
SS	*Sung shih* 宋史 (Peking: Chung-hua Shu-chü, 1977).
SYHA	*Sung Yüan hsüeh-an* 宋元學案.
SYHAPI	*Sung Yüan hsüeh-an pu-i* 宋元學案補遺.
SYTWC	Tai Piao-yüan 戴表元, *Shan-yüan Tai hsien-sheng wen-chi* 剡源戴先生文集 (SPTK ed.).
SZ	*Shodō zenshū* 書道全集 (Tokyo, 1958–66).
THPC	Hsia Wen-yen 夏文彥, *T'u-hui pao-chien* 圖繪寶鑑 (Taipei: Commercial Press, 1970, *Jen-jen wen-k'u* 人人文庫 ed.).
TLTC	*Ta-lu tsa-chih* 大陸雜誌.
TSCC	*Ts'ung-shu chi-ch'eng* 叢書集成.

WHC

T'an Yao 談鑰, comp., *Wu-hsing chih* 吳興志 (rpt. 1914).

WHCKC

Hsü Hsien-chung 徐獻忠 (1483–1559), comp., *Wu-hsing chang-ku chi* 吳興掌故集 (1615 ed. [first ed. 1560]).

WHCSC

Lu Hsin-yüan 陸心源 (1834–1894), ed., *Wu-hsing chin-shih chi* 吳興金石記 (1890 ed., rpt. Taipei: Hsin-wen-feng Ch'u-pan Kung-ssu 新文豐出版公司, 1977, *Shih-k'o shih-liao hsin-pien* 石刻史料新編).

WWC: 1756

Wu Ch'eng 吳澄, *Wu Wen-cheng kung ch'üan-chi* 吳文正公全集 (1756 ed.).

WWC: *chen-pen*

Wu Ch'eng, *Wu Wen-cheng chi* 吳文正集 (*Ssu-k'u ch'üan-shu chen-pen* 四庫全書珍本 ed., series 2).

YS

Yüan shih 元史 (Peking: Chung-hua Shu-chü, 1976).

YTC

Yüan tien-chang 元典章.

YYKYL

Chou Mi 周密, *Yün-yen kuo-yen lu* 雲烟過眼錄 (ISTP ed.).

I. INTRODUCTION

Introduction

JOHN D. LANGLOIS, JR.

I. The Founding of the Yüan by Khubilai

On a date which corresponded to January 18, 1272, Khubilai, grandson of Chinggis Khan, proclaimed the edict which determined that the Mongol regime in China would thenceforth bear the title Yüan. The edict reads as follows:[1]

"[We] have nobly accepted the splendid mandate covering the entire world and giving a place of abode to the exalted ruler. There must be an elegant title to link the many kings [who will follow] and to record [the deeds of] the succession. The origin of [the practice of giving titles to dynasties] is found in antiquity, and is not something only our house has done. Thus the word *t'ang* 唐, which conveys the idea of vastness (*tang* 蕩), was taken by the sage-king Yao 堯 as the name by which he was known, and the word *yü* 虞, which conveys the idea of happiness (*lo* 樂), was taken by Shun 舜 as his title. Coming down to the ages when Yü 禹 and T'ang 湯 arose, their respective dynastic titles Hsia 夏 and Yin 殷 convey the ideas 'great' and 'central.' As the generations followed, the practice [of naming dynasties] came to differ greatly from that of antiquity. Some availed themselves of opportunities and founded dynasties, but they did not take their titles on the basis of ideas (*i* 義). The Ch'in 秦 and the Han 漢 took names based on the places at which they arose. The Sui 隋 and the T'ang 唐 took names from the appanages with which [their founders] had been enfeoffed. In all these cases, they fell prey to the ingrained habits of common people. In essence, they adopted

---

[1] Written for Khubilai by T'u-tan Kung-lü 徒單公履, an adviser of Jurchen descent, the edict incorporated the suggestion of the scholar Liu Ping-chung 劉秉忠 (1216–1274). Liu was fully conversant with both the Mongolian and Chinese political institutions and traditions. Liu is said to have suggested the word *yüan* 元 as the name of the dynasty. For the edict, see YS 7:138; *Ta Yüan sheng-cheng kuo-ch'ao tien-chang* 大元聖政國朝典章 (Taipei: Ku-kung Po-wu-yüan 故宮博物院, 1976; rpt. of Yüan edition), 1:2b. The text in the latter version is the superior. For Liu Ping-chung, see Hok-lam Chan, "Liu Ping-chung (1216–74): A Buddhist-Taoist Statesman at the Court of Khubilai Khan," *T'oung Pao*, 53:1–3 (1967), pp. 98–146, esp. p. 133. The name of the author of the edict is supplied in Su T'ien-chüeh 蘇天爵, ed., *Kuo-ch'ao wen-lei* 國朝文類 (SPTK ed.), 9:4a. The edict is discussed by Herbert Franke in *From Tribal Chieftain to Universal Emperor and God: The Legitimation of the Yüan Dynasty* (München: Bayerische Akademie der Wissenschaften, 1978), pp. 26–29.

momentary measures of expediency for the sake of control. To evaluate all of them with utmost fairness, can they be free from criticism?

"Our Great Progenitor, the Sagelike Martial Emperor [Chinggis Khan], grasped the sign of the Creative (*ch'ien* 乾) and arose in the northern land. With a spirit-like martiality he accepted the imperial design. Majestically, he stirred the heavenly sound; he greatly expanded the territory of the realm to a breadth never before equalled. Presently the venerable worthies have come to the court to present memorials conveying their requests, saying that since the grand enterprise has already been completed it is appropriate to promulgate a magnificent title. According to the ancient institutions, that is so, and it is no different in Our Mind.

"Ta Yüan 大元 ['Great Yüan'] shall be the title of the dynasty. As such, it derives from the principle of *ch'ien-yüan* 乾元 ["the original creative force"] in the *Book of Changes*.[2] The great government gives forms to a multitude of things, but who is it that assigns a title to the great deed of establishing the beginning?[3] We alone have brought peace to the myriad lands. This is particularly in accord with the essential importance of embodying benevolence.[4] In our endeavors there are continuities and discontinuities, but our Way connects Heaven and humanity. Indeed! The taking of a title from an idea is not for the sake of lavishing praise upon ourselves. May the dynasty abide in prosperity forever so as not to be unworthy of the difficult efforts [of the founder]. Let all join efforts to match what Heaven endows. Together we will make this great title celebrated. That the multitude will comprehend our perfect compassion, this edict is promulgated, thinking that it will facilitate complete understanding."

This edict is of great value in any effort to understand the way in which Khubilai and his advisers sought to justify and define the new order in China.

Naming the dynasty "Yüan" was part of a deliberate policy to set historical precedent. By seizing an ideologically sound and prestigious symbol from the *Book of Changes*, Khubilai avoided the use of a place-name. Had he clung to Chinese tradition, he would have taken a name from his point of origin, in his case perforce one somewhere outside China, and that in turn would have been a constant reminder to the Chinese that the regime was a regime of conquest. By naming the dynasty Yüan, "the origin," Khubilai in effect let the dynasty set its own

---

[2] From the first hexagram in the *I ching*, *ch'ien* or "the creative." For a translation, see Richard Wilhelm and Cary F. Baynes, *The I Ching or Book of Changes* (Princeton: Princeton University Press, 1967 [Third edition]), p. 4.

[3] The words "establishing the beginning" (*tzu shih* 資始) appear in the *I ching* in the "commentary on the decision." See Wilhelm and Baynes, *The I Ching*, p. 370.

[4] These words also appear in the *I ching*, as explained below.

precedent. Identifying the dynasty with the generating principle of the cosmos enabled Khubilai to extend the universal pretensions of traditional Chinese monarchy to their natural limits. His attempt to cite classical precedent (the references to Yao and Shun) may have softened the surprise caused by his departure, but it did not undo the nature of the startlingly new notion of what a dynasty was.

The allusion to the *Book of Changes* brilliantly served Khubilai's plan to win acceptance in China as a legitimate ruler. The words in the edict "embodying benevolence" (*t'i jen* 體仁) appear in the *wen-yen* 文言 or "commentary on the text" attached to the first hexagram in the *Book of Changes*. In this commentary, which formed the "seventh wing" of the ancient classic, it states that "Of all that is good, sublimity (*yüan* 元) is supreme.... Because the superior man embodies humaneness (*t'i jen*), he is able to govern men." [5] In other words, the allusion to this passage in the *Book of Changes* implies that precisely because the ruler Khubilai has fulfilled the requirements suggested by the word *yüan*, he is qualified to hold the Mandate of Heaven and to rule *t'ien-hsia* 天下, "All under Heaven."

The step taken in 1272 had actually been anticipated much earlier. About six weeks after Khubilai had held his *khuriltai* (acclamation ceremony) in 1260, he promulgated an edict in Chinese in which a Chinese-style reign-name was pronounced. From that year, the Mongols in China used the Chinese system of dating. The reign-name taken was Chung-t'ung 中統 or "Pivotal Succession." [6] The edict announcing the adoption of this reign-name was drafted by the scholar Wang O 王鶚 (1190–1273). [7] In it the ruler explained that the name was designed to convey the principle of an empire united under one house. Furthermore, he stated that "it takes as its model the orthodox beginning (*cheng-shih* 正始) [of a ruler's suzerainty] found in the *Spring and Autumn Annals*, and embodies the original creative force (*ch'ien-yüan* 乾元) found in the *Book of Changes*." [8]

---

[5] See Wilhelm and Baynes, *The I Ching*, p. 376.

[6] This translation was suggested by Professor Hok-lam Chan in a private communication.

[7] For a detailed biography of Wang O, see Hok-lam Chan, "Wang O (1190–1273)," *Papers on Far Eastern History*, 12 (Sept. 1975), pp. 43–70.

[8] The edict is discussed in Herbert Franke, *From Tribal Chieftain to Universal Emperor and God*, pp. 27–28. For the text of the edict, see YS 4:65. The allusion in the lines quoted here is to the interpretation of the *Spring and Autumn Annals* (*Ch'un-ch'iu* 春秋) as found in the *Kung-yang chuan* 公羊傳. In the latter commentary, it is argued that the *Spring and Autumn Annals* teaches the principle that a proper commencement, i.e. a "new beginning" (*keng shih* 更始), of a reign will lead to success in "amplifying the union of the kingdom" (*ta i-t'ung* 大一統). See James Legge, *The Chinese Classics* (rpt. Hong Kong: Hong Kong University Press, 1960), vol. 5, prolegomena, p. 55.

In other ways, too, Khubilai astutely set out to develop supplementary sources of legitimacy. These sources, he hoped, would enhance the ability of his regime to induce the willing compliance of his subjects. Just six weeks after the new dynastic title had been proclaimed, on the date corresponding to March 4, 1272, an edict issued by Khubilai renamed the Yüan capital city Ta-tu 大都, "the great capital." This city had been one of the capital cities of the preceding Jurchen Chin 金 dynasty and was on the site of modern Peking. K'ai-p'ing fu 開平府 (near the modern city of Dolon in a bend of the Luan 灤 River in Inner Mongolia), where Khubilai had been elevated to the position of *khaghan* ("khan of khans") in 1260, was renamed Shang-tu 上都, "the upper capital." Construction of the palaces in Ta-tu received high priority from the khaghan. The design of the new city had been drawn up on the basis of the capital city outlined in the ancient Chinese classic of government, the *Chou li* 周禮 (*The Rites of Chou*). The *Yüan shih* 元史 (*Yüan History*) notes that construction of palace buildings on the site of the capital began as early as the spring of 1266.[9] Walls and other buildings were constructed during the ensuing years, and in early spring 1272 quarters for the Chung-shu sheng 中書省 (Central Secretariat) were completed, a full four years before the capture of the Southern Sung capital Lin-an 臨安 (modern Hangchow 杭州), and seven years prior to the defeat of the last remnants of the Sung loyalists.

Khubilai's dynasty, after it had become entrenched on the soils of both sedentary China and nomadic Mongolia, naturally took on a complex nature. As a conquest dynasty, it depended heavily on military supremacy. But as a dynasty which drew upon the collective experience of the Jurchens, the Khitans, and other non-Han peoples who had ruled parts of China, it saw and attempted to exploit the advantages of civil legitimacy that were uniquely well developed in the Chinese political and intellectual tradition.

The transformation of the idea of a dynasty by Khubilai in 1272 was an important innovation designed to enhance the regime's civil legitimacy. By this effort the symbolic importance of the throne of China was universalized—more fully so than any preceding Chinese dynasty had ever succeeded in doing.

The dynasty also sought to develop religious legitimacy that would appeal to peoples outside the settled regions of China—to the Uighurs and Tibetans and any Han Chinese who inhabited Inner Asia and who were heavily influenced by Buddhism. In the religious sphere, the role of

[9] See Hok-lam Chan, "Liu Ping-chung," pp. 133–134; YS 7:140.

the khaghan was universalized by a process that Herbert Franke describes as "sacralization." [10]

The religious aura of the khaghan which derived from his role as a Buddhist cakravartin king was expressed in the languages of the Tibetans, Uighurs, and other Inner Asians. It was thus directed primarily outside China to the larger Mongol empire, although Chinese Buddhists would also have been part of the audience. The political and ideological legitimacy which employed Chinese imagery and allusions and which was expressed in Chinese writing was aimed towards the Chinese and sinicized peoples of the Chinese cultural region. Throughout the Yüan era, then, these two systems of legitimacy coexisted, giving the regime in China a split or double image.

II. The Successors of Khubilai

The rulers after Khubilai inherited the latter's schema, according to which the Yüan was a universal empire coeval with the cosmos. Some rulers were able to enhance that schema further. Tugh Temür, for example, whose posthumous temple name was Wen-tsung 文宗 ("the cultivated ancestor") (r. 1328–1332), founded the K'uei-chang Ko 奎章閣 (Pavilion of the Star of Literature). The pavilion served as the imperial library and art collection and housed the compilation project that produced the *Ching-shih ta-tien* 經世大典 ("Great Compendium for Governing the World").[11] But most of the Yüan rulers after Khubilai were unable or disinclined to enhance the dynasty's legitimacy in this way, and instead had a very poor grasp of the stabilizing effect that ideological and symbolic legitimation can bring to bear on a political regime.

Mongol succession practices, however, worked against sound dynastic principles, even though the Chinggisid line was never challenged as the legitimate source of heirs to the throne. The history of Mongol succession in Yüan times is one of assassinations, coups d'état, enthronements of youthful incompetents, fratricide, and domination by non-Chinggisid warlords. The Chinese sources naturally tend to understand these events

---

[10] See the essay by Herbert Franke in this volume.

[11] For a discussion of Tugh Temür's K'uei-chang Ko, see my "Yü Chi and His Mongol Sovereign: The Scholar as Apologist," *Journal of Asian Studies*, 38:1 (Nov. 1978), pp. 99–116; Fu Shen 傅申, "Yüan Wen-tsung yü K'uei-chang ko 元文宗與奎章閣," *Ku-kung chi-k'an* 故宮季刊, 13:2 (1978), pp. 1–24; and Chiang I-han 姜一涵, "Yüan-tai K'uei-chang ko ho Hsüan-wen ko chung ti ch'i-wei chien-shu po-shih 元代奎章閣和宣文閣中的七位鑒書博士," *Chung-kuo hsüeh-jen* 中國學人, 6 (Sept. 1977), pp. 97–117.

in the light of Chinese dynastic history. The *Yüan shih* does this, in part
because its compilers clearly thought of the Yüan as a legitimate Chinese
dynasty, and in part because the Mongols to some degree had adopted
Chinese dynastic principles and had upheld them in some instances.
Nevertheless, the legacy of what Joseph Fletcher has dubbed "bloody
tanistry" was so deeply imbedded in political practices that echoes of it
can be traced throughout later Chinese history.[12]

Khubilai was the first Mongol ruler of China to designate an heir
apparent. He named his son Chen-chin 眞金[13] the heir in order to
predetermine the succession and thereby avert the armed struggles that
were endemic in Mongol political life. But Chen-chin died before
Khubilai, and although Khubilai later named another heir apparent, the
chances for a smooth succession by a groomed heir were reduced. Nevertheless, after Khubilai's death succession remained within the line of
descent from Chen-chin. Chen-chin's son Temür succeeded Khubilai.
The succession at this juncture was peaceful only because Temür's elder
brother Kammala agreed to go along with the selection of Temür in a
show of grace, and also to avoid a showdown with two very powerful
Mongol leaders who supported Temür's candidacy.[14]

Temür saw the need for choosing an heir apparent, but the man he
chose (his son) died before him. The succession then passed to his second
elder brother's sons, one after another (Fig. 1). These were Hai-shan
海山[15] and Ayurbarwada, sons of Darmabala. Both men were supported
by a powerful Mongol leader.[16] Hai-shan, who was the elder son, named
his brother heir apparent, and because Hai-shan's powerful sponsor
favored Ayurbarwada's succession, the transfer of power upon Hai-

[12] See Fletcher's "Bloody Tanistry: Authority and Succession in the Ottoman, Indian
Muslim, and Later Chinese Empires," presented at the Conference on the Theory of
Democracy and Popular Participation, Bellagio, Italy, September 3–8, 1978; and the same
author's "Turco-Mongolian Monarchic Tradition in the Near East, India, and China," in
Eucharisterion (essays in honor of Omeljan Pritsak), forthcoming.

[13] This name, although Chinese in origin, is often transliterated Jingim as though it were
a Mongolian name. (I am indebted to Professor Joseph Fletcher for this point.)

[14] Yanai Watari 箭内亘, *Mōkoshi kenkyū* 蒙古史研究 (Tokyo: Tōkō Shoin 刀江書院,
1930 [reprinted 1966]), pp. 419–420. See also Chao I 趙翼, "Yüan chu-ti to yu ta-ch'en
yung-li 元諸帝多由大臣擁立" ("Most Yüan emperors were enthroned through the efforts
of powerful ministers"), in *Nien-erh shih cha-chi* 廿二史劄記 (*Ts'ung-shu chi-ch'eng*
叢書集成 ed.), 29:612–614.

[15] Hai-shan's name is of Chinese origin, and the quasi-Mongolian transliteration
Khaishan should be avoided. (I am again indebted to Professor Joseph Fletcher for this
point.)

[16] Yanai Watari, *Mōkoshi kenkyū*, pp. 421–423; John W. Dardess, *Conquerors and
Confucians: Aspects of Political Change in Late Yüan China* (New York: Columbia
University Press, 1973), pp. 13–18.

shan's death was peaceful. Similarly the son of Ayurbarwada assumed
the throne without incident upon the latter's death. This man, whose
name was Shidebala, had been named heir apparent, thus carrying
forward the Chinese-style principle of dynastic succession. But things
changed abruptly in 1323, when Shidebala was assassinated. His
assassins put the son of Kammala on the throne. The accession of
Kammala's son Yesün Temür was proclaimed by an edict in colloquial
Chinese.[17]

Yesün Temür, in trying to continue the semblance of order, named his
son Aragibag the heir apparent. When Yesün Temür died in Shang-tu in
1328, Aragibag ascended the throne there, backed by a powerful faction.
At the same time, however, a rival faction led by El Temür had different
plans for the empire. Evidently wanting to repay debts he had incurred
under Hai-shan, El Temür established Hai-shan's son Tugh Temür as the
new ruler. Tugh Temür ascended the throne in Ta-tu, and a civil war
erupted between the two contending factions. Meanwhile Tugh Temür
also faced a rival in his brother Khoshila, who marched towards Ta-tu
from the far west. Tugh Temür yielded the throne to his elder brother
and went forth into the steppe to greet him. At their meeting, Khoshila
died, probably killed at El Temür's command. El Temür then attacked
Shang-tu and eliminated Aragibag's faction, capturing the throne again
for Tugh Temür, who reascended it in 1329.[18]

Three years later Tugh Temür died, whereupon another struggle for
succession erupted. Tugh Temür's designated heir had died prematurely.
The crisis was resolved unsatisfactorily with the accession of the seven-
year-old Irinjibal. Irinjibal, the son of Khoshila, ruled for less than two
months before an abrupt demise. Irinjibal's elder brother Toghōn Temür
was elevated after a half a year of wrangling between the rival sponsors.
He was thirteen, and he was the last Yüan emperor of China. Toghōn
Temür ruled from 1333 to 1370, although the last year or more of his
reign was spent fleeing from Chinese troops in Mongolia after the
Chinese took Ta-tu in the summer of 1368.

Mongol rule in China, like Mongol rule elsewhere, was the rule of
conquerors. The Mongols' aim was to enrich themselves.[19] Their perception of how best to accomplish that aim changed over time, but Mongol
superiority and enrichment remained their chief concerns in China. They
were careful in their early years to keep police and surveillance activities

---

[17] YS 29:638–639.

[18] These events are summarized in Dardess, *Conquerors and Confucians*, chapter 2; and
in Langlois, "Yü Chi and His Mongol Sovereign."

[19] Otagi Matsuo 愛宕松男, *Chūgoku no rekishi: Gen to Min* 中国の歴史：元と明
(Tokyo: Kodansha, 1974), p. 204.

functioning effectively; at the same time, they were reluctant to accept Chinese arguments for the establishment of a standard penal code. In 1272 Khubilai abolished the Chin *T'ai-ho lü* 泰和律 (Code of the T'ai-ho Reign), first promulgated in 1206, at the same time that he proclaimed the new dynastic title. The reason for this was probably that a Chinese code (the *T'ai-ho lü* was based on the *T'ang Code*) would have conflicted with the universal and pluralistic pretensions of the new dynasty. Thus the Yüan became the only major dynasty in Chinese history to rule without the benefit of a formal *lü* or penal code. This fact may well have been seen as an advantage by the Mongols.[20] It was one of a number of choices the Mongols made in which they selected a "universal" element in preference to a pariochially Chinese one; other such choices were made in the state religion (Buddhism), in the script chosen for writing Mongolian, and the like.

While the Mongols may have been primarily concerned with enriching themselves and with preserving their privileged standing, many Chinese kept trying to transform the Mongols into benevolent rulers with more "civilized" aims than those of gathering booty. Chinese scholars frequently advised the Mongols to pay closer attention to the ideological and moral bases of politics. Hsü Heng 許衡 (1209–1281) was an indefatigable spokesman in this regard and is today the most famous of the Yüan scholars who dedicated themselves to "sinicizing" the Mongols. A less well-known contemporary of Hsü's was Hu Chih-yü 胡祇遹 (1225–1293), who diagnosed the chief cause of the defects of Mongol rule in the following words: "[The rulers] are honoring military prestige and financial aggrandizement as priority matters."[21] Hu was outspoken in his direct criticisms of the regime. He devoted strenuous efforts towards reeducating those in power, mapping out strategies for the handling of criminal proceedings and disciplining the thousands of clerical and legal functionaries in the bureaucracy.

The Mongols in China had little anti-Mongol "nationalism" to contend with in administering their realm. In the north, the former Han-Chinese subjects of the Jurchens and the Khitans had grown accustomed

[20] Iwamura Shinobu 岩村忍, *Mongoru shakai keizaishi no kenkyū* モンゴル社会経済史の研究 (Kyoto: Jimbun Kagaku Kenkyūjō, 1968), p. 277. See also Paul Heng-chao Ch'en, *Chinese Legal Tradition under the Mongols: The Code of 1291 as Reconstructed* (Princeton: Princeton University Press, 1979); and Uematsu Tadashi 植松正, "Gendai jōkō kō 元代条画考," *Kagawa Daigaku kyōikugakubu kenkyū hōkō* 香川大學教育學部研究報告, 1:45 (October 1978), pp. 35–73; 1:46 (March 1979), pp. 75–104; and 1:47 (October 1979), pp. 103–137. Uematsu argues that the Mongols ruled China with the aid of the issuance of regulations and other forms of legislation that were promulgated in Chinese. A code or *lü* had no meaning for them.

[21] Hu Chih-yü, *Tzu-shan ta ch'üan chi* 紫山大全集 (1924 ed.), 12:8a.

to rule by non-Han conquerors, and therefore the Mongols had little to fear on their account. In the south, the former territory of the Southern Sung dynasty, there was strong resistance to the conquest. Sung loyalism was politically and morally motivated, by and large, but it was not entirely free of anti-Mongol hostility of an ethnic or quasi-racist nature. Han Chinese literati who experienced the Mongol takeover in the south were at first greatly distressed by the defeat of their dynasty, and many wrote poems in which they expressed strong emotions of this sort. But, as the years went by, they came to realize that the Mongol dominance was not to be an ephemeral event. Many then became more willing to co-operate with the rulers in order to put their learning and ambitions to good use in society. Many of them became instructors at academies, and not a few became government personnel. Although the complex emotions that the conquest had provoked in their hearts were not easily subdued or harmonized, most literati worked out a creative *modus vivendi* under the Mongol order.[22]

One of the strongest reasons behind Han Chinese support of the Mongol regime was the reunification of their country that the Mongols had accomplished. Not even the Northern Sung at its height had controlled all of the land of the Middle Kingdom, for some sixteen prefectures in the north had remained under Khitan domination. The Mongols, by contrast, had brought all of Chinese proper under unified rule. The years of separation of north and south that had been experienced by Chinese since the Jurchen conquest in the 1120s were ended by the Mongol defeat of the Southern Sung in the 1270s. Communication between the two regions became easier, and this had an impact on the literati, providing the Mongols with an aura of legitimacy.

There were important differences between the two regions which reunification could not obliterate. Parts of the north had experienced non-Han rule for more than a century, while the south had never before experienced it. In part as a consequence of that long separation, the northerners had a literary and cultural tradition that, while sharing common origins and language with that of the south, stemmed more directly from that of the T'ang and the Northern Sung. The southerners, on their part, possessed a refined and elegant cultural and intellectual heritage, with brilliant achievements in the arts, philosophy, and letters. Southern Han-Chinese were not wholly trusted by their northern Han-Chinese counterparts who served in the Mongol administration.

---

[22] For a subtle discussion of this topic, see Lao Yen-hsüan 勞延煊 [Lao Yan-shuan], "Yüan-ch'u nan-fang chih-shih-fen-tzu 元初南方知識份子," *Chung-kuo wen-hua yen-chiu-suo hsüeh-pao* 中國文化研究所學報, 10 (1979), pp. 127–156.

Yet these differences only heightened the impact of the reunification, for the rejoining of north and south allowed a mutual discovery that provoked great excitement.

III. The Problem of Appraisal

Identifying areas of enduring Mongol impact on Chinese civilization is extremely difficult. Such a question presupposes a knowledge of what China would have been like if the Mongols had not conquered China. Specific institutional innovations can be easily attributed to the Mongols. The establishment of a rapid postal relay system throughout China proper, linked to Inner Asia, is an obvious example.[23] The creation of the *hsing-sheng* 行省, or "branch secretariats," which evolved into the Ming and Ch'ing provinces, is another.[24] But is hard to demonstrate the existence of causal links between Mongol rule and specific cultural innovations. It is better to think in terms of cultural responses to the special circumstances of Yüan dynasty rule than in terms of Mongol impact on China and the Chinese.

In the early years of Mongol rule in the north before Khubilai founded the Yüan state, some Mongols had advocated the unbridled seizure of wealth in China and the conversion of the land to grazing fields for the herds. Yeh-lü Ch'u-ts'ai 耶律楚材, the son of a Khitan noble, persuaded Chinggis Khan that greater wealth could be obtained by administering China as a conquered territory. This story is well known.[25] Once the Mongols accepted the idea that toleration of and accommodation to the Chinese ways of administration were profitable, the continued vitality of Chinese civilization no longer faced any real danger from Mongol rule. This fact is manifested in many ways, one of which is the emergence of *tsa-chü* 雜劇, an important genre of drama, under the Jurchens and its flourishing under the Mongols.[26] Similarly, in painting, intellectual concerns, and religion, Mongol rule led to no ruptures; indeed, much to

[23] See Peter Olbricht, *Das Postwesen in China unter der Mongolenherrschaft im 13. und 14. Jahrhundert* (Wiesbaden: Otto Harrassowitz, 1954).

[24] See Charles O. Hucker, "The Yüan Contribution to Censorial History," *Bulletin of the Institute of History and Philology, Academia Sinica*, extra vol. no. 4 (1960), pp. 219–227.

[25] See Igor de Rachewiltz, "Yeh-lü Ch'u-ts'ai (1189–1243): Buddhist Idealist and Confucian Statesman," in Arthur F. Wright and Denis Twitchett, ed., *Confucian Persuasion* (Stanford: Stanford University Press, 1962), pp. 189–216.

[26] This is discussed by Stephen West in the article in this volume. See also Chung-wen Shih, *The Golden Age of Chinese Drama: Yüan Tsa-chü* (Princeton: Princeton University Press, 1976); and Ching-hsi Perng, *Double Jeopardy: A Critique of Seven Yüan Courtroom Dramas* (Ann Arbor: Center for Chinese Studies, University of Michigan, 1978).

the contrary, the general picture is one of continuity and development.[27]

The Yüan was a pluralistic society, as all Chinese dynasties have been, but it was more so than any other. Not even the Ch'ing era surpasses it in this respect. Foreign or non-Han rule, China's ties with the larger Mongol empire, and the Mongol practice of employing non-Han peoples, particularly Muslims from Western Asia, as middlemen to assist in administration and tax collection, all served to increase the pluralistic nature of Yüan society. Under the Mongols, wide variations of dress and eating habits, languages and patois and religions, were the stuff of life in China.[28]

The Yüan era is thus one of two remarkably different aspects, the Chinese and the Mongol, with many other dimensions lodged betwixt these two. Each tried to understand the other, and each was partially successful. Both accepted the principle that they shared the same world; the notion of something called the Yüan transcended both groups, and drew a bond between them. In studying the history of this era, one must strive to see both sides. In exploring the responses of the Chinese to their Mongol rulers, one must not forget that the Mongols had their own interests and rationalizations, and displayed their own resilience in adapting to the problems of ruling over the world's largest, and wholly sedentary, society.

During the Yüan period the interaction between Han-Chinese and non-Han peoples was greater than in times of Han-Chinese rule. In that respect Yüan civilization was pluralistic. Yet a striking fact is that there is little evidence to suggest that most Chinese were stimulated to show awareness of that pluralism or to accept it as normal. The art and music of T'ang times show more Inner Asian influences than those of the Yüan. The reasons for this have yet to be explored.

Studies by various modern Chinese scholars have stressed the theme of sinicization. Ch'en Yüan 陳垣 in his important *Yüan hsi-yü-jen hua-hua k'ao* 元西域人華化考, rendered expertly into English by L. C. Goodrich and Ch'ien Hsing-hai under the title *Western and Central Asians in China under the Mongols*, marshalled considerable anecdotal data to show that Chinese culture had largely absorbed its alien conquerors during the era

---

[27] Painting under the Mongols is surveyed in James Cahill, *Hills Beyond a River: Chinese Paintings of the Yüan Dynasty* (New York and Tokyo: Weatherhill, 1976). See also Sherman E. Lee and Wai-kam Ho, *Chinese Art under the Mongols: The Yüan Dynasty (1279–1368)* (Cleveland: The Cleveland Museum of Art, 1968).

[28] For a discussion of one of these dimensions see F. W. Mote, "Yüan and Ming," in K. C. Chang, ed., *Food in Chinese Culture: Anthropological and Historical Perspectives* (New Haven: Yale University Press, 1977), pp. 193–257.

of Mongol rule.[29] Yao Ts'ung-wu 姚從吾 in his studies tended also to
look to sinicization as a useful way of understanding the era.[30] A slightly
different approach has been taken by Professor Sun K'o-k'uan 孫克寬.
In his studies *Yüan-tai Han-wen-hua chih huo-tung* 元代漢文化之活動
(*Han-Chinese Cultural Activities in the Yüan Period*) and *Yüan-tai Chin-hua hsüeh shu* 元代金華學述 (*The Learning of Chin-hua Prefecture in
Yüan Times*),[31] he sets forth the hypothesis that Confucian literati
shielded Chinese culture from any untoward effects of Mongol rule by
engaging actively in public service, both in government and in education.
Here the emphasis is not on sinicization, but rather on efforts of the
literati to "preserve the race and culture" (*pao chung ts'un wen*
保種存文) in the face of potentially destructive rule by the Mongols. In
Sun's analysis, Chinese civilization faced an unprecedented challenge to
its existence during the era of Mongol domination. He attributes its
continued vitality despite that challenge to the elasticity and dynamism
of the cultural tradition and to its protection by great scholars and
officials during the Yüan era. Professor Sun's views, some of which are
presented for the first time in English in this volume, owe a certain debt
to modern Chinese nationalism and the reading of Chinese cultural
history in the light of that.

All of these writings thus shed light on the question of why Chinese
civilization was not fundamentally altered by Mongol rule, and on the
civilization's resources for the reconstitution of the dynastic order under
the leadership of Chu Yüan-chang 朱元璋, scion of a humble farming
family, founder of the Ming Dynasty.

The Ming founder himself held the view, shared by some modern
Chinese historians, that Han Chinese civilization had been partially
despoiled during the Yüan period.[32] One of his expressed aims, announced
early in his reign, was to restore the integrity of that civilization. He
ordered that Mongol forms of dress and Mongol names, both of which

[29] Los Angeles: Monumenta Serica Institute, 1966. The Chinese version was published in
two parts in Peking in 1923 and 1927.

[30] See his study of the question of sinicization in Khubilai's time: "Hu-pi-lieh tui-yü
Han-hua t'ai-tu ti fen-hsi 忽必烈對於漢化態度的分析," *Ta-lu tsa-chih* 大陸雜誌 (July,
1955), pp. 22–31.

[31] Taipei: Chung-hua Shu-chü, 1968; and Taichung: Tung-hai Ta-hsüeh, 1975.

[32] See Wu Han 吳晗, *Chu Yüan-chang chuan* 朱元璋傳 (Peking: San-lien Shu-tien,
1965), pp. 129–130; and Henry Serruys, *The Mongols in China during the Hung-wu Period*
(Bruxelles: *Mélanges chinois et bouddhiques*, vol. 11, 1959), pp. 129–130. A modern scholar
whose views are similar to these is Ch'ien Mu 錢穆. See his "Tu Ming-ch'u k'ai-kuo chu-
ch'en shih-wen-chi 讀明初開國諸臣詩文集," *Hsin-ya hsüeh-pao* 新亞學報, 6:2 (Aug.
1964), pp. 245–326. Chu Yüan-chang also expressed favorable views of Yüan rule on a
number of occasions, and he expressly included Khubilai in the shrine to previous

had in his eyes been adopted by many Chinese, should be banned; violators, he directed, would be punished.[33] If the Ming founder's perspective is correct, then acculturation in Yüan times was hardly a one-way phenomenon, for Chinese people were affected by Mongol customs just as Mongols and Central Asians were affected by Chinese culture. Yet there is little evidence in the literary and artistic sources for this dimension of the acculturation process. Is it possible that it was more evident among non-elites, and that is why the sources are silent? Or is it simply that the Ming founder was hypersensitive to this problem and that he exaggerated its significance for ideological purposes of his own? These are questions that have yet to be studied carefully.

These matters aside, there can be no doubt that in some ways the dominant Han Chinese culture thrived under Mongol rule. As noted above, continuity in letters is a very striking characteristic of Sung-Yüan history. In part this is to be expected, for the Mongols and their Western and Central Asian helpers were a small minority in China's large population.[34] In Yüan times, also, the state had less need for learned literati to serve as officers, and thus the literati were left to pursue their scholarly energies in other careers. Unpublished research by Professor Yan-shuan Lao has documented the establishment of hundreds of private academies (shu-yüan 書院) in Yüan times. There is also evidence that in some areas common descent groups or clans were organizing themselves in order to utilize their resources for self-governance and for support of education in the Confucian classics.[35] Chinese civilization, in short, evidences considerable resiliency during Yüan times.

---

emperors in which he or his delegates offered sacrifices. These materials (with the systematic exclusion of T'ai-tsu's unfavorable views) are included in Li Tse-fen 李則芬, Yüan shih hsin chiang 元史新講 (Taipei: Chung-hua Shu-chü, 1979), preface. For a balanced presentation of T'ai-tsu's views, see John W. Dardess, "Ming T'ai-tsu on the Yüan: An Autocrat's Assessment of the Mongol Dynasty," Bulletin of Sung and Yüan Studies, 14 (1978), pp. 6–11.

[33] See Wu Han, Chu Yüan-chang chuan, p. 156.

[34] A rough estimate of the population, based on the Yüan census of the 1290s, is the following: Mongols, 1,000,000; se-mu jen (Western and Central Asians), 1,000,000; nan-jen 南人 ("southerners," referring primarily to former subjects of the Southern Sung as they were designated after the Mongol conquest), 60,000,000; and Han-jen 漢人 (designating primarily the Han and other nationalities of North China who were subjects of the Jurchens prior to the Mongol conquest), 10,000,000. For these figures I follow Murakami Masatsugu 村上正二, Chūgoku no rekishi, 6: Yūboku minzoku kokka: Gen 中国の歴史, 6: 遊牧民族国家：元 (Tokyo: Kodansha, 1977), p. 142.

[35] See John W. Dardess, "The Cheng Communal Family: Social Organization and Neo-Confucianism in Yüan and Early Ming China," Harvard Journal of Asiatic Studies, 34 (1974), pp. 7–52.

In some ways Mongol rule may even have been rather benign. The Mongols did not perceive the need for, nor did they have the ability to exercise, ideological control over the Chinese populace. They were too few in number and too limited in their understanding of the Chinese literary tradition to be able to exercise ideological control. Since their rule was assisted by many Western and Central Asians, commonly known as *se-mu-jen* 色目人 ("people of the various categories"), their ability to police the administration at all levels was indirect, and often rather tenuous. Thus the bureaucracy in Yüan times, while theoretically governed by numerous codes of regulations, was largely ungovernable.[36] This meant, in practice, that there were many opportunities for corruption. Illicit practices by bureaucratic personnel, the un-ranked "clerks" (*li* 吏), in fact became the chief complaint that the Ming founder lodged against Yüan rule.[37] Put another way, the defect of Yüan rule was the laxity of government surveillance over its own personnel and the concomitant ineffectiveness of the government in dealing with popular disturbances. This partially explains the large number of such disturbances recorded in the Shantung and Lower Yangtze regions in Yüan times.[38] The relative unimportance of the examination system in Yüan times also meant that the dynasty was not engaged in systematic efforts to channel and govern thought in ways it deemed socially constructive.[39] This presented a challenge to literati trained to think in terms of social service; it also left them the freedom, or compelled them, to engage in occupations other than those associated with officialdom. Many literati engaged in pharmacy, medicine, fortune-telling, play-writing, and Taoist pursuits; and many became government clerks.[40]

Modern Chinese scholars of the Yüan period have sometimes con-

[36] For a discussion of these codes, and for a translation of one of them, see Paul H. C. Ch'en, *Chinese Legal Tradition under the Mongols: The Code of 1291 as Reconstructed.*

[37] Numerous pronouncements by the emperor to this effect can be found in the *Veritable Records.* See, for example, *Ming T'ai-tsu shih-lu* 明太祖實錄 (rpt. Taipei: Academia Sinica, 1968 [2nd printing]), pp. 0419–0420, and p. 1288. One must also consider Paul Ch'en's discussion of "legal professionalism" in the Yüan period in his *Chinese Legal Tradition under the Mongols.* What the Chinese called *li-hsüeh* 吏學, "the learning of clerks," was a well developed field in Yüan times, and would have countered the tendency to corrupt behavior that may have been promoted by the absence of careful supervision of the bureaucracy.

[38] See Huang Ch'ing-lien 黃清連, "Yüan-ch'u Chiang-nan ti p'an-luan 元初江南的叛亂," *Chung-yang yen-chiu yüan Li-shih yü-yen yan-chiu-suo chi-k'an* 中央研究院歷史語言研究所季刊, 49:1 (1978), pp. 37–76.

[39] The examination did not serve as the primary recruitment institution in Yüan times, and prior to 1313 it was completely defunct.

[40] See Wai-kam Ho, "Chinese under the Mongols," in Sherman Lee and Wai-kam Ho, ed., *Chinese Art under the Mongols*, pp. 73–87, ff.

tended that the Han Chinese despised being ruled by the Mongols and that throughout the Yüan period the desire to drive them out was a hidden but continually felt wish.[41] It is true that the Ming founder issued a proclamation in which he stated that Mongol rule was a cause of "shame" (ch'ih 恥). But in the same edict he explicitly welcomed all Mongols and other non-Han peoples to continue to live within the territory of the Middle Kingdom.[42] In practice many Mongols did remain, and not a few were retained in key military units defending the Ming court and extending Ming control over the border areas.[43] Therefore the notion that the Yüan and early Ming Chinese were anti-Mongol racists seems extremely dubious. It is far more probable that the Han-Chinese themselves accepted the Mongols as legitimate holders of the Mandate of Heaven. The Ming founder said precisely this in various edicts and letters.[44]

Historians in the People's Republic of China now argue that it is incorrect to describe Yüan rule as the rule of aliens who invaded China. Following the lead of Wu Han 吳晗, who had argued that Mongols, Manchus and other non-Han peoples were fully a part of Chinese history,[45] these scholars now claim that the primary contradiction in Yüan times was not one of ethnicity, but rather one of socio-economic class.[46]

These views serve political expedients in today's China, to be sure, yet

[41] Many scholars cite the T'ieh-han Hsin-shih 鐵函心史, attributed to the late Sung-early Yüan painter Cheng Ssu-hsiao 鄭思肖, for its bitter denunciations of the "barbarians." The work was allegedly found in an iron box in a well at the Ch'eng-t'ien Ssu 承天寺 in Soochow in late Ming times. Cheng's preface to a part of this work refers to the Mongols as "dogs and goats," and describes them as fei jen-lei 非人類, "not human." See Hsin-shih 心史 (in Yang Chia-lo 楊家駱, ed., Min-tsu cheng-ch'i ts'ung-shu 民族正氣叢書 [Taipei: Shih-chieh Shu-chü, 1956]), shang 上, 71b. Parts of this work are probably forgeries, and since its denunciations of the Mongols are not echoed in reliable Yüan writings known at this time it may be best to reserve judgment on it. For discussions of the problems of the text see Yao Ts'ung-wu 姚從吾, "Cheng Ssu-hsiao yü 'T'ieh-han hsin-shih' kuan-hsi ti t'ui-ts'e 鄭思肖與「鐵函心史」關係的推測," in Ch'ing-chu Chiang Wei-t'ang hsien-sheng ch'i-shih jung-ch'ing lun-wen-chi 慶祝蔣慰堂先生七十榮慶論文集 (Taipei: Hsüeh-sheng Shu-chü, 1968), pp. 19–24; and Liu Chao-yu 劉兆祐, "Hsin-shih ti chu-che wen-t'i 心史的著者問題," Shu-mu chi-k'an 書目季刊, 3:4 (Summer 1969), pp. 25–32.

[42] The edict is quoted in Wu Han, Chu Yüan-chang chuan, pp. 128–130. It was probably written by Sung Lien 宋濂. For a partial translation see Henry Serruys, The Mongols in China during the Hung-wu Period, pp. 44–45, 56–57.

[43] On this topic see Henry Serruys, The Mongols in China during the Hung-wu Period, pp. 89–120.

[44] [Ming T'ai-tsu] yü-chih wen-chi [明太祖] 御製文集 (rpt. Taipei: Hsüeh-sheng Shu-chü, 1965), 1:1a, 5:4b, ff.

[45] Chu Yüan-chang chuan, p. 130.

[46] See my notes on this topic in Bulletin of Sung and Yüan Studies, 15 (1979), pp. 103–105.

they are not without their truthful component. While it is anachronistic
to view Yüan history from the perspective of contemporary politics, it is
foolish to deny the fact that the "Yüan" dynasty was a Chinese inven-
tion. All the ideas inherent in the name of the dynasty were derived
directly from the mainstream Chinese literary and political heritage. It is
true that they were brought together in this way at the insistence of the
Mongol conqueror Khubilai. But that does not alter the fact that they
were purely Chinese in origin. A dynasty is much more than a simple
structure of symbols, of course. The Yüan was a complex amalgam of
Jurchen, Mongol, Khitan, and Chinese institutions. The many sources of
Yüan institutions remind us that Chinese civilization was never simply
the civilization of the Han ethnic group, despite the frequent identification of the Hsia 夏 (China) side of the "sino-barbarian" polarity with
the Han people. The history of Chinese civilization is one of constant
enrichment of the "Hsia" tradition by elements from outside, just as
Chinese civilization enriched the surrounding civilizations of Japan,
Korea, Inner Asia, and elsewhere. The degree to which Chinese civilization was so enriched by its contacts with outside peoples and by non-
Han peoples within varied from one age to another, but the process must
have been continual.

It is encouraging to hear that scholars in the People's Republic of
China are reassessing the history of the Yüan period. And it is interesting
that that reassessment is being made at the same time that scholars in
Taiwan and in this country have increased their interest in the Yüan
period. Recently a research conference on the intellectual history of the
Yüan period was held in Seattle, and it is hoped that the papers will soon
be published. In Taipei a voluminous study of the Yüan, entitled *Yüan
shih hsin chiang* 元史新講, by Li Tse-fen 李則芬 recently appeared,[47] and
in its preface the author makes it clear that he sees little value in earlier
prejudicial or anti-Mongol views of Yüan history. In Li's view, the
eighty-nine years of Mongol rule, from Khubilai to near the end of
Toghōn Temür's reign, were years of great peace and prosperity. The
Yüan was more humane than the Sung government, in Li's view, in
respect to its relatively infrequent use of capital punishment. Yüan
taxation was, in his view, less subject to irregular exactions than were
other governments in Chinese history. There were no "literary in-
quisitions" (*wen-tzu yü* 文字獄) in Yüan times; and there was greater
religious freedom in Yüan times than in later times. Yüan classical
scholarship, in Li's view, should be considered worthy of attention. He

---

[47] This five-volume work appeared late in 1979, too late for consideration by the authors
of the papers included in this volume.

counted 213 works on the *I ching* (*Book of Changes*), 149 works on the *Four Books*, and 127 studies of the *Ch'un-ch'iu* (*Spring and Autumn Annals*), not to mention works on the other classical texts. He argues, as Professor Chan does in the essay included in this volume, that the early Ming scholars and the Ming founder had a highly favorable view of the Yüan and that the unfavorable view of the Yüan in Chinese historical scholarship emerges only after the ill-fated adventure of 1449, when the Ming emperor was captured by the Oirat Mongols (the so-called "T'u-mu Incident"). The strong anti-Mongol bias of Chinese historiography appears as a response to this act of humiliation inflicted on the Ming throne by the Mongols.

It would probably be a mistake to wax rhapsodic about the merits of Mongol rule, however, despite the materials cited in Li Tse-fen's enormous study. We still do not have enough detailed monographic studies of Yüan local government, for example, to sustain generalizations about Yüan rule. Even studies of court politics are hard to come by. We know that the Mongols employed the practice of *t'ing-chang* 廷杖 ("court beatings") of ministers when the emperors were displeased. While they did not invent this crude form of intimidation,[48] they seem to have employed it more often than earlier rulers in China. F. W. Mote's view that Mongol rule led to a "brutalization" of politics which in a sense bore tragic fruit in Ming times has still to be dealt with by detailed studies. Paul H. C. Ch'en's study of the *Chih-yüan hsin-ko* 至元新格 (*New Code of the Chih-yüan Era* [1291]) and the surrounding legal practices of the Yüan period puts forth an argument similar to that of Li Tse-fen's, namely that Yüan justice was more lenient than Sung or Ming justice. But Dr. Ch'en's materials are formal, published legal codes. They are not records of actual judicial practice. And, therefore, while his case is extremely well argued and supported, we need more information before we can draw general conclusions about Yüan rule. Who were the darughachis and how did they conduct themselves? What was it like to live under the rule of Western and Central Asians (*se-mu jen*), men who likely had little commitment to the values of Chinese civilization? There are materials for studies of these questions in the writings of Yüan scholars and in other sources. Unfortunately this volume does not contain an essay dealing with local government. Professor Franke's study of the behavior of the Tibetan clerics in China is an eye-opening

[48] On the *t'ing-chang* and its employment by the Jurchens, see Jing-shen Tao, *The Jurchen in Twelfth-Century China: A Study of Sinicization* (Seattle: University of Washington, 1976), pp. 45–46.

[49] See his "The Growth of Chinese Despotism: A critique of Wittfogel's Theory of Oriental Despotism as Applied to China," *Oriens Extremus*, 8:1 (Aug. 1961), pp. 1–41.

examination of one of the oddities of Yüan history, reminding us that it was not a "normal" period of China's long history. The atrocities and corruption engaged in by the Tibetan clerics undoubtedly affected the general quality of life in Yüan times, and no official code or set of imperial proclamations can shed light on this. Professor Farquhar has argued in the essay in this volume that Yüan rule was not nearly as centralized as it has often been made out to have been, and that the Yüan exercised direct, reliable control only over a relatively small section of the realm in the vicinity of the capital and perhaps in a few other limited areas.

Social and economic studies are needed before we can satisfactorialy explain the demographic mystery of Yüan times.[50] Ho Ping-ti's research on the history of China's population suggests that a massive decline in China's population occurred under Mongol rule. The combined population in Sung and Chin times, he calculates, was well in excess of 100,000,000, while in 1393 the population of China had dropped to a little over 60,000,000.[51] Since the Yüan fiscal records of the 1290s indicate a population of roughly 70,000,000,[52] we see a steadily declining population under Mongol rule. One is challenged to explain this. If, as some argue, the Yüan was an era of benevolent and peaceful rule, why did the population drop so drastically? Disease may explain the decline to some extent. We know, for example, that disease took many lives in the 1340s in the Huai basin.[53] But we require more information before the demographic mystery is resolved.

In view of these historiographical questions, not dealt with in the secondary literature in depth, the reader will perhaps forgive the authors of the essays in this volume for their reluctance to make pronouncements about the general nature of Yüan rule. To be sure, each essay embraces an implicit understanding of Yüan rule, one which in most cases is not all unfavorable to the Mongols for their part in the administration of an era of cultural creativity. But no single essay undertakes to establish this as a thesis, for each essay deals with only a limited facet of Yüan history.

[50] Witold Rodzinski, in his *A History of China*, vol. 1 (Oxford: Pergamon Press, 1979), pp. 184–185, has argued that the social and economic consequences of Mongol rule were disastrous. He cites the vastness of the lands confiscated by the state for the Mongol aristocracy and its bad effects on productivity and population.

[51] For the Sung-Chin figures, see Ho Ping-ti, "An Estimate of the Total Population of Sung-Chin China," in Françoise Aubin, ed., *Études Song*, Series 1, Vol. 1 (Paris: Mouton, 1970), p. 52; for the Ming figures, see Ho Ping-ti, *Studies on the Population of China, 1368–1953* (Cambridge: Harvard University Press, 1959), p. 258.

[52] Murakami Masatsugu, cited in n. 34 above.

[53] Most of Ming T'ai-tsu's family was killed by disease at this time. See Wu Han, *Chu Yüan-chang chuan*, pp. 1–2. But this is long after the sharp decline from Sung-Chin times.

We can and should draw conclusions from these essays, and it is likely that the verdict will be in the Mongols' favor, so to speak. But not all the evidence is in, nor are we really very close to the point where we can draw conclusive assessments of the era. The essays here are presented in the spirit of, as the Chinese might say, *chi wang k'ai lai* 繼往開來. We have drawn freely on work done before us, hoping that our work will similarly be drawn upon by later scholars.

The volume is the product of a research conference sponsored by the American Council of Learned Societies. The conference was held in the summer of 1976 at Bowdoin College's Breckinridge Public Affairs Center in York, Maine. All the papers except Professor Franke's were originally presented at that conference. Revisions were made by the authors in the light of criticisms and suggestions offered by the members of the conference. Special thanks should be addressed to Professor Franke, who attended as a discussant, and to Professor James T. C. Liu of Princeton University, who sent written comments on all the papers. Professor Franke's paper was contributed subsequent to the conference at the request of the editor. We are also indebted to Dr. Paul Buell and Ms. Nancy Shatzman for their contributions to the conference as rapporteurs. Dr. Paul Balaran, Professors Timothy Wixted, Perng Ching-hsi, and Thomas Allsen made important contributions to the discussions, and these are hereby acknowledged with gratitude. Dr. Susan Bush assisted the editor on a number of technical questions, and gratitude is hereby recorded. Papers by Mr. David A. Sensabaugh, Dr. Wai-kam Ho, and Dr. S. Kuczera are not included here, but their presentations at the conference were nevertheless extremely valuable. Professors F. W. Mote and Joseph Fletcher read the manuscripts and offered innumerable suggestions and corrections to the editor and to the individual authors. The introduction was read carefully by the members of the conference and by most of the others named above, although their many suggestions are too numerous to list individually. To all the scholars named above, the editor and individual authors are deeply indebted. Errors of fact and interpretation, however, remain the responsibility of the authors themselves, with the exception of Professor Sun's paper. In that instance any distortion of his ideas introduced by the translation and adaptation of his essay should be attributed to the editor.

The editor is grateful to the Committee on Studies of Chinese Civilization of the ACLS, and to the Faculty Research Fund of Bowdoin College, for financial assistance in the editing of these papers.

The Great Khans of the Yüan (figure 1)

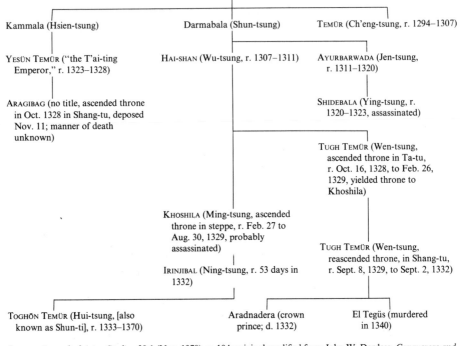

KHUBILAI (Shih-tsu, r. 1260–1294)

|

Chen-chin (Yü-tsung, d. 1285)

Kammala (Hsien-tsung)

Darmabala (Shun-tsung)

TEMÜR (Ch'eng-tsung, r. 1294–1307)

YESÜN TEMÜR ("the T'ai-ting Emperor," r. 1323–1328)

HAI-SHAN (Wu-tsung, r. 1307–1311)

AYURBARWADA (Jen-tsung, r. 1311–1320)

ARAGIBAG (no title, ascended throne in Oct. 1328 in Shang-tu, deposed Nov. 11; manner of death unknown)

SHIDEBALA (Ying-tsung, r. 1320–1323, assassinated)

TUGH TEMÜR (Wen-tsung, ascended throne in Ta-tu, r. Oct. 16, 1328, to Feb. 26, 1329, yielded throne to Khoshila)

KHOSHILA (Ming-tsung, ascended throne in steppe, r. Feb. 27 to Aug. 30, 1329, probably assassinated)

TUGH TEMÜR (Wen-tsung, reascended throne, in Shang-tu, r. Sept. 8, 1329, to Sept. 2, 1332)

IRINJIBAL (Ning-tsung, r. 53 days in 1332)

TOGHŌN TEMÜR (Hui-tsung, [also known as Shun-ti], r. 1333–1370)

Aradnadera (crown prince; d. 1332)

El Tegüs (murdered in 1340)

Source: *Journal of Asian Studies*, 38:1 (Nov. 1978), p. 104; original modified from John W. Dardess, *Conquerors and Confucians: Aspects of Political Change in Late Yüan China* (New York: Columbia University Press, 1973), p. 176.
Note: Names of those who ascended a throne are in caps and small caps.

II. INSTITUTIONS

Structure and Function in the
Yüan Imperial Government

DAVID M. FARQUHAR

We are so accustomed to hearing of the autocratic, highly centralized, bureaucratic character of governments in imperial China, that it is extremely difficult to view them in any other way, except during those periods of disintegration or disunion when serious talk about a central government is clearly impossible.[1] The Yüan dynasty of the Mongols, in particular, has been pointed out as a "tightly centralized régime" with a "centrally controlled bureaucracy."[2] One writer has even said that the Yüan was a state in which "power was absolutely lacking at the local level; it lay only at the center...."[3] Centralizing and bureaucratic tendencies certainly existed in the Yüan government, but that is different from saying that the imperial government was a central government by design. In this essay I intend to examine the structure of this government, to discover its character and functions in the administration of the empire.

At first glance, the imperial government seems well served by the centralized model: it proclaimed itself superior over all local governments, chains of successively smaller units, each with its own chief

[1] This essay is based on research for a comprehensive survey of the institution of Yüan government which I am presently preparing. The American Council of Learned Societies and the Humanities Foundation of the University of California supported some of this research with grants, for which I am grateful. In addition to the members of the Conference on the Yüan Dynasty, who gave me valuable criticism, I would like to thank Professor Okada Hidehiro 岡田英弘 of the Tōyō Bunko 東洋文庫 for suggesting some of the ideas developed here, and colleagues and students at U.C.L.A. who criticized an early version of this paper, especially Professors Philip C. C. Huang and Richard Baum. These persons should not be held responsible for any errors of fact or interpretation in this paper.

[2] See, for example, John W. Dardess, *Conquerors and Confucians: Aspects of Political Change in Late Yüan China* (New York and London, 1973), p. 21, and the same author's "From Mongol Empire to Yüan Dynasty: Changing Forms of Imperial Rule in Mongolia and Central Asia," *Monumenta Serica*, 30 (1972–73), pp. 117–165; Charles O. Hucker, *The Censorial System of Ming China* (Stanford, 1966), p. 25.

[3] Ch'ien Mu 錢穆, *Chung-kuo li-tai cheng-chih te-shih* 中國歷代政治得失 (Hong Kong, 5th printing, 1968), p. 97.

officers; it was huge, complex, and rationally organized, and it seemed to cover every conceivable aspect of governing; it used laws and regulations, which it purported to generate for the entire empire; and most of its chief organs, if not all, had "constitutions" summarizing their purposes and functions and laying down their complements of officers and clerks.[4]

These constitutions, perhaps more than any other single factor, have influenced our conception of the nature of Chinese imperial governments. When we read in our sources that a certain organ of government was responsible for all governmental ordinances relating to the registration of the population, to taxation, and to land throughout the entire empire; that the management of the receipt and expenditure of tribute and tax revenues, the rules concerning the circulation of currency, the verification of stocks in government warehouses and treasuries, the regulation of the prices of goods, and the auditing of records of receipt and disbursement to determine their correctness—all of these— lay within the purview of that organ, the need to understand it as a modern national ministry of finance becomes overwhelming.[5] When we discover that the staff overseeing these far-reaching charges consisted of only ten senior officers, eight service officers (*shou-ling-kuan* 首領官, who supervised the clerks and the office routine), and 136 clerks and other sub-officials, we might be inclined to change our assessment, but reading a bit further and noting this organ's twenty-one subordinate agencies with *their* numerous subordinate granaries, yards, treasuries, works, banks and convoys, confirms us in our original impression. After one has read a hundred such constitutional descriptions, the only analogues to fourteenth-century Ta-tu seem to be twentieth-century Paris or Tokyo.

I. Organs of the Imperial Government

To begin a critical examination of this impression, it may be useful to give a survey of the Yüan imperial government's chief organs. The most important systematic source is the treatise on the official system in the *Yüan History* (*Yüan shih* 元史) (1370), which was based on the "institutes" of the Yüan dynasty, the *Ching-shih ta-tien* 經世大典 of 1332,

---

[4] These are described most fully in *Yüan shih* 元史 (Peking: Chung-hua Shu-chü, 1976, hereafter YS), *chüan* 85–92.

[5] This is a paraphrase of the constitution of the Yüan dynasty Ministry of Revenue (II.A.l.b. in the list of bureaus given below), YS 85:2126, translated by Paul Ratchnevsky, *Un code des Yuan* (2 vols., Paris, 1937, 1972), I, pp. 127–128.

now mostly lost.[6] By 1332 the Yüan government may be said to have reached its mature form, having evolved very substantially since Emperor Khubilai (Shih-tsu) began to build a Chinese-style government in 1260, and it changed thereafter very little until the disintegration of the last few years of Mongol rule.[7] In 1332, the imperial government consisted of 121 principal agencies which might be called independent or quasi-independent, to which were subordinated 474 other agencies, under which, in turn, were 398 and 211 agencies at a second and third level of subordination.[8] I have organized the independent agencies and a very few of the more important subordinate ones under five rubrics, which in some measure reflect modern analytical requirements, the way in which people in Yüan times envisaged the functions of government, and the way in which the government is presented in the *Yüan History*. As in all governments, many organs had overlapping or dual functions and could be listed under two rubrics. Brief characterizations are given where the translated title seems insufficiently suggestive.

I. *The Imperial Establishment*

The emperor (*huang-ti* 皇帝, M. *khaghan*) was the capstone of the state, with the nominal authority to decide most political, administrative, legal, and moral questions. To rule and reign over such a huge empire with the proper magnificence required enormous resources of people and treasure. Agencies to dispose these can be divided into two groups:

A. Agencies which met the physical and creature needs of the emperor, his court, the government buildings in the capitals at Ta-tu and Shang-tu and the capital cities themselves

1. The Bureau for Imperial Household Provisions, *hsüan-hui yüan* 宣徽院 . An enormous organization responsible for feeding the court.[9]

2. The Bureau for Imperial Manufactures, *chiang-tso yüan* 將作院.

---

[6] The imperial government is dealt with in YS 85–90; I have found no entry in these chapters postdating 1332. See Herbert Franke, *Geld und Wirtschaft unter der Mongolen-Herrschaft* (Leipzig, 1949), pp. 17–18, 20–23.

[7] Changes in the governmental structure after 1332 are discussed in YS 92.

[8] There are many difficulties in making such enumerations and in identifying degrees of dependence and independence. The *Yüan shih* occasionally uses expressions like "subordinate to [this organ] were five bureaus...," but usually one must rely on the indenting used in the first edition of the *Yüan shih* to infer independence or subordination; in some places it appears to be in error and I have adopted the suggestions of K'o Shao-min 柯邵忞, *Hsin Yüan shih* 新元史 (Tientsin, 1922).

[9] YS 87:2200; Ratchnevsky, *Un code*, I, pp. 143–146. In presenting this list I give only minimal citations: the main YS entry and one translation or discussion in a modern work when it exists.

Supervised workshops making textiles, clothing, jewellery and other precious things for imperial use.[10]

3. The Court of the Imperial Stud, *t'ai-p'u ssu* 太僕寺. In charge of the state horse herds and provider of the emperor's mare's milk wine.[11]

4. The Court for the Imperial Tack, *shang-ch'eng ssu* 尚乘寺.[12]

5. The Imperial Treasuries Directorate, *t'ai-fu chien* 太府監.[13]

6. The Directorate for Animal Feeds, *tu-chih chien* 度支監.[14]

7. The Directorate for Leathers and Furs, *li-yung chien* 利用監.[15]

8. The Directorate for Felt Manufactures, *chung-shang chien* 中尚監.[16]

9. The Directorate for the Imperial Accessories, *chang-p'ei chien* 章佩監.[17]

10. The Directorate-General for the Imperial Residence at Tung-liang-t'ing 東涼亭, *shang-kung tsung-kuan-fu* 尚供總管府.[18]

11. The Directorate-General for the Imperial Residence at Chaghan-naghur, *yün-hsü tsung-kuan-fu* 雲需總管府.[19]

12. The Office for the Supervision of Attendants, *shih-cheng fu* 侍正府.[20]

13. The Ta-tu Construction and Protection Office, *ta-tu liu-shou ssu* 大都留守司.[21]

14. The Shang-tu Construction and Protection Office, *shang-tu liu-shou-ssu* 上都留守司.[22]

15. The Directorate-General of Ta-tu Circuit, *ta-tu lu tu tsung-kuan-fu* 大都路都總管府. This and the following office formed the basis of the local government in Ta-tu.[23] a. The General Commandery of the Ta-tu Circuit Constabulary, *ta-tu lu ping-ma tu-chih-hui shih-ssu* 大都路兵馬都指揮使司.[24]

[10] YS 88:2225.

[11] YS 90:2288; Paul Ratchnevsky, "Über den mongolischen Kult am Hofe der Grosskhane in China," in Louis Ligeti, ed., *Mongolian Studies* (Amsterdam, 1970), pp. 420–421.

[12] YS 90:2289; Ratchnevsky, "Über den mongolischen Kult," pp. 420–421.

[13] YS 90:2292; Ratchnevsky, "Über den mongolischen Kult," p. 430 n. 74.

[14] YS 90:2292; Francis W. Cleaves, "Bökesün-bökegül," *Ural-Altaische Jahrbücher*, 35D (1964), p. 384.

[15] YS 90:2293.

[16] YS 90:2294; Ratchnevsky, "Über den monglischen Kult," p. 430 n. 75.

[17] YS 90:2294.

[18] YS 90:2299.

[19] YS 90:2300.

[20] YS 88:2224.

[21] YS 90:2277.

[22] YS 90:2297.

[23] YS 90:2300.

[24] YS 90:2301.

B. Agencies which provided the emperor with advice and expertise, and organized for him religious, ideological, and intimate political functions

1. The Han lin and National History Academy, *han-lin (chien) kuo-shih yüan* 翰林 (兼) 國史院. A body of elite literary experts.[25]

2. The Mongolian Han lin Academy, *meng-ku han-lin yüan* 蒙古翰林院. In charge of translating the emperor's edicts and preparing final copies of them; it also managed the Mongolian National College, *meng-ku kuo-tzu hsüeh* 蒙古國子學 in the capital, a school for the sons of Mongolian nobles and officials.[26]

3. The Academy of Worthies, *chi-hsien yüan* 集賢院. A body of learned men which managed the Chinese National College, *kuo-tzu hsüeh* 國子學, and also watched over the Taoist clergy.[27]

4. The Academy of Scholars in the K'uei-chang Pavilion, *k'uei-chang ko hsüeh-shih yüan* 奎章閣學士院. The emperor's librarians.[28]

5. The Academy of Calendrical Studies, *t'ai-shih yüan* 太史院.[29]

6. The Institute of Astronomy, *ssu-t'ien chien* 司天監.[30]

7. The Institute of Muslim Astronomy, *hui-hui ssu-t'ien chien* 回回司天監.[31]

8. The Imperial Academy of Medicine, *t'ai-i yüan* 太醫院.[32]

9. The Directorate for the Diffusion of Confucian Texts, *i-wen chien* 藝文監.[33]

10. The Archives, *mi-shu chien* 祕書監.[34]

11. The Academy of Imperial Sacrifices and Rituals, *t'ai-ch'ang li-i yüan* 太常禮儀院.[35]

12. The Bureau for the Imperial Cults, *ta-hsi tsung-yin yüan* 大禧宗禋院. Its main function was managing the financial affairs of the imperial monasteries and temples.[36]

13. The Bureau of the Imperial Insignia, *tien-jui yüan* 典瑞院.[37]

---

[25] YS 87:2189; Ratchnevsky, *Un code*, I, pp. 148–149.
[26] YS 87:2190, 2191; Ratchnevsky, *Un code*, I, pp. 149–151, II, pp. 22–23.
[27] YS 87:2192; Ratchnevsky, *Un code*, II, pp. 23–26.
[28] YS 88:2222; Ratchnevsky, *Un code*, II, pp. 33–34.
[29] YS 88:2219.
[30] YS 90:2296.
[31] YS 90:2297.
[32] YS 88:2220; Ratchnevsky, *Un code*, II, pp. 46–47.
[33] YS 88:2223.
[34] YS 90:2296.
[35] YS 88:2217; Ratchnevsky, *Un code*, II, p. 1 n. 5.
[36] YS 87:2207.
[37] YS 88:2218.

14. The Imperial Diarists, *chi-shih-chung* 給事中. Kept the official record of the emperor's activities.[38]

II. *General Administration*

A. Civil Administration

1. The Central Secretariat, *chung-shu sheng* 中書省. Contained the emperor's most powerful and highest ranking councillors, and served as the empire's message center. Subordinate to it were six ministries:[39] a. The Ministry of Personnel, *li-pu* 吏部.[40] b. The Ministry of Revenue, *hu-pu* 戶部.[41] c. The Ministry of Rites, *li-pu* 禮部.[42] d. The Ministry of War, *ping-pu* 兵部.[43] e. The Ministry of Punishments, *hsing-pu* 刑部.[44] f. The Ministry of Works, *kung-pu* 工部.[45]

B. Service agencies of the imperial administration

1. The Office of the Grand Supervisors of Agriculture, *ta ssu-nung ssu* 大司農司.[46]

2. The Bureaus for Transmission Services, *t'ung-cheng yüan* 通政院. There were two, one in each capital. They operated the state postal system.[47]

3. The Directorate of Waterways, *tu-shui chien* 都水監.[48]

III. *Survellance and Judicial Agencies*

1. The Censorate, *yü-shih t'ai* 御史臺. Investigated official conduct and the performance of government; had the power of impeachment.[49]

2. The High Court for Mongols, *ta tsung-cheng fu* 大宗正府.[50]

3. The Court of Justice for Uighurs, *tu-hu fu* 都護府.[51]

IV. *The Military Establishment*

1. The Bureau of Military Affairs, *shu-mi yüan* 樞密院.[52]

---

[38] YS 88:2225.

[39] YS 85:2120–2121; Ratchnevsky, *Un code*, I, pp. 117–118, 122–124.

[40] YS 85:2125–2126; Ratchnevsky, *Un code*, I, pp. 126–127.

[41] YS 85:2126; Ratchenvsky, *Un code*, I, pp. 127–128.

[42] YS 85:2136; Ratchnevsky, *Un code*, I, p. 128.

[43] YS 85:2140; Ratchnevsky, *Un code*, I, pp. 130 ff.

[44] YS 85:2142; Ratchnevsky, *Un code*, I, pp. 131 ff.

[45] YS 85:2143; Ratchnevsky, *Un code*, I, pp. 132 ff.

[46] YS 87:2188; Ratchnevsky, *Un code*, I, pp. 189–191.

[47] YS 88:2230; Peter Olbricht, *Das Postwesen in China unter der Mongolenherrschaft im 13. und 14. Jahrhundert* (Wiesbaden, 1954), p. 44 ff.

[48] YS 90:2295; Ratchnevsky, *Un code*, I, pp. 267–268.

[49] YS 86:2177; Ratchnevsky, *Un code*, I, pp. 153–161.

[50] YS 87:2187; Ratchnevsky, *Un code*, I, pp. 52–56.

[51] YS 89:2273.

[52] YS 86:2155; Ratchnevsky, *Un code*, I, pp. 140–141.

2. The Chief Military Commission, *ta tu-tu fu* 大都督府. Supervised four guards units made up mostly of Kipchaks.[53]

3. The Armaments Court, *wu-pei ssu* 武備寺. Manufactured and stored weapons.[54]

V. *Agencies for the Administration of Fiefs, Fief-like Territories, and Other Special Populations*

A. The Heir Apparent's Establishment

1. The Bureau for the Heir-apparent's Household, *ch'u-cheng yüan* 儲政院.[55]

2. The Left Metropolitan Martial Guards, *tso tu wei-wei shih-ssu* 左都威衛使司.[56]

3. The Right Metropolitan Martial Guards, *yu tu wei-wei shih-ssu* 右都威衛使司.[57]

4. The General Commandery of the Guards-in-Waiting, *wei hou-chih tu-chih-hui shih-ssu* 衛候直都指揮使司.[58]

5. The Office of Provisions for the Heir-apparent, *nei-tsai ssu* 內宰司.[59]

6. The Directorate-General for the Management of Artisan-serfs[60] and Civil Artisans in the Original Appanages,[61] Ta-tu, and Other Circuits,

---

[53] YS 86:2175.

[54] YS 90:2284; Ratchnevsky, "Über den mongolischen Kult," p. 431 n. 76.

[55] YS 89:2243.

[56] YS 89:2248.

[57] YS 89:2249.

[58] YS 89:2250.

[59] YS 89:2250.

[60] It is difficult to find satisfactory translations for the term *ch'ieh-lien-k'ou* 怯憐(怜) 口, M. *ger-ün köbegüd*; in an early thirteenth-century Mongolian environment, it meant "domestic slave," a meaning which it undoubtedly continued to have in Mongolia for the next century (see *Yüan-ch'ao pi-shih* 元朝秘史, ed. B. I. Pankratov, *Iuan'-chao bi-shi* (Moscow, 1962), par. 232, p. 459, where *ger-ün kö'üd* is defined as *chia-jen* 家人); in Yüan times in China, however, the term developed a quite different meaning: displaced and other declassé persons who had been rounded up and forced to work at various artisan tasks. My translation is based on this meaning. See YS 89:2254: "In 1264, it was ordered that displaced persons, freed slaves, Buddhist and Taoist monks who had returned to the lay condition, and other kinds of households, be assembled together to practice various sorts of arts and crafts. There was established a directorate-general for the management of *ch'ieh-lien-k'ou* to supervise their manufactures." On the identity of *ch'ieh-lien-k'ou* and *ger-ün köbegüd* see Francis W. Cleaves, "The Sino-Mongolian Inscription of 1335," *Harvard Journal of Asiatic Studies*, 13 (1950), pp. 51–52 n. 170.

[61] The original appanages were the appanages of the descendants of the fourteen tribal cheftains who had helped Chinggis Khan in the conquest years. The tribes were the Barulas, the Uriyangkhan, the Besüd, the Uriyangkhadai, the Arulad, the Jalayir, the Üüshin (Hüüshin), the Süldüs, the Urughud, the Mangghud, the Khonggirad, the Ikires,

kuan-ling pen t'ou-hsia ta-tu teng-lu ch'ieh-lien-k'ou min-chiang tsung-kuan-fu 管領本投下大都等路怯憐口民匠總管府.[62]

7. The Directorate-General for the Management of Artisan-serfs and All Classes of Civil Artisans, *kuan-ling ch'ieh-lien-k'ou chu-se min-chiang tu tsung-kuan-fu* 管領怯怜口諸色民匠都總管府.[63]

8. The Directorate-General for Civil Administration in Pien-liang and Other Circuits, *pien-liang teng-lu kuan-min tsung-kuan-fu* 汴梁等路管民總管府.[64]

9. The General Commission for the Myriarchy of the Heir-apparent's Retinue, *chao-kung wan-hu tu tsung-shih-ssu* 昭功萬戶都總使司.[65]

B. The Empress' Establishment

1. The Bureau for Services to the Empress' Palace, *chung-cheng yüan* 中政院.[66]

2. Directorate-General for the Management of Artisan-serfs and Civil Artisans in the Various Circuits, *kuan-ling chu-lu ch'ieh-lien-k'ou min-chiang tu tsung-kuan-fu* 管領諸路怯憐口民匠都總管府.[67]

3. Directorate-General for Revenue in Chiang-huai and Other Places, *chiang-huai teng-ch'u ts'ai-fu tu tsung-kuan-fu* 江淮等處財賦都總管府.[68]

C. The Establishments of the Dowager Empresses, the Ordos. It was the Mongolian rulers' custom to leave their personal pastures and camping grounds (M. *ordo*) to their widows as estates. The subjects residing on them were included.

1. The Council for the Territories of the Four Ordos of Chinggis Khan, *nei-shih fu* 內史府. Five other agencies shared in the administration of these territories, all of the sort mentioned in V.A.6 above.[69]

2. The Court for Khubilai's Ordos, *ch'ang-hsin ssu* 長信寺.[70]

3. The Court for Wu-tsung's Ordo, *ch'ang-ch'iu ssu* 長秋寺.[71]

4. The Court for Jen-tsung's Ordo, *ch'eng-hui ssu* 承徽寺.[72]

---

the Önggüd, and the Uighur. See Murakami Masatsugu 村上正二, "Genchō ni okeru tōka no igi 元朝に於ける投下の意義," *Mōkogakuhō* 蒙古学報, 1 (1940), p. 183.

[62] YS 89:2257.

[63] YS 89:2252.

[64] YS 89:2259.

[65] YS 89:2262.

[66] YS 88:2230.

[67] YS 89:2258.

[68] YS 89:2260.

[69] YS 89:2266–2667, 2270, 2269, 2267, 2257, 2268.

[70] YS 90:2289; Yanai Watari 箭内亙, *Yüan-ch'ao ch'ieh-hsüeh chi o-erh-to k'ao* 元朝怯薛及斡耳朵考, Ch'en Chieh 陳捷 and Ch'en Ch'ing-ch'üan 陳清泉, trs. (Taipei, 1963), pp. 72–78, 117–118.

[71] YS 90:2290; Yanai, *Ibid.*, pp. 78–79, 90.

[72] YS 90:2290; Yanai, *Ibid.*, pp. 79–80.

5. The Court for Ying-tsung's Ordo, *ch'ang-ning ssu* 長寧寺.[73]
6. The Court for Ch'eng-tsung's Ordo, *ch'ang-ch'ing ssu* 長慶寺.[74]
7. The Court for Ming-tsung's Ordo, *ning-hui ssu* 寧徽寺.[75]

D. Bureaus for the Administration of Other Fiefs and Special Populations

1. The Directorate-General for the Hunters, Falconers, and Artisans of Various Classes in the Several Circuits, *sui-lu ta-pu ying-fang chu-se min-chiang tsung-kuan-fu* 隨路打捕鷹房諸色民匠總管府.[76]

2. The Directorate for Mongolian Pastures, *ching-cheng chien* 經正監. Managed the assignment of grasslands among fief-holders in Mongolia and resolved legal conflicts which arose over pasture rights.[77]

3. Directorate-General for Various Categories of Artisans in the Several Circuits, *sui-lu chu-se jen-chiang tu tsung-kuan-fu* 隨路諸色人匠都總管府.[78]

4. The Directorate-General of the Mews, *jen-yü tu tsung-kuan-fu* 仁虞都總管府.[79]

5. Princely administrations, *wang-fu* 王府 (also called the Preceptors to the Princes, *chu-wang fu* 諸王傅). There were forty-five of these established by and for princes with large fiefs to help them govern. The largest of them was the Advisorate to the Prince of Chou, *chou-wang ch'ang-shih-fu* 周王常侍府, in Yün-nan.[80]

6. The Bureau of Tibetan and Buddhist Affairs, *hsüan-cheng yüan* 宣政院.[81]

7. The Office for Christian Clergy, *ch'ung-fu ssu* 崇福司.[82]

In this system, the Central Secretariat (II.A.1) was the key bureau, integrating the three levels of local government into which the country-side was divided: The Circuits (*lu* 路, M. *chölge*) which were the seats of both military units (the Myriarchies, *wan-hu fu* 萬戶府) keeping order, and civil governments (the Directorates-General, *tsung-kuan-fu* 總管府) performing judicial, revenue, educational and welfare functions;[83] the

[73] YS 90:2291; Yanai, *Ibid.*, p. 91.
[74] YS 90:2291; Yanai, *Ibid.*, p. 78.
[75] YS 90:2291.
[76] YS 89:2271.
[77] YS 90:2295.
[78] YS 89:2254.
[79] YS 34:768, 44:921–922.
[80] YS 89:2272–2273; *Hsin Yüan shih*, 60:22b.
[81] YS 87:2193; F. W. Cleaves, "The Sino-Mongolian Inscription of 1346," *Harvard Journal of Asiatic Studies*, 15:1–2 (1952), p. 41, n. 39.
[82] YS 89:2273.
[83] YS 98:2507–2508; 91:2316 ff, trans. P. Ratchnevsky, *Un code*, I, pp. 34–36 n. 6.

Prefectures of various sorts (*fu* 府, *chou* 州, *chün* 軍);[84] and, finally, the Districts (*hsien* 縣).[85] These units integrated by the Central Secretariat formed the Metropolitan Province (Fu-li 腹裏), an area comprising modern Hopeh, Shantung, Shansi, and the eastern part of the Inner Mongolian Autonomous Region.[86] In the same manner, eleven other provinces were created throughout the empire by the establishment of replica central secretariats (*hsing chung-shu-sheng* 行中書省, usually called "branch" central secretariats), each of which tied together its own subordinate Circuits, Prefectures, and Districts.[87] An additional administrative unit of large size, the Region (*tao* 道), was created by instituting Pacification Offices (*hsüan-wei ssu* 宣慰司)[88] at key places within the provinces, coordinating many civil and some military activities between the Secretariat and the District.[89] The Regions were also the territories of the Regional Investigation Offices (*su-cheng lien-fang ssu* 肅正廉訪司), field bureaus of the Censorate, which watched over the conduct of government.[90]

II. THE STRUCTURES AND FUNCTIONS OF THE BUREAUS

It seems reasonable to begin the exploration of the imperial government with the organs of general administration (II), since they were the most broadly conceived and had the clearest mandates to deal with the empire at large. The method I have chosen is to examine the subordinate bureaus of each and to note the division of functions and the geographical extent of its authority. Such information—it is often the only

[84] YS 91:2317–2318.

[85] YS 91:2318.

[86] For the political geography of Yüan China, see Albert Hermann, *An Historical Atlas of China* (revised edition, Chicago, 1966), p. 41.

[87] These were: the Ho-nan-Chiang-pei 河南江北 Secretariat (modern Honan, Hupeh, Kiangsu, Anhwei); the Chiang-che 江浙 Secretariat (modern Chekiang and Fukien); the Chiang-hsi 江西 Secretariat (modern Kiangsi and eastern Kwangtung); the Hu-kuang 湖廣 Secretariat (modern Hunan, Kwangsi, and parts of Kwangtung and Kweichow); the Shan-hsi 陝西 Secretariat (modern Shensi); the Ssu-ch'uan 四川 Secretariat (modern Szechwan); the Liao-yang 遼陽 Secretariat (modern Liao-ning and Chi-lin); the Kan-su 甘肅 Secretariat (modern Kansu); the Ling-pei 嶺北 Secretariat, which was not broken into administrative units (modern Mongolian People's Republic); the Yün-nan 雲南 Secretariat (modern Yunnan); and the Cheng-tung 征東 Secretariat (modern Korea). The territories comprising these provinces were not settled until after 1287. See YS 91:2305–2308.

[88] The term is a collective one; there were eight different types of pacification offices used in different parts of the empire, each with its characteristic name. See YS 91:2308–2310.

[89] YS 91:2308.

[90] YS 86:2180–2182; Ratchnevsky, *Un code*, I, pp. 169–170, 179.

information we possess—gives a much better notion of the effective administrative authority of an agency than can fanciful imperial constitutions. As both an example of the method and a sample of a bureau in a modern central government with which Yüan bureaus can be compared, the Federal Trade Commission of the United States government in 1969 may serve; it had thirteen subordinate bureaus, seven of which were concerned with in-house management (General Counsel, Hearing Examiners, Program Review, Administration, Comptroller, and so forth), while six were operating bureaus designed to fulfill the Commission's mission (Deceptive Practices, Economics, Industry Guidance, Restraint of Trade, Field Operations, and Textiles and Furs). The Field Operations Bureau coordinated the activities of the Commission's eleven field offices, located in key cities in every section of the country; however, the Bureau of Textiles and Furs—clearly the busiest of the bureaus—maintained its own field stations in twenty cities. Such information, I would suggest, tells us, when properly pursued, as much about this agency's character and its effective centralizing tendencies as does its formal charge "to prevent the free enterprise system from being stifled or fettered by monopoly or corrupted by unfair or deceptive trade practices."[91]

In Yüan China, the Central Secretariat (II.A.1) was the paramount organ in the imperial government and, together with the Bureau of Military Affairs (IV.1) and the Censorate (III.1), was the most important in implementing the emperor's will. Virtually every page of the compilation of administrative acts, the Yüan tien-chang 元典章, (Compendium of Statutes and Sub-Statutes of the Yüan)[92] contains decisions which have in some fashion gone through its hands and bear its name. It had been granted extensive powers by the emperors: all memorials to the throne had to come through it, unless the memorialist was in one of the privileged bureaus entitled to address the emperor directly (the Bureau of Military Affairs [IV.1], the Censorate [III.1], the Bureau for the Heir-apparent's Household [V.A.1], and the Bureau of Tibetan and Buddhist Affairs [V.D.6]);[93] it could make recommendations for official appoint-

---

[91] From United States Government Organization Manual, 1969–70 (Office of the Federal Register, National Archives and Records, General Services Administration, Washington, D.C., 1969), pp. 440–445, 617.

[92] Ta-Yüan sheng-cheng kuo-ch'ao tien-chang 大元聖政國朝典章 (Shen Chia-pen 沈家本 ed., Taipei, 1967, 2 vols.), hereafter Yüan tien-chang.

[93] Yüan tien-chang, 2:2a; Yang Shu-fan 楊樹藩, "Yüan-tai-ti Chung-shu-sheng 元代的中書省," Yu-shih hsüeh-chih 幼獅學誌, 6:2 (1967), p. 8. The heir-apparent's bureau is called the hui-cheng yüan 徽政院 in this passage.

ments to virtually all positions lower in rank than its own;[94] it could resolve legal cases involving capital crimes, and had a staff of judges (*tuan-shih kuan* 斷事官, M. *jarghuchi*) to help in this work;[95] it drafted administrative regulations to implement edicts, which it passed on to its sister central secretariats in other provinces; and it rendered decisions on hundreds of administrative problems submitted to it by other organs. However, it was, with its relatively small staff of fourteen councillors of various ranks, mainly an executive agency, not an administrative one. Its two subordinate offices, the Office of the Left, *tso ssu* 左司, and the Office of the Right, *yu-ssu* 右司, each elaborately subdivided, appear to have been primarily for record-keeping, since their complements of officers (six in each) and clerks (fifty-three in the Office of the Left and twelve in the Office of the Right) would hardly have allowed for many other activities.[96]

What of the Central Secretariat's several ministries (II.A.1.a-e) which were supposed to help it to govern the empire? The Ministry of Revenue (II.A.1.b), whose charge I have summarized above, was indeed deeply involved in administration. Its twenty-one subordinate bureaus divide naturally into four areas: (1) state treasuries; (2) the currency; (3) taxes and their transport; and (4) industrial activities controlled by the government. In the first group were several treasuries, the officers of which had no other responsibilities than the obvious ones of guarding the contents and recording receipts and disbursements.[97] The desire to establish an empire-wide paper currency, on the other hand—as the Yüan emperors clearly desired to do by 1260—[98]required the development of a considerable administrative network, and the Ministry of Revenue had six agencies dealing with currency, the highest-ranking and most important of which was the Superintendency for Paper Currency in the Several Circuits;[99] but its area of concern seems to have been limited to North China, for identically or similarly named superintendencies were established in other parts of the empire—the southeast, west China,

---

[94] There were exceptions: the Bureau of Military Affairs (IV.1), the Censorate (III.1), the Bureau of Tibetan and Buddhist Affairs (V.D.6), and the Bureau for Imperial Household Provisions (I.A.1) could select their own officials, as could some of the vassal lords. YS 22:486; Ratchnevsky, *Un code*, I, p. 145 n. 1; Yang Shu-fan (see n. 93), pp. 8–9.

[95] YS 85:2124.

[96] YS 85:2123; Ratchnevsky, *Un code*, I, pp. 122–125. The Office of the Left was divided into six departments, with thirty-one sections spread among them; the Office of the Right had four departments, with sixteen sections spread among them.

[97] YS 85:2127–2128.

[98] Herbert F. Schurmann, *Economic Structure of the Yüan Dynasty* (Cambridge, Mass., 1956), p. 133 ff.

[99] *Chu-lu pao-ch'ao tu t'i-chü-ssu* 諸路寶鈔都提舉司, YS 85:2128.

Turkestan, and Mongolia—none of which is included among the agencies of the Ministry of Revenue.[100] Under the Ministry of Revenue, the printing of paper currency was done by a special office, the Paper Currency Printing Treasury,[101] but it cannot be established that it was the exclusive printer of currency and that the other superintendencies of paper currency did not have that right; at certain exceptional times, on the other hand, during the Mongol invasion of south China in 1276, and at the very end of the dynasty, paper currency was definitely printed elsewhere.[102] The burning of worn currency was managed, according to our sources, by two Currency Disposal Treasuries,[103] but they served only the capital, since this function was otherwise managed by the regional investigation offices of the Censorates (*su-cheng lien-fang ssu*— see below)[104] or by the officials of the "branch" Central Secretariats.[105] Currency reached the public through exchange banks, at least 156 of which are known to have been established in all parts of the country; only six of these—those in the city of Ta-tu itself—are listed as part of the structure of the Ministry of Revenue.[106]

In view of its deep interest in the collection of taxes, the Ministry of Revenue had very few subordinate bureaus concerned with tax management. The Ta-tu Commodity Tax Collection Superintendency[107] was exactly as area-specific as its name suggests: it managed a number of markets in Ta-tu city, and did not even supervise all commodity or sales tax collections in the Metropolitan Province. The same was true of the Ta-tu Alcohol Tax Superintendency.[108] Similarly, no network of agencies regulated the empire's supposedly important state-controlled industries for the empire's wealth; the Ministry of Revenue's bureaus involved

[100] See Maeda Naonori 前田直典, "Gendai ni okeru shō no hakkō seido to sono ryūtsū jōtai 元代に於ける鈔の発行制度とその流通状態," in his *Genchōshi no kenkyū* 元朝史の研究 (Tokyo, 1973), pp. 50–55. The exact number of these is difficult to decide; Maeda feels that there were four outside of the Metropolitan Province, but there may have been more.

[101] YS 85:2129, *yin-tsao pao-ch'ao k'u* 印造寶鈔庫.

[102] YS 9:183; Maeda, "Shō no hakkō seido," pp. 49–55.

[103] YS 85:2129, *shao-ch'ao k'u* 燒鈔庫.

[104] Ratchnevsky, *Un code*, I, pp. 169–170.

[105] YS 93:2370; Schurmann, *Economic Structure*, p. 140.

[106] Maeda, "Shō no hakkō seido," pp. 59–66; YS 85:2129; Ratchnevsky, *Un code*, I, p. 254, n. 1. Banks were called *p'ing-chun k'u* 平準庫 or *hsing-yung k'u* 行用庫.

[107] *Ta-tu hsüan-k'o t'i-chü-ssu* 大都宣課提舉司, YS 85:2129. The term "commodity tax" translates *k'o-(ch'eng)* 課 (程), which included taxes on products under some sort of government control, as well as sales taxes, *shang-shui* 商税. See *Yüan tien-chang*, 22:1a; Schurmann, *Economic Structure*, p. 219.

[108] *Ta-tu chiu-k'o t'i-chü-ssu* 大都酒課提舉司, YS 85:2130; Schurmann, *Economic structure*, p. 210.

with them were insignificant and restricted in their activities to the Metropolitan Province: one gold-mining and iron smelting superintendency[109] and two salt distribution commissions;[110] a third salt commission, the Salt Distribution Commission for Ho-tung, Shan-hsi and Other Places,[111] might appear from its name to have been located partly outside of the Metropolitan Province, but, by 1332 at least, its subordinate salt works were all in the area of modern Shansi province, and were thus in the Metropolitan Province. The only hint of a centralized function in government-regulated industry is the Commodity Voucher Printing Office,[112] which printed the forms which were claims for legal loads of state-controlled commodities like salt, tea, alum, and iron, for both the Metropolitan and the other provinces.

Two enormous bureaus subordinate to the Ministry of Revenue ran the vital business of transporting tax grain to the capital and the Metropolitan Province and storing it there,[113] but only one of these, the General Grain Transport Commission,[114] had concerns outside of the Metropolitan Province: it supervised some grain convoys in northern Ho-nan-Chiang-pei 河南江北 Province.[115]

The Ministry of Works (II.A.1.f) was even larger than the Ministry of Revenue, with fifty-two subordinate offices, which in turn had forty-four others subordinate to them; it was charged with regulating all manner of construction and manufacturing in the empire, the repair of fortifications, the regulation of artisans, and the evaluation of artisan officers in government ateliers.[116] An examination of its subordinate agencies reveals a different picture, however. Only one of them, the Metropolitan Wall Repair Superintendency,[117] could be said to be involved in public works, as that term is generally understood, and its concerns were restricted to the imperial capital at Ta-tu; all of the others managed government workshops which produced articles in metals, wood, leather, hair, fine textiles, and ceramics—in other words, the Ministry of Works differed little from the Bureau for Imperial Manufactures (I.A.2), the

---

[109] YS 85:2134.

[110] YS 85:2134, trans. Ratchnevsky, *Un code*, I, p. 258 ff.; and YS 85:2135, trans. Ratchnevsky, *Un code*, I, pp. 260–261.

[111] YS 85:2135, trans. Ratchnevsky, *Un code*, I, p. 261, *ho-tung shan-hsi teng-ch'u chuan-yün yen shih-ssu* 河東陝西等處轉運鹽使司.

[112] YS 85:2130, *yin-tsao yen ch'a teng yin chü* 印造鹽茶等引局.

[113] YS 85:2130, trans. Ratchnevsky, *Un code*, I, p. 270 ff; YS 85:2132, trans. Ratchnevsky, *Ibid.*, p. 273.

[114] *Tu ts'ao-yün shih-ssu* 都漕運使司.

[115] YS 85:2132.

[116] YS 85:2143; Ratchnevsky, *Un code*, I, p. 132 ff.

[117] YS 85:2148, *t'i-chü tu-ch'eng so* 提舉都城所.

workshops of which made similar things for the emperor's personal use.[118] Furthermore, all but three of the subordinate bureaus can with some certainty be identified as being located in, and having concerns restricted to, the imperial capitals or the Metropolitan Province. One of the exceptions was the Weaving and Dyeing Office of Ta-ning Circuit[119] located in Liao-yang 遼陽 Province; two others, both called the Bish-balikh Office,[120] may have been located at or controlled artisan activities in the city of Bishbalikh in Turkestan.[121] For an executive bureau for the empire, the Ministry of Works seems not to have been very significant: while it can occasionally be found making decisions on affairs outside of the Metropolitan Province,[122] most of its activities were local, and the regulations governing its work were trivial.[123]

The other ministries subject to the Central Secretariat present some-what different profiles. One, the Ministry of Rites (II.A.1.c), had very restricted charges relating to ritual matters at the imperial court, which did not generally involve it in empire-wide administration,[124] although one of its bureaus, the Seal Manufacturing Office,[125] was indeed an example of the centralization of an imperial administrative function, for it produced all official seals used by Yüan officers.[126]

Another, the Ministry of Punishments, was active in the drafting of the criminal law, but, like many high judicial bodies, including others in the Yüan government (III.2,3), its work was carried on in a cloistered atmosphere, and did not require numerous subordinate bureaus: cases presented to it came through the normal district-prefecture-circuit-secretariat route.[127] A third, the Ministry of War (II.A.1.d), was an empty relic, a descendant of an ancient bureau which had lost its impor-tance in Sung times; in the Yüan period, until 1320, its only significant

---

[118] YS 85:2144–2152.

[119] YS 85:2151, *ta-ning lu chih-jan chü* 大寧路織染局.

[120] Ys 85:2149, 2151, *pieh-shih-pa-li chü* 別失八里局.

[121] It is not usually necessary to guess about the geographical extent of the authority of most subordinate agencies since the area is often mentioned in the agency's name.

[122] *Yüan tien-chang*, 58:15a.

[123] *Yüan tien-chang*, ch 58–60; those relating to bridge-, road-, and dike-building are of some importance, *Yüan tien-chang*, 58:1a–4a.

[124] YS 85:2136; Ratchnevsky, *Un code*, I, pp. 128–129.

[125] *Chu-yin chü* 鑄印局, YS 85:2140.

[126] Yüan dynasty official seals are invariably inscribed "manufactured by the Ministry of Rites of the Central Secretariat." See David M. Farquhar, "The Official Seals and Ciphers of the Yüan Period," *Monumenta Serica*, 25 (1966), pp. 362–393.

[127] YS 85:2142–2143; Ratchnevsky, *Un code*, I, p. 131 ff; *Yüan tien-chang*, ch. 41–57. The ministry had only two small subordinate offices, a Prison, *ssu-yü ssu* 司獄司, and a case review office, *ssu-chi so* 司籍所, both located in the capital. YS 85:2143.

duty was the control of the postal station managers in China proper, a responsibility traditionally ascribed to the military establishment, but thereafter even that passed to the Bureau for Transmission Services (II.B.2);[128] otherwise, it had nothing to do with military matters, which had long been taken over by the Bureau of Military Affairs (IV.1). Of its five subordinate bureaus, one handled the transport of grain to the two capitals, while four others administered groups of artisans, hunters, and falconers on territories which once belonged to princes.[129]

The Ministry of Personnel (II.A.1.a) had no subordinate bureaus at all, not because it was unimportant, but because of the restricted character of its charges, which related to the nomination, appointment, transfer, evaluation, and promotion of nearly all civil officials occupying the empire's 26,690 positions, and the recording of their titles; the sub-officials as well were under its regulation.[130] The right to create and place officials and dispense titles and privileges has always been one of the most important powers of Chinese emperors, and the Yüan rulers cherished it; although they delegated the authority to appoint all but the highest officers, it was kept within the top levels of the imperial government.[131] Indeed, there is good evidence that imperial control over personnel appointments was even more extensive in Yüan times than before; there are at any rate complaints by a Yüan scholar that those in local government were unable to select subordinates as officials in earlier times had.[132]

Just as replicas of the Central Secretariat were established throughout the empire, so replicas of some of the ministries were also created for special purposes. A "branch" Ministry of Revenue (hsing hu-pu 行户部) was created in 1263 in Shan-hsi 陝西 to take charge of that area;[133] another was established at Ta-ming 大名 in the Metropolitan Province to manufacture paper currency in preparation for the invasion of Chiang-nan in 1276.[134] Several "branch" Ministries of Works were created: one to build

---

[128] YS 88:2230; Ratchnevsky, *Un code*, I, p. 277; Olbricht, *Postwesen*, pp. 46–47.

[129] YS 85:2140; Ratchnevsky, *Un code*, I, p. 130 ff; YS 85:2141–2142.

[130] YS 85:2125–2126; Ratchnevsky, *Un code*, I, pp. 126–127. The number of officials, from the year 1317, is recorded in *Yüan tien-chang*, 7:38a.

[131] See n. 94 above.

[132] Wu Lai 吳萊 (1297–1340), *Wu Yüan-ying chi* 吳淵穎集 (*Ssu-pu ts'ung-k'an* reprint of 1352 ed.), 12:9b–10a. On this man, see Lien-sheng Yang, "Ming local administration," in Charles O. Hucker, ed., *Chinese Government in Ming Times* (New York, 1969), p. 10; and the essay in this volume by J. D. Langlois.

[133] YS 5:90.

[134] YS 9:183, 157:3697.

the capital at Ta-tu,[135] and another in 1307 by the Emperor Khaishan (Külüg, Wu-tsung) to build a new capital, Chung-tu 中都, in the Mongolian steppe (it was never completed).[136] The replication of bureaus in this fashion, a common feature of Yüan government, suggests that the administrative responsibilities of the parent bureau were both routine and local. Unlike the "branch" Central Secretariats, however, the "branch" Ministries never became permanent fixtures in the governmental landscape.

The Office of the Grand Supervisors of Agriculture (II.B.1) was a high-ranking bureau charged with the oversight of agriculture, sericulture, and water resources; it had its origins in an Office for the Stimulation of Agriculture, ch'üan-nung ssu 勸農司, which had been created already in 1261 to help restore the ruined condition of agriculture in North China.[137] With its reorganization in 1270 as the Office of the Supervisors of Agriculture (ssu-nung ssu), a genuinely centralized bureaucratic structure was created to carry out its mission. Adopting the Regions (tao) of the censorial system as its chief administrative units, subordinate Mobile Offices for the Stimulation of Agriculture (hsün-hsing ch'üan-nung ssu 巡行勸農司) were established in each to survey the local units of the system;[138] the latter were the "communes," she 社, units of fifty families headed by a commune chief, she-chang 社長, formed out of natural villages, and intended to improve agricultural techniques, raise production, develop irrigation, organize charitable functions for the member families, and recommend lazy farmers to the local magistrate for discipline.[139] But by 1290, the Mobile Offices had been abolished and their duties transferred to the already overworked Regional Surveillance Offices (t'i-hsing an-ch'a ssu 提刑 案察司) of the Censorate;[140] the bureaucratic link between local com-

---

[135] YS 90:2277; it was abolished in 1282. This was probably the same "branch" Ministry of Works which, in 1274, was given charge of runaway slaves whose masters could not be found; YS 8:158.

[136] YS 22:484; Dardess, Conquerors and Confucians, p. 24.

[137] YS 93:2354; Schurmann, Economic structure, p. 50; Ratchnevsky, Un code, I, p. 188.

[138] Ta-Yüan kuan-chih tsa-chi 大元官制雜記 (Kuang-wen Shu-chü ed. under title Shih-liao ssu-pien 史料四編, Taipei, 1972), pp. 61–64; Schurmann, Economic Structure, pp. 47–48.

[139] YS 93:2354–2355; Schurmann, Economic Structure, pp. 46–53. There is a substantial modern literature on the she; see especially Yang Ne 楊訥, "Yüan-tai nung-ts'un she-chih yen-chiu 元代農村社制研究," in Ts'un-ts'ui hsüeh-she 存萃學社, ed., Yüan-tai she-hui ching-chi shih lun-chi 元代社會經濟史論集 (Hong Kong, 1975), pp. 1–18.

[140] These were later called Regional Investigation Offices, su-cheng lien-fang ssu. The Censorate is discussed below.

munes and the Grand Supervisors of Agriculture in Ta-tu was thus effectively severed.[141]

That the Office of the Grand Supervisors of Agriculture was a distincly local bureau, concerned with the Metropolitan Province, or, at best, North China, is shown by the establishment in 1293 of a replica Office of the Grand Supervisors of Agriculture in Yang-chou to deal with South China after its conquest. The reason in this case was only marginally to revive agriculture, since the south had suffered little of the damage experienced by the north; instead, it was to control the powerful landlords who had been concealing their rent incomes and illegally occupying government land. The region and commune units were also introduced in South China, but there is some doubt as to whether the communes were ever really operative. In any case, the "Branch" Office and its apparatus were abolished three years later in 1295, not because the government wished to restore administrative control to the parent office in the capital, but because it was determined that "cases of [landlord] concealment were not numerous, and the [office] had become irrelevant."[142]

A similar bureau, the Directorate of Waterways (II.B.3), was indeed occupied with water conservancy as its description in the *Yüan History* tells us,[143] and its activities are reported to an unusual degree in that source.[144] But examination shows that its work was restricted to the control of the Yellow River, which means that its activity lay mainly in the Metropolitan Province. Dike work in other provinces (and even in the Metropolitan Province, where conditions were exceptional) was performed by replica Directorates of Waterways (*hsing tu-shui chien* 行都水監).[145] In 1308, however, one such directorate in Chiang-che 江浙 Province was abolished at the request of the Secretariat there and the conservancy responsibilities were turned over to local officials at the circuit, prefecture, and distict levels.[146] At various times between 1301 and the end of the dynasty there was established in Chiang-che Province a separate, related bureau, the Commission for Waterways and Land Management, *tu-shui yung-t'ien shih-ssu* 都水庸田使司, to deal with the dredging of the Sung and Wu Rivers and like matters, but it was at least some of the time under the control of the Chiang-che Central Secretariat,

---

[141] *Ta-Yüan kuan-chih tsa-chi*, pp. 62–64; Schurmann, *Economic Structure*, p. 54. The date given in YS 93:2356 is 1292.

[142] *Ta-Yüan kuan-chih tsa-chi*, pp. 59–61.

[143] YS 90:2295; Ratchnevsky, *Un code*, I, p. 267 n. 2.

[144] See, for example, YS 14:297, 17:362, 64:1588 and *passim*.

[145] YS 21:459, 29:655, 140:3368.

[146] YS 22:494.

and hence not a part of the imperial government, although it was of course established by imperial edict. It seems to have been somewhat ineffectual, and, when abolished, its duties were given back to the units of local government, in particular to the Sung-chiang 松江 Superior Prefecture.[147]

The two Bureaus for Transmission Services (II.B.2), one in Ta-tu and the other in Shang-tu, directed the movement of official papers, goods and baggage, and supplied those on official business with transport, food, and lodgings. These functions were obviously of great importance in holding together the empire, and the Mongols' understanding of this is indicated by their early concern for the system, which dates back to the times of Chinggis and Ögödei, the extensive regulations they designed for its management, and their efforts to keep control of it near the center;[148] the Central Secretariat itself had two sections which dealt with postal matters.[149] In 1292, after the conquest of South China, a replica Chiang-nan Bureau for Transmission Service (*chiang-nan hsing t'ung-cheng yüan* 江南行通政院) was established to manage post stations there, but was abolished soon thereafter in 1303.[150] Despite this attempt at centralized direction, the postal system shows some of the defects of the organs previously discussed: it lacked effective intermediate-level overseers between the executive bureaus at the capitals and the post station officers (*chan-ch'ih* 站赤, M. *jamchi*) at the local level. It is true that the Mongols had early appointed Postal Relay Inspectors (*t'o-t'o-ho-sun* 脱脱禾孫, M. *todkhaghul*, *todkhosun), high-ranking independent officers charged with searching out fraudulent use of the system, but they appear to have been employed only in important cities;[151] the real middle-level supervisors were the local officials at the relatively high circuit level, the Directors-General (*tsung-kuan*) and their Mongol associates, the Agents (*ta-lu-hua-*

---

[147] *Ta-Yüan kuan-chih tsa-chi*, pp. 64–67; YS 29:657, 39:833, 92:2335.

[148] YS 101:2583–2594; *Yüan tien-chang*, ch. 36 and 37; *Chan-ch'ih* 站赤 (Taipei, 1972), 9 *chüan*, are the important sources. Secondary studies, besides Olbricht, *Das Postwesen*, are the still valuable article by Haneda Tōru 羽田亨, "Genchō ekiden zakkō 元朝駅傳雜考," in his *Haneda hakase shigaku rombunshū* 羽田博士史學論文集 (Kyoto, 1957), I, pp. 32–114; and Yüan Chi 袁冀, "Yüan-tai-ti chan-ch'ih 元代的站赤," in his *Yüan-shih yen-chiu lun-chi* 元史研究論集 (Taipei, 1974), pp. 236–265.

[149] Ratchnevsky, *Un code*, I, pp. 124–125; Olbricht, *Das Postwesen*, p. 44.

[150] YS 21:448, 88:2230. YS 24:538 says it was abolished in 1311.

[151] YS 91:2318; Olbricht, *Das Postwesen*, p. 82; Haneda, "Genchō ekiden," pp. 70–71. On the term *t'o-t'o-ho-sun* see A. Mostaert and F. W. Cleaves, "Trois documents mongols des Archives Secrètes Vaticanes," *Harvard Journal of Asiatic Studies*, 15:2 (1952), pp. 436–437. The term *jamchi*, "post station officers," includes those low-ranking managers of stations bearing the Chinese titles *i-ling* 驛令, "postal manager," and *t'i-ling* 提領, "director." Olbricht, *Das Postwesen*, p. 60.

ch'ih 達魯花赤, M. *darugha*, *darughachi*), the representatives of the
Mongol imperial power, found not only at the circuit, but at all levels of
government, wherever populations were directly administered and exploited. This was an effort to keep the postal system in responsible
hands.[152] Perhaps inevitably, and despite warnings, the post stations
were given over to the prefects and to the district magistrates, and the
higher authorities were unable to prevent abuse of the postal households
(*chan-hu* 站戶) who provided the services and provisions, or abuse of the
system by those using it. Attempts to remedy these faults may perhaps be
found in the numerous reorganizations which the post underwent,
sometimes being put under the Bureau for Transmission Services, sometimes under the Ministry of War (II.A.1.d), sometimes under both
(Mongolian post stations with the former, Chinese stations with the
latter).[153] Despite structural weakness and the strange dual bureaus, the
purpose of which remains obscure, the postal system remains one of the
few centralized governmental functions in the Yüan empire.

Other departments of the imperial government may be treated more
briefly, since their charges did not involve them in large-scale administration. The fourteen imperial advisory bodies described under I.B were
by their nature bound to the court, and their duties were generally
confined to the capitals at Ta-tu and Shang-tu. Only two of them, the
Imperial Academy of Medicine (I.B.8) and the Bureau for the Imperial
Cults (I.B.12), had subordinate offices concerned with areas outside
those cities. The former had a Superintendency of Medicine[154] to which
were attached seventeen Superintendencies of Official Physicians[155]
which supervised physician households in fourteen circuits and three
other territories in the performance of their obligations to the government, and took care of their legal cases; fifteen of these were located in
the Metropolitan Province, but two were in Liao-yang Province in the
Northeast.[156] One must conclude either that the Imperial Academy
of Medicine was intended to administer primarily the Metropolitan
Province's physicians, or that, for some reason, it was unconcerned with

---

[152]Haneda, "Genchō ekiden," pp. 59 ff. On the Agent, see Meng Ssu-ming 蒙思明,
Yüan-tai she-hui chieh-chi chih-tu 元代社會階級制度 (Peking, 1938, reprinted Hong Kong,
1967), pp. 39–40; Jagchid-sechen 札奇斯欽, "Shuo chiu *Yüan-shih*-chung-ti ta-lu-hua-
ch'ih 說舊元史中的達魯花赤," *Wen-shih-che hsüeh-pao* 文史哲學報, 13 (1964), pp. 293–
441; Igor de Rachewiltz, "Personnel and Personalities in North China in the Early
Mongol Period," *Journal of the Economic and Social History of the Orient*, 9 (1966),
pp. 134 ff.

[153]Haneda, "Genchō ekiden," pp. 63, 52 ff.

[154]*I-hsüeh t'i-chü-ssu* 醫學提舉司, YS 88:2222.

[155]*Kuan-i t'i-chü-ssu* 官醫提舉司.

[156]YS 88:2222.

physicians in the other provinces of China—which was not the case, for legislation was issued which affected them,[157] and Superintendencies of Official Physicians were found in Ho-nan-Chiang-pei, Chiang-che, Chiang-hsi, Hu-kuang, and Shan-hsi 陝西, although they were not part of the Imperial Academy of Medicine.[158] The Bureau for the Imperial Cults (I.B.12), on the other hand, is a rare example of a bureau which appears to have supervised a single function in all parts of the imperial realm; it was an umbrella for most of the state monasteries and temples, their landholdings, serfs, administrations, and endowment offices (*kuei-yün ssu* 規運司), which were found in Ho-nan-Chiang-pei, Chiang-che, Hu-kuang, and Ssu-ch'uan Provinces, as well as in the Metropolitan Province.[159]

Of the sixteen organs which met the physical needs of emperor, courts, and capitals (I.A), only three controlled areas or activities outside the Metropolitan Province. The enormous Bureau for Imperial Household Provisions (I.A.1) had twenty-eight subordinate offices, of which two were not in the Metropolitan Province: the Directorate-General for Agricultural Colonies and Hunting in Huai-tung and Huai-hsi,[160] which administered populations in Ho-nan-Chiang-pei Province; and the General Superintendency of Tea Groves in Ch'ang-chou, Hu-chou, and Other Places,[161] which managed 23,000 households in Chiang-che Province. The Bureau for Imperial Manufactures' (I.A.2) Directorate-General for Precious Metal and Jewel Artisans in the Several Circuits[162] had a sub-office, the Fu-liang Porcelain Office,[163] in Chiang-che Province; there was also a replica Directorate-General in Hang-chou in the same province, which was slightly lower in rank than the parent Directorate-General.[164] The Court of the Imperial Stud (I.A.3) did a good deal more than meet the emperor's personal need for horses and milk; it supplied horses for the imperial guards (under the Bureau of Military Affairs [IV.1,2]) and for the postal system. It had no subordinate bureaus, but it did obtain horses from areas outside the Metropolitan Province, mostly in the North: Korea, Shan-hsi, Kan-su,

---

[157] See *Yüan tien-chang*, 32:2a ff. Some of these orders affecting provinces in the South and elsewhere do not mention the Imperial Academy of Medicine.

[158] YS 91:2312.

[159] YS 87:2207, 2208–2213. Some state monasteries were administered by the Bureau of Tibetan and Buddhist Affairs (V.D. 6).

[160] *Huai-tung huai-hsi t'un-t'ien ta-pu tsung-kuan-fu* 淮東淮西屯田打捕總管府, YS 87:2204–2206. This office had sixten subordinate offices.

[161] *Ch'ang-Hu teng-ch'u ch'a-yüan tu t'i-chü-ssu* 常湖等處茶園都提舉司, YS 87:2206.

[162] *Chu-lu chin-yü jen-chiang tsung-kuan-fu* 諸路金玉人匠總管府, YS 88:2225.

[163] *Fu-liang tz'u chü* 浮梁磁局, YS 88:2227.

[164] YS 88:2228.

Yün-nan, and especially Ling-pei (Mongolia); there were fourteen such areas, nearly all of them fiefs of imperial princes, for whose subjects the providing of horses was a tax obligation.[165]

The agencies included under the "fief-like" rubric (V) are really quite various. The numerous bureaus belonging to the heir-apparent and the empress (V.A,B) should perhaps be considered simply other parts of the emperor's own government, especially the very extensive holdings of artisan-serfs under the Bureau for Services to the Empress' Palace (V.B.1), which produced goods and services for the government. However, in some cases at least, income from these holdings remained under the control of the heir-apparent's or empress' chief bureau.[166] That seems not to have been the case with true fiefs (V.C; V.D.5),[167] where the rights of the fief-holders began to be restricted by the time of Emperor Ögödei (T'ai-tsung, r. 1229–1241). Quite quickly, they became much like the nobility in native Chinese dynasties—recipients of annual grants from the emperor, and thus stipendiaries rather than rent-collecting feudal lords.[168] Still, they retained considerable authority, for they were allowed to nominate the officials of their own administrations (if they had them) and the officials in the local governments in which their fiefs lay. These powers, too, were nibbled away gradually over the years,[169] as were the nobles' subjects, who either absconded or were put under the authority of local governments.[170]

[165] YS 100:2555–2558. The Court also obtained horses by purchase and outright requisition. Jagchid-sechen and C. R. Bawden, "Some Notes on the Horse-Policy of the Yüan Dynasty," *Central Asiatic Journal*, 10:3–4 (1965), pp. 254–263.

[166] See, for example, YS 94:2394, trans. Schurmann, *Ecomomic Structure*, p. 199, where certain tea districts in Chiang-hsi 江西 were declared in 1308 to be an appanage of the empress, the taxes from which were to go directly to the *hui-cheng yüan* 徽政院, a bureau at that time controlled by the empress, although at other times it was controlled by the heir apparent. The histories of these two establishments are the most complicated and confusing in the Yüan government.

[167] I am here using the term "fief" to cover a large number of different Chinese and Mongolian terms: *fen-ti* 分地, land grants; *ying-p'an* 營盤, M. *nuntugh*, territories; *shih-i* 食邑 or *t'ang-mu i* 湯沐邑, fiefs (usually to females); *kuo* 國, M. *khari, gui*, principalities; *pu-lo* 部落, *chih-erh* 枝兒, *ai-ma* 愛馬, M. *aimagh*, tribes; *wei-hsia* 位下, *t'ou-hsia* 投下, appanages (these last two terms referred originally to the grantee, but were also used for their holdings). The very broad Mongolian term *khubi*, "share," included fiefs. On this complicated matter see Meng Ssu-ming, *Yüan-tai she-hui*, pp. 101 ff, 115; Paul Ratchnevsky, "Zum Ausdruck 't'ou-hsia' in der Mongolenzeit," *Collectanea Mongolica, Festschrift für Professor Dr. Rintchen* (Wiesbaden, 1966), pp. 173–177; Murakami Masatsugu, "Genchō ni okeru tōka no igi," pp. 169–216; Erich Haenisch, *Wörterbuch zu Mongol un Niuca Tobca'an (Yüan-ch'ao pi-shi)* (Wiesbaden, 1962), pp. 62, 120. These grants included both lands and peoples.

[168] YS 95:2411, trans. Schurmann, *Economic Structure*, pp. 19–20.

[169] *Yüan tien-chang*, 9:9a–17a; Murakami, "Tōka no igi," p. 204.

[170] YS 95:2414 and *passim*.

Virtually all of these agencies and their subordinate offices were confined to the Metropolitan Province or to areas immediately surrounding it. Of the twenty-six bureaus under the Bureau for the Empress' Palace (V.B.1), fourteen were within the Metropolitan Province, seven were at least in part outside of it (one in Shan-hsi and Kan-su Provinces, three in Ho-nan-Chiang-pei, one in Chiang-che, and two in Liao-yang), while five cannot be exactly located.[171] The Directorate-General for Revenue in Chiang-huai (V.B.3) had seven subordinate offices in Chiang-che, one in Ho-nan-Chiang-pei, and one in Shan-hsi.[172]

In the heir apparent's establishment, seven of its agencies had no interests beyond the Metropolitan Province (V.A.2,3,4,5,6,7,9); the Bureau for the Heir-apprent's Household (V.A.1) had had six offices which were located in Chiang-hsi, but all were abolished in 1322 or 1323.[173] The Directorate-General for Civil Administration in Pien-liang (V.A.8), with twenty subordinate offices, was entirely within Ho-nan-Chiang-pei Province.[174] The establishments of the dowager empresses (V.D) all seem to have been located in the Metropolitan Province, particularly the northern, Mongolian, part of it, but one of them had 40,000 households assigned to it in the southern provinces, Chiang-che and Hu-Kuang.[175]

The Bureau of Tibetan and Buddhist Affairs (V.D.6) represents a fusion in 1329 of the functions of two quite different organs established earlier, one for the local government of Tibet (which was largely in the hands of the Sa-skya family), and another for the regulation of the Buddhist clergy in China, the Buddhist Affairs Commission.[176] All but eight of the bureau's twenty-six subordinate offices were located in Tibet. Like many other important offices in the imperial government, this bureau had replicas of itself created as the need arose: in Tibet proper when military emergencies occurred, and in several places in South China after its conquest, but only one of them, that at Hang-chou in Chiang-che Province, became permanent.[177] There was a host of local

---

[171] YS 88:2232, 2233, 2234, 2235, 2236, 2237–2238, 2238. Through an error YS 88:2239–2240 recopies subordinate bureaus of the Bureau for the Empress' Palace which it has already recorded on YS 88:2234–2235.

[172] YS 89:2260–2261. A few other bureaus and sub-bureaus, the locations of which cannot be determined, may have been outside the Metropolitan Province.

[173] YS 89:2246–2248.

[174] YS 89:2259–2260.

[175] This was the Court for Jen-tsung's Ordo (V.C. 4), YS 27:610.

[176] *Kung-te shih-ssu* 功德使司, YS 87:2193–2194, trans. Ratchnevsky, *Un code*, I, pp. 151–52; YS 33:744. YS 36:802 mentions the separate reestablishment of the Buddhist Affairs Commission in 1332, but no trace of its activities can be found.

[177] YS 87:2194; 16:350. YS 24:538 mentions the abolition of a Chiang-nan "Branch" Bureau of Tibetan and Buddhist Affairs in 1311, which I take to be a different bureau from

offices throughout the land to handle legal cases involving Buddhist
monks, but these were not parts of the Bureaus of Tibetan and Buddhist
Affairs, and they were in any case all abolished in 1311, after such legal
cases were referred to the local civil magistrates.[178] In a sense, then,
control of Buddhist clergy became more centralized within the provinces,
although not on an empire-wide level. For three short years, however,
the Bureau of Tibetan and Buddhist Affairs had a structure which
approached the model of the American bureau described earlier, and
which is almost unique among important imperial offices in Yüan China.
In 1331 there was established for it sixteen regional Directorates-General
for Religious Affairs, *kuang-chiao tsung-kuan-fu* 廣教總管府, one in each
region (or area of comparable size), in every section of the empire (only
Ling-pei Province is not mentioned, and it was undoubtedly included in
the assignment of one of the Metropolitan regional offices). The
Direcorates-General were high-ranking (3A), and had four officials each,
including an Agent (*ta-lu-hua-ch'ih*), who were nominated to the emperor
by the Bureau of Tibetan and Buddhist Affairs at Ta-tu. Because of the
Directorates' short life (the reasons for their sudden demise are, as usual,
unclear), no hints of their activities can be found in the record; they were
replaced by a revived "branch" Bureau of Tibetan and Buddhist
Affairs.[179]

A similar profile is presented by the Office for Christian Clergy
(V.D.7). From its creation in 1289 until 1315, it presided over seventy-
two local Offices for the Management of the Christian Religion, *yeh-li-
k'o-wen chang-chiao ssu* 也里可溫掌教司, the locations of which are
unknown; but in the latter year all of them were abolished and their
activities—probably the handling of legal cases involving priests—
reverted to the parent office in Ta-tu. This may sound like the centralization of a governmental function, but it is more akin to the amputation
of limbs from a body: the ten regular officers, three service officers, and
seven clerks at Ta-tu could not be expected to exert much supervision
over the empire's scattered Nestorian clergy without local representatives. One suspects in this case that the local bureaus were abolished as

---

the one at Hang-chou, since the latter was abolished in 1326 (YS 30:672), only to be
reestablished again in 1342 (YS 92:2335).

[178] YS 24:539, *Yüan tien-chang*, 33:1a ff. These local offices included the Buddhist
Registry Offices, *seng-lu ssu* 僧錄司, and others.

[179] YS 35:776; 92:2335; 38:820. In 1342, the Chiang-che "Branch" Bureau of Tibetan
and Buddist Affairs established bureaus called *ch'ung-chiao so* 崇教所, which resolved legal
cases involving monks, but nothing is known of their number or distribution. YS 92:2335,
142:3407.

an economy measure because they had little to do in the first place, while the Office for the Christian Clergy continued, as it had from the start, to attend to the clergy in the capital and the management of the Christian cathedral there.[180]

Of all branches of government, one would expect the military system to be among the most centralized and unified in its organization because of its intimate connection with the Mongols' conquest and the maintenance of their control, but that is only partially true. The Bureau of Military Affairs (IV.1) did have access to the imperial person and considerable independence, and it established norms for military units throughout the empire, but its direct administrative responsibilities were limited to thirty-five imperial guards units and other military organizations, all but three of which were located in the Metropolitan Province (the three exceptions had some troops stationed in Ho-nan-Chiang-pei, Shan-hsi, and Liao-yang Provinces),[181] the task of which was to maintain the security of the Metropolitan Province and the emperor.[182]

In other provinces, military activities by the emperor's troops were controlled by replica Bureaus of Military Affairs (*hsing shu-mi-yüan* 行樞密院), at least ten of which are known to have been established at various times; they were often the first high-level Yüan administrations to appear in a newly conquered area. However, these "branch" bureaus were intended as temporary, to be abolished or replaced by "branch" Central Secretariats as soon as order had returned,[183] although some of them, like the Ssu-ch'uan "Branch" Bureau of Military Affairs, became permanent and apparently influential features of the governmental scene in West China until 1338, when all "branch" bureaus were abolished.[184]

---

[180] YS 89:2273, 15:320.

[181] These were, respectively, the General Myriarchy of Mongolian Troops in Ho-nan-Huai-pei, *ho-nan huai-pei meng-ku chün tu wan-hu-fu* 河南淮北蒙古軍都萬戶府; the Directorate-General for Hunting in Yen-an Colony, *yen-an t'un-tien ta-pu tsung-kuan-fu* 延安屯田打捕總管府; and the Hunting Office for the Colonies at Ta-ning, Hai-yang, and Other Places, *ta-ning hai-yang teng-ch'u t'un-t'ien ta-pu-so* 大寧海陽等處屯田打捕所. YS 86:2166, 2169–2170. The Chief Military Commission (IV.2) had one myriarchy with some troops stationed in Ho-nan-Chiang-pei Province. YS 86:2177. For this discussion of the Bureau of Military Affairs I have depended, unless otherwise indicated, on the dissertation of Gunther Mangold, *Das Militärwesen in China unter der Mongolen-Herrschaft* (Bamberg, 1971!), pp. 4–15.

[182] Mangold, *Das Militärwesen*, pp. 4–5.

[183] YS 86:2156; Mangold, *Das Militärwesen*, pp. 5–7, which describes the five most important branch bureaus (others which preceded them are also included).

[184] YS 86:2156; Mangold, *Das Militärwesen*, p. 6. The order abolishing the branch bureaus of military affairs mentions, besides the Ssu-ch'uan bureau, three others in Ho-nan-Chiang-pei, Chiang-hsi, and Chiang-che. YS 39:843. A branch bureau was established in Ling-pei Province in 1329, but there is no record of its abolition. YS 86:2157.

The natural habitat of the imperial troops thus seems to have been the Metropolitan Province and its fringes, and there they were indeed organized in a highly centralized manner. Military security in the other provinces, however, when no imperial troops were on duty there, was the responsibility of the myriarchies located at the circuit level, and these were under the control of the "branch" secretariats, not the Bureaus of Military Affairs; the Pacification Offices at the Region level also seem to have been influential in local military affairs, although they did not directly control troops.[185] The agricultural colonies (*t'un-t'ien* 屯田) which contributed to the support of troops in Yüan China were, in provinces other than the Metropolitan, also controlled by the "branch" secretariats; in the Metropolitan Province, most of them were controlled by the Bureau of Military Affairs, but some were under the Central Secretariat or other bureaus.[186]

The Armaments Court (IV.3) was a local, not a national, agency, undoubtedly supplying the bows, arrows, and armor to the imperial troops in the Metropolitan Province and in adjacent areas. Of its thirty-nine subordinate offices with their subject artisans, only eleven were outside that province, six in northern Ho-nan-Chiang-pei, one in Chiang-hsi, and the rest in Liao-yang.[187] In the other provinces of the empire, arms manufacture was carried on as an activity of local government.[188]

III. GENERAL FEATURES OF YÜAN RULE

Having surveyed virtually the entire Yüan imperial government, we now find it possible to make a few statements about its nature. First, it is clear that its bureaus were principally organs for the governance of the Metropolitan Province, and their administrative competence was over-whelmingly within that province's boundaries; where it exceeded them was in the two provinces to the north, Liao-yang and Ling-pei, thinly settled areas with largely non-Chinese populations and rudimentary official systems,[189] in the adjoining northern parts of Ho-nan-Chiang-pei

---

[185] Mangold, *Das Militärwesen*, p. 9 ff.

[186] YS 100:2558–2579; Mangold, *Das Militärwesen*, pp. 37–43.

[187] YS 90:2284–2288.

[188] See *Yüan tien-chang*, 35:12ab, trans. Mangold, *Das Militärwesen*, pp. 228–229.

[189] I cannot agree with John W. Dardess, "From Mongol Empire to Yüan Dynasty," p. 156, that any substantial bureaucratization of Mongolia (Ling-pei) occurred in Yüan times, despite the governmental activities there which he describes. He writes, "The main difference between this new Mongolian province... and those of China was that the steppes were not further subdivided into the usual local administrative hierarchy of prefectures, subprefectures and counties." But surely such subdivision lies at the very heart of bureau-cratization.

and Chiang-che provinces, and in a few other spots in North China. This characteristic—the intimate involvement of the imperial government with the administration of a particular territory within the empire—distinguishes it greatly from modern central governments, and makes it resemble the government of a royal domain instead. With the important exception of the appointment of officials, its engagement in empire-wide administration was at best transitory or limited to very restricted activities. In yet another way is it unlike a central government: it did not simply manage a group of techniques, institutions, and facilities to assist the units of local government in the administration and exploitation of the population, but was itself directly involved in such administration and exploitation, and its subjects were governed by special bureaus, not by the usual district magistrates. Of the seventy-six most important primary government bureaus[190] twenty-one or 27.5 percent directly governed subjects as their principal activity;[191] of the remaining fifty-five which did not, nineteen (or 34.5 percent) had bureaus at the first level of subordination which governed subjects, and these numbered ninety-nine or 20.8 percent of all first-level subordinate bureaus.[192]

The elaborate division of labor which appears in the list of bureaus of the emperor's government is only partly real; there is much duplication of function, a fact which was not lost on contemporaries. One Wang Chieh 王結 (1274–1336) noted:

"We have a Ministry of Revenue [for financial matters], and yet we have an Office of the Grand Supervisors of Agriculture, too; we have a Ministry of Rites [for ritual matters], and yet we have an Academy of Imperial Sacrifices and Rituals, a Court for State Wine Affairs, *kuang-lu ssu* 光祿寺, an Office for State Ceremonial, *shih-i ssu* 侍儀司, and a College for Foreign Reception, *hui-t'ung kuan* 會同館; we have a Ministry of War [for postal affairs, official transport, and remount service], yet we also have the Bureau for Transmission Services, the Court of the Imperial Stud, and the Court for the Imperial Tack; [we have a Ministry of Punishments] [for legal matters], yet we have the Grand Judge, *i-k'o cha-erh-ku-ch'i* 伊克扎爾固齊 (M. *yeke jarghuchi*), too;[193] we have a Ministry of Works [for construction and manufactures], yet we have a Bureau for

[190] I exclude the forty-six princely administrations (V.D. 5).

[191] This can be determined in several ways: the descriptions in the *Yüan shih* may specifically state as much, giving the number of households; it may be clear by the name of the bureau (V.D. 1 for example); or by the presence of an Agent (*ta-lu-hua-ch'ih*) in the list of officials.

[192] In making this determination, I do not include forty-four military units, although technically they meet the criteria mentioned in the previous note.

[193] The words "we have a Ministry of Punishments" (*yu hsing-pu* 有刑部) have been inadvertently omitted. The Grand Judge was the chief of the judges attached to the Central Secretariat (II.A.1).

Imperial Manufactures, an Armaments Court, a Directorate of Palace Workshops, *shao-fu chien* 少府監, a Directorate for Felt Manufactures, and a Directorate for Leathers and Furs, too.... In the circuits outside [the Metropolitan Province] we have the 'branch' secretariats, but we also have Pacification Offices and Directorates-General." [194]

The emperor's device for extending his authority outside of his domain was the creation of replicas of his own metropolitan bureaus. These are often termed "branch" or "local" bureaus by modern writers, but they were not true branches, for they had their own independent officials, and ranks equal to, or only slightly lower than, the prototypes at Ta-tu, and they were no more local than their parent bodies. With two exceptions—the "branch" Censorates and Central Secretariats discussed below—all were considered temporary expedients, and all but a few were eventually abolished. This means that the "branch" Central Secretariats were virtually the only significant conduits for imperial power into provincial territories; but, in fact, as we have seen, the emperors gave them enormous powers in all sectors of government. Furthermore, the "branch" secretariats created, with imperial approval, their own administrative bureaus much as the imperial government did. Some examples are the Maritime Trade Superintendencies in Chiang-che Province, which collected the maritime customs revenues, [195] the Kuang-tung Salt Tax Superintendency in Chiang-hsi Province, [196] and the Ssu-ch'uan Tea and Salt Distribution Office in Ssu-ch'uan Province. [197]

The late Maeda Naonori has correctly observed that the "branch" secretariats were not organs of local government like the circuit (*lu*) bureaus of Sung times, but governments of external territories, separate vassal states surrounding a nuclear state, the emperor's domain—an idea of political order which he traces to the pre-dynastic period of the Mongols' history. [198] This view is given further support by the writings of two contemporary visitors from other cultures, Rašīd al-Dīn of Iran and

---

[194] Wang Chieh, "Shang Chung-shu tsai-hsiang pa-shih shu 上中書宰相八事書," *Wen-chung chi* 文忠集 (*Ssu-k'u ch'üan-shu chen-pen*, first series, ed.), 4:7b, quoted by Meng Ssu-ming, *Yüan-tai she-hui*, p. 156. Some of the bureaus mentioned in this passage later became absorbed by others or subordinated to the Ministries (II.A. 1. a–f). On Wang Chieh, see *Hsin Yüan shih*, 208:10a–12b.

[195] *Shih-po t'i-chü-ssu* 市舶提舉司, YS 91:2315, trans. Ratchnevsky, *Un code*, II, p. 175 n. 3; YS 94:2401–2403; Schurmann, *Economic Structure*, pp. 230–236.

[196] *Kuang-tung yen-k'o t'i-chü-ssu* 廣東鹽課提舉司, YS 91:2314, 94:2392, trans. Schurmann, *Economic structure*, pp. 185–186.

[197] *Ssu-ch'uan ch'a-yen chuan-yün-ssu* 四川茶鹽轉運司, YS 91:2314.

[198] Maeda Naonori, "Genchō kōshō no seiritsu katei 元朝行省の成立過程," in his *Genchōshi no kenkyū*, pp. 145–202, especially pp. 182 ff. The Mongols called the nuclear state the *ghol-un ulus*, the vassal states *khari*.

Marco Polo of Venice, who often prefer to call the provinces of China "kingdoms" or "countries."[199] Rašīd noted, too, that the provinces did not all bear the same relation to the emperor: some, like Korea, Kan-su, and Yün-nan, were "separate" countries, much more independent of his authority than the others.[200] Thus the provinces, while internally centralized and integrated by their powerful Central Secretariats, were only loosely bound to the imperial province, and were liable to dangerous regional and separatist forces—forces which ultimately appeared and brought down the dynasty.[201]

The emperor had several devices at his disposal to fight these forces. Some of the most important derived from his traditional constitutional supremacy: his power to appoint and remove officials, to issue edicts with the force of law on any topic, and to act as a court of last resort in all criminal or administrative matters. He also exploited ethnic solidarity, reserving all important posts for Mongols and for his Central and Western Asian allies.[202] He promoted the organs of his government as the supreme normative bodies of the empire, but, as we have seen, gave them too little administrative machinery and personnel to be effective beyond the Metropolitan Province. He tried to make the "branch" central secretariats inferior by having them address him through his own Central Secretariat, and by sometimes refusing to appoint their top officials.[203]

The only agency of the imperial government which helped the emperors to counter the decentralization which the "branch" central secretariat system brought, was the Censorate (III.1). It has been called monolithic, centralized, and an example of extreme integration,[204] but it seems to fall far short of that because it embodies the same pattern of prototype and replicas which we have encountered before. Still, the Censorate organization did transcend the provincial system, for it divided the country into only three areas instead of the usual twelve. The Censorate at Ta-tu reserved for itself the Metropolitan Province, Ho-

---

[199] See John Andrew Boyle, trans., *The Successors of Genghis Khan* (New York, 1971), pp. 281–284, 323; and A. C. Moule and Paul Pelliot, *Marco Polo, The Description of the World* (London, 1938), I, p. 275.

[200] Boyle, *The Successors*, pp. 282–283, 325–326.

[201] See Dardess, *Conquerors and Confucians*, p. 119 ff.

[202] This theme has been extensively treated by Meng Ssu-ming, *Yüan-tai she-hui*, pp. 25–67.

[203] See the tables of provinical officials in *Hsin Yüan shih, chüan* 32, which often show the Chief Councillor's (*ch'eng-hsiang* 丞相) position empty. See also YS 91:2305–2306.

[204] Charles O. Hucker, "The Yüan Contribution to Censorial History," *Chung-yang yen-chiu yüan Li-shih yü-yen yen-chiu-so chi-k'an* 中央研究院歷史語言研究所集刊, 4:1 (1960), pp. 219–227, and his *Censorial System*, pp. 25–29.

nan-Chiang-pei, and presumably Liao-yang and Ling-pei.[205] A Shan-hsi "Branch" Censorate covered Shan-hsi, Kan-su, Ssu-ch'uan, and Yün-nan Provinces,[206] while the Chiang-nan "Branch" Censorate looked after Chiang-che, Chiang-hsi, and Hu-kuang.[207] Each of the Censorates had subordinate to itself an Office of Surveillance, *ch'a-yüan* 察院, with from twenty to thirty-two investigating censors assigned to it,[208] and from four to ten regions (*tao*) under its jurisdiction, in each of which was a Regional Investigation Office, *su-cheng lien-fang ssu*,[209] with several Investigation Commissioners.[210] Although all three Censorates were of equal rank, the Metropolitan Censorate seems to have assumed general management of the others.[211] With its extensive powers of investigation and impeachment, its privileged relations with the emperor, and its relatively integrated structure, the Censorate, along with the Central Secretariat and the Bureau of Military Affairs, was among the most important imperial bureaus.[212]

It is widely believed by students of late imperial Chinese history that the Ming and Ch'ing epochs embody a greater tendency towards centralization, autocracy, and bureaucratization than is to be found in Sung times or before. The origins of the new trend have sometimes been attributed to the Mongol presence in China, but support for that view seems hard to find, at least among the formal political institutions. Ming T'ai-tsu's abolition of the "branch" Central Secretariats in 1376 was a much more important step in the centralization of political authority in China than was the Mongols' creation of them.[213] The Ming reorganization of the Ministry of Revenue also exemplifies an important step towards the development of an authentic central governmental bureau. It had thirteen subordinate offices to deal with the fiscal administration of

---

[205] YS 86:2178; Ratchnevsky, *Un code*, I, p. 179. Neither Liao-yang nor Ling-pei were organized into Regions (*tao*), the key subordinate territorial units of the censorates, although there had at one time been a Region established in Liao-yang called Hai-hsi Liao-tung 海西遼東. Hucker, "The Yüan Contribution," p. 221; Ratchnevsky, *Un code*, I, pp. 169–170.

[206] YS 86:2179; Ratchnevsky, *Un code*, I, p. 162.

[207] YS 86:2179; Ratchnevsky, *Un code*, I, p. 161 f.

[208] YS 86:2178, 2179, 2180; Ratchnevsky, *Un code*, I, pp. 175–176.

[209] YS 86:2180; Ratchnevsky, *Un code*, I, pp. 169–170, 179.

[210] YS 86:2180.

[211] Hucker, "The Yüan Contribution," p. 223. See YS 86:2178.

[212] See Sa Meng-wu 薩孟武, *Chung-kuo she-hui cheng-chih shih* 中國社會政治史 (Taipei, 1968, 4 vols.), IV, pp. 187 ff.

[213] Charles O. Hucker, "Governmental Organization of the Ming Dynasty," John L. Bishop, ed., *Studies of Governmental Institutions in Chinese History* (Cambridge, Mass., 1968), p. 39.

the empire, one office for each of the thirteen provinces.[214] Among the
hundred-odd chief bureaus of the Yüan imperial government, there is
not one which reflects in its structure a concern for empire-wide administration to this extent.

[214] Ray Huang, *Taxation and Governmental Finance in Sixteenth-century Ming China*
(Cambridge, England, 1974), pp. 15–17. It is worth noting, however, that the Ministry of
Revenue in Ming times had no regional offices in the provinces. It was also woefully
understaffed by modern standards.

Chinese Official Historiography
at the Yüan Court:
The Composition of the Liao,
Chin, and Sung Histories

HOK-LAM CHAN

1. INTRODUCTION*

One of the most ambitious projects ever undertaken in the history of official Chinese historiography was the compilation of the "standard histories" (*cheng-shih* 正史) of the Liao (906–1125), Chin (1125–1234), and Sung (960–1279) dynasties under the auspices of the Mongol rulers of the Yüan dynasty (1260–1368).[1] It was an extraordinary undertaking not only because of its grandiose attempt to deal with the heritage of three different ruling houses with diverse backgrounds, but also because of the haste under which their records were brought to order amid decades of heated discussions over the ideological principles for these historical compilations. Within three years, or between 1343 and 1345, the Yüan National History Office successfully produced a massive volume of histories of over seven hundred *chüan*: the *Liao-shih* 遼史 (*History of the Liao*), 116 *chüan*; *Chin-shih* 金史 (*History of the Chin*), 135 *chüan*, and the *Sung-shih* 宋史 (*History of the Sung*), 496 *chüan*, encompassing a time span in excess of three centuries.[2] It was, moreover, a significant enterprise in view of the fact that these history projects were sponsored

---

*In this essay, the archaic spelling Tsin is adopted for the native Chin 晉 dynasty (265–420) in order to avoid confusing it with the Jurchen Chin 金 dynasty (1115–1234).

[1] For a general survey of the composition of the Liao, Chin, and Sung histories under the Yüan dynasty, see Chin Yü-fu, pp. 106–111; Naitō Torajirō 內藤虎次郎, *Shina shigaku shi* 支那史学史 (Tokyo, 1953), pp. 321–334; Otagi Matsuo, pp. 315–322; Ch'en Fang-ming; and Herbert Franke, "Chinese Historiography," *passim*. On the Liao history, see Feng Chia-sheng, pt. 1; on the Chin history, see Hok-lam Chan, *Chin Historiography*, ch. 1. There is not yet a similar study for the Sung history.

[2] This order of the three histories was the standard usage by the Yüan historiographers; it was based on the time of their completion and not necessarily on ideological and political grounds. Later scholars, favoring the Sung as the legitimate ruling house over the Liao and Chin, usually put the Sung history ahead of the latter two. See the works of Ch'ien Ta-hsin, Chao I, and of modern scholars such as Chin Yü-fu and Hsü Hao, *passim*.

by the alien Mongol rulers. The Mongols had conquered China as nomads, and as such they attempted to respond to the demands of the distinctly different cultural tradition of the subjugated population to enhance their political stature in the consolidation of the Chinese territories.

The successful completion of this massive historical compilation was one of the most outstanding examples of the strenuous efforts exerted by the Mongol conquerors over several decades to address themselves to the problems and difficulties confronting them as rulers of China. In this particular case, the Mongol conquerors, who did not possess a literary culture, adopted Chinese practice and sponsored the compilation of the chronicles of the regimes they had subjugated. In so doing, they were beset with the issue in Chinese historiography known as *cheng-t'ung* 正統 ("legitimate" or "orthodox succession"). This issue had great political implications, as the Mongols were alien conquerors succeeding to a native ruling house.[3] The task was not only to ascertain the legitimate status of the three defunct dynasties—Liao, Chin, and Sung—but also to accommodate the Mongol conquerors within the Chinese dynastic order. The question was how to make them succeed to the regimes that they had replaced as the legitimate rulers of all China. This issue of "legitimate succession" may have been of little concern to the Mongol rulers during their early phase of conquest, for they considered their legitimacy to have stemmed from the *tengri*, the universalistic heavenly mandate of their nomadic tradition. But as they steeped themselves further in the Chinese tradition and gradually alienated themselves from the rest of the Mongol empire in their late phase of rule, the issue became more relevant and significant.[4] It was primarily the difficulty of formulating appropriate guidelines for the three histories in order to accommodate the interests of the Mongol rulers that prolonged the execution of the historical composition. Finally, the Yüan historiographers had to cope with the multitude of source materials that were relevant to the successful completion of the histories. The problem was not one of locating the sources, for the compilers had ready access to the archives of these defunct regimes. Rather, the difficulty lay in reducing the diversified, voluminous data to a format that was both well attuned

[3] On the controversy over the issue of legitimate or orthodox succession in Chinese historiography, see the references cited in n. 35, 38 below.

[4] For a general background of these developments, see Herbert Franke, *From Tribal Chieftain to Universal Emperor and God: The Legitimation of the Yüan Dynasty. Bayerische Akademie der Wissenchaften Phil.-Hist. Klasse Sitzungsbericht. Jahr.* 1978, Heft 2 (München, 1978), and John W. Dardess, *Conquerors and Confucians: Aspects of Political Change in Late Yüan China* (New York, 1973), *passim*.

to the ideological demands of the Mongol rulers and consistent with the Chinese historiographical tradition.[5]

With these considerations in mind, an investigation into the composition of the standard histories of the Liao, Chin, and Sung would not only instruct us about the perpetuation of the Chinese historiographical tradition under foreign rule, but also help us to understand the Mongol impact on the Chinese cultural tradition as well as the Chinese intellectual response to Mongol domination in general. In the following sketches, I shall try to document the composition of the three standard histories in the context of the development of Yüan official historiography, and supplement this overall review with a discussion of the evaluation of these histories by later Chinese historians. In doing so, my aim will be to enhance our appreciation of the real achievements of Yüan historiography and to further our understanding of their impact on historical writings on the Liao, Chin, and Sung dynasties in later periods.

2. HISTORIOGRAPHICAL BACKGROUND

To introduce our subject, it is desirable to delineate the main features in the background of the development of Chinese-style official historiography during the Yüan period. The Mongol conquerors, like many other nomadic peoples who had ruled over China, did not possess a literary culture. The conception of historical recording was alien to them until they came under the influence of sinicized non-Chinese peoples and eventually of the Chinese themselves.[6] The establishment of the National History Office in the early 1260s and its charge to preserve and compile historical records and documents, therefore, marked the beginning of a significant phase in the Mongol response to the Chinese cultural tradition.[7] This institutional innovation underscored the recognition by the

[5] See the references cited in n. 1.

[6] The Mongols possessed a semi-folkloristic historical narrative of their ancestors beginning with Chinggis Khan called *Chinggis-gahan-u huja'ur*, later known by its Chinese title as *Yüan-ch'ao mi-shih* 元朝秘史 or *The Secret History of the Mongols*. It is believed to have been compiled, according to Igor de Rachewiltz, around 1228, sometime after they possessed a writing script. No more chronicles in Mongolian, however, were written during the reigns of the later emperors (1229–1259), since they were preoccupied with military campaigns and conquests. They resumed their historiographical activities after Khubilai's accession in 1260, when he came under the influence of the Chinese tradition of historical record and compilation. For an account of the pre-Yüan phase of Mongol historiography, see Kobayashi Takashirō 小林高四郎, *Genchō hishi no kenkyū* 元朝秘史の研究 (Tokyo, 1954), *Intro.*; William Hung, "The Transmission of the Book Known as the Secret History of the Mongols," HJAS, 14 (1951), p. 467 ff; and Igor de Rachewiltz, "The Dating of the Secret History of the Mongols," *Monumenta Serica*, 24 (1965), p. 200 ff.

[7] See the references cited in n. 18 below.

Mongol rulers of the value of keeping historical records and of the purpose in compiling the chronicles of the ruling regimes that they had subjugated. We may speculate about their motives. Were the Mongol rulers truly impressed by the grandeur of the Chinese historiographical tradition, or were they more concerned with utilitarian objectives? It would be presumptuous to endorse the former, and the latter assumption may be closer to the truth. The reason was that, as will be shown in the ensuing discussions, the Mongol rulers were little attracted to Chinese culture until the later stage, for they were more concerned with rallying the support of the Chinese literati in the initial phase of consolidation.[8] Nevertheless, the Mongol restoration of the traditional Chinese organization of official historiography laid the institutional groundwork for the composition of the standard histories of the Liao, Chin, and Sung, the compilation of the Mongols' own reign chronicles, and the perpetuation of the Chinese historiographical tradition.

The organization of Chinese official historiography at the Yüan court followed the system and procedure which had evolved from the Han and had become a standard pattern during the T'ang dynasty. This system provided for the establishment of an independent organ, known as the National History Office (kuo-shih yüan 國史院), functioning alongside the Office of Records (ch'i-chü chu 起居注), in charge of the compilation of imperial chronicles and the records of the preceding dynasties.[9] The names of these offices may have varied over time, but their basic functions and operational principles remained relatively unchanged. One of the most notable features in the T'ang system was the practice of appointing special commissions of historiographers to take charge of the historical composition. This marked the beginning of the commissioned compilation of histories under which the group responsibilities of bureaucrat-historians replaced the singular efforts of an individual historian. It was the T'ang procedure that set the pattern for the organization of official historical compilations under the Sung and the conquered dynasties.[10]

---

[8] See Otagi Matsuo, p. 318; Herbert Franke, "Chinese Historiography," p. 19.

[9] For a general survey of the organization of Chinese official historiography from Han to T'ang, see, among others, Chin Yü-fu, ch. 5, 6; Naitō Torajirō, ch. 7, 8; Fu Chen-lun 傅振倫, "Chung-kuo li-tai hsiu-shih chih-tu k'ao 中國歷代修史制度考," Shuo-wen yüeh-k'an 說文月刊, 4 (1944), pp. 383–398; Chao Kang 趙岡, "T'ang-tai shih-kuan k'ao 唐代史館考," Wen-hua hsien-feng 文化先鋒 (Nanking), 8:10 (May 1948), pp. 17–21; and Lien-sheng Yang, "The Organization of Chinese Official Historiography...," in Historians of China and Japan, ed. W. G. Beasley & E. G. Pulleyblank (London, 1961), pp. 44–59.

[10] The T'ang procedure of appointing commissioned historical bureaus for compilations found a severe critic in the eminent historian Liu Chih-chi (661–721). He summed up the defects of the system in the last chapter of his Shih-t'ung (Comprehensive Survey of

The Sung dynasty developed an elaborate and complicated set of organizations which were responsible for official historiography. They assumed various names under different periods, but generally they performed functions similar to those of their T'ang predecessors.[11] There was, first of all, the Office of Records, which produced the records of the emperor's daily activities known as *Ch'i-chü chu* (*Diaries of Activity and Repose*). These became the basic sources for more extensive chronicles such as the *Jih-li* 日曆 (*Daily Calendars*), *Jih-lu* 日錄 (*Daily Records*) and the *Shih-lu* 實錄 (*Veritable Records*, i.e., *Reign Chronicles*) compiled by the National History Office.[12] In addition, there were special bureaus responsible for the compilation of imperial edicts and memorials submitted to the court. Their compilations were known as *Shih-cheng chi* 時政記 (*Records of State Affairs*). The National History Office, subordinate to the Imperial Library (*mi-shu chien* 秘書監), was nominally headed by the chancellor and staffed by scholars from the Hanlin Academy. In addition to the *Veritable Records*, the most important chronicles compiled by this office were the dynastic histories (*kuo-shih* 國史) of the reigning emperors.[13] Together with the *Veritable Records* and the above-mentioned imperial records, they constituted the basic sources for the composition of the official Sung history under the auspices of the Yüan historiographical office.

Following the Chinese precedents, the Liao state developed a system of official historiography as early as the founding of the Khitan kingdom in the tenth century. Officials in charge of historical composition had already been appointed by A-pao-chi 阿保機 (T'ai-tsu 太祖, r. 907–926),

---

Historiography). This has been translated by William Hung under the title "A T'ang Historiographer's Letter of Resignation," in HJAS, 29 (1969), pp. 5–52. For general remarks on the subject, see Lü Ssu-mien 呂思勉, *Shih-t'ung p'ing* 史通評 (Hong Kong, 1964), p. 53 ff, and E. G. Pulleyblank in *Historians of China and Japan*, p. 139 ff.

[11] For a general survey of Sung official historiography, see Chin Yü-fu, ch. 6; Naitō Torajirō, ch. 9; and the references cited in n. 12, 13 below.

[12] For a survey of these Sung historical works, see NESCC 23:306; Chin Yü-fu, p. 101. On the *Daily Records*, see Ting Tse-liang 丁則良 in *Ch'ing-hua hsüeh-pao* 清華學報, 13:2 (1941), pp. 1–12; on the *Veritable Records*, see, among others, Chiang Fu-ts'ung 蔣復璁, *Sung-shih hsin-t'an* 宋史新探 (Taipei, 1965), pp. 61–72; Huang Han-ch'ao 黃漢超, in *Hsin-ya hsüeh-pao* 新亞學報, 7:1–2 (1966), pp. 363–409, 157–195; and Wang Te-i 王德毅, *Sung-shih yen-chiu lun-chi, ti-er-chi* 宋史研究論集, 第二集 (Taipei, 1972), pp. 71–118. There survives in the SPTK series a fragmentary edition of the *Sung T'ai-tsung shih-lu* 宋太宗實錄, in 12 *chüan*.

[13] For studies on the Sung national histories, see Wang Te-i, "Shen-Che-Hui-Ch'in ssu-ch'ao kuo-shih hsiu-tsuan k'ao 神哲徽欽四朝國史修纂考," *Yu-shih hsüeh-chih* 幼獅學誌, 2:1 (Jan. 1963), pp. 1–7; and Sudō Yoshiyuki 周藤吉之, "Sōchō kokushi no hensan to kokushi retsuden 宋朝国史の編纂と国史列傳," in *Sōdai shi kenkyū* 宋代史研究 (Tokyo, 1969), pp. 513–565.

the dynastic founder, before the formal establishment of a National History Office based on the T'ang pattern. It was staffed by members of the Hanlin Academy, comprising both Chinese and sinicized Khitan scholar-officials. Its main duty was the recording of the emperor's daily activities and the compilation of the imperial records. The most important chronicles composed by the Liao historiographical office were the *Veritable Records* of the reigning emperors. Some of these escaped destruction at the fall of the dynasty and constituted the main source for the Liao standard history compiled at a later date.[14]

Similarly, the Chin state had an elaborate organization of official historiography in the Office of Records and the National History Office, following the T'ang and Sung models. The National History Office, established as an independent organization, was staffed by members of the Hanlin Academy, including Chinese, sinicized Khitan and Jurchen scholar-officials.[15] Its main duty was the compilation of imperial reign records such as the *Daily Calendars, Daily Records*, and, most important of all, the *Veritable Records* of the reigning emperors. In addition, the National History Office undertook the composition of an official history of the defunct Liao state in conformity with the Chinese historiographical tradition. Two sets of the official Liao history were compiled. The first, completed in 1148 and attributed to Hsiao Yung-ch'i 蕭永祺, a former Liao official, in 75 *chüan*, was rejected by the court as inadequate, and a new version was ordered by Emperor Wan-yen Ching 完顏璟 (Chang-tsung 章宗, r. 1189–1208) in 1201.[16] The composition of the second version, however, was impeded by the issue of whether the Chin should succeed the Liao or the Northern Sung as the legitimate ruling order. A series of discussions on dynastic legitimacy were held between 1194 and 1202 in the context of the Five Agents theory. The outcome of the discussions was that it was ruled that the Chin should proclaim the Earth Power in succession to the Sung, and that the Liao was rejected as a legitimate ruling house. In consequence, the Liao history composition was given a low priority. Its completion under the supervision of Hanlin Academician Ch'en Ta-jen 陳大任 was delayed until 1207, and the final

[14] LS 47:781–82. See Feng Chia-sheng, part 1; Karl A. Wittfogel and Feng Chia-sheng, *History of Chinese Society: Liao (907–1125)* (Philadelphia, 1949), pp. 28, 610; Otagi Matsuo, p. 296 ff; and Li Chia-ch'i 李家祺, "Pu Liao-shih lieh-chuan Shih-kuan p'ien, 補遼史列傳史官篇," *Yu-shih yüeh-k'an* 幼獅月刊, (Nov. 1970), pp. 49–52.

[15] CS 55:1245. See Otagi Matsuo, p. 300 ff; Feng Chia-sheng, p. 11 ff; and Hok-lam Chan, *Chin Historiography*, p. 3 ff.

[16] For details of the compilation of the Liao history under the Chin, see Otagi Matsuo, pp. 300–306; Karl A. Wittfogel and Feng Chia-sheng (n. 14), p. 610 ff; Feng Chia-sheng, pp. 10–15; and Ch'en Fang-ming, pp. 10–13.

product still fell short of the standard for a dynastic history.[17] Nevertheless, these two official Liao histories, together with remnants of Liao government archives and literary works, contributed significantly to the source materials for the composition of the third official history during the later years of the Yüan dynasty.

The Mongol restoration of traditional Chinese official historiography to its position as an integral function of state activities began shortly after the enthronement of Khubilai Khaghan (Shih-tsu 世祖, r. 1260–1294) as founder of the Yüan dynasty early in 1260. This was the result of the petition of the senior Hanlin Academician Wang O 王鶚 (1190–1273), an ex-Chin official who had earlier made a similar recommendation to Khubilai when he was summoned to the audience of the future Mongol emperor at Karakorum in 1244. In August 1261, Wang submitted a lengthy memorial on the importance and desirability of compiling the historical records of the early Mongol emperors, as well as those of the Liao and Chin.[18] He stated emphatically that it had been a time-honored practice in China to compile historical records of the merits and faults of the former rulers for transmission to posterity; it was also at the heart of the Chinese tradition that even though a state had been vanquished, its history should be written by the succeeding dynasty, since judgment and evaluation can be impartial only in later generations. It was desirable, he argued, to compile the records of the great Chinggis Khan (1167–1227) in order to show the magnificence of his conquests and the reasons that had enabled him to pacify so many states, including

[17] This series of discussions on dynastic legitimacy was collectively known as *Te-yün i* 德運議 or "Discussions on the 'Cyclical Domination of the Cosmic Powers or Virtues'" in the context of the Five Agents theory. It was inaugurated by Emperor Wan-yen Ching in 1194 to designate the cosmic patron of the Chin state in the cyclical production formula of the Five Agents and to legitimize its succession to the past dynasties in the Chinese political tradition. This resulted in the pronouncement by the emperor in 1202 that the Chin state commanded the Earth Power in succession to the Sung. These discussions were resumed during the reign of Emperor Wan-yen Hsün 珣 (Hsüan-tsung 宣宗, r. 1213–1223) in 1214, but they reaffirmed the adoption of the Earth Power. The basic documents on these episodes have been preserved in a compendium called *Ta-Chin te-yün t'u-shuo* 大金德運圖説, 1 *chüan*, available in several editions. For details, see my forthcoming study: *Theories of Legitimacy in Imperial China: Discussions on "Legitimate Succession" under the Jurchen-Chin Dynasty (1115–1234)* (Seattle: University of Washington, in press). On the Chin's declaration of succession to the Sung, bypassing the Liao as the legitimate dynasty, and its effects on the composition of the Liao History, see Otagi Matsuo, pp. 304–306; Feng Chia-sheng, pp. 13–15; and Ch'en Fang-ming, pp. 10–13.

[18] For details, see Wang Yün 王惲, *Ch'iu-chien hsien-sheng ta-ch'üan-chi* 秋澗先生大全集 (SPTK ed.), 93:3b; Su T'ien-chüeh 蘇天爵, *Kuo-ch'ao ming-ch'en shih-lüeh* 國朝名臣事略 (Shanghai, 1962 ed.), 12:12a; YS 160:3757. These data have been summarized in Hok-lam Chan, "Wang O (1190–1273)," *Papers on Far Eastern History* (Canberra), 12 (Sept. 1975), pp. 43–70.

the Liao and Chin. Such records could provide lessons for the present. He then proposed reorganizing the Hanlin Academy by incorporating within it the traditional National History Office. The new office, known as the *Han-lin kuo-shih yüan* 翰林國史院, would not only be charged with recruiting talented scholars for government services, but also with compiling historical records. He further submitted a roster of former Chin officials and distinguished men of letters who he thought would serve well as Hanlin scholars and historiographers.[19] In this endeavor, it is significant that Wang O proposed the compilation of the Liao and Chin records in subordination to those of the early Mongol khans, and that he recommended the establishment of the National History Office within the Hanlin Academy. The former appears to have been a skillful device to impress Khubilai with the importance of the history projects and to justify the official sponsorship of the Liao and Chin records. The latter was an institutional innovation, apparently aimed at utilizing the influence of the Hanlin academicians, who were mostly Khubilai's advisers, to expedite the completion of the history projects.

Khubilai heartily endorsed Wang O's proposal and ordered the formation of the proposed National History Office within the Hanlin Academy and the composition of the historical records as recommended. It would be far-fetched to assume that Khubilai was unduly impressed by the magnificence of Chinese culture, since he aspired to be the universal ruler of the Mongol empire in the footsteps of Chinggis Khan. Instead, it seems more likely that he initiated the historical composition in order to learn more about the regimes conquered by his ancestors, to placate the Chinese literati, and to enhance his stature in the Chinese political tradition.[20] In any case, no matter what the motivations may have been, the re-establishment of the traditional historiographical office

[19] For a list of these scholars, see the Yüan sources cited above, and Hok-lam Chan, "Wang O," p. 55.

[20] When Khubilai ascended the throne in 1260, the only Mongolian chronicle he had in possession was probably that of the *Chinggis-gahan-u huja'ur*, which did not record events beyond 1227. It was upon Wang O's recommendation that Khubilai gave the order for the compilation of the reign chronicles of Tolui, Ögödei, Güyüg, and Möngke; they were composed in Mongolian and were presented by the *ssu-t'u* 司徒 Sarman in 1288 and 1290. See YS 15:309; 16:338; 16:341–342. They were then translated into Chinese and revised by the National History Office, and were later used for the composition of the *Wu-ch'ao shih-lu* 五朝實錄, i.e., the reign chronicles of the first five Mongol rulers in China. They were completed and presented to Emperor Temür (Ch'eng-tsung 成宗, r. 1295–1307) in 1303. See YS 21:455. For details, see Ichimura Sanjirō 市材瓃次郎, "Genchō no jitsuroku oyobi keisei daiten ni tsuite 元朝の実録及び経世大典に就きて," in Yanai Watari 箭内亙, *Mōkoshi kenkyū* 蒙古史研究 (Tokyo, 1929), Appendix. See also William Hung (n. 16), p. 473 ff; and Igor de Rachewiltz (n. 6), p. 200 ff.

as an integral part of Yüan governmental institutions had far-reaching implications. It provided the institutional mechanism not only for the composition of the three standard histories, but also for the compilation of the reign chronicles of the Mongol rulers in both Mongolian and Chinese. In this way the Mongol conquerors were invested with a historical record of their own that lay completely beyond their indigenous tradition and that guaranteed the continuity of the imperial sponsorship of historical composition under foreign domination.

3. STAGES IN THE COMPOSITION

Three distinct stages in the composition of the standard Liao, Chin and Sung histories under the auspices of the National History Office at the Yüan court may be enumerated as follows:

(a) *The First Phase: under Khubilai Khaghan (1260–1294)*

The proposal for compiling the historical records of the regimes subjugated by the Mongols was first presented to Khubilai by two Chinese scholars long before his enthronement as founder of the Yüan dynasty. They were Wang O, whose name has already been mentioned, and Liu Ping-chung 劉秉忠 (1216–1274). Both scholars recommended the composition of a history of the defunct Chin state.[21] An *optimus* on the *chin-shih* examination in 1233, Wang O served in the Presidential Council (*shang-shu sheng* 尚書省) of the last Chin emperor Wan-yen Shou-hsü 守緒 (Ai-tsung 哀宗, r. 1224–1234). Late in 1244, upon the recommendation of Chang Jou 張柔 (1190–1268), a myriarch commander of the Chinese forces in the Mongolian army, Wang O was summoned to Karakorum by Khubilai Khaghan to lecture on the Chinese classics. Shortly afterwards, he submitted to Khubilai his plan for compiling an official Chin history, the first such public proposal since the Jurchen capitulation to the Mongols in spring 1234.[22] Following this, in 1249, when Liu Ping-chung, a Buddho-Taoist disciple, received a similar invitation to Khubilai's quarters to offer counsel on state affairs, he also recommended the composition of a Chin history. The recommendation was incorporated in his lengthy memorandum on the adoption of the Chinese model for governmental reforms. "'A state may be vanquished, but its history remains'; this is a saying of the sages," he said. "An

---

[21] For Liu Ping-chung's biography, see YS 157:3691. His recommendation of the composition of the Chin history is mentioned in Hok-lam Chan, "Liu Ping-chung (1216–1274): A Buddhist-Taoist Statesman at the Court of Khubilai Khan," *T'oung Pao*, 53:1–3 (1967), p. 121.

[22] *Ch'iu-chien hsien-sheng ta-ch'üan-chi*, 82:11b.

official·history of the defunct Chin state should be compiled, so that [the record of] the merits and deeds of its ministers will be transmitted to future generations."[23]

The proposals of these two scholars were similar in tone, although their motives may have differed. Wang O, as a former official of the Chin, would naturally have been eager to see the composition of the history of his former state out of loyalty or nostalgia. Liu Ping-chung, however, who had had no previous connection with the Chin, probably made his proposal as a part of a scheme to transform the Mongol regime into a traditional Chinese state in conformity with Confucian principles of government. Their recommendations, however, received a negative response, since Khubilai was not yet in a position of authority.

Subsequently, however, in August 1261, a year after Khubilai's enthronement, Wang O became a senior Hanlin academician and was entrusted with making many institutional reforms on the traditional Chinese models. It was at this juncture, as previously stated, that he urged the composition of the Liao and Chin histories together with the reign chronicles of the early Mongol rulers. He further urged that these tasks be placed in the hands of the National History Office. Khubilai approved his request, whereupon Wang recommended that Wang Wen-t'ung 王文統, then director of political affairs in the Central Secretariat (chung-shu sheng 中書省), be ordered to supervise the historical composition.[24] Before long, however, Wang Wen-t'ung was executed (Feb. 1262). He had been implicated in the rebellion of his son-in-law Li T'an 李壇, the chief military administrator of Shantung, and the resultant political situation temporarily stalled the history project.[25] In 1264, when the Hanlin Academy with its National History Office was transferred to the new capital Ta-tu 大都 (modern Peking), Wang O submitted another memorial pleading for the revival of the historical composition. His effort was subsequently joined by another Hanlin academician, Shang T'ing 商挺 (1209–1288), who memorialized Khubilai on the importance of compiling the chronicles of the early Mongol rulers. He also urged the joint composition of these records alongside the Liao and Chin histories.[26] This clever strategy, like Wang O's before

[23] YS 157:3691.

[24] See n. 18 above.

[25] For Wang Wen-t'ung's biography, see YS 206:4594. For details of Li T'an's rebellion and Wang Wen-t'ung's demise, see Otagi Matsuo, "Ri Dan no hanran to sono seijiteki igi 李壇の叛乱と其の政治的意義," Tōyōshi kenkyū 東洋史研究, 6:4 (1931), pp. 1–26; Sun K'o-k'uan 孫克寬, "Yüan-ch'u Li T'an shih-pien ti fen-hsi 元初李壇事變的分析," TLTC, 13:8 (1956), pp. 7–15; and Hsiao Ch'i-ch'ing 蕭啓慶, Hsi-yü jen yü Yüan-ch'u cheng-chih 西域人與元初政治 (Taipei, 1966), pp. 159–161.

[26] YS 159:3740.

him, was designed to arouse the enthusiasm of the Mongol emperor for the compilation and to push through the Liao and Chin history projects. From then on, the composition of the Liao and Chin histories remained an integral part of the Mongol reign-chronicle compilation project under the auspices of the National History Office.

Under Wang O, some progress was made in the Chin history project, much more than in the Liao. He recommended sixteen former Chin scholar-officials to staff the National History Office, drafted a general outline for the Chin history, and prepared several chapters of the history himself.[27] In this way, a solid foundation was laid for the composition of the standard Liao and Chin histories during the early years of Khubilai Khaghan's reign.

The need to compile a Sung history came to official attention soon after the end of the Southern Sung dynasty in 1279. During the fall of the Southern Sung capital Lin-an 臨安 (modern Hangchow) in February 1276, Tung Wen-ping 董文炳 (1216–1277), a Chinese myriarch in the Mongolian army who took part in that campaign, recovered portions of the Sung government archives and kept them in his custody. When the Hanlin academician Li P'an 李槃 arrived in Lin-an with an order from Khubilai Khaghan to recruit former Sung scholar-officials for service in the Yüan government, Tung said to Li: "A state may be vanquished, but not its history," and turned over to him the Sung archives he had captured.[28] Thereupon the task of collecting and compiling the Sung dynasty records was assigned to the National History Office, although the only noticeable progress made during this period seems to have been on the Liao and Chin histories; as to the Sung history, the office's activities were probably limited to the collection of source materials.

In this context, a pertinent question may be raised. If one of the objectives of the composition of the Liao, Chin, and Sung histories was to inform the Mongol rulers about the regimes they had subdued, why were there no proposals to include a separate history for the Hsi-Hsia 西夏, the Tangut kingdom that had existed in northwest China between 1032 and 1227 and which had been a powerful rival of all these three states and even of the Mongols? The main reasons, I think, are the following. First, the Hsi-Hsia was never considered by its adversary

---

[27] *Ch'iu-chien hsien-sheng ta-ch'üan-chi*, 93:3b; 100:12a. Cf. Hok-lam Chan, *Chin Historiography*, pp. 10–12; and *id.*, "Wang O," pp. 50–57.

[28] YS 156:3672. This is based on Tung's family biography by Yüan Ming-shan (1269–1322) included in *Ch'ing-ho chi* 清河集 (*Ou-hsiang ling-shih* 藕香零拾 ed., 1895), 7:1a (also in Su T'ien-chüeh, *Kuo-ch'ao wen-lei* 國朝文類 [SPTK ed.], 70:10b). For an account of Tung Wen-ping, see Sun K'o-k'uan, *Yüan-tai Han wen-hua chih huo-tung* 元代漢文化之活動 (Taipei, 1968), p. 309 ff.

rulers or by Chinese historians as a legitimate state that should or could be incorporated into the traditional dynastic succession pattern. Second, the Tanguts were not as sinicized as the Khitans and Jurchens. They did not develop a Chinese-style tradition of historical recording, and most of their surviving documents were written in the Tangut script. Lastly, the Hsi-Hsia never found a patron among the scholar-officials in Mongol service, whether Chinese or non-Chinese, to speak for the need of compiling its history in the Chinese historiographical fashion. These factors account for the fact that no separate standard history of the Hsi-Hsia was compiled under the Yüan. Instead, the Hsi-Hsia was accorded only a brief monograph appended to each of the three standard histories. Yet these accounts were based entirely on contemporary records written in Chinese. As such they are sketchy and riddled with errors. They are inadequate representations of the historical importance of the Hsi-Hsia. It appears that the Yüan historiographers either did not bother to translate the Tangut documents and make use of them, or they did not have access to the original source materials at all.[29]

(b) *The Second Phase: From Emperor Ayurbarwada (Jen-tsung, r. 1312–1320) to Tugh Temür (Wen-tsung, r. 1328–1332)*

Between the reigns of Emperors Ayurbarwada and Tugh Temür, several officials submitted memorials recommending that the Liao, Chin, and Sung histories be compiled. During the reign of Ayurbarwada, Li Meng 李孟 (1255–1321), who had tutored the emperor when he was the heir apparent, submitted a plea for the composition of the Sung history, but the proposal aroused little enthusiasm.[30] During the next reign, that of Shidebala (Ying-tsung 英宗, r. 1321–1323), the chancellor of the Central Secretariat, Baiju (d. 1323), a scholar of Turkish descent who concur-

---

[29] The two most important works on Hsi-Hsia compiled by Ch'ing historians based on traditional Chinese sources are: Wu Kuang-ch'eng 吳廣成, *Hsi-Hsia shu-shih* 西夏書事, 42 *chüan* (1825); and Tai Hsi-chang 戴錫章, *Hsi-Hsia chi* 西夏記, 28 *chüan* (1924). For a brief survey of the Ch'ing historical compilations see Chu Hsi-tsu 朱希祖, "Hsi-Hsia shih-liao k'ao 西夏史料考," *Shuo-wen yüeh-k'an* 說文月刊, 3:11 (Nov. 1942), pp. 25–30. Some of the earlier Tangut documents of the Hsi-Hsia have been studied by Wang Ching-ju 王靜如 in *Hsi-Hsia yen-chiu* 西夏研究, 3 vols. (Peiping, 1932–33). The best account of Hsi-Hsia's history in Chinese is Lin Lü-chih 林旅之, *Hsi-Hsia shih* 西夏史 (Hong Kong, 1975). For recent studies on the Tangut documents in Western languages, see Françoise Aubin, "Travaux et tendances de la Sinologie Soviétique récente," *T'oung Pao*, 58 (1972), pp. 166–171; Eric Grinstead, "Hsi-Hsia," in *Sung Studies Newsletter* (Supplement 1), 10 (1974), pp. 38–42; and Luc Kwanten, "Tangut Miscellanea," *Journal of the American Oriental Society*, 97:3 (July-Sept. 1977), pp. 333–335.

[30] See Huang Chin 黃溍, *Chin-hua Huang hsien-sheng wen-chi* 金華黃先生文集 (SPTK ed.), 27:8b; YS 175:4084. Cf. Herbert Franke, "Could the Mongol Emperors Read and Write Chinese?" *Asia Major*, 3 (1952), p. 32.

rently served as supervisor-director of the National History Office, expressed considerable interest in the Liao, Chin, and Sung history project. He entrusted Yüan Chüeh 袁桷 (1266–1327), a Hanlin academician serving in the same office, with the task of formulating principles for the historical composition and setting the criteria for the collection of source materials for the three histories.[31] The time seemed ripe for a breakthrough in the history project; unfortunately, Shidebala was assassinated in a coup d'état in 1323, and the project was again prematurely terminated in the ensuing political turmoil.[32] Following this, under Emperor Yesün Temür (r. 1324–1328), an attempt was made by Chang Kuei 張珪 (1264–1327), chancellor of the Central Secretariat, to resuscitate the historical compilation project. He submitted a memorial in 1325 recommending the renowned Confucian scholar Wu Ch'eng 吳澄 (1249–1333) to take charge of the composition of the three histories as well as of the reign chronicle of the demised emperor Shidebala. But the court again failed to respond.[33] During the reign of Tugh Temür, upon the urging of some Confucian scholars, the emperor promulgated several edicts in an effort to re-activate the history project, but little progress was made. It appears that the main obstacles by this time lay, not in the paucity of source materials nor in insufficient imperial support, but in the formulation of principles for historical composition.[34] With respect to the latter, the efforts were impeded by the controversy over the issue of cheng-t'ung. The controversy surfaced during the later years of Khubilai Khaghan's reign, when attempts were made to determine the legitimacy of the Liao, Chin, and Sung dynasties, as well as to settle the status of the Mongol emperors as the legitimate rulers of all China.

The term cheng-t'ung, which has been conventionally rendered in

[31] See Su T'ien-chüeh, "Yüan Wen-ch'ing kung mu-chih 袁文清公墓誌," in Ch'ing-jung chü-shih chi 清容居士集 (I-chia t'ang ts'ung-shu 宜稼堂叢書 ed., 1840), Appendix, 3a. Yüan Chüeh's memorandum on the collection of source materials for the three histories entitled "Hsiu Liao-Chin-Sung shih sou-fang i-shu t'iao-li shih-chuang 修遼金宋史搜訪遺書條列事狀" is preserved in Ch'ing-jung chü-shih chi (SPTK ed.), 41:31a–40b. For an account of Baiju, see YS 136:3300; see also Louis Hambis, Le chapitre CVII du Yuan-che (Leiden, 1954), pp. 74, 79.

[32] On the coup d'état against Shidebala (Ying-tsung), see YS 28:632–633; K'o Shao-min 柯劭忞, Hsin Yüan shih 新元史 (Shanghai, 1921), 114:5b. See also Ch'en Pang-chan 陳邦瞻, Yüan-shih chi-shih pen-mo 元史紀事本末 (Shanghai, 1955), ch. 20, and Louis Hambis (n. 31), p. 76.

[33] See Yü Chi 虞集, "Lin-ch'uan hsien-sheng Wu kung hsing-chuang 臨川先生吳公行狀," in Tao-yüan hsüeh-ku lu 道園學古錄 (SPTK ed.), 44:9b. For Chang Kuei's biography, see YS 175:4071.

[34] See "Chin Chin-shih piao 進金史表," in CS, Appendix, 2900; Yü Chi (n. 32), 32:5a; T'ao Tsung-i 陶宗儀, Cho-keng lu 輟耕錄 (SPTK ed.), 3:3b; and Wang Ch'i 王圻, Hsü Wen-hsien t'ung-k'ao 續文獻通考 (1602), 176:11a.

English as "legitimate" or "orthodox succession" and identified with the Western concept of legitimacy, originated as two separate words, *cheng* and *t'ung*, in the expressions "ta chü-cheng 大居正" and "ta i-t'ung 大一統" in the Kung-yang Commentary to the *Ch'un-ch'iu* 春秋公羊傳 (Annals of the Spring and Autumn Period, 722–481 B.C.) composed during the third century B.C. *Cheng-t'ung* emerged as a compound in the Later Han literature, such as the *Han-shu* 漢書 (*History of the [Former] Han Dynasty*), at the dawn of the Christian era, and subsequently came to be applied in the theory of legitimacy of imperial rulers and political regimes in an interdynastic linkage scheme of uninterrupted succession. In its inception, the Chinese concept of legitimacy is traceable to the "mandate of heaven" (天命) theory in the Chou antiquity. It was reinforced by the Confucian notion of moral preponderance as expounded in the *Spring and Autumn Annals*. But the specific criteria for designating the legitimacy of rulership underwent successive changes in the course of time.[35] During the Ch'in and Han, under the influence of the Five Agents theory of cosmological and political changes espoused by Tsou Yen 鄒衍 (305–240 B.C.?), the various imperial rulers each declared their legitimacy by proclaiming the acquisition of a specific cosmic force or power: water, fire, metal, wood, or earth, according to the cyclical pulsation sequence of these mystical forces or powers. But by the Later Han, the possession of the proper blood relationship in the imperial genealogy emerged as the most important qualification for legitmacy. The expression *cheng-t'ung* was then coined with the specific meaning of "correct filiation" and was frequently invoked to legitimize the imperial claimants. In the post-Han period, however, the term generally meant "legitimate" or "orthodox succession," and thus the criteria for postulating the legitimacy of rulership in a continuous line of succession included, in addition to the possession of the proper blood relationship, moral integrity, political unification, and cultural achievement, with or without reference to the Five Agents theory.[36] During the Northern Sung, *cheng-t'ung* theories enjoyed renewed popularity under the rise of the rational, moralistic

[35] For a general discussion of the evolution of the *cheng-t'ung* theories in Chinese political thought and their application for political legitimation, see Naka Michiyo 那珂通世, "Shina seitōron 支那正統論" (1898), in *Naka Michiyo isho* 那珂通世遺書 (Tokyo, 1915), pp. 1–14; Liu I-cheng 柳詒徵, *Kuo-shih yao-i* 國史要義 (Shanghai, 1948), pp. 50–66; Chao Ling-yang 趙令揚, *Kuan-yü li-tai cheng-t'ung wen-t'i chih cheng-lun* 關於歷代正統問題之爭論 (Hong Kong, 1976), *passim*; Jao Tsung-i 饒宗頤, *Chung-kuo shih-hsüeh shang chih cheng-t'ung lun* 中國史學上之正統論 (Hong Kong, 1977), Intro.; and Hok-lam Chan, *Theories of Legitimacy in Imperial China* ... , Intro.

[36] See Liu I-cheng (n. 35) p. 54 ff; Jao Tsung-i (n. 35), p. 2 ff.

philosophies of Neo-Confucianism. The criteria of legitimacy then shifted to those of moral right and political unification as expounded by Ou-yang Hsiu 歐陽修 (1007–1072) and Chu Hsi 朱熹 (1130–1200), both of whom rejected the cosmic pulsation scheme of the Five Agents formulation and the notion of an uninterrupted line of succession of legitimate rulers and dynasties. The last attempt by imperial rulers to invoke the Five Agents theory for legitimation was, as mentioned earlier, that of the Jurchen emperors of the Chin dynasty. They proclaimed the acquisition of Earth Power in succession to the Northern Sung as the legitimate rulers of China.[37]

In the course of time, the *cheng-t'ung* concept in its general meaning of "legitimate succession" became a prominent ideological principle for the writing and interpretation of Chinese history. It was first applied in this way by Hsi Tso-ch'ih 習鑿齒 (d. 384) of the Eastern Tsin in his *Han-Tsin ch'un-ch'iu* 漢晉春秋 (*Spring and Autumn Annals of the Han and Tsin*). In this work he invoked the criteria of correct bloodline, moral superiority, geo-political advantages, and cultural preponderance to posit the legitimacy of the ruling houses from the Later Han to the Tsin dynasties, without reference to the Five Agents theory. In so doing, he restored legitimacy to the Shu 蜀 kingdom (221–263) during the Three Kingdoms Period, and rejected its two principal rival states, Wei 魏 (220–265) and Wu 吳 (222–280), as usurpers. He sought thereby to rectify the injustice done by the pro-Wei historian Ch'en Shou 陳壽 (233–297) in his *San-kuo chih* 三國志 (*Chronicles of the Three Kingdoms*). The precedent was thus set for the application of the concept of legitimate succession to historical writing.[38] It was further developed by Sung scholar-historians

---

[37] On the development of the Neo-Confucian interpretation of the *cheng-t'ung* theories with reference to Ou-yang Hsiu, Chu Hsi and others, see, in particular, Nishi Junzō 西順蔵, "Hoku-Sō sonota no seitō ron 北宋その他の正統論," *Hitotsubashi ronsō* 一橋論叢, 30:5 (1953), pp. 48–70; Rolf Trauzettel, "A Discussion on the Legitimate Line of Succession in Northern Sung Time," *Cina* 8, (1964), pp. 56–58; *Id.*, "Ou-yang Hsiu's Essays über die Legitime Thronnachfolge," *Sinologica*, 9:3–4 (1967), pp. 236–258; Ch'en Fang-ming 陳芳明, "Sung-tai cheng-t'ung lun ti hsing-ch'eng pei-ching chi ch'i nei-jung 宋代正統論的形成背景及其內容," *Shih-huo yüeh-k'an*, 1:8 (Nov. 1971), pp. 16–28; and Shigezewa Toshio 重沢俊郎, "Oyōshū no seitōron 歐陽修の正統論," in *Tōhō gakkai sōritsu nijūgo shūnen kinen tōhō gaku ronshū* 東方学会創立二十五周年紀念東方学論集 (Tokyo, 1972), pp. 395–406.

[38] For a general account of the application of the *cheng-t'ung* theories for the writing and interpretation of Chinese history since the post-Han era, see, among others, Wei Ying-ch'i 魏應麒, *Chung-kuo shih-hsüeh shih* 中國史學史 (Shanghai, 1941), pp. 94–96, 109–113; Naitō Torajirō, *Shina shigaku shi*, pp. 321–334; Liu I-cheng (n. 35), pp. 50–66; Otto van der Sprenkel, "Chronologie et historiographie chinoises," *Mélanges publiés par l'Institut des Hautes Études Chinoises*, 2 (Paris, 1960), pp. 407–421; as well as Chao Ling-yang and Jao Tsung-i's works cited in n. 35 above, *passim*. On the historiography of the *Han-Tsin ch'un-*

culminating in Chu Hsi's *magnum opus, Tzu-chih t'ung-chien kang-mu*
資治通鑑綱目 *(Outline of the Comprehensive Mirror for Aid in
Government).* This was a digest of a chronology compiled by Ssu-ma
Kuang 司馬光 (1019–1086), covering the period from Eastern Chou to
the Five Dynasties. In this work Chu Hsi classified the imperial regimes
of the Chinese past as either legitimate or illegitimate, called *cheng* 正
(orthodox) and *jun* 閏 (irregular) respectively. He based these classifications on the criteria of moral right and political unification as elucidated in Ou-yang Hsiu's interpretation of the Kung-yang Commentary
on the *Spring and Autumn Annals.* Chu Hsi's work provided the
inspiration and the guidelines for the application of the theories of
legitimate succession in Chinese historical writings until the present
century.[39]

In the light of this background, it is not surprising that the issue of
legitimate succession became a heated topic of discussion when the
scholar-historians under the Yüan attempted to formulate principles for
the composition of the three histories. The discussions were complicated
and burdened by political overtones since two of the dynasties, Liao and
Chin, were alien conquerors, whereas the Yüan court that sponsored the
history project was also of foreign origin and had destroyed a legitimate
Chinese dynasty, the Southern Sung.[40] Shortly after the Mongol conquest of China, there appeared a number of essays and treatises on the
issue of legitimate succession, and towards the last reign of the Yüan
dynasty the number of such essays proliferated greatly. Some of these
were drafted by scholar-historians in response to requests from the court,
while others were written by private historians concerned with the
application of the moralistic principles to historical writing. The more
important ones include: Yang Huan 楊奐 (1186–1255), *Cheng-t'ung shu
正統書 (Documents on Legitimate Succession),* 60 *chüan;* Yao Sui 姚燧

---

ch'iu and *San-kuo chih,* see Wei Ying-ch'i, pp. 109–113; Hsü Hao, pp. 69–83; and Rafe
R.C. de Crespigny, *The Records of the Three Kingdoms: A Study in the Historiography of
the San-kuo chih* (Canberra, 1970).

[39] On the historiography of *Tzu-chih t'ung-chien* and *Tzu-chih t'ung-chien kang-mu* with
reference to their positions on the legitimate succession issue, see Otto Franke, "Das Tse
Tschi T'ung Kien und das T'ung Kien Kang Mu," *Sitz. d. Preuss. Ak. d. Wiss.; Phil. Hist.
kl* (1930), pp. 103–156; Nakayama Kyūshirō 中山久四郎, "Shushi no shigaku, toku ni
sono Shichitōkan kōmoku ni tsuite 朱熹の史学, 特にその資治通鑑綱目について,"
Shichō 史潮, 1:3 (Oct., 1931), pp. 33–60, and 2:1 (Oct., 1932), pp. 72–98; Ch'ien Mu
錢穆, "Chu-tzu chih T'ung-chien kang-mu 朱子之通鑑綱目," in *Essays in Chinese Studies
Presented to Professor Lo Hsiang-lin* 壽羅香林教授論文集 (Hong Kong, 1970), pp. 1–11;
and Ming K. Chan, "The Historiography of the *Tzu-chih t'ung-chien:* A Survey,"
Monumenta Serica, 30 (1974–75), pp. 1–38.

[40] See Otagi Matsuo, pp. 315–322; Ch'en Fang-ming, pp. 1–14.

(1239–1314), *Kuo-t'ung li-ho piao* 國統離合表 (*Configurations of Dynastic Rule*); Hsiu (or Hsieh) Tuan 修(謝)端, "Pien Liao, Sung, Chin cheng-t'ung 辯遼宋金正統" ("Distinguishing the Legitimate Succession of Liao, Chin and Sung"); Ni Shih-i 倪士毅, *Li-tai ti-wang ch'uan-shou t'u-shuo* 歷代帝王傳授圖説 (*Diagrams Illustrating the Succession of Emperors of All Ages*); Feng I-weng 馮翼翁 (*chin-shih* 1324), *Cheng-t'ung wu-te lei-yao* 正統五德類要 (*Classified Essentials on Legitimate Succession and the Five Cosmic Powers*), 34 *chüan*; Wang Li 王理, "San-shih cheng-t'ung lun 三史正統論" ("On Legitimate Succession and the Three Histories"); and Wang Wei 王禕 (1322–1373), "Cheng-t'ung lun 正統論" ("On Legitimate Succession").[41]

These writings fall into two categories: (a) those based on purely theoretical discussions, and (b) those which applied theory to the concrete cases of the Liao, Chin, and Sung. In the latter category, we would include Hsiu (Hsieh?) Tuan's discourse. There he records a discussion that transpired in 1294 between two schools of concerned scholars. The argument went as follows:[42]

The first school advanced the example of the *Tsin-shu* 晉書 (*History of the Tsin Dynasty*), which created a special section for the "barbarian" kingdoms, entitled *tsai-chi* 載記 (*Contemporaneous Records*). The "barbarians" were thus kept apart from the Basic Annals of the legitimate imperial house of the Tsin (265–420).[43] Proponents of this approach maintained that although the Northern Sung had been brought to an end by the Jurchens in 1126, the Chinese ruling house still survived for more than a century in the south as a legitimate dynasty. The Liao and Chin, which had established themselves as independent kingdoms partly inside

---

[41] Yang Huan's *Cheng-t'ung shu* has been lost, but its preface is preserved in his *Huan-shan i-kao* 還山遺稿 (*Shih-yüan ts'ung-shu* 適園叢書 ed., 1916), *shang*: 7b. The works of Yao Sui, Ni Shih-i, and Feng I-weng have not been transmitted; they are mentioned in *Yüan i-wen chih* 元藝文志, in *Liao-Chin-Yüan i-wen chih* 遼金元藝文志 (Shanghai, 1958), p. 239. The preface to Yao Sui's treatise is preserved in his *Mu-an chi* 牧庵集 (SPTK ed.), 3:2a ff. Hsiu (Hsieh?) Tuan's discourse is included in Su T'ien-chüeh, *Kuo-ch'ao wen-lei*, 45:3a, and Wang Yün, *Ch'iu-chien hsien-sheng ta-ch'üan-chi*, 100:1a. Wang Li's work is mentioned in Pi Yüan 畢沅, *Hsü Tzu-chih t'ung-chien* 續資治通鑑 (*Ssu-pu pei-yao* 四部備要 ed.), 208:13a. Wang Wei's essay is available in his *Wang Chung-wen kung chi* 王忠文公集 (*Chin-hua ts'ung-shu* 金華叢書 ed., 1869), 1:1b–13b. Cf. Feng Chia-sheng, pp. 17–18; Hok-lam Chan, *Chin Historiography* pp. 13–14; and Jao Tsung-i (n. 35), pp. 39–42.

[42] See Hsiu (Hsieh?) Tuan's essay cited in n. 41 above.

[43] *Tsin-shu*, 130 *chüan*, covers the years 265–419. It includes 30 *chüan* of *Tsai-chi* (ch. 101–130). It was compiled by Fang Hsüan-ling 房玄齡 (578–648), *et al.*, under imperial auspices. For an account of its historiography, see Hsü Hao, pp. 79–91, and Lien-sheng Yang, *Studies in Chinese Institutional History* (Cambridge, Mass., 1963), pp. 119–124.

China proper, were, in their opinion, comparable to the "barbarian" kingdoms in North China during the Tsin dynasty. Therefore, they argued, if the Sung, Liao, and Chin were to be grouped together into a single history, the Sung should be accorded a place in the Basic Annals, whereas the Liao and Chin should be relegated to the Contemporaneous Records.

The second school upheld the example provided by the *Nan-shih* 南史 (*History of the Southern Dynasties*) and the *Pei-shih* 北史 (*History of the Northern Dynasties*), which classified the kingdoms, both Chinese and non-Chinese alike, according to their geographical locations.[44] Proponents of this school held that the Liao, which had arisen in the north toward the last days of the T'ang, had expanded during the Five Dynasties and had co-existed with the Northern Sung, was a legitimate northern state. They averred that the history of the Liao, together with that of the Chin (which succeeded the former as rulers of north China), should be entitled *Pei-shih*. The Northern Sung should be treated independently in a *Sung shih* (*History of the Sung*) whereas the Southern Sung, a legitimate dynasty in South China, should have a separate history entitled *Nan-shih*.

Aside from theoretical considerations, the respective positions taken by these scholars inevitably bore political implications. Those who invoked the precedent of the *History of the Tsin* thereby placed the accounds of the Sung in the Basic Annals and those of the Liao and Chin in the Contemporaneous Records. This implied the recognition of the legitimacy of the Sung house, and the dismissal of the Yüan, along with the Liao and Chin, as usurpers in the Chinese dynastic tradition. Meanwhile, those who followed the example of the histories of the Southern and Northern Dynasties, thereby according Liao and Chin legitimate status alongside the Sung, essentially offered a compromise to placate the Yüan court. That is, they implied that the Mongols were legitimate claimants to the throne of China even prior to their conquest of the Southern Sung. It is not certain what the political pretensions of the individual scholars who professed these diverse opinions may have been; nevertheless, it is quite obvious that those who proposed the latter solution were willing to extend legitimacy to the non-Chinese conquerors even at the expense of the Chinese rulers of the Sung.

The conflicts between these views brought the composition of the three histories to a standstill. The issue of the legitimate sucession of the Liao,

---

[44] *Nan-shih*, 80 *chüan*, covers the years 420–589; *Pei-shih*, 100 *chüan*, covers the years 368–618. They were compiled by Li Yen-shou 李延壽 (*ca*.629), *et al.*, under imperial auspices. For an account of their historiography, see Hsü Hao, pp. 133–142, 143–156.

Chin, and Sung states even became a subject of public concern. It was raised, for example, in a civil service examination at the county level. The question, drafted by the Hanlin Academician Sung Pen 宋本 (1218–1334), reads as follows:

"The Sung dynasty, founded by the Chao 趙 family, lasted over three hundred years. The Liao and Chin were its contemporaries.... The court is deliberating over the joint compilation of their chronicles.... Shall we follow the *Tso chuan* 左傳 [i.e., the chronological style of the *Tso Commentary*] or the *Shih chi* 史記 [i.e., the annual-biographical style of the *Records of the Historian*]? And how shall we decide on the adoption or rejection of the principles [governing historical composition] and those [concerning the designation of] the correct calendar?"[45]

The last part of this question, in fact, was directed at the issue of dynastic legitimacy, since the designation of a correct chronology for these three histories would have required a settlement of the problem of the legitimate succession of the three states. The issue, moreover, had serious political implications for the Mongol regime in China. If the Liao and the Chin were treated as illegitimate rulers, it would imply that the Mongols were similarly illegitimate. A related question, which was no less pertinent, emerged from the political and historiographical points of view. That is, which year should mark the founding of the Mongol dynasty in China? Should it be the year 1206, when the Mongol hegemony began under Chinggis Khan, even though both the Chin and the Sung still existed? Or should it be as late as 1276, the year the Southern Sung capital fell to the Mongol forces? Since Mongol legitimacy was the real issue at stake, it seems that the only viable alternative would have been to make all three ruling houses simultaneously legitimate, thereby allowing the Mongols to become the legitimate successor of each state in turn as they unified all China under their rule.[46]

(c) *The Third Phase: Completion under Emperor Toghōn Temür (Shun-ti, r. 1333–1368)*

The three histories project was finally launched with full vigor under Emperor Toghōn Temür after decades of lethargy due to political and ideological polemics over the issue of legitimate succession. The initiative reportedly came from Nao-nao 巎巎 (1295–1345), a sinicized scholar of Turkish descent, who expounded on the need to compose the Liao, Chin,

---

[45] Sung Pen, "Hsiang-shih ts'e-wen 鄉試策問," included in *Kuo-ch'ao wen-lei*, 47:4a. For Sung Pen's biographies, see Sung Chiung 宋褧, *Yen-shih chi* 燕石集 (Taipei, 1971 ed.), 15:1a, and YS 182:4203.

[46] This was Yang Wei-chen's view; see n. 103, 106 below.

and Sung histories in the midst of a lecture on the *Comprehensive Mirror for Aid in Government* that he delivered before the throne.[47] His proposal received instant support from Chancellor Toghto 脱脱 (1314–1355) and the latter's pro-Chinese faction at the Yüan court. This group considered such an undertaking a timely device to enhance their political stature to rally the support of the Chinese literati. In April 1343, Toghto memorialized Toghōn Temür, proposing the establishment of a special bureau for the three histories project. His argument echoed the views of traditional historians on the importance of historical composition. It reads in part:

"These three kingdoms had been taken over by our holy regime. Their statutes and institutions, and the causes of their rise and fall, may vanish as time goes by.... [Their historical chronicles] will reveal the glory and virtue of our ancestors and the reasons for our succeeding to the Liao, Chin and Sung [as the legitimate rulers of the empire]. These will serve as a mirror for later generations ... and will be the great work of our dynasty."[48]

The Yüan emperor heartily endorsed Toghto's proposal and issued a decree appointing him director-in-chief of the history project. The decree also charged him with the recruitment of scholar-officials to staff the historical commissions. His appointments included not only Chinese but also sinicized Mongols and Central Asians.[49] The same decree ordered local officials throughout the empire to collect miscellaneous historical data for the project, promising rewards for those who submitted such material.[50] To finance this enormous undertaking, the court assigned

---

[47] For Nao-nao's biography, see YS 143:3413; see also Ch'en Yüan, *Western and Central Asians in China Under the Mongols*, tr. and annotated by Ch'ien Hsing-hai and L.C. Goodrich (Los Angeles, 1966), pp. 24–25. On the correct reading of his name, see F. W. Cleaves in HJAS, 10 (1947), pp. 1–12. See also Marilyn Wong Fu's essay in the present volume.

[48] LS, Appendix, pp. 1553–1554.

[49] A complete list of scholar-officials appointed to the respective history commission is given in the preface to each individual history. These have been included in the appendices to LS, CS and SS in the Chung-hua Shu-chü 中華書局 ed. of the three histories. It should be noted, however, that whereas the top echelon of supervising officials remained the same for all three histories, those in the lower echelon, i.e., compilers and supporting staff, differed from one history to another with only few exceptions. The result was that unless there was close coordination among the three groups of compilers, it would have been difficult to avoid discrepancies and inconsistencies in their work. Unfortunately, this was exactly what happened. There are detailed accounts on the appointment of compilers for the three histories in the collected works of Wei Su 危素 (1303–1372), one of the compilers of the Sung history. See *Wei T'ai-p'u wen-chi* 危太樸文集 (1914 ed.), *ch.* 3, 7, 8, 9; *ibid.*, *hsü-chi* 續集, *ch.* 4, 7, 8, 9.

[50] See LS, Appendix, p. 1554.

the income of the *kung-t'u-chuang* 貢土莊, the former holdings of rich Sung families confiscated by the Mongol rulers.[51]

In view of the overall political scene, the time would seem to have been ripe for such a major undertaking. The northern borderlands of China had been stabilized by the 1320s and the menace from the disenchanted anti-Chinese factions of the Mongol tribes had been eliminated. Furthermore, the civil service examinations had been re-instituted, and, by the time of Toghōn Temür's accession, there already existed a nucleus of non-Chinese *chin-shih* degree holders. Conversely, many Chinese literati had made their way into the bureaucracy, and after the fall of the violently anti-Chinese Chancellor Bayan in 1340, there was even a growing number of southern Chinese admitted to high offices in the Yüan government.[52] Under these conditions, Toghōn Temür, with the assistance of the pro-Chinese Toghto, tried to emulate Khubilai, and the Yüan court gradually gave way to a steady process of Confucianization. In this respect, as Herbert Franke has observed, the decision to push forth the compilation of the three histories may be seen as a deliberate move to enhance the respectability of the Yüan court in the eyes of the Confucian scholars, Chinese and non-Chinese alike, and to bolster the Mongol claim to legitimacy in the Chinese political tradition.[53]

The main obstacle to the completion of the historical composition, however, remained the deadlock in the bipolar dispute over the issue of legitimate succession. At this juncture, a third school arose with a compromise. It held that neither the Liao, the Chin nor the Sung was exclusively the legitimate dynasty, for the era was one of division comparable to the Three Kingdoms Period during the third century A.D. The opinion of the proponents of this view was elucidated by Wang Wei in his essay entitled "On Legitimate Succession":

"Though they occupied North China, the Chin could not be accepted as having taken the legitimate position [as rulers of] the empire. Because the Sung had moved to the south, it cannot be said to have unified the empire. The situation is similar to that of the period of Wei, Shu, Wu, the Eastern Tsin, and the Later Wei [founded by the Toba tribe]. In that

---

[51] This is shown in the imperial edict promulgated in April 1343 ordering the compilation of the three histories, and the directive issued by the Central Secretariat in 1346 concerning the printing of the Sung History. They have been included in LS, Appendix, p. 1554, and SS, Appendix, p. 14261. See also Ch'üan Heng 權衡, *Keng-shen wai-shih* 庚申外史 (*Hsüeh-chin t'ao-yüan* 學津討原 ed., 1922), 15a, and the translation of this passage in Helmut Schulte-Uffelage, *Das Keng-shen Wai-shih* ... (Berlin, 1963), pp. 48–51.

[52] For details, see John W. Dardess (n. 3), ch. 3–5.

[53] See Herbert Franke, "Chinese Historiography ... ," pp. 18–19.

period right and wrong were difficult to define, and the line of legitimate succession was thus broken. After the Liao had been vanquished by the Chin, and both the Chin and the Southern Sung conquered by the Yüan, [the Yüan] took the legitimate position [as rulers of] the empire, unified the empire, and restored the legitimacy of the line of succession." [54]

In other words, the Mongols succeeded in becoming the legitimate rulers only by conquering the Liao, the Chin and the Sung, although each had separately regarded itself as legitimate. Toghto accepted this solution despite continued opposition. He recommended that special history commissions be formed and that scholars of exceptional talent be invited to take charge of the historical composition. [55] There remained, however, the question of formulating the principles for the composition of the three histories based on the official guidelines with respect to the issue of legitimate succession.

During this time, a leading Hanlin academician named Liu Yüeh-shen 劉岳申 (1260–1346?) proposed the adoption of the format of Ou-yang Hsiu's *Hsin Wu-tai shih* 新五代史 (*New History of the Five Dynasties*) for the composition of the Liao and Chin histories, and that of his *Hsin T'ang-shu* 新唐書 (*New History of the T'ang Dynasty*) for the Sung history. [56] This formula, however, could not be applied, since Ou-yang Hsiu's *New History of the Five Dynasties* relegated the Liao and the Chin to the "Monographs of Barbarian Kingdoms," an option which had been ruled out by Toghto's decision to accord legitimacy to these two states along with the Sung ruling house. The director-general of the three histories project, the Chinese scholar Ou-yang Hsüan 歐陽玄 (1283–1357), then proposed a compromise by retaining Ou-yang Hsiu's *New History of the T'ang* as one of the models of composition. He drew up the following guidelines:

a. *Ti-chi* 帝紀 (Imperial Annals)
The style of the three histories shall follow that of the *Records of the*

---

[54] Wang Wei, *Wang Chung-wen kung chi*, 1:13a. For Wang Wei's biographies, see MS 289:7414, and A. R. Davis' contribution in *Dictionary of Ming Biography*, eds. L.C. Goodrich and Chaoying Fang (New York, 1976), pp. 1445–1447.

[55] See n. 48 above.

[56] Liu Yüeh-shen 劉岳申, "Ts'e-wen hsiu Liao-Chin-Sung san-shih 策問修遼金宋三史," in *Shen-chai Liu hsien-sheng wen-chi* 申齋劉先生文集 (Taipei, 1970), 15:1a. He proposed following the model of *Hsin Wu-tai shih* for the composition of the Sung history because he felt that only by adopting Ou-yang Hsiu's interpretive approach would it be possible to synthesize the mountainous source materials into a slender volume of history. See Ch'en Fang-ming, p. 17. For a brief account of Liu Yüeh-shen's biography, see the introductory remark to his collected works by Ch'ang Pi-te 昌彼得 included in the photo-lithographic reproduction by the Commercial Press.

Historian, History of the Former Han and the *New History of the T'ang*.
The dynastic titles will accord with the examples of the standard histories
of the Southern and Northern Dynasties.

b. *Chih* 志 (Treatises)

The treatises should record the important events of each dynasty.

c. *Piao* 表 (Chronological Tables)

Same principles as above.

d. *Lieh-chuan* 列傳 (Biographies)

The biographies are to be classified into Empresses and Ladies-in-
waiting, Royal Families, Imperial Relatives, Ministers, and
Miscellaneous Biographies. Each meritorious official will have a separate
biography, even when his father or son already has one. Group biographies are warranted. Accounts in the three histories that conflict with
those of the present dynasty must be reported without concealment.
Martyrs of the Chin and Sung are entitled to biographies. Questions not
covered by principles thus far have to be discussed jointly by the
directors and compilers.

e. In following the criteria of the *Spring and Autumn Annals*, doubts
which cannot be settled shall remain as doubts, and truth, when as-
certained, shall be transmitted as such.[57]

By this time, scores of scholar-officials had already been appointed to
the respective commissions in charge of the historical composition. Most
of the compilers were Chinese scholar-officials since the bulk of the
documents were written in Chinese, but a few non-Chinese were also
recruited to handle the linguistic problems arising from the transcription
of the Khitan, Jurchen, and Mongolian nomenclature. The latter were
also equally at home in Chinese. There were four compilers for the Liao
history, including a Uighur; six compilers for the Chin history, with two
being Uighur; and twenty-three compilers for the Sung history, only
three of whom were non-Chinese of Tangut and Mongolian origin. The
distribution of the personnel in these historical commissions, as mentioned below, was by and large dictated by the scope and requirement of
the respective histories.[58]

Thereupon, the composition of the three histories went ahead with full
speed; the Liao history was completed in April 1344, the Chin history in
November of the same year, and the Sung history in December 1345.[59]

---

[57] LS, Appendix, p. 1557: "San-shih fan-li 三史凡例." For details of Ou-yang Hsüan's
biographies, see YS 182:4196, and his "Account of Conduct" by Wei Su included in Ou-
yang's collected works, *Kuei-chai wen-chi* 圭齋文集 (SPTK ed.), Appendix, 16:11a.

[58] See Herbert Franke, "Chinese Historiography . . . ," pp. 16–17.

[59] See the memorials on the presentation of the three histories included in the respective
histories (i.e., LS, Appendix, pp. 1555–1556; CS, Appendix, pp. 2899–2901, and SS,

In the meantime, Toghto relinquished the post of director-in-chief following his resignation as the senior chancellor in June 1344. The Liao history still listed him as director-in-chicf,[60] whereas the Chin and Sung histories were entrusted to Arughtu (fl. 1313–37), the newly appointed chancellor of the right, and his deputy, Berke Bukha, chancellor of the left.[61] There were also changes in the junior staff.[62] The project, therefore, was rushed to completion after decades of inaction. This haste resulted in violations of the basic principles for compilation as outlined above, and thus numerous flaws and defects in the three histories exist.[63] The need for a speedy conclusion was probably due to the Yüan authorities' fear that if they procrastinated further, unforeseeable events such as political dissension and financial crises might threaten to dissolve the project. The personal ambition of Toghto, who wished to see the three histories completed under his directorship, was probably a contributory factor.[64] Nevertheless, it was quite possible that if the project had not been pushed through vigorously, it might never have been completed, for in less than two decades after its completion the Mongol empire had begun to disintegrate.[65]

4. SOURCES AND FORMAT

To supplement the foregoing survey of the composition of the Liao, Chin, and Sung histories undertaken by the Yüan National History Office, it is desirable to scrutinize the source materials used and the methods by which they were compressed into the format of a standard history. During the earlier stages, lack of source materials, particularly

---

Appendix, pp. 14253–14255), and in *Kuei-chai wen-chi*, 13:2a–8a. They were composed by Ou-yang Hsüan in the name of Arughtu. T'ao Tsung-i, however, gave a set of slightly different dates in *Cho-keng lu*, 3:1a. They were April 1344 for LS, December 1344 for CS, and December 1345 for SS.

[60] LS, Appendix, pp. 1556, 1558. It is said in *Keng-shen wai-shih* (15a) that Toghto insisted that he be listed as Director-in-chief when the histories were presented to the throne. This is not true, however, since Toghto had already been appointed to this position by the imperial decree of April 1343. See Feng Chia-sheng, pp. 22–23.

[61] See their biographies in YS 139:3361, 140:3365.

[62] See the list of compilers and supporting staff given in the preface to the three histories, i.e., LS, Appendix, pp. 1557–1559; CS, Appendix, pp. 2902–2904; and SS, Appendix, pp. 14256–14260.

[63] See n. 109, 112, 113 below.

[64] See n. 51 above.

[65] The uprising of the White Lotus-Maitreya sect in May 1351 in the Huai River valley marked the start of all-out rebellions leading to the collapse of the Mongol empire. See YS 42:981.

for the Sung dynasty, had been one of the factors that repeatedly impeded the efforts of composition.[66] The problem of sources, nevertheless, was not insurmountable, since the National History Office later acquired a substantial collection of government archival materials and a large quantity of private literary works. From the start of the project in the early 1260s until its final execution in 1343, the Yüan court had issued serveral edicts ordering the public to present materials, with the promise of reward. The last such order was decreed shortly after Toghto resolved the dispute over the legitimate status of the Liao, Chin, and Sung states.[67]

The main body of source materials for the three histories were government archives. These were written exclusively in Chinese and had been procured by Yüan officials in the course of their search for the literary remains of the defunct regimes before and after the announcement of the compilation of the three histories. The *Veritable Records* of the Liao emperors, for example, had been kept intact in the home of Yeh-lü Ch'u-ts'ai 耶律楚材 (1189–1243), the illustrious chief of the secretariat under Ögödei (r. 1229–1241), and were turned over to the National History Office by his descendents.[68] The same records for the Chin were rescued from destruction by Chang Jou, the myriarch commander of the Chinese forces in the Mongolian army, amid the chaos during the fall of the Chin capital Pien 汴 (modern Kaifeng), early in 1233.[69] These archival materials were later supplemented by other official works and private literary writings collected at various stages. The nature of the source materials at the disposal of the Yüan historiographical bureau, therefore, conditioned the quality and outlook of the three histories.

The limited scope of this essay does not allow a full account of the sources used for the three histories, but a summary of these may be of use in assessing the achievements of the Yüan historiographers. In general, the Liao history is the most deficient in sources, whereas the Sung history, particularly as regards the Northern Sung, is overburdened by source materials to the extent that a balanced synthesis became a

---

[66] See n. 51 above.

[67] See *Ch'iu-chien hsien-sheng ta-ch'üan-chi*, 84:6a; *Ch'ing-jung chü-shih chi*, 41:3a; LS, Appendix, p. 1554.

[68] Su T'ien-chüeh, *Tzu-ch'i wen-kao* 滋溪文稿 (*Shih-yüan ts'ung-shu* ed.), 25:5a.

[69] Su T'ien-chüeh, *Kuo-ch'ao ming-ch'en shih-lüeh*, 6:9a; YS 147:3474. See also Sun K'o-k'uan, "Yüan-ch'u Han-chün Chang Jou hsing-shih k'ao 元初漢軍張柔行事考," *Tung-hai hsüeh-pao* 東海學報, 4:1 (1962), p. 61 (also in *Yüan-tai Han wen-hua chih huo-tung*, pp. 279–280).

problem to the historiographers.[70] The main sources for the Liao history were (a) the *Veritable Records* of the Liao emperors compiled at various stages, (b) an incomplete official Liao history composed by Ch'en Ta-jen under the auspices of the Chin emperor, and (c) the *Ch'i-tan kuo-chih* 契丹國志, an account of the history of the Khitans, the early Liao kingdom, written by the Sung scholar Yeh Lung-li 葉隆禮 (*chin-shih* 1247) under imperial auspices.[71] In addition, there were numerous (d) official records, statutes, legal codes, treatises on rites, astronomy, and the like that the Chin historiographical bureau inherited and that survived the Mongol conquest. No less important were (e) private records, such as the collected works of bellettrists which included biographical materials such as tomb-inscriptions and epitaphs.[72] Other works consulted were (f) the standard histories of the previous periods, and also the most important chronicle compiled during the Northern Sung, the *Comprehensive Mirror for Aid in Government* of Ssu-ma Kuang, which contains much useful information on the early years of the Khitan state.[73]

The sources for the Chin history were more voluminous and diversified than their Liao counterparts, not only because the Chin historiographical bureau was more productive but also because these sources had been better preserved and organized through the dedication of ex-Chin scholar-officials such as Wang O and Yüan Hao-wen 元好問 (1190–1257) after the fall of the dynasty.[74] The main sources were the reign chronicles of the Chin emperors—*Diaries of Activity and Repose*, the *Daily Records*, the *Veritable Records*—and collections of imperial decrees, such as the *Ssu-ch'ao sheng-hsün* 四朝聖訓 (Holy Instructions of Four Emperors) for the record of the early Chin rulers.[75] Supplementing these were collections of statutes, law codes, and treatises on rites such as

---

[70] NESCC 23:308; Hsü Hao, p. 218 ff.

[71] See Feng Chia-sheng, pp. 25–37. For a bibliographical note on the *Ch'i-tan kuo-chih*, see SKTY 50:5a; see also Wou Hsiao-ling, "Index du K'i-tan kouo tche," in *Silver Jubilee Volume of the Zinbun-kagaku-kenkyūsyo* (Kyoto University) (Kyoto, 1954), p. 175 ff.

[72] *Tzu-ch'i wen-kao*, 25:6b; cf. Feng Chia-sheng, pp. 38 ff, 50 ff.

[73] These include *Wei-shu* 魏書, *Pei-Chou shu* 北周書, *Sui-shu* 隋書, *Pei-shih* 北史, *Hsin T'ang-shu* 新唐書, *Chiu Wu-tai shih* 舊五代史 and *Wu-tai shih-chi* 五代史記. See Feng Chia-sheng, p. 64. Cf. Feng, pp. 40–50.

[74] On the contribution of Wang O and Yüan Hao-wen to Chin history, see Hok-lam Chan, *Chin Historiography*, ch. 1 & 2. See also Yao Ts'ung-wu 姚從吾, "Chin-Yüan chih chi Yüan Hao-wen tui-yü pao-ch'üan chung-yüan ch'uan-t'ung wen-hua ti kung-hsien 金元之際元好問對於保全中原傳統文化的貢獻," TLTC, 26:3 (1963), pp. 1–11; and Hok-lam Chan, "Wang O," *passim*.

[75] Cf. Hok-lam Chan, *Chin Historiography*, ch. 1. See also Fujieda Akira 藤枝晃, "Kinchō no jitsuroku 金朝の実録," in *Seifuku ōchō* 征服王朝 (Akitaya, 1947), pp. 30–54.

the *Ta-Chin chi-li* 大金集禮 (*Rites of the Great Chin*), an incomplete version of which still survives in printed form.[76] Private works supplied an important segment of sources for the biographical section. The more important ones were the collections of biographical materials contained in Yüan Hao-wen's *Chung-chou chi* 中州集 (*Anthology of the Central Kingdom*) and in his collected works, the *I-shan hsien-sheng wen-chi* 遺山先生文集 (*Literary Collection of Master I-shan*).[77] Other important private sources for the Chin period, particularly for the last years of the dynasty, were the *Kuei-ch'ien chih* 歸潛志 (*Records Written on Returning to Retirement*) by Liu Ch'i 劉祁 (1203–1250), and the *Ju-nan i-shih* 汝南遺事 (*Reminiscences of Ju-nan*) by Wang O.[78] These authors were first-rate bellettrists and historians, and their writings hence contributed to the excellence of those portions of the Chin history that utilized their materials.[79]

Of the three histories, the sources for the Sung were perhaps the most voluminous and diversified. The reasons are threefold: the Sung covered the longest period of history; its historiographical bureau was more productive; and, due to the proximity of time, most of its records were available to the Yüan National History Office.[80] Besides, the Sung had marked one of the most brilliant periods of literary achievement, producing numerous volumes of diversified works of literature which supplied profuse data for its historical record. The main body of the official records ranged from the *Daily Records*, *Daily Calendars*, *Diaries of Activity and Repose*, and *Records of State Affairs*, to the voluminous *Veritable Records* of most of the reigning emperors.[81] In addition, compiled under imperial orders were the national histories known as *kuo-shih* for all the nine emperors of the Northern Sung, and for four emperors of the Southern Sung.[82] The last items alone not only shaped

[76] For a bibliographical note on the *Ta-Chin chi-li*, see SKTY 82:2a; Wang Ming-sheng 王鳴盛, *I-shu pien* 蛾術編 (Peking, 1958 ed.), p. 171. See also Mikami Tsugio 三上次男, *Kinshi kenkyū* 金史研究, Vol. 2 (Tokyo, 1970), pp. 35–40; and Hok-lam Chan, *Chin Historiography*, pp. 25, 59, n. 107.

[77] For these works, see SKTY 166:2a, 188:1a. Cf. Hok-lam Chan, *Chin Historiography*, pt. 1 & 2.

[78] For these works, see SKTY 141:9b, 51:66. See also Hok-lam Chan, *Chin Historiography*, ch. 1 & 3; and *id.*, "Prolegomena to the *Ju-nan i-shih*: A Memoir on the Last Chin Capital under the Mongol Siege of 1234," *Sung Studies Newsletter*, 10 (Supplement 1) (Dec. 1974), pp. 2–19.

[79] See Ku Yen-wu 顧炎武, *Jih-chih lu chi-shih* 日知錄集釋 (*Ssu-pu pei-yao* ed., 1926), 26:25b; NESCC 27:372; Li Tz'u-ming 李慈銘, *Yüeh-man t'ang tu-shu chi* 越縵堂讀書記 (Peking, 1963 ed.), p. 343. Cf. Hok-lam Chan, *Chin Historiography*, p.39.

[80] NESCC 23:306; Hsü Hao, p. 219.

[81] See n. 12 above.

[82] See n. 13 above.

the format but also supplied the principal sources for the Sung history.

Sung archives of various kinds, such as statutes, legal codes, treatises on rites, astronomy, and others constituted another major source for the Sung history, particularly for the treatises. The wealth of data preserved in the *Sung hui-yao* 宋會要 (*Essential Documents of the Sung*) and the *Ch'ing-yüan tiao-fa shih-lei* 慶元條法事類 (*Statutes and Cases of the Ch'ing-yüan Reign* [*1195–1200*]) alone serve to indicate the value of this kind of sources.[83] Supplementing these records was the Sung section of a Yüan work on government institutions, the *Wen-hsien t'ung-k'ao* 文獻通考 (*Comprehensive Survey of Literary Remains*) by Ma Tuan-lin 馬端臨 (1250–1324/25), which supplied a major source for the Treatises on Civil Offices and Food and Money.[84] No less important as sources for this period were the numerous private histories composed by individual scholar-historians. To name but a few, they include: Li T'ao 李燾 (1115–1184), *Hsü Tzu-chih t'ung-chien ch'ang-pien* 續資治通鑑長編 (*Long Draft for the Continuation of the Comprehensive Mirror for Aid in Government*), 520 *chüan*; Hsü Meng-hsin 徐夢莘 (1126–1207), *San-ch'ao pei-meng hui-pien* 三朝北盟會編 (*Comprehensive Accounts of the Northern Alliance under Three Sung Emperors*), 250 *chüan*; Wang Ch'eng 王偁 (d. ca.1200), *Tung-tu shih-lüeh* 東都事略 (*Brief Account of the Eastern Capital*), 130 *chüan*; and Li Hsin-ch'uan 李心傳 (1166–1243), *Chien-yen i-lai hsi-nien yao-lu* 建炎以來繫年要錄 (*Chronicles of the Years Since the Chien-yen Reign* [i.e., 1127]), 200 *chüan*.[85]

Private works of varied contents and diverse origins supplied equally important sources for the Sung history. They ranged from the collected

---

[83] The *Sung hui-yao*, preserved in the *Yung-lo ta-tien* 永樂大典, was extracted and edited in 1809 by the Ch'ing scholar Hsü Sung 徐松, and entitled *Sung hui-yao chi-kao* 宋會要輯稿, in 460 *chüan*. A modern photolithographic reproduction in 8 volumes was published by Chung-hua Shu-chü in 1957. For details, see T'ang Chung 湯中, *Sung hui-yao yen-chiu* 宋會要研究 (Shanghai, 1931). The *Ch'ing-yüan t'iao-fa shih-lei* was recently reproduced from a manuscript transcription in 36 *chüan* preserved at Seikadō Bunko 靜嘉堂文庫 in one volume (Tokyo, 1969). The section on regulations governing the Buddhist and Taoist establishments has been translated by W. Eichorn in *Beitraag zur Rechtlichen stellung des Buddhismus und Taoismus im Sung-staat* (Leiden, 1970).

[84] On the relation between the Treatises on Civil Offices, Food and Money in SS and the *Wen-hsien t'ung-k'ao*, see Teng Kung-san 鄧恭三, "Sung-shih chih-kuan chih chüeh-yüan k'uang-miu 宋史職官志抉原匡謬," in *Wen-shih tsa-chih* 文史雜誌, 2:4 (1942), pp. 27–38; Sudō Yoshiyuki, "Sanchō kokushi shikashi to Sōshi shikashi to no kankei 三朝国史食貨志と「宋史」食貨志との関係," in *Sōdaishi kenkyū*, pp. 569–634 (see also *Memoirs of the Research Department of the Tōyō Bunko*, 19 [1960], pp. 63–110).

[85] For these works, see SKTY 47:6b, 49:1b, 50:4a, 47:8b. See also Sudō Yoshiyuki in *Sōdaishi kenkyū*, pp. 469–512; Ch'en Lo-su 陳樂素 in CYYY 6:2–3 (1936), pp. 193–279, 281–341; Ch'en Shu 陳述 in CYYY 8:1 (1939), pp. 129–138; and Fang Chuang-yu 方壯猷 in *Shuo-wen yüeh-k'an*, 4 (1944), pp. 465–492.

works of bellettrists, travelogues, diaries, personal memoirs, miscellanies, and even works of fictional disposition—amounting to several hundreds of items and thousands of volumes. A modern scholar who has scrutinized an extensive amount of Sung miscellaneous literature concludes that the following six were extensively consulted by the Yüan historiographers in the composition of the Sung history.[86] They include: Ou-yang Hsiu, *Kuei-t'ien lu* 歸田錄 (*Records Compiled in Retirement*), 2 *chüan*; Ssu-ma Kuang, *Su-shui chi-wen* 涑水紀聞 (*Notes from Su-shui*), 16 *chüan*; Shen Kua 沈括 (1031–1095), *Meng-ch'i pi-t'an* 夢溪筆談 (*Jottings from the "Dream River" Studio*), 26 *chüan*; Shao Po-wen 邵伯溫 (1057–1134), (*Shao-shih*) *Wen-chien ch'ien-lu* (邵氏) 聞見前錄 (*First Record of Findings* [by Mister Shao]), 20 *chüan*; Wang Kung 王鞏 (1048–1102?), *Wen-chien chin-lu* 聞見近錄 (*Recent Record of Findings*), 1 *chüan*; and Wang Chih 王銍 (d. *ca.*1154), *Mo-chi* 默記 (*Notes in Silence*), 3 *chüan*.[87]

In retrospect, only the Southern Sung reigns from Emperor Li-tsung 理宗 (r. 1225–1265) to the last emperor were deficient in source materials for their records. The main reason for this is that only a few reign chronicles compiled for these emperors survived, and most of their archival records were destroyed during the war with the Mongols. The sources for this period had to be drawn from semi-official works and from private accounts of scholar-officials composed during the late Sung and early Yüan.[88] Because of the nature of the sources, the accounts of the last years of the Southern Sung in the *Sung shih* 宋史 (*History of the Sung*) are particularly sketchy and confusing, falling short of the standard set by previous dynastic histories.

The question of source materials having been resolved, it remained the task of the Yüan historiographers to find the ways and means to compress these materials into the format of a dynastic history on the basis of the official guidelines.[89] Although we have no records of the exact operation of the historical commissions and the responsibilities of the individual members, it seems that they adopted the same procedures

---

[86] See Chao T'ieh-han 趙鐵寒, "Yu Sung-shih chih ch'ü-ts'ai lun ssu-chia chuan-chi ti shih-liao chia-chih 由宋史之取材論私家傳記的史料價值," TLTC, 12:12 (1956), pp. 20–28.

[87] For these works, see SKTY 140:10a, 9a; 120:4b; 141:5b; 140:12a; 141:4b.

[88] See Ch'ien Ta-hsin 錢大昕, *Shih-chia chai yang-hsin lu* 十駕齋養新錄 (Shanghai, 1957), 7:149; NESCC 23:309; Hsü Hao, p. 222. For a list of imperial records compiled for these last Sung emperors, see Chin Yü-fu, p. 97. For a survey of the private works on the last Sung emperors, see Chang Yin-lin 張蔭麟, "Nan-Sung wang-kuo shih pu 南宋亡國史補," *Yen-ching hsüeh-pao* 燕京學報, 20 (1936), pp. 159–175; Jao Tsung-i, *Chiu-lung yü Sung-chi shih-liao* 九龍與宋季史料 (Hong Kong, 1959).

[89] See n. 57 above.

as those developed by the T'ang historiographical bureau and subsequently elaborated upon in later periods. In view of the exigency, the
Yüan historiographers did not enjoy the leisure of their predecessors and
had to adopt more drastic attitudes and stringent procedures. Instead of
attempting a new synthesis of the existing materials, they resorted to a
"scissors-and-paste" formula, summarizing the ready-made materials
and re-arranging them to fit the prescribed pattern.[90] They could do this,
not only because the historiographers of the preceding periods had done
considerable spade-work, but also because some of the original materials
had already been put into forms which could be used in a standard
history.[91] Otherwise, it would not have been possible for the Yüan
historiographers to achieve the desired result within such a tight
schedule.

The speedy completion of the three histories was aided not only by the
semi-finished nature of the source materials, but also by the stringent
methods of the officials in charge of the composition. In general, the
supervisors clung to the official guidelines, shying away from the innovative suggestions of conscientious scholars, and exhorting the compilers to adhere to the established rules instead of expressing their
individual opinions.[92] According to his standard biography, when Ou-
yang Hsüan assumed the directorship of the three histories some of
the historiographers were found to be quarrelsome, ostentatious, or
biased.[93] Instead of arguing with them, he simply made changes in their
draft chapters when these were presented to him for editing. Another
director of composition, Chang Ch'i-yen 張起巖 (d. 1345), reportedly
adopted the same austere attitude in suppressing dissident opinion.[94]
This somewhat authoritarian method, though accounting for much of

[90] NESCC 23:308; 26:362.

[91] *Ibid*, 23:305, 27:362, 372; Chao I 趙翼, *Kai-yü ts'ung-k'ao* 陔餘叢考 (Shanghai,
1967), 13:235.

[92] Shortly after the Yüan court announced the compilation of the three histories, Su
T'ien-chüeh (1294–1352), a leading scholar-historian who did not receive an invitation to
join the project, submitted a lengthy memorandum to his friend Ou-yang Hsüan, then a
newly appointed director-general in charge of the composition. In his memorandum, Su
outlined a number of special points regarding the principles of composition and selection of
sources for the histories, and invited the historiographers to give consideration to his
recommendation. Many of his points were highly instructive and should have deserved
serious consideration by the Yüan historiographical office. However, as it turned out, few
of his recommendations were adopted. Su's memorandum on the three histories is included
in *Tzu-ch'i wen-kao*, 25:5a–10b. Cf. Hok-lam Chan, *Chin Historiography*, pp. 18–20. For
Su T'ien-chüeh's biography, see YS 183:4224; see also Sun K'o-k'uan (n. 28), pp. 382–413.

[93] See Ou-yang Hsüan's biographies cited in n. 57 above; see also Lien-sheng Yang's
article in *Historians of China and Japan*, p. 54.

[94] YS 182:4195.

the infelicity in style and defects in content, seems to have been the only possible way to ensure the completion of the three histories within the prescribed time limit.

While adhering strictly to the official guidelines for expediting the history project, the Yüan historiographers did introduce certain innovations and alterations in the format and contents of the three histories. They were not, however, the result of a change in the basic concept and methods of history-writing that had been imposed by the alien rulers. Rather, they reflect the accommodation of the historical data to the changing patterns in the political development of the three defunct states within the traditional framework of dynastic histories. In addition, the evaluation and judgment of individuals and events as expressed in the *tsan* 贊 (encomiums) attached to the Basic Annals and Biographies of the individual histories frequently varied from those of the preceding era. These are particularly apparent in the treatment of the last Chin and Sung rulers and individuals, which was prejudicial and unfavorable, because the historiographers were obliged to express the viewpoints of the Mongol conquerors who had subdued these regimes.[95]

A few noticeable innovations and alterations in the three histories were made in order to accommodate historical realities. In this effort the historians were facilitated considerably by the flexible framework of the dynastic history format which allowed for a wide range of subject matter in the Monographs (*chih*) and Tables (*piao*). This can be shown, first of all, in the Liao and Chin histories. The chronological table of embassies between the Chin, on the one hand, and the Sung, the Hsi-Hsia and Korea, on the other hand, found in *chüan* 60 and 61 of the Chin history,[96] for example, may be regarded as a formal innovation, reflecting the multi-state relations of northern East Asia in the twelfth and thirteenth centuries. There is also a similar parallel for this in *chüan* 69 of the Liao history.[97] The largely tribal structure of Liao rule is reflected in the list of tribes in *chüan* 45 and again in *chüan* 68, where the annual and seasonal sojourns of the Khitan emperors are recorded, or again in *chüan* 31, where we can find a description of the *ordo* and *na-po* 捺鉢 residences of a still non-sedentary sort of rulership.[98] Another

---

[95] See Herbert Franke, "Chinese Historiography," pp. 15–18; Wang Gungwu, "Some Comments on Later Standard Histories," in Donald Leslie, *et al.*, eds, *Essays on the Sources for Chinese History* (Canberra, 1973), pp. 58–63.

[96] CS, *ch*. 60–61: "Chiao-p'in piao 交聘表"; cf. Hok-lam Chan, *Chin Historiography*, p. 29 ff.

[97] LS, *ch*. 69, "Pu-tsu piao 部族表." This has been expanded by Chang Liang-ts'ai 張亮采 in *Pu Liao-shih chiao-p'in piao* 補遼史交聘表 (Shanghai, 1958).

[98] LS, *ch*. 45, "Pai-kuan chih 百官志"; LS, *ch*. 68, "Yu-hsing piao 遊幸表"; and *ch*. 31, "Ying wei chih 營衛志." See Karl A. Wittfogel and Feng Chia-sheng (n. 14), Sec. 1, 15.

innovation, which has met with the enthusiastic welcome of modern linguists, is found in the vocabularies of Khitan and Jurchen nomenclature in the closing chapters of the Liao and Chin histories. They reveal the historiographers' awareness of the alien elements of the respective states, something which is absent in earlier histories but which is made possible in these histories because they were written under alien rule and within a largely bilingual administration.[99] This is a unique achievement, especially in view of the fact that when the *Yüan shih* 元史 (*History of the Yüan*) was compiled soon after the founding of the Ming, the historiographers did not bother to include foreign vocabularies, although many non-Chinese terms are explained in the body of the text. Unfortunately for modern historians, a "reform" of the orthography of non-Chinese names and terms in the standard histories was carried out under imperial auspices during the Ch'ien-lung 乾隆 reign (1736–1796). The new transcriptions were introduced in the imperial editions of the standard histories of the Liao and Chin dynasties in 1739. They have caused great confusion in the identification of their original foreign referents.[100]

In the case of the Sung history, there were relatively few significant innovations in format. Some changes in the contents of the Basic Annals and Biographies were made which reflect the prejudice and ideological commitment of the Yüan historiographers. In the Basic Annals, for example, although the third to last Sung ruler, Chao Hsien 趙㬎, was formally enthroned as emperor (r. 1275–1276), he was not accorded an imperial title since he surrendered to the Mongols; instead, he came to be known as Ying-kuo kung 瀛國公 (the Duke of Ying-kuo) in his chronicle, after the title invested upon him by Khubilai Khaghan. The last two Sung rulers, Chao Cheng 趙昰 (Tuan-tsung 端宗, r. 1276–1278), and Chao Ping 趙昺 (Prince Wei 衛王, r. 1278–79), were likewise denied legitimacy by the Yüan court; each therefore received only a short notice appended to Chao Hsien's chronicle. They were all given rather

---

[99] They are the "[Liao] kuo-yü chieh 遼國語解," in LS 116:1533–49; "Chin kuo-yü chieh 金國語解," in CS, Appendix, pp. 2891–2897. Cf. Herbert Franke, "Chinese Historiography," p. 18.

[100] This orthography "reform" was introduced not only to the Liao and Chin histories, but also to the standard Yüan history compiled under the Ming. It resulted in the publication of several new lists of *yü-chieh* 語解 [explanations on nomenclature] for the three histories. These lists, which underwent at least three revisions since 1747, reached their final form in 1781. They were subsequently published together in a compendium entitled [*Ch'in-ting*] *San-shih yü-chieh* [欽定] 三史語解, and each list was also included as an appendix to the respective imperial edition of the three histories in 1824 and later reprints. For a brief note on these lists, see Hok-lam Chan, *Chin Historiography*, pp. 42, 65 (n. 184), and, for the *Chin-shih yü-chieh*, see the critical examination by Li Hsüeh-chih 李學智 in *Hsin-ya hsüeh-pao*, 5:2 (Aug. 1963), pp. 377–429.

unfavorable appraisals by the historiographers, as were the last two Chin emperors, because they had resisted the Mongol conquerors and been defeated.[101]   In the Biographical section, the most significant innovation was the addition of the category of *Tao-hsüeh* 道學 (the School of the True Way) for the biographies of the school of Neo-Confucian scholars, in *chüan* 427–438, so labelled because this school championed the *Tao*, or the Established Way of Confucianism. This is to be distinguished from the category of biographies known under the rubric *Ju-lin* 儒林 (Confucian scholars), which applied to the accounts of learned individuals who were not associated with this particular school. This section was edited by Chang Ch'i-yen, a member of the Yüan True Way school. The school's interpretation of the classics enjoyed the sanction of the Yüan court as the standard for the civil-service examinations.[102]

In summation, the innovations and alterations introduced to the Liao and Chin histories met with the general approval of later historians since they did not involve sensitive ideological issues applied to historical writing. In the case of the Sung history, however, much of the disposition in both format and substance aroused the ire of later historians. The Sung history was held to have violated the principle of legitimacy in favor of the Mongol rulers, and hence it became the target of attack by proto-nationalistic historians in the late Ming who undertook to revise the Sung history. In so doing, they tried not only to rectify the injustice done to the Sung, but also to make the Sung the only legitimate dynasty by relegating both the Liao and the Chin to the status of usurper. This they did by accommodating all three dynasties in a single history, as is shown in the following section.

5. CRITICISMS AND EVALUATION

The arbitrary decision taken on the issue of legitimate succession for the principles governing the composition of the three histories by the Yüan historiographical office, and the great haste under which the project was executed, caused numerous defects in style and contents. These became foci of criticism by later historians. They disputed the ideological basis of the project, reopening the debate on legitimate succession, and criticized

[101] For accounts of the historiography of this period, see the studies by Chang Yin-lin and Jao Tsung-i cited in n. 88 above.

[102] See Chang Ch'i-yen's biography cited in n. 94 above. For the general background of the development of the *Tao-hsüeh* school in the Sung and Yüan period, see James T. C. Liu, "How Did a Neo-Confucian School Become the State Orthodoxy?" *Philosophy East and West*, 23:4 (Oct. 1973), pp. 483–505.

the format and contents of the three histories. These historians not only expressed their dissatisfaction on paper, but also attempted to rewrite or amend the existing histories.

The ideological guidelines adopted by Toghto for the composition of the three histories, whereby each ruling house was accorded the status of legitimacy, found several vocal critics of the day, including Yang Wei-chen 楊維楨 (1296–1370), a literary celebrity who also specialized in the *Spring and Autumn Annals*.[103] In 1343 Yang emerged from retirement when he, together with a score of other scholars, received a summons to the capital for consultation. An impasse over the legitimate succession issue had impeded several attempts to expedite the history project. In response, Yang stated that only the Sung deserved recognition as a legitimate dynasty, that the Liao and the Chin were usurpers, that there should be only one history, namely the one for the Sung, and that the accounts of the Liao and the Chin should be relegated to an appendix therein. Two other contemporary scholars, Hsieh Kuan 解觀 (1310–1360) and Chou I-li 周以立 (1307–1360), both from Kiangsi, who also had arrived in the capital for participation in the history project, expressed a similar opinion.[104] Yang Wei-chen's daring proposal, how-ever, ran counter to the position of the Yüan authorities, who feared that an extended controversy over the ideological issue would further delay the execution of the historical composition. As a result, Yang was excluded from the historical commission and denied an official appoint-ment.[105] Undaunted, he composed an essay entitled "Cheng-t'ung pien 正統辨" ("On Legitimate Succession") and continued freely to expound his view on the subject. The instant popularity of this essay prompted his friend T'ao Tsung-i 陶宗儀 (*ca.* 1316–1402) to include it in his miscellany, *Cho-keng lu* 輟耕錄 (*Notes Taken during Breaks from Ploughing*).[106]

In essence, Yang Wei-chen elaborated the viewpoint advanced by a group of scholars at the end of Khubilai's reign and summarized in Hsiu (or Hsieh) Tuan's discourse on legitimate succession. But he defined it more precisely by positing that only with the downfall of the Sung

[103] For Yang Wei-chen's biographies, see Pei Ch'iung 貝瓊, *Ch'ing-chiang Pei hsien-sheng wen-chi* 清江貝先生文集 (SPTK ed.), 2:3a; Sung Lien 宋濂, *Sung hsüeh-shih wen-chi* 宋學士文集 (SPTK ed.), 16:6a; MS 285:7308; and Edmund Worthy, Jr.'s contribution in *Dictionary of Ming Biography*, pp. 1547–1553.

[104] See their biographies by Hsieh Chin 解縉 (1369–1425) included in his *Hsieh Ch'un-yü hsien-sheng wen-chi* 解春雨先生文集 (preface 1562), 8:4b, 59a. For additional comments, see Yeh Sheng 葉盛, *Shui-tung jih-chi* 水東日記 (Taipei, 1965 ed.), 24:7b.

[105] Yang Wei-chen, *Tung Wei-tzu wen-chi* 東維子文集 (SPTK ed.), 27:4b.

[106] *Cho-keng lu*, 3:1a; summarized in Worthy's biography of Yang Wei-chen cited in n. 103.

dynasty was legitimacy conveyed to the Mongol ruling house. He rested his argument primarily on the theory of *cheng-t'ung* as developed in the *Outline of the Comprehensive Mirror for Aid in Government* by Chu Hsi. Briefly stated, Yang asserted that under the Chin there had been no *cheng* 正, for the affairs of state were not right and correct; furthermore, there had been no *t'ung* 統, because the entire realm had not been unified. On the other hand, the Southern Sung had acquired its legitimacy directly from the Northern Sung. To substantiate his argument, he introduced two new dimensions to the theory of *cheng-t'ung*: the Chu Hsi-influenced concepts of *tao-t'ung* 道統 (moral succession) and *chih-t'ung* 治統 (political succession), which actually are interrelated and indivisible. Pursuing Chu's line of reasoning, Yang traced the transmission of the *tao* from the ancient sage rulers Yao and Shun through various stages, passing through Chu Hsi and ending with the Yüan Confucianist Hsü Heng 許衡 (1209–1281). He maintained that the *tao* never passed through the Liao and the Chin. In conclusion he boldly pointed out that the reason why the Yüan officials had set on an arbitrary solution to the dispute was that they were anxious to extend the legitimacy of the Mongol supremacy in China. In holding that the Yüan had succeeded the Liao and the Chin as the legitimate ruling house, they conferred legitimacy on the fifty years of the pre-dynastic phase of Mongol rule in China, although many contemporary Confucian scholars viewed this scheme as a violation of the principles of the *Spring and Autumn Annals*.[107]

It is obvious that Yang Wei-chen's argument ran against the temperament of the time, because denying legitimacy to the Liao and the Chin would have cast a bad light on the Mongols. Moreover, by positing that legitimacy was conveyed to the Yüan exclusively through the Sung, the argument suggested that Mongol rule before 1279 was somehow illegitimate. Thus in one way or another, it would have had serious political repercussions for Mongol rule in China. Nevertheless, Yang Wei-chen stood as a towering figure in expounding the principles of the *Spring and Autumn Annals* in this way, even at the risk of offending the Mongol authorities.

Added to this challenge of the ideological principles governing the composition, historians in the Ming and Ch'ing expressed much dissatisfaction with the format and contents of the three histories. Although few dynastic histories won the universal acclaim of historians, their criticism of the Liao, Chin, and Sung histories was perhaps the most

---

[107] Cf. Edmund Worthy (n. 103); Jao Tsung-i (n. 35), pp. 22–25.

severe. The great haste taken in the completion of the histories and the overhelming quantity of source materials to be digested, coupled with the mediocrity of the historiographers, perhaps explain the numerous defects in the three histories. Traditional historians' evaluation of these three histories is best represented by Ch'ing scholars such as Ch'ien Ta-hsin 錢大昕 (1728–1804) and Chao I 趙翼 (1727–1814) in their respective works *Nien-er-shih k'ao-i* 廿二史考異 (*Study of Discrepancies in the Twenty-two Standard Histories*) and *Nien-er-shih cha-chi* 劄記 (*Critical Notes on the Twenty-two Standard Histories*).[108] Their criticisms may be conveniently summarized under the following headings:

a. *Narratives*

The narratives in the three histories are the first target of criticism by these Ch'ing historians. Various forms of discrepancies, such as inconclusive statements, erroneous accounts, duplication of sources, inconsistent transcription of foreign names, and other infelicities are noted. In many cases, statements occurring in the Basic Annals are contradicted elsewhere in the same text; similarly, a certain account in one history may be disputed by a similar account in another. A casual checking of the Liao history against the Chin, or the Chin against the Sung history, would yield many such examples. The inconsistency in the transcription of non-Chinese names is also a serious defect. This could have been due to the absence of a standard system of transcription, or simply that the names in one text were never checked against those in another. In any case, a person may be known under different names or he may be erroneously identified with another in a different context. This discrepancy is the more glaring when one examines the names that appear in the Liao and Chin histories against those in the Sung.[109]

b. *Style*

In regard to style, of the three histories the Liao history was downgraded for its coarseness and simplicity, whereas the Sung history, which abounds in primary source materials, was criticized for being clumsy and repetitious. Only the Chin history received relatively favorable comment in this respect. The biographical section in the Chin history, in particular, was praised for its elegant and concise literary style. This is because this section based its sources on the works of bellettrists such

[108] NESKI, *ch.* 66–85; NESCC, *ch.* 23–27; *Shih-chia chai yang-hsin lu*, *ch.* 7, 8; *Kai-yü ts'ung-k'ao*, *ch.* 13. Cf. Hsü Hao, pp. 218–258.

[109] NESKI, *ch.* 66, 80; NESCC, *ch.* 26, 27; *Shih-chia chai yang-hsin lu*, *ch.* 7; *Kai-yü ts'ung-k'ao*, *ch.* 13. Cf. Hsü Hao, pp. 233, 247, 254.

as Yüan Hao-wen and Liu Ch'i, who in this way indirectly contributed to the quality of the Chin history. In the opinion of a contemporary critic, the Chin history is the only standard history that has inherited the fresh and expressive style of the grand historian Ssu-ma Ch'ien 司馬遷 (145?–90? B.C.).[110]

c. *Judgment*

Two areas of criticism of the three histories are (a) their inaccurate, biased judgment, and (b) their distorted representation of historical facts in violation of the principle of objectivity. On certain occasions the Yüan historiographers suppressed or distorted facts for fear of offending the ruling authorities. At other times their inaccurate or biased judgment was due to the necessity to uphold the viewpoints of the Mongol rulers and to the uncritical acceptance of opinions derived from the original source materials. The most obvious example in the first category was the evasion or suppression of unfavorable comments in the treatment of the early relations between the Mongol rulers and those of the three ruling houses. Examples of the second category can be found in the pejorative treatment of the rulers and personalities of the later Chin and Sung in their respective histories, as well as of the many Sung official-statesmen who were leading figures in factional strifes in the biographies of the Sung history. In the former cases, the Yüan historiographers deliberately downgraded their achievements to buttress the grandeur of the Mongol conquest, and, in the latter, instead of conveying their own opinion, they often passed on the somewhat conventional, one-sided views formulated by the biased Sung authors.[111]

d. *Classifications*

The biased classifications in the three histories, particularly in the Biographies and Tables, were also an object of the historians' criticism. The Sung history, in particular, was criticized for the exclusion of biographies of certain notable personalities, the inclusion of unworthy ones, the duplication of material, and misarrangement in the order of the

---

[110] NESCC 27:362, 374; Shih Kuo-ch'i 施國祁, *Chin-shih hsiang-chiao* 金史詳校 (*Kuang-ya ts'ung-shu* ed., 1894), 1a; Li Tz'u-ming, *Yüeh-man t'ang tu-shu chi*, p. 343; Ch'ien Chi-po 錢基博, *Hsü Tung-shu tu-shu chi* 續東塾讀書記 (Shanghai, 1936), pp. 52–53.

[111] *Shih-chia chai yang-hsin lu*, 7:150; NESCC 27:377, 23:309. On the taboo of the Yüan authorities against revealing the unfavorable relation between the Mongols and the three ruling houses, see Ch'ien Ta-hsin, *Ch'ien-yen t'ang wen-chi* 潛研堂文集 (1884 ed.), 31:10a; Wang Kuo-wei 王國維, *Kuan-t'ang chi-lin* 觀堂集林 (Shanghai, 1927), 15:1a. Cf. Hsü Hao, pp. 234, 256.

biographical accounts. In addition, the three histories were blamed for inappropriate classification of personalities and for grouping unrelated individuals into various categories. Some of these charges, however, are disputable, since the rationale for these classifications and their ideological basis may have varied from one period to another. The inconsistent standard of judgment of individuals in general also accounted for much of the infelicities in the categorization of these personalities. Aside from the Biographies, both the Chin and Sung histories have been faulted for inadequate presentation of Tables. The Sung history, for example, has only two Tables (32 *chüan*) out of 496 *chüan*, whereas its Liao counterpart has eight Tables (8 *chüan*) out of 116 *chüan*. In the latter case, the Tables partially compensated for the inadequacy of its Biographies, but were considered misused in the light of the established framework of the standard dynastic histories.[112]

e. *Sources*

Ch'ing historians have also criticized the omission and uncritical selection of source materials by the compilers of the three histories. In the case of the Liao history, they noted the absence of Chin archival and private sources, as well as the failure to employ Sung works such as those by Li T'ao, Hsü Meng-hsin, Wang Ch'eng, and others listed above. The omission of the latter sources applies also to the Chin history. As to the Sung history, in view of the sheer volume of materials available, only the last reigns of the dynasty have been criticized for inadequate sources. Instead, historians blamed the Yüan historiographers for indiscriminate selection of source materials, such that all available data were often lumped together despite their dubious reliability and lack of consistency. In many cases they fused the ascertainable data with fictional materials, and perpetuated the bias and prejudice of the Sung authors. These facts account for much of the discrepancies not only in the Sung history, but also in the other two histories, since so little cross-checking was done for the three histories taken as a whole.[113]

The main flaws of the Liao, Chin, and Sung histories, therefore, lie in the lack of coherence or consistency, not only in one history but in all three. The fault seems to have been due to the haste in composition, which denied the historiographers the opportunity to scrutinize the work of each other. Since this occurred even within one history commission, it

[112] *Shih-chia chai yang-hsin lu*; NESCC 26:356, 27:365; *Kai-yü ts'ung-k'ao*, 13:240. Cf. Hsü Hao, pp. 228, 245.

[113] *Shih-chia chai yang-hsin lu*, 7:149; NESCC 23:308, 27:362; *Kai-yü ts'ung-k'ao*, 13:237. Cf. Feng Chia-sheng, p. 57 ff; Hok-lam Chan, *Chin Historiography*, p. 38 ff.

cannot be expected that historiographers from different commissions would have cross-checked their results, although some members concurrently served on two or three entirely different commissions.

In retrospect, these Ch'ing historians developed their criticisms of the three histories largely from the viewpoint of traditional historical scholarship. There was, it seems, little appreciation of the problems and dilemmas confronting the Mongol rulers in sponsoring the historical compilation. On the issue of legitimate succession, the position adopted by Toghto making all three states—Liao, Chin, and Sung—legitimate dynasties, although severely denounced by later historians, was in fact a practical and sensible settlement from the standpoint of the Mongols. Under this scheme, the Mongols became legitimate rulers of China not as late as 1279, when they conquered the Southern Sung, but several decades earlier, when they replaced both the Khitans and the Jurchens as rulers of north China.[114] From the historiographical point of view, making both the Liao and the Chin legitimate ruling houses on a par with the Sung had far greater significance than could have been envisaged in those days. This is because if Liao and Chin had not been accorded such a status and were denied their individual histories, as was the Hsi-Hsia, their accounts would have been condensed to appendices in the Sung history, whereupon many details of their historical records would have been sacrificed.[115] This would have greatly impaired our understanding of the history of these two alien conquest dynasties in north China, and would have been a disservice to the tradition of Chinese historiography.

It has been generally agreed that the unremitting speed taken in the completion of the three histories project accounted for much of the infelicities and defects in the final product. The main reason for expediting the composition has been explored. It has been suggested that the authorities feared that further procrastination would have allowed unforeseeable events, both political and financial, to impede the compilation. The personal ambition of Toghto, who was anxious to see the histories completed under his directorship, may have been a contributory factor. This accelerated pace inhibited the historiographers and was damaging to the refinement of the finished product. It prevented them from closely scrutinizing the sources and cross-checking the relevant entries in the three histories, let alone carefully polishing their literary style. From the hindsight of later events, however, if the histories had not been finished on schedule, they may not have been completed at all,

---

[114] Cf. Feng Chia-sheng, p. 18 ff.   [115] Cf. Chu Hsi-tsu (n. 29), p. 25.

for in less than two decades the Mongol regime was teetering on the edge of collapse.

On the other hand, the low caliber of the scholars chosen for the historical composition also accounted for the impoverishment of the three histories. In his reply to Toghōn Temür, who inquired about the composition, Ou-yang Hsüan stressed two essential requirements: adequate source materials, and men of scholastic distinction.[116] Apparently he did not have the latter, since he was forced to act on his own initiative while being hard-pressed to complete his assignment within a tight schedule. The mediocrity of the historiographers was also a cause of concern to Huang Chin 黃溍 (1277–1357), a leading scholar-official from Chin-hua 金華 who was appointed to the three histories project in 1343, for he once lamented: "Even if Ssu-ma Kuang were reborn, he would hardly have been able to work with them!"[117] The historiographers' incompetence, aggravated by the mountains of documents to be digested, naturally made it difficult for the meticulous screening of the sources and for the exercise of critical, objective judgment. The taboo of the Mongol rulers against statements that seemed derogatory to them in their earlier relations with the regimes they had subjugated was yet another inhibiting factor in the perfection of the three histories.

6. REVISIONS AND EMENDATIONS

Dissatisfied with what they regarded as the misguided principles and the irregular composition of the three histories, numerous scholar-historians in subsequent centuries devoted themselves to the revision and emendation of the three histories. They were concerned not only with rectifying the issue of dynastic legitimacy, to restore the Sung as the only legitimate ruling house, but also with eliminating the infelicities of the three histories and upholding the standard of Chinese historiography. In the following I shall examine, first of all, the attempts to rewrite the histories on principles geared to a reassessment of the legitimate succession issue, and, secondly, the efforts to uncover and emend the lacunae and errors in the three histories.

In the rewriting of the three histories, the focus fell on the Sung

---

[116] See Wei Su's biography of Ou-yang Hsüan cited in n. 57 above. Another compiler, Chieh Hsi-ssu 揭傒斯 (1274–1344), expressed a similar view; see *Kuei-chai wen-chi*, 10:30a.

[117] Huang Chin, *Chin-hua Huang hsien-sheng wen-chi*, 21:9b. For Huang Chin's biographies, see his "Account of Conduct" written by Sung Lien (1310–1381) included in Huang's collected works, Appendix, and YS 181:4187. According to Sung Lien, Huang Chin did not take up this assignment because of the death of his mother.

history, since these historians considered Sung the only legitimate ruling
house. The Liao and the Chin were considered usurpers, and it was
therefore held that their records should be treated in the category of
contemporaneous alien states appended to the Sung history.[118] The first
to apply this scheme to rewrite the Sung history was Hsieh Kuan, who, as
already noted, was invited by the Yüan historiographical office, together
with his friend Chou I-li, to participate in the historical composition. But
these two men both refused to take office after disagreements with the
authorities over ideological principles. Hsieh then engaged himself in
writing his own Sung history, but his effort was cut short by his death in
1360.[119] It was during the Ming dynasty (1368–1644), however, that
scholars made notable advances in the revision of the Sung history. The
pioneer was Chou Hsü 周敍 (1392–1452), a great grandson of Chou I-li,
who served as a Hanlin expositor at the court of Emperor Ying-tsung
英宗 (r. 1436–49; 1457–64). He submitted a memorial in June 1448,
requesting the court to undertake the revision of the Sung history, but
received no favorable response. He then initiated his own project but
died shortly later without much accomplishment.[120] Nevertheless, his
effort set a precedent for later scholars and inspired them to write a new
history of the Sung dynasty on the basis of different ideological
principles.

It is important to note, at this juncture, that the renewal of interest in
the Sung history coincided with a political incident that significantly
altered the Chinese perception of the historical relations between Sung,
Liao, Chin, and the Mongols. This was the debacle of the Chinese
campaign led in person by Emperor Ying-tsung against the Oirat-
Mongols at the battle of T'u-mu 土木 outside the Great Wall northwest of Peking in September 1449. The battle ended in a colossal defeat
for the Chinese, with the loss of quarter of a million soldiers and the
capture of the Ming emperor by the enemy.[121] The result of this

---

[118] For a useful summary of the revisions of the Sung history in Ming and Ch'ing times,
see NESCC 23:305, and *I-shu pien*, p. 154. See also Chin Yü-fu, pp. 139–144, and Huang
Yün-mei 黃雲眉, "Yü Hsia Ch'ü-ch'an lun kai-hsiu Sung-shih chu-chia shu
與夏瞿禪論改修宋史諸家書," *Wen-lan hsüeh-pao* 文瀾學報, 2:1 (1936), pp. 1–6.

[119] See their biographies cited in n. 104 above.

[120] This is recorded in *Ming Ying-tsung shih-lu* 明英宗實錄 (Taipei, 1965 ed.), p. 3196,
under 1448/5/16. For Chou Hsü's biographies, see Ch'en Hsün 陳循, *Fang-chou wen-chi*
芳洲文集 (1619), 8:17b, and MS 152:4198.

[121] For a detailed account of the Chinese debacle in the battle of T'u-mu, see Lai Chia-tu
賴家度 and Li Kuang-pi 李光璧, *Ming-ch'ao tui Wa-la ti chan-cheng* 明朝對瓦剌的戰爭
(Shanghai, 1954), and F. W. Mote, "The T'u-mu Incident of 1449," in *Chinese Ways in
Warfare*, eds. Frank A. Kierman, Jr. and John K. Fairbank (Cambridge, Mass., 1974),
pp. 243–272, 361–369.

humiliating setback was a wave of sentiment against the Mongols, and
by extension, against all the alien conquerors in Chinese history. This
upsurge of proto-nationalism was manifested not only in memorials to
the throne denouncing the Mongols, but also in historical writings,
belles lettres and folklore. In this context, the renewed efforts at rewriting
the Sung history, making the Sung the only legitimate ruling house over
the Liao and the Chin, were evidently inspired, if not conditioned, by
this outburst of anti-foreignism. They served, in a sense, as psychological
compensation for the Chinese humiliation at the hands of the Mongol
descendants.

It is not surprising, therefore, that serious attempts were made during
the following century to revise the Sung history that had been compiled by the Yüan historiographers. The initiative came mainly from
nationalistic private historians, but their efforts also had a significant
impact on the Ming court. In response to the prevailing opinion,
Emperor Shih-tsung 世宗 (1522–1566) issued a decree in 1536 appointing Yen Sung 嚴嵩 (1480–1565), the Minister of Rites, to head a special
commission for rewriting the Sung history. But the plan was abandoned
due to financial difficulties.[122] This abortive attempt sealed the fate of
the imperial sponsorship of a new Sung history, but it nevertheless encouraged several distinguished scholars to undertake their own projects.
It was under such inspiration that the leading bellettrist Kuei Yu-kuang
歸有光 (1506–1571) initiated his Sung history project. While he did not
succeed in producing a complete history, he left in his collected works
twenty odd chapters of "encomiums" for the biographies of eminent
personalities of the Sung.[123]

In the meantime, two contemporaneous Ming scholars, working
independently, finally produced a complete new version of the Sung
history. The first was Wang Chu 王洙 (chin-shih 1521), whose work, the
Sung-shih chih 宋史質 (Verified History of the Sung), 100 chüan, contains
a preface dated 1546. The other was K'o Wei-ch'i 柯維騏 (1497–1574),
who produced a work entitled Sung-shih hsin-pien 宋史新編 (The Newly

---

[122] This is recorded in Ming Shih-tsung shih-lu 明世宗實錄 (Taipei, 1965 ed.), p. 3951,
under 1536/5/20. For Yen Sung's role in the project, see MS 308:7914, and So Kwan-wai's
biography of Yen Sung in Dictionary of Ming Biography, p. 1586.

[123] For a brief note of Kuei Yu-kuang's Sung history project, see Chen-ch'uan hsien-
sheng chi 震川先生集, ch. 5: "Sung-shih lun-tsan 宋史論贊;" cf. Huang Yün-mei (n.
118), p. 2. For his biographies, see MS 287:7382, and Chao-ying Fang's account in
Dictionary of Ming Biography, pp. 757–761. Following Kuei, a scholar by the name of
Chao Ta-chou 趙大周, a contemporary of the renowned writer Ho Liang-chün 何良俊
(1506–1573), also thought of launching a Sung history project but without success. See Ho
Liang-chün, Ssu-yu chai ts'ung-shuo 四友齋叢説 (1573; Shanghai, 1959 ed.), p. 48.

Edited Sung History), 200 *chüan*, published around 1557. Both these works are available in modern reproductions.[124]

Wang Chu, a native of T'ien-t'ai, Chekiang, who had served in various minor offices in the central and provincial governments under Emperor Shih-tsung, devoted sixteen years to the writing of his new Sung history.[125] Following Yang Wei-chen's scheme, Wang Chu rehabilitated the exclusive legitimacy of the Sung rulers in the Basic Annals and relegated the Liao and the Chin to the Monographs on foreign nations. His *Verified History* is distinguishable not only for its radical departure in the layout of the contents and the treatment of subject matter, but also for the overt anti-foreign propaganda directed against the Mongol rulers of the previous dynasty. The work begins with the basic imperial annals covering all the Sung rulers. This section is called *T'ien-wang cheng-chi* 天王正紀 (*Orthodox Annals of the Celestial Kings*) (12 *chüan*), alluding to the legitimacy of the succession of the Sung house to the heavenly mandate. It concludes with the biographies of Neo-Confucian scholars, called *Tao-t'ung* (4 *chüan*), in deference to Yang Wei-chen's criteria of "moral succession" for postulating the legitimacy of the Sung dynasty.[126] The most unorthodox feature of Wang's history, however, was the introduction of the category of *Jun-chi* 閏紀 (*Irregular Annals*), immediately following the *Orthodox Annals of the Celestial Kings*, for the accounts of the Mongol rulers of the Yüan dynasty. In this case, Wang Chu tried to deny the legitimacy of the Mongol rulers and to create an impression of the continuation of native Chinese rule after the fall of the Southern Sung. He accomplished this by deleting from the records all the reign titles of the Yüan emperors. In place of Yüan rule from 1280 to 1351, he substituted a fabricated chronology based upon the ancestral line of Chu Yüan-chang 朱元璋 (1328–1398), founder of the Ming

[124] For a bibliographical note on these two works, see SKTY 50:10a, 15a; Chin Yü-fu, pp. 142, 139. The *Sung-shih chih* has been reprinted by photolithographic reproduction in one volume by Ta-hua Shu-chü 大華書局, Taipei, in 1977. It has been studied by Liu I-cheng in "Shu 'Sung-shih chih' 述「宋史質」," *Shih-hsüeh tsa-chih* 史學雜誌 (Nanking), 1 (1929), pp. 1–4, and by Wang Te-i in "Yu Sung-shih chih t'an-tao Ming-ch'ao jen ti Sung-shih kuan 由宋史質談到明朝人的宋史觀," *Kuo-li T'ai-wan Ta-hsüeh li-shih hsüeh-hsi hsüeh-pao* 國立臺灣大學歷史學系學報, 4 (May 1977), pp. 221–234. The *Sung-shih hsin-pien* was reproduced in a modern edition in one volume in 1939 and was reprinted by Lung-men Shu-tien 龍門書店, Hong Kong, in 1973. It has been studied by Mary Ferenczy in "Chinese Historiographers' Views on Barbarian–Chinese Relations (14th–16th C.)," *Acta Orientalia* (Budapast), 21:3 (1968), pp. 352–362.

[125] For an account of Wang Chu's career, see his autobiography appended to the last chapter of the *Sung-shih chih*; see also Liu I-cheng (n. 124), pp. 1–2, and Wang Te-i (n. 124), pp. 228–229.

[126] On Yang Wei-chen's criteria for postulating dynastic legitimacy, see the sources cited in n. 105, 106, 107 above.

dynasty, and elevated Chu's line to the status of direct successor to the Sung house.[127] In order to dramatize the rise of Chu Yüan-chang in rebellion against the Mongols in 1352, Wang designated this year, which actually corresponded to the twelfth year of the Chih-cheng reign (1341–1368) of the last Yüan emperor Toghōn Temür, as the founding date of the Ming dynasty. Thus the Ming was effectively antedated by sixteen years.[128] This was a radical attempt to apply Chu Hsi's categories of "orthodox" and "irregular" rulers to rehabilitate the exclusive legitimacy of Chinese rule from Sung to Ming. The Mongol rulers were thus dismissed as illegitimate in this scheme.

In the treatment of subject-matter, Wang Chu applied the principles expounded in the *Spring and Autumn Annals* to assert the supremacy of Chinese rule over the Mongols, and by implication over all the alien conquerors in China's past. Similarly, in praising meritorious and virtuous individuals and stigmatizing treacherous and corrupt officials, he proved himself an overzealous adherent of *Annals*-type methodology. In addition, while he aimed at producing a more concise version of Sung history by eliminating redundant and ornamental material, he stopped short of scrutinizing the evidence. He merely synthesized what was available in the existing histories.

In general, Wang Chu's *Verified History of the Sung* received more criticism than praise from later historians, precisely because his unorthodox manner of denouncing the alien rulers violated the principle of

---

[127] The chart in Appendix 1, based on *Sung-shih chih*, 12:36a, 13:41a, shows how Wang Chu tried to deny the legitimacy of Mongol rule by replacing the Yüan chronology with one of his own. The ancestors of the Ming founder, whose posthumous honorifics were used as reign names in Wang's new chronology, began with Chu Yüan-chang's 朱元璋 great grandfather Te-tsu, went through I-tsu, and Hsi-tsu, and terminated with Chu's father Jen-tsu. They were supposed to have reigned over the period 1279–99, 1299–1318, 1318–38, and 1339–51. These reign periods, however, were artificially contrived since there is no record of their precise chronology nor are there details of their life. In fact, Jen-tsu died in 1344, thereby leaving a vacuum of seven years in the chronology until Chu Yüan-chang's rise against the Mongols. They were accorded these posthumous honorifics by Chu Yüan-chang in February 1368, shortly after he was enthroned as founder of the Ming dynasty. See *Ming T'ai-tsu shih-lu* 明太祖實錄 (Taipei, 1962), p. 479; Chu Yüan-chang, *Kao huang-ti yü-chih wen-chi* 高皇帝御製文集 (colophon 1582), 16:1a; Hsieh Chin, *T'ien-huang yü-tieh* 天潢玉牒 (ca.1403) (Shanghai, 1938 ed.), la. Liu I-cheng, however, states in his review of the *Sung-shih chih* (n. 124, p. 3) that Wang Chu's attempt to deny the legitimacy of Mongol rule by eliminating from the annals the reign names of the Yüan emperors already had a precedent in the *Han-shu*. He shows that Pan Ku 班固 (32–92) had tried to dismiss the imperial status of Wang Mang 王莽, the usurper who founded the Hsin 新 dynasty (A.D. 9–25), by eliminating his reign name and relegating his annals to a monograph, in *Han-shu*, ch. 99. Liu contends that Wang Chu's device was not an innovation in the Chinese historiographical tradition.

[128] *Sung-shih chih*, 13:49a.

impartial judgment in the Chinese historiographical tradition. The most severe condemnation came from the compilers of the Ch'ing Imperial Catalogue on order of the Ch'ien-lung emperor during the 1770s; they denounced his work not only for its ideological deviation, but also for its deliberate distortion of historical facts.[129] It has received a more generous appraisal from nationalistic modern historians, but they have also shared the view that his approach was extreme and failed to reach the standard of a balanced dynastic history.

K'o Wei-ch'i, author of *The Newly Edited Sung History*, was a native of P'u-t'ien, Fukien, and received his *chin-shih* in 1523; he never held an official appointment but instead devoted the better part of his life to the writing of his new Sung history. He began working on the project in 1530 and did not complete it until twenty-five years later.[130] Following in the footsteps of Wang Chu, K'o Wei-ch'i rehabilitated the Sung as the sole legitimate ruling house, placing the accounts of the Liao and the Chin in the monographs on foreign nations in the same category as the Hsi-Hsia kingdom. Similarly, he conferred imperial titles on the two last Sung rulers and accorded each a biography in the Basic Annals, something that had been denied them by the Yüan historiographers. In addition, he rearranged the categories of the Biographies, assigning first place to the Neo-Confucian philosophers (*Tao-hsüeh*) instead of to the exemplary officials (*Hsün-li* 循吏) in the official history; also, as a corollary to rehabilitating the exclusivity of Sung legitimacy, he extolled the deeds of Sung loyalists and condemned those who surrendered to the Chin and the Yüan. Unlike Wang Chu's work, however, K'o Wei-ch'i's new history has been commended for its correction of errors, its addition of new biographies, and its incorporation of supplementary source materials.[131] Though criticized by the compilers of the Ch'ing Imperial Catalogue for its prejudice in favor of the Sung ruling house, it remains the standard reference for later revisions of the Sung history.

During the next century, another scholar, Wang Wei-chien 王惟儉 (*chin-shih* 1595), produced yet a different version of the Sung history, called *Sung-shih chi* 宋史記 (*Historical Records of the Sung*), in 250 *chüan*. This work was never printed but was transcribed by the Ch'ing

---

[129] SKTY 50:10a.

[130] For an account of K'o Wei-ch'i's life, see MS 287:7366; *P'u-t'ien hsien chih* 莆田縣志 (1879), 13:27a, 16:27a, 17:33a; and my biography of him in *Dictionary of Ming Biography*, pp. 721–722.

[131] For remarks of Ch'ing historians, see *I-shu pien*, p. 157; Chu I-tsun 朱彝尊, *P'u-shu-t'ing chi* 曝書亭集 (SPTK ed.), 45:7b; Ch'ien Ta-hsin, *Ch'ien-yen t'ang wen-chi*, 28:15a; for modern scholars' appraisal, see the studies of Chin Yü-fu and Huang Yüan-mei cited in n. 118 above.

bibliophiles. Two manuscript versions still survive in major libraries today.[132]

Wang Wei-chien, a native of Hsiang-fu, Honan, had held several minor offices in the ministries of War and Public Works before retiring to devote himself to his Sung history project in 1602, but it is not certain when he completed his work.[133] In general, Wang Wei-chien followed K'o Wei-ch'i's *Newly Edited Sung History* by incorporating the accounts of the Liao, Chin, and Hsi-Hsia into the Sung annals, elevating the last three Sung rulers to imperial status, and including new biographies for several imperial princesses and other royal dignitaries. The *Historical Records of the Sung*, however, is distinguished by several innovations and revisions in organization and in the treatment of subject matter. Wang eliminated the Treatises on Astronomy (*T'ien-wen* 天文), Five Agents (*Wu-hsing* 五行) and Literature (*I-wen* 藝文) in conformity with the criticism of Liu Chih-chi's 劉知幾 *Shih-t'ung* 史通 (*Comprehensive Survey of Historiography*). He also combined the Biographies of *Tao-hsüeh* and those of *Ju-lin*, incorporated the Treatise on Ceremonial and Guards (*I-wei* 儀衛) with that on the Rituals (*Li* 禮), and enlarged the Tables by including the accounts for the Southern T'ang kingdom, the Liao, the Chin and the Hsi-Hsia in the original histories.[134] Wang also deleted many of the redundant and purely ornamental materials in the original narratives. He thereby condensed the three histories to approximately one-third their former length. In addition, he incorporated major edicts and memorials in the annals and biographies that were absent in the original *Sung History*, and amended the narratives of the Mongol invasion of South China which had been rendered obscure by the taboos observed by the Yüan biographers. He placed greater emphasis on the

[132] For a bibliographical note on the *Sung-shih chi*, see Ch'ien Ch'ien-i 錢謙益, *Mu-chai ch'u-hsüeh chi* 牧齋初學集 (SPTK ed.), 84:4b; Chu I-tsum, *Ching-chih-chü shih-hua* 靜志居詩話 (1819 ed.), 16:23a; and Wang Shih-chen 王士禎, *Ts'an-wei chi* 蠶尾集, in *Yü-yang san-shih-liu chung* 漁洋三十六種 (1710 ed.), 10:10a. There survive two manuscript transcriptions of the *Sung-shih chi*. The first, in complete form, is preserved in the Peking Library; see *Kuo-li Pei-p'ing t'u-shu-kuan shan-pen shu-mu* 國立北平圖書館善本書目 (Peiping, 1933), Series A, *mu* 2:13b. The other copy, containing only the first 75 *chüan*, is available at the Fung Ping Shan Library of the University of Hong Kong, Hong Kong; see Jao Tsung-i, *Hsiang-kang Ta-hsüeh Feng P'ing-shan t'u-shu-kuan shan-pen shu-lu* 香港大學馮平山圖書館善本書錄 (Hong Kong, 1970), p. 125. For a modern appraisal of this work, see Chang Sui-ch'ing 張邃青, "Tu Sung chiao-pen Wang-shih Sung-shih chi 讀宋校本王氏宋史記," *Kuo-feng pan-yüeh-k'an* 國風半月刊, 5:10–11 (Dec. 1934), pp. 51–55.

[133] For an account of Wang Wei-chien's biography, see MS 288:7399, and Chang Sui-ch'ing's article cited in n. 132 above.

[134] See *Sung-shih chi*, "fan-li 凡例," and Chang Sui-ch'ing's study cited in 132 above.

exposure of inept and corrupt officials, and exercised the principles of the *Spring and Autumn Annals* in extolling the loyal and meritorious officials of the Southern Sung, and repudiating those who surrendered and served the Mongol rulers.[135]

These novel features notwithstanding, Ch'ing historians generally snubbed the *Historical Records of the Sung* as falling short of the standard of a refined and balanced historical annal. They contended that Wang Chu's arrangement of the contents left much to be desired, and that his indiscriminate revision of the substance had eliminated much useful information from the original histories. They also criticized him for over-indulgence in applying the principles of praise and blame which, they felt, tended to be farfetched and prejudicial, and for his excessive concern with literary elegance, which they said, accounted for much of his obscure phraseology and the distortion of historical facts.[136] It was probably because of these unfavorable impressions that the work failed to attract serious scholarly attention and was never published.

In various ways, therefore, these new versions of the Sung history failed to satisfy later scholars. Efforts to rewrite the history continued. The dissatisfaction with these works seems to lie, not in the question of the pattern of dynastic succession which these Ming historians established, but in the format and substance of the histories. During the late Ming and the early Ch'ing, several scholars, including T'ang Hsien-tsu 湯顯祖 (1550–1616) and Ku Yen-wu 顧炎武 (1613–1682), devoted themselves to revising the Sung history, but the results of their work do not seem to have survived.[137] During the Ch'ing period, a number of scholars carried on the Ming efforts to refine the Sung history, but here again few were able to fulfill their goals. These include Ch'üan Tsu-wang 全祖望 (1705–1755), Hang Shih-chün 杭世駿 (1696–1773), Shao Chin-han 邵晋涵 (1743–1796), Chang Hsüeh-ch'eng 章學誠 (1783–1801), and others.[138] It was only during the Ch'ien-lung period that Ch'en Huang-chung 陳黃中 (1704–1762) succeeded in producing a new history, called *Sung-shih kao* 宋史稿 (*Draft Sung History*), in 219 *chüan*. The *Draft Sung History* was not printed and seems to have been lost; fortunately the

[135] *Ibid.*

[136] See n. 132 above.

[137] See T'ang Hsien-tsu, *T'ang Hsien-tsu chi* 湯顯祖集, ed. Hsü Shuo-fang 徐朔方 (Shanghai, 1962), 44:1232; see also Ch'üan Tsu-wang. *Chieh-ch'i t'ing chi, wai-pien* 鮚埼亭集, 外編 (SPTK ed.), 43:4b. The latter has been analyzed by Ch'eng Kuang-yü 程光裕 in "Chieh-ch'i t'ing chi chung Sung-shih shih-liao k'ao-shih chü-li 鮚埼亭集中宋史史料考釋舉例," TLTC, 21:5 (1960), p. 12.

[138] See Chu I-tsun, *P'u-shu t'ing chi*, 45:6b; Liang Yü-sheng 梁玉繩, *Ch'ing-pai-shih chi* 清白士集 (1800), 21:15b; Chang Hsüeh-ch'eng, *Chang-shih i-shu* 章氏遺書 (Shanghai, 1936.), *wai-pien* 外編, 3 (Bk. 1), pp. 313, 315; *wen-chi* 文集, 21 (Bk. 5), p. 134. Cf. Chin Yü-fu, p. 144; Huang Yün-mei (n. 118), p. 4.

preface is preserved in the author's collected works.[139] Ch'en's history was essentially modelled on that of Wang Chu and K'o Wei-ch'i; it was noted, however, for certain rearrangements of the contents, correction of errors, elimination of duplications, and incorporation of new source materials.

It can be seen, therefore, that the main aim of these revisions of the Sung history was to rehabilitate the Sung as the only legitimate ruling house, relegating the Liao and the Chin to the status of alien usurpers. In this respect K'o Wei-ch'i's *Newly Edited Sung History* stood out as the most highly regarded achievement. Later historians, while correcting the mistakes and supplementing the sources of the original Sung history, generally followed his guidelines. K'o's model, aside from ideological considerations, had one exceptional feature. By appending the accounts of the Liao and the Chin in monographs in the Sung history, he provided a more comprehensive view of the relations between the Sung and its contemporary alien states than that which is given in the original histories. This arrangement, however, would have been commendable only when the records of both the Liao and the Chin were otherwise present in an individual history along with that of the Sung ruling house. If K'o's scheme had been adopted by the Yüan historiographers, the voluminous accounts about the Liao and the Chin would have had to have been reduced to the size of a monograph like that on the Hsi-Hsia, and much of the record of their existence would have been sacrificed. This would not only have destroyed the historiographical integrity of the Liao and Chin as rulers of North China, but would also have distorted our understanding of the relations between the Sung and these two ruling houses.

During the Ming and Ch'ing, there also appeared several works devoted to supplementing or simplifying the existing Sung history, or to integrating the Sung records with those of the Liao and the Chin. The first was the *Hung-chien lu* 弘簡錄 (*Great Outline of Historical Records*) by Shao Ching-pang 邵經邦 (1491–1561), 254 *chüan*. This work is a chronological synthesis of the dynastic histories from the T'ang through the Sung, intended as a continuation of the *T'ung-chih* 通志 (*Comprehensive Treatise*) by Cheng Ch'iao 鄭樵 (1102–1160).[140] The second

---

[139] Ch'en's preface to *Sung-shih kao* is preserved in his collected works, *Tung-chuang i-chi* 東莊遺集 (early Ch'ing ed.), ch. 2, and quoted in *Ch'ien-yen t'ang wen-chi*, 28:15b. A manuscript copy of Ch'en's collection, extremely rare, is available at the Seikadō Bunko, Tokyo. Chin Yü-fu suspects that Ch'en hesitated to publish his work for fear that it might implicate the Manchu rulers. See Chin, pp. 143, 214, n. 25.

[140] First engraved in 1561, and reprinted in 1688, see *I-shu pien*, p. 182. Later his son Shao Yüan-p'ing 邵遠平 (*chin-shih* 1664) compiled a continuation of his work entitled *Hsü Hung-chien lu*, 42 *chüan*, better known as *Yüan-shih lei-pien* 元史類編, printed in 1693.

was the *Sung-shih chi-shih pen-mo* 宋史紀事本末 (*Topical Sung History*) by Ch'en Pang-chan 陳邦瞻 (d. 1623), 109 *chüan*, being an annal of Sung history in a simplified style, integrating the records of the Liao and the Chin.[141] One outstanding feature of these two works is that the accounts of both the Liao and the Chin are relegated to the status of contemporaneous alien usurpers, evidently following K'o Wei-ch'i's model. In addition to these, two other works should be mentioned: the *Nan-Sung shu* 南宋書 (*History of the Southern Sung*) by Ch'ien Shih-sheng 錢士升 (1575–1652), 68 *chüan*, a chronicle devoted exclusively to the Southern Sung;[142] and the *Sung-shih i* 宋史翼 (*Wings to the Sung History*) by Lu Hsin-yüan 陸心源 (1834–1894), 40 *chüan*, a supplement to the biographies of the Sung history.[143] None of these works, however, made a serious effort to evaluate the existing source materials, and hence none made any significant breakthroughs in the rewriting of the Sung history.

Along with these ambitious attempts to restructure the Sung history, historians also sought to uncover the discrepancies, correct the errors, and restore the omissions in the Liao amd Chin histories. In this branch of scholarship, the most distinguished contributions came from Ch'ing historians such as Ch'ien Ta-hsin and Chao I, whose main works have already been mentioned.[144] In the case of the Liao history, the pioneering scholar was Li O 厲鶚 (1692–1752), whose collection of critical notes, the *Liao-shih shih-i* 遼史拾遺 (*Repairs of Omissions in the Liao History*), 24 *chüan*, is indispensable for the study of Liao history.[145] Li's work was brilliantly supplemented by the researches of modern scholars such as Feng Chia-sheng 馮家昇, Lo Chi-tsu 羅繼祖, Chang Liang-ts'ai 張亮采, and others.[146] In the field of the Chin history, the authority is

[141] See SKTY 49:2b. First engraved in 1605, later editions include a commentary by Chang P'u (1602–1641).

[142] See SKTY 50:12b. It was printed from manuscript possessed by Hsi Shih-ch'en 席世臣 in 1797.

[143] Printed by members of his family in the late Kuang-hsü period; see Chin Yü-fu, pp. 144, 169.

[144] See n. 108 above.

[145] Preface 1743, KYTS ed., 1900. This work was later supplemented by Yang Fu-chi 楊復吉, in *Liao-shih shih-i pu* 遼史拾遺補 (preface 1794), 5 *chüan*, also available in the KYTS collection. These two works, together with those cited in n. 146 below, have been fully utilized by the editors of the punctuated edition of the *Liao shih* published by the Chung-hua Shu-chü in 1974.

[146] I.e., Feng Chia-sheng, *Liao-shih cheng-wu san-chung*; Lo Chi-tsu 羅繼祖, *Liao shih chiao-k'an chi* 遼史校勘記 (Shanghai, 1958); Chang Liang-ts'ai, *Pu Liao-shih chiao-p'in piao* (Shanghai, 1958). These works have been reprinted, together with those cited in n. 145 and other items, in *Liao-shih hui-pien* 遼史彙編, 10 volumes, edited by Yang Chia-lo 楊家駱 (Taipei, 1973), being a comprehensive and indispensable collection of sources for the study of Liao history.

Shih Kuo-ch'i 施國祁 (1750–1824), whose works, *Chin-shih hsiang-chiao* 金史詳校 (*Detailed Corrections to the Chin History*), 10 *chüan*, and *Chin-yüan cha-chi* 金源箚記 (*Textual Notes on the Chin History*), 2 *chüan*, marked one of the highest achievements in traditional textual criticism.[147] Modern scholars such as Mao Wen 毛汶, Chu Hsi-tsu 朱希祖, and Ch'en Shu 陳述, among others, have also made substantial contributions to the textual criticism of the Chin history.[148]

The greatest problem confronting students of the Liao, Chin, and Sung histories, however, leaving aside the traditional disputes on legitimate succession, remains the lack of consistency in the sources and of cross-references among the three histories. The contributions by Ch'ing scholars in this field have been noted, but most of them focused only on individual cases, or on subjects of parochial interest.[149] There is no work that offers a comprehensive collation of the diverse data in all the three distories. Until this is done, we shall not gain a clear picture of the records of any one of the ruling houses, let alone of the interrelationships among all three in their respective histories.[150]

7. CONCLUSION

Despite the infelicities and defects of the Liao, Chin, and Sung histories composed under the auspices of the Yüan National History Office, the successful completion of this massive history project must be hailed as a unique achievement by the Mongol rulers who in this respect were noble successors to the Chinese political and cultural traditions. It is a tribute to the Mongol adaptation to the Chinese historiographical tradition, to their appreciation of the value of historical records, and to their acceptance of the obligation to compile the history of the regimes they had

[147] Preface 1811. The first work is available in the KYTS ed.; the second has been included in *Yang-shih ch'ien-ch'i-pai er-shih-chiu ho chai ts'ung-shu* 仰視千七百二十九 鶴齋叢書, ed. Chao Chih-ch'ien 趙之謙 (1880). These two works have been fully utilized by the editors of the punctuated edition of *Chin shih* published by the Chung-hua Shu-chü in 1975.

[148] I.e., Mao Wen 毛汶 in *Kuo-hsüeh shang-tui* 國學商兌, 1:1 (1933), pp. 33–36; *Kuo-hsüeh lun-heng* 國學論衡, 3 (1934), pp. 52–57; *ibid.*, 6 (1935), pp. 57–72; Chu Hsi-tsu 朱希祖 in *Kuo-li Chung-shan Ta-hsüeh wen-shih-hsüeh yen-chiu-so yüeh-k'an* 國立中山大學 文史學研究所月刊, 2:3–4 (1934), pp. 1–8; *id.*, in *Yen-ching hsüeh-pao*, 15 (1934), pp. 101–161; Ch'en Shu 陳述, *Chin-shih shih-pu wu-chung* 金史拾補五種 (Peking, 1960).

[149] Cf. Ch'ien Ta-hsin, *Sung-Liao-Chin-Yüan ssu-shih shuo-jun k'ao* 宋遼金元四史 朔閏考 (1884); Wang Hui-tsu 汪輝祖, (*Liao-Chin-Sung*) *San-shih t'ung-ming lu* (遼金宋) 三史同名錄 (1920); and Feng Chia-sheng, pt. 3.

[150] The modern historian Fang Chuang-yu made an attempt to collate the data in the Liao, Chin and Sung histories to produce a new Sung history, but without success. He left an outline of his project in his article "Sung-shih lei-pien chi Sung-shih chiao-chu 宋史類編及宋史校注," in *Shuo-wen yüeh-k'an*, 3:11 (1943), pp. 21–23.

subjugated. In the course of this endeavor, they faced many obstacles as nomadic conquerors with a totally different heritage. The solutions they adopted were to condition the format and substance of the final product.

In a nutshell, the main problem confronting the Mongol rulers was the dispute over the application of the *cheng-t'ung* theories in historical composition, for they carried not only ideological but also political implications. The issue at stake was which of the three states they had subjugated—the Liao, the Chin, or the Sung—should be considered as legitimate, and to which of these the Mongols should claim to be the legitimate successor in the Chinese dynastic order. That they adopted the proposal granting all three states the status of legitimacy, whereby the Yüan succeeded all three as legitimate ruler, was a practical solution both ideologically and politically, from the Mongol standpoint. This decision was also important from the historiographical point of view, for making all the three states legitimate guaranteed that each of them was to have an individual history. If, on the other hand, only the Sung had been considered legitimate, there would then have been only one history, one in which the Sung would occupy the dominant position, and the Liao and the Chin would survive merely as appendices to the Sung history. This would have been detrimental to our knowledge of the Liao and Chin dynasties.

The other chief problem facing the Mongols, that of the organization of the commissions of historiographers and the search for source materials for the three histories, was less demanding. With strenuous efforts and the cooperation of the Chinese literati, the Yüan historiographical bureau accumulated voluminous source materials and succeeded in fulfilling its task within a specified time limit. The great haste with which the Mongol authorities pushed forth the completion of the history project was a cause of the numerous defects in the histories, and it therefore became the general target of criticisms by later historians. This expediency, however, also reflected the dilemma of the Mongol administrators. They had wasted considerable time in the search for a solution to the central ideological dispute; once this was settled, they had to expedite the project, for otherwise unforeseeable events might, as they feared, threaten the completion of the enterprise.

All in all, credit must go to the Mongol rulers for their sustained efforts in preserving, albeit inadvertently, the chronicles of the Liao, Chin, and Sung ruling houses, and in according each an individual history within the framework of Chinese traditional historiography. The difficulties faced by a nomadic people ruling over a sedentary people with a sophisticated and long-standing literary tradition, deserve consideration in any appraisal of the Mongols' historiographical undertaking.

Southern Chinese Scholars and Educational Institutions in Early Yüan: Some Preliminary Remarks

YAN-SHUAN LAO

Throughout the history of China's traditional period, scholars often heeded the saying of Confucius that "the way of a superior man remains constant, whether he serves in public or lives in retirement."[1] This was further modified and amplified by his disciple Tzu Hsia, when the latter stated: "when one has attained excellence in office, he should study; when one has attained excellence in learning, he should serve in office."[2] From the Han dynasty on, this calling to office seemed irresistible to great numbers of literati. While such a tendency has been characterized as worldly or vulgar because of the primary emphasis on office and emolument, admittedly it is difficult to distinguish it from the goals of true learning.[3] In any case, it would not be incorrect to say that the Confucian insistence on learning, civil-service examination, and public life have been so intertwined that to try to separate them would be extremely difficult, if not impossible.

Ostensibly, the civil service examination system which the T'ang dynasty initiated could enable scholars to combine learning and the official career. But, in practice, it had many inherent deficiencies.[4] Although in the early Northern Sung large numers of scholars could become officials, by the time of the Southern Sung the supply of accomplished scholars had far exceeded existing official positions. Under such circumstances, many a scholar chose not to serve in any official capacity but remained in private life and concerned himself with academic and pedagogical ac-

---

[1] *Chou i* 周易 (SPTK ed.), 7:6a. See also James Legge, *Chinese Classics* (Hong Kong: University of Hong Kong Press, 1960) I, p. 632, and Richard Wilhelm/Carry F. Baynes, *The I Ching* (Princeton, N.J.: Princeton University Press, 1950), p. 305.

[2] *Lun-yü* 論語 (SPTK ed.), 10:4b. Cf. also Legge, *Chinese Classics*, I, p. 344.

[3] See Ying-shih Yü, "Some Preliminary Observations on the Rise of Ch'ing Confucian Intellectualism," *Ch'ing-hua hsüeh-pao* 清華學報, N.S. 11 (1975), pp. 137–138.

[4] Teng Ssu-yü 鄧嗣禹, *Chung-kuo k'ao-shih chih-tu shih* 中國考試制度史 (Taipei: Hsüeh-sheng Shu-chü, 1967), pp. 76–134, especially, pp. 113–121.

tivities.[5] In other words, owing to both the political environment and the intellectual atmosphere, from the twelfth century on, Chinese scholars often failed to regard the civil service examinations highly. Indeed, many of them perceived that in such examinations the emphasis put on mere literary skills and on current discussion of the classics rather than on the classic texts themselves and the traditional commentaries could in no way assure the acquisition of virtuous and capable officials.[6] This kind of criticism, however, was ignored by the Southern Sung government.

The last Southern Sung metropolian examination was held in 1274, and the Yüan did not reinstate the examination system until 1315. In between there were four full decades when the southern scholars could not utilize their literary skills for advancement. To be sure, a small number of them could and did obtain official appointments through various other means (see below), but for the majority the important question was: in order to keep themselves occupied intellectually, what should they do? Actually, this was not a new question brought about only by Mongol domination, because even in the prosperous times of the Sung, there had always been far more people who failed in the examinations than those who passed them. Among those whose hopes for an official career were dashed by their failure in civil-service examinations at various levels, many often "collected their thoughts and devoted themselves to serious learning, or released their feelings through poetry."[7] In other words, dabbling in literature (especially poetry) and engaging in serious studies of the classics had already become two principal outlets for the unsuccessful candidates during the Sung. The former led to a great outpouring of poetry; the latter evolved into the ever-increasing emphasis on the reinvestigation and reinterpretation of fundamental Confucian works, resulting in the blossoming of numerous master-pupil relationships.

If anything, the Mongol conquest seems to have intensified both of the above-mentioned tendencies. So far as the popularity of poetry composition was concerned, precisely because the suspension of the civil-service examinations freed the literati from necessity to prepare for narrow examination subjects, they had more leisure time at their disposal. And the recent sad events concerning the destruction of the Southern Sung undoubtedly provided much for them to write about. Therefore, one of them commented: "when the *k'o-chü* 科舉 [exami-

[5] See James T. C. Liu, "How did a Neo-Confucian School Become the State Orthodoxy?" *Philosophy East and West*, 23 (1973), pp. 483–504, esp. pp. 484–485.

[6] The most typical views are found in Chu Hsi 朱熹, "Hsüeh-hsiao kung-chü ssu-i 學校貢舉私議," *Chu Wen-kung wen-chi* 朱文公文集 (SPTK ed.), 69:20a–28b.

[7] See Shu Yüeh-hsiang 舒岳祥, *Lang-feng chi* 閬風集 (SKCSCP ed.), 10:6b.

nation system] was abolished, there was not a single scholar who did not compose poetry. Now that the *k'o-chü* has been suspended for twelve years, poetry has become even more popular."[8] Similar statements abound in the writings of others.[9] One exemplary statement which helps to deepen our insight into this phenomenon is the following:

"Since the fall of the dynasty, the literary route leading to examinations has been cut off. As candidates have nothing with which to put their skills to use, by the faraway seashore or on top of some distant mountains they often tap the literary techniques in parallelism and rhyming which they are versed in, and apply them to poetry, so as to express their grief and describe their sufferings. But this is not their original goal of literary study.... Alas! When the *k'o-chü* was at its height, scholars of high calibre all exerted their efforts in current literature (*shih-wen* 時文). If one fortunately passed the *chin-shih* 進士 examination, he would gain glory and apply himself to current affairs. He would be extremely proud of himself. Only those who are not so skillful with their pen—with which to compete against thousands of others for the top spot—would join the ranks of poets. And the examination candidates actually looked down upon them. Now, as the *k'o-chü* is abolished, the formerly arrogant ones have turned around and are trying to master what they had despised. This indeed is lamentable!"[10]

Considering such statements, although we can say that the literati at the time probably pursued poetry with a vengeance, they cannot lead us to believe that composing poetry had become *the* major part of their intellectual activities. Granted that in poetry they found a suitable vehicle to vent their emotions and frustrations, how many poems could one compose in one day before boredom set in? And how many different allusions could one use for such expressions as the "demise of the dynasty" before one had to repeat oneself? Further, while the mechanics of poetry composition may not be difficult to master, it does not follow that everyone who has mastered them can automatically become a good poet. Under such circumstances, they often relied on novelty and gimmickry in order to distinguish themselves. Many observant critics deplored such trends. A typical criticism reads: "Ever since the *k'o-chü* was abolished, scholars have seized upon poetry as their avocation.... Most of them follow the styles of the late T'ang and

[8] Liu Ch'en-weng 劉辰翁, *Hsü-ch'i chi* 須溪集 (SKCSCP ed.), 6:9b.

[9] See, e.g., Chao Meng-fu 趙孟頫, *Sung-hsüeh chai chi* 松雪齋集 (SPTK ed.), 6:11a–11b; Tai Piao-yüan 戴表元, *Shan-yüan Tai hsien-sheng wen-chi* 剡源戴先生文集 (SPTK ed.), 9:2b; Ch'en Li 陳櫟, *Ting-yü chi* 定宇集 (SKCSCP ed.), 17:22b.

[10] Shu Yüeh-hsiang, *Lang-feng chi*, 12:3b–4b.

frequently strive for eccentricity to such an extent that their works are unreadable. Do these have the quality of profundity and subtlety? Can they touch one's conscience and rectify one's frivolous feelings?"[11]

It is easy to see that while poetry indeed served a definite need for these people in a limited way, it could not be expected to provide them with enough challenge and mental stimulation during a time when much was in a state of flux. It is small wonder that although we still can read a large number of prefaces to such early Yüan poetry collections (included in the works of more prominent authors), few of them are extant— mostly because their quality did not justify the cost of printing or even the preservation in manuscript form.

Furthermore, while composing poetry naturally could not provide these literati with sustenance and livelihood, the Confucian tradition of "serving in office" no doubt was constantly on their minds. Yet, the route to officialdom was now full of obstacles. Before the Mongols conquered the Southern Sung, they had already organized a bureaucracy which absorbed a large number of scholars and ex-bureaucrats from the defunct Jurchen-Chin.[12] Therefore, in the early Yüan, those who were appointed to high offices in the south were invariably northerners. Southern scholars for the most part lived in retirement.[13]

For the southerners who were really eager to serve, it was a common practice to go north to the capital "to seek official emolument." Far too often, however, those who went to the capital were opportunists. They expected positions which may not even have existed.[14] As for the truly learned and gifted ones, unless they were fortunate enough to be discovered by some dignitaries, their journey north frequently came to naught. The famed poet Fan P'eng 范梈 (1272–1330) is a case in point. He was from an impoverished family but studied very diligently until he was versed in literature in general and poetry in particular. Still, there was little chance for him to distinguish himself in his native place. So he went to the capital Ta-tu, making a living by telling fortunes at the market place. Eventually, Tung Shih-hsüan 董士選 (1253–1321) learned

---

[11] Ch'en Li, *Ting-yü chi*, 17:22a–22b.

[12] See T'ang Chang-ju 唐長孺, "Meng-ku ch'ien-ch'i wen-jen chin-yung chih t'u-ching chi ch'i chung-shu tsu-chih 蒙古前期文人進用之途徑及其中樞組織," *Hsüeh-yüan* 學原, 2:7 (1949), pp. 75–94, esp. pp. 83–87. See also Igor de Rachewiltz, "Personnel and Personalities in North China in the Early Mongol Period," *Journal of the Economic and Social History of the Orient*, 9 (1966), pp. 88–142.

[13] Chang Po-ch'un 張伯淳, *Yang-meng hsien-sheng wen-chi* 養蒙先生文集 (SKCSCP ed.), prefaces, 2a.

[14] Wu Ch'eng 吳澄, *Wu Wen-cheng chi* 吳文正集 (SKCSCP ed.), 26:5b–6a.

about him and hired him as the family tutor. It was only through Tung's assistance that Fan P'eng gradually became famous.[15] Similarly, Fang Chung-ch'üan 方中全, a son of Fang Hui 方回 (1227–1307),[16] was outside officialdom for some twenty years after the Mongol conquest. Then on some "eminent person's" recommendation he went to the capital. After a while, he was appointed the prefect of Yen-kuan 鹽官.[17] It is also true that many high officials, such as Ch'eng Chü-fu 程鉅夫 (1249–1318) and Kao K'o-kung 高克恭 (1248–1310), recommended qualified persons to the court.[18] Yet there must have been a large number of individuals who could not find any sponsors readily. If such an individual wanted to secure even a low government position, he would have to "put on a fawning appearance, wait at the door of an influential official from early dawn on, and humor the servants before he can get anywhere. And this is precisely what those with principles can not do."[19]

Thus, before the reinstitution of civil-service examinations during the reign of Ayurbarwada, the only reliable and respectable route to officialdom for most southern literati was through government posts connected with education, starting with those at the district (*hsien* 縣) level.[20] According to the *Yüan shih* 元史 (*Yüan History*), an imperial edict was issued in 1291, regulating the founding of public schools and academies (*shu-yüan* 書院) in different localities. The most important feature of this edict is that it made detailed stipulations for the appointment of teaching and non-teaching personnel in these schools, and the sequence of promotion from one level to the next was carefully specified.[21] The meticulous and thorough treatment of these matters in this

[15] Chieh Hsi-ssu 揭傒斯, *Chieh Wen-an kung ch'üan-chi* 揭文安公全集 (SPTK ed.), 8:8b.; see also Wu Ch'eng, *Wu Wen-cheng chi*, 85:15a–17a, and YS 181:4183–4184.

[16] For his life, see Fang Hui, *T'ung-chiang chi* 桐江集 (Taipei: National Central Library, 1970), which includes a biography by Hung Yen-tsu 洪焱祖; see also Sun K'o-k'uan 孫克寬, "K'uei-hsin tsa-chih chi Fang Hui shih shu-cheng 癸辛雜識記方回事疏證," in *Meng-ku Han-chün yü Han wen-hua yen-chiu* 蒙古漢軍與漢文化研究 (Taipei: Wen-hsing Shu-tien, 1958), pp. 107–132.

[17] Tai Piao-yüan, *Shan-yüan Tai hsien-sheng wen-chi*, 13:14b–15a; Chen Li, *Ting-yü chi*, 2:30b.

[18] See Ch'eng's funeral inscriptions which are included in his collected works, *Ch'eng Hsüeh-lou wen-chi* 程雪樓文集 (Taipei: National Central Library, 1970), Appendix, la-12a; and Kao's Account of Conduct in Teng Wen-yüan 鄧文原, *Pa-hsi chi* 巴西集 (SKCSCP ed.), *hsia* 下, 23a. Some of Ch'eng's recommendations will be discussed below.

[19] Yü Ch'üeh 余闕, *Ch'ing-yang wen-chi* 青陽文集 (SPTK ed.), 4:9a.

[20] Wu Ch'eng, *Wu Wen-cheng chi*, 30:9a–9b.

[21] YS 81:2032–2033.

edict is a good indication that personnel in charge of education formed a significant source for other types of officials.[22]

The 1291 edict may have been an honest attempt to attract southerners into official positions. But, in practice, it took interminable periods to obtain needed promotions to become ranked officials. Many persons received only a single ranked official appointment during their entire lives.[23] And few educational officials ever attained prominence.[24] Comparing the Sung situation with that of the early Yüan, Fang Hui points out that during the Sung, while it was difficult to enter the realm of officialdom, official advancements were much easier to obtain than in the early Yüan. This is owing to the fact that although only five to six hundred *chin-shih* degrees were conferred every three years in the Sung, once the person has secured the degree, advancement could be rapid. In the early Yüan dynasty, it was the other way around: from the position of public-school instructor at the district level, one could gradually advance to that at the subprefecture (*chou* 州), prefecture (*fu* 府) and circuit (*lu* 路) levels, and thereby "enter the current."[25] But, from there on, the process became slow. The appointment to the office of a circuit governor (*tsung-kuan* 總管) or even to that of a district magistrate, not to mention appointments in the central government, would be extremely difficult to obtain.[26] Actually, official records show that Fang Hui's appraisal was quite optimistic, and the reality was considerably harsher. For instance, in March of 1305, there were eighty-nine openings for Confucian school instructors at the subprefecture and prefecture levels in the whole nation. Yet there were more than five hundred qualified candidates for these openings, many of whom had waited for such openings for as long as eight or nine years.[27]

---

[22] The sequence of promotion set in the 1291 edict tallies well with the official careers of many individuals; see, e.g., Huang Chin 黃溍, *Chin-hua Huang hsien-sheng wen-chi* 金華黃先生文集 (SPTK ed.), 33:1a–1b; Sung Lien 宋濂, *Sung hsüeh-shih chi* 宋學士集 (SPTK ed.), 65:5b–6b; Fang Hui, *T'ung-chiang hsü-chi* 桐江續集 (SKCSCP ed.), 33:23b–24b.

[23] Wu Shih-tao 吳師道, *Wu Cheng-ch'uan hsien-sheng wen-chi* 吳正傳先生文集 (Taipei: National Central Library, 1970), p. 418.

[24] Su T'ien-chüeh 蘇天爵, ed., *Kuo-ch'ao wen-lei* 國朝文類 (SPTK ed.), 40:10b.

[25] In fact, after serving one term of subprefecture or prefecture instructorship, it would qualify a person for the official rank of 9a; see YTC 9:13a, and YS 81:2032–2033; see also YS 91:2316.

[26] Fang Hui, *T'ung-chiang hsü-chi*, 34:17a–18a. The number of triennial *chin-shih* graduates which Fang cites here obviously refers to those during the last decades of the Southern Sung; see E. A. Kracke, "Family vs. Merit in Chinese Civil Service Examinations under the Empire," HJAS, 10 (1947), pp. 115–119.

[27] YTC 9:14a.

Since there were far more candidates than openings, the Ministry of Personnel sometimes took the unusual step of appointing scholars as District Chief of Police (*hsün-chien* 巡檢). Even though they were ill-prepared for the position, they eagerly grabbed it and were extremely glad to have it.[28] The situation did not improve much after the civil-service examinations were reintroduced, because in 1317 there were still cases in which persons took more than thirty years to become a circuit-school instructor and thereby qualify to become a ranked official. By then, they were already close to the age of retirement.[29] For many, this meant that the circuit-school instructorship would be the highest post that they held during their entire lives. Be that as it may, many southern scholars still rushed toward such posts if only because they had little other choice.

Since the public-school instructors had considerations other than pedagogy and scholarship, teaching and learning were not always seriously carried out. In fact, matters pertaining to money seem to have been constantly on their minds. Those who were honest simply spent much time on book-keeping so as to win trust and praise from local officials upon whom their future careers depended. The corrupt ones, on the other hand, "consorted with lowly persons and worthless rogues. Together they measured and counted [the school] money and grain day and night. They committed pilferage and theft, and contended with one another with disputes and lawsuits. Thus, although the schools exist, it is as if they had been done away with."[30] The shift of attention from academic matters to such extracurricular activities no doubt resulted in the decline of the quality of education. On the one hand, those who were in charge of education simply waited out their terms for other official posts. Few were truly devoted or even interested in their vocation.[31] They were "often troubled by the fact that moral principles are not salable, so they must make all the efforts in attending to the influential people and make rounds in order to benefit themselves." In the end, they could no longer keep up with what they had been trained for.[32] As a matter of fact, because too many individuals were contending for too few

---

[28] Wu Ch'eng, *Wu Wen-cheng chi*, 30:8b, 33:8b.

[29] *Wu Wen-cheng chi*, 9:16b–17a; for an actual case, see Huang Chin, *Chin-hua Huang hsien-sheng wen-chi*, 32:3b–4a.

[30] Wu Shih-tao, *Wu Cheng-ch'uan hsien-sheng wen-chi*, p. 424; see also Ch'eng Chü-fu, *Ch'eng Hsüeh-lou wen-chi*, 15:7b; and Wu Ch'eng, *Wu Wen-cheng chi*, 34:6a–7b. Kuo Pi in his famous *Diary* speaks of embezzlement of the instructor from one circuit school land; see *Kuo T'ien-hsi jih-chi* 郭天錫日記 (*Ku-hsüeh hui-k'an* 古學彙刊 ed.), 3:1b.

[31] Wu Ch'eng, *Wu Wen-cheng chi*, 27:15b–16a.

[32] Chang Po-ch'un, *Yang-meng wen-chi*, 2:11b.

available positions, it was common to use fraudulent means in order to secure such positions. This condition is reflected clearly in a communication issued by the Chiang-nan Censorate in 1312:

"In recent years, as far as educational personnel of various places is concerned, accomplished scholars are truly few while frivolous persons are numerous. This is due to the fact that these individuals can cleverly make connections with those who wield power and influence, and take shortcuts with deviousness. Some depend on their abundant wealth; others rely on [those who have] high office or power. Some impress people with artful but petty skills; others utilize their flattery and glibness to make themselves known. Therefore, famous and virtuous scholars withdraw and hide in the countryside, as flippant and boastful persons calmly take up the instructorships. It is indeed difficult for us to expect the schools to flourish and to train men of ability." [33]

This indictment is well corroborated by other sources. For instance, the famous Neo-Confucian scholar Wu Ch'eng 吳澄 (1249–1333)[34] made a sarcastic analogy between the duties of local-school instructors in the south and those of the servant of a businessman or the assistant of an architect, because the former, in his view, were constantly preoccupied with matters pertaining to money and the physical plants of the schools.[35] Kuo Pi 郭畀 (1280–1335), the famous painter and calligrapher, vividly described the scholastic incompetency of a Chen-chiang Circuit School intructor with the following words: "I listened to the lecture of Instructor Chang. He was virtually like a roadside story-teller in the North. At present, academic standards have fallen by the wayside to such an extent. How can I lament enough, how can I lament enough!" Again: "Instructor Chang lectured. His talk was so vulgar that I simply could not listen any longer. I therefore went out." [36]

Such being the case, it is not difficult to see why that, although by the year 1288 there already were more than 24,400 public schools scattered throughout the empire,[37] few good scholars were produced by these schools. Therefore, it was only natural for the serious-minded scholars in the south to view these educational establishments with scorn.[38] Many of those who were so inclined often would forgo public-

[33] YTC 9:16a.

[34] For Wu Ch'eng's life, see his Account of Conduct in Yü Chi 虞集, *Tao-yüan hsüeh-ku lu* 道園學古錄 (SPTK ed.), 44:2b–14b, and his biography in YS 171:4011–4014; see also David Gedalecia's article in this volume for Wu's philosophy.

[35] Wu Ch'eng, *Wu Wen-cheng chi*, 34:6b–7a.

[36] Kuo Pi, *Kuo T'ien-hsi jih-chi*, 3:13a and 4:11a.

[37] YS 15:318.

[38] Needless to say, not all public schools were substandard and many learned Southern scholars did teach in public schools in early Yüan. For a discussion of some of these

school teaching and give instruction to a handful of pupils at or near their own dwellings, or become headmasters (*shan-chang* 山長) of academies. But before we examine the activities of some individuals in this group, it will be useful to say a word about the status of academies in Yüan times.

First of all, *shu-yüan* or academies had already undergone a long period of development before the Yüan. Their origin can be traced back to the ancient *ching-she* 精舍 ("house of refinement"), which was a term for small buildings erected by some scholars in Later Han times for the express purpose of giving private lessons to students.[39] From the T'ang dynasty on, this institution underwent further development. Some of them came to be known as *shu-yüan*, but their number was rather limited. During the Northern Sung, among the scores of academies, the "Four Great Academies" were especially famous. Yet prominent scholars of the time taught mostly in private rather than at any of the academies. In the Southern Sung, not only did the number of academies multiply, but it had become common for reknowned scholars such as Chu Hsi 朱熹 (1130–1200) and Lü Tsu-ch'ien 呂祖謙 (1137–1181) to teach or to give lectures in them. Chu Hsi, in fact, did much to popularize the *shu-yüan* institution, including his efforts in restoring and renovating the Pai-lu Academy.

Generally speaking, the basic guidelines for study in an academy can be reduced to the following four: (1) setting up a high goal (*shang chih* 尚志), (2) holding fast to seriousness (*chü ching* 居敬), (3) searching for the ultimate principles (*ch'iung li* 窮理), and (4) applying what one has learned to oneself (*fan shen* 反身).[40] The main reason why the academies adopted such an approach was that "the teachings in the prefecture and district schools were infatuated with vulgar learnings, and the practice of

---

scholars, see Chou Tsu-mo 周祖謨, "Sung wang hou shih Yüan chih ju-hsüeh chiao-shou 宋亡後仕元之儒學教授," *Fu-jen hsüeh-chih* 輔仁學誌, 12 (1946), pp. 191–214, esp. pp. 198–203.

[39] Huang Chung-yüan 黃仲元, *P'u-yang Huang Chung-yüan Ssu-ju hsien-sheng wen-kao* 莆陽黃仲元四如先生文稿 (SPTK ed.), 1:9a. For further discussion of the term *ching-she*, see James T. C. Liu, "How Did a Neo-Confucian School," p. 409.

[40] These were what Jao Lu 饒魯 (SYHA 83:1a–1b) provided for his pupils, which in turn were based on Chu Hsi's "Pai-lu shu-yüan chiao-kuei 白鹿書院教規," and "Ch'eng [Tuan-meng] (1143–1191) Tung [Shu] (1152–1214) erh hsien-sheng hsüeh-tse 程 [端蒙] 董 [銖] 二先生學則." Both sets of rules can be found in Ch'eng Tuan-li 程端禮, *Ch'eng-shih chia-shu tu-shu fen-nien jih-ch'eng* 程氏家塾讀書分年日程 (SPTK ed.), "Kung-ch'eng kang-ling 工程綱領," 1a–7a. They are also included in the Collectanea *Hsüeh-hai lei-pien* 學海類編. Ch'eng Tuan-li's *Jih-ch'eng* contains detailed reading guides for the *Four Books* and the *Five Classics*. Although the *Jih-ch'eng* was compiled to guide those who wished to take the Yüan civil service examinations, it was based on Fu Kuang's *Chu-tzu tu-shu-fa* 輔廣朱子讀書法, a work widely used in the academies.

using the *k'o-chü* as an inducement deluded the minds of scholars. There-fore, it is hoped that scholars can assemble together and discuss the Tao 道 [in an academy]."[41] It is clear from this that the academies were expected to rectify the wrong tendencies perpetuated in the local schools.

In regard to the financial and other non-curricular aspects of the academies, it is probably safe to say that there existed no uniform system. The majority of the Sung academies were founded by private individuals, with a smaller percentage of them founded by local officials. The academies generally had their own "school land" from which stipends, fellowships, and other expenditures were derived. But, from time to time, they received grants from the government in the forms of land, money, or books, or a combination of these. And it was not uncommon for the emperor to issue "name tablets" (*e* 額) for the academies.[42]

The Mongol conquest of the south exerted little negative impact on local public schools there,[43] and the *shu-yüan* tradition also continued on without much difficulty. Jen Shih-lin 任士林 (1253–1309),[44] who served as the headmaster of a number of academies in the early Yüan, discussed the development of such institutions thus:

"Not until Master Chu had the old practices at Pai-lu-tung 白鹿洞 [Academy] been restored.... Thereafter, those who founded academies in places where prominent Confucian scholars had expounded the Tao became more numerous. After Master Chu passed away, in all the localities where he had sojourned or served, they honored him and thereby studied his teachings. Thus, academies have become more flourishing. Students in such places did not engage in monthly tests and quarterly examinations. What they studied was the essence of acquiring exhaustive knowledge of the principles (*li* 理) and the inner human nature (*hsing* 性). The official in charge [of an academy] was senior to the Prefectural Instructor.[45] As for their stipends, either they were paid from

[41] Wu Ch'eng, *Wu Wen-cheng chi*, 37:2b.

[42] This brief description of the Sung academies is based on the following works: (1) Chou Shu-ling 周書齡, "Shu-yüan chih-tu chih yen-chiu 書院制度之研究," *Shih-ta yüeh-k'an* 師大月刊, 1 (1932) pp. 1–22; (2) Sheng Lang-hsi 盛朗西, *Chung-kuo shu-yüan chih-tu* 中國書院制度 (Shanghai: Chung-hua Shu-chü, 1934); (3) Ts'ao Sung-yeh 曹松葉, "Sung Yüan Ming Ch'ing shu-yüan kai-k'uang 宋元明清書院概況," *Yü-yen li-shih yen-chiu-so chou-k'an* 語言歷史研究所週刊, 10:111 (1929), pp. 4425–4453.

[43] Wu Ch'eng, *Wu Wen-cheng chi*, 36:7b.

[44] His funeral inscription can be found in Chao Meng-fu, *Sung-hsüeh chai chi*, 8:18b–20a.

[45] This appears to be a reference to late Southern Sung practices only; see Pan Shu-ko 班書閣, "Shu-yüan chang-chiao k'ao 書院掌教考," *Nü-shih hsüeh-yüan ch'i-k'an* 女師 學院期刊, 1:2 (1933), pp. 12–16.

the land granted by the government, or by those who were philanthropic and well-to-do and were willing to support them with their own resources.

"After Emperor Shih-tsu (Khubilai) unified the entire domain, [public] schools in prefectures and districts have become bigger and more important. And the authorities have not discouraged persons who wished to establish academies with their own resources. The censors reviewed them and the provincial governments appointed officials to be in charge of them. Their qualifications were comparable to those for the *hsüeh-cheng* 學正 and *hsüeh-lu* 學錄 [local government education officials]."[46]

Then Jen Shih-lin goes on to describe the physical and financial aspects of Wen-kung 文公 Academy (in Feng-hua 奉化) which he headed. According to him, the founding of the academy was enthusiastically supported by the *darughachi*, the prefect and their subordinates. They ordered government workers to construct the buildings with private contributions so that "the government is not burdened by the costs of wood and stone at all." After the completion, local gentry agreed to spend one-third of their charitable grain to support the expenditures of the academy. The whole endeavor was duly reported to the provincial officials, presumably to seek their authorization of the appointment of the headmaster.

What Jen Shih-lin described in this account was quite typical, because it was a common practice for people in a given locality to chip in to build or to restore an academy with the active participation or assistance of the local officials. The financial contribution could come in a variety of forms: grain, land, interests drawn from an accumulated trust fund, etc.[47] Therefore, in the majority of instances, the foundation or restoration of an academy during Yüan times may be considered as a joint effort between the officials and the people in the same locality. Moreover, once an academy was established, the local government sometimes would make further subsidies, but not necessarily on a very regular basis.[48] The government appointment of academy headmasters was distinctly a Yüan feature, for it was not carried out so extensively either before or after the dynasty,[49] although there were a large number of

---

[46] Jen Shih-lin, *Sung-hsiang chi* 松鄉集 (SKCSCP ed.), 1:6a–6b; see YS 81:2032–2033 for similar descriptions.

[47] See, e.g., Tai Piao-yüan, *Shan-yüan Tai hsien-sheng wen-chi*, 1:3b, 5a; Fang Hui, *T'ung-chiang chi*, 1:132; Wu Ch'eng, *Wu Wen-cheng chi*, 37:11a–12a; Yü Chi, *Tao-yüan hsüeh-ku lu*, 8:10b; Liu Yüeh-shen 劉岳申, *Shen-chai Liu hsien-sheng wen-chi* 申齋劉先生文集 (Taipei: National Central Library, 1970), 6:16a.

[48] See Wu Ch'eng, *Wu Wen-cheng chi*, 41:2a–2b.

[49] See Pan Shu-ko, "Shu-yüan chang-chiao k'ao," p. 15.

instances in which some academies received no support or control from the government during the Yüan.

The headmasters were by and large serious and accomplished scholars, for otherwise they would not have wanted to endure such an appointment, which bordered on poverty. Thus it is said that those who did not have their minds on their jobs would simply neglect their duty and leave their charge in financial ruins.[50] Conversely, those who had a genuine interest in their work often showed a surprising degree of dedication, as witnessed by the following words from a letter addressed to Wu Ch'eng by Hu Ping-wen 胡炳文 (1250–1333):

"Of the three hundred and sixty days of a year, I have approximately some ten days of leisure. Diligently and perseveringly, I investigate the learning in the Classics with [the pupils] day and night. . . . I am seventy now; I do not know how many more years I shall have in this world. With all desires turning cold as ashes, I do not search for anything else: if only I can accomplish such matters as pertain to the academy, then I shall die without regret."[51]

This kind of dedication is indeed a far cry from the attitude of public-school instructors described above.

Something else worth mentioning in connection with the academies is their location and their collection of books. As a rule, academies were located in the countryside: on a mountain, by a stream, or at some rural place of note. This was intended to provide an environment for quiet studying. And, from the Sung dynasty on, many academies became repositories of books or small-scale libraries.[52] During Yüan times, this practice not only continued but seems to have gone one step further. That is, in addition to maintaining a collection of books, some academies also kept the printing blocks of certain books at hand so that such books could be printed readily as the need arose.[53] In fact, among the many sets of printing blocks deposited at Hsi-hu 西湖 Academy in Hangchow, there were included the blocks for the important Yüan anthology *Kuo-ch'ao wen-lei* 國朝文類 (*Our Dynasty's Literature by Genre*) compiled by Su T'ien-chüeh 蘇天爵 (1294–1352).[54] Such a practice further illustrates the serious nature of the academies.

[50] Liu Chiang-sun 劉將孫, *Yang-wu chai chi* 養吾齋集 (SKCSCP ed.), 15:25b–26a.

[51] Hu Ping-wen, *Yün-feng chi* 雲峯集 (SKCSCP ed.), 1:4a–5a.

[52] See Sheng Lang-hsi, *Chung-kuo shu-yüan chih-tu*, pp. 47–49.

[53] See, e.g., Fang Hui, *T'ung-chiang chi*, 3:291; Liu Yüeh-shen, *Liu hsien-sheng wen-chi*, 6:25a–25b; Cheng Yüan-yu 鄭元祐, *Ch'iao Wu chi* 僑吳集 (Taipei: National Central Library, 1970), 9:11b–12a.

[54] See *Kuo-ch'ao wen-lei*, "Kung-wen 公文." This work was first printed in 1335. The Hsi-hu Academy edition, now in SPTK, dates from 1342.

As the number of academies grew, however, the quality of some of them went down. It is said of such academies that "their increase in various places in recent years has been numerous. They merely copy the names of academies in the previous dynasty. There is no advantage in having them, and no harm in not having them."[55] Further, when it became the responsibility of the government to appoint the headmasters, not all the selections were made with great care. As a result, many appointees were not interested in what they were assigned to do. And, in other instances, even government subsidies were not enough to cover the deficits. Thus, many had to close their doors subsequently.[56] On top of these problems, some rich persons simply utilized their wealth to establish academies and regarded them as stepping stones to officialdom.[57] In other words, many academies fell into the old public-school rut, and scholastic failures were often due to too much government interference.[58] Be that as it may, such failure only occurred after the Yen-yu era (1314–1320), not during the first few decades of the Yüan. And even when some of the government sponsored academies were failing, more privately sponsored academies were founded, avoiding the pitfalls.[59]

Now, let us take a look at some of the southern scholars who either taught privately or served as headmasters in the early years of the Yüan. What follows cannot but be a cursory list.

Fang Feng-ch'en 方逢辰 (1221–1291, chin-shih, 1250): served as ping-pu shih-lang 兵部侍郎 (Vice Minister of War) in the Southern Sung, remained in retirement and taught at Shih-hsia 石峽 Academy (in Ch'un-an 淳安) in early Yüan until his death.[60]

Wang I-lung 汪一龍 (1230–1282, chin-shih, 1268): refused official Yüan appointment, but consented to teach at Tzu-yang 紫陽 Academy (in Hsi-hsien 歙縣, modern Anhwei) in early Yüan.[61]

Ts'ao Ching 曹涇 (1234–1315, chin-shih, 1268): served as headmaster of Tzu-yang Academy.[62]

Shu Yüeh-hsiang 舒岳祥 (1236–?, chin-shih, 1256): after the fall of the Sung, he lived in retirement and regarded pedagogy as his responsibility.

---

[55] Wu Ch'eng, *Wu Wen-cheng chi*, 36:15b.

[56] *Wu Wen-cheng chi*, 41:2a.

[57] Liu Yüeh-shen, *Liu hsien-sheng wen-chi*, 5:26a.

[58] Ch'eng Chü-fu, *Ch'eng Hsüeh-lou wen-chi*, 13:16b.

[59] *Ch'eng Hsüeh-lou wen-chi*, 13:17a–17b.

[60] Huang Tsung-hsi 黃宗羲 and Ch'üan Tsu-wang 全祖望, SYHA 2:12a–14a; Huang Chin, *Chin-hua Huang hsien-sheng wen-chi*, 30:1a–6b.

[61] SYHAPI 80:44a.

[62] SYHA 89:2a. Ts'ao succeeded Wang as headmaster of Tzu-yang Academy; see Fang Hui, *T'ung-chiang chi*, 1:132; 3:289.

Both Tai Piao-yüan 戴表元 (1244–1310) and Yüan Chüeh 袁桷 (1266–1327) were his pupils.[63]

Wu Ssu-ch'i 吳思齊 (1238–1301): served as deputy magistrate of Chia-hsing 嘉興 in Southern Sung; led a private life in early Yüan, scholars vied to study with him.[64]

Ho Meng-kuei 何夢桂 (1240–1319, chin-shih, 1265): declined Ch'eng Chü-fu's recommendation, associated closely with Fang Feng-ch'en and his brother Fang Feng-chen 方逢振 at Shih-hsia Academy.[65]

Wei Hsin-chih 魏新之 (1242–1293, chin-shih, 1271): after the fall of the Sung, established Ch'ui-yün 垂雲 Academy (in T'ung-lu 桐廬, modern Chekiang) and taught there; declined Yüan official appointment.[66]

Sun T'ung-fa 孫潼發 (1244–1315, chin-shih, 1268): declined Ch'eng Chü-fu's recommendation, led a retired life and was a close associate of Wei Hsin-chih.[67]

Shih Meng-ch'ing 史蒙卿 (1247–1306, chin-shih, 1265): declined to serve officially after the fall of the Sung and taught students instead.[68]

Hsiung Ho 熊禾 (1253–1312, chin-shih, 1274): was acquainted with Hsieh Fang-te 謝枋得, founded two academies and taught a large number of students.[69]

Jen Shih-lin 任士林 (1253–1309): served as headmaster of two academies; was closely associated with the Sung loyalist T'ang Yü-ch'ien 唐玉潛.[70]

Wei Fu-i 衛富益: refused to seek office after the demise of Sung; taught at an academy where he set up rules forbidding those who served the Yüan to attend any lectures.[71]

Chao Chieh-ju 趙介如 (chin-shih, 1253): served as headmaster of an academy and had many students.[72]

Fang Feng-chen (chin-shih, 1262): declined Ch'eng Chü-fu's recommendation, became headmaster of Shih-hsia Academy after the death of his brother Fang Feng-ch'en.[73]

Chang Ch'ing-pi 張卿弼 (chin-shih, 1268): declined a recommendation

---

[63] Yüan Chüeh, Ch'ing-jung chü-shih chi 清容居士集 (SPTK ed.), 33:13a–13b; SYHA 55:17b; SYHAPI 55:62b.

[64] SYHA 56:16b–17a.

[65] Ho Meng-kuei, Ch'ien-chai wen-chi 潛齋文集 (SKCSCP ed.), 11:21b–22a.

[66] Sung Lien, Sung hsüeh-shih chi, 3:22b.

[67] Huang Chin, Chin-hua Huang hsien-sheng wen-chi, 30:11b–13b.

[68] Yüan Chüeh, Ch'ing-jung chü-shih chi, 28:27b.

[69] SYHA 64:9a–9b.

[70] Chao Meng-fu, Sung-hsüeh chai chi, 8:19b.

[71] SYHA 82:39b–40a.

[72] SYHA 70:9a; Chiang-hsi t'ung-chih 江西通志 (1881 ed.), 23:8a.

[73] SYHA 82:15a; Fang Feng-ch'en, Chiao-feng wen-chi 蛟峯文集 (SKCSCP ed.), 8:12b–13a.

to the court, founded Lan-shan 藍山 Academy (in I-yang 宜陽, in modern Honan) and served as its first headmaster.[74]

Ting I-tung 丁易東 (*chin-shih*, 1268): declined repeated summonses to offices in early Yüan, founded a private school and then accepted the appointment of headmaster of an academy.[75]

Tseng Tzu-liang 曾子良 (*chin-shih*, 1268): declined Ch'eng Chü-fu's recommendation, taught both the Classics and literature in retirement.[76]

Huang Chung-yüan 黃仲元 (*chin-shih*, 1271): After the Sung debacle, he even changed his name so as to avoid the character *yüan*, taught students in retirement until his death.[77]

Liu Ying-li 劉應李 (*chin-shih*, 1274): declined to serve after the fall of the Sung, taught with Hsiung Ho (see above) first, then founded an academy and attracted a large number of pupils.[78]

Poring over the above list, one cannot help but notice immediately the high percentage of *chin-shih* degree holders who declined government service in favor of private scholastic pursuit and teaching in early Yüan. This is all the more surprising because it is said that Khubilai personally esteemed the Sung *chin-shih* degree holders and wished to appoint large numbers of them to offices. Yet few were appointed.[79] Surely, for most of them, their original purpose of passing all the hurdles to earn the highest civil-service examination degree in the Southern Sung was to obtain the qualification for official positions. Unlike their contemporary, the reknowned Neo-Confucian scholar Chin Lü-hsiang 金履祥 (1232–1303), who had already spurned the possibility of an official career and who was committed to serious learning while young,[80] the very fact that they held the *chin-shih* degree is a good indication that they were oriented towards government service at first. Furthermore, in order to prepare for the examinations, what they had to study in the Southern Sung certainly differed both in content and in emphasis from what they studied and taught their pupils in these early years of the Yüan.[81] This shift merits some scrutiny.

Additionally, there is one other interesting phenomenon. According to

[74] Yü Chi, *Tao-yüan hsüeh-ku lu*, 8:6a.

[75] SYHAPI 37:12b; Lu Hsin-yüan 陸心源, *Sung-shih chi-shih pu-i* 宋詩紀事補遺 (Taipei: Chung-hua Shu-chü, 1971), 75:18a.

[76] *Chiang-hsi t'ung-chih*, 151:39b; Wu Ch'eng, *Wu Wen-cheng chi*, 20:4b.

[77] Huang Chung-yüan, *Huang Chung-yüan wen-kao*, *chüan-ch'üan* 卷全: *wen-hsien* 文獻 and *p'u* 譜; SYHA 70:10a.

[78] SYHA 70:9a; Li Ch'ing-fu 李清馥, *Min-chung li-hsüeh yüan-yüan k'ao* 閩中理學淵源考 (SKCSCP ed.), 37:21b.

[79] See Yü Chi, *Tao-yüan hsüeh-ku lu*, 18:15b.

[80] See Liu Kuan 柳貫, *Liu tai-chih wen-chi* 柳待制文集 (SPTK ed.), 20:1b–2b. For more on Chin Lü-hsiang, see the paper by J. Langlois in this volume.

[81] See, e.g., Chao Wen 趙文, *Ch'ing-shan chi* 青山集 (SKCSCP ed.), 3:31b.

the Yüan government regulations, the headmaster of an academy could be promoted to fill the post of instructor at the sub-prefecture and prefecture levels, which carried the official rank of 9b, thereby qualifying for further official appointments.[82] But many headmasters, after they had completed their terms of appointment, declined to serve in the posts of instructor to which they had been promoted. Such occurrences are too numerous to be regarded as isolated cases. Before we examine the motives behind their decisions, it will be helpful to cite some examples:

(1) Huang Tse 黃澤 (1260–1346): "At the age of twelve or thirteen, he had already mastered the learning in the classics and essays for the *chin-shih* [examination] of the time. When he came over to our dynasty [i.e., when the Mongols conquered the Sung], he was sixteen. Resolutely, he urged himself to comprehend the classics, to emulate the ancient ways, to purify his ambitions, and to carry them out with vigor ... He taught at Ching-hsing 景星 Academy in Chiu-chiang 九江 [in modern Kiangsi] and Tung-hu 東湖 Academy in Hung-chou 洪州 [modern Nan-ch'ang]. When the terms were completed, he immediately returned home and taught pupils in private to support himself."[83]

(2) Yeh T'ien-yü 葉天與: "served as the headmaster of Mei-hua 美化 Academy [in Chin-yün 縉雲 (Chekiang)] in the imperial dynasty. When the term was completed, he was qualified to serve as the Prefecture Instructor. But he did not take up the post."[84]

(3) Yüan I 袁易 (1262–1306): "His Excellency Hsü [Shih-lung] 徐世隆 of Tung-p'ing 東平 went on a mission [to the south] and heard about his name and was greatly pleased after a talk with him. When [Hsü] was about to recommend him to the court, he vigorously protested.... Subsequently the provincial authorities appointed him headmaster of Shih-tung 石洞 Academy [in Sung-chiang 松江]; he thereupon elatedly went to the post. After returning from that post, he always lived in retirement and never served officially."[85]

(4) Yüan P'ou 袁裒 (1260–1320): "As the headmaster of An-ting 安定 Academy [in Hu-chou 湖州 (i.e. Wu-hsing)], he was appointed the Hai-yen 海鹽 Prefecture School Instructor. But he did not accept the post."[86]

(5) Hu Ping-wen (1250–1333): "On recommendation, he became the headmaster of Tao-i 道一 Academy in Hsin-chou 信州 [in modern

[82] YTC 9:13a; YS 91:2316.
[83] Chao Fang 趙汸, *Tung-shan ts'un-kao* 東山存稿 (SKCSCP ed.), 7:5b–6a.
[84] Huang Chin, *Chin-hua Huang hsien-sheng wen-chi*, 36:6b.
[85] *Chin-hua Huang hsien-sheng wen-chi*, 33:3a.
[86] Yüan Chüeh, *Ch'ing-jung chü-shih chi*, 30:20a.

Kiangsi]. When he was transferred to the post of school instructor in Lan-ch'i 蘭溪 Prefecture [in Chekiang], he did not go." [87]

(6) Ch'en P'u 陳普 (1244–1315): "When the Sung fell, he decided to withdraw to his own world. The [Yüan] court sent envoys three times to appoint him Provincial School Instructor, but he did not accept the appointment. He opened up his place and gave instructions to pupils.... Liu Ch'un-fu 劉純甫 [88] of Chien-chou 建州 [in Fukien] invited him to head Yün-chuang 雲莊 Academy [in Chien-yang 建陽]." [89]

In all the abovementioned instances, the individuals concerned consented to serve as academy headmasters. But once they had served out their terms and were entitled to be promoted to the position of Prefecture School Instructor, which carried the official rank of 9b, they all turned it down. In the case of Huang Tse, we learn from his biography that he decided to forgo any official career immediately after the fall of the Sung. Thus, after his headmaster's term was over, even though he was living in reduced circumstances, he did not seek official appointment but taught pupils in private in order to supplement the meager pension which a sympathetic prefect was kind enough to grant him. In the case of Yüan I, he "elatedly" took up the headmaster appointment but never wished to serve in any official capacity after that appointment. In the case of Ch'en P'u, he repeatedly declined the court appointment to a Provincial School Instructorship, but willingly accepted the invitation of a friend to fill the vacancy of a headmaster. And in the case of Hu Ping-wen, although we have already seen the kind of deep commitment he had made to an academy, the fact remains that he declined any official appointment. All these point to a basic fact: namely, the headmastership did not carry any official rank and was appointed by the provincial authorities or the *hsüan-wei ssu* 宣慰司 in the south. But if a headmaster was to be promoted to become the instructor in a sub-prefecture school, the appointment had to come directly from the imperial court. [90]

The phenomenon of large numbers of *chin-shih* degree holders serving as headmasters in early Yüan may be looked at from two different angles. One is that since such persons have always commanded respect, their presence could add more prestige to those academies to which they

---

[87] SYHA 89:10a. According to YS 189:4322, he took the Lan-ch'i post, but this statement contradicts his own account found in his collected works, the *Yün-feng chi*, 1:3b.

[88] I.e., Liu Ching 劉涇; see SYHA 67:57a–57b.

[89] Li Ch'ing-fu, *Min-chung li-hsüeh yüan-yüan k'ao*, 40:2a; SYHA 64:6a.

[90] See YS 81:2032–2033. The importance of the fact that the headmastership was not a court appointment has been emphasized by the Ch'ing scholar Ch'üan Tsu-wang (1705–1755) in his *Chieh-ch'i t'ing chi* 鮚埼亭集 (SPTK ed.), 19:8a–8b; see also Chou Tsu-mo, "Sung wang hou shih Yüan chih ju-hsüeh chiao-shou," p. 198.

had been appointed, no matter whether such appointments were made
by the government or by private individuals. But far more importantly,
this phenomenon was probably due the fact that these persons, for one
reason or another, had given up their previous hopes of pursuing an
official career.

Furthermore, the fact that large numbers of *chin-shih* degree holders
declined to come out and serve in government and that many southern
scholars were quite willing to serve as headmasters but declined the
promotion to instructor appear to be related. We have already pointed
out that duties of instructors in public schools included some aspects that
tended to be unacademic and even undignified. And because appointments to such posts could lead to further official careers (at least in
theory), they often attracted persons of low scholastic calibre. Such
factors must have had some dampening effects on at least some serious
southern scholars. Yet, there are other factors that may have affected
their decisions not to serve. It would appear that they harbored deeply
felt loyalty for the fallen dynasty, together with a certain measure of
uncertainty about the new dynasty. To some extent, this kind of
sentiment can already be discerned in the brief descriptions of the
individuals given above, but we may be able to gauge it more accurately
by sampling the southern scholars' literary works.

In 1287, Ch'eng Chü-fu persuaded his friend, the famous Neo-
Confucian philosopher Wu Ch'eng, to accompany him on his trip to Ta-
tu. Although Wu consented, he left the capital after only a short stay.
Upon departure, he composed twenty-four quatrains which were addressed to Chao Meng-fu 趙孟頫 (1254–1322)[91] and other newly made
acquaintances at the Yüan court. In the following, we shall quote five of
these quatrains which have a direct bearing on the matter under
discussion:

Innundating waves ushered in the Three Dynasties,	洪流啓三聖
Burning flame emblazed the *Six Classics*,	烈焰顯六籍
Clay and wooden idols in this world,	世間土水偶
Can't escape the perils of water and fire.	不度水火厄
Chang Liang 張良 has devoted himself to the cause of the Han	子房爲韓心

[91] See biography in YS 172:4018–4033; Account of Conduct in Chao Meng-fu, *Sung-hsüeh chai chi*, "hsing-chuang," 1a-12a; see also Li Chu-chin 李鑄晉, "Chao Meng-fu ch'üeh-hua ch'iu-se t'u 趙孟頫鵲華秋色圖," *Ku-kung chi-k'an* 故宮季刊, 3:4 (1969), pp. 22–33 and 4:1 (1969), pp. 59–63.

Chu-ko Liang 諸葛亮 made the restoration
    of the Han [Dynasty] his career.
孔明興漢事

Although they lived long after the Three
    Dynasties,
三代以後人

Their greatness is forever manifested.
卓偉表萬世

Yang Hsiung stooped to serve Wang Mang
    王莽,
揚雄莽大夫

While T'ao Ch'ien lived in retirement loyal
    to Tsin.
陶潛晋處士

A man's life can't be judged,
男兒百歲中

Until after his death.
蓋棺事乃已

Crossing the Chi River, grackles built nests,
踰濟巢鴝鵒

Coming to Loyang, cuckoos cried.
入洛啼杜鵑

Great events are thus portented,
大事可知已

As fowls are first to perceive the terrestrial
    ether.
禽鳥得氣先

Whitecaps appear truculent against the
    wind,
風前白浪惡

The current is yellow and turbid after the
    rain.
雨後黃流渾

Sir, please don't go 'cross the river,
公無渡河去

As Heaven will not let this culture perish![92]
天未喪斯文

In the first poem quoted above, Wu Ch'eng states in the most
definitive terms that the civilization of China became crystalized only
after a natural disaster, and that it can withstand more disasters: the
burning of books ordered by the First Emperor of the Ch'in not only
had not destroyed Confucianism, but had brought it greater attention
and had deepened its profundity. The clay idols, on the other hand,
suggest that alien Buddhism, especially the Lamaism espoused by the
Yüan court, cannot endure the kind of calamities which Confucianism
endured.

In the second poem, Wu indicates that he would like to emulate Chang
Liang and Chu-ko Liang. In his case, it would be to avenge the cause of
the Sung and then to restore it.[93] By contrasting the lives of Yang
Hsiung and T'ao Ch'ien, he is in fact pointing out his preference and

[92] Wu Ch'eng, *Wu Wen-cheng chi*, 91:2a–4a.
[93] Even before the fall of the Sung, Wu already indicated that he wished to emulate Chu-
ko Liang; see Yü Chi, *Tao-yüan hsüeh-ku lu*, 44:5a.

advising his southern friends at the court that the decision as to whether to serve in government should be made in a historical perspective. In other words, they should not merely take the present situation into consideration, lest they be criticized by future generations.

While these poems are addressed to southerners, the fourth poem brings the question of north versus south into focus. Both the *Ch'un-ch'iu* 春秋 (*Spring and Autumn Annals*) and the *Chou-li* (*Rites* [or *Institutes*] *of Chou*) state that the northern grackle normally does not fly south of the Chi River but stays only in the Central Plain,[94] while, according to the philosopher Shao Yung 邵雍 (1011–1077), the southern cuckoo should not have reached Loyang (and this reflected Shao Yung's personal prejudice against the southerners and against Wang An-shih 王安石 in particular).[95] Obviously, by alluding to these passages Wu's intention was to remind his southern compatriots that similar sentiments existed in their own times and to caution them not to harbor the illusory expectation of a good relationship with the Mongols and the northerners.

With all these in mind, Wu concluded the last poem by drawing an analogy between the current affairs in Ta-tu and the truculence and turbidity of the river, brought about by a storm, which reminds the reader of the "innundating waves" contained in the first quoted poem. Does he imply that China was now undergoing another kind of "flood" which would eventually usher in another auspicious era? The phrase "white caps appear truculent" is also worth noting because white was the favorite color of the Mongols.[96] Alluding to a line in the famous Han ballad "K'ung-hou yin 箜篌引"[97] and a statement in the *Analects*,[98] he at once warns his friends about the danger of "going to the other side" and assures them that the Chinese cultural tradition shall continue despite the Mongol conquest. We can almost hear him say: "Since Heaven will not let this culture perish, what can the Mongols do to us?"

Viewed as a whole, these poems delineate with great clarity Wu

[94] *Ch'un-ch'iu ching chuan chi-chieh* 春秋經傳集解 (SPTK ed.), 25:6a; *Chou-li* 周禮 (SPTK ed.), 11:3a; Legge, *The Chinese Classics*, V, p. 707.

[95] For the discussion of the cuckoo's flying north and its "portent," see Shao Po-wen 邵伯溫, *Ho-nan Shao-shih wen-chien-lu* 河南邵氏聞見錄 (*Hsüeh-chin t'ao-yüan* 學津討原 ed.), 19:6b–7a.

[96] I am indebted to Professor Herbert Franke, who pointed this out at the Yüan Conference held in York, Maine. For a discussion of the Mongols' color preference, see T'ao Tsung-i 陶宗儀, *Cho-keng lu* 輟耕錄 (Taipei: Shih-chieh Shu-chü, 1963), 1:32.

[97] See Ts'ui Pao 崔豹, *Ku chin chu* 古今注 (SPPY ed.), 2:1b–2a; for a rather free English translation of this particular ballad, see Burton Watson, *Early Chinese Literature* (New York: Columbia University Press, 1962.), p. 291.

[98] See Legge, *The Chinese Classics*, V, pp. 217–218.

Ch'eng's personal feelings at this particular juncture about the pressing question of "to serve or not to serve" at the Mongol court. It was apparently his wish that by expressing his innermost thoughts to his friends in Ta-tu, he might thereby cause them to feel a greater empathy for his rejection of office. Additionally, he was pointing to a possible alternative for them to ponder and to choose. Of course, Wu Ch'eng later did come out of retirement and served at court, but these poems undoubtedly represented the lingering loyalty towards the Sung which was widely shared by the southern literati.

It is regrettable that we have no way of knowing how his friends—especially Chao Meng-fu—responded to these poems. In the collected works of Chao Meng-fu, however, we can detect some strikingly similar sentiments, although they are perhaps expressed more subtly. On the eve of Wu Ch'eng's departure, Chao lamented that since his own talents simply could not measure up to those of Wu Ch'eng, "now that Mr. Wu is going, what am I to do?"[99] (吳君且往則余當何如也) And after Wu returned to Kiangsi, Chao sent him a poem containing the couplet "crossing to the north, I commiserate with Chiang Tsung (519–594); Returning east, I remembered Kuan Ning 管寧 (158–241)."[100] (北度憐江摠 [i.e. 總], 東歸憶幼安) That he had sympathy for Chiang Tsung was because he and Chiang Tsung[101] shared a common destiny: both were highly cultivated and both were compelled to serve in a new dynasty. By making an analogy between Wu Ch'eng and Kuan Ning (Kuan was able to flee to Liao-tung and teach after the Yellow Turban Rebellion),[102] Chao in fact showed his envy of them both. Unlike them, Chao had to endure the most direct consequence of the demise of his own dynasty as a result of not being able to get away from the political arena.

Elsewhere, Chao manifested even stronger feelings in the lines "Of personages of the Central Plain, I remember Wang Meng (325–375); Regarding achievements made in the south, it mortifies me to think of Hsieh An (320–385)."[103] (中原人物思王猛, 江左功名愧謝安) The reason that he felt this way, of course, was that, on the one hand, Wang Meng advised Fu Chien 符堅 (r. 357–385) of the Former Ch'in 前秦 (351–394) not to attack the Tsin, and, on the other hand, Hsieh An was

---

[99] Chao Meng-fu, *Sung-hsüeh chai chi*, 6:10a.

[100] *Sung-hsüeh chai chi*, 4:3b.

[101] See his biography in the *Ch'en shu* 陳書 (Peking: Chung-hua Shu-chü, 1972). 7:343–347.

[102] See Kuan's biography in the *San-kuo chih, Wei chih* 三國志魏志, (Peking: Chung-hua Shu-chü, 1973, 5th printing), 11:354.

[103] Chao Meng-fu, *Sung-hsüeh chai chi*, 4:10a.

instrumental in repelling Fu Chien's famous but ill-fated attack against
the Tsin in A.D. 383.[104] The message here is that Chao regrets that he
was neither able to follow Wang Meng's suit to dissuade the Mongols
from attacking the Sung, nor to help to repulse their attacks against the
Sung, as Hsieh An did for the Tsin. Instead, he was now like a "caged
bird" (*lung chung niao* 籠中鳥),[105] an ornament at the Yüan Court with
a feeling of helplessness, when he wrote to his friend:

> My classmates and old friends are now few,
> I repeatedly lament that my deeds run counter to my will.
> While I fully realize that I am of no value to worldly affairs,
> Alas! the emperor still does not favor my resignation.

> 同學故人今已稀
> 重嗟出處寸心違
> 自知世事都無補
> 其奈君恩未許歸

> Oft dreaming about the cranes at my hide-away by the river,
> Jade belt and goldfish [bag] are not in my thoughts.
> I'm planning to beg for my leave next year,
> We then shall fish together again on the old moss-covered
>   jetty.[106]

> 滄洲白鳥時時夢
> 玉帶金魚念念非
> 準擬明年乞身去
> 一竿同理舊苔磯

Of course, his wish of voluntary retirement was never fulfilled. And,
although his thoughts are expressed in these lines with much restraint,
the elements of disaffection and despair can still be detected. Had he
been outside the court, he might have expressed these thoughts more
bluntly.

Unlike Chao Meng-fu, Shu Yüeh-hsiang (*chih-shih* 1256), the teacher
of Tai Piao-yüan and Yüan Chüeh mentioned above, remained outside
the Yüan government. Therefore, he could afford to be more straight-
forward. In the poem entitled "Two Confucians in Lu" (*Lu erh ju*
魯二儒), he really let his feelings flow forth:

---

[104] See *Chin shu* 晉書 (Peking: Chung-hua Shu-chü, 1974), 114:2929–2933, and
79:2072–2077, for accounts of Wang and Hsieh.
[105] Chao Meng-fu, *Sung-hsüeh chai chi*, 2:12b.
[106] *Sung-hsüeh chai chi*, 4:16b.

When Shu-sun [T'ung] served the Ch'in,   叔孫事秦
He used flattery to deceive the foolish [Second   以諛蔽愚
    Emperor].
Upon his submission to the Han,   至於歸漢
He recommended crafty fellows.   薦進狡夫
The damage he caused to our Confucian Way,   滅我王道
Is more excessive than that done by the Burning   甚於焚書
    of the Books.
For this reason, the two Confucians   是以二儒
Have their place in history secured.[107]   確乎其居

Without any doubt, we may characterize this poem as a typical example of "borrowing the past to criticize the present." Shu Yüeh-hsiang was not talking about the two Confucians of Lu at all but was commenting on contemporary Yüan circumstances. In addition to serving the second emperor of the Ch'in and Emperor Kao-tsu of the Han, Shu-sun T'ung[108] also served King Huai of Ch'u 楚懷王 and Hsiang Yü 項羽, shedding his allegiance like old clothes. When he was entrusted with the responsibility of designing court ceremonies for the Han, he asked some thirty Confucians from Lu to assist him. Of those, two refused to go with him, accusing him of not being in accord with the ancient tradition. Thus, Shu Yüeh-hsiang draws a parallel between Shu-sun T'ung's actions and those of his contemporaries: whoever recommended scholars to the Yüan court would be like Shu-sun T'ung and is to be condemned. (Could this be a reference to Ch'eng Chü-fu?) On the other hand, those who refuse to have anything to do with the new dynasty are to be commended, and will secure their places in history.

That Shu Yüeh-hsiang was speaking of his own times rather than those of the Han is most clear: although Shu-sun T'ung's frequent change of allegiance was looked down upon, to the best of my knowledge no one else has *ever* accused him of doing more harm to the Confucian tradition than did Ch'in Shih Huang-ti! On the contrary, the court ceremonies he designed for the Han were often regarded as having bolstered that tradition, for they actually caused Emperor Kao-tsu to have greater respect for the Confucians around him. In addition, the "two Confucians of Lu" have nowhere else been praised as highly as Shu does here. This unmistakably indicates that since Shu felt a strong

---

[107] Shu Yüeh-hsiang, *Lang-feng chi*, 1:1b–2a.
[108] His biography is contained in *Han shu* 漢書 (Peking: Chung-hua Shu-chü, 1975), 43:2124.

affinity towards them, he deliberately elevated their status in order to justify the action that he had taken and perhaps even to persuade some of his close friends to join this imaginary league of non-collaborators throughout history, as it were.

Like Shu Yüeh-hsiang, Jen Shih-lin did not secure a government position in the early Yüan. While Shu only gave private instructions to pupils, Jen did become a headmaster. If we think his discussion on *shu-yüan* quoted above is at best lukewarm towards the Yüan court, then the following lines from a poem may help us understand why:

> In this world, the lofty deeds of holly planting are few,
> In the mountains there are the many good poems you
>   composed daily.
> When there are white clouds and a bright moon, I recall Hsieh
>   An,
> Out in drizzling rain and side wind, I grow old like Chang
>   Chih-ho.[109]

世上冬青高誼少
山中日錄好詩多
白雲明月懷安石
細雨斜風老志和

It must be pointed out first that the poem in question was addressed to the Sung loyalist T'ang Yü-ch'ien, who supposedly planted hollies on top of the mounds after he had interred the scattered bones of the Southern Sung emperors.[110] Thus, the first two lines are in praise of both T'ang's loyalty and his literary skills. The remaining two lines reflect Jen Shih-lin's own deep emotions. Because there was no one who could resist the onslaught of the Mongols as Hsieh An did against the Former Ch'in (as we have seen, this very allusion is also used in the poem by Chao Meng-fu quoted above), all Jen could do now was to reflect upon that feat. And, in order not to betray his loyalty to the Sung, he was now leading the life of a recluse, like the T'ang poet Chang Chih-ho 張志和 (730–810), who enjoyed being with nature so much that he did not have to return home even "in drizzling rain and side wind."[111] Herein lie two extremely interesting points: (1) Jen considered his life as a headmaster a kind of

[109] Jen Shih-lin, *Sung-hsiang chi*, 9:1b.

[110] Many writings have dwelt on this subject. See, e.g., T'ao Tsung-i, *Cho-keng lu*, 4:63–69; Lin Ching-hsi 林景熙, *Chi-shan wen-chi* 霽山文集 (SKCSCP ed.), 3:25b–30a; Ch'eng Min-cheng 程敏政, *Sung i-min lu* 宋遺民錄 (*Chih-pu-tsu-chai ts'ung-shu* ed.), 6:1a–15b, 14:1a–2a and 15b–16b.

[111] For this famous poem by Chang, see Huang Sheng 黃昇, *T'ang Sung chu-hsien chüeh-miao tz'u-hsüan* 唐宋諸賢絕妙詞選 (SPTK ed.), 1:4a.

eremitism, similar to that of Chang Chih-ho, (2) unlike Chang Chih-ho, his own eremitism was not chosen freely but rather was brought about by the lack of capable people to defend the Sung against the Mongol invasion. Such feelings probably also occurred in the minds of many other early Yüan academy headmasters who may have approached their careers in the same way that Jen Shih-lin did.

Much attention has been centered on the recruitment of southern scholars authorized by Khubilai and carried out by Ch'eng Chü-fu,[112] although the extent of Ch'eng's success was limited. It has been pointed out that of the twenty-odd persons whom Ch'eng recruited,[113] most served as censors at different levels in the Yüan government.[114] Further, there is some evidence indicating that some simply did not wish to be considered for office in the first place and even refused to see him in person,[115] while others whose names he submitted to the court simply ignored his recommendations and subsequent appointments. Take Fang Feng-chen and Ho Meng-kuei, for example. On Ch'eng Chü-fu's recommendation, the court appointed them to the offices of Assistant Surveillance Commissioner of Huai-hsi Chiang-pei Circuit[116] and Superintendent of Confucian Schools of Kiangsi,[117] respectively, but neither actually took office. They hinted in their own writings, including some poems composed in response to Ch'eng Chü-fu, that they could not completely forget their loyalty to the vanquished Sung, and that, therefore, it would be best to find other "talents" to serve the new regime while they themselves remained as recluses.[118] In other words, they had imposed on themselves what F. W. Mote has called "compulsory eremitism."[119] Unlike the Sung loyalists Hsieh Fang-te (?–1289) and Cheng Ssu-hsiao 鄭思肖, however, whose cases Professor Mote has used

[112] See Yao Ts'ung-wu 姚從吾, "Ch'eng Chü-fu yü Hu-pi-lieh p'ing Sung i-hou ti an-ting nan-jen wen-t'i 程鉅夫與忽必烈平宋以後的安定南人問題," *Wen-shih-che hsüeh-pao* 文史哲學報, 17 (1968), pp. 357–379; Sun K'o-k'uan, "Chiang-nan fang hsien yü yen-yu ju-chih 江南訪賢與延祐儒治," in *Yüan-tai Han wen-hua chih huo-tung* 元代漢文化之活動 (Taipei: Chung-hua Shu-chü, 1969), pp. 345–355.

[113] For a partial list of their names, see Ch'eng Chü-fu, *Ch'eng Hsüeh-lou wen-chi*, Appendix, 3a.

[114] Sun K'o-k'uan, *Yüan-tai Han wen-hua chih huo-tung*, pp. 353–354.

[115] Yü Chi, *Tao-yüan hsüeh-ku lu*, 43:3a–3b; Huang Chin, *Chin-hua Huang hsien-sheng wen-chi*, 30:12b.

[116] SYHA 82:15a.

[117] Ho Meng-kuei, *Ch'ien-chai wen-chi*, 11:21b.

[118] See such writings in Fang Feng-ch'en, *Chiao-feng wen-chi*, 8:12b–13a; and Ho Meng-kuei, *Ch'ien-chai wen-chi*, 1:10a–10b.

[119] See Frederick W. Mote, "Confucian Eremitism in the Yüan Period," in Arthur F. Wright, ed., *The Confucian Persuasion* (Stanford: Stanford University Press, 1960), pp. 202–240, esp. pp. 229–236.

as illustrations in his well-developed article on Confucian eremitism in the Yüan, their eremitism was not tantamount to a total rejection of the Mongol regime for the simple reason that they both elected to serve in Shih-hsia Academy. Furthermore, unlike Huang Tse and others who refused offices *after* they served as headmasters, Fang Feng-chen declined a much higher official appointment *before* he settled for the headmaster's job. In either case, they had no qualms about serving in that capacity. Why?

Previously, we have pointed out the fact that the position of headmaster at an academy was neither ranked in the bureaucracy nor was it appointed by the court. Indeed, many such appointments were made through private arrangements. In the words of one of their contemporaries, "The headmaster is an emaciated scholar who guides the students. His stipend is tiny and his function little, his position is humble and his affairs few. Unlike the officials who govern the people, his place is seldom visited. There is nothing for him to appropriate, so he is uncorrupt. And there is nothing which is difficult for him to handle, so why shouldn't he be diligent in his studies?"[120] The implication here is that the duty of a headmaster truly transcends politics and worldly affairs. Such being the case, coupled with the fact that the position had nothing to do with the court, the reason why these southern scholars had little objection to this particular appointment now becomes clearer. By accepting such appointments, they may have achieved all or some of the following goals: (1) remaining loyal to the cause of the defunct Sung dynasty, or, at least, by keeping themselves out of the true official circle, avoiding the necessity to pledge their allegiance to the new dynasty, (2) not wasting their time on bureaucratic routines which may have been incompatible with their dispositions, (3) in their self-imposed isolation, being able to keep on studying and transmitting the Tao in a time of great uncertainty, and to project their hopes to future generations. And, precisely because of this, they repeatedly brought out the motto: "The world is lost, the Way is not!"[121]

Once they had made peace with themselves and with their surroundings, they began to accept the status quo with equanimity. Thus, we find that they often took outings to scenic spots and composed poetry to express their thoughts.[122] Of more interest is the fact that Ho Meng-kuei had renamed his dwelling the "Nest of Tranquility and Happiness" (An-lo

---

[120] Fang Hui, *T'ung-chiang chi*, 3:334.

[121] Ho Meng-kuei, *Ch'ien-chai wen-chi*, 1:7a, 11b.

[122] Sung Lien, *Sung hsüeh-shih chi*, 3:22b.

wo 安樂窩),[123] after the name of the Sung philosopher Shao Yung's habitat in Loyang. But while Shao Yung considered himself a recluse living in a time of great peace, Ho Meng-kuei probably used his retreat as a device signifying that he was cut off from current affairs. Yet, by the same token, it also betrayed his feeling that living under alien rule was far more than just bearable. In fact, he thought he could lead the life of a Yüan Ku 轅固 or a Shen Kung 申公[124] in the Yüan dynasty.[125]

From the above discussions, we can see that lingering Sung loyalism at least played some appreciable part in the building up of the *shu-yüan* institution in the early years of the Yüan, which in turn served as the fountainhead of Yüan Neo-Confucianism. And when we speak of the Yüan Neo-Confucian tradition, one aspect which always comes to mind is the martyrdoms of Cheng Yü 鄭玉 (1298–1358)[126] and Yü Ch'üeh 余闕 (1303–1358),[127] since both men had been deeply imbued with that tradition. Yet we normally do not stop and reflect on the contributions which the Sung loyalists have made to that tradition. Herein lies a great historical irony.[128]

[123] Ho Meng-kuei, *Ch'ien-chai wen-chi*, 3:25a–25b; Fang Feng-ch'en, *Chiao-feng wen-chi*, 6:6b.

[124] Both were accomplished scholars in Former Han times who lived to an old age without having been troubled by politics. See *Han shu* 88:3612 and 88:3608, biographies of Yüan Ku and Shen Kung, respectively.

[125] Ho Meng-kuei, *Ch'ien-chai wen-chi*, 1:12a.

[126] See YS 196:4432–4433.

[127] See YS 143:3426–3429.

[128] See the essay by J. Langlois in this volume, which touches on the topic of loyalism and the apparent irony alluded to here.

III. THOUGHT

Political Thought in Chin-hua
under Mongol Rule[1]

JOHN D. LANGLOIS, JR.

Wu-chou Circuit 婺州路 (modern Chin-hua Prefecture 金華府) in central Chekiang 浙江 was the center of Yüan China's perhaps most distinguished tradition of political thought. It provided much of the philosophical and intellectual continuity between the Sung and the Ming eras. Scholars from Chin-hua were noted for their support of *tao-hsüeh* 道學, the teaching of "the True Way" of the Sung master Chu Hsi 朱熹 (1130–1200). But, beyond their dedication to the transmission of Chu Hsi's teachings, the Chin-hua scholars faced the problems of government in an age when "sage kings" did not occupy the throne of the Son of Heaven and when the persuasive relevance of rhetorical models of sage emperors was extremely curtailed owing to the fact of rule by persons other than Han Chinese.

Chin-hua scholars responded to these problems by formulating the notion of the "authentic scholar" (*chen-ju* 眞儒). The "authentic scholar" was a scholar-official who was both a master of traditional Confucian learning and of the law. The "authentic scholar," in short, was both a scholar of ethics and a well-trained jurist and bureaucrat.

Yüan government, at levels below the Mongol rulers, was dominated by clerks (*li* 吏), whose expertise in government was defined in bureaucratic and legal rather than in ideological terms. They were not trained or tested in traditional Confucian learning and had very little stake in its preservation or continuity. By reformulating the role of the scholar as they did, the Chin-hua scholars fused together the moral teachings of Chu Hsi and the "utilitarian" teachings of the Eastern Chekiang school of Ch'en Liang 陳亮, Yeh Shih 葉適, and others.[2] They provided the

[1] I am grateful for valuable assistance in the preparation of this paper from the members of the research conference for which it was produced, the members of the Regional Seminar in Neo-Confucian Studies at Columbia University, where it was presented in October 1976, and from the following individuals: Professor F. W. Mote, Dr. Wm. S. Atwell, Professor Robert M. Somers, and Ms. M. Nylan. Errors and other shortcomings of this paper are my sole responsibility.

[2] "Utilitarian" is commonly used by Western scholars as a rough equivalent of the term *kung-li* 功利 (lit., "merit and profit"). For a discussion of this school, see Hsiao Kung-ch'üan 蕭公權, *Chung-kuo cheng-chih ssu-hsiang shih* 中國政治思想史 (Taipei: Chung-hua Wen-hua Ch'u-pan Shih-yeh She 中華文化出版事業社, 1954), pp. 449–481.

Confucian literatus with a rationale supporting government service in an age when government did not give the scholar top priority. And they provided the literatus with a methodology that enabled him to acquire and esteem the bureaucratic skills and knowledge that were crucial for service as agents of the Mongols.

Chin-hua (the modern name will be used interchangeably with the Yüan name Wu-chou in this paper) was not the only important intellectual area in Yüan China. Other key areas included Hui-chou 徽州 (modern Hsin-an 新安 in Anhwei province) and Lin-ch'uan 臨川 (in Kiangsi province). Hui-chou was a thriving economic center, and had been since Sung times.[3] It was the ancestral place of Chu Hsi, and as such it retained a measure of his influence. (More of that influence, however, was retained in Fukien, where Chu Hsi taught, and in Chin-hua as will be explained below.) Hui-chou literati were deeply involved in the study of classical texts, including in particular the *Spring and Autumn Annals* (*Ch'un-ch'iu* 春秋).[4] This ancient work was allegedly compiled by Confucius in order to convey his "righteous decisions."[5]

Lin-ch'uan had qualities which were strikingly different from those of either Chin-hua or Hui-chou, qualities which derived from the powerful presence in Lin-ch'uan of organized religious Taoism. Lin-ch'uan was one of the major national centers of this religious movement, as Professor Sun K'o-k'uan 孫克寬 shows elsewhere in this volume. Lin-ch'uan was characterized by syncretism (or, better, eclecticism), as Confucians and Taoists came into close contact with one another and had great mutual respect.

Chin-hua thought occupies an important place in Chinese cultural history, owing to contributions it made both to Yüan rule and to the Ming dynasty that succeeded the Yüan. Chin-hua literati played roles in the development of the Ming state in the 1360s. And two Chin-hua literati supervised the compilation of the official *Yüan shih* 元史 (*Yüan History*),[6] thus leaving an eternal imprint on our assessment of Yüan

---

[3] For a study of Hui-chou's economic growth in Sung times, see Shiba Yoshinobu 斯波義信, "Sōdai Kishu no chi-iki kaihatsu 宋代徽州の地域開発," in *Yamamoto hakushi kanreki kinen tōyōshi ronsō* 山本博士還暦記念東洋史論叢 (Tokyo: Yamagawa Shuppansha 山川出版社, 1972), pp. 215–229.

[4] See my biography of Chao Fang 趙汸 (1319–1369) in L. C. Goodrich and Chaoying Fang, ed., *Dictionary of Ming Biography* (New York: Columbia University Press, 1976), pp. 125–128.

[5] This is what Mencius tells us. See James Legge, tr., *The Chinese Classics* (Hong Kong: University of Hong Kong Press, 1960), vol. 1, p. 327; *Meng-tzu* 孟子 4B/21.

[6] I refer to Sung Lien 宋濂 (1310–1381) and Wang Wei 王禕 (1323–1374). For their biographies, see F. W. Mote's and A. R. Davis' entries in *Dictionary of Ming Biography*, pp. 1225–1231 and 1444–1447, respectively.

history. The extent to which Ming T'ai-tsu 明太祖 was indebted to China-hua literati has not been explored in modern scholarship. Certainly he was not indebted to Chin-hua literati alone. But many such literati contributed their prestige and learning to the regime of the Ming founder and thereby helped to transform the itinerant-monk-turned-warlord into an emperor.

Mongol rule in China went through various transformations. By the time Khubilai Khaghan conquered South China in the 1270s, Mongol rule had already been altered by the encounter with Chinese civilization. In its new form, Mongol rule was not simply an occupation by nomads bent on seizure of booty from the sedentary people of China. It had become a hybrid form of government, partly bureaucratic, partly colonial and military, partly bent on seizing booty, and partly bent on developing wealth and income in the ruled territories, and never compromising on the principle of Mongol superiority. The monarchy remained Mongolian, despite certain evidences of Chinese influence.[7] Contenders for the throne fought each other in bloody battles. Brothers fought and killed brothers, nephews fought and killed uncles. Succession practices were brutal. Assassinations were common. But underneath it all, governement went on. The literate helpers of the Mongols—the Uighurs and other *se-mu-jen* 色目人 (Central Asians) who served under the Mongols as administrative assistants and tax collectors, and the northern and southern Chinese (*Han-jen* 漢人 and *Nan-jen* 南人 in the terms used then)[8] who provided lower-level administrative expertise, handling documents, keeping financial records, and so forth—these people actually held power on a day-to-day basis. The Mongols themselves remained largely illiterate and were therefore dependent on the literate helpers who made it possible for something resembling a Chinese dynasty to exist. All of these points were made a generation ago by Meng Ssu-ming 蒙思明 in his classic study of the classes in Yüan society.[9] Meng pointed out that the Mongols had had to rely on Uighurs and other literate persons for assistance in managing the financial and other technical aspects in the regions controlled by Mongol armies. These

[7] See Joseph Fletcher, "Bloody Tanistry: Authority and Succession in the Ottoman, Indian Muslim, and Later Chinese Empires," paper presented at The Conference on the Theory of Democracy and Popular Participation, September 1978. (Cited with the author's permission.) See also my "Yü Chi and His Mongol Sovereign: The Scholar as Apologist," *Journal of Asian Studies*, 38:1 (November 1978), pp. 99–116.

[8] *Han-jen* and *Nan-jen* are usually interpreted as Chinese who were subjects of the Chin 金 prior to the Mongol conquest, and Chinese who were subjects of the Sung prior to the conquest. Hence they are often identified as northerners and southerners, respectively.

[9] *Yüan-tai she-hui chieh-chi chih-tu* 元代社會階級制度 (Peiping: Harvard-Yenching Institute, 1938 [special issue no. 16 of *Yen-ching hsüeh-pao* 燕京學報]).

skills, which the Mongols did not possess to any significant degree, were chiefly bureaucratic. The Mongols had no choice but to rely upon selected members of the conquered peoples in order to rule the subjugated populations. As Meng put it, "This was because the Mongols did not understand government matters, did not comprehend the written word, were not competent in the law (*hsing-ming* 刑名),[10] did not understand government documents, and therefore had no choice [but to employ Han-jen and Nan-jen]."[11]

As a result, many Han-jen and Nan-jen came to enjoy a great deal of *de facto* power. Entrance to positions of influence in government were three, according to the scholar Yao Sui 姚燧 (1283–1313), a native of Liu-ch'eng 柳城 (in modern Liao-ning 遼寧 province):

"Nowadays there are only three avenues to officialdom. One is the *su-wei* 宿衛 (imperial guards), another is as a scholar (*ju* 儒), and another is as a clerk (*li* 吏). One out of ten do so as a guardsman, half of one out of ten do so as a scholar, and nine and a half out of ten do so as a clerk."[12]

The Chin-hua scholars understood that for them to make a difference in society they had to work within the existing power structure. They saw that the power structure left open to the clerks many opportunities for corruption. Their Mongol rulers were not always fully apprised of the complexities of administration. They did not always concern themselves with the moral quality of their agents, so long as the agents were able to deliver sufficient amounts of monies and goods. The Chin-hua scholars were concerned about this, and they saw that the solution to the problems lay in reeducating the scholar class. By defining the role of the scholar as one that encompassed the duties of clerical functionaries, the Chin-hua scholars were able to reassert the values of Confucianism within the constraints imposed by Mongol rule.

Owing to pioneering studies of Chin-hua thought by Professor Sun K'o-k'uan,[13] it is now possible to attempt an assessment of Chin-hua thought within the context of Mongol rule. Until we have similar studies of Lin-ch'uan, Hui-chou, and other key intellectual areas of Yüan China, we will be handicapped in any effort to make intelligent comparisons between those areas and Chin-hua.

[10] *Hsing-ming* usually has this meaning in modern Chinese, although in antiquity its meaning was "performance and title," according to H. G. Creel, "The Meaning of *Hsing-ming*," reprinted in Creel, *What Is Taoism? and Other Studies in Chinese Cultural History* (Chicago: University of Chicago Press, 1970), pp. 79–91.

[11] *Yüan-tai she-hui chieh-chi chih-tu*, p. 78.

[12] Yao Sui, *Mu-an chi* 牧庵集 (SPTK ed.), 4:10a; quoted in Meng, *Yüan-tai she-hui chieh-chi chih-tu*, p. 51 note 290.

[13] See *Yüan-tai Chin-hua hsüeh shu* 元代金華學述 (Taichung: Tung-hai Ta-hsüeh 東海大學, 1975).

The seat of Wu-chou Circuit was located about 110 kilometers south of Hangchow 杭州, formerly the capital of the Sung after the retreat of the Sung court to the south in 1126. Situated along a major transportation route, Wu-chou, now known as Chin-hua, is today an important station on the railway line from Shanghai and Hangchow to points south. The name Wu-chou derives from the traditional association of the region with the Wu-nü 婺女 constellation, one of the twenty-eight *hsiu* 宿 or lunar lodges which were assigned "responsibilities" for segments of the Chinese world. Wu-chou Circuit was one of thirty circuits administered by the Chiang-che Regional Secretariat (Chiang-che teng-ch'u hsing chung-shu sheng 江浙等處行中書省), of which the capital was located at Hangchow. Overlapping supervision was provided by the Che-tung Hai-yu Regional Surveillance Office (Che-tung Hai-yu tao su-cheng lien-fang ssu 浙東海右道肅政廉訪司). Altogether some six *hsien* 縣 (districts) and one *chou* 州 (sub-prefecture) were administered by Wu-chou Circuit. These included Chin-hua 金華, Tung-yang 東陽, I-wu 義烏, Yung-k'ang 永康, Wu-i 武義, and P'u-chiang 浦江 districts, and Lan-ch'i 蘭溪 sub-prefecture.[14] According to one source, the population of the entire circuit in Yüan times was 221,118 households and 1,077,540 persons.[15] Another source cites figures for the year 1290, according to which there were 216,228 households and 1,088,569 persons.[16] During the early Yüan the walls around the district and sub-prefecture settlements were taken down on order from the Mongol rulers, but in later years of dynastic decline a number of these settlements rebuilt their walls for self-protection. The walls of Chin-hua district, for example, were rebuilt in 1352 at the command of Po-chia-na 伯嘉納, the vice-censor for the region[17] and the son of the famous A-sha Pu-hua 阿沙不華 (d. 1309), elder brother of the Khangli Toghto 康里脫脫 (d. 1327).[18]

A special quality was early recognized in Chin-hua literati history. The martyr Fang Hsiao-ju 方孝孺 (1357–1402), who stubbornly refused to do the bidding of the Ming Prince of Yen when the latter usurped the Ming throne, observed this in several statements that bear repeating. Fang noted that, "At the heights of the Sung and the Yüan, the All-under-Heaven (*t'ien-hsia* 天下) was a great community (*ta-t'ung* 大同). The exalted officers and great scholars were all dragons among hu-

---

[14] YS 62:1497 provides information on the administration of Wu-chou Circuit.

[15] YS 62:1497.

[16] *Chin-hua fu-chih* 金華府志 (1909 woodblock ed.), 5:5a.

[17] *Chin-hua fu-chih*, 2:3a.

[18] On these brothers, see John W. Dardess, *Conquerors and Confucians: Aspects of Political Change in Late Yüan China* (New York: Columbia University Press, 1973), pp. 16–17, 43–46. For the biography of A-sha Pu-hua (Bukha), see YS 136:3295–3300.

manity."[19] This statement was made by Fang in memory of the Chin-hua scholar Hu Han 胡翰 (1307–1381), and it indicates that for Fang Hsiao-ju, Mongol rule did not prevent Chinese civilization from establishing and maintaining a near-Utopian community. The fact that Hu Han is singled out for praise in this context suggests that Chin-hua played an important role in this achievement. Fang also noted in connection with another Chin-hua literatus that, "This Way (*ssu-tao* 斯道, alluding to Confucius' commitment to preserving the Way) moved to the southeast along with the Sung [Court]; as for letters and great scholars (*wen-hsien* 文獻), Wu 婺 [i.e., Chin-hua] was held in high esteem."[20]

Finally, referring to still another Chin-hua literatus, Fang noted: "After the Sung perished, the great line of orthodox legitimate rule (*ta-t'ung* 大統) was interrupted. Yet if one looked toward Chin-hua, [one could have seen there] a glow that was uninterrupted."[21] Fang Hsiao-ju was no impartial observor, for although he was a native of Ning-hai 寧海 on the Chekiang coast, he had long since become an "adopted" disciple of Chin-hua learning when as a boy he engaged in studies under Sung Lien 宋濂 (1310–1381), the leading late-Yüan literatus from Chin-hua.[22] But despite the partiality of Fang's views of Chin-hua's importance, they nevertheless present a good starting point for the discussion in this essay. In his view, the Sung and Yüan had both constituted "Great Communities," a notion which comes from the ancient *Book of Rites* and which describes an ideal community of peace and harmony.[23] Fang also notes that the Sung and the Yüan differed from one another in terms of the legitimacy or illegitimacy of the respective ruling houses. In Fang's eyes, the Mongols had severed the chain of legitimate rule that had linked the Sung with the preceding eras. The Mongol conquest, in

---

[19] Fang Hsiao-ju, *Hsün-chih chai chi* 遜志齋集 (SPTK ed.), 20:8b.

[20] Fang, *Hsün-chih chai chi*, 20:9b. This statement was made in memory of Tai Liang 戴良 (1317–1383), a native of P'u-chiang who was a Yüan loyalist. See my biography of Tai Liang in *Dictionary of Ming Biography*, pp. 1234–1237. For Confucius' concern for "this Way," see *Lun-yü* 論語 VI/17. Arthur Waley, tr., *The Analects of Confucius* (New York: Knopf, 1938), p. 119. The expression *wen-hsien* comes from *Lun-yü*, 3/9; Waley, tr., *Analects*, p. 96.

[21] Fang, *Hsün-chih chai chi*, 20:12a. This statement was made in memory of Cheng T'ao 鄭濤 (1315–ca.1384), a native of P'u-chiang and the leader of the Cheng clan. For more on the clan see below.

[22] See F. W. Mote's biography of Fang Hsiao-ju in *Dictionary of Ming Biography*, pp. 426–433. His biography of Sung Lien has been cited above (n. 6).

[23] See the *Li yün* 禮運 chapter of the *Li chi* 禮記. For a translation, see James Legge, *The Li Ki* (Sacred Books of the East, Oxford: Oxford University Press, 1885), vol. 1, pp. 364–393.

other words, marked a fundamental political rupture of the tradition.[24]

Yet the illegitimacy of the non-Han rulers of the Yüan had had little to do with the uninterrupted flow of culture throughout the era. Alien rule did not cause a rupture on the cultural level. Furthermore, it was Chin-hua which, more than any other area, continuously generated a "glow" of cultural achievements. By juxtaposing the Mongol interruption of the line of legitimate political succession, and the unbroken line of cultural achievements in Chin-hua, Fang celebrates the learning of his adopted locale. It is viewed as having performed a sacred act of cultural preservation, enabling the Ming to enjoy cultural roots in the past that it might have been denied otherwise. It is ironic indeed that it was the Chinese emperor Yung-lo who, by executing Fang Hsiao-ju, closed the chapter of Chin-hua history. No Mongol ruler did this.

Chin-hua had been settled since post-Han times, but its economic development accelerated during the Sung. Recent research has shown that in Chin-hua the employment of mountainous land-reclamation techniques was relatively more active than elsewhere in South China. In fact, in terms of investment in water conservation techniques for the improvement of agricultural productivity in hilly and mountainous locales, Chin-hua was very advanced when compared against other locales at the same time. These techniques entailed primarily the construction of irriguous reservoirs on the slopes for storage of water and control of erosion.[25]

But all this did not add up to great concentrations of wealth. By comparison with wealthy areas in Chiang-nan 江南, Chin-hua in Southern Sung times was relatively insignificant economically. This was observed by the classicist Wang Po 王柏 (1197–1274), one of the "Four Masters of Chin-hua," who wrote, "Indeed, the so-called rich families and great houses of Chin-hua are really not even the match of the lowest families among the impoverished houses in Chiang-hsi 江西 and Che-hsi 浙西."[26] Wang Po undoubtedly exaggerated the poverty of Chin-hua in order to emphasize the purity of Chin-hua people. But the comparison nonetheless indicates that relatively speaking Chin-hua was not a prosperous economic center.

---

[24] For Fang's ideas of legitimacy, see Hsiao Kung-ch'üan, *Chung-kuo cheng-chih ssu-hsiang shih*, pp. 526–530; and John Fincher, "China as a Race, Culture and Nation: Notes on Fang Hsiao-ju's Discussion of Dynastic Legitimacy," in David C. Buxbaum and F. W. Mote, ed., *Transition and Permanence: Chinese History and Culture* (Hong Kong: Cathay Press, 1972), pp. 59–69.

[25] Honda Osamu 本田治, "Sōdai Bu-shu no suiri kaihatsu 宋代婺州の水利開発," *Shakai keizai shigaku* 社会経済史学, 41:3 (1975), pp. 211–234.

[26] Cited in Honda, p. 226.

Chin-hua surrendered in 1276 to the chiliarch Kao Hsing 高興, a northern Chinese who had joined Bayan's camp when the latter was leading the Mongol invasion of the Sung. Bayan charged Kao with mopping up areas of the south that still had not surrendered when the Sung capital at Hangchow was taken. Shortly after Chin-hua surrendered to Kao, a certain Chang Yü 章焴 revolted and set himself up as the governor of Wu-chou. Kao attacked with 5,000 troops. The series of seven engagements that ensued finally ended after forty days with the beheading of 5,000 "rebels" and the execution of Chang Yü. Kao Hsing proved extremely useful to the Mongols in Chin-hua and elsewhere in Chekiang and Fukien. He was therefore rewarded by the court in 1277 and appointed to the post of Chao-t'ao-shih 招討使 (pacification commissioner) for Wu-chou and Ch'u-chou 處州.[27]

CHIN-HUA STATECRAFT IN THE SOUTHERN SUNG

Two important Sung scholars hailed from Chin-hua. These were Lü Tsu-ch'ien 呂祖謙 (1137–1181), from Chin-hua district, and Ch'en Liang 陳亮 (1143–1194), from Yung-k'ang. Lü, of course, is well known today as the co-compiler (with Chu Hsi) of the *Chin-ssu lu* 近思錄 (*Reflections on Things at Hand*),[28] an anthology of Neo-Confucian writings that encapsulated the philosophy of the Northern Sung Neo-Confucians and that became a standard reference and teaching device of the "orthodox" tradition in the later imperial era. Lü was pragmatic in orientation, and had a deep interest in history and the development of the institutions of society. As Wing-tsit Chan has shown, Lü's contributions to the *Chin-ssu lu* included the incorporation of the passage on law, quoting Wang An-shih 王安石.[29] Lü's thought falls within the parameters of the Chekiang school in Southern Sung intellectual history. This school, as indicated above, is usually labelled the *kung-li* 功利 or "merit and profit" school, an expression which some translators render "utilitarian." Their thinking stressed the betterment of the material conditions of social life through coordinated institutional regeneration and reform.[30] Lü's affinity for these statecraft concerns was observed by Chu Hsi, who wrote:

"The learning of Po-kung [Lü Tsu-ch'ien] unifies the learning of Ch'en

[27] YS 162:3803–3804.

[28] Wing-tsit Chan, tr., *Reflections on Things at Hand* (New York: Columbia University Press, 1967).

[29] *Reflections on Things at Hand*, pp. 325–326. See section IX/20.

[30] Hsiao Kung-ch'üan points out that their main ideological tenet was the "enrichment of the state and the strengthening of its military" (*fu-kuo ch'iang-ping* 富國強兵). See *Chung-kuo cheng-chih ssu-hsiang shih*, vol. 4, p. 461.

Chün-chü [Ch'en Fu-liang 陳傅良 (1137–1203)] and Ch'en T'ung-fu [Ch'en Liang]. The Yung-chia 永嘉 [school of] learning [of Ch'en Fu-liang] understood regulations and measures (*chih-tu* 制度 ["institutions"]), and was inclined towards the investigation of trivial matters. Chün-chü was the only one to pursue [learning] with some achievement. As for Cheng-tse [Yeh Shih 葉適 (1150–1223)], he was disorganized and incoherent. T'ung-fu discoursed on antiquity and modernity, and on true kings (*wang* 王) and military dictators (*pa* 霸). Po-kung combined the respective strengths of both men."[31]

Chu had but modest respect for his colleague's attachment to the Chekiang school. That school he criticized because in his eyes it failed to place the priority in the moral sphere and instead concerned itself with studies of history, the *Spring and Autumn Annals* and the *Tso Commentary*, the nature of imperial rule, military defense and economic livelihood. A "debate" transpired between Chu Hsi and the Chekiang thinkers over the issue of priorities.[32] Ch'en Liang stressed the importance of pragmatic recognition of the institutional and military bases of social order, while Chu Hsi maintained that any set of ideas which did not place a premium on moral cultivation as the only true and lasting basis of social order was inherently defective. Ch'en Liang ultimately became known as one of the greatest "heretics" in Chinese thought,[33] for, compared to Lü Tsu-ch'ien, he was far stronger as a spokesman of this point of view. Ch'en's arguments, based thoroughly on Confucian texts, for strong national defense, rational state planning for economic well-being, and a powerful emperor based on the model of T'ang T'ai-tsung rather than on the mythical models of the ancient sage-kings, were in many ways antithetical to those of Chu Hsi.

Chu Hsi's thought ultimately became the official doctrine of the Chinese state. As Wm. Theodore de Bary has recently shown,[34] this event took place in Yüan times, in part because Chu Hsi's preference for stressing moral cultivation was accepted by most Chinese scholars and teachers in the private academies. But the importance of Chu Hsi's school in post-Yüan times has caused scholars to overlook the legacy of the Southern Sung statecraft school that had been centered in Chin-hua.

[31] *Sung Yüan hsüeh-an* 宋元學案 (*Ssu-pu pei-yao* 四部備要 ed.), 51:15b–16a.

[32] See Hoyt Cleveland Tillman, "Divergent Philosophic Orientations Toward Values: The Debate Between Chu Hsi (1130–1200) and Ch'en Liang (1143–1194)," *Journal of Chinese Philosophy*, 5 (1978), pp. 363–389.

[33] Hellmut Wilhelm, "The Heresies of Ch'en Liang," *Asiatische Studien*, 11 (1957–58), pp. 102–112. For a discussion of Ch'en Liang's thought, see Wu Ch'un-shan 吴春山, *Ch'en T'ung-fu ti ssu-hsiang* 陳同甫的思想 (Taipei: Taiwan University, 1971).

[34] "The Rise of Neo-Confucian Orthodoxy in Yüan China," paper presented at University Seminar in Neo-Confucian Studies, Columbia University, November 1979.

Another scholar from Chin-hua who was associated with strong utilitarian demands for military and economic preparedness was T'ang Chung-yu 唐仲友 (*chin-shih* 進士 1151). T'ang was a strong-willed individualist who was unable to get along with his rivals Chu Hsi and Ch'en Liang. Yet he nevertheless exerted a powerful influence on later Chin-hua thinkers. Appraising T'ang and the other Chin-hua scholars, the great Ch'ing historian Ch'üan Tsu-wang 全祖望 (1705–1755), him-self a proponent of a latter-day Eastern Chekiang school, wrote:

"During the Ch'ien-tao 乾道 and Ch'un-hsi 淳熙 reigns [1165–1189] the learning of Wu [Chin-hua] was at its height. The brothers of Tung-lai 東萊 [i.e., Lü Tsu-ch'ien and Lü Tsu-chien 呂祖儉 (d. 1196)] became known for their philosophy of human nature and destiny, T'ung-fu [Ch'en Liang] for practical achievements (*shih-kung* 事功), and Yüeh-chai [T'ang Chung-yu] for his learning of regulations and institutions (*ching-chih* 經制)." [35]

Ch'üan goes on to note that the Yung-chia school, referring mainly to Yeh Shih, was the strongest in "the learning of regulations and insti-tutions." This school, which was a part of the larger Eastern Chekiang school, stressed the study of historical and canonical texts that focused on government institutions, including expecially those that pertained to monarchical institutions and national defense. Lü Tsu-ch'ien, Ch'üan suggests, was the broadest of all the Chin-hua thinkers because his writings touched on the philosophical as well as the purely utilitarian. But while the individual emphases of the various thinkers varied, at least one crucial notion drew them together: the belief in the importance of maintaining a strong state, particularly against outsiders like the Jurchens, who had established control over all of North China after the flight of the Sung court in 1126.

T'ang Chung-yu's major works were the 150-*chüan Liu ching chieh* 六經解 (*Explanations of the Six Classics*), *Chu-shih ching-i* 諸史精義 (*Pearls from the Histories*) in 100 *chüan*, *Lu Hsüan-kung tsou-i chieh* 陸宣公奏議解 (*Explanations of the Memorials of Lu Chih* 陸贄 [754–805]), and *Ti-wang ching-shih t'u-p'u* 帝王經世圖譜 (*Charts and Programs for Emperors Governing the World*) in sixteen *chüan*. All of these scholarly writings were well within the developing tradition of statecraft (*ching-shih* 經世), of which Eastern Chekiang was the center. T'ang's major point was that institutions had to function by adaptation to immediate and changing circumstances, for only then could they be successfully financed through taxation and be well supported by the people. T'ang Chung-yu, like his Eastern Chekiang confreres, sought to

---

[35] *Sung Yüan hsüeh-an*, 60:2b.

make "emperorship" (*ti-wang* 帝王) a subject of rational and non-magical study, divorced from the idealized notions of emperors that had characterized much of Confucian thought.

Ni P'u of P'u-chiang District

Lü, Ch'en, and T'ang were justly famous in their day and later, although T'ang's biography was excluded from the *Sung shih* 宋史 (*Sung History*) because of an alleged moral deficiency.[36] Still, Chin-hua statecraft formulae were not, of course, the exclusive preserve of these men. One of the most interesting of their local contemporaries was the eccentric P'u-chiang scholar Ni P'u 倪樸.[37] During the Shao-hsing 紹興 reign (1131–1162), when the Sung was troubled by military incursions launched by the Jurchens, Ni P'u took it upon himself to devise schemes for dealing with them. For generations Ni's family had been farmers and had not produced an official (although they claimed one among their ancestors in T'ang times). Ni P'u became outraged by the presumed ineffectiveness of the Sung court in handling the Jurchens. An educated man whose grandfather had been on excellent terms with the P'u-chiang magistrate and had helped to lead local militia to quell bandits there, Ni P'u in 1157, with no official standing at all, sent a communication to Emperor Kao-tsung. In that year Ni had heard that the court was planning to send troops "to sweep clean the Ho-Lo 河洛 [i.e., the Loyang region of Honan]." Ni was delighted at the prospect of a Sung revival, and in his

[36] Ch'üan Tsu-wang discusses this problem in a preface to a collection of T'ang's writings. See *Chieh-ch'i t'ing chi, wai-pien* 鮚埼亭集外編 (SPTK ed.), 24:2a–3b. Sung Lien wrote a biography of T'ang in an attempt to rehabilitate the man's reputation. See Chang Tso-nan 章作楠, "Pa Sung Ch'ien-hsi 'T'ang Chung-yu pu-chuan'" 跋宋潛溪「唐仲友補傳」," cited in Ho Ping-sung 何炳松, *Che-tung hsüeh-p'ai su-yüan* 浙東學派溯源 (Shanghai, 1933), pp. 201–202. The Ch'ing scholar Chang Hsüeh-ch'eng 章學誠 (1738–1801) criticized Sung Lien for failing to have the *Yüan shih* include a biography of T'ang to make up for the *Sung shih's* lack. See his "Chih fei jih cha 知非日札" in *Chang-shih i-shu wai-pien* 章氏貴書外編, 4:2b. For an inscription to Sung Lien's biography of T'ang (which is not extant), see Chu Yu 朱友 (1314–1376), "T'i [Yüeh-chai] hsien-sheng pu-chuan 題[説齋]先生補傳," in *Sung Yüan hsüeh-an pu-i* 宋元學案補遺, 60:32b–33a. For a preface by Su Po-heng 蘇伯衡 (b. 1329) to a collection of T'ang Chung-yu's writings, see Su's collected works, *Su P'ing-chung wen-chi* 蘇平仲文集 (SPTK ed.), 5:1a–2b.

[37] Wu Lai 吳萊, in *Yüan-ying chi* 淵潁集 (SPTK reprint of 1352 edition), 10:13a–15b, discusses the miscellaneous writings of Ni P'u. See also Sung Lien, *P'u-yang jen-wu chi* 浦陽人物記, included in *Sung Wen-hsien kung ch'üan-chi* 宋文憲公全集 (Ssu-pu pei-yao ed.), 53:13a–13b; Wu Shih-tao 吳師道, *Ching-hsiang lu* 敬鄉錄, chüan 6; Kao Po-ho 高伯和, *P'u-yang i-wen k'ao* 浦陽藝文考 (Taipei: Li-chih Shu-chü 立志書局, 1968), pp. 69–70; *Sung Yüan hsüeh-an*, 56:10a–11a; *Sung Yüan hsüeh-an pu-i*, 56:18b–19a.

letter to Kao-tsung, which was thousands of characters in length, he set forth his analysis of the military situation.[38] He proposed maneuvers to counter the mobile strength of the Jurchens, and he argued that the Chin 金 state could be extinguished. In his view, history demanded that it be wiped out.

Ni P'u's arguments were based on studies of geography and population distribution. His treatise on historical geography entitled *Yü-t'u hui-yüan chih* 輿圖會元志 (*The Restoration of the Realm*) was never printed and consequently by Yüan times was lost. But the maps evidently were extant, for the scholar Wu Lai 吳萊, who is discussed below, saw them and commented on them. Early Yüan observers noted that the work was an exhaustive historical and strategic, political and physical geography of the realm. A series of maps indicated the relative positions of Chinese and non-Chinese over the centuries. Ni is said to have posted the maps on the walls of his dwelling, where he operated an unofficial war command headquarters. He ordered battles and defenses at key points and cities in his imaginary campaigns against the Jurchens.

Ni P'u was known and appreciated by Ch'en Liang, and may even have been the inspiration for the latter's own outspoken statements to the court demanding a more aggressive policy towards the Jurchens. In 1169, when Ch'en Liang was twenty-six, Ch'en sent a letter to Emperor Hsiao-tsung urging vigorous attempts by the state to restore the empire's lost territories in the north. Aside from this obvious similarity between Ni and Ch'en, both men experienced difficulties with the local officials of Chin-hua. Ch'en was jailed three times in his life, and Ni P'u was sentenced to penal servitude in Yün-yang 筠陽 (in modern Kiangsi) during the Ch'un-hsi reign (1174–1189) because he had angered the P'u-chiang magistrate.

In their individual ways, both Ni and Ch'en were courageous and innovative men dedicated to the restoration of China's dignity. But neither man actually went forth and engaged in direct confrontation with the Jurchens. P'u-chiang had one hero who did just that, the martyr Mei Chih-li 梅執禮 (1079–1127). Mei was a characteristic activist Confucian whose career spanned martial and civil duties. He received the *chin-shih* in 1106 under Emperor Hui-tsung, and advanced through a series of civil offices until he was appointed *wu-hsüeh po-shih* 武學博士 (Erudite for Martial Studies), a position he is said to have accepted with zeal and alacrity despite suggestions that he, a scholar of letters, should avoid such a position. During his career he twice was asked by the throne to compile the emperor's edicts (*ch'ih-ling* 敕令), the formal legislation of

---

[38] Ni's letter to the emperor is partially reproduced in *Kuang-hsü P'u-chiang hsien-chih kao* 光緒浦江縣志稿 (1916 woodblock), 9 (*wen-yüan* 文苑 section), 6b–17a.

the realm which in Sung times was regularly revised in accordance with changing circumstances. Under Emperor Ch'in-tsung 欽宗 (r. 1125–27), Mei urged the throne personally to lead an expedition to chastise the Jurchens. He advised the empress, the royal mother, and the heir apparent to leave the palace for a safe haven. The advice was not taken. The emperor eventually surrendered to the Jurchens, who had laid siege to the capital for a second time. The surrender took place in 1126. The Sung were ordered to ransom their emperor back from his captives, but the enormous fortune they offered was deemed insufficient. (After a hasty search they came up with 308,000 ounces of gold, six million ounces of silver, and other precious things. Pressed further, they produced another 70,000 ounces of gold and 1.1 million ounces of silver, plus a large quantity of other precious things, such as bolts of silk cloth.) So Mei Chih-li, who had accompanied the emperor into captivity and who had attempted to negotiate the ransom, was beheaded. The execution was sudden and brutal and was carried out with a concern for the psychological impact it would have on other Sung Chinese. His head was mounted on a pole for all to see.[39]

Mei's example of heroism and active service by itself was not unique. He was not the only scholar to die in an attempt to devise a way to allow the Sung to prevail over the Jurchens. Others were executed with him on the same occasion. But the memory of him, and of Ch'en, Ni, and Lü, formed part of the tradition of Chin-hua. It is this tradition we must keep in mind as we examine the Chin-hua response to Mongol rule.

TAO-HSÜEH AND THE "FOUR MASTERS"

During the waning years of the Southern Sung, the school of thought known as *tao-hsüeh* ("the learning of the [true] Way") gradually assumed the position of the predominant orthodox wisdom.[40] So powerful did the movement become that it provided a large part of the curriculum for the growing private academies in which most of Yüan China's higher education took place. In Chin-hua, the tradition of *tao-hsüeh* took deep

[39] On Mei Chih-li, see Sung Lien, *P'u-yang jen-wu chi*, in *Sung Wen-hsien kung ch'üan-chi*, 53:1b–3a; *Sung Yüan hsüeh-an pu-i*, 35:38b–39b; Kao Po-ho, *P'u-yang i-wen k'ao*. pp. 67–68. On the execution and surrounding events, see Liu Po-chi 劉伯驥, *Sung-tai cheng-chiao shih* 宋代政教史 (Taipei: Chung-hua Shu-chü 中華書局, 1971), vol. 1, pp. 273–277; see also Mei Chih-li's biography in *Sung shih* 宋史 (Peking: Chung-hua Shu-chü, 1977), 357:11232–11234.

[40] On the rise to prominence of *tao-hsüeh*, see James T. C. Liu, "How Did a Neo-Confucian School Become the State Orthodoxy?" *Philosophy East and West*, 23:4 (October 1973), pp. 483–505; Conrad Schirokauer, "Neo-Confucians under Attack: The Condemnation of Wei-hsüeh," in John W. Haeger, ed., *Crisis and Prosperity in Sung China* (Tucson: University of Arizona Press, 1975), pp. 163–198.

root.[41] Yet, despite this fact, it did not displace the indigenous "utilitarian" orientation of Chin-hua statecraft. In Chin-hua, the *tao-hsüeh* school of Chu Hsi merged with the local tradition, producing a mix of Chu Hsi idealism and the pragmatic attention to methodologies for achieving social and political order in an age when the kings were not sages or even Chinese.

The agent by which Chu Hsi's teachings were transmitted to Chin-hua was Ho Chi 何基 (1188–1268), a native of Chin-hua district. When he was a young man he was taken by his father to Lin-ch'uan in Kiangsi, where the father had been appointed as a district officer. It happened that Chu Hsi's disciple and son-in-law Huang Kan 黃榦 (1152–1221) was teaching there. Huang was not merely a bookish scholar, for he had served nobly on behalf of the Sung when the Jurchens invaded the city of An-ch'ing on the north shore of the Yangtze River. Just before Chu Hsi died in 1200, Chu had presented his formal robe to Huang Kan and had asked the latter to carry on his work and teaching. Huang accepted the task and the honor and remained faithful to the obligation he incurred.[42] Ho Chi became Huang Kan's student and thus, when he returned to Chin-hua, he formed the link that joined Chu Hsi's teachings with the tradition of Chin-hua.

Ho Chi taught that the student should concentrate on the *Four Books* (*Analects, Mencius, The Great Learning*, and *The Doctrine of the Mean*), and that Chu Hsi's *Ssu-shu chi-chu* 四書集註 (*Collected Commentaries on the Four Books*) should be the primary text for the student. Chu Hsi's *Yü-lu* 語錄 (*Recorded Sayings*) should also be studied carefully, Ho taught, but, because the *Yü-lu* was merely based on notes taken by many different hands, it was sometimes unreliable and was generally not tightly written.[43] Huang Tsung-hsi 黃宗羲, the seventeenth-century historian of Sung and Yüan thought, noted that Ho Chi's main philosophical and pedagogical position was simply that Chu Hsi's *Ssu-shu chi-chu* occupied central importance.[44]

Ho Chi was the first of the "Four Masters of Chin-hua" (*Chin-hua ssu-tzu* 金華四子).[45] Ho Chi and his successors all sought to be the true and faithful adherents of the True Way taught by the master. After Ho, the succeeding three "masters" were Wang Po 王柏, Chin Lü-hsiang 金履祥 (1232–1302), and Hsü Ch'ien 許謙 (1270–1337). In that order, the

[41] For a summary of early *tao-hsüeh* in Chin-hua, see Sun K'o-k'uan, *Yüan-tai Chin-hua hsüeh shu*, pp. 15–49.

[42] *Sung Yüan hsüeh-an*, 63:1a–2a..

[43] *Sung Yüan hsüeh-an*, 63:1a–2a.

[44] *Sung Yüan hsüeh-an*, 63:1a–2a.

[45] The Four Masters are the central figures of *chüan* 82 in *Sung Yüan hsüeh-an*.

teachings were passed from scholar to scholar and from scholar to hundreds of students.

The writings of the Four Masters were attempts to systematize Chu Hsi's teachings so that they could be taught easily to large numbers of students. Ho Chi's major efforts all bore the label *fa-hui* 發揮, "elaborations." One example is his *Ta-hsüeh fa-hui* 大學發揮 (*Elaborations of the Meaning of the Great Learning*). Wang Po, first Ho's student and later his colleague, shared this desire to remain faithful to the texts and to Chu Hsi's interpretations, and he was like the following two masters in this regard.

But Wang Po's breadth of scholarly concerns far outstripped Ho's. In this respect Wang reveals the influence of his father, who had been a disciple of Lü Tsu-ch'ien. Wang Po himself is said to have been an admirer of the great military and political hero of the Three Kingdoms era, Chu-ko Liang 諸葛亮 (181–234). Thus, while one can discern in Wang Po's intellectual concerns the enormous import of Chu Hsi's True Way teachings, there is also a broad horizon which included pragmatic statecraft and the active heroism that was classically exemplified by Chu-ko Liang.[46]

THE MONGOLS

Wang Po did not live to hear about the capture of Hangchow in 1276 or about the death of the loyalist Lu Hsiu-fu 陸秀夫 and the heir to the throne in 1279. But he certainly was aware of the growing Mongol threat and the increasing likelihood of a Sung collapse. The reign of Emperor Tu-tsung (1265–1274) saw the failure of the Sung defense of Hsiang-yang 襄陽 after a five-year siege, and it was during his reign as well that Khubilai issued his proclamation of the final expedition against the Sung. Thus while Wang Po never experienced Mongol rule, he certainly felt the looming specter of Sung defeat.

The statecraft orientation which underlay much of Wang Po's thought was carried on by his student Chin Lü-hsiang.[47] Chin's biography in the

---

[46] On Wang Po, see Ch'eng Yüan-min 程元敏, *Wang Po chih sheng-p'ing yü hsüeh-shu* 王柏之生平與學術 (Taipei: Hsüeh-hai Ch'u-pan-she 學海出版社, 1975); and the same author's *Wang Po chih shih-ching hsüeh* 王柏之詩經學 (Taipei: Chia-hsin Shui-ni Kung-ssu Wen-hua Chi-chin-hui 嘉新水泥公司文化基金會, 1968); *Sung Yüan hsüeh-an*, 82:3a–5b; *Sung Yüan hsüeh-an pu-i*, 82:23a–83a.

[47] On Chin, see Ch'eng Yüan-min 程元敏, "Chin Lü-hsiang ho t'a-ti i-chu 金履祥和他的遺著," *Sung shih yen-chiu chi* 宋史研究集, vol. 4 (Taipei: Chung-hua ts'ung-shu pien-shen wei-yüan-hui 中華叢書編審委員會, 1969), pp. 63–94; Ho Shu-chen 何淑貞, "Chin Lü-hsiang ti li-hsüeh 金履祥的理學," *Ssu yü yen* 思與言, 13:2 (July 1975), pp. 6–11; Sun K'o-k'uan, *Yüan-tai Chin-hua hsüeh shu*, pp. 25–34.

Yüan shih 元史 (*Yüan History*) indicates that Chin sent proposals to the
Sung court for dealing with the Mongol siege of Hsiang-yang. He
proposed that a large army be transported north by sea for an attack on
the area of Yen-ching 燕京 (modern Peking). This would force the
Mongols to lift the siege of Hsiang-yang, he believed.[48] Chin presented
these proposals in Hangchow, where he had gone for the express purpose
of offering himself for the service of the dynasty.[49] Chin thus upheld the
spirit of constructive thought and effort directed against the foreign
invaders that had characterized the Chin-hua literati.

Chin Lü-hsiang's wide learning embraced astronomy, geography, rites,
music, penal law, the keeping of public lands, Yin and Yang, fortune
telling, and calendrical studies. When the catastrophic capitulation of the
Sung occurred, Chin moved his family into the Chin-hua mountains to
avoid soldiers and bandits. Near the end of his life he took stock of his
life's experiences and put his writings in order in a manner that reflected
his assessement. The writings were grouped chronologically into four
periods, each of which was given an appropriate heading. Works written
before he reached the age of forty *sui* he collected under the title *Tso-fei
ts'un-kao* 昨非存稿 (*Manuscripts of Past Mistakes*), a rubric which
evokes the memory of the ancient Taoist recluse T'ao Ch'ien 陶潛 and
his poetic statement *Kuei-ch'ü-lai tz'u* 歸去來辭 (*The Return*). T'ao had
written:

> To get out of this and go back home!
> My fields and garden will be overgrown with weeds—I must go
>   back.
> It was my own doing that made my mind my body's slave.
> Why should I go on in melancholy and lonely grief?
> I realize that there's no remedying the past
> But I know that there's hope in the future.
> After all I have not gone far on the wrong road
> And I am aware that what I do today is right, yesterday
>   wrong.[50]

[48] YS 189:4316.

[49] See the *hsing-chuang* 行狀 (record of conduct) by Liu Kuan, included in Chin's *Jen-shan chi* 仁山集 (*Kuo-hsüeh chi-pen ts'ung-shu* 國學基本叢書 ed.), p. 97.

[50] Tr. by James Robert Hightower, "The *Fu* of T'ao Ch'ien," *Harvard Journal of Asiatic Studies*, 17 (1954), p. 220. Hightower cites a passage from *Chuang Tzu* (SPTK ed.), 9:13b–14a, which T'ao may have had in mind: "When Confucius was in his sixtieth year, in that year his views changed. What he had before held to be right, he now ended by holding to be wrong; and he did not know whether the things which he now pronounced to be right were not those which he had for fifty-nine years held to be wrong." (Tr. by James Legge.)

Works written during the period 1271–1275 Chin entitled *Jen-shan hsin-kao* 仁山新稿 (*New Manuscripts from Jen Mountain*), referring to the place where he kept his library and studio. This period was one of active efforts by Chin to assist the Sung to stave off the Mongol conquest.

Manuscripts dating from the fall of Hangchow in 1276 were collected under the title *Jen-shan luan-kao* 仁山亂稿 (*Manuscripts of Chaos from Jen Mountain*), while those dating from 1292 were entitled *Jen-shan i-kao* 仁山噫稿 (*Manuscripts of Regret from Jen Mountain*). He explained the reasons for these last two titles as follows, according to the record made by his student Liu Kuan 柳貫 (1270–1342): "From the catastrophe of 1276, my lifelong hopes were shattered. From the sadness of weeping for my [deceased] son, my hopes for posterity were orphaned. [The words] 'chaos' and 'regret' [in the titles] indicate those feelings."[51]

Unfortunately, the extant editions of Chin Lü-hsiang's works are not organized according to these four categories, so it is therefore difficult to appraise his intellectual development. Yet one can document one important philosophical assumption of Chin's that bears upon his response to the Mongol conquest.

In his lecture "Fu ch'i chien t'ien-ti chih hsin chiang-i 復其見天地之心 講義" (Lecture on "In the Hexagram *Fu* [*Return*] One sees the Mind of Heaven and Earth"),[52] we can detect the idea that, while cyclical change inevitably brings times of order and disorder, in times of decay the scholar has an obligation to lay the groundwork for the inevitable recovery that lay ahead. Chin's essay is a commentary on a famous statement by the Northern Sung scholar Ch'eng I 程頤 that pertained to the hexagram *Fu* in the *Book of Changes*. Ch'eng's statement, which was included in the *Chin-ssu lu* by Chu Hsi and Lü Tsu-ch'ien, went as follows: "Former scholars have all contended that the mind of Heaven and Earth is seen in tranquillity. They did not know that the mind of Heaven and Earth is seen in the beginning of activity. How can those ignorant of the Way know this?"[53] Ch'eng I's words suggest that cyclical unfolding of natural processes entails a priority on activity, and that tranquillity is but the preparatory stage for the crucial events of creation and growth.

---

[51] *Jen-shan chi*, pp. 97–101.

[52] The words in quotation marks appear in the commentary to the hexagram *Fu* in the *Book of Changes*. See the translation by Richard Wilhelm and Cary F. Baynes, *The I Ching or Book of Changes* (Princeton: Princeton University Press, 1967, third edition), p. 505. The text of Chin's essay is incomplete in *Jen-shan chi*. For the complete text see *Sung Yüan hsüeh-an*, 82:8b–10a.

[53] *Chin-ssu lu* (*Ssu-pu pei-yao* ed.), 1:5b. See Wing-tsit Chan. tr., *Reflections on Things at Hand*, p. 12.

The lecture by Chin Lü-hsiang provides an illuminating commentary on Ch'eng I's statement and aims to imbue the student with the very same activist values that Chin and the Chin-hua school stood for. In the lecture Chin ties *kung-fu* 功夫 or "effort" to the potentiality that is inherent in the process of change. The concluding passage of the lecture develops this point in a powerful manner:

Thus we know that the meaning of the hexagram *Fu* 復 [☷☳ (Return)] is the beginning of this mind [of Heaven and Earth]. Once [the point of] Return has passed, and there has been nothing to grow or to nourish it, then the meaning of Return is lost. This is what the Master Chu [Hsi] meant by "the Return that is not firm brings on repeated failure and repeated Return." [54] Ever since Heaven and Earth had this Return, times have grown more prosperous, so that there was an advance to [the situation described by] the hexagram *Lin* 臨 [☷☱ (Approach)], another advance to the hexagram *T'ai* 泰 [☷☰ (Peace)], once again to the hexagram *Ta-chuang* 大壯 [☳☰ (The Power of the Great)], again to the hexagram *K'uai* 夬 [☱☰ (Resoluteness)], and then again to the hexagram pure *Ch'ien* 乾 [☰☰ (The Creative)]. The mind of the human being that has this Return necessarily increases and grows day by day. Advancing, he achieves "The Power of the Great" as well as the fortitude and resolve of "Resoluteness." The "Creative" does not tire, but combines its virtue with Heaven and Earth. This is [the result of] effort (*kung-fu*) after the "Return." Now, in all events there is the "Return," so is this not important? For example, the renewal of schools that have been abandoned: this is the "Return" that pertains to schools; or the illumination of the ethical principles (*kang-ch'ang* 綱常) that have been obscured: that is the "Return" of the Way of the world; or the making secure of a dynasty (*kuo-chia* 國家) that has been tottering:[55] that is the "Return" of the power of the dynasty (*kuo shih* 國勢). Worthy ministers and generals go forth to pacify the great land (*ta-pang* 大邦) to establish schools, to exalt and maintain the Ming-lun t'ang 明倫堂 (Halls for Illuminating the Ethical Relations)[56] [in the schools], and that is the "Return" appropriate to schools. As to the "Return" to brightness of the human relations that were in decay and the "Return" to strength of

[54] Chu Hsi, *Chou-i pen-i* 周易本義 (*Liu-shih ch'uan-ching t'ang ts'ung-shu* 劉氏傳經堂 叢書 ed., 1875), 1:24b.

[55] The word "tottering" (*wei* 危) alludes to *Lun-yü*, 8/13: Confucius said a gentleman "will not enter a tottering state, nor dwell in a disorganized one...." James Legge, tr., *The Chinese Classics*, vol. 1, p. 212.

[56] Cf. *Mencius*, 3A/3. Legge, tr., *The Chinese Classics*, vol. 2, pp. 242–243.

a dynastic power that was tottering, these all depend upon you gentlemen (*chün-tzu* 君子). Among you there must be some who can capture the principle of "Return" and fulfill the meritorious function (*kung-yung* 功用) of the "Return." Please do not waste this.[57]

Chin Lü-hsiang declined to serve the new regime after the fall of the Sung. Under the Mongols he lived as a scholar and a teacher, withdrawn from any formal or institutional involvement with Yüan government. But, as this lecture on the "Return" makes clear, he believed that the superior human being was one who committed himself to the betterment of the community. With a knowledge of the nature of change, the superior person will draw strength from tranquillity and go forth at the proper moment to transform adversity into advantage. This is what Chin taught his disciples.

Chin's most famous disciple was Hsü Ch'ien, the fourth and last of the Chin-hua "masters." Among Hsü's main scholarly accomplishments is his study of the *Four Books* and their commentaries, a work which he entitled *Tu Ssu-shu ts'ung-shuo* 讀四書叢説 (*The Many Interpretations for the Study of the Four Books*). Hsü Ch'ien refused offers of official employment that were tendered from time to time by Yüan officials. But he was no isolated recluse. He was one of the most sought-after scholars in the Chekiang region. Hsü's door was always open to callers, and he carried on an active correspondence with people in government.[58] Hsü even had non-Han Chinese disciples, such as the Mongol Khara Bukha 合剌不花 who had served in T'ai-chou 泰州 as the *darughachi* (agent of the khaghan) prior to becoming Hsü's follower.[59]

Hsü Ch'ien's approach to the *Four Books* was that of the faithful disciple of the master Chu Hsi. In all his discussions of key passages in the texts, he attempted to uncover and to articulate clearly the "correct" interpretations. It was not his intention to introduce novel ideas or interpretations, for his primary task was to ensure the accurate transmission of Chu Hsi's teachings.

But the act of preservation, which requires that the ideas be re-articulated, changes those ideas, if ever so slightly. The literal representation of the ideas may not change if the disciple merely mouths the same

[57] *Sung Yüan hsüeh-an*, 82:10a. I am indebted to Dr. Fang Chao-ying for assistance in translating the last part of this passage.

[58] Sun K'o-k'uan, *Yüan-tai Chin-hua hsüeh shu*, p. 40.

[59] *Sung Yüan hsüeh-an*, 82:41b–42a. For the biography of Khara Bukha, see YS 193:4384–4386. See also Dardess, *Conquerors and Confucians*, p. 204 note 60. The taking of Mongol disciples was an extremely rare event, according to *Sung Yüan hsüeh-an*, 82:42a.

words of the master. But, even then, the context of the restatement will be different from that which prevailed at the time of their original uttering. At the worst, the collection and preservation of a master's ideas may turn them into stony convention. Rearticulation and clarification of a master's ideas which iron out inconsistencies and correct or improve vague and imprecise statements may transform the ideas. The changes thus introduced may not be perceived as changes, but many possible changes can nevertheless be introduced. The original ideas may lose their mysterious attraction by the process of restatement, or they may become more persuasive. Emphases may change as well.

Hsü Ch'ien's restatement of the master's ideas did indeed introduce a subtle change of emphasis. This can be shown by an examination of one rather obvious instance. It concerns the important passage in the *Analects* (passage II/3) in which Confucius presented the notion that the state should be governed by men of superior moral quality. The passage as translated by James Legge reads as follows:

"The Master said, 'If the people be led by laws and uniformity sought to be given them by punishments, they will try to avoid [the punishments], but have no sense of shame.

"'If they be led by virtue, and uniformity sought to be given them by the rules of propriety (*li* 禮), they will have the sense of shame, and moreover will become good.'"[60]

The word rendered "laws" (*cheng* 政) is controversial. It is sometimes translated as "regulations," to convey a somewhat softer notion of control by the use of governmental restraints.[61] In using the word "laws" in his translation, Legge followed Chu Hsi's exegesis as found in the *Ssu-shu chi-chu*: "*Cheng* means legal measures and prohibitionary statutes" (*fa-chih chin-ling* 法制禁令).[62] Chu Hsi explained the passage in his own words:

"In my humble view, laws are the tool of government, and punishments the methods for assisting government. Virtue and the rules of propriety are those things which issue from the root of government, while virtue is the root of propriety. Thus they exist in a relationship of end and beginning. While it is not permissible to discard the one, laws and punishments can do no more than cause the people to remain far away from crime. The efficacy of virtue and the rules of propriety is such as to cause the people constantly to move closer to the good without being aware of the fact. Therefore he who governs the people must not

[60] James Legge, tr., *The Chinese Classics*, vol. 1, p. 146.

[61] Cf. Wing-tsit Chan, *A Source Book in Chinese Philosophy* (Princeton: Princeton University Press, 1963), p. 22: "governmental measures." Cf. also Arthur Waley, tr., *Analects of Confucius*, p. 88: "regulations."

[62] *Ssu-shu chi-chu* (*Ssu-pu pei-yao* ed.), *Lun-yü*, 1:6b.

merely depend upon the branch; he must also deeply seek out the root." [63]

The "Confucianization of the law" in the history of Chinese political theory has been well recognized, [64] but it is also well known that Confucius himself did not insist on the complete abandonment of punishments. He taught that punishments should be employed only as a regretted but necessary supplemental measure to ensure the furtherance of good government. As a practical matter, of course, no dynasty ever contemplated the dismantling of the penal system. In Sung times, Confucian statecraft naturally assigned a place to penal matters. Chu Hsi was no exception, for he saw clearly the importance and indispensability of laws and punishments.

Hsü Ch'ien restated Chu Hsi's views on punishments in his commentary on the preceding passage from the *Analects*, and in doing so he introduced a subtle shift in emphasis. In Hsü Ch'ien's restatement, the emphasis on punishments is greater than in the original. This can be seen in Hsü's own words:

"Fu-tzu [Confucius] said in the *Wei-cheng* 為政 [chapter on government in the *Analects*] that one should employ virtue and the rules of propriety [in administering the realm]. If one solely employed laws and punishments and disregarded the root, that would be insufficient to establish good government. But he merely meant that one must not rely solely on punishments and laws. He did not mean that one need merely employ virtue and the rules of propriety and that laws and punishments were not required. Virtue and the rules of propriety are indeed capable of transforming the people, but if laws are not instituted then the purpose of virtue will not flow universally below. Therefore to bring peace to the world one must employ 'the principle of the measuring square' [65] [to compel the recalcitrant to behave as good people]. When there are 'legal measures and prohibitionary statutes,' [66] then the benefits of virtue will be able to flow downwards. Even in the age of the sage rulers Yao and Shun, there were 'the four wicked ones' [who had to be banished]. [67] Punishments then could not be abolished. Wen-kung [Chu Hsi] feared

---

[63] *Ssu-shu chi-chu, Lun-yü*, 1 : 6b.

[64] See Ch'ü T'ung-tsu 瞿同祖, *Law and Society in Traditional China* (The Hague: Mouton and Co., 1965), pp. 267–279; Hsiao Kung-ch'üan, "Legalism and Autocracy in Traditional China," *Ch'ing-hua hsüeh-pao* 清華學報, N.S. 4 : 2 (February 1964), pp. 108–121.

[65] *Hsieh-chü chih tao* 絜矩之道. See the *Great Learning*, commentary, part 10. Legge, tr., *The Chinese Classics*, vol. 1, p. 373.

[66] *Fa-chih chin-ling* are the words Chu Hsi used to define the term *cheng* 政 (government [or laws]). See above, p. 156.

[67] On the "four wicked ones," see *Tso chuan* 左傳, eighteenth year of Duke Wen (608 B.C.); Legge, tr., *The Chinese Classics*, vol. 5, p. 283.

that students would say that the Sage's intention was that the first paragraph [of the text of the *Analects* cited above] was not as important as the second. [He feared] they would merely view the matter as one involving virtue and the rules of propriety and would slight laws and punishments. Therefore outside the circle [i.e., in his commentary notes] he clarified the meaning. The Sage was originally of this mind. Wen-kung was not forcing the two paragraphs into one." [68]

In this passage Hsü Ch'ien implies a tendency among contemporary students of Confucian learning to overlook the political importance of laws and punishments. Chu Hsi, he claims, fought that tendency, and Hsü Ch'ien sees no less a need to do the same. But in restating Chu Hsi's views in this manner, he gave greater emphasis to the necessity of laws and punishments. This gave added ideological legitimacy to their use in society by the rulers of China.

THE NEXT GENERATION

Hsü Ch'ien had many students, and a few became influential in their own rights as scholars. But none carried on the line of teachings in the same way that the Four Masters had done. There was no Fifth Master of Chin-hua. Yet the followers of Chin and Hsü became or attempted to become active participants in the affairs of Yüan government. They worked closely with Mongols and other non-Han persons in control of the empire. They devoted themselves to establishing the "Return" for the fundamental moral and political institutions of society.

Liu Kuan, whose ideas on law will be discussed below, addressed precisely this point in his *hsing-chuang* 行狀 for Chin Lü-hsiang.[69] A *hsing-chuang* is a "record of conduct" written as a laudatory bio-graphical record of a deceased person. In this piece Liu wrote that some 1,500 years had elapsed between the time when the learning of the sages became obscured and the time when it was reilluminated by the five Northern Sung philosophers (Chou Tun-i 周敦頤, Ch'eng I 程頤, Ch'eng Hao 程顥, Chang Tsai 張載, and Shao Yung 邵雍). After 1,500 years the Way of the Six Classics once again shone brightly in the world. Human beings were once again able to rely on the teachings to establish the best in themselves, to assist their rulers, and to nourish social life. This brilliant illumination in Northern Sung times came about suddenly, Liu wrote, but, like all phenomena it was potentially ephemeral. Days of sun and fair winds are few, while stormy and dark changes are numer-

---

[68] *Tu Ssu-shu ts'ung-shuo* (SPTK ed.), *Lun-yü*, 1:10b–11a.
[69] Cited in n. 49.

ous. Crowds of inauspicious creatures like the owl and the snake are
more numerous than tortoises, dragons, unicorns, and phoenixes! The
very instant before illumination and expansion contains the possibility of
harm and disintegration. If the possibility becomes a reality, the minds of
the people will be trapped in a state of ignorance "in which inquiry is
impossible." [70] Such times are viewed by the superior person as times of
severe vicissitudes for scholarship. But at such times superior persons
will arise to preserve and continue the precious teachings of the Sage. [71]
Liu Kuan said all this in the context of remarks on the career and
scholarship of his mentor Chin Lü-hsiang. Liu could not possibly have
failed to take his remarks seriously in his own scholarly and political
pursuits.

To sum up the intellectual and moral dimensions of the Chin-hua
heritage in early Yüan times: it was directly linked to the prestigious
synthesis of Confucian philosophy and scholarship of Chu Hsi. Beyond
this, it was heir to the pragmatic statecraft scholarship of the Southern
Sung Eastern Chekiang school. Chin-hua literati were profoundly sensitive to the creative potential of the turbulence of their era. While this
turbulence was not desirable, since it disturbed people's lives, it nevertheless contained within it the potential for a reversal and for the establishment of a better moral and political order. If that was to happen,
however, they knew it could come about only if committed individuals
dedicated themselves to the task of regeneration.

P'U-CHIANG IN THE EARLY YÜAN: SUNG LOYALISM

The chilling crisis of Mongol conquest and domination was felt sharply
in Chin-hua, as has been noted above. Chin-hua, however, soon became
a center of Confucian activism, constructively dedicated to reforming
and improving the institutions that governed China. One of sources of
the emotional intensity with which Chin-hua literati sought to improve
Yüan rule was paradoxically found in loyalism, which in turn was
manifested in Chin-hua as loyalism to the Sung. Sung loyalism centered
on Chin-hua in the form of literary gatherings, Confucian eremitism, and
the historical commemoration of Sung martyrs. It was directed not so
much against the Mongol conquerors, however, as towards the ideal of
loyalty to one's ruling dynasty. The incentive and commitment that

---

[70] *Lao tzu* 老子, 14. Cf. Wing-tsit Chan, *A Source Book in Chinese Philosophy*, p. 146.

[71] The foregoing is a close paraphrase of passages from Liu's *hsing-chuang*. See *Jen-shan chi*, p. 102. Parts of these passages also appear in *Sung Yüan hsüeh-an pu-i*, 82:164a–b; and Sun K'o-k'uan, *Yüan-tai Chin hua hsüeh shu*, p. 71.

underlay the impressive Confucian activism in Chin-hua during the high Yüan (roughly 1310–1355) derived part of its energy from the exemplary behavior of Sung loyalists.

This can be demonstrated by a closer study of the literati of P'u-chiang district. Also known in some sources by its literary name P'u-yang 浦陽, P'u-chiang was the home of some of the most fascinating individuals in the Confucian activist tradition of Chin-hua. Some have already been mentioned above.

P'u-chiang is located in the northeastern quarter of Chin-hua prefecture, and is a mountainous, relatively remote, region of Chekiang. P'u-chiang bordered on Chu-chi 諸暨 sub-prefecture in the neighboring administrative area Shao-hsing Circuit 紹興路. Shao-hsing and Wu-chou circuits had been established under Khubilai Khaghan in the year 1276 immediately following the surrender of Hangchow and the takeover of all of Chiang-nan by the Mongols. P'u-chiang lay roughly midway between Chin-hua and Chu-chi. From the Chin-hua district seat, formerly surrounded by a wall of about one *li* 里 (about a third of a mile) in circumference, to the Chin-hua district border, straight south, was a distance of about 55 or 60 *li*. It was about the same distance to the border of Chu-chi sub-prefecture directly east, and roughly the same distance again to the Chu-chi seat. P'u-chiang was ovoid in shape, measuring approximately 102 *li* from east to west and 140 *li* from north to south. To the Yüan capital city Ta-tu 大都, it was about 3,600 *li*.[72] In mid-Yüan times the population of P'u-chiang was estimated at about 120,000.[73] While not extremely wealthy, the area was prosperous and supported at least two large extended clans (the Wangs and the Chengs),[74] and sent forth a continuous stream of talented literati. Population declined markedly in early Ming times, perhaps due to epidemics, pests, and the wars of the late Yüan, and perhaps also due to emigration. By 1391 the population is said to have dropped to under 100,000.[75]

[72] *Kuang-hsü P'u-chiang hsien-chih kao*, 1:41a–42a; *Chin-hua fu-chih*, 1:11a–12a.

[73] Sung Lien, *Sung Wen-hsien kung ch'üan-chi*, 53:3a. Cf. *kuang-hsü P'u-chiang hsien-chih kao*, 11:4a.

[74] On the Chengs, see John W. Dardess, "The Cheng Communal Family: Social Organization and Neo-Confucianism in Yüan and Early Ming China," *Harvard Journal of Asiatic Studies*, 34 (1974), pp. 7–52. Dardess mentions the Wangs in passing. See also Su Po-heng, *Su P'ing-chung wen-chi*, 12:26b–28b, for a tomb inscription for a deceased member of the Wang clan; 7:2a–3b, for a note on the "ritual land" held by the clan (about 50 *mu* of first-grade fields); and 15:1a–2a, for a poem about the clan. The Wangs modeled themselves after the Chengs, as Dardess points out. See also Sung Lien, *Sung Wen-hsien kung ch'üan-chi*, 23:4a–5a; and Fang Hsiao-ju, *Hsün-chih chai chi*, 13:27b–29a, esp. 28b.

[75] *Kuang-hsü P'u-chiang hsien-chih kao*, 11:4a.

P'u-chiang was accessible in Yüan times only by foot or by animal. The P'u-yang River that arose in Shen-niao 深臬 mountain, northwest of P'u-chiang, was too shallow for boats until it reached well inside Chu-chi. It flowed eastwards, cutting across P'u-chiang just south of the district seat. Two other small streams flowed out of P'u-chiang, in whose mountains they originated. One flowed west into Lan-ch'i, and the other north into Fu-yang 富陽. The district was not far from Hangchow, which was but a few days' journey, but it was nevertheless felt that P'u-chiang was remarkably free of the hassle of urban life. Liu Kuan, a native, wrote that "P'u-chiang in Wu is a mountainous district, not a place where travelers and merchants rush to converge."[76] The *daru-ghachi* of P'u-chiang, a Mongol named Hsieh-yün-shih Pu-hua 寫雲石不花, who assumed his post in 1358 in the twilight of Yüan rule there,[77] and Wu-chou circuit vice-governor Chao Ta-ne 趙大訥,[78] described P'u-chiang in a letter jointly written to the scholar Sung Lien to request a commemoratory essay:

"P'u-yang is an insignificant district in Wu.[79] It is encircled by great mountains and long ranges, and is a place that cannot be penetrated by boats and carts. In a bygone year, Great General Chao Yeh-hsün-t'ai 趙野遜台 led the first army into this region in search of roads.[80] Because of their military equipment they did not travel easily. En route whatever farmers, merchants, Buddhists and Taoists they met, without asking whether they were able, were bound by the neck with streamers and forced to shoulder the equipment. Some shed blood and could not do the deed, and these were instantly killed as a warning [to the others]. The people were very hard pressed [by this]."[81]

P'u-chiang was thus not untouched by the military aspects of Mongol rule. Yet, on the whole, the geography tended to protect the region, giving it a special character. It became the refuge of many poets who remained loyal to the Sung. The Yüeh-ch'üan yin-she 月泉吟社, a loyalist poetry society, held gatherings at the Yüeh-ch'üan *ching-she*

[76] Liu Kuan, *Liu Tai-chih chi* 柳待制集 (SPTK ed.), 12:9b.

[77] *Kuang-hsü P'u-chiang hsien-chih kao*, 7:25a.

[78] For Chao's biography see Sung Lien, *P'u-yang jen-wu chi*, in *Sung Wen-hsien kung ch'üan-chi*, 53:9a–b; and the inscription on 42:1a–3b.

[79] Cf. *Tso chuan*, 533 B.C.; Legge, tr., *The Chinese Classics*, vol. 5, p. 618.

[80] For Chao Yeh-hsün-t'ai, see YS 195:4423; and *Hsin Yüan shih*, *chüan* 149. He was the son of Chao Shih-yen 趙世延 (1260–1336), a sinicized Onggud whose family had adopted a Chinese surname. Chao Shih-yen served in government for nearly half a century and received many honors. He was a compiler of the *Ching-shih ta-tien* 經世大典 (*Compendium for Governing the World*). See YS 180:4163–4167. The orthography of Chao Yeh-hsün-t'ai's name in the *Yüan shih* is given as Yeh-chün 峻-t'ai.

[81] Sung Lien, *Sung Wen-hsien kung ch'üan-chi*, 43:7b.

精舍, a meditation retreat just two *li* northwest of the district seat.[82] The spring after which it was named was said to rise and fall with the phases of the moon, hence the name "moon spring."

As Sun K'o-k'uan has shown in a recent study, a number of prominent Sung loyalist poets gathered in P'u-chiang in the early years of the Yüan.[83] These included Hsieh Ao 謝翱 (1249–1295), who had raised militia on his own to fight the Mongols and who had aided Wen T'ien-hsiang 文天祥 (1236–1282) in the latter's efforts against the invaders; Wu Ssu-ch'i 吳思齊 (1238–1301), a native of Yung-k'ang district; and Fang Feng 方鳳 (1240–1321), from P'u-chiang.[84] Fang Feng was the key figure in this gathering, for both Wu and Hsieh relied upon him for support for a time. When Hsieh died, Fang and Wu buried him at Tiao-t'ai 釣台 where Hsieh had built a shrine to Wen T'ien-hsiang. Wu Ssu-ch'i, a grandson of Ch'en Liang's daughter, had sought to reform Sung military institutions by submitting carefully written memorials to the emperor. Following the Sung defeat, he adopted the style-name Ch'üan-kuei-tzu 全歸子, "the wholly loyal one." Fang Feng, on his part, had been acquainted with Ch'en I-chung 陳宜中, the chief minister of the Sung who fled Hangchow in 1276 with two princes in a last-ditch loyalist effort. In Foochow one of the princes was set up as Emperor, with Ch'en as his chief minister. The Mongols attacked, driving the loyalists farther south for the final battle at sea off Canton. Ch'en fled to Champa, and later, in 1282, following Mongol attacks there, to Siam. He died in Siam at an unknown time. Fang Feng heard of these events through an envoy sent by Ch'en prior to the latter's departure for Siam.[85]

The loyalist feature of the P'u-chiang heritage in early Yüan times gave the area an added aura of prestige. But the impetus it inspired there

---

[82] On the Yüeh-ch'üan loyalist poets, see the brief note in F. W. Mote, "Confucian Eremitism in the Yüan Period," in Arthur F. Wright, ed., *The Confucian Persuasion* (Stanford: Stanford University Press, 1960), p. 235 note 55. See also Yokota Terutoshi 横田輝俊, "Getsusen ginsha ni tsuite 月泉吟社について," *Hiroshima Diagaku bungakubu kiyo* 廣島大學文學部紀要, 14 (1958), pp. 99–125; Hu Huai-ch'en 胡懷琛, "Yüeh-ch'üan yin-she chi ch'i-t'a 月泉吟社及其他," *Yüeh-feng pan-yüeh-k'an* 越風半月刊, 6 (January 1936), pp. 22–25; Ch'üan Tsu-wang, *Chieh-ch'i t'ing chi*, 33:8b, 34:6b–7a. For their poems, see Wu Wei 吳渭, ed., *Yüeh-ch'üan yin-she kao* 月泉吟社稿 (*Chin-hua ts'ung-shu* 金華叢書 ed.).

[83] *Yüan-tai Chin-hua hsüeh shu*, pp. 50–55.

[84] See *Hsin Yüan shih*, chüan 241, for biographies of Hsieh, Wu, and Fang.

[85] For a biography of Ch'en I-chung (ca.1228–ca.1285), see Chan Hok-lam in Herbert Franke, ed., *Sung Biographies* (Wiesbaden: Franz Steiner, 1976), pp. 138–146. For Fang Feng's friendship with Ch'en I-chung, see Sung Lien, *P'u-yang jen-wu chi*, in *Sung Wen-hsien kung ch'üan-chi*, 53:14a.

was not hostile to the Mongols; rather, it was an impetus of dedicated service to the prevailing regime, no matter what it happened to be. But the service was not born of loyalty to the *rulers*; instead, it was born of loyalty to the Way and to the community of people over whom the rulers prevailed. Sung loyalism, plus the line of teachings stemming directly from Chu Hsi, plus the other line of teachings in the statecraft school, formed the unique character of Chin-hua thought in Yüan times.

P'u-chiang literati went forth to serve the Mongol government. Several ultimately became Yüan loyalists in the 1360s and in the early Ming. This fact supports the notion that P'u-chiang and, more generally, Chin-hua literati accepted the Mongols as more than mere de facto rulers. Loyalty to the culture of China transcended mere political configurations and supported active service in Yüan rule even by individuals who may have felt a disliking for domination by an ethnic minority. At the end of the Yüan, P'u-chiang district produced one of the most notable Yüan loyalists, the scholar Tai Liang 戴良 (1317–1383). He was the student of Wu Lai, Liu Kuan, and Huang Chin 黄溍 (1277–1357), and a scholar of the *Spring and Autumn Annals*.[86] The aforementioned Chao Ta-ne (1278–1358), descendant of a Sung prince and a native of P'u-chiang, was learned in written Mongolian. He had a long career of government service under the Yüan, and when Chin-hua was conquered in 1358–1359 by the armies of the future Ming founder, Chao stubbornly refused to surrender.[87] Three members of the illustrious Cheng 鄭 clan of P'u-chiang, who had served Mongol chancellor Toghto 脱脱 in the 1340s and 1350s, remained loyal to the Yüan in the years of transition to Ming rule.[88]

Chin-hua was a key intellectual area, one which Chu Yüan-chang 朱元璋, the future Ming founder, naturally sought to control early in his rise to orthodox power as the emperor of a Chinese dynasty. Chu's general Hsü Ta 徐達 first took P'u-chiang in July of 1358. Chin-hua district, the headquarters of Wu-chou Circuit, was not taken until January of the following year. Chu personally directed the conquest of Chin-hua and supervised the reestablishment of political order there. The takeover was carefully staged by Chu to include the display of legitimiz-

---

[86] My biography of Tai Liang has been cited above (n.20).

[87] Sung Lien quoted him as having said, "I am an old official of the Yüan court. I have only one death with which to requite the dynasty." See the inscription cited in note 78.

[88] These were Cheng Shen 鄭深 (1314–1361), Cheng T'ao, and Cheng Yung 鄭泳 (lived into the early Ming). For a study of the sources, see my "Chin-hua Confucianism under the Mongols, 1279–1368," Ph.D. diss., Princeton University, 1974, pp. 236–264, 268–289, and 289–292, respectively.

ing cultural symbols, designed to assist the effort to win over literati support.[89] The scholars who eventually joined him not only loaned him their considerable prestige in the elite culture, but they helped him to assemble the formal structure of the Ming dynasty as it was constructed in the late 1360s.

THE PROBLEM OF DOMINATION

For the scholar with a penchant for political thought, the rule of the Mongols presented him with a new problem, that of domination by a power that was largely out of the scholar's control or influence and perhaps even out of his ken. Any scholar who was dedicated to active public service now faced the challenge of a monarchy which followed behavioral norms that were alien to the Han Chinese tradition. The Mongols ruled China as though it were a colony of their larger empire; the native Chinese were dealt with on that basis, and hence were not granted ready access to positions of influence in government. The need for clerical personnel to staff government offices was undiminished by Mongol rule, and consequently many literati entered into government service through that route. To some degree Yüan government was "Chinese" in that it allowed existing bureaucratic procedures to continue. This fact of course represented the mature Mongol policy towards the Chinese realm, since at the outset Chinggis Khan had thought to convert China into pasturage for his animals. Mongol rule was far from static. The reign of Khubilai was marked by continual pressure to expand the territory, while the reigns of the subsequent emperors in Yüan China were marked by struggles to retain the spoils that Khubilai

---

[89] During the siege of the city, he had a metal tablet held up high with the following words written thereon: "Obeying Heaven to govern all of China" (*feng-t'ien tu-t'ung Chung-hua* 奉天都統中華). After the city was taken, Chu had a pair of banners in imperial yellow placed at the entrance to his new "branch central secretariat" (hsing chung-shu-sheng 行中書省). On the banners appeared the words: "Mountains, rivers, all the territory of China / Sun and Moon unfold again the Heaven of the Great Sung." Two wooden tablets were also placed beside the entrance with the words: "Ninefold Heaven, Sun and Moon, open the cosmic ecliptic / Rivers and Mountains of the Sung are restored to the territory of China." Immediately after the takeover of Chin-hua and the restoration of order there, he commanded that the Confucian school be reopened. Thirteen famous local scholars were summoned and ordered to deliver lectures on the teachings of the classics and histories. He appointed a Master of the Five Classics and two instructors. Sung Lien joined with the scholars to instruct Chu Yüan-chang. For the sources, see Ch'ien Ch'ien-i 錢謙益, *Kuo-ch'u ch'ün-hsiung shih-lüeh* 國初群雄事略 (reprinted Taipei: Chung-hua wen-shih ts'ung-shu 中華文史叢書, second series, volume 9, 1966 [?]), p. 52; Wang Ch'ung-wu 王崇武, *Ming pen-chi chiao-chu* 明本紀校注 (1945; reprinted, Hong Kong: Lung-men Shu-tien 龍門書店, 1967), pp. 61–63, 75.

had won for them. There were constant battles between contenders to the throne. Some emperors tolerated a relatively energetic support of Han Chinese institutions, such as the examination system which was reinstated in 1315. Other emperors had no interest in Chinese methods of rule. One emperor was probably quite literate in Chinese, while nearly all the others were virtually illiterate in Chinese. The reign of the last emperor went through many phases. In the early years of his reign the emperor's throne was dominated by powerful grandees who were inimical to native Chinese interests, while these were subsequently overthrown by others who were pro-Chinese. These pro-Chinese were heavily supported by Chin-hua scholars, until their Mongol patrons lost power and were killed. These events marked the beginning of the end of Yüan rule as rebels began to eat away at Mongol control over Chinese territory. Thus Mongol rule was protean, and the response of the Chinese in turn reflected that moving target.

One approach seems to have informed Chin-hua literati's attitudes toward the political problems fostered by Mongol rule, despite the continually changing nature of that rule. This was the stress on the employment of law as a means of transforming Mongol domination into orderly government. Law in pre-modern China meant first of all the will of the sovereign—the commands of the emperor issued in the form of edicts. Law also meant the regulations that were set down to guide the behavior of persons in their various social and political roles in the hierarchical order. It also meant penal law, the specified criminal acts for which society demanded punishment in accordance with the hierarchical principles of Confucian ethics.

During the Yüan period the study of legal texts and their dissemination became an astonishingly widespread practice. Important "Confucian" thinkers urged their students to study the law, to become well versed in the principle and practice of its various kinds. There were efforts to codify the laws of the sovereign and the regulations of the bureaucracy; and there were efforts to promote the understanding of the penal laws. A recent study has in fact argued that "legal professionalism" was a characteristic of many Yüan scholar-officials. Chin-hua scholars were well within this developing tradition, for they took the lead in calling on literati to become legal experts.

This trend emerged in part because the increasingly bureaucratic nature of government in China demanded it. The trend had begun in Sung times and was not reversed simply because of Mongol rule. Indeed, the Mongols put it to good use. In many territories administered by the Mongols, resort was made to agents who were not Mongols but instead were literate Central Asians. Central Asians were employed as agents in

China, but many Han Chinese were called upon to fill the manpower needs of government offices.

By advocating that scholars who participated in Mongol administration should become legal experts, the P'u-chiang theorists sought to reduce the level of constraints on human livelihood that unbridled Mongol rule often entailed. Since many legislative acts were not directly made by the Mongol rulers, although they were subject to veto by those rulers, scholars who participated in legislation and in legislative interpretation could exert a leavening effect on the conduct of Mongol rule as it affected the larger community. The printing of legislation and the mastery of its purposes and methods by scholar-interpreters can do much to confer order and rationality to an entire political system (including the legal system), and this seems to have been the unstated premise of the P'u-chiang theorists.

LIU KUAN AND WU LAI

The Chin-hua intellectual and moral achievement in Yüan times was to a great extent built on a core provided by the literati from P'u-chiang. Two names stand tallest in this regard: Liu Kuan 柳貫 (1270–1342) and Wu Lai 吳萊 (1297–1340). A saying traditionally ascribed to Liu Kuan provides an insight into his motivations: "The Six Classics were handed down through the centuries, and the words with which they established the moral teachings must never for a single day fail to shine bright in the world."[90] Liu pursued this aim relentlessly throughout his life. He did so both through long and active service in government and as a teacher during his later years of retirement.

As a young man in P'u-chiang, Liu[91] studied under Chin Lü-hsiang, Fang Feng, Wu Ssu-ch'i, and Hsieh Ao. Later he went to Hangchow and to other urban centers to meet the elder scholars who had lived under the Sung and who therefore had experienced and survived the Mongol conquest. Among the people he sought out was the poet and painter Kung K'ai 龔開, who was a biographer of the loyal Sung martyrs Wen T'ien-hsiang and Lu Hsiu-fu.[92] Liu's official career began in 1300, when he took up an appointment as an instructor in Chiang-shan 江山, southeast of Chin-hua, setting a pattern of service that was largely devoted to educating others or administering educational institutions.

[90] *Sung Yüan hsüeh-an pu-i*, 82:192a.

[91] Sun K'o-k'uan indicates the main sources for Liu's biography in *Yüan-tai Chin-hua hsüeh shu*, pp. 55–60.

[92] For this material see Langlois, "Chin-hua Confucianism under the Mongols, 1279–1368," pp. 61–69.

Between 1311 and 1326 he spent most of his time in Ta-tu on various appointments.[93] From 1326 to 1341 Liu Kuan served in a series of positions in Chiang-nan, save for an interruption beginning in 1329 to mourn his father. In 1341 he was recalled to the capital to serve in the newly constituted court under the patronage of Toghto. He received appointment to the Hanlin Academy as *tai-chih* 待制 (rescript attendant), with a concurrent appointment as compiler in the Bureau of Dynastic History.[94] In the fifth moon of 1342 Liu travelled to the capital, where he died before the year was out. Funeral arrangements were taken care of by three scholars, one of whom was Wu Chih-fang 吳直方 (1275–1356), the father of Wu Lai and long-term personal adviser and mentor of the chancellor Toghto.

When Liu Kuan died he was one of the most highly regarded literary stylists in the land. He was not a major philosopher, for there were few such figures in the Yüan period. Rather, his energies were directed towards the aims set forth in the adage quoted above. His writings reflect a deep concern with statecraft, and especially with the methodology for transforming arbitrary rule into orderly administration. An excellent example of the analyses he made is found in his preface to the *T'ang-lü shu-i* 唐律疏議 (*T'ang Code with Commentary*). The *T'ang-lü shu-i* was the formative legal code in traditional China. It had been compiled by the T'ang scholar Chang-sun Wu-chi 長孫無忌 (d. 659) and others and was the most influential legal text ever compiled in pre-modern China.

In the history of legal codification in China, the *T'ang Code* is a major watershed.[95] All later codes were either directly modeled on it or fundamentally influenced by it. Sung codifiers had prepared the Sung *Hsing-t'ung* 刑統 (*Penal Tradition*), which derived directly from the *T'ang Code*. Day-to-day legislation in Sung times, however, was enacted by imperial fiat. Laws therefore changed rapidly, and this required that the dynasty issue periodic supplementary compilations of edicts. When appropriate, all obsolete legislation was weeded out or revised.[96]

---

[93] In 1319 he was assistant instructor in the National College (Kuo-tzu hsüeh 國子學), with court rank and with the forty-second of the forty-two civil honorary titles, bearing rank 8B; in 1321 he advanced to the fortieth honorary title, with rank 8A; in 1324 he advanced to the thirty-seventh title and rank 7B; and in 1326 to the thirty-fifth title and rank 7A.

[94] He also received the thirty-fourth of the forty-two honorary titles and rank 6B.

[95] For some notes and references on this point, see Niida Noboru 仁井田陞, *Chūgoku hōseishi* 中国法制史 (rev. and enlarged edition, Tokyo: Iwanami, 1975), pp. 62–73. For a translation of the first fifty-seven articles, see Wallace S. Johnson, tr., *The T'ang Code, Volume I, General Principles* (Princeton: Princeton university Press, 1979).

[96] On Sung legal codification, see Hsü Tao-lin 徐道隣, "Sung-ch'ao ti hsing-shu 宋朝的刑書," in Hsü's *Chung-kuo fa-chih shih lun-chi* 中國法制史論集 (Taipei: Chih-wen Ch'u-pan-she 志文出版社, 1975), pp. 273–304.

Under the Yüan there were similar efforts to codify the laws,[97] although no formal code (*lü* 律) was ever proclaimed. A further aspect of Chinese efforts under the Mongols to establish and to maintain a good legal system was the collation and publication of texts of the *T'ang Code with Commentary*. In this effort, Yüan literati continued the work begun earlier under the Jurchens. During the Yüan, however, two editions of the *T'ang Code with Commentary* were published under court auspices. The first was under Yesün Temür (the T'ai-ting Emperor [r. 1323–1328]), and the second under the last ruler Toghōn Temür (r. 1333–1370) during the Chih-cheng 至正 reign (1341–1368).[98]

In view of these facts, Liu Kuan's interest in the *T'ang Code* with Commentary may be seen as representative of a concern among Yüan scholars and officials about the state of the legal system. Liu's P'u-chiang colleague Wu Lai also studied the text and even made an abridgement of it for official use.

An unsung but crucial linchpin in the P'u-chiang response to Mongol rule, and a key element in the P'u-chiang interest in law, was Wu Lai's father Wu Chih-fang.[99] He left no writings for us to examine today, and it is therefore virtually impossible to form more than a vague understanding of his thought. The Wu clan home in P'u-chiang, headed by a cousin of Wu Chih-fang's, was not badly off, to judge from the facts that a number of the Wus, including Wu Lai's mother, were well educated by contemporary elite standards and that the clan was able to host the well-known Sung loyalist poets of whom mention has already been made. But the clan was not powerful, for they were bullied by other families more powerful than they. Wu Chih-fang launched his public career at P'u-chiang district office as a clerk. There he developed an interest in penal law, a field in which the *li* or clerical functionaries were traditionally closely involved. He subsequently headed for Hangchow, where he attempted to acquire a mastery of the law of punishments and to obtain higher employment in government. After a few years in Hangchow,

[97] Paul Heng-chao Ch'en, in *Chinese Legal Tradition under the Mongols: The Code of 1291 as Reconstructed* (Princeton: Princeton University Press, 1979), pp. 3–40, traces the development of Chinese codes during the Yüan period.

[98] A third edition was published by the Shan-nan Chiang-pei Regional Surveillance Office 山南江北道 at Pien-liang 汴梁 (formerly K'ai-feng 開封). Only one extant edition is attributed to Sung provenance, and that attribution is actually in dispute. It may be a Yüan edition. See Niida Noboru, *Chūgoku hōseishi kenkyū: hō to kanshū, hō to dōtoku* 中国法制史研究: 法と慣習, 法と道徳 (Tokyo: Tōkyō Daigaku Tōyō Bunka Kenkyūjo 東京大学東洋文化研究所, 1964), pp. 65–81, esp. 68.

[99] The following discussion is based primarily on Sung Lien's *hsing-chuang* for Wu Chih-fang, in Sung's works, *Sung Wen-hsien kung ch'üan-chi*, 41:5a–8b. See also 53:8b–9a and 46:16a–16b. For a modern study, see Sun, *Yüan-tai Chin-hua hsüeh shu*, pp. 77–78.

which were marked by little success and much frustration, he left abruptly for Ta-tu, the capital of the empire.

In Ta-tu, things did not go well for Wu at the start. Friends accordingly urged him to give up his ambitions and return home to Chekiang. Wu refused, reportedly saying: "Life is being dependent, and death is being abandoned. Both amount to the same thing: death. What difference does it make whether I am in Chi-pei 冀北 [the Ta-tu region] or Chiang-nan?"[100] Sometime during the Ta-te 大德 reign (1297–1308) he was chosen by the Ministry of Rites to do part of the calligraphy for a copying of the Buddhist sutra of Vairocana in gold ink. The project was cancelled, however. During the Yen-yu 延祐 period (1314–1321) Wu was recommended as classics instructor for Khoshila 和世瓎 (1300–1329), a Mongol prince then dwelling in his vassal residence in Ta-tu. As a son of Hai-shan 海山, Khoshila was a potential heir to the throne of the khaghan, but in 1315 rivals had him sent out of the capital, ending Wu Chih-fang's association with him.[101] (Khoshila became emperor in 1329 and ruled for a few months until his assassination by his brother's supporters. He was the father of Toghōn Temür, last Mongol ruler of China.)

We next hear of Wu Chih-fang in the year 1324, when he was appointed an instructor in the Confucian school in Shang-tu 上都, the summer capital. In Shang-tu he did not actually obtain the position, because someone else beat him to it, but he did eventually win an interview with the governor of the city, Majartai 馬札兒臺. This interview changed his life. Majartai was impressed by Wu and hired him as a private instructor in the Chinese classics for his two sons, Toghto and Esen Temür. Toghto was to become the leading Mongol advocate of a pro-Han Chinese system of rule during the early years of Toghōn Temür's reign. At this time he was but a teenager. Wu Chih-fang became his Chinese righthand man and confidant. During Toghto's stormy career Wu Chih-fang stood by his side, providing advice and counsel. He was there when Toghto staged the coup d'état of 1340, brilliantly driving out the anti-Chinese grandees who had dominated Toghōn Temür's reign during the first seven years.[102]

Following the coup, Wu was awarded court rank of 4B and a position in the Chi-hsien yüan 集賢院, the Academy of Worthies, plus a prestige title bearing rank 3B. This was later raised to rank 2B, for which the emperor personally offered his congratulations. During the next seven

---

[100] Sung Lien, *Sung Wen-hsien kung ch'üan-chi*, 53:9a.

[101] For the politics of this period see Dardess, *Conquerors and Confucians*, pp. 18 ff.

[102] Wu quoted the *Tso-chuan* 左傳 to justify Toghto's maneuvers against his uncle Bayan. See Dardess, *Conquerors and Confucians*, p. 201 note 13.

years Wu remained active in Ta-tu as a scholar and a planner. Upon his retirement, following an indictment by a rival of Toghto's in 1347, he was awarded a prestige title of 1B and a stipend for the rest of his life. Declining the offer of 1,900 *mu* of land, he returned to P'u-chiang, where he remained until 1354. In that year at the venerable age of eighty *sui* he travelled back to Ta-tu to mourn the death of Toghto's mother, whom he must have known very well. Meanwhile in P'u-chiang he founded an academy of learning known as the Sung-lin shu-yüan 松林書院, which was located some forty *li* west of P'u-chiang town at the foot of Sung-lin Mountain.

The career of his son Wu Lai in no way resembled that of Wu Chih-fang's. His mother taught him some basic texts (such as the *Analects*, the *Hsiao ching* 孝經 [*Classic of Filial Piety*], and the *Spring and Autumn Annals* and its commentaries) before he reached the age of seven *sui*. Fang Feng, who resided at the Wu compound, changed the orthography of his name from *lai* 來 ("to come") to *lai* 萊 ("goosefoot grass"), in a deliberate allusion to an ode from the *Shih ching* 詩經:

> On the southern hills grows the nutgrass;
> On the northern hills the goosefoot.
> Happiness to our lord,
> This is the groundwork of land and home!
> Happiness to our lord!
> May he live forever.[103]

The allusion suggests that Fang Feng expected Wu Lai to become a great literatus and a pillar of society who would help an enlightened ruler to establish peace and prosperity in the realm. Fang was so impressed with the boy's progress that he betrothed his granddaughter to him and personally guided him in his studies. Wu Lai's readings were chosen from a broad range of materials, including political institutions, Yin and Yang and fortune telling, geography, and etymology.

Wu Lai attempted to pursue a career in government by entrance through the examination system.[104] This system had been reinstituted in 1315, and in 1318 local officials recommended him for a seat in the regional civil service examination to be held at Hangchow. He competed in the field of the *Spring and Autumn Annals*, was successful, and went off to Ta-tu to sit for the *chin-shih* examination. He did not pass. Departing from Ta-tu, he returned to P'u-chiang in 1320, never to attempt the examination again. His movements after 1320 are not

---

[103] Arthur Waley, tr., *The Book of Songs* (New York: Grove, 1960), p. 179.

[104] His career is outline in Sun, *Yüan-tai Chin-hua hsüeh shu*, pp. 83–88.

documented. Sun K'o-k'uan has uncovered some literary evidence suggesting that he visited Ta-tu in the late 1330s, and perhaps even in 1340, the year of the coup and of Wu Lai's death.[105] But little can be pinned down with certainty.

Wu Lai devoted a number of years to teaching at clan schools in the vicinity of P'u-chiang. He began in the 1320s at such a school in Chu-chi, where he had among his students Sung Lien, Cheng Shen 鄭深, and Cheng T'ao 鄭濤. The latter were members of the Cheng clan from P'u-chiang, while Sung Lien was a native of Chin-hua district who later transferred his residence to P'u-chiang to be near the Chengs. In 1333 or thereabouts the Cheng clan established its own *i-hsüeh* 義學 ("charitable school") in P'u-chiang, and Wu Lai was invited to become the instructor there. In 1334 Sung Lien also went to P'u-chiang to continue his studies under Wu, and Sung took over as instructor in 1335 when Wu Lai's health grew too poor to permit him to carry on. Sung Lien's formal relationship with the Cheng clan lasted well into the 1350s. The Cheng clan rules,[106] which were compiled and revised over a period of twenty or thirty years, were undoubtedly written with the advice of the clan's two teachers, Wu Lai and Sung Lien. Since Sung Lien was also a student of Liu Kuan's, it is likely that Liu Kuan's influence also came to bear in the compilation process. The clan rules, which cited Chu Hsi's *Chia-li* 家禮 (*Household Rules of Propriety*) as a precedent, were very legalistic in that they carefully prescribed punishments and procedures for dealing with infractions of various kinds.

LIU'S PREFACE

Liu's preface to the *T'ang Code with Commentary*[107] presents a view of the importance of law and punishments that fits cleanly into the Chin-hua tradition. Similarly, Wu Lai's preface to *T'ang-lü shan-yao* 唐律刪要 (*Essentials of the T'ang Code*)[108] presents a rationale for simplifying the exemplary *T'ang Code* and for using it as an aid in reinvigorating the dynastic institutions. Liu composed his preface on the occasion of a Kiangsi provincial publication of the *T'ang Code with Commentary*,

[105] Sun, *Yüan-tai Chin-hua hsüeh shu*, p. 86.

[106] The earliest edition extant is the 1397 woodblock edition of *P'u-chiang Cheng-shih ching-i pien* 浦江鄭氏旌義編, held in the National Central Library, Taipei. A microfilm is held by the Gest Library, Princeton University.

[107] The text appears in Su T'ien-chüeh 蘇天爵 (1294–1352), ed., *Kuo-ch'ao wen-lei* 國朝文類 (SPTK ed., reprint of original 1342 edition), 36:10a–12a. The text does not appear in Liu's collected works.

[108] For the text see Wu Lai, *Yüan-ying chi*, 11:4b–6a.

whereas Wu Lai likely wrote his essay somewhat later, perhaps as a response to one of the Yüan publications of the *Code*.

In his preface Liu Kuan observes that in the history of codification of penal codes the T'ang was far from the first. But in terms of the T'ang era's high civilization and ceremonial standards, the T'ang dynasty was unparalleled. T'ang Emperor T'ai-tsung (r. 626–649), at the urging of his chief adviser Wei Cheng 魏徵 (580–643),[109] ordered his officials to compile a benevolent code. After many revisions, a code was approved. T'ai-tsung's desire not to have "legal prohibitions" (*fa-chin* 法禁) predominate at the expense of "moral transforming influence" (*te-hua* 德化) was, Liu Kuan claims, on the same order as that of the most compassionate and sympathetic scholar at court. The *Commentary* to the *Code* appeared in 650, and later standardizations of the statutes, regulations, and ordinances were compiled from time to time. These traced their origins to the *Code*, which formed the permanent basis of the T'ang legal system. The *T'ang Code*, Liu argues, although it was set down in an age long ago, is nonetheless timeless in its thorough understanding of "the mutability of human feelings and the principles of law" (*jen-ch'ing fa-li chih pien* 人情法理之變). In recent times, he continues, dynasties have usually turned to the T'ang regulations (*T'ang chih* 唐制) when establishing their own institutional structures, and hence they have all taken the *T'ang Code* as their primary statutory basis. Adding his own personal assessment, Liu notes:

"Now I have often been on the tail end of court deliberations, and I have observed the clerks hugging their printed laws, standing out in front saying, 'The *Code* is like this, not like that,' arguing with crafty skill. The officials generally go along with them. But when you study their arguments, you find that they justify the status quo on the basis of the T'ang and rationalize changes on the basis of earlier emperors' decisions. [But I say,] if one insists on referring to T'ang precedents, then be sure to hit the mark. If you add to them, then you are wrong; and if you subtract from them, you are wrong. In either case, the loss is the same. Alas! The codes of the Legalists are just like the canons of the Confucians. The Five Classics convey the Way and guide the behavior of human beings for countless generations. The *Code* in twelve parts [i.e., the *T'ang Code*] hands down the law and rectifies the hearts of people. The Way must not be destroyed. And the law—can that be destroyed?"[110]

---

[109] On Wei Cheng, see Howard J. Wechsler, *Mirror to the Son of Heaven* (New Haven: Yale University Press, 1974).

[110] *Kuo-ch'ao wen-lei*, 36:11a–b.

Liu explained that he had requested the commissioner of Kiangsi to publish the Code and Commentary because students in Kiangsi, with abundant supplies of the standard Confucian canons, lacked sufficient texts of the *T'ang Code* to study. That situation, he felt, was most unfortunate. His instructions to the commissioner read as follows:

"The rules of propriety and the penal laws stem originally from the same source. The theory about 'what is not governed by the rules of propriety (*li*) is governed by the law (*fa*),' is one that pertains to the regulations of the people. It has nothing to do with the relentless deceit of the people [that is associated with harsh Legalism]. I am going to have the Lung-hsing 龍興 school in Lung-hsing [modern Nan-ch'ang 南昌, Kiangsi] publish a corrected edition of the *T'ang Code with Commentary*. I hope thereby to restore the ancient practice of studying the law (*tu fa* 讀法)." [111]

In Liu Kuan's view, penal codes should be granted a stature that was formally equivalent in value to the Confucian canons. They are fundamentally alike, he argued, in respect to the establishment of good social norms. Beyond this, Liu also argued that good government exists only when the officials are thoroughly knowledgeable legal experts. In his view, government should be administered by professionals versed in ethics and jurisprudence, and by reference to published standards, regulations, and penal codes.

WU LAI'S PREFACE

Similar ideas are evident in Wu Lai's preface. He commenced by observing that the plethora of articles in the *T'ang Code* was distressing. Furthermore, he noted that some of the articles were incomprehensible. He therefore was moved to prepare an abridgment in which he pared away the non-essentials and left in clear relief the crucial parts. In doing this he sought "to inquire into the depth of legislation in antiquity and modernity and the weights assigned to the employment of penal law." [112] Wu's abridgment is no longer extant, nor do there appear to be any extant inscriptions or colophons that would tell us about its contents. But Wu Lai revealed his theoretical premises in his preface: "The kings of old employed virtue in the governing of people and assisted that with punishments. Governors of people in later times have only employed punishments." [113]

[111] *Kuo-ch'ao wen-lei*, 36:11b–12a.
[112] *Yüan-ying chi*, 11:4b.
[113] *Yüan-ying chi*, 11:4b.

Wu Lai implies that his work on the *T'ang Code* is undertaken in order to redress the excessive reliance on penal laws in the dynasties of post-classical times. But, as his argument unfolds, it becomes clear that in his eyes the reason for this excessive reliance on punishments is the lack of professional legal expertise among the officials in charge of administering the law.

Tracing the origins of the legal systems of the later dynasties, Wu Lai observes that punishments had been instituted during the period of decline in the era of the Three Dynasties. Later, during Warring States times, Li K'uei 李悝 (ca.455 to ca.395 B.C.) of the state of Wei 魏 compiled the first penal code, the *Fa ching* 法經 (*Canon of Laws*).[114] When Lord Shang served as minister to the ruler of Ch'in, he employed that code, and Ch'in laws and institutions as then established were carried on by the Han Dynasty, which succeeded the Ch'in. In turn, from dynasty to dynasty, those laws and institutions were transmitted to the Sui. During the Sui, the *K'ai-huang lü* 開皇律 (*Code of the K'ai-huang Reign Period* [581–600]) was compiled. "This is why," Wu Lai writes, "the *T'ang Code*, which was based on that of the Sui, and the *Han Code*, which was based on that of the Ch'in, actually shared a common origin, [the *Canon of Laws* of] Li K'uei of the Warring States era, and is also why they were simply extensions [of the *Canon*'s articles dealing with] theft, violence, criminals under detention and arrests."[115] Consequently, the legal tradition began in China on principles having very little to do with the honesty and compassion that had characterized the administrations of the ancient sage-kings. The sage-kings' attitude towards law had been summed up in the old adage, "through punishments there may come to be no punishments."[116] In other words, the proper aim of punishments was to make people fear them. Fearing them, the people would behave properly, leaving no cause to employ punishments.

But the Ch'in had spoiled this ancient ideal, Wu Lai argues, by burning the ancient books and burying the scholars in an orgy of violence. The Ch'in ordered all persons in the realm to study "laws" (*fa*-

---

[114] On the *Fa-ching*, first attested in the *Chin shu* 晉書, compiled in early T'ang, see T. Pokora, "The Canon of Laws by Li K'uei: A Double Falsification," *Archiv Orientalni*, 27 (1959), pp. 96–121; and Kobayashi Shigeki 小林茂樹, "Ri Ke hōkyō kō 李悝法経考," *Tōhō gakuhō* 東方学報 (Kyōto), 4 (1934), pp. 266–314.

[115] *Tao* 盗, *tsei* 賊, *ch'iu* 囚, and *pu* 捕 were categories of articles in the *Fa-ching*, supposedly. There were two others: *tsa* 雜 (miscellaneous) and *chü* 具 (general). For a survey of early codes, see Derk Bodde and Clarence Morris, *Law in Traditional China* (Cambridge: Harvard University Press, 1967), pp. 52–60.

[116] From the *Book of Documents* (*Shang shu* 尚書), tr., Legge, *The Chinese Classics*, vol. 3, pp. 58–59.

ling 法令) and "to take *li* 吏 [clerks or legal functionaries] as their teachers." In later times the Sui resembled the Ch'in most closely, in terms of its reliance on laws for governing the realm. But the Ch'in and Sui differed in the nature of the historical background of their respective rises to power. The Ch'in arose after the death of Confucius in an age of "heterodox teachings" (*i-tuan* 異端). Contradictory and irresponsible notions were peddled widely and highest regard was paid to military exploits (*shou-kung* 首功 or "head counts"). Governing was accomplished by clerks who applied the laws.

Different conditions affected the nature of the Sui legal system. At the time of the Sui founding, the region of Chiang-tso 江左 (the area of modern Nanking), where the Ch'i 齊 (479–502) and Liang 梁 (502–557) dynasties had been located, was an area of utter decadence. In the north, the region formerly occupied by the Northern Chou (556–581) and the Northern Ch'i 北齊 (550–577), people "adopted the practices of the western barbarians" (*hsi fan-i* 習蕃夷). The fortuitous reunification by the Sui did not completely purify the realm of these two kinds of pernicious influences, and this was because the officials who deliberated on policy matters at court were typically "pedestrian clerks" (*su-li* 俗吏) and "petty bureaucrats" (*mi-yen chih t'u* 米鹽之徒). They administered the realm harshly and failed to exercise sufficient "discipline" (*chi* 紀). The Sui rulers despised the frivolity of such people, but were unable to do anything about it because they failed to perceive the importance of the "authentic" scholar. Consequently, the Sui rulers, like those of the Ch'in, "governed by employing laws and clerks."

Ch'in and Sui were thus deficient, not because the employment of laws in the administration of the realm was inherently wrong. Rather, both dynasties failed because both failed to staff the government with scholars who knew the laws. The Ch'in ignored the scholar altogether, which was tantamount, Wu says, to "doing violence to oneself" (*tzu-pao* 自暴). The Sui, however, failed to acknowledge the nature of "the authentic scholar" (*chen-ju* 真儒), and therefore was unable to employ him properly in the pursuit of good administration. This was equivalent to "throwing away oneself" (*tzu-ch'i* 自棄).[117]

A comparison of the two states Ch'in and Sui reveals that the Ch'in was more violent than the other when it relied on laws exclusively; but the Sui employed the *Code* in a manner that was, in effect, "the copying of the old wisdom of the Ch'in, and perhaps much worse." Both dynasties collapsed after very short reigns, "as though they came down

---

[117] *Tzu-pao* and *tzu-ch'i* are terms from *Mencius*, IV/11. See Legge, tr., *The Chinese Classics*, vol. 2, pp. 301–302.

the same track." Both exalted the pedestrian clerk and both established the laws as rules for all to follow. Both proclaimed "the great detail of the laws" (*fa-lü chih mi* 法律之密) and "the intensity of their surveillance and castigation" (*tu-tse chih chün* 督責之峻).[118] And both gave full expression to the techniques of repression ("iron collars and rope bonds" [*ch'ien-chih shu-po* 鉗制束縛]).[119] In those times, conniving and jealous individuals at court were suspicious of the entire empire. The ruin that brought down the two dynasties was a product of inadequate "moral transforming influence" and the excessive employment of punishments.

The falls of Ch'in and Sui being such, "the Han gathered together the Ch'in laws with magnanimity and benevolence, and the T'ang transformed the Sui code with benevolence and justice. They intended to reverse at once the policies of Ch'in and Sui," Wu wrote. This kind of reversal, however, is something only the scholar can perform. "Pedestrian clerks" could not fathom such a task. Only the scholar could "establish the dynastic laws (*kuo fa* 國法) and embellish the court ceremonies." Although the Han and T'ang rulers had not been sage kings of great compassion and sympathy, they still were able to restore orderly administration to their realms. Their reigns may have been marked by entrapments and falsified indictments of innocent officials, and the people may have been driven to great hardship. But because these rulers had followed the scholars in constructing their dynasties, they managed to circumvent the massive chaos that would otherwise have beset the empire. Soon after their dynasties were established, scholars of the laws appeared, and they put the legal texts in order. This in turn made possible the real achievements of the Han and the T'ang; without the scholars who were experts in law, neither era would have accomplished anything worthwhile.

In the Han the scholars Ma Jung 馬融 (79–166) and Cheng Hsüan 鄭玄 (127–200) prepared editions of the codes. In the T'ang it was primarily Chang-sun Wu-chi who compiled the important commentary to the *T'ang Code*. Revisions and deletions were made as appropriate. Hence, in the Han, cases were frequently decided by reference to the canons, whereupon "the root of the laws (*fa-lü chih pen* 法律之本) was reached"; and, in T'ang, the civil-service recruitment system induced

---

[118] Li Ssu 李斯, in his letter to the Second Emperor of Ch'in, referred to these techniques of control. See *Shih chi* 史記 (Peking: Chung-hua Shu-chü, 1972), 87:2554. See also Derk Bodde, *China's First Unifier* (Leiden: Brill, 1938), pp. 12–55, 205; and Hsiao Kung-ch'üan, "Legalism and Autocracy."

[119] On the *ch'ien* or "iron collar" used in Han times on persons sentenced to penal servitude, see Niida Noboru, *Chūgoku hōseishi kenkyū: keihō* 中国法制史研究: 刑法 (Tokyo: Tōkyō Diagaku Tōyō Bunka Kenkyūjō, 1959), pp. 75–77, 607.

scholars to become acquainted with the concrete aspects of the laws and to avoid thereby "empty talk" about things of which they were ignorant. Achievements of this order, Wu Lai says, are attributable to "the meritorious deeds of the scholars who served in government." The ancient sage-kings had been "intelligent in the use of the punishments" and had "assisted in moral education,"[120] so their great achievements cannot be remotely matched by the Han and the T'ang. But, given the absence of sage-kings in the real world of Yüan China, the models of the Han and T'ang rulers are the only relevant ones, not the ideal types of the ancient past. Wu observes that the true scholar should never be ignorant of the matters that are normally handled by the "pedestrian clerks," nor should clerks themselves fail to comprehend the affairs of the scholars. In short, in the absence of sage-kings, the administration of the realm depended upon the scholars and the clerical functionaries. To the extent that the scholars are "authentic" and well versed in both ethics and jurisprudence, the dynasty will stand a chance of being well administered. Summing up his message, Wu wrote: "In placing the primary value on moral transforming influence, one cannot but depend upon punishments. And in depending upon punishments, one cannot but endeavor to promote moral transformation. This is where the Han and the T'ang succeeded, and where the Ch'in and the Sui failed. Here indeed is the lesson for our later times."[121]

Wu's remarks are of course oblique commentaries on the *wei-cheng* chapter of the *Analects* quoted above. In tone they echo the teachings of the Chin-hua master Hsü Ch'ien. But they go still further to articulate the importance of legal studies to scholars who wish to serve in government. In Wu's view, as in Liu Kuan's, legal studies and "moral transformation" go hand in hand.

One of Wu Lai's regrets in life was his inability to serve in government as an official. A premature baby, Wu Lai had started life with a physical frailty that he never overcame. But he compensated for his infirmity by urging his students to go forth to serve. In his own words, "How can the ways of the world and the affairs of human beings be fathomed? For the methods of the scholars and the principles of government, it is necessary to climb high." These were his words of advice to his students Cheng Hsüan 鄭玄 and Cheng T'ao 鄭濤 when they were starting on their journey to Ta-tu to take up positions there.[122] "Climbing high" (*p'an-*

---

[120] From the *Book of Documents*, tr., Legge, *The Chinese Classics*, vol. 3, p. 58.

[121] *Yüan-ying chi*, 11:6a.

[122] From a poem written on the occasion of their departure from P'u-chiang. *Yüan-ying chi*, 2:7b.

yüan 攀援) suggests hanging onto the coattails of the noble in order to ascend to a higher position. This should be done, Wu Lai urges, in order to advance "the methods of the scholars" (*ju shu* 儒術), i.e., the Confucian principles of government. Wu Lai's students accomplished this, since with the patronage of Toghto they obtained access to the *Ching-yen* 經筵 or "Classics Mat" in Ta-tu, the setting for Confucian instruction of the emperor.

HUANG CHIN'S EXAMINATION QUESTIONS

Huang Chin 黃溍 (1277–1357), a native of I-wu district in Wu-chou Circuit, was perhaps the most distinguished Chin-hua scholar in Yüan government. Most of his career was undertaken in the capacity of "clerk," which meant that he was deeply involved in penal matters.[123] Huang Chin is the best example of a scholar who carried out the teachings of the Chin-hua school.

As a young man Huang studied poetry under Fang Feng, the loyalist poet mentioned above as a teacher also of Wu Lai. He had no career to speak of prior to 1315, when, at the age of thirty-eight *sui*, he obtained the *chin-shih* degree in the first year of the examination system. From then until 1331 he served in a series of positions that did not exceed clerical status. In that year Emperor Wen-tsung invited him to court as a compiler in the Dynastic History Bureau in the Hanlin Academy. He retired shortly to mourn the death of his father, but under the succeeding emperor he became an Erudite (*po-shih* 博士) in the Kuo-tzu hsüeh 國子學 (National College), a position he held for six years. From 1340 to 1350 he held a series of important positions in and out of the capital. He retired from active service in 1350, spending the last seven years of his life at home.

Huang Chin combined all the characteristics of the Chin-hua school. He was an avid supporter of the teachings of Chu Hsi, and he was an expert in the law. During his career, particularly during the years of prominence after 1340, Huang had occasion to draft questions to be used in the examining of candidates for degrees. The Yüan examination system set separate standards of achievement for Han Chinese and non-Han Chinese in an effort to ensure chances for success for the Mongols and Central Asians, who were less likely to master the subtleties of Chinese classical learning. Huang Chin wrote questions for both categories.[124] And in both categories he insisted that the candidate have a

---

[123] For Huang's life and career, see Sun, *Yüan-tai Chin-hua hsüeh shu*, pp. 109–126.

[124] *Chin-hua Huang hsien-sheng wen-chi* 金華黃先生文集 (SPTK ed.), *chüan* 20, contains Huang's examination questions. For this statement see 20:1b.

profound grasp of the moral priorities of Tao-hsüeh and of the prag-matic priorities of legal institutions.

A series of questions (*ts'e-wen* 策問) for Mongols and Central Asians in the capital examinations given in Shang-tu includes the exhortation "Do not indulge in extremely lofty discourses,"[125] meaning, of course, that the candidates should do their level best to stay close to reality in their answers. Another series for the same category of examinees includes eighteen questions on the following topics (among others): Why are there bandits today despite the enlightened rule of the court? How should the people be best treated so that they do not become bandits? How can the army of clerks who staff the bureaucratic offices be kept incorrupt? What is the best plan for equalizing the distribution of wealth?

Huang's questioning demanded a good deal of sophistication from the candidates. In the question about how to keep the clerks incorrupt, Huang inquired as follows: Some say that if the regulations are strict and salaries are adequate, then the clerks will not become corrupt. And yet today regulations are strict and salaries are adequate, but the func-tionaries are still corrupt. "How do you explain this?" he asked.[126]

Huang expected his examinees to question the relevance of the models of antiquity. In a question on governance (*chih* 治), Huang noted that the sages and worthies always took examples from antiquity. Confucius, he pointed out, told Yen Yüan 顏淵 about the rites and music for the four generations, and Mencius told Duke Wen of T'eng 滕文公 about the ancient well-field system and the schools. But Yen Yüan had no position from which he could exercise Confucius' advice and Duke Wen of T'eng had not the will (*chih* 志) to act on the advice of Mencius. In later historical times rulers had occasionally tried to carry out such advice, but they never succeeded to the full. Today, Huang asked, is there still the same need to advocate the old theories?[127]

Another question written by Huang Chin addresses the priorities that rulers should establish in instituting the regulations of government. Huang noted that the establishment of institutions (*fa* 法) required a proper order. One who knows the priorities, he said, will be best prepared to manage the institutions. In antiquity, he noted, there were ten priorities that went as follows:

1. Clarity in promotion and demotion.
2. Relying on the fortunate.
3. Excellence in operation of the tribute recruitment system.

---

[125] *Chin-hua Huang hsien-sheng wen-chi*, 20:3a–7a.
[126] *Chin-hua Huang hsien-sheng wen-chi*, 20:5b.
[127] *Chin-hua Huang hsien-sheng wen-chi*, 20:5b–6a.

4. Selection of office chiefs.
5. Equalization of public lands.
6. Care given to agriculture and sericulture.
7. Cultivation of military preparedness.
8. Reduction of *corvée* duties.
9. Extension of grace to all the people.
10. Upholding the commands and laws.

Nowadays, Huang asked, which of these items should be regarded as most urgent, which the least?[128]

Huang also demanded a critical understanding of the teachings of the classics. One question written for Mongols and Central Asians required that the examinee demonstrate the relationship between the teachings of the classics and the needs of actual government. In his question Huang noted that Hu Yüan 胡瑗 (993–1059), one of the founders of Northern Sung Neo-Confucianism, had said: "If one exhausts the meaning of the Classics (*ch'iung ching* 窮經) without being able to apply it, then the Classics are merely empty words." Hu also said, "If in doing things one does not study the ancient lessons, then the things will be done carelessly." Huang then called on the examinees to answer the question: All the scholars of by-gone days spoke about "the meaning of the Classics" (*ching-i* 經義), but what did they actually accomplish in the way of good government?[129]

A series of questions for *Han-jen* 漢人 (a special category of Chinese, referring mainly to northerners) who were students in the National College required the candidates to analyze the ancient ways of doing things and the ancient ways of studying the Classics.[130]

Huang asked them to answer the question, Why have not Legalists and Taoists disappeared in Yüan times despite the predominance of Confucian statecraft (*ju-shu* 儒術)? When Shen Pu-hai 申不害 and Han Fei Tzu 韓非子 were in favor in Ch'in times, rule was extremely harsh on the people. And when the Taoists Chuang Tzu and Lieh Tzu 列子 were the rage during the Chin 晉 period, people indulged in decadent pursuits. But "in our dynasty" (*wo kuo-chia* 我國家) priority has been given to Confucian techniques of government, of which the radiance has spread to the four corners of the world. The scholar-elite (*chin-shen hsien-sheng* 搢紳先生), Huang stated, uphold the ritual conventions of the Classics, but they "dare not bring up the theories of the Legalists." Nor, he added, dare they mention the teachings of the Taoists. And yet the heterodox

---

[128] *Chin-hua Huang hsien-sheng wen-chi*, 20:6b.
[129] *Chin-hua Huang hsien-sheng wen-chi*, 20:6a–b.
[130] *Chin-hua Huang hsien-sheng wen-chi*, 20:7a–16b.

philosophies of the non-Confucian schools have made an indelible imprint on the minds of men. Is this because, he asked, men of high purpose are blind to the needs of the times?[131]

On the matter of statecraft, Huang Chin's questions are equally probing. In one question[132] he noted that in antiquity there were four institutional aspects of a state: 1. the well-field system; 2. the enfeoffment system (*feng-chien* 封建); 3. the school system; and 4. the system of corporal punishments (*jou-hsing* 肉刑). In contemporary times, Huang said, only the school system still obtained in society, while the other three elements of the state had withered away. He then presented three questions:

1. In the absence of the well-field system, how is the state to ensure that the people are not utterly impoverished, i.e., that wealth is fairly distributed?

2. In the absence of the enfeoffment system, in which fiefs were permanently designated and were in turn staffed by permanent officer corps, how is the state to ensure that the clerks who staff the local government offices are not turned over so frequently that they cannot normalize governance?

3. In the absence of a strict system of corporal punishments for misdeeds, and of the replacement of the old system by a set of regulations governing conduct, how is the state to ensure that people do not unconcernedly engage in illicit behavior?

But Huang questioned even the school system. Noting that it "exists tenuously by virtue of statute" (*i chu ling chin ts'un* 以著令僅存), it nevertheless is inadequately developed. As a consequence of this, the sacred teachings are insufficiently spread among the people. In such a condition, he asked, how is the state to ensure that people will be allowed to bring their natural endowments to perfect and full development? Concluding, Huang exhorted the candidate: "You have studied in the schools and have been devoted to learning that is useful (*yu yung chih hsüeh* 有用之學). Have you not studied discussions of this? Answer by evaluating the appropriate aspects of [the systems of] past and present."

Huang was especially concerned about the problems of institutional change, and he was accordingly hard on those scholars who insisted that antique institutions retained their validity timelessly. In a question written for Mongols and Central Asians, he indicated his assumptions clearly at the outset: "The government of an age must have laws (*fa* 法) [that are appropriate] to that age. The theories (*lun* 論) of Confucian

---

[131] *Chin-hua Huang hsien-sheng wen-chi*, 20:14b.
[132] *Chin-hua Huang hsien-sheng wen-chi*, 20:9a–b.

scholars commonly assume that government in antiquity purely employed the *tao*, while government of later times purely employed or law."[133] The question for the candidates, then, was whether or not the standard Confucian theories about government were correct. As Huang put it, "Does the empire really have laws which lie outside the *tao*?"

Huang Chin started out his career in government as a clerk (*li*) and consequently he was fully conversant with legal matters. He saw clearly the importance of professional expertise in the law. This understanding is reflected in his examination questions, of which the best example is the following question for *Han-jen* 漢人 in the National College:

"Question: Among the great scholars (*ta ju* 大儒) of ancient times are those who are recorded in the histories for their expertise in legal matters (*wen-fa li shih* 文法吏事 [lit. 'written codes and the affairs of clerks']). And so, legal matters are also matters of which the gentleman (*chün-tzu* 君子) should be knowledgeable. How may he ignore them? Confucius said, 'Legal experts of antiquity were able to reduce punishments, and that was the root. Legal experts of today never fail to get the guilty, and that is the branch [i.e., the pursuit of the wrong goal].' Now, causing there to be no lawsuits and thereby reduce punishments is indeed a difficult thing.... The Studies of Law Codes (*lü-hsüeh* 律學) have been abolished for a long time. [Note: T'ang and Sung both established *lü-hsüeh* as a field of study for the examination system.] What the judicial officer (*li-kuan* 理官) is responsible for is not something the students [today] learn about. But the intentions of the former sage kings in instituting the laws (*li-fa chih i* 立法之意) can be discerned by investigating the books [i.e., the classics]."[134]

Huang then asked the Mongols and Central Asians who were sitting for the examination to answer the question by drawing on their knowledge of these matters as best they could.

There seems little room for doubt that Huang Chin and his Chin-hua colleagues believed in the importance of professional legal studies by the officialdom. Efficient administration required it. A just legal system required it. And the dynasty required it if it was to function properly. Legal learning lay at the heart of what the official did as the agent of the emperor.

The law also lay at the heart of the role of the emperor. Wu Lai had made this clear in his discussion of the reign of T'ang T'ai-tsung. Wu argued that the reign of T'ai-tsung was a valuable lesson to rulers of later

[133] *Chin-hua Huang hsien-sheng wen-chi*, 20:16b.
[134] *Chin-hua Huang hsien-sheng wen-chi*, 20:14b.

times, more valuable in fact than the examples of the sage kings of antiquity. In a preface to the *Ti-fan* 帝範 (*Plan for an Emperor*) of T'ang T'ai-tsung, which had been presented to the court when Yüan armies were attacking the Po 僰 tribe in Yunnan, Wu Lai noted that T'ai-tsung had ensured the success of his dynasty by enshrining the institutions and laws (*fa-tu tien-chang* 法度典章) in the ancestral temple of the ruling house.[135]

T'ang T'ai-tsung knew that his successors might not be great rulers, and for that reason he set forth in the the *Ti-fan* the principles and laws by which his successors could rule. Wu Lai believed that in this way the T'ang founder made it possible for the T'ang dynasty to thrive. The basis of T'ang success, then, was the continuity of its institutions and laws, and this in turn permitted mediocre rulers to govern effectively.

The laws of a dynasty, Wu Lai noted, are the product of the founding age. They are born in times of crisis. "The Han received the chaos of the Ch'in Dynasty, whereupon Emperor Kao-tsu established the laws (*fa* 法) of the Han house. The T'ang succeeded to the chaos of the Sui Dynasty, whereupon T'ai-tsung established the regulations of the T'ang house."[136] Both the Han and the T'ang, he suggested, succeeded by humanizing the harsh legalistic states that had preceded them. But more than that, both the Han and the T'ang discovered ways to prolong the institutions that the respective founders had devised in the course of the wars and struggles of the founding periods. Similarly, the Yüan Dynasty should pay careful heed to the lessons of the founder, in this case Khubilai Khaghan.

The Chin-hua approach to government was quite "utilitarian" in its endorsement of the historical models rather than of the mythical sage models, and in its down-to-earth stress on the importance of the legal bases of orderly administration. But these attitudes were also in accord with the teachings of Chu Hsi. This in turn is one reason why Chu Hsi's teachings were revered in Chin-hua. Chu Hsi had never claimed that utilitarian values were wrong. What distinguished him was his stress on moral reform that began with the heart or mind of the individual, whether ruler or private subject. As Hsiao Kung-ch'üan has shown, Chu Hsi disputed the naive claim that the institutions of the Three Dynasties of antiquity were suited to contemporary times. In Chu's words, "Even if

[135] For a note on the *Ti-fan*, see *Ssu-k'u ch'üan-shu tsung-mu* 四庫全書總目 (Taipei: Yeewen, 1969, 3rd. printing), 91:27a; it is noted here that the expedition against the Po took place in 1325. For Wu Lai's essay, "Tu T'ang T'ai-tsung *Ti-fan* 讀唐太宗帝範," see *Yüan-ying chi*, 10:1a–3a.

[136] Wu Lai, *Yüan-ying chi*, 10:2b–3a.

they were forcefully applied, one fears that unforeseen evils would arise...."[137] Chu Hsi believed that, since the times had changed, even the sages would do things differently if they were reborn in the present.

A fundamental issue separated the Yüan Chin-hua scholars from Chu Hsi, however, and this was the willingness of the Chin-hua scholars to recognize that dynastic institutions could be made to function well even in the absence of moral rulers. It did not matter to the Chin-hua scholars that the rulers may have been incapable of transforming themselves into superior beings or of fully accepting the moral judgments and injunctions of the Confucian scholars. They could live with that. What mattered to them was that the rulers permit the "authentic scholars" to administer the realm on the rulers' behalf. In that case, the empire would be well managed, and the efficiency or non-efficiency of the ruler himself would matter little. This is not to say that the Chin-hua scholars were totally indifferent to the moral quality of their rulers—far from it. But they were fully capable of accommodating themselves to the contrary situation. This made the Yüan administration more humane, they thought, than it would otherwise be.

When Chu Yüan-chang established his supremacy in Chekiang, Chin-hua scholars were ready to supply expertise and advise. The fact that Chu was not a well-educated Confucian gentleman mattered little, since by that time the Chin-hua scholars had already worked out their political philosophy of pragmatic accommodation. Chin-hua scholars did not have a monopoly on this form of thinking. There were other scholars in the realm who similarly served the Mongols, and Chu Yüan-chang, with pragmatic dedication to the goal of improving administration. But it was the Chin-hua scholars who articulated these values most clearly. They stood out in Yüan times, and they continued to stand out in the early Ming period. They gave the Yüan-Ming transition a degree of continuity it might otherwise have lacked. They helped to make it possible for Mongols and Chu Yüan-chang, who had in common the military origins of their regimes and their status as outsiders to the elite cultural tradition of China, to establish and maintain regimes that were accepted by the literati as legitimate.

One of the hallmarks of Yüan government was its reliance on non-scholar clerks to administer even the most important agencies. The Mongol rulers severely curtailed the role of the traditional Chinese scholar in government. Recruitment into government service did not take place chiefly through the examination system, although after 1315 it did serve to bring a small number of scholars into government. The vast

[137] See Hsiao Kung-ch'üan, *Chung-kuo cheng-chih ssu-hsiang shih*, vol. 4, p. 504.

majority of persons serving in government received their positions through recommendation. Such functionaries, whether Han Chinese or not, were literate. Certainly they were aware of the Confucian tradition. But they were not committed necessarily to the preservation of that tradition. In a sense, they were technicians who espoused no ideology. They held important duties and responsibilities in the legal system. They knew the laws from experience. They even had their own professional literature consisting of handbooks like the *Li-hsüeh chih-nan* 吏學指南 (*Guide to Bureaucratic Learning*).[138]

In this context it was essential, in the eyes of scholars who were committed to the Confucian tradition, to reformulate the role of the scholar. Since the alternative of abandoning the scholarly Confucian tradition was not openly contemplated, the task for these literati was to devise a means of merging the roles and learning of the scholar and the clerk. If that could be done, the scholar would find a valid and useful role in government, one that would mesh with the realities of Mongol rule.

The stakes in this reformulation were high. They went beyond the simple issue of "bread and butter" for the scholarly class. Behind Wu Lai's and Liu Kuan's formulations of the role of the scholar lay a sharp dissatisfaction with the notion of a professional clerk class that administered the realm without firm commitments to Confucian beliefs and ideology. Without those commitments, the clerical functionaries remained the servants of the Mongol rulers. For the Chin-hua scholars it was essential that a way be found to avert the complete takeover of administration by un-Confucian bureaucrats. The Chin-hua scholars found the answer in their reformulation of the scholar role as one that combined the learning and expertise of the clerk with those of the Confucian scholar.

---

[138] The full title of this work is *Hsi-li yu-hsüeh chih-nan* 習吏幼學指南 (*A Guide in Beginner's Studies for Learning How to be a Clerk*). It is discussed in Miyazaki Ichisada 宮崎市定, "Sō Gen jidai no hōsei to saiban kikō 宋元時代の法制と裁判機構," *Ajiashi kenkyū* アジア史研究, vol. 4 (Kyoto: Tōyōshi Kenkyūkai 東洋史研究会, 1964), pp. 245–249. For further notes on this text see Paul Ch'en, *Chinese Legal Tradition under the Mongols*, p. 60 note 62. The *Li-hsüeh chih-nan* was one of many handbooks for clerks in Yüan times.

Wu Ch'eng and the Perpetuation of the Classical Heritage in the Yüan

DAVID GEDALECIA

Wu Ch'eng 吳澄 (1249–1333), the premier classical scholar and Neo-Confucian thinker during the Yüan period, lived a long and productive life spanning both the late Sung era and a good portion of the Yüan. His prolific scholarship involved him in searching and influential explications of all of the major Confucian classics and in revitalizing philosophic trends, so as to preserve and enrich the cultural heritage. His life is testimony to this unified intellectual outlook.

This essay discusses the importance of Wu Ch'eng in the intellectual history of the Yüan by examining the nature and development of his scholarly achievements, how those achievements were grounded in particular philosophic viewpoints, and his perception of the continuity of the tradition to which those achievements made a contribution.

I. SCHOLARSHIP IN THE LIFE AND CAREER OF WU CH'ENG[1]

Wu Ch'eng's earliest years, as described by his principal biographer and disciple, Yü Chi 虞集 (1272–1348), manifest quite typical strains in Confucian hagiography. While one is hard-pressed to accept the apocryphal events surrounding his birth, the descriptions of his precocious studiousness from his fifth to his seventh years are nevertheless revealing,

---

[1] The biographical sketch in this section is based on the four major sources for the life of Wu Ch'eng: the funeral tablet (*shen-tao-pei* 神道碑) composed by Chieh Hsi-ssu 揭傒斯 (1274–1344); the record of conduct, or family biography (*hsing-chuang* 行狀) completed by Yü Chi 虞集 in 1335; the chronological biography (*nien-p'u* 年譜) completed by Wei Su 危素 (1295–1372) in 1365; and the standard treatment in *Yüan shih* 元史. All of these appear in WWC: 1756, as well as in the last volume of WWC: *chen-pen*. Yü Chi's piece also appears in his collected works, *Tao-yüan hsüeh-ku lu* 道園學古錄 (SPTK ed.), 44:2b–14b. For the standard biography see YS 171:4011–4014.

Of the four, Yü Chi's work is the earliest and most definitive source; all others derive from it in varying degrees. Extensive information on Wu's classical work appears in its last four pages. Shao Yüan-p'ing 邵遠平 (*chin-shih* 1664), in *Yüan-shih lei-pien* 元史類編, provides excerpts from some of Wu's prefaces to his *Observations* on the classics.

The sketch here, since it is a composite, shows documentation only for quoted passages or for viewpoints particular to one of the individual biographers.

and it is likely that he was gifted. We learn that for fear of disturbing his mother, who was concerned about his excessive diligence, he shielded the light from his candle while he committed to memory substantial portions of the *Analects*, *Mencius*, and the Five Classics.

After these two years of effort, Wu Ch'eng placed well in the county-level examinations at his village school in Ch'ung-jen 崇仁, southeastern Kiangsi, and soon progressed to the study of the commentaries of Chu Hsi 朱熹 (1130–1200) on the *Great Learning* and other works. Later in his life he would comment on this period of classical study:

"In my tenth year [1258], by chance among my old books, I discovered Chu Hsi's commentaries on the *Great Learning* and the *Doctrine of the Mean*. I was so overjoyed upon reading them that from this time on I made a point of reciting the former from memory more than twenty times early each day. For three years it was this way, and later on, when I studied the *Doctrine of the Mean* and the various classics, it was like having the power of splitting bamboo, without the slightest resistance or obstruction in understanding." [2]

It was during these early years that Wu so impressed a local bookseller with his budding erudition that the latter loaned him books for study because Wu's family could not afford to buy them.[3] In his fifteenth year (1263), a year after he took the examination in the prefectural seat in Fu-chou 撫州 (Lin-ch'uan 臨川), Wu wrote four admonitions on such themes as reverence (*ching* 敬) and harmony (*ho* 和), as well as cautionary pieces on self-cultivation. These all reflect the ideas of the major Sung dynasty Neo-Confucian thinkers, and indicate that Wu was leaning in this direction prior to assuming any formal academic training under a Neo-Confucian master.

In 1264, Ch'eng Jo-yung 程若庸 (*chin-shih* 1268) was engaged to lecture at the Lin-ju 臨汝 Academy in Fu-chou. Ch'eng was a scholar in the Chu Hsi lineage, having learned Confucian doctrine from Jao Lu 饒魯, a native of Kiangsi and himself a disciple of Chu Hsi's son-in-law, Huang Kan 黃榦 (1152–1221).[4] Wu became a student at the academy under Ch'eng, and made a lifelong acquaintance when he befriended the master's young cousin, Ch'eng Chü-fu 程鉅夫 (1249–1318).

As a student at the Lin-ju Academy, Wu demonstrated his growing mastery of the classical tradition by pressing his mentor on the relationship between the *Great Learning* and the *Lesser Learning* (*Hsiao-hsüeh*

---

[2] WWC: 1756, *shou*: 22a (*nien-p'u*).

[3] WWC: 1756, 22b.

[4] On Ch'eng Jo-yung, note Huang Tsung-hsi 黃宗羲, *Sung Yüan hsüeh-an* 宋元學案 (Shanghai, 1933), 83: 92–97. Ch'eng's principal work is the *Hsing-li tzu-hsün* 性理字訓.

小學); the sources say that this pleased Ch'eng Jo-yung and that a
master-disciple relationship soon developed between the two men.

During the first three years of his discipleship, Wu Ch'eng prepared an
edition of the *Classic of Filial Piety* (*Hsiao-ching* 孝經) and completed a
supplementary commentary which drew together various writings on the
subject of filiality.[5] At this same time Wu also composed a sketch of the
Confucian line of transmission of the *tao*, entitled *Tao-t'ung t'u* 道統圖,
in which he revealed that he had accepted at this young age the burden
of continuing the Sung heritage.[6] At this juncture Wu was firmly
dedicated to classical scholarship, and the next twenty years proved to be
his first productive period in this area.

Wu's dedication to scholarship also involved his own understanding of
tao, of which he later confessed he had not as yet become fully aware: "I
truly utilized all my energies in this and suddenly I seemed to gain
understanding and was freely able to put it into practice. However,... I
certainly did not self-righteously presume that my understanding surpassed that of others."[7] Between 1267 and 1280 we cannot accurately
date Wu's intellectual development. But we do know that sometime prior
to 1280 he commenced study under the scholar Ch'eng Shao-k'ai 程紹開
(d. 1280). This scholar introduced Wu to the ideas of Lu Hsiang-shan
陸象山 (1139–1192) and attempted to harmonize them with the teachings of Chu Hsi. This no doubt widened Wu's intellectual range.[8]

Wu's dedication becomes all the more meaningful when we learn that
he had become diffident about pursuing an official career through the
examination system, despite strong family pressure in that direction.
Thus he never advanced beyond the provincial examination (*hsiang-shih*
鄉試). Wei Su 危素 (1295–1372), another of Wu's biographers, attributes
Wu's failure to capture the *chin-shih* degree to a non-competitive streak
in his personality.[9] Yü Chi, however, attributes it to the malaise which
overtook young scholars whose intellectual world was in transition as the
fortunes of the Sung declined in the decade of the 1270s.[10] Yan-shuan
Lao's essay in this volume also comments on this trend of the times.

In 1280, after the Mongol conquest, the scholar Cheng Sung 鄭松
invited Wu to live in the mountains southwest of Ch'ung-jen in Kiangsi.
Like Wu, Cheng had also failed to pass the examination for the *chin-shih*

---

[5] WWC: 1756, *shou*: 24a (*nien-p'u*).

[6] The actual passage is given in *Tao-yüan hsüeh-ku lu*, 44:4a–b, and in YS 171:4013, but
only named in WWC: 1756, *shou*: 24b (*nien-p'u*).

[7] *Tao-yüan hsüeh-ku lu*, 44:4b–5a.

[8] *Sung Yüan hsüeh-an*, 94:1, 84:120; Lien Chu 連柱 comp., *Kuang-hsin fu-chih*
廣信府志 (1783 ed.), 17:48a, 16:45b–46a.

[9] WWC: 1756, *shou*: 25a.

[10] *Tao-yüan hsüeh-ku lu*, 44:3b, 5a.

degree. But he had become well known for his study of the *Huang-chi ching-shih shu* 皇極經世書 (*Book on the Supreme Principles Governing the World*), composed by the Sung Neo-Confucian Shao Yung 邵雍 (1011–1077). This was a cosmological treatise which Wu had studied himself more than a decade before.[11]

Cheng's work in extending Shao's scheme of periodization and dynastic succession involved isolating the Sung from the alien Liao, Chin and Yüan.[12] This may have had a bearing on Wu's uncertainties concerning Mongol rule and the course of "the transmission of the Way" (*tao-t'ung*), but, whatever the effect, Wu accomplished a prodigious amount of textual collation and punctuation during these years in retreat. He completed his earlier work on the *Classic of Filial Piety* (in 1281) and prepared textual studies of the *Book of Changes, Book of Poetry, Spring and Autumn Annals, Classic of Rites and Ceremonies* (*I-li* 儀禮), as well as emendations of the *Record of Ritual* (in 1282). He returned home in 1283. During these three years of voluntary retreat, Wu's studies of the classical texts formed the basis of his subsequent efforts to refurbish and reinvigorate the classical heritage.

In 1286, his boyhood friend Ch'eng Chü-fu, under imperial decree, sought out worthies in Chiang-nan for service to the Yüan.[13] Although Ch'eng could not persuade Wu Ch'eng to serve in the capital (which Wu visited for several months in 1287), he eventually requested that Wu's classical editions be transcribed and disseminated: "Although Wu Ch'eng is unwilling to serve, the classics which he has edited convey the essentials of the sages and can be used to teach the students of the National College. Thus they should be transmitted throughout the realm."[14] In this way, Ch'eng Chü-fu balanced his friendship for Wu with his official duties. Ch'eng's recognition of Wu's achievements brought Wu into the scholarly limelight.

Thus in 1295, when Wu traveled near the present-day city of Nan-ch'ang (in Kiangsi), he was approached by scholars interested in the classics. Among them was Yüan Ming-shan 元明善 (1269–1322) who, after inquiring about the *Spring and Autumn Annals*, was so impressed by Wu's explications that he told Wu: "Your teaching is the teaching of

---

[11] A biography of Cheng can be found in Chu K'uei-chang 朱奎章 and Hu Fang-hsing 胡芳杏 , comps., *Lo-an hsien-chih* 樂安縣志 [Kiangsi] (1871 ed.), 8:18a, in the section on Sung literati. The date 1280 is given in WWC: 1756, *shou*:26a (*nien-p'u*). Wu Ch'eng has a preface to Shao's work in WWC: 1756, 10:4b–5b.

[12] *Lo-an hsien-chih*, 8:18a.

[13] The date here is that given by Yü Chi in *Tao-yüan hsüeh-ku lu*, 44:5b. In YS 172:4016 the year given is 1287. See Yan-shuan Lao's paper in this volume for a discussion of this topic.

[14] *Tao-yüan hsüeh-ku lu*, 44:5b, and WWC: 1756, *shou*: 28a (*nien-p'u*).

Master Ch'eng,"[15] referring to the great Northern Sung scholar Ch'eng I 程頤 (1033–1107). At this time, large numbers of students began to flock to hear Wu's animated lectures on the critical importance of reverence (*ching*) in self-cultivation.

Wu's knowledge of the classics soon became publicly recognized. In 1296, the general Tung Shih-hsüan 董士選, who was then serving as an official in the provincial secretariat, engaged Wu to teach at his family school. Tung soon recommended Wu to the throne, feeling that no one could match Wu in the use of textual evidence from the classics. In 1301, when Wu was appointed to a position in the Hanlin Academy, Tung urged him to accept the position. Wu hesitated, however, and by the time he arrived in Ta-tu the following year, the post had already been taken by someone else.[16] Even so, during his brief stay in the capital, he was sought out by students there.

In 1307, Wu wrote commentaries on the Taoist works *Lao-tzu* 老子 and *Chuang-tzu* 莊子, as well as on the *T'ai-hsüan ching* 太玄經 (*Classic of the Great Mystery*) by Yang Hsiung 揚雄 (53–18 B.C.). Wei Su suggests that Wu's avowed purpose in dealing with these works was to prevent students from being misled by them,[17] while Yü Chi indicated that Wu wished to correct misconceptions in setting down his own explanations.[18] Wu's intent, however, was not necessarily polemical, for the commentaries were thorough and broad in their approach.

Wu had several "flirtations" with government service before he actually accepted a post in 1309. These took place in 1286, 1302, and 1304. He was almost sixty when he reluctantly accepted a post as Proctor (and later, in 1311, Director of Studies) in the National College. Whether he accepted the appointment because public recognition prevented him from again turning it down, or because a sense of scholarly obligation compelled him to serve, one cannot be certain. Possibly a combination of the two entered into his decision.[19]

We do know, however, that when Wu arrived in Ta-tu in 1309, he became discouraged by what he perceived to be the low level of scholarly practice in the National College. Wu is said to have observed that during the forty years after Hsü Heng 許衡 (1209–1281) ended his career as

---

[15] *Tao-yüan hsüeh-ku lu*, 44:6a.

[16] In the reply Wu sent to Tung, he likened himself to the retiring Confucian disciple Ch'i-tiao K'ai 漆雕開 and also quoted a poem by Shao Yung mentioning how the sage-emperors Yao and Shun had freed the two recluses Ch'ao Fu 巢父 and Hsü Yu 許由 from service. See *Tao-yüan hsüeh-ku lu*, 44:6b; complete text in WWC: 1756, 7:21a–22a.

[17] WWC: 1756, *shou*:32b (*nien-p'u*).

[18] *Tao-yüan hsüeh-ku lu*, 44:7a.

[19] Wei Su comments that while Wu did not want to serve, he was informed that he could not disobey the imperial edict. See WWC: 1756, *shou*:33a (*nien-p'u*).

Chancellor there, using especially the *Lesser Learning* to instruct his disciples, the educational methods had deteriorated: "When the Master [Wu Ch'eng] arrived, he bemoaned the fact that the students daily engaged themselves in frivolous practices and were motivated by personal gain." [20] In encouraging careful investigation of the classics and emphasizing self-mastery, Wu Ch'eng's pedagogical techniques apparently became quite popular with the students, who lined up in the early morning to await his instruction. [21]

Using the writings of Hu Yüan 胡瑗 (993–1059), Ch'eng Hao 程顥 (1032–1085) and Chu Hsi, Wu Ch'eng attempted to institute a four-part curriculum in the National College: classical studies (*ching-hsüeh* 經學), concrete practice (*hsing-shih* 行實), literary arts (*wen-i* 文藝) and administration (*chih-shih* 治事). These categories of instruction were broken down as follows:

1. *Ching-hsüeh* (classical studies), in which the student would be required to study the major classics and master the *Lesser Learning* (*Hsiao-hsüeh*) and the Four Books.

2. *Hsing-shih* (concrete practice), in which the student would be required to practice concretely the teachings of *hsiao* 孝 (filial piety) towards parents, *ti* 弟 (brotherliness) towards brothers, and so forth.

3. *Wen-i* (literary arts), in which the student would be required to master *ku-wen* 古文 (ancient-style prose) and poetry.

4. *Chih-shih* (administration), in which the student would be expected to master the details of civil-service recruitment examinations, economic institutions, rituals, musical laws, arithmetic, accounting, astronomy, and irrigation; for these areas the student relied on compilations such as the *T'ung-tien* 通典 (a collection of institutional materials), the *Hsing-t'ung* 刑統 (the official penal code of the Sung dynasty), and the *Suan-ching* 算經 (a mathematical encyclopedia). [22]

---

[20] *Tao-yüan hsüeh-ku lu*, 44:7a; in the same work, 5:14a–15b, Yü Chi bemoans Wu's short stay, feeling that Wu had assumed the post at an inopportune time.

[21] *Tao-yüan hsüeh-ku lu*, 44:7a.

[22] The description of the four instructional methods is given in WWC: 1756, *shou*:34b (*nien-p'u*), which is somewhat fuller than the one found in WWC: 1756, (supplementary *chüan*) 1:1b–8b; the categories are outlined in YS 171:4012.

Wu was interested in Hu Yüan's educational reforms, some of which had been adopted by Fan Chung-yen 范仲淹 (989–1052) in the latter's proposals regarding the National College, where Hu served as Proctor (see Wang Chien-ch'iu 王建秋, *Sung-tai t'ai-hsüeh yü t'ai-hsüeh-sheng* 宋代太學與太學生 [Taipei, 1965], pp. 10–11). Ch'eng Hao's memorials on the school system (see, for example, *Ming-tao wen-chi* 明道文集 [SPPY ed.], 2:6a–7b) and Chu Hsi's criticism of examination practices in his day (found in *Hui-an hsien-sheng Chu Wen-kung wen-chi* 晦菴先生朱文公文集 [SPTK ed.], 69:20a–28b) were also utilized by Wu.

Although Wu's plan was never implemented, we can get a glimpse of the kind of instruction in which he is said to have excelled from the outline given.

Wei Su points out that Wu decided to resign before he had fully consolidated his instructional method. According to Wei, this was because Wu wished to place less emphasis on a competitive grading system (which was in fact implemented) than did some of his colleagues. Whether or not this was the ultimate reason,[23] Wu departed from Ta-tu early in the year 1312. Clearly there were disagreements as to the merits of his ideas. Some felt that Wu wrongly favored the "heterodox" approach of Lu Hsiang-shan[24] rather than that of Chu Hsi. They argued that Wu stressed self-cultivation to the detriment of inquiry and study.[25] Even as he surprised many by departing, did he also sadden many scholars who had been close to him.

Although Wu was evidently broadminded in his approach to education, he was also a tireless student of the classics. In addition, he emphasized to his disciples lively practical experience. As we shall see further in the third section of this essay, the ideas of Chu and Lu formed complementary parts in Wu's philosophy of life. While this obviously relates to his training with both Ch'eng Jo-yung and Ch'eng Shao-k'ai, Wu himself struck a balance experientially: he agreed that the classics were the ultimate points of reference, yet he insisted that the mere repetition of phrases (as for example on a competitive examination) was not synonymous with genuine understanding.

Wu's first period of service in Ta-tu lasted only about two and one-half years, and it was in the end rather disappointing to him. One senses that although Wu was reluctant to serve at the outset, he eventually took up the post with some hope of accomplishment. He nevertheless became frustrated and came into conflict with his colleagues; thus, having put in some service, he withdrew. The conclusion of this term of service marked the beginning of his second period of productive scholarship.

In 1316, while staying at a monastery in the mountains southeast of Ch'ung-jen, Wu worked intensively on his *Observations on the Book of*

---

[23] From an essay written later in Wu's career we note that Wu was critical of those who studied the classics only to obtain the *chin-shih* degree; such an attitude possibly relates to his frustration with examination procedures or to a cynicism resulting from his own failure to obtain the *chin-shih* degree (WWC: 1756, 42:14a–b).

At the time Wu was serving in the National College, there was a purge of the *Shang-shu sheng* 尚書省 shortly before its abolition in 1311. See YS 85:2121, and Herbert Franke, *Geld und Wirtschaft in China unter der Mongolen-Herrschaft* (Leipzig, 1949), p. 89.

[24] Sun K'o-k'uan 孫克寬, *Yüan-ch'u ju-hsüeh* 元初儒學 (Taipei, 1953), p. 84.

[25] See section three of this essay for Wu's parting statement.

Changes (*I tsuan-yen* 易纂言) (which he eventually completed in 1322). In the following year, while presiding at the provincial examination in Kiangsi, we once again get a glimpse of Wu's approach to the classics. In that year he set forth an interesting question calling for an analysis of the concept of human nature in the *Analects* and the *Mencius* which was to serve as a springboard for an exposition of the Neo-Confucian idea of the unity of the nature. On this occasion, Wu came into conflict with his co-examiners, who thought his approach too facile.

Soon after this, Wu settled near Chien-k'ang (modern Nanking), where, in the year 1318, he completed his *Observations on the Book of History* (*Shu tsuan-yen* 書纂言). In this and in his *Observations on the Book of Changes* we see Wu's original approach to classical commentary emerging against the background of his earlier efforts at textual study and emendation. This creative building on the foundation of his earlier philological work was continued right up until the end of his life.

Wu's second period of service took place between 1323 and 1325, when he served as Chancellor of the Hanlin Academy. During these years he became involved, against his wishes, in two sensitive projects. The first was the transcribing of the Buddhist canon, for which he was asked to write a preface. He managed to get out of it by arguing cleverly that such a project, undertaken to assist in the salvation of the imperial ancestors, in fact slandered those individuals, because the need for assistance implied unworthiness.[26]

The second project was the compilation and editing of the *Veritable Record of the Emperor Ying-tsung* (r. 1321–1324), who had recently been assassinated by Mongol rivals for the throne.[27] Wu countered with much stalling and frequent requests for sick leave. These tactics ultimately brought about his precipitate exit from the capital. As it turned out, the project, which was for the most part completed during his tenure, was never presented to the throne.[28]

Between these two projects, in 1324 the court opened the *ching-yen* 經筵 or "Classics Mat," the hall for classical exposition (where emperors listened to lectures on Confucian principles). Wu became a lecturer in

---

[26] The text of Wu's statement can be found in *Tao-yüan hsüeh-ku lu*, 44:8b–9a, and in YS 171:4012–4013.

[27] The minister who assassinated Ying-tsung was also responsible for killing the minister Baiju (1296–1323), Wu's promoter in the Secretariat when Wu was made Chancellor in the Hanlin Academy. See YS 136:3305, 28:633. The successor to Ying-tsung, after much factional struggle, was Yesün Temür (r. 1324–1328), who, because he never received a posthumous title, became known as "the T'ai-ting emperor."

[28] YS 171:4013. Apparently the *Veritable Record*, although complete, was still in draft form awaiting final editing. See *Tao-yüan hsüeh-ku lu*, 44:10b.

charge of classical studies. Had it not been for the controversial nature of the *Veritable Record* project (the reigning emperor owing his position to the assassination of his predecessor), Wu might have remained longer in Ta-tu. Apparently the emperor had taken pleasure in Wu's lectures on the relationship between the ruler's virtue and heavenly favor in the *Doctrine of the Mean* (chapter 17) and several passages in *Tzu-chih t'ung-chien* 資治通鑑 (*General Mirror for the Aid of Government*).[29] The fact that he was already past seventy-five, of course, somewhat qualifies this judgment.

The last eight years of Wu's life may be considered his third period of scholarship. He completed his other principal commentaries during this period. These included the *Observations on the Spring and Autumn Annals* (*Ch'un-ch'iu tsuan-yen* 春秋纂言) in 1328, the *Supplementary Appendix to the Observations on the Book of Changes* (*I tsuan-yen wai-i* 易纂言外翼) in 1329, and the *Observations on the Record of Ritual* (*Li-chi tsuan-yen* 禮記纂言) written just prior to his death in 1333.[30]

In the *Yüan shih* 元史 (*Yüan History*), Wu's prolific scholarship is praised as follows: "In his moments of leisure, he set about writing books, and up to the time when he was about to die, he still did not lay them aside."[31] We learn as well from Yü Chi that, in these waning years, Wu's faculties remained acute. Wu even made sure that he met with all those numerous scholars who came to be instructed.

Thus did his enthusiasm for scholarship and dedication to teaching remain with him up to the very end of his eighty-five years. Indeed, throughout his entire life under Mongol rule he relentlessly pursued his goal of ensuring the continuity of the Chinese cultural tradition.

II. THE NATURE OF THE CLASSICAL SCHOLARSHIP OF WU CH'ENG

As we have seen, Wu Ch'eng's scholarly work involved an evolution from textual study to original commentary. Yü Chi may have had precisely this in mind when he stated that Wu's renditions of the classics, called *tsuan-yen* 纂言, or observations, "cleared up the confusions of former scholars and formed the pronouncements of a single school."[32]

[29] WWC: 1756, *shou*: 38b–39a (*nien-p'u*).

[30] Yü Chi's biography of Wu Ch'eng mentions that the work was completed in 1331 and that this was the year of his death (a mistake perpetuated in *Yüan shih*). Wei Su gives the correct date of death, 1333, and says that the work was completed in 1332. See WWC: 1756, *shou*: 43a–b (*nien-p'u*).

[31] YS 171:4014.

[32] *Tao-yüan hsüeh-ku lu*, 44:12a–b.

While Wu's educational and scholarly emphasis on the Five Classics did not indicate opposition to any of the Four Books, it did represent a desire to resurrect the authority of the classics in a critical way. Wu's aims were counterposed against the institutionalized Four Books trend in the Yüan.

Wu Ch'eng was interested in restoring the proper arrangement of chapters in his work with classical texts. In certain cases, this involved judgments which he made after classifying topics and dividing up the given work thematically. In others, Wu first had to reconstruct the text itself, or make emendations before drawing general conclusions.

In the case of the *Book of Changes*, Wu began work on the text in his early thirties, though as was the case with the other four of the Five Classics, he had studied it in his youth. Wu recollated the text of the *Book of Changes* which Lü Tsu-ch'ien 呂祖謙 (1137–1181) had established in a reliable edition, and in his *Observations on the Book of Changes*[33] (completed about a decade before his death) he collected various commentaries from the distant and recent past. As for meaning and interpretation, Wu's own commentary relied on the work of Chou Tun-i 周敦頤 (1017–1073) and Ch'eng I. He followed Chu Hsi's explanations of the use of the text for prognostication and divination, but, as Yü Chi notes, he greatly improved on the subtlety of Chu Hsi's theories.[34] Wu also composed a *Supplementary Appendix to the Observations on the Book of Changes*[35] in 1329, which distinguished themes and set forth examples for further study.[36]

Wu Ch'eng devoted much effort to a critical evaluation of the so-called *ku-wen* 古文 ("ancient text") portions of the *Book of History* in his *Observations* on that work.[37] Yü Chi mentions that Wu relied on the *chin-wen* 今文 ("modern text") version of Fu-sheng 伏勝 (b. 260 B.C.),[38] but it is clear as well that his judgments owe much to Chu Hsi's doubts about the twenty-five *ku-wen* portions. Whereas Chu Hsi had raised questions as to why the simpler *ku-wen* texts had not been transmitted in

---

[33] The (*Chou*) *I tsuan-yen* (周) 易纂言 can be found in *T'ung-chih t'ang ching-chieh* 同志堂經解(1863 ed.), *ts'e* 92–93.

[34] *Tao-yüan hsüeh-ku lu*, 44:12b. Lü's works on the *I-ching* include the *Ku Chou-i* 古周易 and the *Ku-i yin-hsün* 古易音訓. In the *Ssu-k'u ch'üan-shu tsung-mu* 四庫全書總目 (Shanghai, 1926), 4:1b, there is also mention of Wu's use of Lü's works.

[35] The *I tsuan-yen wai-i* 易纂言外翼 is found in *Yü-chang ts'ung-shu* 豫章叢書 (1916 ed.), *ts'e* 1–3.

[36] Cf. *Ssu-k'u ch'üan-shu tsung-mu*, 4:2a.

[37] The *Shu tsuan-yen* 書纂言 is found in *T'ung-chih t'ang ching-chieh*, *ts'e* 175–178.

[38] *Tao-yüan hsüeh-ku lu*, 44:12b.

the Former Han (while the *chin-wen* had), Wu Ch'eng went a step further in declaring that the *ku-wen* texts were forgeries.[39]

The Ch'ing scholar Tseng Lien 曾廉 (b. 1860) emphasized that until Wu no one had doubted the *ku-wen* texts thoroughly enough simply to discard them. By doing precisely that, Wu Ch'eng followed Chu Hsi's lead to its logical conclusion.[40] Wu arrived at this conclusion on a quite personal and introspective basis, for his own experience with the text had raised basic questions. Furthermore, the conclusion came as a great shock, as his own words make clear: "I could not obscure from my vision the fact that I had honestly come to disbelieve the veracity of the twenty-five ancient text chapters."[41]

His decision to accept only the twenty-eight *chin-wen* chapters, and to exclude altogether the twenty-five *ku-wen* chapters, was reaffirmed by Wang Keng-yeh 王耕野 in the Yüan,[42] Mei Tsu 梅鷟 in the Ming (sixteenth century),[43] and Yen Jo-ch'ü 閻若璩 in the Ch'ing.[44] Yen, as we know, used linguistic techniques of analysis which represented a more exacting approach than that of either Wu or Chu. The recognition that a text which most scholars considered a classic was partially a forgery, however, must surely have been disturbing to Wu, and his judgment manifested a clear independence of mind.

Wu's *Observations on the Spring and Autumn Annals*[45] has unique features as well. He cut through older, forced interpretations in the commentaries and annotations of traditional schools associated with the text and arrived at a compromise by using the *Tso* 左, *Kung-yang* 公羊, and *Ku-liang* 穀梁 commentaries simultaneously in explicating the text. Wu's threefold eclectic approach diverged from the sole reliance on the *Tso* by Chu Hsi. Chu had felt that the other two commentaries differed from the *Tso* merely in respect to technical niceties, such as the names of peoples and places.[46]

---

[39] *Chu-tzu yü-lei* 朱子語類 (1473 ed.), 78:2a (*passim*); Hu Shih, "The Scientific Spirit and Method in Chinese Philosophy," in Charles Moore, ed., *The Chinese Mind* (Honolulu, 1967), pp. 118–119; Joseph Needham, *Science and Civilisation in China*, Vol. 2 (Cambridge, England, 1956), pp. 391–392.

[40] *Yüan shu* 元書 (1911 ed.), 88:11b; cf. P'i Hsi-jui 皮錫瑞, *Ching-hsüeh li-shih* 經學歷史 (Hong Kong, 1961), p. 235.

[41] WWC: *chen-pen*, 1:6a.

[42] James Legge, tr., *The Chinese Classics* (Hong Kong, 1960), Vol. 3 (*Shoo King*), preface.

[43] Hu Shih, "The Scientific Spirit and Method," p. 119.

[44] Needham, *Science and Civilisation*, Vol. 2, pp. 392–393.

[45] *Ch'un-ch'iu tsuan-yen* 春秋纂言, rpt. in *Ssu-k'u ch'üan-shu chen-pen* series. A notice on the work appears in the *Ssu-k'u ch'üan-shu tsung-mu*, 28:1a–b.

[46] WWC: *chen-pen*, 1:8a.

Wu Ch'eng, though supporting Chu Hsi's search for *ta-i* 大義 or "general meaning" in the text, felt that the *Kung-yang* and *Ku-liang* commentaries often served this purpose better than did the *Tso*, primarily because they represented an oral tradition. Because the *Tso* relied on written records, it was authoritative for nomenclature and language; but in Wu's view, when the meaning was obscured in the *Tso*, the other two served a corrective purpose.[47]

Yü Chi pointed out that Wu "...allowed others to know that the writings...contained the principles of a single age and that all the specific instances in this classic could be subsumed under such principles. He selected out these various statements and joined them to the classic."[48] Clearly Yü Chi grasped and endorsed Wu Ch'eng's stress on general meaning, alluded to above, and the Confucian emphasis on discovering the connecting thread running through the *Spring and Autumn Annals*.

Wu Ch'eng set up seven major headings toward this end, two of which, *t'ien-tao* 天道 (the way of heaven) and *jen-chi* 人紀 (human regulations), were his own innovations. The other five were patterned after the ideas of Chang Ta-heng 張大亨 of the Sung.[49] For the details of his study, Wu relied on the T'ang commentators Chao K'uang 趙匡, Tan Chu 啖助 (725–770), and Lu Ch'un 陸淳, especially the classificatory methods of the first. He was critical of commentators who had preceded them.[50]

Wu adopted a "praise and blame" approach to the work in pointing out those instances in which propriety (*li* 禮) was transgressed. He stressed that those persons who transgressed propriety came into the provenance of criminal law.[51] Thus, for him, the didactic import of the work involved both ethical and legal considerations. This blend appears to be quite in line with the varied curriculum he suggested while teaching in the National College.

Wu Ch'eng did much work in reconstructing the ritual texts. He preserved the standard *chin-wen* version of the *Classic of Rites and Ceremonies* (*I-li*) and emended the so-called "Lost Classic" (*I-ching* 逸經) by selecting various sections from the ritual texts compiled by the Elder and Younger Tai (Tai Te 戴德 and Tai Sheng 戴聖) of the Former Han, as well as some nomenclature from Cheng Hsüan 鄭玄 (127–200)

[47] WWC: *chen-pen*, 1:8b.

[48] *Tao-yüan hsüeh-ku lu*, 44:12b.

[49] *Ssu-k'u ch'üan-shu tsung-mu*, 28:1b; Chang Ta-heng's work is known as the *Ch'un-ch'iu wu-li li-tsung* 春秋五禮例宗.

[50] WWC: *chen-pen*, 1:9a; *Tao-yüan hsüeh-ku lu*, 44:12b.

[51] *Tao-yüan hsüeh-ku lu*, 44:13a.

of the Latter Han.[52] His own commentary on the work[53] involved the incorporation of material from the two Tais, as well as from the Sung classicist Liu Ch'ang 劉敞 (1019–1068).[54]

Wu is more prominently known for his *Observations on the Record of Ritual*,[55] a commentary he completed in or near the last year of his life. Again, the work stands out for the tight structure by which it orders the various sections of the classical text in order to highlight its meaning.[56] To do this, Wu Ch'eng removed certain sections (for example the *T'ou-hu* 投壺 and *Pen-sang* 奔喪) from the *Record of Ritual* and restored them to the *Classic of Rites and Ceremonies*. In Wu's view, these sections had been wrongly included in the former text by the Younger Tai.[57]

In his work on the *Record of Ritual*, Wu did not include the chapters "Great Learning" and "Doctrine of the Mean." This is because he followed the lead of Ch'eng I and Chu Hsi with respect to them and probably left them a part of the Four Books,[58] even though he did not emphasize this particular classical grouping as much as he did the Five Classics.

Wu also wrote a commentary (his earliest) on the *Classic of Filial Piety*[59] and, as has been indicated, explicated Taoist texts as well.[60] As early as 1267 (his eighteenth year) he had taken an interest in the numerology of Shao Yung in writing his sequel to the latter's *Supreme Principles Governing the World* (see the first section of this essay);[61] he was to continue his interest in and study of the work in his later years as well.[62]

---

[52] *Tao-yüan hsüeh-ku lu*, 44:13a; see also *Ssu-k'u ch'üan-shu tsung-mu*, 20:3a–b.

[53] The *I-li ching-chuan* 儀禮經傳 is found in *T'ung-chih t'ang ching-chieh*, ts'e 403.

[54] *Tao-yüan hsüeh-ku lu*, 44:13a.

[55] The *Li-chi tsuan-yen* 禮記纂言 is found in *Ts'ang-shu shih-san chung* 藏書十三種 (1736 ed.), ts'e 30–43. Wang Yang-ming 王陽明 (1472–1529) wrote a preface to the work in 1520 in which he praised Wu highly for his new ideas on the ritual text (*Wang Wen-ch'eng kung ch'üan-shu* 王文成公全書 [SPTK ed.], 7:27a–28a).

[56] *Tao-yüan hsüeh-ku lu*, 44:13a–b.

[57] *Ssu-k'u ch'üan-shu tsung-mu*, 21:2a.

[58] *Tao-yüan hsüeh-ku lu*, 44:13a; *Ssu-k'u ch'üan-shu tsung-mu*, 21:2a. In general, Wu felt that Chu Hsi's commentaries on the Four Books were distinguished. Nevertheless he was not afraid to point out instances where he had some differences in matters of interpretation (WWC: *chen-pen*, 20:5b).

[59] *Ssu-k'u ch'üan-shu tsung-mu*, 32:3a–b.

[60] The commentary on *Lao-tzu* 老子 can be found in the *Tao-tsang* 道藏 (Shanghai, 1924–1926), ts'e 392–393, and that on the *Chuang-tzu* 莊子 in the same work, ts'e 497. See also *Tao-yüan hsüeh-ku lu*, 44:13b.

[61] WWC: 1756, *shou*:24b (*nien-p'u*).

[62] Yü Chi mentions his work on the text in 1305 in *Tao-yüan hsüeh-ku lu*, 44:7a. A preface to Shao's work is found in WWC: 1756, 10:4b–5b; also see Wu's descriptive

The breadth of his classical study is staggering, for one finds structural outlines of all the major classics in his collected works. These chart out in simplified form his own reconstructions and emendations, indicate to which traditional commentators he was indebted, and give his general approaches to, and theories regarding, the great books of antiquity.[63]

The image of Wu Ch'eng as teacher is sharply reflected in his broad approach to classical study. Wu had little use for academic sectarianism and this was exemplified in the two curriculum programs which he wrote, entitled *Hsüeh-chi* 學基 (*The Foundation of Learning*) and *Hsüeh-t'ung* 學統 (*The System of Learning*).[64] Yü Chi attempts to explain the rationale behind these two works in stating that they were designed to guide students of differing abilities in their progress to adulthood: "Scholars from poor villages or who were latecomers, and who had the ambition to study yet were without good mentors, could hardly go wrong if they followed and studied these [two works]."[65] Yü observed that the two pieces embodied Wu Ch'eng's dual emphasis on cultivation (*tsun te-hsing* 尊德性 or "honoring the virtuous nature") and learning (*tao wen-hsüeh* 道問學 or "pursuing inquiry and study").[66] Wu's syncretic inclination in philosophy and classical studies, which will be discussed in the following section of this essay, is here reflected in his approach to education.

Hsüeh-chi is a pastiche of quotations. They are arranged in two parts, with twenty passages in each. The first part consists of quotations from ancient works, while the second consists entirely of quotations from the writings of Sung philosophers. To be more precise, part one includes the following: *Book of Changes*, two quotations; *Analects*, five; *Doctrine of the Mean*, one; *Record of Ritual*, seven; and *Mencius*, five. In part two we find: Chou Tun-i, three; the Ch'eng brothers, twelve (Ch'eng Hao, two and Ch'eng I, ten); Chang Tsai 張載 (1020–1077), two; Hsieh Liang-tso 謝良佐 (1050–1103), one; Yin T'un 尹焞 (1071–1142), one; and Chu Hsi, one.

The stress in Wu's selections in both parts of *Hsüeh-chi* appears to be on the importance of the mind and reverence (*ching*) in one's conduct and cultivation of character. Fifteen of the twenty passages from the Sung Neo-Confucians in part two are from the anthology of Neo-

---

outline in WWC: 1756, 24b–25a. Yü Chi comments on Wu's special affinity for Shao's ideas in *Tao-yüan hsüeh-ku lu*, 44:13b (cf. n. 16, above).

[63] These pieces can be found in WWC: 1756, 1:1a–14b.

[64] The two pieces can be found in WWC: 1756, (supplementary *chüan*) 1:1b–8b.

[65] *Tao-yüan hsüeh-ku lu*, 44:13b.

[66] *Tao-yüan hsüeh-ku lu*, 44:13b. The ideas are found in the *Doctrine of the Mean*, chapter 27.

Confucian writings which was compiled by Chu Hsi and Lü Tsu-ch'ien, namely *Chin-ssu lu* 近思錄 (*Reflections on Things at hand*).[67]

Fourteen of these fifteen Neo-Confucian passages are taken from chapter four of *Chin-ssu lu*, which is entitled "Preserving One's Mind and Nourishing One's Nature." A quotation from Chang Tsai seems to capture this theme quite well: "When one's mind is clear, one's vision is clear and his hearing intelligent, and his four limbs are naturally respectful and careful without any rigid control."[68] The emphasis on reverence is exemplified in a quotation from Ch'eng I: "Concentration on one thing is reverence and not being distracted is concentration on one thing."[69] Wu's citing of this quotation in *Hsüeh-chi* lends support to Yü Chi's idea that the work emphasized the honoring of the virtuous nature, since Chu Hsi himself had defined it by referring to this same passage from Ch'eng I.[70]

Hsüeh-t'ung can best be described as a curriculum and is divided into four parts: part one is entitled *pen-yen* 本言 or "root teachings." These consist of the *Book of Changes*, the *Book of History*, the *Book of Poetry*, the various ritual texts (*I-li, Chou-li,* and so forth), the *Spring and Autumn Annals* and its three major commentaries, the *Analects*, the *Classic of Filial Piety*, the *Great Learning*, the *Doctrine of the Mean*, and *Mencius*.

Part two, entitled *kan-yen* 幹言 or "trunk teachings," consists entirely of Sung philosophers' writings, in the following order: Shao Yung, Chou Tun-i, the Ch'eng brothers, and Chang Tsai.

The third part is entitled *chih-yen* 支言 or "branch teachings." Included here are eight categories, listed as follows (the numbers are added here): 1. *Kuo-yü* 國語; 2. *Kuo-ts'e* 國策; 3. *Shih-chi* 史記 and *Han-shu* 漢書; 4. *Lao-tzu* 老子; 5. *Chuang-tzu* 莊子; 6. *Sun-tzu* 孫子 and the *Pa-chen-t'u* 八陣圖; 7. *Ch'u-tz'u* 楚辭 and *Hou-yü* 後語; 8. *T'ai-hsüan* [*ching*] 太玄[經] and *Ch'ien-hsü* 潛虛.

Finally, the fourth part, entitled *mo-yen* 末言 or "branch-tip teachings," consists of six items: 1. *Yin-yang ta-lun* 陰陽大論; 2. *Nei-ching* 內經, *Su-wen* 素問, and *Ling-shu* 靈樞; 3. *Pa-shih-i nan ching*

---

[67] *Chin-ssu lu chi-chu* 近思錄集註, commentary by Chiang Yung 江永, (SPPY ed.); see also Chan Wing-tsit, tr., *Reflections on Things at Hand* (New York, 1967).

[68] WWC: 1756, (supplementary *chüan*) 1:2b; *Chin-ssu lu chi-chu*, 4:12a (translation in Chan, *Reflections on Things at Hand*, pp. 151–152). The original quotation can be found in *Chang-tzu ch'üan-shu* 張子全書 (SPPY ed.), 7:1b. The passage is also quoted by Wu Ch'eng in an essay on mind in WWC: 1756, 5:26a.

[69] WWC: 1756, (supplementary *chüan*) 1:2b; *Chin-ssu lu chi-chu*, 4:8a (cf. translation in Chan, *Reflections on Things at Hand*, p. 144). The original quotation is found in *Erh-Ch'eng ch'üan-shu* 二程全書 (SPPY ed.), *I-shu* 遺書, 15:20a.

[70] *Chu-tzu yü-lei*, 64:23b.

八十一難經; 4. *Shang-han lun* 傷寒論; 5. *Chou-i ts'an-t'ung ch'i* 周易參同契; 6. *Tsang-shu* 塟書.

As a general observation on this curriculum of Wu Ch'eng's, it is clear that while he places priority on traditional "orthodox" texts, he is extremely broad and eclectic in his choice of supplementary teaching materials, even more so than in the curriculum he proposed for the National College around 1309. The items in the third and fourth parts run the gamut from standard historical writings (Ssu-ma Ch'ien's *Shih-chi*) and Taoist philosophical texts (*Lao-tzu* and *Chuang-tzu*), to military writings (*Sun-tzu*) and medical texts (*Nei-ching* and *Shang-han lun*). The *Pa-shih-i nan ching*, a medical treatise dealing with such themes as acupuncture, was highly praised in Yüan times and was annotated by the Ningpo scholar Hua Shou 滑壽 (d. Hung-wu reign, Ming period).[71] The *Chou-i ts'an-t'ung ch'i* is a fourth-century Taoist text on immortality which was important to the Taoists discussed in the essay by Sun K'o-k'uan in this volume.

Although the Confucian classics are given due attention as core teaching texts in Wu Ch'eng's curriculum in *Hsüeh-t'ung*, they constitute no more than a quarter of the entire program. If, as Yü Chi says, *Hsüeh-t'ung* was designed to emphasize the pursuit of inquiry and study, we may say that it does so through a broadminded approach which is firmly rooted in a traditional Confucian context.

The fact that Wu listed the *Great Learning* and the *Doctrine of the Mean* as separate items in this curriculum indicates that he did not disagree with the Ch'eng-Chu stress on the Four Books; yet the absence of a specific reference to the Four Books in his curriculum here suggests that he looked beyond them in his estimation of worthwhile literature. It is likely that he did not want his students to be circumscribed by that one small collection of texts.

In terms of the work of textual commentators from former times, Wu also demonstrated an independence in outlook which made him quite selective. He clearly recognized value in the works of Tung Chung-shu 董仲舒 (179?–104? B.C.) in the Han period and Han Yü 韓愈 (768–824) in the T'ang. Nevertheless, he felt that they had failed to grasp essential truths through their scholarly endeavors.[72] Similarly, in the early Sung, he recognized the influence of Hu Yüan and Sun Fu 孫復 (992–1057) in elucidating the classics, yet he viewed them as barely surpassing Tung and Han in fundamentals.[73]

---

[71] See *Ssu-k'u ch'üan-shu tsung-mu* 四庫全書總目 (Yeewen ed.), 103:4b–6b.

[72] WWC: 1756, 22:1a; WWC: *chen-pen*, 2:4a.

[73] WWC: 1756, 22:1a.

In the cases of Cheng Hsüan and Liu Ch'ang, mentioned in connection with Wu's work on the *Classic of Rites and Ceremonies*, Wu's indebtedness mostly involved classification, for he was critical of the fact that they, like Tung, Han, Hu, and Sun, never quite transcended the words of the texts themselves.[74]

The limitations of these scholars were overcome, in Wu's eyes, by Chou Tun-i, Shao Yung, Chang Tsai, the Ch'eng brothers, and Chu Hsi. No doubt Wu felt that classical study was vital, but he saw it as ultimately a springboard for the moral perfection of the individual; thus for many commentators his praise is qualified. To explore this further, the following section will relate Wu's classical work to his philosophical development. In doing so, we will see that his criticism of certain textual scholars parallels his criticism of the late Southern Sung followers of the Chu Hsi school.

III. Scholarship and Philosophy in Wu Ch'eng

In addition to Wu's importance as a prolific classical scholar, he was an important thinker in the Neo-Confucian tradition itself. The burden of propagating the Confucian classics reflected a preservationist mentality, to be sure, but it had as a goal the ethical transformation of society.

The fact that prior to 1315 the route into government through the civil-service examination was cut off did not prevent the Mongol establishment from selecting scholars such as Wu Ch'eng for special appointment. Nevertheless, the situation further complicated the relationship between scholarship and social service. It is to be remembered, of course, that Wu's pessimism about that relationship antedated the Mongol conquest itself and was not uncommon among his late Sung peers.

Similarly, as a southerner who had declined to serve at all in the late 1280s, Wu felt uncomfortable in the north during his first period of service some thirty years later. For him, at least, the transition to Mongol rule exacerbated earlier feelings about service. In any case, the tension between Wu and some of his northern colleagues was also founded on conflicting approaches to scholarship and education.

In this regard, Yü Chi's comment on Hsü Heng, who had served in the National College at an earlier time, is rather telling:

"Before north and south were united, his excellency Hsü Wen-cheng [Heng] first obtained the works of Master Chu in the remote regions, studying them with great care.... He made use of this teaching in service to the Emperor Shih-tsu [Khubilai] and thus the *tao* of the Confucians

---

[74] WWC: *chen-pen*, 2:4a.

was not destroyed ... Yet in terms of one who could be measured successfully against the sages and worthies and whose teachings could be passed down a hundred generations, ... people who discussed these matters were still discontented." [75]

Yü felt that this discontent was in some sense alleviated once Wu Ch'eng appeared on the scene:

"When the Master [Wu] was born, the Chinese tradition was about to expire. From the time he was about seven years of age, he was quite an extraordinary individual. He obtained fragments from [the writings] which had survived and discovered new ideas through his outstanding insight. In the prime of his life he excelled in his abilities and assumed for himself the burden of the cultural tradition of the world." [76]

In tracing Wu's short terms of service (as a not-too-willing servitor), and exploring his respectability as a teacher, Yü concluded that scholars of later generations would be able to examine and learn from the distinctiveness of Wu's writings for a long time to come. [77] The contrast between Hsü and Wu is important. Yü was being properly circumspect since Wu's direct scholarly conflicts were with Hsü's disciples.

Just as Wu's approach to service was conditioned by the late Sung milieu in which he grew up, and was later reinforced under the Yüan, so were his feelings about scholarship and educational practices in the early Yüan conditioned by a broad critical view of post-Chu Hsi scholarship. Furthermore, while in the first instance Wu may have resolved his dilemma by deciding to contribute something through brief service in the capital, in the second, the dilemma could be addressed through the exercise of imaginative philosophical reconciliation.

The roots for this philosophical reconciliation in Wu Ch'eng must be discovered in the context of the training he received from Ch'eng Jo-yung in the Chu Hsi lineage (via Huang Kan and Jao Lu), and from Ch'eng Shao-k'ai, who exposed Wu to the teachings of Lu Hsiang-shan by attempting to reconcile Chu and Lu.

In an essay probably written around the time Wu was serving in the National College, Wu spoke of his scholarly heritage as follows: "I myself did exegetical research [on the classical texts], analyzing in great detail, although I still felt that Ch'en [Ch'un] 陳 [淳] (1153–1217) was not subtle enough and that Jao [Lu] was not exacting enough. I fell into this mold for forty years, and then for the first time I realized that it was wrong.... I am troubled that I have wasted so much time." [78]

While Wu himself had been devoted to textual research, he nonetheless

---

[75] *Tao-yüan hsüeh-ku lu*, 44:12a.
[76] *Tao-yüan hsüeh-ku lu*, 44:11b–12a.
[77] *Tao-yüan hsüeh-ku lu*, 44:12b.
[78] WWC: 1756, 22:2a–b.

felt that it had moral and intellectual limitations: a true scholar had to consider the meaning of the texts he studied. He was thus presenting a rather ringing indictment of his own scholarly development in the preceding passage. He attacked his excessive refinement in textual criticism as no more than inches away from "the vulgar scholarship of memorization and literary composition" (*chi-sung tz'u-chang chih su-hsüeh* 記誦詞章之俗學).[79] He also revealed a generalized dislike for the scholarship in which he had once been caught up:

"After four generations the teachings of the Ch'eng brothers were passed down to Chu Hsi. As for the fine points of meaning, each sentence and word was discussed so that since [the time of] Mencius there had never been such learning. His [Chu's] disciples, however, would often cling to this practice, obscuring their minds, so that while they considered memorization and literary composition of the scholars of the day as vulgar scholarship, their own method of learning was not set apart from trivial [matters of] words and writing. They even clung only to a single literary craft (*i-i* 一藝) and did not make use of other writings. They gathered together worthless doctrines without being able to say anything of their own.... These, then, were the defects of the Chu school after the Chia-ting reign period (1208–1224). No one was able to remedy them."[80]

In addition to clarifying Wu's sense of mission, discussed in the first section of this essay, and supporting Yü Chi's judgments on Wu's uniqueness in the context of scholarship in the Yüan given at the beginning of this section, the preceding passage reflects a broad critical outlook. While obviously addressed toward the late Sung figures Ch'en Ch'un and Jao Lu, the criticism nevertheless does not exclude scholars of the Chin and Yüan.

Read in the context of Wu Ch'eng's *Hsüeh-t'ung* curriculum, this passage delivers the message that true disciples of the master Chu Hsi must read widely and not be constrained by a single craft, a narrowly defined program of learning and scholarship constructed around the master's words. Wu Ch'eng wanted his students to read the master's words, but he wanted them to read much more than those alone. He had discovered this limitation after four decades of study himself. We shall see a similar sentiment expressed by Wu in discussing his views on the value of studying the ideas of Lu Hsiang-shan without blind adherence to Lu's words in the fourth section of this essay.

Elsewhere, Wu continued his attack on those who fell into the trap of

[79] WWC: 1756, 22:2a.
[80] WWC: 1756, 22:1b.

exegesis for its own sake. In this way he conveyed the importance, as he saw it, of striking the necessary balance between the dual pursuits of study and self-cultivation:

"'Breadth through learning and restraint [acquired] through propriety' [alluding to the *Analects*, VI:25] were the methods passed down by the sages and worthies. For fifteen-hundred years or more after the Chou, this tradition continued. Since the Masters Chou [Tun-i], Ch'eng [Hao and I], and Chang [Tsai], and the demise of Master Chu, this learning has been lost. Every household of the present age has the works of Master Chu and everyone repeats his theories from memory...."[81]

As an antidote to a narrow devotion to Chu Hsi's ideas, Wu stressed the importance of balancing cultivation and study in the public statement he made before his departure from the National College (probably in 1310 or 1311):

"Master Chu [Hsi] was pre-eminent in the practice of 'maintaining constant inquiry and study' (*tao wen-hsüeh*) while Lu Tzu-ching [Hsiang-shan] regarded the 'honoring of the virtuous nature' (*tsun te-hsing*) as the primary thing. If [the pursuit of] inquiry and study is not rooted in the virtuous nature, then its flaw will be an unbalanced attention to trivial [matters of] linguistic and textual exegesis. Surely this is comparable to what Lu Tzu-ching has said. Learning today must take the virtuous nature as its basis; only then can one succeed."[82]

While in the statement before his departure from the National College Wu may have deliberately provoked criticism from his northern colleagues by invoking Lu's name as a pretext for leaving the capital, it is nevertheless true that the broadmindedness he wished to promote in scholarship, in or out of official position, was inclusive of the ideas of both Chu and Lu.

It was sectarianism that Wu disliked, and it is apparent that in the thirteenth century scholars were beginning to choose sides. Wu defended Lu Hsiang-shan against the Chu Hsi critics. Answering the question, "What kind of man was Master Lu?" Wu wrote as follows:

"In Master Chu's teaching of others, one must first study and investigate. In Master Lu's teaching of others, he caused them to know genuinely and to practice concretely. Study and investigation surely are the foundation of genuine knowledge and concrete practice,

---

[81] WWC: 1756, 7:18a–b; the passage from *Analects*, 6:25, can be found in Legge, tr., *The Chinese Classics*, Vol. I, p. 193.

[82] This passage is quoted in the *hsing-chuang* by Yü Chi. See *Tao-yüan hsüeh-ku lu*, 44:7b–8a; YS 171:4012 (abbreviated version). The internal quotations from the *Doctrine of the Mean*, chapter 27, can be found in Legge, tr., *The Chinese Classics*, Vol. 1, pp. 422–423.

just as genuine knowledge and concrete practice must also be attained through study and investigation. What the two teachers taught is one, yet the mediocre and base followers of the two schools in each case set up placards with which they defamed and reviled each other to the point where scholars today are as though deluded." [83]

As a scholar with wide-ranging interests, Wu perceived that such sectarianism could be remedied by reconciling the ideas of Chu and Lu. After all, neither had viewed cultivation and study as mutually exclusive. Their differences were a matter of emphasis and of the extent to which one might rely on either objective or subjective knowledge in pursuing one's moral development.

The inability to strike a proper balance in scholarship by the scholars of the late Sung and Yüan (compounded by north-south differences in the latter) in fact caused Wu Ch'eng to emphasize the theme of original mind (*pen-hsin* 本心), so prominent in Lu's philosophy, as an intellectual corrective:

"To seek for knowledge only in the Five Classics and not return to one's own mind for it is like buying a box and discarding the pearl.... As for students who come here requesting instruction, I first have them make reverence (*ching*) the ruling consideration in honoring the virtuous nature. Afterwards I have them study books and exhaust principle (*ch'iung-li* 窮理) in pursuing inquiry and study.... It is necessary to seek first within one's mind and afterwards in the Five Classics." [84]

Thus we see an ideological predisposition behind the classical studies of Wu Ch'eng which is framed in the context of intellectual history. His philosophic methodology enlivened the Neo-Confucian picture in the Yüan and provided direction for scholarship. The searching clarification in which he was engaged was part of an openminded approach to inquiry in general.

Furthermore, Wu's openmindedness had a preservationist motivation. Just as Wu restructured and clarified the classical foundations so as to establish continuity with the past, so did he encourage philosophic reconciliation to preserve the depth and richness of the Sung intellectual heritage.

Even as one senses a double-edged approach with respect to textual investigation and personal cultivation, Wu Ch'eng's intellectual predispositions may be seen in high relief in his views of intellectual history.

[83] WWC: 1756, 15:31b.

[84] WWC: 1756, 3:22b–23a; the pearl simile is from *Han Fei Tzu* 韓非子 and the statement on reverence from *Erh-Ch'eng ch'üan-shu* (1908 ed.), 15:7a, 28a.

His view of the declining intellectual current in his own era, his doubts about the Confucian lineage after Chu Hsi, and his efforts to counteract the effects of sectarian divisiveness, all indicate that he bore a heavy burden—the responsibility of preserving the true classical heritage.

His classical and philosophical inclinations dovetail nicely in his evaluations of historical writing. With Wu's ideas about the necessity of elucidating "general meaning" in studying the *Spring and Autumn Annals* in the background,[85] we see this dovetailing in his opinions on the *General Treatise* (*T'ung-chih* 通志) of the Sung historian Cheng Ch'iao 鄭樵 (1102–1160). The *T'ung-chih* is an encyclopedic historical text incorporating materials on eras from antiquity through the T'ang. Wu's comments on this treatise served to raise some general questions on historical learning.

Wu prefaces his remarks by criticizing several classical and literary figures. He argues that Cheng Hsüan of the Han and Liu Ch'ang of the Sung practiced learning rooted chiefly in rote memorization, and that Han Yü of the T'ang and Ou-yang Hsiu 歐陽修 (1007–1070) of the Sung devoted themselves principally to the pursuit of fine literary style. The former he called *chi-sung chih hsüeh* 記誦之學 and the latter *tz'u-chang chih hsüeh* 詞章之學. These criticisms, of course, resemble those which Wu leveled at Ch'en Ch'un and Jao Lu in terms of the late Chu school. Thus Wu is careful to distinguish the above four individuals from the Sung Neo-Confucian philosophers, whose learning he characterizes as pertaining to "the Confucian scholars" (*ju-che chih hsüeh* 儒者之學).[86]

This sets the stage for the criticism of Cheng Ch'iao. Wu holds that Cheng, in attempting to write objective history, and thereby to avoid the pitfalls of the moralistic approach held to be characteristic of the *Spring and Autumn Annals*, instead became superficial. This was because he rooted his historical studies in that which could be committed to memory.[87] Instead of uniting the inner and outer spheres of learning, Cheng had drifted excessively into an external approach which tended to becloud true knowledge and render one's writing virtually meaningless. Cheng's work took account of concrete historical facts but failed to penetrate fundamental truths; he attacked the "skin rather than the flesh."[88]

---

[85] See the discussion of Wu's *Observations on the Spring and Autumn Annals* in section two of this essay.

[86] WWC: *chen-pen*, 2:4a. A similar distinction between form and content in learning can be found in the writings of Ch'eng I, in *Erh-Ch'eng ch'üan-shu, I-shu* 遺書 (SPPY ed.), 18:4b.

[87] WWC: *chen-pen*, 2:4b–5a.

[88] WWC: *chen-pen*, 2:5b–6a.

In Wu's view, the approach to historical investigation which Cheng Ch'iao represented was based on perceptual (or intellectual) knowledge (*wen-chien chih chih* 聞見之知) alone and was therefore set apart and divorced from moral knowledge (*te-hsing chih chih* 德性之知: literally, "knowledge based on the virtuous nature").[89] To achieve a proper balance, Neo-Confucian ethical and metaphysical ideas had to be made central.

In commenting on the *Classic of Rites and Ceremonies*, for example, Wu Ch'eng put the painstaking nature of his textual work in the context of moral uplift:

"Preserve sincerity, emphasize reverence (*ching*), extend knowledge, practice with effort, and let your studies lie low so as to penetrate the higher. Study much and [grasp] the unifying thread with which one will attain the mind of the sages Yao, Shun, Yü, T'ang, Wen, Wu, the Duke of Chou and Confucius. Then the later followers of the school of our Master Chu will not do the things that the Han scholars did."[90]

In seeking to divest himself and his disciples of textual formalism and sectarian intellectual impulses, Wu Ch'eng trod a path which could become morally subjective. This, however, touches on a perennial problem in Chinese intellectual history: how can one ground thought on a firm textual basis while yet preserving the personal ethical experience? Wu Ch'eng attempted to address this problem in unique ways.

Wu felt that historical and classical study achieved ultimate fruition in moral knowledge. For him, the unity of creative textual study and ethical fulfillment was the message he derived from a synthesis of the methodologies of Chu and Lu: study was no handicap to moral enlightenment and the two were identifiable if inspiration could overcome rote formalism.

IV. THE CONTINUITY OF TRADITION IN WU CH'ENG

In examining Wu Ch'eng's views on history, we have found them couched in a classical approach and informed by a broad intellectual outlook. We next confront the issue of Wu's place in Chinese intellectual history. To consider this, one must first address the issue of *tao-t'ung*, or the transmission of the Confucian way, a problem which Wu himself was deeply aware of as he viewed his own age.

Chu Hsi emphasized the preeminence of Chou Tun-i in the Confucian

---

[89] WWC: *chen-pen*, 2:5a; cf. Yü Ying-shih, "Some Preliminary Observations on the Rise of Ch'ing Confucian Intellectualism," *Ch'ing-hua hsüeh-pao*, N.S. 11 (1975), p. 110.

[90] WWC: *chen-pen*, 1:12a–b. Cf. *Analects*, 14/35.

line of succession after Mencius. Thus he completed the scheme of Han Yü, which had begun with the sage-emperor Yao and ended with Mencius.[91] This was the interpretation adopted in the *Sung shih* 宋史 (*Sung History*)[92] and was one which routed the Confucian lineage along a particular ideological path.

As mentioned in the first section of this essay, Wu composed a rather precocious sketch of the line of succession (*Tao-t'ung t'u*) to reinforce his scholarly commitment as he entered manhood. In his sketch there are three stages, high, middle and recent antiquity, each in turn having a four-fold division based on a scheme of classification taken from the *Book of Changes*. In Wu's sketch, as in the scheme of Chu Hsi, the link between the stages of middle and recent antiquity occurs in the transmission from Mencius to Chou Tun-i. Wu's sketch then continues the transmission of *tao* thereafter:

"In the succession of recent antiquity (*chin-ku* 近古), Master Chou [Tun-i] was its [i.e., the Way's] inception (*yüan* 元), Chang [Tsai] and the Ch'eng brothers its ripening (*heng* 亨), and Master Chu [Hsi] its flowering (*li* 利). Who represents the fruition (*chen* 貞) today? As yet no one does, but will there never be one to whom we can turn? There will certainly be someone who cannot but accept this position."[93]

Wu's rhetorical question, and his implied certainty that a scholar of heroic importance will eventually step forward to assume the burden, perhaps suggests that he himself hoped to perform the needed task. In a later passage on this subject Wu explained:

"For more than a thousand years after the demise of Mencius, there was a decline into the base practices of vulgar scholarship, as well as into excesses in the heterodox teachings of Taoism and Buddhism. In this period, not a single distinguished scholar (*hao-chieh chih shih* 豪傑之士) was born. As for the coming forth in one age of Chou, Chang, the

[91] W. T. Chan, "Chu Hsi's Completion of Neo-Confucianism," *Études Song: Sung Studies in Memory of Étienne Balazs*, Françoise Aubin, ed. (series two, number 1, Paris: Mouton, 1973), p. 74.

[92] W. T. de Bary, "A Reappraisal of Neo-Confucianism," in Arthur Wright, ed., *Studies in Chinese Thought* (Chicago, 1953), pp. 88–89.

[93] *Tao-yüan hsüeh-ku lu*, 44:4a–b. The four terms translated in the quotation represent the opening words of the *Book of Changes*. See *Chou-i* in [*Sung k'an-pen*] *Shih-san ching chu-shu fu chiao-k'an chi* [宋刊本] 十三經注疏附校勘記 (1815 ed.), 1:1a. Cf. James Legge, tr., *The Yî Kîng, The Texts of Confucianism, The Sacred Books of the East* (Oxford, 1882), Vol. 16, p. 57, where these are rendered as "great and originating, penetrating, advantageous, correct and firm," respectively; and Chu Hsi's commentary on Chou Tun-i's *T'ung-shu* 通書 in *Cheng-i t'ang ch'üan-shu* 正誼堂全書 (1868 ed.), 5:3b, from which one may derive the nouns origination, penetration, completion and correction for the four terms.

Ch'engs and Shao, who but a distinguished scholar could be their peer? When a hundred years later Master Chu gathered together the great works of these masters, we then had the appearance once again of a distinguished scholar. Is there today someone who will take upon himself the task of handing down the legacy of Master Chu?" [94]

In the first section of this essay it was stressed that Wu was urging himself on in his early sketch of *tao-t'ung*; in the above passage it would seem that this sense of obligation began to be coupled with grave doubts about post-Chu Hsi scholarship, as detailed in the preceding section. Thus the criticisms of late Sung scholarship were related to a generalized outlook about the inheritance from the Sung patriarchs, as well as to specifically objectionable features. The phrase itself, *hao-chieh chih shih*, with its heroic and martial nuances, reflects Wu's feeling that only heroic scholarly achievement could preserve the Confucian *tao*.

In the context of the basic scheme of Neo-Confucian *tao-t'ung* found in Chu Hsi, Wu Ch'eng elsewhere emphasized the role of original mind (*pen-hsin*), a theme from Lu Hsiang-shan, in terms of thematic inheritance:

"If one turns and seeks for the origin in himself, he is using the mind for learning. Not only is it the case that Master Lu did so. Yao, Shun, T'ang, Wen, Wu and the Duke of Chou, Confucius, Yen [Hui], Tseng [Tzu], [Tzu] Ssu, Mencius, and on down through the philosophers Shao, Chou, Chang, the Ch'engs: all of them did so. Hence if one only points to the learning of Master Lu as that of the original mind, one does not understand the Way of the sages. . . . This mind is the mind of Master Lu. This Way is the Way of the sages." [95]

While this passage includes the usual sages and worthies, it omits the name of Chu Hsi from the Neo-Confucian lineage, whereas Lu's name is placed precisely on the main track of the Confucian intellectual tradition.

This is not to suggest that Wu neglected Chu Hsi, for in the same essay in which Wu describes his break with Ch'en Ch'un and Jao Lu (in section three, above), the apostolic line does devolve on Chu. [96] Wu did not entirely desert the traditional approach to *tao-t'ung*. His view of ideal scholarly accomplishments in previous Neo-Confucians prevented that. He did, however, begin to feel that Lu Hsiang-shan deserved a niche as well, as his intellectual outlook broadened and came to stress reconciliation.

The preservation of the Sung tradition itself could not have been

---

[94] *Tao-yüan hsüeh-ku lu*, 44:4a–b.
[95] WWC: 1756, 26:11a.
[96] WWC: 1756, 22:1b.

complete without the emphasis which Lu gave to the mind. Wu felt that Lu's learning had been lost and that it was his task to revive it. As Wu said: "In the closing years of the Sung ... there was no one who was able to grasp the method of mind (hsin-fa 心法) of Master Lu. The learning of Lu was isolated, cut off, and not handed down. How regrettable this is!"[97]

Naturally the concept of a Lu *school* was a problem, since Lu did not want his students to follow him blindly. The independent spirit in Lu's teaching was incompatible with a unilinear scheme of ideological transmission. Wu also felt that the ineffable qualities of Lu's thought could survive the dearth of disciples. As he pointed out in a preface to Lu's *Collected Sayings*:

"The learning of Master Lu of Ch'ing-t'ien cannot be transmitted in words.... If one is able to turn around and discover it [tao] in oneself, one will then know what heaven has given to us. Since we certainly possess it, we do not need to go outside [of ourselves] to discover it. If we can expand and complete it, it is not necessary to add onto it.... That one should not seek to find it in oneself but seek to discover it in the words of others is [something] that the Master [Lu] deeply grieved about. Today those who talk about the Master and admire him are numerous. Is there, however, a single individual who is able to know the teachings of the Master? Is there a single individual who is capable of putting them into practice? ... One must not think that the teachings of the Master are merely in his words."[98]

While it is possible to view the sage-mind as a central feature of tao-t'ung, emerging more clearly in the Lu-Wang school,[99] Wu Ch'eng's linkage of Lu's concept of mind to the traditional tao-t'ung scheme is a departure which vastly broadened the definition of the Confucian intellectual inheritance.[100]

It can be said that during the Yüan era, Wu Ch'eng's trenchant classical scholarship and imaginative philosophic methodology provided for the preservation and continuity of the Neo-Confucian line of succession. It is true, of course, that this was not so patently clear to Wu himself, who assumed a life-long burden in a solitary way during a time of transition and, eventually, in the context of alien rule. His achievements in scholarship and philosophy assure him an important position in a tradition he labored long and hard to perpetuate.

[97] WWC: 1756, 42:14b.
[98] WWC: 1756, 10:26b–27b.
[99] J. Ching, "The Confucian Way (Tao) and Tao-T'ung," *Journal of the History of Ideas*, 35 (1974), p. 386.
[100] This theme is picked up by Yü Chi in *Tao-yüan hsüeh-ku lu*, 44:11b.

Yü Chi and Southern Taoism during the Yüan Period

K'O-K'UAN SUN[1]

Some of Yüan China's leading Han Chinese literati were extremely close to leaders of southern Taoism. Yü Chi 虞集 (1272–1348), a Confucian-trained scholar reared in Kiangsi, and his famous mentor Wu Ch'eng 吳澄 (1249–1333), also from Kiangsi, are perhaps the most prominent examples of this phenomenon. Wu Ch'eng and Yü Chi wrote numerous laudatory essays on behalf of Taoist leaders such as the hereditary Celestial Masters (T'ien-shih 天師). And both men were highly regarded by the patriarchs of Hsüan-chiao 玄教. Hsüan-chiao, "the sublime teaching," was in effect a branch of southern T'ien-shih Taoism that had been created by the edict of the Mongol rulers. Hsüan-chiao was purely a Yüan religious phenomenon, for the Hsüan-chiao patriarchy was obliterated by the founder of the Ming dynasty, Ming T'ai-tsu. What is more important, from the standpoint of the history of Yüan literati, is that Hsüan-chiao, a Taoist religious movement replete with beliefs in magic, divination, and immortality, was the product, not of Taoists

---

[1] This essay has been adapted by the editor from several publications by Professor Sun K'o-k'uan. The bulk of its contents was presented at the ACLS research conference and then published in Chinese: "Yüan Yü Chi yü nan-fang tao-chiao 元虞集與南方道教," *Ta-lu tsa-chih* 大陸雜誌, 53:6 (Dec. 1976), pp. 1–12. Additional materials have been incorporated from the following writings: "Yüan-ch'u cheng-i chiao yü chiang-nan shih-ta-fu 元初正一教與江南士大夫," in Sun K'o-k'uan, *Yüan-tai Han wen-hua chih huo-tung* 元代漢文化之活動 (Taipei: Chung-hua Shu-chü, 1968), pp. 199–208; *Yüan-tai tao-chiao chih fa-chan* 元代道教之發展 (Taichung: Tung-hai Ta-hsüeh, 1968); "Yüan-tai ti i-ko wen-hsüeh tao-shih: Chang Yü 元代的一個文學道士: 張雨," *Ta-lu tsa-chih*, 46:4 (April 1973), pp. 1–10; "Ming-ch'u t'ien-shih Chang Yü-ch'u chi ch'i *Hsien-ch'üan chi* 明初天師張宇初及其峴泉集," *Shu-mu chi-k'an* 書目季刊, 9:4 (March 1976), pp. 3–17. Several of these essays have been conveniently reprinted in *Han-yüan tao lun* 寒原道論 (Taipei: Lien-ching Ch'u-pan Shih-yeh Kung-ssu, 1977). The editor is extremely grateful to Professor Yan-shuan Lao and Hsin-i Fan Langlois for assistance in the preparation of this text. The author's original footnotes have been expanded, and new references added, to serve the interests of our readers. The editor bears responsibility for any distortion of Professor Sun's ideas that may have been introduced in the process of translation and adaptation.

acting on their own, but of Taoists working with the active cooperation of prominent Confucian literati and under the endorsement and sponsorship of the ruling Mongols. Hsüan-chiao was a distinctive form of Tao-chiao 道教, and from the standpoint of traditional elite Han Chinese culture it was highly refined and literary. It was also highly political. In effect, Hsüan-chiao Taoist culture and the culture of the Han Chinese literati were overlapping phenomena, and in some cases they were one. They spoke and wrote the same language; they shared the same political arena. A study of Yü Chi's life will show this.

One impression this writer has gained after studying the history of Yüan Taoism over many years is that the arm-in-arm mutuality of Taoism and Confucianism, which was characteristic of southern Chinese, particularly those from Kiangsi, seems to have represented the Han Chinese urge to preserve their culture during the time of non-Han rule. The people in the south had never experienced rule by non-Han people and were therefore shocked by the Mongol conquest. They felt that their culture was threatened by that conquest and they sensed the great cultural gap that separated their ways from the ways of the nomads and of the Mongols' Central Asian helpers. Southern Chinese, whether Taoists or Confucians or whatever, were alike in that they were the conquered. To that extent their destiny was indivisible. The emergence of Hsüan-chiao is symptomatic of this, for it had no function once Mongol rule was ended.

Yü Chi possessed eminent literary and Confucian credentials. He was the descendant of a Sung general who had fought the Jurchens.[2] Under the Mongol rulers of the first three and a half decades of the fourteenth century, Yü Chi served as a loyal and dedicated official, leading the ranks of Chinese officials at Ta-tu 大都 (modern Peking). His mentor Wu Ch'eng was not as devoted an official at court, but as an intellect and a scholar he was the brightest light of Yüan times. Both men were close to Hsüan-chiao Taoists, and both benefitted from the help of those Taoists in the political sphere. The Taoists had an avenue of influence which led to the Mongol court, an avenue unto which ordinary Confucian scholars lacked entry. In return for the Taoists' assistance, the Confucian scholars lent them their orthodox prestige within the Han Chinese world order. As a consequence, the Taoist religious movement in Yüan times was raised to a higher cultural level than it had previously

---

[2] This was Yü Yün-wen 虞允文 (1110–1154), who fought and defeated the Jurchen Chin emperor Wan-yen Liang 完顏亮 in 1161. See Tao Jing-shen's entry in Herbert Franke, ed., *Sung Biographies* (Wiesbaden: Franz Steiner, 1976), pp. 1264–1266.

attained. Yü Chi was instrumental in this effort, and it is this subject which the present essay attempts to explore.

In the Yüan period a multiplicity of religious forms thrived. Because the Mongols were religious people, and because they had their own shamanistic tradition, they were receptive to certain Taoistic practices when they came into contact with Chinese civilization. Eventually Taoism took a back seat to Lamaism, as far as Mongol religious patronage was concerned, but it nevertheless played an influential role. Yüan Taoism can be divided into two main branches, the northern and the southern. The northern included Ch'üan-chen 全眞 ("Complete Realization"), T'ai-i 太一 ("Grand Unity"), and Chen-ta 眞大 ("Realization [Made] Great"). In the south the main form of Taoism was the ancient school of the Celestial Master, known as Cheng-i 正一 ("Correct Unity"). All four schools had close ties with Han Chinese literati and all four in Yüan times exerted efforts to nourish and protect Han Chinese culture. A number of prominent Taoist leaders emerged with literary abilities that rivalled those of the traditional literati elite. Wang Ch'ung-yang 王重陽 (1113–1170), an early leader of Ch'üan-chen Taoism in the north, is one such example.[3] Ch'iu Ch'u-chi 丘處機 (1148–1227), successor of Wang Ch'ung-yang, who travelled to Samarkand and beyond to instruct Chinggis Khan in the 1220s, is another.[4] And Li Tao-ch'ien 李道謙, the Yüan compiler of *Kan-ho hsien-yüan lu* 甘河仙源錄 (*Record of the Immortals' Spring at Kan River*),[5] preserved many important literati writings about the early Ch'üan-chen movement begun by Wang Ch'ung-yang.

Literary attainment was characteristic as well of southern Taoists. The Celestial Master's school of Taoism was centered at Mao Shan 茅山 in Kiangsu. The peak was also known as San-mao Feng 三茅峯, after the legendary "Three Mao Brothers." Taoism had been centered there since Ch'i 齊 and Liang 梁 times (late fifth century to early sixth), when the

---

[3] Also known as Wang Che 王嚞, he was educated in Confucian learning, eventually studying Buddhism and Taoism. He is considered the founder of Ch'üan-chen Taoism. Collections of his prose and poetry are available in the *Tao tsang* 道藏. See the entry by Kubo Noritada in *Ajia rekishi jiten* アジア歴史事典 (Tokyo: Heibonsha, 1975, 7th printing), vol. 2, p. 24. See also Arthur Waley, tr. and introd., Li Chih-ch'ang, *Travels of an Alchemist: The Journey of the Taoist Ch'ang-ch'un from China to the Hindukush at the Summons of Chingiz Khan* (London: Routledge, 1931), pp. 13–16.

[4] Ch'iu Ch'u-chi's collected works are also available in the *Tao tsang*. For a Western-language study, see Arthur Waley, *Travels of an Alchemist*.

[5] This work appears in the *Tao tsang*. The title alludes to Wang Ch'ung-yang's meeting with an immortal at Kan-ho chen 甘河鎮. He drank the water and the illness he had been suffering from was cured. For a note on this collection of writings, see *Ssu-k'u ch'üan-shu tsung-mu* 四庫全書總目 (Taipei: Yeewen reprint, 1969, third printing), 147:35b–36b.

great Taoist scholar T'ao Hung-ching 陶弘景 (456–536) resided there as
a hermit.[6] After T'ao a continuous succession of Taoist luminaries was
associated with Mao Shan, and during the Yüan period, as in earlier
times, literati frequently went there for retreats and for enlightenment.

The history of official patronage of southern Taoism in the Yüan
period commences in the thirteenth year of the Chih-yüan 至元 reign
period. This corresponds to the year 1276, the year of Khubilai's
subjugation of most of Chiang-nan 江南 and the conquest of the
Southern Sung capital at Hangchow 杭州 (then known as Lin-an 臨安).
In that year the north and south were reunited after many years of
separation. Khubilai issued an edict in which he summoned to Shang-tu
上都, his steppe capital, the titular head of the southern Taoist clergy,
the thirty-sixth Celestial Master, Chang Tsung-yen 張宗演 (d. 1292).[7]
This event marks a turning-point for southern Taoism, for, despite its
second-rank status with respect to Buddhism, Taoism from this time on
until the end of the dynasty held a major position in the religious life of
the rulers. And from this time on southern Taoism had formal spokes-
men in the north.

In Chinese history, Han Chinese scholars typically looked down on
what they called "the heterodox teachings" of Buddhism and Taoism.
This contempt was particularly true with respect to the practitioners of
religious Taoism, whose *fu-lu* 符籙 (prognostications), *chai-chiao* 齋醮
(fasts and prayer ceremonies), elixir alchemy, and pursuit of immortality
they severely criticized and attacked. But, after the Mongol conquest of
China, these traditional prejudices lessened considerably. Following the
conquest, many of the *i-min* 遺民 (loyal survivors) of the Southern Sung
sought refuge in Taoist monasteries. This tended to promote the blending of Confucian and Taoist concerns, and in turn gave added impetus to
the notion that "the three teachings are one" (*san chiao i chih* 三教一致),
an idea that had emerged as early as late T'ang times.[8]

---

[6] For biographies see *Nan shih* 南史 (Peking: Chung-hua Shu-chü, 1975), 76:1897; and
Liang shu 梁書 (Peking: Chung-hua Shu-chü, 1973), 51:742. T'ao was the author of the
famous Taoist scripture, *Chen kao* 真誥.

[7] *Yüan shih* 元史 (Peking: Chung-hua Shu-chü, 1976) [hereafter abbreviated YS], 9:182.
See also YS 14:295, for the year 1287, where we read that Khubilai sent an agent bearing
incense and gifts to the three big Taoist monasteries in Kiangsi and Kiangsu: Lung-hu
Shan 龍虎山, Yü-ssu 玉笥 and Ko-tsao 閤皁 (a pair of monasteries), and San-mao 二茅.
Fasting and prayer ceremonies were held, and the emperor summoned the Celestial Master
to Shang-tu for a second visit.

[8] See *Chi ku-chin fo-tao lun-heng* 集古今佛道論衡, by Tao-hsüan 道宣, in *Fo-tsang*
佛藏; biography of Ch'en T'uan 陳摶, *Sung shih* 宋史 (Peking: Chung-hua Shu-chü,
1977), 457:13420; Ch'en Teng-yüan 陳登原, *Chung-kuo wen-hua shih* 中國文化史 (repr.
Taipei: Shih-chieh Shu-chü, 1955–56), vol. 2, pp. 48–49.

In Yüan society we observe the emergence of what one might call "lay Taoists," who in reality were both Confucian and Taoist. At the same time, Manichaeism, Maitreyaism, and other religious movements which had usually been regarded as "heterodox" and uncivilized by the traditional Confucian scholarly elite, began to flourish. The intellectual and religious world of the Chinese thus became increasingly turbulent, so that individual identification with Confucian or non-Confucian schools of thought grew rather ambiguous. Furthermore, a certain amount of ethnocentric thought[9] became evident, for the various intellectual and religious currents that became active were all in part manifestations of the greater Han Chinese struggle against the non-Han nationality that had conquered China proper. Eventually these movements played a role in the military uprisings at the end of the Yüan, driving the Mongol rulers back into the steppe. They played a strong role, as well, in the establishment of the Ming dynasty, proclaimed in 1368.

The Taoist religious movement, known in Chinese as Tao-chiao 道教, "the teaching of the Way," claimed Lao Tzu 老子 as its founder and raised high the banner of Huang-Lao 黃老, the Yellow Emperor and Lao Tzu. It incorporated the ideals of the worthies and immortals, the Yin-Yang mystical techniques that had evolved since Warring States times, the prognostication techniques of the *ch'an-wei* 讖緯 (prognostication texts and apocrypha) of the Later Han, and the efficacy of shamans or witches (*wu-hsi* 巫覡). It was founded as an organized movement by Chang Ling 張陵 (or Chang Tao-ling 張道陵) in the late part of the second century A.D. Its name was The Way of the Five Pecks of Rice (*wu tou mi tao* 五斗米道). This movement gradually merged with the Way of the Great Peace (*t'ai-p'ing tao* 太平道), inspired by Chang Chüeh 張角 (d. A.D. 184). The scriptural authority of this movement was the *T'ai-p'ing ch'ing-ling shu* 太平青領書, which was probably the forerunner of the extant text known as the *T'ai-p'ing ching* 太平經.[10] The T'ai-p'ing and Five Pecks of Rice Taoist movements were separate, but both played roles in the Yellow Turban rebellion at the end of the Han. The Taoist religious movement thus had a powerful political component, and this was certainly not absent in Yüan time, despite the fact that it was a time of peace.

Religious Taoism claimed descent from Lao Tzu, as already mentioned, but it was quite distinct from philosophical Taoism. In Chinese this latter current is known as Tao-chia 道家 to distinuish it from Tao-chiao. The former refers to a philosophical school of thought, whereas the latter refers mainly to a popular structure of belief. Although both

---

[9] *Min-tsu ssu-hsiang*　民族思想.
[10] This work is found in the *Tao tsang*.

claimed an affiliation with Lao Tzu's doctrine of "purity and non-action" (*ch'ing-ching wu-wei* 清淨無爲),[11] the founding of religious Taoism as an important political and social movement occurred in the latter part of the Later Han. The first large-scale popular rebellion in Chinese history was the Yellow Turban rebellion, and it was motivated by a revolutionary organization which upheld the *T'ai-p'ing ching* as its scriptural inspiration.

Chang Chüeh's movement had attempted to institute a structure under the rubric "the thirty-six districts (*fang* 方)," and in this it was paralleled by "the twenty-four parishes (*chih* 治)" of the Way of the Five Pecks of Rice. These "parishes" served as Taoist monasteries and political agencies and had been instituted by Chang Lu 張魯, the grandson of Chang Ling, in an effort to regularize his control. Chang Lu did not succeed, for Ts'ao Ts'ao 曹操 (A.D. 155–220) defeated Chang's followers. But in a sense these Taoist movements were not defeated, for they re-emerged in later times. The rebellions of Sun En 孫恩 and Lu Hsün 盧循 during the Eastern Chin 東晉 period are cases in point.[12]

Taoism was a multifaceted religious movement, of which the Five Pecks of Rice was but one. Literati and scholars had their own form of religious Taoism, and this may be viewed as another facet of religious Taoism in general. This line began with Ko Hung 葛洪 (283–343), author of the *Pao-p'u tzu* 抱朴子, which teaches one how to attain immortality by consuming elixirs.[13] This line in turn thrived under the influence of T'ao Hung-ching at Mao Shan. Literati Taoists in this sphere were not willing to engage in revolutionary activities, but rather sought ties with the ruling establishments in their day and obtained sponsorship from the rulers. Eventually, however, K'ou Ch'ien-chih 寇謙之 (362–448) and other powerful Taoist leaders engaged the Buddhists in a struggle and brought greater power and prestige to religious Taoism.[14]

Because the basic nature of religious Taoism was political (although

---

[11] These terms are frequently associated with philosophical Taoism.

[12] For Sun En (d. 402), see *Chin shu* 晉書 (Peking: Chung-hua Shu-chü, 1974), 100:2631. Sun's family for generations had upheld the teaching of the Way of the Five Pecks of Rice. For Lu Hsün (d. 411), see *Chin shu*, 100:2634. He was Sun's successor, but his life ended in suicide.

[13] For translations, see James R. Ware, *Alchemy, Medicine, Religion in the China of* A.D. *320: The* NEI P'IEN *of Ko Hung* (PAO-P'U TZU) (Cambridge: The M.I.T. Press, 1966), and Jay Sailey, *The Master Who Embraces Simplicity: A Study of the Philosopher Ko Hung, A.D. 283–343* (San Francisco: Chinese Materials Center, 1978).

[14] K'ou Ch'ien-chih succeeded to the position of the Celestial Master, and it was under his influence that Taoism became the state religion of the Northern Wei. See *Wei shu* 魏書 (Peking: Chung-hua Shu-chü, 1974), 114:3049–3054. See also Miyakawa Hisayuki's entry in *Ajia rekishi jiten*, vol. 3, p. 222.

not exclusively so), the history of Tao-chiao over the centuries is one of political struggle. The T'ang emperor Wu-tsung 武宗 (r. 840–846) sought to eradicate Buddhism in part due to the advice of his trusted Taoist adviser Chao Kuei-chen 趙歸真 (d. 846).[15] Similarly, Emperor Hui-tsung 徽宗 (r. 1100–1125) of the Sung was under the influence of the Taoist adept Lin Ling-su 林靈素 (d. 1119), who induced the emperor to spend enormous sums on Taoist rituals. The emperor, in fact, took a Taoist title for himself, *Tao-chün huang-ti* 道君皇帝.[16]

Tao-chiao experienced a transformation in North China after the Jurchen conquest. Under Sung Hui-tsung, organized religious Taoism had been largely a movement associated with the court. But under the Jurchens it began to gain a popularity that it had not enjoyed since pre-T'ang times. Under the Jurchens this reinvigorated religious Taoism rallied its followers around the cries "save the world" (*chiu-shih* 救世) and "restore the dynasty" (*fu-kuo* 復國). The rise of Ch'üan-chen Taoism as well as of T'ai-i Taoism during this period is indicative of this larger trend. But the content of religious Taoist teachings changed as well. Elements of *li-hsüeh* 理學, the Neo-Confucian philosophy of "principle" (*li* 理), were absorbed into religious Taoism, as were elements of the teachings of the Buddhist Ch'an (or Zen) school. Learned literati joined this new movement, which incorporated both philosophical and religious dimensions, as it gained wider appeal among the popular masses.

All the khans, beginning with Chinggis, believed in shamans or witches and in fortune-telling and divination. Before undertaking military actions, the Mongols nearly always engaged in divination to determine auspicious moments for action. For this reason Tibetan monks' incantations and spells (*chin chou* 禁咒) and Chinese Taoists' apparent control over spirits and ghosts, their prayers for rain, and their prayer ceremonies (*chiao* 醮), not to mention the Chinese literati's divination and theories of the Five Agents (*wu hsing* 五行) and Yin-Yang, were all compatible with the Mongols' own original religious beliefs.

The *Yüan shih* 元史, an "official" history of the Yüan dynasty compiled in the early years of the Ming using extant documents, notes

---

[15] Chao Kuei-chen was beheaded by the subsequent ruler, who reinstated Buddhism. See Kubo Noritada's entry in *Ajia rekishi jiten*, vol. 6, p. 277. See also the brief note on the Taoist-Buddhist rivalry in T'ang times in Denis Twitchett and Arthur F. Wright, ed., *Perspectives on the T'ang* (New Haven: Yale University Press, 1973), pp. 23–25.

[16] *Sung shih* 宋史, 462:13528, biography of Lin Ling-su. See also the entry by Kubo Noritada in *Ajia rekishi jiten*, vol. 9, p. 332. According to the *Sung shih*, Hui-tsung took this title when he enthroned his heir apparent and retired to the Lung-te Kung 龍德宮 in 1125. See *Sung shih*, 23:421. For a biography of Hui-tsung in German, see Yoshida Tora's entry in Herbert Franke, ed., *Sung Biographies*, pp. 461–464.

that Yeh-lü Ch'u-ts'ai 耶律楚材 (1189–1243), a sinicized Khitan noble-man who advised Chinggis Khan, performed divination on behalf of Chinggis before the latter launched troops into the field.[17] Liu Ping-chung 劉秉忠 (1216–1274), an adviser to Khubilai Khaghan, was an expert on the *Book of Changes* and was, for this expertise, particularly well favored by the emperor.[18] Divination was one medium through which Chinese and Mongols were able to communicate.

This partially explains the new and close links that developed between literati in the south and the religious Taoist establishment there. When Khubilai conquered the Southern Sung, reunifying China, the political structure of the Mongol regime was already well established. Confucian scholar-ministers among the Han Chinese serving Khubilai at the time of the conquest of the south were dominated by persons from the advisory group which Khubilai had assembled at Chin-lien ch'uan 金蓮川 when he was still a prince, prior to taking the throne of the *khaghan* in 1260. Chin-lien ch'uan was in the steppe, where the city Dolon is today, in Inner Mongolia. Khubilai was ordered by the reigning khaghan to establish a headquarters preparatory to the conquest of China. It was renamed K'ai-p'ing fu 開平府. Later, after Khubilai became khaghan, he renamed it Shang-tu 上都, "the upper capital," to distinguish it from Ta-tu 大都, "the great capital," on the site of modern Peking. Among the Chin-lien ch'uan group of advisers were a number of influential Han Chinese. These included Hsü Heng 許衡 (1209–1281), Yao Shu 姚樞 (1203–1280), Tou Mo 竇默, and Sung Tzu-chen 宋子貞. All of them were northerners and all were adherents of Chu Hsi's *tao-hsüeh* 道學, or fundamentalist Confucian philosophy. As such they tended to prefer solid and simple literary styles over the ornate and showy. To some degree they had little sympathy for the ornate and refined literary styles of their southern literati brethren. Southerners had a hard time support-ing themselves in the north, partially because of the rift that separated them from their northern Han Chinese colleagues.[19] This fact lay behind the heightened solidarity among southern literati and Taoists that was characteristic of the Yüan period.

Alternatives for southern literati were limited. A number of scholars

---

[17] YS 146:3456.

[18] YS 157:3688. See also Hok-lam Chan, "Liu Ping-chung (1216–74), A Buddhist-Taoist Statesman at the Court of Khubilai Khan," *T'oung Pao*, 53 (1967), pp. 99–146.

[19] Chao Meng-fu 趙孟頫 (1254–1322) is an important and obvious exception. But most members of the Sung house of Chao fared poorly. Chao Yü-p'iao 趙與𤧬 (1242–1303), for example, devoted many years of his life to service in the northern capital, but he was impoverished when he died. See the *hsing-chuang* 行狀 (record of conduct) by Yüan Chüeh 袁桷, in *Ch'ing-jung chü-shih chi* 清容居士集 (SPTK ed.), 32:4a, where it states that he "could not support himself" (*pu neng tzu yang* 不能自養).

simply remained poor and dwelt quietly in anonymity, their lives devoted entirely to scholarship. Ma Tuan-lin 馬端臨 and Wang Ying-lin 王應麟 are two notable examples of this. They were the compilers of the *Wen-hsien t'ung-k'ao* 文獻通考 and *K'un-hsüeh chi-wen* 困學紀聞, respectively, two important encyclopedic compilations frequently used by historians today. We know rather little about the lives of these two scholars, for in their day they remained relatively unprominent.

There were a number of Sung loyalists, too, such as Hsieh Fang-te 謝枋得, Cheng Ssu-hsiao 鄭思肖, and Hsieh Ao 謝翱, who refused to submit to the new rulers.[20] But the greatest number of literati were probably those who chose neither of these two routes of resistance, and instead chose to seek careers in Yüan government. They never climbed very high. The highest any ever reached was into the ranks of some academy or bureau in Ta-tu, and there they wiled away their years. The majority entered careers as unranked bureaucrats, dependent for their positions on the patronage of Mongols or others in power. In Yüan times there were really only two avenues to government service, the military route and the clerkly route. This was observed by Yü Chi in an inscription for Su Chih-tao 蘇志道 (1261–1320), father of Su T'ien-chüeh 蘇天爵 (1294–1352), the prominent literatus of the late Yüan period:

"Our dynasty (*kuo-chia* 國家) in the beginning pacified the realm by means of arms and esteemed ministers of military ability and exploits. But the tasks involving money, grain, grain shipments, deadlines, evaluation of personnel for rewards and sanctions, surveys of the highways and products [of the realm], for these, without the clerks (*li* 吏) and official documents there is no way to keep records and to execute policy. This is why the clerks have come to be advanced into official posts. There was no eagerness [on the part of the rulers] to advance scholars through other (i.e. examination) paths. High officials and military officers in the end have come solely from these two routes!"[21]

Yü Chi was an intelligent observer. Scholars who wanted to pursue government careers had to face the fact that the rulers had use only for functional literacy. That is, aside from the need for generals who could perform exploits on behalf of Mongol expansionism, the Mongols had need only for literate functionaries to keep accurate records and to get

[20] On these see F. W. Mote, "Confucian Eremitism in the Yüan Period," in Arthur F. Wright, ed., *The Confucian Persuasion* (Stanford: Stanford University Press, 1960), pp. 202–240.

[21] On Hsieh Ao see Lo-shu Fu, "Teng Mu: A Forgotten Chinese Philosopher," *T'oung Pao*, 52:1–3 (1965), pp. 46–53; Yü Chi, *Tao-yüan hsüeh-ku lu* 道園學古錄 (SPTK ed.), 15:3a–3b.

things done on time. These were bureaucrats, and such careers were comedowns from the standpoint of scholars who had traditionally prepared for careers in statecraft as ranked officials at court.

Yet, while the scholars from the south met a chilling situation in respect to their ambitions, the Taoists met a warm one. They were well received in the north. Yü Chi noticed that the Celestial Master's disciple Chang Liu-sun 張留孫, when both men went north in response to Khubilai's summons in 1276, had received a most warm welcome and had even later been invited to assist in the khaghan's selection of a minister to succeed the corrupt Sengge. Chang was highly regarded by Emperor Wu-tsung (Hai-shan 海山), Yü Chi added, and his divination expertise was the skill that had won him this favor.

Chang's disciple Wu Ch'üan-chieh 吳全節 was also highly regarded by the emperors. In fact, it was he who first introduced the writings and teachings of the Sung philosopher Lu Hsiang-shan 陸象山 (1139–1192) to the court. And it was he who intervened to support the southern scholar Wu Ch'eng when the latter encountered the intransigence of the Ch'eng-Chu disciples in the north in 1331. Ch'eng-Chu learning at that time was predominant in the north. The emphasis on *tao wen hsüeh* 道問學 (inquiry and study) tended to displace any complementary emphasis on *tsun te hsing* 尊德性 (honoring the moral nature), as David Gedalecia has pointed out in his paper on Wu Ch'eng in this volume. But in Chiang-nan, the scholars tended to favor the broadening of intellectual concerns by elucidating the teachings of Lu Hsiang-shan. Wu Ch'eng was the leading literatus representing this approach. He was discriminated against by the northern scholars who dominated the Han-lin Academy in Ta-tu. But perhaps because the approach taken by Wu Ch'eng and his school, with its non-dogmatic, non-sectarian eclectic nature, meshed well with the learning of the Taoists, or perhaps because Wu Ch'üan-chieh and Wu Ch'eng were from the same home locale, and perhaps because Wu Ch'eng had a slight relationship through marriage with the family of the Celestial Master,[22] perhaps for all of these

---

[22] Wu Ch'eng's relationship with the Celestial Master's household was indirect and posthumous. His grand-nephew was married to the daughter of the forty-third Celestial Master Chang Yü-ch'u 張宇初 (1359–1409). For this fact, see Chang's collected works, *Hsien-ch'üan chi* 峴泉集 (*Ssu-k'u ch'üan-shu chen-pen* 四庫全書珍本 ed., series 5), 3:61b–62b and 3:62b–63b. [The editor is indebted to Professor Lao Yan-shuan for this reference.] For a study of Chang Yü-ch'u see Sun K'o-k'uan, "Ming-ch'u t'ien-shih Chang Yü-ch'u chi ch'i *Hsien-ch'üan chi*," *Shu-mu chi-k'an*. 9:4 (March 1976), pp. 3–17.

Wu Ch'eng's wife was the aunt of a lay Taoist named Yü Hsi-sheng 余希聖. Wu revealed this in a funerary inscription for his wife, Yü Wei-kung 余維恭 (1255–1291). For the inscription, see *Wu Wen-cheng kung chi* 吳文正公集 (1756 woodblock ed.), 36:8b. Yü Chi confirms this fact in *Tao-yüan hsüeh-ku lu*, 50:18b. For more on this lay Taoist, whose

reasons, Wu Ch'üan-chieh and other Taoists were inclined to assist Wu
Ch'eng and other southerners of his school when they were in the north.

When the Celestial Master travelled north to Ta-tu in 1276 at the
summons of Khubilai, he took with him his disciple Chang Liu-sun, a
native of Kui-hsi hsien 貴溪縣 in Hsin-chou 信州, Kiangsi. In the
following year the Celestial Master returned south, and he left Chang
Liu-sun behind in the north to act as his representative. According to
contemporaneous records, the Celestial Master left the north because he
did not like the northern climate: "The northern land is high and cold
and all [the others] were unable to live there, so [the Celestial Master]
deputed [Chang Liu-sun] to take charge of his affairs." [23]

Chang Liu-sun soon became well regarded by Khubilai's son Chen-
chin 真金, the heir apparent. In 1278 Khubilai grew so fond of him that
he wanted to award Chang the title Celestial Master. But Chang declined
out of respect for his former lord. Khubilai then conferred a new title,
Hsüan-chiao tsung-shih 玄教宗師, "Patriarch of the Sublime Learning."
Thus was this new school of Taoism born. Its birth was primarily a
political matter, not religious, because Chang Liu-sun was put in charge
of all Taoist activities in the south. This new position evidently was
regarded by the khaghan as one that displaced the position of the
Celestial Master.

Chang Liu-sun enjoyed great prominence as the leading Taoist in Ta-
tu. He was able to utilize his close and good tie with Chen-chin
(Khubilai's son and heir), for example, to have the ban on Taoist writings
relaxed. This ban had been in force ever since the defeat of the Taoists in
the debates with the Buddhists in the 1270s. [24] In 1279 Chen-chin
attempted to "explain" the teachings of the Taoists, at Chang's urging,

---

Taoist cognomen was Fei-fei-tzu 非非子, see Wang I 王沂, *I-pin chi* 伊濱集 (*Ssu-k'u
ch'üan-shu chen-pen* ed., 1st series), 50:17a; and Ch'en Ming-kuei 陳銘珪, *Ch'ang-ch'un
tao-chiao yüan-liu k'ao* 長春道教源流考 (*Chü-te t'ang ts'ung-shu* 聚德堂叢書 ed.), 1:12a.

Wu Ch'eng's collected works are replete with writings about Taoist subjects. *Chüan* 46 in
the *Ssu-k'u ch'üan-shu chen-pen* edition of his works is devoted to writings about Taoist
monasteries. And he even referred to a stage in his life as the time when he "donned the
robes of the Taoist." See the preface to three poems in his collected works, *Wu Wen-cheng
chi* 吳文正集 (*Ssu-k'u ch'üan-shu chen-pen* ed.), 96:4b; quoted in Lao Yen-hsüan 勞延煊
[Yan-shuan Lao], "Yüan-ch'u nan-fang chih-shih-fen-tzu 元初南方知識份子," *Chung-kuo
wen-hua yen-chiu-suo hsüeh-pao* 中國文化研究所學報, 10 (1979), p. 142.

[23] Yüan Chüeh, "Hsüan-chiao ta tsung-shih Chang kung chia-chuan 玄教大宗師
張公家傳," *Ch'ing-jung chü-shih chi*, 34:14b–22a; see 15b. This text is reproduced in Sun
K'o-k'uan, *Yüan-tai tao-chiao chih fa-chan*, pp. 416–420.

[24] See Paul Demiéville, "La situation religieuse en Chine au temps de Marco Polo," in
Oriente Poliano (Rome: Instituto Italiano per il Medio ed Estremo Oriente, 1957), pp.
193–234.

to the khaghan. Evidently his explanations had some effect, for the ban on Taoist writings was never strictly enforced.

Chang even played a role in the selection of Mongolian names for Emperors Wu-tsung and Jen-tsung 仁宗, born in 1281 and 1285 respectively. In both instances the Mongolian names were chosen after advice was received from Chang Liu-sun with respect to the auspicious qualities of various suggestions. Although Chang knew no Mongolian, Khubilai nevertheless felt it advisable to solicit his advice.

Eventually Chang won a more solid institutional base for his activities when the Han-lin Chi-hsien yüan 翰林集賢院 was split into its component parts, the Hanlin Academy and the Academy of Worthies. This event took place in 1281, and at Chang's suggestion the Academy of Worthies was assigned the responsibility, among others, of overseeing Taoist activities throughout the realm. Under Emperor Ch'eng-tsung 成宗, who succeeded Khubilai in 1294, the patronage of religious Taoism grew deeper. Ch'eng-tsung was personally very fond of Taoism, and so in 1295 he appointed Chang Liu-sun the co-director of the Academy of Worthies. It was Ch'eng-tsung who in 1299 elevated Chang's title to *Hsüan-chiao ta tsung-shih* 玄教大宗師, "Great Patriarch of Hsüan-chiao." Ch'eng-tsung also ordered Chang to deliver lectures on the meaning of the Taoist text *Nan-hua ching* 南華經, better known as the *Chuang Tzu* 莊子.

Honors of this sort kept coming to Chang Liu-sun right up until his death on the *jen-tzu* 壬子 day of the twelfth month of the first year of the reign of Emperor Ying-tsung 英宗, which corresponds to January 1, 1322. Because of his eminence, two of Chang's nephews were enrolled in the *su-wei* 宿衛, the Imperial Guard, which, among other duties, guarded the palace.[25]

Chang Liu-sun was succeeded as Hsüan-chiao head by his disciple Wu Ch'üan-chieh. Wu had begun the study of the Tao when he was thirteen *sui* 歲 (i.e., about twelve by Western reckoning), and by the age of sixteen *sui* he was already a *tao-shih* 道師 (Taoist adept).[26] After 1287, the year in which he was invited north by his master Chang Liu-sun, Wu Ch'üan-chieh spent most of his time in the northern capitals, Shang-tu and Ta-tu. Winning the favor of the rulers, he was asked to greet the new khaghan Ch'eng-tsung in 1295 on the occasion of the latter's arrival at

---

[25] On the *su-wei*, see Hsiao Ch'i-ch'ing, *The Military Establishment of the Yüan Dynasty* (Cambridge: Harvard University Press, 1978), p. 210, note 1. For this information, see Yüan Chüeh, *Ch'ing-jung chü-shih chi*, 34:21b.

[26] See Yü Chi, funerary inscription for Chang Liu-sun, in *Tao-yüan hsüeh-ku lu*, 50:13b; quoted in Nogami Shunjō 野上俊静, *Genshi shakurōden no kenkyū* 元史釈老傳の研究 (Kyoto: Hoyu Shoten 朋友書店, 1978), p. 102. See also Lo-shu Fu, "Teng Mu," p. 43.

the capital from the steppe. Wu presided over the *chiao* (prayer ceremonies) at Shang-tu at that time, in celebration of the accession of the
new sovereign. The ceremonies lasted five days and nights without
interruption. Wu's career from that date on was a series of imperial
recognitions. In 1307, for example, Emperor Wu-tsung conferred upon
him the title *Hsüan-chiao ssu-shih* 玄教嗣師 or "Heir to the Hsüan-chiao
Patriarchy." This meant that he was officially recognized as the successor
to Chang Liu-sun as the head of Hsüan-chiao Taoism. When Chang died
in 1322, Wu indeed succeeded him as Great Patriarch of Hsüan-chiao.
At the same time, he was appointed head of Taoist affairs under the
Academy of Worthies. Between that year (1307) and the year of his
death there were many occasions when the rulers issued edicts demanding "the protection of [the Taoist] religion" (*hu chiao* 護教). These
proclamations were directly connected with imperial favors which were
conferred upon him.

Chang Liu-sun's and Wu Ch'üan-chieh's influence came of course
from their easy ties, through their Taoist practices, with the Mongol
court. But their influence in society at large depended to a great extent
on the administrative and demonstrative aspects of their favor at court.
By designating the Patriarch of Hsüan-chiao as the head of Taoist
religion in the lower Yangtze Valley, the Mongols effectively regionalized
their influence, using the Hsüan-chiao as a means of assisting their rule
over south China. In return, the southern Chinese obtained a channel of
communication with the rulers. The Academy of Worthies served as the
institutional setting of much of that communication near the top of the
pyramid of power.

According to the *Yüan History*, the Academy of Worthies had a range
of responsibilities including both Taoism and Confucianism. Under its
aegis were the Kuo-tzu chien 國子監 (National College), Yin-Yang,
sacrifices, divination, recluses, and Hsüan-chiao. Yü Chi noted
that the Academy of Worthies, when it was separated from the Hanlin
Academy in 1285, was given the responsibility of appointing Tao officers
in all the local districts, presumbly in the south. These officers possessed
rank at court and were empowered to use official seals corresponding to
rank five. The Academy of Worthies was also given authority over
administrators (*chu-chang* 主掌) at all Taoist monasteries. Thus the
Academy of Worthies was the Taoist equivalent of the Hsüan-cheng
yüan 宣政院 (Bureau of Buddhist and Tibetan Affairs).[27]

Chang Liu-sun and Wu Ch'üan-chieh evidently were quite successful

---

[27] For discussions of the Hsüan-cheng yüan, see the essays by David Farquhar and
Herbert Franke in this volume.

in reinvigorating the monasteries of religious Taoism in Chiang-nan, if
not even throughout China. The Taoist monasteries in the lower Yangtze
and Han river regions were virtually all rebuilt and restored during this
period. The monasteries Yü-ssu 玉笥 and Ko-tsao 閣皁 in Kiangsi, the
Wu-tang 武當 monastery in Hupei, and the T'ien-t'ai 天臺 and Tung-
hsiao 洞霄 monasteries in Chekiang were all restored. They were able
eventually to rival the great monasteries of Buddhism.

Wu Ch'üan-chieh was known as a tireless supporter of southern
literati. He was commemorated for his "chivalrous" character by the
authors of the *Yüan History*:

"[Wu] Ch'üan-chieh elegantly favored making friends with literati
(*shih-ta-fu* 士大夫), and there were no favors he would not perform [for
them]. In his relations with his elders, he was especially considerate and
respectful, and in promoting [the careers of] talented persons, he feared
only that he did not exert all his strength. As for helping those in poverty
or in dire straits, he never let his mind be altered by personal debts or
grudges. In his day he was highly regarded for his endowment of
chivalric spirit (*hsia ch'i* 俠氣)."[28]

Wu was so fondly regarded by Confucian scholars that not even the
scholars' traditional antipathy for religious Taoist pursuits prevented
them from appreciating him. The scholar Hsü Yu-jen 許友壬 (1287–
1364), who became prominent in the 1330s and 1340s, confessed that he
had a general dislike for "the affairs of spirits and immortals" (*shen-hsien
chih shih* 神仙之事), meaning Taoist matters, because "they undermine
the great ethical relationships" (*luan ta lun* 亂大倫). Despite these
reservations, however, Hsü saw in Wu Ch'üan-chieh great depths of
loyalty and filial piety.[29]

Yü Chi's career was undertaken within the context of the careers of
the two Kiangsi Taoists discussed above. He was close to them, and as
such he and they inevitably exerted influence upon one another. Yü Chi,
for his part, became quite learned in Taoist lore and thought. The
Taoists, for their part, were to some degree taught how to function with
distinction in the refined literary world of the scholars.

Yü Chi's career at court was impressive, although to be sure he never
became a key decision-maker among the Mongols. No southern Chinese
ever assumed the role of decision-maker at court in Yüan times. Yet Yü
Chi did manage to climb high in the Confucian academies at court. His
career reached its summit during the reign of Wen-tsung, a man who

---

[28] YS 202:4529; for a Japanese annotated translation, see Nogami Shunjō, *Genshi
shakurōden no kenkyū*, p. 108.
[29] For the text, see Sun K'o-k'uan, *Yüan-tai tao-chiao chih fa-chan*, p. 178.

may have acquired some measure of literacy in Chinese. Yü Chi stood at the head of Wen-tsung's prestigious academy, the K'uei-chang ko 奎章閣 (Pavilion of the Star of Literature).[30] A man of impressive attainments in poetry, prose, and song, Yü Chi's great influence can be seen in the general refinement of the literary capabilities of the religious Taoists in the south. Through his literary influence, the social position of religious Taoism in the south was significantly improved, to the extent that it even exceeded that of the other sects of Taoism in the north (i.e., Ch'üan-chen and T'ai-i).

Yü Chi's accomplishments were multi-faceted. He had great abilities in politics, as evidenced by his career, virtually uninterrupted despite the frequent battles between Mongol factions.[31] In poetry he was acclaimed widely. In fact, even today people still refer to "the poetry of the four Yüan masters," of which Yü Chi is one.[32] It was partly due to Yü Chi's literary eminence that he became the director of the *Ching-shih ta-tien* 經世大典 compilation project in 1331.[33] This work was an encyclopedia of Yüan institutions and served, among other things, to justify the reign of Emperor Wen-tsung. Wen-tsung, it will be recalled, obtained the throne upon the assassination of his brother.

Within religious Taoism as practiced during Yü Chi's time there were two major camps, differentiated on the basis of their approach to immortality. One may be designated the Tan-ting 丹鼎 or "Elixir Vessel" school.[34] This was a blend of a number of currents within the broad Taoist tradition. It was particularly characterized by *fang-hsien* 方仙 (immortals), and was virtually a cult of immortality which pursued its aim through the ingestion of elixirs. Within this Elixir school there was a sub-current which we may designate the *I-shu* 易數 or numerology school. This school was actually an offshoot of classical learning which

[30] For this aspect of Yü Chi's career, and his relation with Wen-tsung and Wen-tsung's effort to achieve legitimacy following his accession to the throne over the dead body of his brother, see John D. Langlois, Jr., "Yü Chi and His Mongol Sovereign: The Scholar as Apologist," *Journal of Asian Studies*, 38:1 (November 1978), pp. 99–116.

[31] See his biography in YS 181:4177, where it relates that at one point Yü Chi unsuccessfully requested a position outside the capital, and on another occasion his proposals regarding the opening of the salt fields in Yen-nan were disregarded.

[32] The others were Yang Wei-chen 楊維禎 (1296–1370), Fan Ch'un 范梈 (1272–1330), and Chieh Hsi-ssu 揭傒斯 (1274–1344). For Yang, see Edmund H. Worthy's entry in L. C. Goodrich and Chaoying Fang, ed., *Dictionary of Ming Biography* (New York: Columbia University Press, 1976), pp. 1547–1553. For Fan and Chieh, see YS 181:4183–4187.

[33] This work is discussed briefly in Langlois, "The Scholar as Apologist." It is not fully extant today.

[34] This expression was coined by Liang Ch'i-ch'ao 梁啓超 (1873–1929). See *Yin-ping shih wen-chi* 飲冰室文集 (Taipei: Chung-hua Shu-chü, 1960), volume 3, *chüan* 7, p. 59.

focussed on the *Book of Changes*. Another subcurrent within the larger
Elixir school was that begun by Wei Po-yang 魏伯陽 (fl. A.D. 140), the
eminent alchemist and scholar of Eastern Han times[35], and continued by
Ko Hung of the Eastern Chin. This current represented a philosophical-
literary approach, and has already been alluded to earlier in this essay. A
fourth sub-current within the Elixir school was that of *hsüan-hsüeh* 玄學,
"the sublime learning" or Neo-Taoist metaphysics. Taoist scholars of
this sort included Juan Chi 阮籍 (210–262) and Chi K'ang 嵇康 (223–
262), who were among the most active of the *ch'ing-t'an* 清談 ("pure
talk") Taoists in the third century. With the participation of these Taoist
literati, the Tan-ting or Elixir school took on the appearance of an
eremitic scholar movement. T'ao Hung-ching, an official of the Southern
Ch'i, had resigned office to take refuge at Mao Shan. He thus entered the
eremitic Taoist school, and his writings, such as the *Chen kao* 眞誥
(*Declarations of Perfected Ones*), gave the Elixir school a new prestige.

The second major camp may be designated The Way of the Five Pecks
of Rice. This was the Taoist school headed by the Celestial Master.
Unlike the Elixir school, it tended to have roots in the common people
and to be relatively free of elite influence. But in time it was susceptible
to a certain amount of insincere manipulation of superstitious people by
use of their belief in *fu-lu* (prognosticatory texts).

These two general camps must be kept in mind when examining the
history of Taoism in the period of non-Han rule. When the Jurchens
invaded and occupied North China in 1126, an element of Han Chinese
ethnocentrism became a part of the popular reaction by the Han people.
This in turn affected the nature of religious Taoism, since Taoism,
particularly the popular forms of religious Taoism, was prone to identify
with the root emotions and desires of the masses. Under domination by
non-Han peoples, the Han people to some degree evolved a determination to guard and preserve the Han Chinese cultural tradition. The
Taoists naturally were no exception to this trend.

In North China under the Jurchens this new spurt of ethnocentrism
promoted the emergence of a reformed Taoism. This is the religious

---

[35] Wei Po-yang was the author of *Ts'an-t'ung-ch'i* 參同契, a title which Joseph Needham
renders *The Kinship of the Three*. See *Science and Civilisation in China* (Cambridge:
Cambridge University Press, 1959-), volume 5, part 3 (1976), pp. 50–75, for a discussion of
Wei Po-yang. For a study of the *Ts'an-t'ung-ch'i*, see Wang Ming 王明, "Chou-i ts'an-
t'ung-ch'i k'ao-cheng 周易參同契考證," *Chung-yang yen-chiu-yüan li-shih-yü-yen yen-chiu-
suo chi-k'an* 中央研究院歷史語言研究所集刊, 19 (December 1948), pp. 325–366. For a
biography of Wei, see Chang Chün-fang 張君房 (fl. ca.1010), ed., *Yün chi ch'i ch'ien*
雲笈七籤 (SPTK, reduced-size reprint ed.), 109:744. For a discussion of Ko Hung's
thought, see Hou Wai-lu 侯外廬, *Chung-kuo ssu-hsiang t'ung-shih* 中國思想通史 (Peking:
Jen-min Ch'u-pan-she, 1957), vol. 3, pp. 263–325.

Taoism which the late Ch'en Yüan 陳垣 has dubbed "the new Taoism of the northern provinces." [36] With Ch'üan-chen Taoism at its center, a movement to preserve the cultural heritage of the Han people during the Chin-Yüan period developed and thrived. Through the simple missionary activities of the Ch'üan-chen Taoists and their ascetic style of training and cultivation in the manner of the well-known "Seven Perfected Ones" (ch'i chen 七真), their teachings were quickly accepted by the common people, who in turn offered worship and protection. [37] During this period, the ancient political activism of religious Taoism asserted itself. As the only native Chinese religion in North China under the Jurchens and the Mongols, it came into competition with the foreign religions in the realm of politics. [38]

During the Southern Sung, religious Taoism had been subjected to political repression owing to the backlash against what was seen as Northern Sung Emperor Hui-tsung's excessive fondness for the religion. He had built a great number of Taoist monasteries, and the expenditures were heavily criticized by some. This is why in Southern Sung times no emperor dared openly revere Taoism at court. But in the lower reaches of the Yangtze River, the traditional bastion of Celestial Master Taoism and Elixir Taoism, the Lung-hu 龍虎 Monastery in Kiangsi cast a great spell of influence. The second major center, Mao Shan, was located near Nanking. The dissemination of the myth of the Three Mao Brothers (san Mao chün 三茅君) helped to draw favorable attention in the south towards this center. [39] The favorable reception of religious Taoism in the

[36] See Ch'en Yüan 陳垣, Nan-Sung ch'u ho-pei hsin tao-chiao k'ao 南宋初河北新道教考 (Peking: The Catholic University of Peking, 1941).

[37] See Sun K'o-k'uan, "Ch'üan-chen chiao k'ao-lüeh 全真教考略," Ta-lu tsa-chih 大陸雜誌, 8:10 (May 1954), pp. 21–25; Sun K'o-k'uan, "Chin Yüan Ch'üan-chen chiao ch'uang-chiao shu-lüeh 金元全真教創教述略," Ching-feng tsa-chih 景風雜誌, 19 (December 1968), pp. 42–52; and Sun K'o-k'uan, "Chin Yüan Ch'üan-chen chiao ti ch'u-ch'i huo-tung 金元全真教的初期活動," Ching-feng tsa-chih, 22 (September 1969), pp. 23–46. On the "Seven Perfected Ones," who included Ch'iu Ch'u-chi and Wang Che (Ch'ung-yang) among them, see Li Tao-ch'ien 李道謙, Ch'i-chen nien-p'u 七真年譜 (Tao tsang ed.); Ch'i-chen yin-kuo chuan 七真因果傳 (retitled Pei-p'ai ch'i-chen hsiu-tao shih-chuan 北派七真修道史傳, and included in Tao-tsang ching-hua 道藏精華 (Taipei: 1965).

[38] Foreign religions in Yüan China, other than Buddhism, included Lamaism (actually a Tibetan form of Buddhism), Islam, and Christianity. See Hung Chün 洪鈞 (1840–1893), "Yüan-shih ko-chiao ming k'ao 元世各教名考," in Yüan-shih i-wen cheng pu 元史譯文證補 (TSCC ed.), 29:451–467. See also Ch'en Yüan 陳垣, Western and Central Asians in China under the Mongols, tr. by Ch'ien Hsing-hai and L. Carrington Goodrich (Los Angeles: Monumenta Serica, 1966).

[39] This myth is discussed in Sun K'o-k'uan, Yüan-tai tao-chiao chih fa-chan, pp. 82–92.

south was also in part a product of the incorporation of philosophical Taoist and religious Taoist tenets into Neo-Confucian doctrine by the Sung philosophers. Many of the Sung Neo-Confucian thinkers had been well versed in Taoist philosophy, and this is reflected in their teachings.[40] For these reasons, therefore, the south was fertile ground for the rapid development of religious Taoism under the Mongols.

In the south a branch of the Elixir school shifted in time from its traditional emphasis on aurifaction and laboratory alchemy, sometimes known as exoteric alchemy (*wai-tan* 外丹), to physiological or "esoteric" alchemy (*nei-tan* 內丹). In the latter form of alchemy, the body is construed as a furnace in which one refines one's internal "breath" (*ch'i* 氣).

Esoteric alchemy was the tradition of Taoist cultivation that stemmed from Pai Yü-ch'an 白玉蟾, the alchemist who flourished during the years 1209–1224.[41] As this school became more thriving during the Yüan period, its practitioners turned toward the theories of Wei Po-yang as they were recorded in the *Chou-i ts'an-t'ung-ch'i* 周易參同契 (*The Kinship of the Three and the Book of Changes*). The popularity of this work in Yüan times went hand-in-hand with the increased social and scholarly standing of religious Taoism. This trend had commenced in Southern Sung times, as already indicated, but the Mongol conquest of the south tended to promote its further development.

When the thirty-sixth Celestial Master from Lung-hu Shan was summoned to the capital by the khaghan in 1304 as his predecessors had been since 1276, he was invested as *Cheng-i chiao-chu* 正一教主, "Head of the Cheng-i School."[42] With this investiture, religious Taoism in the south acquired a double nature. This is indicated by the distinction made between the Cheng-i school and the Hsüan-chiao school. Under the new rubric, the Celestial Master set out to bring about the repair of the

[40] See Ch'en Teng-yüan 陳登原, *Chung-kuo wen-hua shih* 中國文化史, vol. 2, p. 49, for a quotation from *Sung Yüan hsüeh-an* 宋元學案 to the effect that the great masters of Neo-Confucian philosophy had all "indulged widely in Buddhism and Taoism." See also *Sung shih*, 427:12716.

[41] Pai Yü-ch'an is preserved in the *Wu-chen p'ien* 悟眞篇, dated 1075. (This title has been translated by Joseph Needham as *Poetical Essay on Realizing [the Necessity of Regenerating the] Primary [Vitalities]*. See *Science and Civilisation in China*, vol. 5, part 2 (1974), p. 360.) Pai was also known by the name Ko Ch'ang-keng 葛長庚. His collected works, *Pai Yü-ch'an ch'üan-chi* 全集, are found in the *Tao tsang*. A somewhat more handy edition is the reprint in *Tao-tsang ching-hua*. See especially P'eng Ssu 彭耜, "Hai-ch'iung Yü-ch'an hsien-sheng shih-shih 海瓊玉蟾先生事實," appended to Pai's collected works, for biographical information on Pai.

[42] YS 202:4526.

decayed monasteries and the construction of new ones.[43] The investiture thus may indicate an effort by the Mongol rulers to ensure the health and viability of southern Taoism. It may also suggest that the rulers wanted to keep southern Taoism from being united under one general leader or school.

There is very little evidence to suggest that the thirty-sixth Celestial Master was himself particularly talented or influential. In fact, the evidence suggests the contrary.[44] Yet the increasing participation by literati like Wu Ch'eng and Yü Chi in Taoist activities tended to cultivate the literary quality and calibre of the Taoists themselves. As this occurred, the mutual alliance of Taoists at court and Confucian scholars seeking advancement in government grew firmer. To some extent scholars such as Yü Chi thereby drifted away from the anti-Mongol attitudes that had characterized a portion of southern literati in early Yüan times. Yü Chi, in fact, gained access to the court of the Mongols with the aid of the Taoists. In turn, Yü Chi helped to open up a path to office and fame for other southern literati. At the same time, however, he compromised the essential integrity of the Confucian scholar. This may have been sensed by his contemporaries and may explain the circulation of the absurd rumor that his eyes were sewn up by the Mongols in order to punish him for some crime.[45]

The greatest point of difference between the styles of the northern and southern schools of Taoism in Yüan times lay eventually in the extremely cultivated airs and skills of the adepts of the south, and the relative lack of these by their northern counterparts. Wu Ch'üan-chieh was a man of administrative and scholarly attainments who directed the construction of three Taoist monasteries in the Hangchow area. These were the K'ai-yüan Kung 開元宮, the Tsung-yang Kung 宗陽宮, and the Ta-ti Tung-hsiao Kung 大滌洞霄宮. Wu compiled a work entitled *Tunghsiao kung t'u-chih* 洞霄宮圖志 (*Gazetteer of the [Ta-ti] tung-hsiao Monastery*), which described the third of the great monasteries just mentioned. Wu also directed the construction of the Pai-shih Kuan 白石觀 atop Chi-ch'ou Shan 計籌山 near Wu-hsing. This monastery

---

[43] These were Lung-hu Shan, Mao Shan, and the pair of monasteries at Lin-ch'uan known as Yü-ssu and Ko-tsao. Collectively they were known as San Shan 三山 ("the three mountains").

[44] See Sun K'o-k'uan, *Yüan-tai tao-chiao chih fa-chan*, p. 54.

[45] The notebook of Ch'ü Yu 瞿祐 (1347–1433), preface dated 1425, indicates that "with leather thongs he was bound at the waist, and his eyes were sewn up with horse's tail. He was pressed between two horses and taken under arrest to Ta-tu." See *Kuei-t'ien shih-hua* 歸田詩話 (TSCC ed.), p. 29. [The editor is indebted to Prof. Yan-shuan Lao for this reference.] This story is not confirmed by earlier sources and would seem to be apocryphal.

became a magnet for southern literati in Yüan times, serving as a place of retreat and cultivation.

Under the influence of the literati and of refined Taoist leaders like Wu Ch'üan-chieh, the succession to the position of Celestial Master devolved eventually upon a man of eminent scholarly attainments, a man who skillfully blended Confucianism and Taoism. This was Chang Yü-ch'u 張宇初 (1359–1410), the forty-third Celestial Master.

The nature of religious Taoism was thus transformed, so that even a great painter emerged from its midst. Fang Ts'ung-i 方從義 was one of the most imaginative painters of the later Yüan era.[46] Other painters like Huang Kung-wang 黄公望 (1269–1354) and Ni Tsan 倪瓚 (1301?–1374) were deeply imbued with the colors of Taoism. Ni Tsan's brother was an official of the Taoist temple Hsüan-miao Kuan in Soochow.

Several factors lay behind Yü Chi's deep personal involvement with the southern Taoists. For one thing, he was born at Heng-yüeh 衡嶽, the sacred mountain Heng-shan 衡山, in Hunan. This area was shrouded in Taoist lore and myth. Since the fifth century, legends about the immortal woman, "Lady Wei of the Southern Peak," had contributed to the Taoist aura of Heng-shan. T'ao Hung-ching had recorded her story in his *Chen kao*. By mid-T'ang times Heng-shan had produced several famous Taoist adepts, including Liu Yüan-ching 劉元靖 and Hsien-yüan Chi 軒轅集.[47] The famous "Taoist immortal prime minister" Li Mi 李泌 (722–789) resided there as a Taoist recluse scholar.[48] The Taoist tradition in Heng-shan remained strong throughout the Sung period, and legends about "the perfected ones of Nan-yüeh [Heng-shan]" were commonplace. From a very young age, Yü Chi was thus surrounded by the mysterious atmosphere of "perfected ones" and immortals, and this partially accounts for his close ties with Taoists later in life.[49]

[46] Fang flourished into the Ming period. The works of Sung Lien 宋濂 (1310–1381) contain many colophons written on Fang's paintings, as well as other writings referring to Fang's literary works.

[47] Liu, who flourished in T'ang Wu-tsung's time, served at court with Chao Kuei-chen, mentioned above as having contributed to the launching of the Hui-ch'ang suppression of Buddhism. Hsien-yüan Chi, a native of Ling-nan 嶺南, served at court under Hsüan-tsung 玄宗. See Sun K'o-k'uan, "T'ang-tai tao-chiao yü cheng-chih 唐代道教與政治," *Ta-lu tsa-chih*, 51:2 (August 1975), pp. 1–37.

[48] Li Mi was a learned Taoist, especially fond of immortality pursuits. See his biographies in *Chiu T'ang shu* 舊唐書 (Peking: Chung-hua Shu-chü, 1975), 130:3620–3623; and *Hsin T'ang shu* 新唐書 (Peking: Chung-hua Shu-chü, 1975), 139:4631–4638. See also Michael T. Dalby, "Court Politics in Late T'ang Times," in Denis Twitchett, ed., *The Cambridge History of China, Volume 3, Sui and T'ang China, 589–906* (Cambridge: Cambridge University Press, 1979), pp. 592–594.

[49] Note Yü Chi's biography in the *Yüan shih*, which reports the fact that his father, upon the birth of Yü Chi, dreamt that a Taoist priest had come forward and was announced by a

Another factor behind Yü Chi's close attachments with Taoists is the fact that his father took him to live in Lin-ch'uan 臨川, Kiangsi, when the father was assigned to a post there. Not only was Lin-ch'uan adjacent to the Taoist center at Lung-hu Shan; it was the location of the two Taoist monasteries already mentioned, Yü-ssu Shan and Ko-tsao Shan. In Lin-ch'uan the Taoist "atmosphere" was extremely thick. When the status of Lung-hu Shan rose after the defeat of the Sung, the prestige of Taoists matched and even surpassed that of Confucian scholars, particularly in Lin-ch'uan.[50] It was natural, therefore, that Yü Chi should acquire an admiration for the Taoists. One source indicates that Yü Chi was capable of writing seventy-two styles of *fu-chuan* 符篆, "talisman" style seal script,[51] a fact which indicates more than a passing acquaintance with Taoist literary forms. Since Taoists were quite numerous in Kiangsi, it is probable that Yü became acquainted with a number of them early in life. This, of course, could well have increased his interest in and admiration for Taoists.

A third factor behind Yü Chi's close Taoist ties was that he was a devoted disciple of the philosopher Wu Ch'eng, as has already been indicated. Wu's learning, which was influenced by the teachings of Lu Hsiang-shan, stressed the *pen-hsin* 本心 (original mind).[52] In emphasis Wu's teaching was not far removed from the doctrines of "emptiness" and "quietude" of Buddhism and Taoism. Thus, as a mode of thought, Wu's philosophy easily absorbed the metaphysical concepts of the *Book of Changes* and the *Lao Tzu*.

Yü eventually established a close rapport with Wu Ch'üan-chieh. When Yü served in Ta-tu as *Ju-hsüeh t'i-chü* 儒學提舉 (overseer of Confucian learning) with Yüan Chüeh 袁桷 (1226–1327), the famous scholar from Ssu-ming 四明 (modern Ningpo), the three men were very close. Wu Ch'üan-chieh at that time was but a young man of twenty-two or twenty-three, although as a Taoist adept he had already established close friendships with several literati. He exchanged verses with Yüan and Yü. In Yüan's collected works one finds a piece which accords Wu Ch'üan-chieh extremely high praise as a Taoist who was profoundly concerned about the affairs of the secular world.[53] It may well be that Yüan

---

guard with the words "The Perfected One from Nan-yüeh has arrived." See YS 181:4174.

[50] When Chiang-nan was conquered by Khubilai, he sent the Taoist adept Tu Tao-chien 杜道堅 and others in search of surviving scholars and "worthy" hermits. See Chao Meng-fu 趙孟頫, *Sung-hsüeh chai wen-chi* 松雪齋文集 (SPTK ed.), 9:12b.

[51] T'ao Tsung-i 陶宗儀, *Cho-keng lu* 輟耕錄 (TSCC ed.), 9:144.

[52] On this subject, see the paper by David Gedalecia in this volume.

[53] Yüan Chüeh, *Ch'ing-jung chü-shih chi*, "Sung Wu Ch'eng-chi kuei-hsing hsü 送吳成季歸省序," 23:10a–b.

became acquainted with Wu Ch'üan-chieh through Yü Chi's introduction, since both Wu and Yü hailed from the same locale. Yü Chi, on his part, wrote a piece in honor of "Wu the Perfected One" after Wu assumed the post of Great Patriarch of Hsüan-chiao.[54] This piece resembles the one by Yüan Chüeh in that it heaps praise upon Wu for his deep sense of filial devotion to his parents and his visit home to see them. Yü's friendship with Wu Ch'üan-chieh did not wane even in old age, for the continuation of their friendship is evidenced by the number of verses exchanged by the two men.[55]

A fourth factor behind Yü Chi's close ties with Taoists is certainly the mutual advantage that Yü Chi and the Taoists enjoyed by virtue of their mutual relationship in the realm of politics. The Cheng-i school's standing jumped rather suddenly in mid-Yüan times due to the favor of the dynasty and the efforts that were made on its behalf by Chang Liu-sun and Wu Ch'üan-chieh. As Yü Chi noted in a commemorative inscription, Chang Liu-sun informed Emperor Ch'eng-tsung that "My disciple Wu Ch'üan-chieh is deeply versed in Confucian learning and is fit to be an adviser."[56] Wu Ch'üan-chieh in turn recommended literati to the court. The scholar Lu Chih 盧摯, for example, was recommended for higher office by Wu after the latter met Lu on a trip through Loyang where Lu happened to be serving.[57] Wu informed Emperor Ch'eng-tsung that Lu Chih was a gifted administrator who administered by the Taoist principle of wu-wei 無為 (non-action). Lu was then appointed to the position of academician in the Academy of Worthies in the capital. Wu Ch'üan-chieh also went to the defense of Wu Ch'eng when the latter's efforts in the capital were stymied by his opponents. When Wu Ch'eng was preparing to quit the capital, Wu Ch'üan-chieh said to the officials in charge that "The master Wu is a great ju 儒 [Confucian scholar], a man of the realm. If you permit him to depart, it will not be to the credit of the court."[58] As a consequence, Wu Ch'eng was immediately promoted to the position of chih-hsüeh-shih 直學士 (attendant academician) in the Academy of Worthies. Wu Ch'eng did not accept the offer, but as Yü Chi noted, "the whole world approved [of the promotion]."[59] Yü Chi's remarks on Wu Ch'üan-

[54] "Sung Wu chen-jen hsü 送吳真人序," Tao-yüan hsüeh-ku lu, 46:1a.
[55] Sun K'o-k'uan, Yüan-tai tao-chiao chih fa-chan, for materials shedding light on this point.
[56] See "Ho-t'u hsien-t'an chih pei 河圖仙壇之碑," Tao-yüan hsüeh-ku lu, 25:12a.
[57] See Tao-yüan hsüeh-ku lu, 25:11a. See also Lu's biography in Hsin Yüan shih 新元史, chüan 237.
[58] Tao-yüan hsüeh-ku lu, 25:11b.
[59] Tao-yüan hsüeh-ku lu, 25:11b.

chieh's career also indicate that the scholar Yen Fu 閻復 (1236–1312) was assisted by Wu when Yen was under attack during the reign of Emperor Jen-tsung. Yü Chi observes that the Mongol court was respectful towards its high ministers and did not insult worthies with offensive language, and he indicates that the reason for this was the beneficent influence of Wu Ch'üan-chieh. Even more striking is Yü Chi's comment that Wu commanded the respect of the outer court, which consisted of the high-ranking officials, both Han Chinese and non-Han, northerners and southerners:

"As for his learning and command of precedents, he was quiet-spoken and helpful, which some people could not comprehend. But the gentlemen of the outer court, dressed in their lofty hats and beautiful gowns as they discoursed on the good administrations of [the sage kings] T'ang and Yü, all followed the lead of his excellency [Wu Ch'üan-chieh], no matter whether they were southerners or northerners."[60]

Wu Ch'üan-chieh achieved this eminence, Yü Chi says, in part because he had a thorough knowledge of "the tao, the virtue, human nature, and [Heaven's] command" (tao te hsing ming 道德性命).

Yü Chi made his own contributions to Taoist activities at court by composing various specialized writings for formal Taoist occasions. These were chiefly ch'ing-tz'u 青詞, prayers written on blue-green paper, and wai-chih 外制, formal pronouncements by the court for chiao ceremonies.[61]

In addition, Yü Chi's stele inscriptions and commemorative essays for Taoists and Taoist monasteries provided for southern Taoism a detailed record of its history under the Mongols. Through his accomplishments in poetic composition, Yü Chi had a refining influence on persons of literary inclination among the Taoists. Individuals such as Chang Yü 張雨 (1276–1341), Hsüeh Hsüan-hsi 薛玄曦 (1289–1345), and Chu Ssu-pen 朱思本 (1273–?) were all Taoist scholars of superb "orthodox" literary credentials.[62] Their achievements in the literary realm were

---

[60] Tao-yüan hsüeh-ku lu, 25:11b.

[61] Tao-yüan hsüeh-ku lu, chüan 26. For ch'ing-tz'u, see Liu Ts'un-yan, "The Penetration of Taoism into the Ming Neo-Confucianist Elite," reprinted in Selected Papers from the Hall of Harmonious Wind (Leiden: E. J. Brill, 1976), pp. 96–114.

[62] For Chang Yü, see Sun K'o-k'uan, "Yüan-tai ti i-ko wen-hsüeh tao-shih: Chang Yü," cited in n. 1. For Hsüeh Hsüan-hsi, see Huang Chin 黃溍, "Hung-wen yü-te ch'ung-jen chen-jen Hsüeh kung pei 弘文裕德崇仁眞人薛公碑," Chin-hua Huang hsien-sheng wen-chi 金華黃先生文集 (SPTK ed.), 29:7b; also in Sun, Yüan-tai tao-chiao chih fa-chan, pp. 463–466. For Chu Ssu-pen, see the entry by Mori Shikazō in Ajia rekishi jiten, vol. 4, p. 319. All of these men were Taoists, but all were known as well for their literary style and their knowledge of the Confucian books. They all left literary collections, although Hsüeh's seems no longer to be extant. Chang Yü's Chü-ch'ü Chang wai-shih shih-chi 句曲張外

accomplished in part through the aid and advice of Yü Chi, whose example taught them how to compose refined verse and prose. Yü even encouraged the establishment of the Celestial Master at Lung-hu Shan to devote some of its energies to "cultural" activities such as building libraries. Yü Chi pointed this out in his "Inscription for the Lung-hu Shan *Taoist Patrology*" (*Lung-hu shan tao-tsang ming* 龍虎山道藏銘):

"Lao Tzu was originally an archivist in the Chou Dynasty library, and that is why his followers issue from the archivists. Today Taoists have storage rooms for storing books. This is thus something that harks back to [important] precedents." [63]

Yü Chi and Yüan Chüeh were admirers of the Taoist scholar Lei Ssu-ch'i 雷思齋, whose knowledge of the *Book of Changes* they held in deep regard. [64] Lei was a Confucian in his early years, but became an instructor in "the sublime learning" (*hsüan-hsüeh*) at Lung-hu Shan later on. Lei was one of the important figures in the convergence of the Taoist and Confucian scholarly currents, a process which by late-Yüan early-Ming times was producing a significant number of learned scholar-Taoists.

Turning to the question of Yü Chi's actual training and achievements as a Taoist, one must say that, despite his ability to compose *ch'ing-tz'u*, his level of attainment was not that of a true Taoist adept. He aimed to blend the world-view of the Neo-Confucian philosopher, the theories of the Great Ultimate (*t'ai-chi* 太極), Principle (li 理) and Material Force (*ch'i* 氣), with the Taoist notions of Emptiness (*hsü* 虛) and Quiessence (*ching* 靜). Despite these lofty aims, Yü remained under the influence of the

---

史詩集 is available in the SPTK series. Chu Ssu-pen's *Chen-i chai tsa-chu* 貞一齋雜著 may be found in the *Shih-yüan ts'ung-shu* 適園叢書. Chu is also known as a cartographer. Naitō Torajirō 內藤虎次郎 studied this aspect of Chu's work in "Chiri gakusha Shu Shi-hon 地理學者朱思本," in *Geibun* 芸文, 11:1–2 (1920); this article was translated into Chinese by Wu Han 吳晗 and published in *Pei-p'ing t'u-shu-kuan kuan-k'an* 北平圖書館館刊, 7:2 (March 1933). See also Walter Fuchs, *The "Mongol" Atlas of China by Chu Ssu-pen, and the "Kuang Yü T'u"* (Peiping: Fu-jen University Press, 1946).

[63] *Tao-yüan hsüeh-ku lu*, 45:1a. The allusion to Lao Tzu as an archivist (*shih* 史) stems from Lao Tzu's biography in Ssu-ma Ch'ien 司馬遷, *Shih chi* 史記 (Takigawa Kametarō 瀧川龜太郎, ed., rpt. Taipei: Yeewen Press, 1972), 63:3. The line about Taoists issuing from the archivists is quoted from the "Treatise on Literature" in the *Han shu* 漢書 (Peking: Chung-hua Shu-chü, 1975), 30:1732.

[64] For Lei Ssu-ch'i, see the tomb inscription in his memory by Yüan Chüeh in *Ch'ing-jung chü-shih chi*, 31:21b. Lei's work on the *Book of Changes*, the *I-t'u t'ung-pien* 易圖通變, is included in the *Tao tsang*. The preface by the Confucian scholar Chieh Hsi-ssu 揭傒斯 (1274–1344) notes: "He discarded the Confucian dress and became a 'Yellow Hat' [i.e., a Taoist] master." The preface by Wu Ch'üan-chieh observes that "the thirty-sixth Celestial Master [Chang Tsung-yen]..., therefore, in full observance of decorum, invited him [i.e., Lei] to become the Hsüan-chiao instructor for young disciples."

unsophisticated, common beliefs of religious Taoism, particularly those suggested by the term *i-shu* 易術 or "the arts [or techniques] of the Changes." This refers primarily to prognostication, but as a category of thought it should be considered to include Elixir Taoism. Yü Chi believed the legends of mysterious demons, and he transmitted the stories about magical feats performed by the magicians of the "Five Thunders" school that had become popular during the waning years of the Southern Sung.[65]

The Five Thunders (*wu lei* 五雷) school of sorcerers is commemorated by Yü Chi in an essay on Wang Shih-ch'en 王侍宸, a magician and rain-maker who lived during the reign of Emperor Hui-tsung (1100–1125).[66] In the essay, Yü Chi writes boldly of mysterious beings and strange happenings. Yü reveals in this essay that during his later years, when he was living in retirement at home in Lin-ch'uan, he supported a Taoist magician named Hu Tao-hsüan 胡道玄. Hu had been introduced to Yü in 1340 by Hsüeh Hsüan-hsi, who told Yü that Hu had mastered the magic skills associated with the teachings of Wang Shih-ch'en. Hu was then about twenty years of age.

It appears that Yü Chi never seriously studied the philosophical teachings of Lao-Chuang, i.e. philosophical Taoism. In this respect he does not reach the high level of learning attained by his mentor Wu Ch'eng. Wu, for example, had annotated the *Lao Tzu*.[67] In fact, most of Yü Chi's writings on Taoist subjects are either poems and songs written on purely social occasions involving Taoist acquaintances or simply records of the cultivation and careers of Taoist adepts. He never went beyond the composition of talisman style seal writings and *ch'ing-tz'u*. Most of the latter, in fact, were written on behalf of Taoist priests for their use in formal ceremonies. Yü Chi did little to develop or amplify the learning of Taoism; and even in regard to his writings about Taoist immortals, he was not the equal of Ko Hung or T'ao Hung-ching. Probably he simply lacked philosophical training, as he never engaged in the analysis of Taoist concepts. Rather, he merely used them as allusions and figures of speech in his poetry and verse.

A few lines from his essay on Wang Shih-ch'en, which he pretends are direct quotations from the mouth of Hu Tao-hsüan, actually appear to be autobiographical:

"He [Hu Tao-hsüan] said, 'I am going to withdraw [to become a

---

[65] See Yü Chi, "Ho-t'u hsien-t'an chih pei," *Tao-yüan hsüeh-ku lu*, 25:9b ff.; also in Sun K'o-k'uan, *Yüan-tai tao-chiao chih fa-chan*, pp. 420–428.

[66] *Tao-yüan hsüeh-ku lu*, 25:15a–18b. This text is included in Sun K'o-k'uan, *Yüan-tai tao-chiao chih fa-chan*, pp. 428–432.

[67] Wu Ch'eng's commentary on the *Lao Tzu* is included in the *Tao tsang*.

hermit]. I must find the right person and teach him [as my disciple]. He must be someone who observes the prohibitions with a mind like ice and frost; who sets his will with a mind of steel and stone; whose heart is like water and the moon; whose spirit (ch'i-hsiang 氣象) is like the sunny spring; who may have been born in a prominent family but [a family that] every generation produces men of hidden virtue; who cultivates himself at the gate of purity and quietude; and whose being is one of good fortune and strength. He is the one I will teach.' If so, is such a one not difficult to find?" [68]

This transparent reference to Yü Chi himself suggests that he thought he was capable of "receiving the Tao." Actually, even if Yü Chi had reached the level of cultivation described or hinted at in this passage, his thinking as revealed here was no more sophisticated than the mere imagining of wealth, fame, and good fortune by the common people. This level of thinking is embodied in the eleventh-century religious text *T'ai-shang kan-ying p'ien* 太上感應篇 (*The T'ai-shang Scripture: Tractate of Actions and Retributions*).[69]

Yü Chi's Taoist writings are typified by his liturgies for *chiao* fasts and his *ch'ing-tz'u*. In his "Manuscripts Written While Serving at Court" (*Tsai ch'ao kao* 在朝稿), a section of his collected works, such writings make up one full *chüan* 卷. Each of these pieces, such as "Chien kuo-chiao chien-t'an ch'ing-tz'u 建國醮建壇青詞 " ("*Ch'ing-tz'u* for the Setting up of the Altar for the Dynastic Prayer Ceremonies")[70] and "Chiao hsing chu wen 醮星祝文 " ("Prayer for the Star Fast"),[71] fit perfectly the formal requirements of Taoist ritual literature. Furthermore, in his "Chin-lu p'u-t'ien ta-chiao ch'ing-tz'u 金籙普天大醮青詞" ("*Ch'ing-tz'u* for the Golden Talisman All-Souls' Prayer Ceremonies")[72] there appear various kinds of written prayers and incantations. All of these writings incorporate beautiful, ornate language to give a handsome appearance to what today would be considered absurd supersitions.

In his stele inscriptions on Taoist subjects, Yü Chi was fond of recording the details of stories about spiritual beings. In his "Manuscripts Written While Transcending the Mundane World" (*Fang-wai kao* 方外稿), another section of his collected works, there appears a piece entitled "Ch'u-chou lu Shao-wei shan Tzu-hsü kuan chi

---

[68] *Tao-yüan hsüeh-ku lu*, 25:18b; *Yüan-tai tao-chiao chih fa-chan*, pp. 431–432.

[69] This was a popular religious work which had a great influence among elites and non-elites in China. For a brief selection in translation, see *Sources of Chinese Tradition* (New York: Columbia University Press, paperback ed., 1964), vol. 2, pp. 287–290.

[70] *Tao-yüan hsüeh-ku lu*, 26:2b.

[71] *Tao-yüan hsüeh-ku lu*, 26:7b.

[72] *Tao-yüan hsüeh-ku lu*, 26:10b.

處州路少微山紫盧觀記" ("Record of the Purple Vacuity Abbey at Shao-
wei Shan in Ch'u-chou Circuit").[73] This work records the fact that the
Taoist Lu Chung-fan 盧仲璠, an adept in that monastery, had precise
foreknowledge of the moment when he would "transform" (hua 化) into
an immortal. It also records the respiratory techniques of a Taoist
named Chang Ssu-lien 章思廉, who was the son of a Confucian scholar.
In the "Pai-yün kuan chi 白雲觀記" ("Record of the White Cloud
Abbey"),[74] about the Taoist monastery of that name in Ta-tu (and still
standing in Peking), Yü repeats the story of "Ch'i the Perfected One"
(Ch'i chen-jen 祁眞人) who became an immortal by employing the
techniques of the Ch'üan-chen sect. Yü Chi evidently believed that in his
day there were people who had become immortals, and stated as much in
his "Chiu-wan P'eng chün chih pei 九萬彭君之碑" ("Inscription for
Master P'eng Chiu-wan"). The subject of the inscription is the Taoist
P'eng Hsüan 彭鉉 (1314–1344). Yü wrote: "I have heard that in recent
times there are those who have become immortals, and one of them is
the master Li Chien-i 李簡易 of Yü-hsi 玉谿 in I-ch'un 宜春 [Kiangsi]."[75]

In his "Ho-t'u hsien-t'an pei 河圖仙壇碑," the long inscription for the
"River Chart Immortals' Altar" that contains valuable information
about Wu Ch'üan-chieh, Yü Chi wrote:

"In Ch'ang-sha 長沙 there was Chao Ch'i 趙淇, the son of Chao K'uei
葵,[76] former minister of the Sung. He was extremely broadly learned,
and was particularly devoted to the pursuit of immortality through the
Way of the Golden Elixir. There was also Li Chien-i of I-ch'un,
descendant of Li Kuan-chu 李觀諸 of Yü-hsi. He encountered an extraordinary person [i.e., an adept] and obtained from him [the teachings
of] tan tao 丹道 [the Way of the Elixir]. The one he encountered was
probably Liu Hai-ch'an 劉海蟾 [Liu Ts'ao 劉操 (d. before 1050)], from
whom he acquired the teachings. [Chao] Ch'i studied under him, but
before he had learned the teachings he [Li Chien-i] transformed [into an
immortal]. [Chao later] encountered him along the road in Yü-shan
玉山, and that is when he acquired his teachings.... When Wu Ch'üan-
chieh was sent by the Son of Heaven to Nan-yüeh [to perform ceremonies at the sacred Southern Peak in Heng-shan], he passed through
Ch'ang-sha. Chao [Ch'i] was impressed by him..., and decided to pass

[73] *Tao-yüan hsüeh-ku lu*, 46:7b.

[74] *Tao-yüan hsüeh-ku lu*, 46:9a.

[75] *Tao-yüan hsüeh-ku lu*, 50:6a. For another inscription dealing with P'eng, see Wei Su
危素, *Wei T'ai-p'u yün-lin hsü-chi* 危太樸雲林續集 (1913 woodblock ed.), 4:1a.

[76] Chao K'uei (1186–1266) was a native of Heng-shan, Hunan. For his biography, see
Sung shih, 417:12498–12504; and the entry by G. v. Mende in Herbert Franke, ed., *Sung
Biographies*, pp. 64–69.

on his *tao* to him. He burned incense in his secluded chamber and brought out his books to teach him [Wu]. What he taught was the secret teaching of [Liu] Hai-ch'an and Yü-hsi [Li Chien-i]." [77]

During this period, the Way of the Elixir, the Tan-ting school in the south, called itself the Southern Sect (*nan-tsung* 南宗). As such it travelled north to carry out its *tao*. Yü Chi was a firm believer in their legends about people who had become immortals, and it would appear that in his later years he devoted himself rather seriously to their teachings. During some of those years he dwelt at the Yü-lung Kung 玉隆宮, a Taoist monastery northwest of Nan-ch'ang 南昌 in Hunan. There he left behind a poem in ancient-style pentasyllabic verse which reveals his deep respect for immortality Taoism. A passage from the poem reads as follows:

> A thousand years, embracing the subtle respiration,
> Moving together with the sun and the moon;
> Looking forward to the time when I well become a yellow-
> haired one,
> Daily awaiting the growth of the purple mushroom. [78]

千載抱微息, 日月共來往.
欲爲黃髮期, 日待紫芝長.

A couplet from one poem in a series celebrating the construction of an "elixir room" (*tan shih* 丹室) for a Taoist recluse indicates that Yü Chi had deep respect for Taoist "interior" alchemy and the pursuit of immortality:

> Henceforth I shall aim at eternity,
> In the grottoes [nearby], I will first submit myself to Taoist cere-
> monies. [79]

從此便爲千載計, 洞天先拜紫霞章.

These lines indicate that Yü Chi, who at the time was about seventy, probably thought of engaging in Taoist techniques to prolong his life. Such an impression is strengthened further by words from his "self-encomium" (*tzu-tsan* 自贊), written for a portrait of himself:

"My ancestral home was at Min-shan 岷山 [in Szechwan], on the south side, but my place of birth was the house at Heng-yüeh [Heng-shan]. I recited the teachings of the sages and climbed the paths traversed

---

[77] *Tao-yüan hsüeh-ku lu*, 25:10b. See Joseph Needham, *Science and Civilisation in China*, vol. 5, part 3, p. 202.

[78] *Tao-yüan hsüeh-ku lu*, 27:4a.

[79] *Tao-yüan hsüeh-ku lu*, 29:1b.

by the carts of the immortals and perfected ones. I cannot paint pictures
of the white snow, the blue sky, the spring breeze, the beautiful fields, or
rain, clouds, dew and thunder. All I can do is gather the magic mush-
room to leave for those from afar."[80] It seems entirely appropriate to
term Yü Chi a lay Taoist.

I TURN NOW to a consideration of the various modes of expression found
among Southern Taoists, and to a few of the more important figures
among them. In general we can distinguish three types. One was the
Taoist in government who was at the same time a professional cleric.
Many of the disciples of the Hsüan-chiao leader and of the Celestial
Master of Lung-hu Shan were of this type. Also in this category were the
adepts of the Three Monasteries.

The second type was the Taoist who appeared in society as an errant
scholar-monk. These "men of rivers and lakes" (chiang-hu yu-shih
江湖遊士), or "Greenwood" types, were adherents of immortality
Elixir Taoism. They are also known as tan-shih 丹師 or "elixir masters"
of the southern sect. Magicians were a part of this group; they were men
who summoned rain by the use of gesticulations and magic techniques
known as fa-shu 法術. They also "subdued demons" (p'ing yao 平妖),
and formed a strong element in the Five Thunders school of magical
Taoism. Some of these were supported by wealthy families, under whose
aegis they engaged in elixir alchemy. Others retreated into the mountains
as hermits, yet seeking by the force of their lofty example to win over
followers.

A third type was the literatus who adopted a Taoist persona, whose
real love was literature, and who depended upon wealthy patrons for
support. These were relatively better educated than those of the former
types. Their literary attainments were often superb, and they often threw
themselves eagerly into the poetry gatherings sponsored by wealthy
families.[81] They were active in society in the modes of the learned
scholar and of the retired or eremitic scholar. They may be termed
"literary Taoists" (wen-hsüeh tao-shih 文學道士).

One can suggest representative figures for each of the three types. With
regard to the first type—the political Taoist—the leading representatives
would naturally be the two Great Patriarchs of Hsüan-chiao, Chang Liu-
sun and Wu Ch'üan-chieh. Two lesser examples would be Tu Tao-chien

[80] Tao-yüan hsüeh-ku lu, 30:16a. For some minor textual variants, see the original Yüan
edition, published in 1340 (reprinted Taipei: Hua-wen Shu-chü 華文書局, 1968 [?]), 32:16b
(p. 1934).

[81] The painter Ku Te-hui 顧德輝 was one of the leading members of the literati elite who
frequently held what were called ya-chi 雅集 or "elegant gatherings." This topic is
discussed in a paper by David Sensabaugh, "Notes on the Life of Ku Te-hui," unpublished.

杜道堅 (1237–1318), a Mao Shan Taoist of late-Sung early-Yüan times, and Wang Shou-yen 王壽衍 (dates unknown), whose position was second only to that of Wu Ch'üan-chieh. These two well-known Taoist leaders both shared reputations for chivalrous behavior. Both did what they could to support and protect southern Confucian literati, and both exerted efforts to ensure the survival of Han Chinese culture.

A prominent representative of the second type, the elixir expert, was Yü Yen 俞琰, a Confucian-turned-Taoist from the city of Soochow. In this category one would also place the magician Mo Ch'i-yen 莫起炎 (1226–1293).

A well-known representative of the third type was Chang Yü, whom I have discussed elsewhere.[82] Two others, whom I will discuss here, were Ma Chen 馬臻, "the poet of the lake" (*hu-shang shih-jen* 湖上詩人), and the cartographer Chu Ssu-pen.

Taoists in Government. The most important forms of activity in Southern Taoism during the period of Mongol rule were those which involved politics. Although the Hsüan-chiao adepts had a great deal of political influence, it was the Mao Shan Taoist Tu Tao-chien who began the tradition of political involvement in Mongol rule. A native of Tang-t'u 當塗 in Anhwei, he was probably quite well known by late Southern Sung times. He enjoyed frequent contacts with powerful men in society, and his literary attainments were excellent. When the Mongol General Bayan marched south at the head of the invading army, stationing his troops at Chien-k'ang 建康 (modern Nanking) in preparation for the attack on Hangchow, Tu travelled north to Ta-tu to plead with Khubilai for lenient treatment of the people of the Sung dynasty. Tu's effort did not alter the fate of the Sung dynasty, but that did not deter him from joining the new regime to become a pacification official in the south. In modern jargon his new role may be described as "united front" work. In the pursuit of his task he called on Chiang-nan literati and asked them to submit to the rule of the khaghan. Tu was placed in charge of the great Hangchow monastery, Tsung-yang Kung 宗陽宮. He also established the T'ung-hsüan Kuan 通玄觀 at Mt. Chi-ch'ou 計籌 in Hu-chou 湖州 (modern Wu-hsing 吳興, Chekiang),[83] and built up a large collection of books there. Many homeless literati gathered at the site in search of refuge from the hardships of the day.

---

[82] See the article cited in note 63.

[83] On the history of Wu-hsing in the Yüan period, see the paper in this volume by Chu-tsing Li. Chi-ch'ou Shan was the legendary site of the home of Chi-jan 計然 in Spring and Autumn times. Tu Tao-chien rebuilt a Taoist temple on the site. See the inscription by Chao Meng-fu entitled "Lung-tao ch'ung-chen ch'ung-cheng chen-jen Tu kung pei 隆道沖眞崇正眞人杜公碑 ," *Sung-hsüeh chai wen-chi*, 9:11b–15a.

Tu was a scholar of the Taoist canon, and in the *Tao tsang* 道藏 (*Taoist Patrology*) one will find an impressive set of his writings.[84] He lived to a ripe old age, dying only during the reign of Emperor Ch'eng-tsung. The famous painter and calligrapher Chao Meng-fu 趙孟頫 (1254–1322) wrote an inscription for him in which Chao stated his belief that Tu's "achievement in learning was profound, his literary cultivation and character both were perfected" (*hsüeh yeh yüan shen, wen hsing chü pei* 學業淵深，文行俱備).[85] The two men, Chao and Tu, were firm friends, and one would therefore presume that Chao's inscription is reliable and accurate, though biassed in Tu's favor. In narrating the stages of Tu's career, Chao wrote:

"When the Celestial Troops [i.e., the invading Mongol army] crossed [the Yangtze] south, . . . he [Tu] went to see the T'ai-fu Huai-an chung-wu wang 太傅淮安忠武王 [i.e., Bayan] in his native locale [Nanking]. He spoke directly and honestly, begging for the life of the people. . . . Therefore, he was permitted to travel [to Ta-tu] on the official courier transport route, and was admitted into the Imperial Palace. His memorial resulted immediately in a summons [to an audience with the Emperor] . . ., and the Emperor bestowed favors upon him. . . . Very soon an edict was sent down, specially dispatching him along the courier transport route to Chiang-nan on the task of gathering in the survivors and hermits. The Perfected One [i.e., Tu Tao-chien] withdrew [from the Emperor's presence] and sent up a memorial which set forth the way in which [the Emperor] should seek out, nourish, and employ worthy men. The Emperor accepted his words with praise [for them]."[86]

Poems written at the Tsung-yang Kung can be found in the literary collections of Yüan writers.[87] It is thus evident that the monastery played an important role in the lives of southern literati.

The figure of Wang Shou-yen appears in the late-Yüan notebook *Cho-keng lu* 輟耕錄 (*Notes Taken during Breaks from Ploughing*) by T'ao Tsung-i 陶宗儀 (fl. 1366). It also appears in the literary collection of the works of Wang Wei 王禕 (1323–1374), the scholar from Wu-chou 婺州 (modern Chin-hua 金華) who served on the commission to compile the *Yüan shih* 元史 (*Yüan History*) in 1368–69, and in the writings of Yü Chi. Huang Chin 黃溍 (1277–1357), another Wu-chou scholar of great

---

[84] These include *T'ung-hsüan chen-ching tsan-i* 通玄真經纘義 and *Tao-te chen-ching hsüan-ching yüan-chih* 道德真經玄經原旨.

[85] *Sung-hsüeh chai wen-chi*, 9:13b.

[86] *Sung-hsüeh chai wen-chi*, 9:12b–13a. See also *Yüan-tai tao-chiao chih fa-chan*, pp. 410–413.

[87] For example, the poem "Tsung-yang kung wang yüeh 宗陽宮望月," in Yang Tsai 楊載 (1271–1323), *Yang Chung-hung shih-chi* 楊仲弘詩集 (SPTK ed.), 6:1a.

literary fame, also wrote about Wang Shou-yen.[88] Wang Wei's inscription for Wang Shou-yen describes the latter's chivalrous spirit: "With regard to the manner in which he dealt with events and people, he was not stuck in conventional patterns,... and by nature he was very generous."[89] Yü Chi's inscription for the K'ai-yüan monastery indicates that Wang Shou-yen was deeply trusted by the court. According to Yü:

"In the first year of the Yen-yu era [1314],... the Emperor [Jen-tsung] commanded him to perform sacrifices at all the important mountains in Chiang-nan. On the day he received his command, the Son of Heaven admitted him to the *pien-tien* 便殿 [the palace for informal audiences] and bestowed upon him [the privilege of] sitting [in the Emperor's presence]. He detained him in discussion for a long time.... He referred to him as 'the perfected one' (*chen-jen* 真人) and gave him the appellation *mei-sheng* 眉生."[90]

Wang Shou-yen and Wu Ch'üan-chieh were roughly the same age and at one time served Kammala, Prince of Chin, a grandson of Khubilai. Wang and Wu were highly respected by the prince and were supported by him and his underlings. The scholar Chang Yü was one of Wang's disciples; Chang in turn was a frequent associate of Yü Chi and Huang Chin. Wang was known for his chivalric spirit, and thus he enjoyed considerable respect and prestige. The K'ai-yüan monastery itself was a newly established Taoist center. The buildings had originally served as the mansion of the Sung Princess of Chou, daughter of Emperor Litsung 理宗 (r. 1225–1264). Yü Chi informs us that after the conquest the mansion had been purchased by a Taoist *chen-jen* 真人 for conversion to a Taoist temple.[91] This suggests something of the power and prominence of the Taoists in the early Yüan period.

The Errant Scholar Monks. These Taoists were not specialists in Taoist fasts and sacrifices, nor were they administrators of Taoist temples. They

---

[88] T'ao's dates were ca.1316–ca.1402. See his biography by Peter Ch'ang in L.C. Goodrich and Chaoying Fang, ed., *Dictionary of Ming Biography* (New York: Columbia University Press, 1976), p. 1268. *Cho-keng lu* was first printed in 1366. See *Cho-keng lu*, 9:144. Wang Wei, *Wang Chung-wen kung chi* 王忠文公集 (TSCC ed.), 13:335, "Yüan ku hung-wen fu-tao ts'ui-te chen-jen Wang kung pei 元故宏文輔道粹德真人王公碑." Yü Chi, "K'ai-yüan kung pei 開元宮碑," *Tao-yüan hsüeh-ku lu*, 47:7a–9b; also found in *Yüan-tai tao-chiao chih fa-chan*, pp. 449–451. See also Huang Chin, "Wang chen-jen ch'i-shih shou hsiang tsan 王真人七十壽像贊," and "Mao chai chi 茅齋記," in *Chin-hua Huang hsien-sheng wen-chi*, 7:20b and 15:7a–8a, respectively.

[89] *Wang Chung-wen kung chi*, 13:339.

[90] The words in the SPTK ed. of *Tao-yüan hsüeh-ku lu*, 47:11a, are incorrect. For the correct words as given here, see the *Ssu-pu pei-yao* 四部備要 edition, 47:8a, or the 1912 woodblock edition, 47:11a (p. 2218).

[91] *Tao-yüan hsüeh-ku lu*, 47:10a.

had little involvement with things political, yet their standing in society was extremely high. They employed two general techniques to improve and maintain their social standing, and both were essentially devices to acquire and hold mass followings. One technique entailed the use of elixir alchemy and the "techniques of immortality." These dated from the Six Dynasties era and had been refined and altered over the centuries since. By Yüan times the ancient practices involved in laboratory alchemy and aurifaction had largely given way to the techniques of internal, physiological alchemy. These were referred to as methods of cultivating one's *hsing* 性 (human nature) and *ming* 命 (life span) and the "internal elixir."[92] The other technique for winning large followings among the people was the use of "magic techniques" (*fa-shu*) in the tradition of the Five Thunders school. These methods were especially successful among the highly superstitious rulers and aristocrats who came from outside China proper.

One of the earliest figures in the development of Elixir Taoism in the south was the thirteenth-century Sung master Pai Yü-ch'an 白玉蟾 (fl. 1209–1224), who was also known by the name Ko Ch'ang-keng 葛長庚. Pai was a "Greenwood" type sorcerer, but he was also a poet and a scholar. He played a crucial role in transmitting the important work *Wu chen p'ien* 悟真篇 (*Poetical Essay on Realizing [the Necessity of Regenerating] the Primary [Vitalities]*) by Chang Po-tuan 張伯端 (d. 1082).[93] The *Wu chen p'ien* describes the method of the cultivation of the internal elixir. Chang's methods were first taught to the immortal Liu Hai-ch'an, who then passed them to the monk Shih T'ai 石泰. Shih T'ai passed them to Hsüeh Shih 薛式 (d. 1191), who had no known disciples. Eventually the teachings, known as the methods of the Golden Elixir (*chin tan* 金丹), were taken up by Ch'en Nan 陳楠 (d. 1213) from Hainan, whose main stock in trade seems to have been the use of "paste pills" (*ni wan* 泥丸) to treat illness. He thus became known by the sobriquet "The Paste Pills Perfected One" (*Ni-wan chen-jen* 泥丸真人). Pai Yü-ch'an learned the methods from Ch'en, who became known then as the last of "the Five Patriarchs" of the southern sect.[94] Chang's *Wu*

---

[92] This is how Joseph Needham renders these concepts in *Science and Civilisation in China*, vol. 5, part 2, p. 331.

[93] Chang's preface discusses his own experiences as a student of the teachings. Three major commentaries to the *Wu chen p'ien* were written in Sung and Yüan times prior to 1333. See Joseph Needham, *Science and Civilisation in China*, vol. 5, part 3, p. 206. The texts are all found in the *Tao tsang*.

[94] The five were Liu Ts'ao 劉操 (i.e., Liu Hai-ch'an), Chang Po-tuan, Shih T'ai, Hsüeh Tzu-hsien 薛紫賢 (i.e., Hsüeh Shih), and Ch'en Nan. For the list see Joseph Needham, *Science and Civilisation in China*, vol. 5, part 3, p. 202.

chen p'ien derives ultimately from Wei Po-yang's *Ts'an-t'ung-ch'i* 參同契 (*The Kinship of the Three*). The elixir-refining method of the latter work is addressed primarily to the refinement of Yellow and White Golden Elixir. Chang Po-tuan, in his *Wu chen p'ien*, proceeds with Wei's techniques, but applies them towards the flowing currents of *ch'i* 氣 or "breath" within the body. Chang's method involves the guidance of the breath and the careful cultivation of the thoughts, seeking thereby "to condense the elixir [within the body] and form the fetus" (*chieh tan ch'eng t'ai* 結丹成胎). This leads ultimately to the transcendance of mundane existence and the achievement of immortality.

These techniques perfectly matched the atmosphere and style of the Southern Sung Neo-Confucian movement known as Tao-hsüeh 道學, "the learning of the [True] Way." This movement's theories regarding "the ultimate of non-being" (*wu-chi* 無極), the supreme ultimate (*t'ai-chi* 太極), principle (*li* 理), and material force (*ch'i* 氣) were absorbed into the newly emergent Taoist movement. Chu Hsi, in his later years, wrote a study of Wei Po-yang's work under the title *Ts'an-t'ung-ch'i k'ao-i* 參同契考異 (*A Textual Study of The Kinship of the Three*), dated 1197. Chu determined that the version of the text which had been edited by the Five Dynasties scholar P'eng Hsiao 彭曉 was the authentic one; and he even adopted the theories of Yin and Yang, water and fire, that are set forth in that text. Yet he employed a pseudonym for this particular study. Following his example, later Tao-hsüeh scholars also studied the work and engaged in the Taoist cult of internal alchemy.

The works of Yüan Chüeh provide a brief description and explanation of the different methods of elixir preparation used by the northern and southern sects. In his essay on the Yeh-yüeh Kuan 野月觀, a Taoist monastery, Yüan Chüeh said of the southern sect that:

"The major tenet of the teachings of the Master of the Southeast, Wei Po-yang, is not-dying (*pu-ssu* 不死). It is based on the Yellow Emperor's method of 'concealing the essence and refining the form' (*t'ao ching lien hsing* 韜精鍊形), and harnesses the six *ch'i* to journey beyond the myriad things. Those whose longevity is greatened are called immortals (*hsien* 仙), and there is indeed a school by which [these teachings] have been transmitted."[95]

Thus, as Yüan Chüeh pointed out, the southern sect's methods were derived from the *Ts'an-t'ung-ch'i*, although a certain amount of deviation had taken place over the centuries. Chang Po-tuan, however, was not a Taoist throughout his entire life. He began as a Confucian scholar, and, according to his preface to the *Wu chen p'ien*, made a point of

---

[95] *Ch'ing-jung chü-shih chi*, 19:9a.

attempting to bring together the Three Teachings.[96] The *Wu chen p'ien* is written entirely in septasyllabic verse. Its contents consist of a description of the key elements of Taoist cultivation. In the early Yüan many of the former subjects of the Sung Dynasty, still loyal to the Sung, took to Chang's methods with great enthusiasm. Hsieh Fang-te 謝枋得 (1226–1289) and Cheng Ssu-hsiao 鄭思肖 (1241–1318), for example, who were staunch loyal supporters of the Sung,[97] are only two of the most prominent individuals who took up these studies. Perhaps the one with the most detailed knowledge of Taoist immortality practices as taught in the *Ts'an-t'ung-ch'i* was the Soochow scholar Yü Yen.[98] Like many others in Taoist alchemy in early Yüan times, Yü Yen was originally raised in a Confucian family. He became a Taoist relatively late in life, adopting the Taoist style-name Ch'üan-yang-tzu 全陽子 ("the Master of Complete Yang"). Yü wrote *Chou-i ts'an-t'ung-ch'i fa-hui* 周易參同契發揮 (*Elucidations of the Kinship of the Three and the Book of Changes*) and *Chou-i ts'an-t'ung-ch'i shih-i* 周易參同契釋疑 (*Clarification of Doubtful Matters in the Kinship of the Three and the Book of Changes*) in the year 1284.[99] Regarding the latter work, the Ch'ing editors of the

---

[96] In the preface he wrote, "When I was young I was fond of the Tao; I read widely in the scriptures of the Three Teachings." (僕幼親善道, 涉獵三教經書). See *Wu-chen p'ien chih-chih* 悟真篇直旨 (1880 ed. [*Tao-shu erh-shih-ssu chung* 道書二十四種 ed.]), preface, 4b.

[97] See F. W. Mote, "Confucian Eremitism in the Yüan Period," in Arthur F. Wright, ed., *The Confucian Persuasion* (Stanford: Stanford University Press, 1960), pp. 232, 234 ff.; Wai-kam Ho, "Chinese under the Mongols," in Sherman Lee and Wai-kam Ho, *Chinese Art under the Mongols: The Yüan Dynasty (1279–1368)* (Cleveland: Cleveland Museum of Art, 1968), pp. 76, 96, and catalogue number 236. Hsieh Fang-te, in his *Tieh-shan chi* 叠山集 (TSCC ed.), 1:6, in a letter to Liu Meng-yen 留夢炎, indicates that at the time of writing he had spent twenty years in such pursuits. Similarly, Cheng notes in "San-chiao chi hsü 三教記序," in *Cheng Suo-nan hsien-sheng wen-chi* 鄭所南先生文集 (*Chih-pu-tsu chai ts'ung-shu* 知不足齋叢書 ed.), 51b: "When I was young I lived in a Confucian family, by middle age I had begun to study immortals, and in my old age I wandered into Ch'an Buddhism."

[98] Yü was the author of many books, including several on the *Book of Changes* and one on alchemy. The latter was entitled *Lu-huo chien-chieh lu* 爐火監戒錄, which James Needham has rendered *Warnings against Inadvisable Practices in Works of the Stove*. Needham indicates that the work was written ca.1285. See *Science and Civilisation in China*, vol. 5, part 2, p. 338. Yü has no biography in either the *Sung shih* or the *Yüan shih*. But see *Hsin Yüan shih* 新元史 (T'ui-keng t'ang 退耕堂 ed.), 1930), 234:12a. Yü is also noted in Lu Hsin-yüan 陸心源 (1834–1894), *Sung shih i* 宋史翼 (repr. Taipei: Wen-hai Ch'u-pan-she, 1967), 35:6a. For a discussion of the problems of Yü's biography, see Sun K'o-k'uan, "Yüan-ch'u Nan Sung i-min shu-lüeh 元初南宋遺民述略," *Tung-hai Ta-hsüeh t'u-shu-kuan hsüeh-pao* 東海大學圖書館學報, 15 (July 1974), pp. 1–21.

[99] These dates are supplied in Needham, *Science and Civilisation in China*, vol. 5, part 2, pp. 319 and 320.

Ssu-k'u ch'üan-shu 四庫全書 (*Complete Library in Four Sections*) noted that: "This work [teaches the methods of] using the body's water and fire, Yin and Yang, in order to develop the Way of the Elixir."[100]

Yü was a prolific author. In the *Tao tsang* (*Taoist Patrology*) we will find his *Ts'an-t'ung-ch'i shih-wei* 參同契釋微 (*Explanation of the Mysteries of the Kinship of the Three*), which is prefaced by Juan Teng-ping 阮登炳, a "surviving elder" (*i-lao* 遺老) of the Sung dynasty. The work is also graced with an encomium in song by Tu Tao-chien. Another of Yü's works found in the *Tao tsang* is *I wai pieh chuan* 易外別傳, a commentary on the *Book of Changes* which uses philosophical Taoism and the *Book of Changes* itself to provide an interpretation of Elixir Taoism.[101]

Most southern Taoists of the Elixir school did not reside in monasteries, but lived instead in the homes of families who acted as private patrons of their teachings. The notion of "temporarily lodging one's traces in the dust [of the secular world]" (*chi chi ch'en chien* 寄迹塵間) while engaging in the refining of elixirs was a part of the tradition of Elixir Taoism. Since the time of T'ao Hung-ching, it had been said that the preparation of elixirs required enormous amounts of wealth.[102] The Elixir Taoists, therefore, had little choice but to depend on wealthy families for support.

Pai Yü-ch'an was among the Taoists who brought together the Three Teachings of Confucianism, Taoism, and Buddhism. In the *Tao tsang* one will find his collected writings, and included in these are several sermons (*fa-yü* 法語) which resemble the interviews given by Ch'an (Zen) monks to their disciples. This Ch'an-like quality in Taoism is also seen in the early Yüan Ch'üan-chen Taoist Li Tao-ch'un 李道純.

Li was a northerner who travelled south and practiced a form of Taoism which was highly reminiscent of Ch'an Buddhism. This can be seen in the style of his "sayings" (*yü lu* 語錄) and of his writings, the *Chung-ho chi* 中和集.[103]

Aside from the Elixir school, southern Taoism also included the Five Thunders school that engaged in, among other activities, the making of

---

[100] *Ssu-k'u ch'üan-shu tsung-mu*, Tao-chia 道家 category, 146:38a.

[101] Yü's preface states that "Change (*i* 易) guides the Yin and the Yang, and that is why [Wei] Po-yang used Change [i.e., the *Book of Changes*] to elucidate his teachings. Its greater import does not go beyond the Hsien-t'ien 先天 chart." The reference is to a diagram of the eight trigrams, probably similar or identical to the one devised by Shao Yung 邵雍 (1011–1077) in his *Huang-chi ching-shih shu* 皇極經世書. The chart was used for divination and prognostication.

[102] See the letter to Emperor Wu of the Liang dynasty, in T'ao's collected works, *Hua-yang T'ao yin-chü chi* 華陽陶隱居集 (*Tao tsang* 道藏 ed.), *shang* 上, 16a.

[103] *Chung-ho chi* (*Tao tsang* ed.), "Wen-ta yü-lu 問答語錄," in *chüan* 3.

rain by magical charms. Mo Ch'i-yen,[104] as has already been noted, was the chief figure in this school. Mo was a unique individual, and it is therefore hard to fit him into a narrowly defined school. He obtained the methods of the Five Thunders, it is said, from Hsü Wu-chi 徐無極. He resided in quarters provided by the Tsou 鄒 family in Nan-feng 南豐 (Kiangsi). From Hsü Wu-chi he obtained the work *Wang Shih-ch'en hsin-p'ien lei-shu* 王侍宸新篇雷書 (*The Book of Thunder, Newly Compiled by Wang Shih-ch'en*), and from this work he acquired knowledge of the techniques of "summoning thunder and rain, vanquishing evil spirits and consorting with Heaven" (*chao lei yü, p'o kuei mei, tung yü t'ien ho* 召雷雨, 破鬼魅, 動與天合).[105] After the fall of the Sung Dynasty, Mo travelled north and received an audience with Khubilai Khaghan. He demonstrated for the Mongol ruler his technique of causing a thunder-clap by throwing a walnut on the floor of the palace. Ceremonious treatment by the Mongol court was his immediate reward, we are told.[106]

Literary Taoists. The third type of Taoist adept in Yüan times was the literary Taoist, and it was this type which most fully represented the character of southern Taoism. These learned individuals expended on the tradition of *hsüan-hsüeh*, i.e. Neo-Taoist metaphysical thought, that had been begun by fourth- and fifth-century Taoists, particularly T'ao Hung-ching. In the Yüan period the active participation in the Taoist move-ment by "high culture" literary men gave inspiration to further develop-ment of what we might call "immortality literature" (*hsien-chen wen-hsüeh* 仙真文學). In the transitional years from Yüan to Ming this trend became so evident that learned Taoist adepts emerged who were virtually indistinguishable, in terms of their literary expertise, from the typical Confucian scholars. Chang Yü of Mao Shan and Hsüeh Hsüan-hsi of Lung-hu Shan were the most prominent of these Taoists.

In effect, all these men were disciples of Yü Chi. Yü Chi may actually have instructed them personally in poetry and prosody. In the collected works of Chang Yü, the preface by Hsü Ta-tso 徐達左 (1333–1395) discusses Chang, Yü Chi, and the poet Fan Ch'un all together, and observes that "Yü and Fan flourished together at court, ... but [Chang] flourished alone in the valleys."[107] Since Hsüeh Hsüan-hsi's literary

---

[104] He is also known by his *tzu* 字, Yüeh-ting 月鼎. See "Biography of Mo Yüeh-ting" in Sung Lien 宋濂, *Sung hsüeh-shih wen-chi* 宋學士文集 (SPTK ed.), *Luan-p'o hou-chi* 鑾坡後集, 1:4b–6a.

[105] Sung Lien, *Luan-p'o hou-chi*, 1:4b.

[106] Sung Lien, *Luan-p'o hou-chi*, 1:5a. Sung Lien notes that Mo also produced rain for the emperor.

[107] Preface to *Chü-ch'ü wai-shih chen-chü hsien-sheng shih-chi* 句曲外史貞居先生詩集 (SPTK ed.), 2a.

collection is not extant, our only means of appraising his literary capabilities is through a limited number of poems and prefaces which Yü Chi wrote and presented to him.[108] One such piece includes the lines: "He loved ancient calligraphy, and in his poetry he had a style that floated lightly on the wind among the clouds."[109]

Turning to Ma Chen, we note that he thrived during Emperor Ch'eng-tsung's reign (1294–1307). He and his contemporary Chu Ssu-pen were Confucian scholars who became Taoists. Their literary collections are extant and can therefore be examined.

Ma Chen's works bear the title *Hsia-wai chi* 霞外集, a title suggestive of Taoist-like soaring beyond the pink clouds. There are no standard biographies of Ma, for all we have are a notice in the catalogue of the *Complete Library in Four Sections*[110] and a short biographical entry in *Yüan shih hsüan* 元詩選 (*Selected Yüan Poetry*) written by its compiler Ku Ssu-li 顧嗣立 (1665–1722).[111] The former tells us that the prefaces in Ma's collection "were all composed in the early years of the Ta-te reign period [i.e., shortly after 1297], so he must have been older than Chang Yü." The notice by Ku Ssu-li is not much more helpful: "When Chiang-nan was pacified, survivors and old scholars frequently sought to hide their traces outside the pale [i.e., by becoming Taoist recluses]. Hsü-chung [i.e., Ma Chen] was probably such an individual." Ma was a disciple of the eminent Southern Sung Taoist Ch'u Po-hsiu 褚伯秀, author of *Chuang-tzu i-hai* 莊子義海 (*The Ocean of Meaning in the Chuang-tzu*).[112]

Ch'u was a man of lofty and pure moral quality, judging from the fact that when the Mongols conquered Chiang-nan he refused to come out and acknowledge the new rulers. Cheng Yüan-yu 鄭元祐 (1292–1364) recorded in his notebook *Sui-ch'ang shan-ch'iao tsa-lu* (*Miscellaneous Notes by the Wood-Cutter of Sui-ch'ang*) that Ch'u adamantly refused to have anything to do with the occupying forces in Chiang-nan.[113] It is likely that Ma Chen shared these qualities. Although Ma's poetry is not discussed by the traditional critics, in this writer's view it is not inferior to the verse of Chang Yü. Ma's poetry is quite powerful and is frequently

---

[108] For a complete listing, see *Yüan-tai tao-chiao chih fa-chan*, pp. 293–297.

[109] *Tao-yüan hsüeh-ku lu*, 46:3a.

[110] *Ssu-k'u ch'üan-shu tsung-mu*, 167:5a.

[111] *Yüan shih hsüan, ch'u-chi* 初集, *jen-chi* 壬集, *Hsia-wai shih-chi* 霞外詩集.

[112] This immense study of Chuang Tzu's philosophy (106 *chüan*) is found in the *Tao tsang*. For notes on the text, see *Ssu-k'u ch'üan-shu tsung-mu*, 146:26b. The full title is *Nan-hua chen-ching i-hai tsuan-wei* 南華眞經義海纂微.

[113] *Sui-ch'ang shan-ch'iao tsa-lu* 遂昌山樵雜錄 (*Pai hai* 稗海 ed., repr. Taipei: Hsin-hsing Shu-chü, 1968), p. 1925.

even better than the poetry of the "rivers and lakes" (*chiang hu* 江湖)
poets of the late Southern Sung.

Ma also excelled in painting. It is said that he painted landscapes of
Lung-men 龍門, a place in the northwest, and Sang-kan 桑乾 river in the
far north.[114] As a poet he was ever mindful of his former dynasty, the
Sung. A poem included in *Yüan shih hsüan* entitled "Shu huai shih
述懷詩" or "Explaining my feelings" contains the following lines:

> Long ago, when there was an enduring peace, life was
> quite lovable.... The seasons passed, and the fragrant
> flowers withered; the era shifted and the Big Dipper
> tilted.... The righteous scholar [i.e., the poet himself] was
> filled with solitary resentment, while the conniving officials
> abused their great powers.[115]

昔際承平久, 生涯足可憐⋯
候轉芳華歇, 時移斗柄偏⋯
義士含孤憤, 謀臣誤大權

But Ma eventually was forced to an accommodation with the Mongols
and to travel north to the capital. He touched on that trip north, which
was not undertaken voluntarily, in the same poem just quoted:

> Wearing feathered dress to match the jasper palaces [in the
> capital],
> The Celestial Kitchens conferred upon me a marvelous
> banquet.
> Within the world the Tao I know is great,
> But here beyond the pale I am sick with myself for having come
> forth.
> My desire to return [south] would startle a Chang Yung[116];
> Dwelling away from home, [I am] an ageing Cheng Ch'ien.[117]
> [Lieh Tzu 列子] rode on the wind, but still had to depend on
> something;
> I only started back home when the time was [already] late.[118]

---

[114] See the notes by Ku Ssu-li in *Yüan shih hsüan*.

[115] *Yüan shih hsüan*, *Hsia-wai chi*, 14b.

[116] This likely refers to Chang Han 張翰, the Chin 晉 dynasty figure who, while serving
under the ruler, grew homesick for his native Wu 吳. He resigned and returned home. See
Chin shu 晉書, 92:2384.

[117] Cheng Ch'ien was a painter and scholar who served under T'ang Hsüan-tsung. When
the An Lu-shan 安祿山 rebellion broke out, he became an officer in the rebel army at
Loyang. See *Hsin T'ang shu*, 202:5766.

[118] *Yüan shih hsüan*, *Hsia-wai chi*, 15a.

羽服陪瑤殿, 天廚錫綺筵.
域中知道大, 物外愧身先.
歸意驚張詠, 離居老鄭虔.
風行猶有待, 歲晚薄言還.

One would gather from these lines that in his heart Ma Chen was an
unwilling participant in Mongol rule. Whatever his feelings, however, he
nevertheless found time to paint and write. His *Hsia-wai chi* contains
several poems which refer to landscapes he painted.[119] Perhaps some of
these paintings are still extant. Ma's works also preserve some thirty
poems in septasyllabic *chüeh-chü* 絕句 entitled "Hsi-hu ch'un-jih chuang-
yu chi-shih 西湖春日壯遊即事" ("Recording an Encounter while on a
Hearty Spring Outing on West Lake"). The preface to the series
indicates that it was written with thoughts of the previous dynasty in
mind, and not as a simple poetic paeon to West Lake. If Ma's verse were
measured by the standard of the Sung loyalists and "survivors," it would
seem that it is even more praiseworthy than the verse of Chang Yü.

Chu Ssu-pen was a Taoist of relatively wide-ranging acquaintances. A
native of Lin-ch'uan, Kiangsi, he did not take up Taoist pursuits until
after the fall of the Sung. Four years younger than Wu Ch'üan-chieh, he
went to Ta-tu and began the study of Taoism at roughly the time Wu
made his first journey north. Wu eventually became familiar with Chu's
writings and commented on them as follows: "He and I studied the Tao
together as 'Yellow Hats' [i.e., as Taoist adepts], and dwelt together at
Lung-hu Shan. When we were at court, we dwelt together in the capital.
Our literary aspirations are the same. I am older than he by four years,
so we are contemporaries."[120]

Chu's poems were prefaced by famous literati other than Wu Ch'üan-
chieh. These included Fan Ch'un, Yü Chi, and Liu Kuan 柳貫.[121] Yü's
preface, which also appears in Yü's collected works, discusses their
relationship in some detail. According to Yü, Chu "made reading books
his task, and the books [he chose to read] were not a random selection.
In studying, he had his own Tao." Yü noted further that Chu was
"especially fond of reading books that recorded administrative geography."[122] Chu Ssu-pen was a geographer and a cartographer. In his

[119] Examples are "The Yangtze River on a Clear Day," "Lung-men Mountain and Sang-
kan River," "Celestial Horses Presented as Tribute by Hai-nan," and "Small Landscapes
and Scrolls."
[120] Preface to Chu Ssu-pen, *Chen-i chai tsa-chu* 貞一齋雜著 (*Shih-yüan ts'ung-shu* 適園
叢書 ed.), preface, 4b.
[121] For more on Liu Kuan, see the paper by J. Langlois in this volume.
[122] See *Tao-yüan hsüeh-ku lu*, 46:4a.

works there appear several writings on geographical terminology.[123] When Chu was in charge of the Yü-lung Taoist monastery at Nan-ch'ang, the Chin-hua scholar Liu Kuan was then serving there as an intendant for Confucian studies. Liu and Chu became rather close friends, as is evident from the preface to Liu Kuan's works which is included in Chu's collected works. At the time of their friendship, Chu was probably sixty or older.

Yü Chi's preface to Chu's writings evaluates Chu's poetry:

"His words fit the thing described, and he does not write strange language to startle the readers and hearers [of his verse]. The facts presented are always described accurately; he does not employ obscure usages in order to appear special and ancient. By nature he is faithful to what is correct, and never flounders wildly, losing his original quality."[124]

The present author's view of Chu Ssu-pen's poetry is that it is somewhat lacking in terms of "refined feeling" (feng-ch'ing 風情), and that it is inferior to the poetry of Chang Yü and Ma Chen. For the purposes of the present study, however, it is sufficient that Chu Ssu-pen was a practicing Taoist and a man of letters, comfortable in the realms of the Taoist and the literatus. After his middle years, he took charge of Taoist activities in Kiangsi at the Yü-lung Kung. Liu Kuan noted in this connection that, "In the first year of the Chih-yüan reign [1321], Chu Ssu-pen of Lin-ch'uan was in actual charge of its affairs.... The work [of construction] began in the second year of the T'ai-ting 泰定 era [1325] and was completed in three years."[125] One would infer that Chu Ssu-pen was not merely a literary Taoist, but a man with considerable political, scientific, and administrative expertise as well.

All of the southern Taoists of the Yüan period with which this writer is familiar had some kind of relationship with Yü Chi. Their poetry and prose are rich in artistic qualities, while they also have a strong eremitic Taoist flavor. In the late Yüan many men of letters and the arts gathered together at the Ch'ing-pi Ko 清閟閣 (Hall of the Pure Mystery), owned by the painter Ni Tsan 倪瓚 (1301?–1374), and at the Yü-shan ts'ao-t'ang 玉山草堂 (The Retreat of Jade Mountain), owned by Ku Te-hui 顧德輝. The Lung-hu Shan Taoist Yü Yen-ch'eng 于彥成 was a poet in Ku's circle, for some of his verses are found in the anthology of poems

---

[123] Examples: a preface to Yü-ti t'u 輿地圖, a map of the realm (see n. 62 above); explanations of the terms North Sea, Ho-ning 和寧, Two Rivers.

[124] Tao-yüan hsüeh-ku lu, 46:4a.

[125] Liu Kuan, "Yü-lung wan-shou kung hsing-hsiu chi 玉隆萬壽宮興修記." Liu Tai-chih wen-chi 柳待制文集 (SPTK ed.), 14:17a.

written by participants in the "elegant gatherings" held there.[126] Ni
Tsan, on his part, wrote a number of affectionate verses to Chang Yü.[127]
Thus the process by which Southern Taoists had come to be exemplified
by refined men of letters had gone a long way in Yüan times. The
southern Taoists traversed a path completely different from that taken
by the Taoists in the north. The Ch'üan-chen Taoists were less cultivated, in the sense of the Han Chinese literati of the south, than were
their southern brethren.

One important factor in this process, one would surmise, was the
institution known as the *Hsüan-hsüeh chiang-shih* 玄學講士 (Instructor in
the Sublime Learning), a lectureship, to use modern terminology, that
had been established at the Shang-ch'ing Kung 上清宮 at Lung-hu Shan.
According to the tomb inscription in Yüan Chüeh's works, the earliest of
such instructors was Lei Ssu-ch'i.[128] It was he whose instruction produced the "Confucian" scholar-Taoist Wu Ch'üan-chieh.

There are a number of indicators that Taoists had become highly
cultivated by late Yüan times. Tomb inscriptions for Taoists indicate
that the Taoists were well cultivated in both literary and ethical concerns.
Sung Lien's works, for example, describe the lofty literary attainments of
the Taoist Teng Chung-hsiu 鄧仲修.[129] And Chang Yü-ch'u, the forty-
third Celestial Master, recorded similar attainments for the Taoist Fu Jo-
lin 傅若霖.[130] Without going into greater detail here, suffice it to say that
the process by which the Taoists of the south became cultivated and
refined in the style of the Confucian literati also tended to detach those
Taoists from their former identification with the mass of common
people. These Taoists were best suited to roles as decoration for an age
of peace, and helped to serve the interests of the rulers, whether Yüan or
Ming, in maintaining a semblance of normality and control. Therefore,
in the late Yüan movement to restore rule to the Han Chinese, the
southern Taoists had very little to offer. They were fit to serve the court,
and did so, but in society at large they sustained themselves only by
providing liturgical services, refining elixirs, and promoting various
physical practices. When the special circumstances that had characterized Chinese civilization during the period of Yüan rule ended, so did
those which characterized southern Taoism.

[126] See *Ts'ao-t'ang ya-chi* 草堂雅集 (*Ssu-k'u ch'üan-shu chen-pen* 四庫全書珍本 ed.).

[127] See *Ni Yün-lin shih-chi* 倪雲林詩集 (SPTK ed.).

[128] Yüan Chüeh, *Ch'ing-jung chü-shih chi*, 31:21b.

[129] "Teng lien-shih shen-ku pei 鄧鍊師神谷碑," in *Sung hsüeh-shih wen-chi, Chih-yüan
hsü-chi* 芝園續集, 3:7a-8b.

[130] *Hsien-ch'üan chi* 峴泉集 (*Ssu-k'u ch'üan-shu chen-pen* ed.), 3:24b-28a.

IV. FOREIGNERS IN CHINA

The Muslims in the Early
Yüan Dynasty[1]

MORRIS ROSSABI

I. INTRODUCTION

The non-Chinese Muslims in China first attained prominent positions in government and finance during the Yüan dynasty. Muslims from Central Asia and from the Middle East, however, had reached China much earlier. Within a century after Muhammad's death, Muslims had travelled by land to China's northwest and by sea to China's eastern coast.[2] During the T'ang and Sung dynasties,[3] a few Muslims led distinguished

---

[1] In revising this paper, I have benefitted from the suggestions of Professors Herbert Franke, John Langlois, and the other participants at the original conference where the paper was presented. I have also benefitted from a critique of the paper by Professor Jonathan Lipman.

[2] On the first contacts between the Muslims and the Chinese, see F. S. Drake, "Mohammedanism in the T'ang Dynasty," *Monumenta Serica*, 7 (1943), pp. 1–40; and Edward H. Schafer, *The Golden Peaches of Samarkand* (Berkeley: Univ. of California Press, 1963), pp. 10–28. One of the major needs in the field of Sinology is a history of Islam in China. In striking contrast to the Chinese Jews (who have been studied by Donald D. Leslie in *The Survival of the Chinese Jews: The Jewish Community of Kaifeng* (Leiden: E. J. Brill, 1972), and by William C. White in *Chinese Jews* (Toronto: Univ. of Toronto Press, 1942), not to mention several hundred articles in various Western languages), the Chinese Muslims have not been accorded a full-scale history in a Western language. Marshall Broomhall's *Islam in China: A Neglected Problem* (London: Morgan and Scott, 1910) is badly out of date. In note 3 of my "Muslim and Central Asian Revolts in Late Ming and Early Ch'ing" (in Jonathan Spence and John Wills, ed., *From Ming to Ch'ing* (New Haven: Yale Univ. Press, 1979), pp. 168–199, I listed some of the major sources that ought to be consulted for such a history of Islam in China. To these I would now add D. D. Leslie's brief bibliographical guide in his "Arabic Sources" in Donald Leslie, Colin Mackerras, and Wang Gungwu, ed., *Essays on the Sources for Chinese History* (Canberra: Australian National Univ. Press, 1973), pp. 147–153, and Leslie's "Islam in China to 1800: A Bibliographical Guide," *Abr-Nahrain*, 16 (1976), pp. 16–48. The most important account in a non-Western language of the Chinese Muslims is Tazaka Kōdō 田坂興道, *Chūgoku ni okeru kaikyō no denrai to sono kōtsū* 中国における回教の伝来とその弘通 (Tokyo: Tōyō bunko ronsō 東洋文庫論叢, vol. 43, parts 1–2, 1964).

[3] Some of these Muslims wrote accounts of their experiences in China. These texts are invaluable for the study of Chinese history. See, for example, Howard S. Levy (tr. and anno.), *Biography of Huang Ch'ao* (Berkeley: University of California Press, 1961), pp. 109–121.

careers in the local and regional administration or prospered as merchants. Yet it was only with the Mongol invasions and the establishment of the Yüan that they were suddenly appointed to high-ranking positions in the central government and played an influential role in the national economy. Muslims directed the financial administration of the empire, served as trade commissioners in the coastal cities of southeastern China, and staffed the Bureau of Astronomy at the imperial court.[4]

Yet the Muslims drew the hostility of their Chinese underlings and their Mongol overlords. Marco Polo reports that "the Cataians [Chinese] hated the rule of the great Kaan because he set over them Tartar, and for the more part Saracen, rulers ...."[5] Marco Polo is, of course, not an unbiased informant. In his accounts of Persia and Central Asia, he repeatedly proclaims his scorn and hatred of the Muslims. In this instance, however, he appears to be a faithful and accurate observer. Many Chinese perceived the Muslims as oppressors. Muslims often served, after all, as tax collectors, usurers, and merchants, occupations which made them adversaries of the Chinese and which designated them, in Chinese eyes, as avaricious, aggressive, and miserly. Their contributions to Chinese architecture, medicine, astronomy, and military technology failed to erase this negative image.

Similarly, their Mongol overlords, who required their expertise, enacted restrictive laws directed at the Muslims. Despite their policy of religious toleration, the Mongols, on occasion, interfered with the practice of Islam. Khubilai Khaghan (Shih-tsu, r. 1260–1294), for example, once issued an edict prohibiting circumcision, and for almost a decade he demanded that the Muslims adopt the Mongol way of slaughtering animals rather than their own religiously prescribed method. Both of Khubilai's prohibitions were serious transgressions on traditional Muslim beliefs and practices.

By serving as intermediaries between the Mongol rulers and their Chinese subjects, the Muslims performed valuable services but simultaneously provoked the wrath of the conquerors and the conquered. This essay suggests that the Mongols, consciously or not, used the Muslims as

---

[4] On Jamāl al-Dīn, the most renowned of the Muslim contributors to Yüan astronomy, see YS 90:2297. On the later history of the Bureau of Astronomy, see Ho Peng-yoke, "The Astronomical Bureau in Ming China," *Journal of Asian History*, 3:2 (1969), pp. 137–157.

[5] A. C. Moule and Paul Pelliot, *Marco Polo: The Description of the World* (London: George Routledge & Sons, Ltd., 1938), p. 215. For more on Marco's views of Muslims, see Leonardo Olschki, *Marco Polo's Asia* (Berkeley: University of California Press, 1960), pp. 242–246. General studies of the religions of China in Yüan times barely allude to Islam. See, for example, Paul Demiéville, "La situation religieuse en Chine au temps de Marco Polo," *Oriente Poliano* (Rome: Instituto Italiano per il Medio ed Estremo Oriente, 1957), pp. 219–20.

scapegoats, thereby diverting Chinese animosity from themselves. Like the European and Middle Eastern Jews of modern times, a large number of Muslims were involved in trade and finance. By employing the Muslims as tax collectors and moneylenders, the Mongols ensured that the Chinese and the Muslims would frequently be at odds.

Also like the Jews in the Western world, the Muslims often lived in self-contained, virtually self-governing communities separated from the Chinese sections of towns and cities.[6] They did so perhaps in order to hear the muezzin's call to prayer more clearly. The Mongols presumably did not force them to live in ghettoes, but it suited their purposes because it raised additional barriers between the Muslims and the Chinese. It should be noted that the Chinese resented the Muslims because of their financial activities and their political manipulation, not because of an antipathy for Islamic theology and practice. The religious doctrines of Islam scarcely perturbed the Chinese. Their distrust of the Muslims stemmed from what they perceived to be the excesses of some Muslim merchants and financial officials.

This is not to imply that the Muslims were merely helpless victims exploited by the Mongols and despised by the Chinese. Some notorious Muslim merchants and officials used their privileged status to victimize the Chinese and to enrich themselves through shady deals. The Chinese sources of the Yüan are replete with examples of such villainous Muslims. In this essay, I will argue that the Mongol court, whether by conscious design or by mere happenstance, placed the Muslims in positions in which they would appear to be exploitative (and some Muslims clearly were). By identifying the Muslims and several other non-Chinese groups as a separate class, the Se-mu jen 色目人, it isolated them from the Han-jen 漢人 (Northern Chinese, Jurchens and Khitans) and the Nan-jen 南人 (Southern Chinese).

The court also lumped all Muslims, be they natives of Central Asia, the Middle East, or China itself, into one group, which blurred the distinctions among them. These Muslims spoke different languages, belonged to different ethnic groups, and represented different religious orders within Islam. They surely had distinct, occasionally conflicting, economic and political interests, but the Yüan sources yield few details about these differences. The court, in addition, frequently did not distinguish between the Muslims and other foreigners, including the Uighurs and the Jews, a fact which poses problems in determining the Mongols' attitudes and specific relations with the Muslims. Most of the

[6] H. A. R. Gibb, tr., *Ibn Battúta: Travels in Asia and Africa, 1325–1354* (London: George Routledge & Sons, Ltd., 1929), p. 283.

Muslims mentioned here will be Central Asian and Middle Eastern
Muslims. There was a sizable Chinese Muslim community, which included the descendants of Chinese who had converted to Islam during
the T'ang and Sung dynasties, but most of the prominent Muslims in the
early Yüan derived from Central Asia or the Middle East. Specific
information about the Chinese Muslims is limited. Within these limitations, a study of the Mongol-Muslim relationship before the founding
of the Yüan illustrates the general development of Mongol policy
towards the Muslims.[7]

II. Early Mongol Court and the Muslims

The nomadic Mongols needed foreign products as well as foreign
craftsmen. Prolonged drought, diseases among their animals, and lack of
grasslands for their flocks forced them at times to rely on food from the
neighboring sedentary agricultural societies.[8] Even when they were
prosperous, they still sought foreign grain. And they always required
manufactured articles from the settled civilizations because their constant migrations prevented the development of an artisan class. Pottery,
clothing, and iron tools, as well as medicines and musical instruments,
were, of necessity, imported into Mongol territory. Commerce was thus
crucial for the Mongols.[9] They traded primarily with the Chinese and
with the Liao and Chin dynasties, foreign rulers who had expelled the
indigenous Sung dynasty from North China in the twelfth century.

Muslims, too, traded with the Mongols before the time of Chinggis
Khan. Muslim merchants and craftsmen from Central Asia travelled in
Mongol territory, offering tools and manufactured articles in return for
animals and animal products.[10] They also supplied information about
Islamic Central Asia and Persia and, perhaps, China to the Mongols.[11]
From the outset of their relationship with the Mongols, therefore, the
Muslims served as intermediaries, in commerce and in gathering of

[7] A useful account of the distinctions between these various classes is Meng Ssu-ming
蒙思明, *Yüan-tai she-hui chieh-chi chih-tu* 元代社會階級制度 (1928; rpt. Hong Kong:
Lung-men Shu-tien 龍門書店, 1967).

[8] Morris Rossabi, *China and Inner Asia* (London: Thames and Hudson, 1975),
pp. 40–41.

[9] Henry Serruys, "Sino-Mongol Relations during the Ming: The Tribute System and
Diplomatic Missions (1400–1600)," *Mélanges chinois et bouddhiques*, 14 (1967), p. 30.

[10] Tazaka (see n. 2 above), pp. 728–730; Hsiao Ch'i-ch'ing 蕭啓慶, *Hsi-yü-jen yü Yüan-
ch'u cheng-chih* 西域人與元初政治 (Taipei: Kuo-li T'ai-wan Ta-hsüeh Wen-hsüeh-yüan
國立臺灣大學文學院, 1966), p. 11.

[11] H. Desmond Martin, *The Rise of Chingis Khan and His Conquest of North China*
(Baltimore: The Johns Hopkins Press, 1950), pp. 122–123.

information, between the ancestors of the Yüan dynasty and the sedentary societies.

The rise of Chinggis Khan and the unification of the Mongols appears at first to have scarcely altered the Mongol-Muslim relationship. Chinggis himself did not object to the practice of Islam. He appears to have been tolerant of other religions unless they directly contravened the Mongol world view or posed an immediate threat to Mongol political hegemony.[12] His tolerance did not, however, extend to the Muslim method of slaughtering animals. The *jasagh*, a Mongol law code which reputedly expressed his viewpoint, noted that "When an animal is to be eaten, its feet must be tied, its belly ripped open and its heart squeezed in the hand until the animal dies; then its meat may be eaten, but if anyone slaughter an animal after the Mohammedan fashion, he is to be himself slaughtered."[13] Slitting an animal's throat, the traditional Muslim ritual, was taboo. Chinggis did not, however, seek to prohibit other Islamic practices and customs.

As a result, some Muslims were favorably impressed. When Chinggis encountered difficulties in seeking to unite the Mongol tribes under his leadership, he received the support of several Muslim merchants. According to the *Secret History of the Mongols*, in 1203 Chinggis and his forces had encamped along the shores of the Baljuna lake (or perhaps a river) to prepare for a difficult campaign against the Kereyid.[14] A Muslim merchant named Hasan (Asan 阿三 in the *Secret History*), riding a white camel and leading a flock of more than a thousand sheep, stopped at the Baljuna to water his animals. Hasan, who wished to trade for Mongol sable furs and squirrel hides, met and was attracted by Chinggis. Abandoning his commercial venture, he, together with eighteen other men, including at least one other Muslim named Jabar Khoje (Cha-pa-erh Huo-che 札八兒火者), ceremoniously joined Chinggis in drinking water from the Baljuna, signifying thus his enlistment in

---

[12] Martin (see n. 11 above) p. 316, writes that "the conqueror [Chinggis Khan] was careful to cultivate the support of all religious bodies." See also Arthur Waley, tr., *The Travels of an Alchemist* (London: Routledge & Kegan Paul Ltd., 1931), pp. 4–26 for more on Chinggis' religious views.

[13] Valentin A. Riasanovsky, *Fundamental Principles of Mongol Law* (rpt. Bloomington: Indiana University Press, 1965), p. 83. Cf. David Ayalon, "The Great 'Yasa' of Chingis Khan," *Studia Islamica* 33 (1971), pp. 97–140; 34 (1971), pp. 151–180; 36 (1972), pp. 113–158; 38 (1973), pp. 107–156, who asserts that the *jasagh* was used as a political ploy in the succession struggles that plagued the Mongols in the middle of the thirteenth century. Thus he argues that part of it may have been added much after Chinggis' death.

[14] Erich Haenisch, *Manghol un niuca tobca'an* (*Yüan-ch'ao pi-shi*): *Die Geheime Geschichte der Mongolen* (Wiesbaden: Franz Steiner Verlag, 1962), p. 51.

Chinggis' cause.[15] Additional Muslim merchants subsequently joined Chinggis, so that the great Mongol conqueror had Muslim followers even before he unified Mongolia.

As Chinggis initiated his military campaigns to the west, however, he began to encounter Muslim adversaries. Though his relations with the Muslims suffered as a result, he did not sanction the persecution of Islam. Yet the Muslims of Central Asia were among his main antagonists. In 1218, after some preliminary exchanges, Chinggis dispatched a caravan "laden with merchandise, consisting of gold, silver, Chinese silk, 'targhu' stuffs, beaver skins, sables, and other articles" to the state of Khorezm to initiate a regular exchange of goods. An avaricious Khorezmian official, who claimed that the mission was sent to gather military intelligence, confiscated these goods and rashly executed the merchants. Chinggis responded by sending an embassy to the Khorezmian ruler Muhammad Shāh, demanding that the governor be punished. Instead Muhammad Shāh executed the envoys. Chinggis thus had a perfect pretext for launching an invasion. Within a year, he began his campaign against Bukhara, Samarkand, and the other renowned commercial centers of Central Asia.[16] According to a somewhat exaggerated modern account, "For the first time the Mongol military machine was set in motion against a Muslim state, and rivers of blood were destined to flow...."[17] The great Persian historians Juvaini and Juzjani have recounted in harrowing detail the horrors and destruction unleashed on Central Asia.[18] These accounts, which tend to magnify the violence and bloodletting, are well known and need not be repeated here. Despite the devastation, there was little overt suppression of Islam. Chinggis dealt harshly with some of the towns of Central Asia because they resisted

[15] The *Secret History* does not mention the drinking of the water. A number of Chinese and Persian sources recount the incident. Francis W. Cleaves in his "The Historicity of the Baljuna Covenant," *Harvard Journal of Asiatic Studies*, 18:2 (1955), pp. 357–421, after an exhaustive examination of the evidence, argues that the incident did indeed take place. For the derivation of the name "Baljuna" and for its possible location, see Paul Pelliot and Louis Hambis, tr., *Histoire des campagnes de Gengis Khan: Cheng-wou ts'in-tcheng lou* (Leiden: E. J. Brill, 1951), pp. 39–49.

[16] W. Barthold, *Turkestan down to the Mongol Invasion* (tr. by T. Minorsky and ed. by C. E. Bosworth) (London: Luzac and Company Ltd., 1968, 3rd. ed.), pp. 393–427, for more on these campaigns.

[17] J. J. Saunders, *The History of the Mongol Conquests* (New York: Barnes & Noble Publishers, 1971), p. 55.

[18] Both of these Persian histories are available in English translations. Juvaini's work is translated by John Andrew Boyle as *The History of the World-Conqueror* (Manchester: Manchester University Press, 1958, 2 vols.); and Juzjani's history is translated by H. G. Raverty as *Ṭabaḳāt-i-Nāṣirī: A General History of the Muhammadan Dynasties of Asia* (rpt. New Delhi: Oriental Books Reprint Corporation, 1970).

his demands for submission, not because their inhabitants were Muslims.

Instead of massacring the Muslims, Chinggis wished to use their skills and expertise. He ordered his troops to spare Muslim craftsmen. Having few artisans among his own people, Chinggis depended upon foreigners, first to produce tools, weapons, and ornaments, and then to collaborate with captured Chinese architects and craftsmen in designing buildings in the Mongol territories. His son and successor Ögödei made even greater use of Muslim and Chinese architects to build the Mongol capital at Karakorum, and his grandson Khubilai employed Muslims in designing and building his capital at Ta-tu (Peking). Chinggis himself deported a large number of Muslims from Central Asia to the east. Juvaini notes that thirty thousand Muslim craftsmen from Samarkand were distributed among Chinggis' relatives and nobles.[19] Many of these artisans were eventually settled in Mongolia or in North China. Chinggis also encouraged Muslim merchants to carry on the East Asia-Central Asia trade that they had engaged in before the Mongol conquests. Finally, Chinggis appointed loyal Muslims to influential and highly visible positions in the administration of the newly subjugated lands.[20] Mahmūd Yalavach, for example, was appointed governor of Transoxiana and later attained even higher ranks at the Mongol court.[21]

Chinggis' death in 1227 and the subsequent enthronement of Ögödei (r. 1229–1241) ushered in a period when Muslims appeared ever more frequently in Mongol society. This is in part due to the expansion, in the last years of Chinggis' reign, of Mongol military control and to the incorporation of Muslim territories. But it may also be attributed to the growing need for Muslim expertise in trade, finance, and crafts. As the Mongols subjugated and sought to administer more territory, they required the assistance of foreigners. The Mongol court began to use Muslims in ruling the conquered populations, a practice that persisted into the fourteenth century. It entrusted them with vast responsibilities and powers, but it controlled these men by periodic purges. That the leading Muslim advisers and confidantes who served the Mongols and whose careers will be studied here—'Abd al-Raḥmān (Ao-tu-la Ho-man 奥都剌合蠻), Fāṭima (Fa-ti-ma 法迪瑪), and Aḥmad (A-hei-ma 阿黑馬)

---

[19] Boyle, *World Conqueror*, vol. 1, p. 122.

[20] See "Chinggis Khan to kaikyōto 成吉思汗と回教徒," *Kaikyō jijō* 回教事情, 2:2 (1939), pp. 79–85, for more details about Chinggis' attitude and policy towards the Muslims.

[21] John Andrew Boyle, tr., *The Successors of Genghis Khan* (New York: Columbia University Press, 1971), p. 94; L. A. Khetagurov, et al., *Rashid ad-Din, Sbornik Letopisei* (Moscow-Leningrad, 1946–1960), vol. 2, p. 64.

—were assassinated or executed is no accident. The court used each of them until they proved to be liabilities. Then it discarded them.

Ögödei himself initiated projects that necessitated the advice of the Muslims, the Chinese, and other foreigners. By 1234, he had crushed the Chin dynasty and added North China (that is, China north of the Huai River) to his domain, which by this time also included much of Central Asia. The Mongols now had an empire, and in 1235 Ögödei established their first capital at Karakorum. He needed Muslim and Chinese artisans and architects to build the town. Like Chinggis, he simply gathered craftsmen from Central Asia and had them dispatched to Mongolia.[22] Muslim and Chinese goldsmiths, metal workers, weavers, and potters were moved to Karakorum, where they settled in specifically designated quarters.[23] One section of the town was reserved for the Muslims and another accommodated the Chinese. William of Rubruck, the Franciscan friar who visited Karakorum in 1254, noticed two mosques in the Muslim quarter, an indication that the Mongols did not prevent the practice of Islam.[24]

The inhabitants of Karakorum relied upon foreign sources for grain, horses, sheep, and many other goods. According to Juvaini, five hundred cartloads of food reached Karakorum every day.[25] William of Rubruck observed four separate markets operating just beyond the four town gates.[26] Trade was essential to the survival of Karakorum, and the Muslims and the Chinese conveyed most goods to and from the town. The recent discovery of quantities of Yüan dynasty money in Karakorum attests to a lively and significant commerce.[27]

[22] Johannes de Plano Carpini, "Incipit Ystoria Mongalorum quos nos Tartaros Appellamus," in Anastasius van den Wyngaert, ed., Sinica Franciscana, vol. 1 (Quaracchi-Firenze: Collegio di S. Bonaventura, 1929), pp. 91–92. During the Ming dynasty, the Mongols persisted in dispatching expeditions to capture foreign artisans. See Henry Serruys, "Chinese in Southern Mongolia during the Sixteenth Century," Monumenta Serica, 18 (1959), pp. 56–57.

[23] Tazaka (see n. 2 above), p. 618; YS 120:2964; S. V. Kiselev, ed., Drevnemongol'skie goroda (Moscow: Izdatelst'vo Nauka, 1965), pp. 274–293, describes some of the craft articles produced by these artisans.

[24] William W. Rockhill, tr., The Journey of William of Rubruck to the Eastern Parts of the World, 1253–1255 (London: The Hakluyt Society, 1900), p. 221; Mouradja d'Ohsson, Histoire des Mongols depuis Tchinguiz Khan jusqu'a Timour Bey ou Tamerlan (The Hague: Les Freres Van Cleef, 1834), vol. 2, p. 304.

[25] Murakami Masatsugu 材上正二, "Genchō ni okeru senfushi to kandatsu 元朝に於ける泉府司と斡脱," Tōhō gakuhō 東方学報 (Tokyo), 13:1 (May, 1942), p. 161.

[26] Christopher Dawson, ed., Mission to Asia: Narratives and Letters of the Franciscan Missionaries in Mongolia and China in the Thirteenth and Fourteenth Centuries (New York: Harper & Row, 1966), p. 184; Rockhill (see n. 24 above), p. 221.

[27] Kiselev (see n. 23 above), pp. 183–187.

Ögödei also moved Central Asian Muslims into other territories in Mongolia and North China. In one instance, which has been studied by the French Sinologist Paul Pelliot, Ögödei ordered Ha-san-na 哈散納, a Kereyid who had been with Chinggis at Baljuna, to settle three thousand Muslims in Hsün-ma-lin 尋麻林, about twenty miles west of modern Kalgan.[28] This community produced grape wine and silk lined with gold thread for the Mongol rulers. Other Muslim merchants and artisans were settled in inhabited towns and cities in North China. Later, with the Mongol conquest of southwestern China, they helped to colonize the province of Yunnan.

Perhaps Ögödei's most pressing need was Muslim expertise in financial administration. The building of Karakorum, the military campaigns against North China (culminating in the fall of the Chin dynasty in 1234), and the luxury goods coveted by the Mongols required vast expenditures. Taxes on the subject peoples of North China were one means of raising the revenues needed to cover such costs. The tax collectors appointed by the Mongols were, for the most part, Muslims, and Ögödei granted tax-farming privileges to them.[29] Yeh-lü Ch'u-ts'ai 耶律楚材 (1189–1243), the sinicized Khitan who was Chief of the Central Secretariat (chung-shu-ling 中書令) in Ögödei's government, had opposed the institution of tax farming. He had already persuaded Ögödei neither to ravage North China nor to turn it into pasture lands for the Mongol flocks; he pointed out that it was more profitable to permit the Chinese to continue to farm the land and then to tax them. As the most powerful official in the early years of Ögödei's reign, he had devised a system of taxation that had "imposed a limit on the fiscal exploitation of Chinese subjects...."[30] Yet the court needed additional revenue. Thus it turned to Muslim merchants to raise sums sufficient to cover its expenses. In 1239, the Muslim trader 'Abd al-Raḥmān suggested that the adoption of the system of tax farming would double annual tax revenues from 22,000 ingots (ting 錠) of silver to 44,000

---

[28] Paul Pelliot, "Une ville musulmane dans la Chine du nord sous les mongols," Journal asiatique, 211 (1927), pp. 261–279, for a study of this community; for Ha-san-na, see YS 122:3016; K'o Shao-min 柯劭忞, Hsin Yüan shih 新元史 (Erh-shih-wu-shih ed. [Shanghai: K'ai-ming Shu-tien, 1935]), p. 6875; T'u Chi 屠寄, Meng-wu-erh shih-chi 蒙兀兒史記 (rpt. Taipei: Shih-chieh Shu-chü, 1962), 40:5a.

[29] Herbert Franz Schurmann, Economic Structure of the Yüan Dynasty (Cambridge, Mass.: Harvard University Press, 1956), p. 4.

[30] Igor de Rachewiltz, "Yeh-lü Ch'u-ts'ai (1189–1243): Buddhist Idealist and Confucian Statesman," in Arthur F. Wright and Denis Twitchett, ed., Confucian Personalities (Stanford: Stanford University Press, 1962), p. 207.

ingots.[31] Ögödei overrode Yeh-lü's objection to this plan and appointed 'Abd al-Raḥmān to be in charge of tax collection for North China. Nonetheless, though the Muslims acted as tax collectors and garnered some profits from tax farming, the Mongols were the principal beneficiaries. The court used Muslim expertise for its own profit.

Perhaps because of his need for their services, Ögödei was well disposed towards the Muslims. The Persian historians are unanimous in their praise of Ögödei. He is portrayed as "exceedingly beneficent and of excellent disposition, and a great friend to the Musulmāns." [32] Anecdotes reflecting his pro-Muslim attitudes appear frequently in the histories of Juzjani, Juvaini, and Rashīd al-Dīn. One such story is worth recounting in detail:

"An Arabic-speaking apostate from Islam came to Qa'an [Ögödei] and, kneeling, said: 'I saw Chingiz-Khan in a dream and he said: "Tell my son to kill many of the Muslims, for they are exceedingly evil people!"' After reflecting for a moment Qa'an asked whether he had spoken to him through an interpreter or personally with his own tongue. 'With his own tongue' said the man. 'Dost thou know the Mongol language' said Qa'an. 'No,' said the man. 'There is no doubt,' said Qa'an, 'that thou art lying. I know for certain that Chingiz-Khan knew no language but Mongol.' And he ordered the man to be put to death." [33]

Ögödei also rewarded Muslim merchants who offered him lavish tribute, and he protected the Muslims from their enemies. Some of his pro-Muslim actions, as reported in the Persian accounts, contravene Mongol customary law. In one case, a Turk reported to the court that he had climbed on his Muslim neighbor's roof and had witnessed this Muslim slaughtering a sheep in the Muslim manner, which the Persian historians cited as a violation of the *jasagh*.[34] By Mongol law and tradition, Ögödei should have executed the Muslim and rewarded the Turk. Instead he pardoned the Muslim and executed the Turk, justifying his decision on the ground that "this poor man [the Muslim] has observed the yasa [*jasagh*] and this Turk infringed it, for he climbed onto the roof of his house." [35]

[31] YS 2:36; Joseph-Anne-Marie de Moyriac de Mailla, *Histoire générale de la Chine ou annales de cet empire*; *traduites du Tong-kien-kang-mou* (Paris, 1779), 9, p. 231.

[32] Raverty (see n. 18 above), p. 1106.

[33] Boyle, *Successors*, p. 79.

[34] Bertold Spuler, *History of the Mongols Based on Eastern and Western Accounts of the Thirteenth and Fourteenth Centuries* (tr. by Helga and Stuart Drummond) (Berkeley: University of California Press, 1972), pp. 61–62.

[35] Boyle, *Successors*, p. 78.

Ögödei's favorable attitude towards the Muslims was not shared by all the Mongol elite. His older brother Chaghadai, portrayed by all the accounts as the stern upholder of Mongol customs and laws, imposed limits on the Muslims and forbad certain Islamic practices. Having taken an active role in the Mongol military campaigns in Central Asia and then serving as ruler of that vast territory, he had encountered stiff resistance from the Muslims and had reciprocated with a bloody and brutal suppression of his Muslim opponents. His repressive acts earned him the wrath of the Persian historians. Juzjani characterized Chaghadai as "a tyrannical man, cruel, sanguinary, and an evil-doer." In comparison with other Mongol rulers, "there was not one who was a greater enemy of the Musulmāns."[36] According to these same Persian accounts, Chaghadai was merciless, and it was only through Ögödei's benevolent influence that he was prevented from persecuting the Muslims. The following incident illustrates, from the Persian standpoint, Chaghadai's severity and Ögödei's more humane attitude toward the Muslims. While on a hunt, the two brothers spied a Muslim washing himself in a stream. The Mongols prohibited anyone from washing in a stream during the spring and summer; they believed that bathing in those months would bring on thunderstorms and lightning. Chaghadai wished to execute the unfortunate Muslim on the spot, but Ögödei won a delay until the next morning. Later that night, Ögödei secretly ordered some of his retainers to throw a silver coin in the stream and to command the Muslim captive to say, in his defense, that he dove into the water to find his last bit of money, which had fallen into the stream. The following morning he told this story to Ögödei. The khaghan pardoned him, and explained his compassionate action in this way: "Who would dare to contravene the great Yasa? But this poor man, because of his distress and helplessness, has sacrificed himself for this wretched amount."[37]

As long as the Muslims performed useful functions for the Mongols, the court protected and, in fact, rewarded them. Yet an undercurrent of hostility, exemplified initially by Chaghadai, persisted. Some of the Mongol ruling elite distrusted the Muslims employed in government. The court often accused Muslim financial administrators of favoritism and corruption. So Muslim officials were alternately offered lavish inducements to serve the Mongols or were purged for malfeasance.

This alternation is evident during the reigns of Ögödei's descendants in the period from 1241 to 1248. Ögödei's immediate successor was his wife Töregene, who served as regent until 1246. She favored the Muslim

[36] Raverty (see n. 18 above), pp. 1145–46.
[37] Boyle, *Successors*, p. 77.

administrators at court, allowing them considerable leeway in financial matters. Reprimanding Yeh-lü Ch'u-ts'ai for his opposition to the Muslims, she repeatedly sought to increase taxes in North China. Even during Ögödei's reign, Yeh-lü had been accused of profiteering and corruption.[38] Capitalizing on his vulnerability, Töregene transferred more and more authority from him to the Muslim merchant 'Abd al-Raḥmān and to her confidante Fāṭima. The latter, who had been captured by the Mongols in Central Asia and had become Töregene's servant, apparently cast a "hypnotic spell" on her mistress. Fāṭima persuaded her patroness to support and promote the financial policies of 'Abd al-Raḥmān and to curb the influence of the Chinese and other non-Muslim advisers at court.[39] Töregene needed little persuasion, for she understood that Muslim financial administration led to increased revenues. Enemies of Fāṭima and 'Abd al-Raḥmān, including the previously powerful Nestorian Christian minister Chinkhai 鎮海, were stripped of their rank. Some were forced to flee to Central Asia to escape harsher punishments. Despite this political turbulence, the Mongols, by using the Muslims, achieved their goal of an increase in state income.

Just as it appeared that the Muslims were well entrenched at court, the leading Muslims in government were suddenly purged in 1246. In that year, Töregene's regency ended. Ögödei's eldest son Güyüg assumed the throne with elaborate ceremonies witnessed by the Papal emissary John of Plano Carpini and described in an account of his travels.[40] The new khaghan, who appeared to favor Nestorian Christians and who surrounded himself with Nestorian advisers and ministers, moved against the Muslims in government. Perhaps he viewed them as a potential fifth column. Or it may be that he was persuaded that their arbitrary exactions, which in fact provided revenue for the Mongols as well, were alienating the subject populations and were thus detrimental to the welfare of his domain. Or, finally, it may be, as the Persian historians suggest, that he simply despised Islam. Whatever the motive, he purged the two most powerful Muslims in his mother's court. 'Abd al-Raḥmān was summarily executed for profiteering and for diverting state revenue to his own use and profit.[41] Fāṭima was accused of sorcery and of having used her nefarious powers to cause the death of Güyüg's cousin. The court tortured her until she confessed to these crimes. Then "her upper

[38] de Rachewiltz (see note 30 above), p. 208. Yeh-lü died shortly thereafter, in 1243.

[39] Hsiao (see n. 10 above), pp. 40–44.

[40] Rockhill (see n. 24 above), pp. 23–30.

[41] René Grousset, *L'empire des steppes* (Paris: Payot, 1939), p. 337; George Vernadsky, *The Mongols and Russia* (New Haven: Yale University Press, 1953), p. 63.

and lower orifices were sewn up, and she was rolled up in a sheet of felt and thrown into the river."[42]

In this case, Muslim authority depended on the support of the Mongol court. Töregene willingly transferred power over financial affairs to the Muslims. Güyüg, reversing Töregene's policy, removed Muslims from positions of authority in his court. Whether his purge extended to and affected the general Muslim population is unclear. One indication that Muslims as a whole were affected by his policies was the constant complaints lodged against the government by Muslim merchants from Central Asia. And Muslim historians repeatedly assert that he was fond of denouncing Islam. Yet there was no general persecution of the Muslims. Nor was there a concerted effort to infringe on Islamic religious practices.

Möngke's accession to the throne prompted a return to a more conciliatory policy towards Islam. In 1248, Güyüg died en route to a confrontation with Batu Khan (d. 1255), the Mongol ruler of the Golden Horde in Russia, who had covertly opposed Güyüg's enthronement as the khaghan. Three years later, after a bitter but brief struggle, power over the Mongol domains shifted from the descendants of Ögödei to the line of his younger brother and Chinggis Khan's youngest son, Tolui (d. 1232), who sired four illustrious sons—Möngke, Khubilai, Hülegü, and Arigh Böke. Tolui's eldest son Möngke (d. 1259) became the khaghan in 1251, wresting control from his cousins, and then systematically executed those who resented his usurpation. Recognizing that Güyüg had alienated influential and potentially useful Muslims, Möngke set forth to regain their confidence and to employ their expertise. He reaffirmed Chinggis' edict exempting them from ordinary taxation.[43] To prove that he trusted them, he reappointed the venerable Maḥmūd Yalavach as governor of northwestern China and of the adjacent territories in Central Asia. Maḥmūd's son Mas'ūd Beg was given jurisdiction over Khorezm and much of western Central Asia.

In Möngke and his younger brother Hülegü, however, one notices the same sharply divergent views of the Muslims evidenced earlier by Ögödei and his brother Chaghadai. Möngke was tolerant of Islam and offered various pecuniary advantages to Muslims who served the court. On the other hand, Hülegü, whose principal wife was a fervent Christian and who had been dispatched to conquer the Muslim lands of Persia and of

---

[42] Boyle, *World Conqueror*, p. 246.

[43] Ernest A. Wallis Budge, tr., *The Chronography of Gregory Abû'l Faraj: The Son of Aaron, The Hebrew Physician Commonly Known as Bar Hebraeus* (London: Oxford University Press, 1932), pp. 420–424.

the Middle East, perceived the Muslims as enemies and treated them accordingly.[44] Möngke subsidized the *madrasa* (a Muslim theological school) in Bukhara to which his mother had donated a substantial amount of silver.[45] He was generous in his gifts to Muslim merchants and compensated those merchants whom Güyüg's court had not paid for their goods and services. And he appointed several Muslim scribes to his entourage. Though no individual Muslim had the power wielded in earlier days by Fāṭima or ʿAbd al-Raḥmān, Möngke created a more favorable milieu for the Muslims. The Persian historians acclaim him for his efforts: "And of all the peoples and religious communities he showed most honor and respect to the Muslims and bestowed the largest amount of gifts and alms upon them."[46] Meanwhile Hülegü was campaigning against the Ismāʿīlī order of Islam (popularly known as the Assassins) and the ʿAbbāsid Caliphate.[47] By 1258, he had occupied the Ismāʿīlī fortress at Alamūt and the Abbāsid capital of Baghdad, massacring thousands of Muslims in the process.[48]

By the time of Möngke's death in 1259, the Mongol-Muslim relationship was well defined. The Mongol rulers employed Muslims in administering North China and Central Asia and would often offer them prestigious positions and lavish rewards. But some in the Mongol elite loathed and feared Islam. Chaghadai, Hülegü, and others who had encountered stiff resistance from the Muslims on the battlefield despised them; some at the Mongol court resented the influence of the Muslim advisers; and others were concerned by the power enjoyed by the Muslims over financial affairs.

III. KHUBILAI KHAGHAN AND THE MUSLIMS

Khubilai Khaghan reflects the same conflicting Mongol attitudes and policies towards the Muslims. Khubilai alternated between entrusting

---

[44] Étienne Marc Quatremère, tr., *Historie des Mongols de la Perse écrite en persan par Raschid-Eldin* (Paris: Imprimerie Royale, 1836), 1, pp. 151–213, for a detailed description of these campaigns.

[45] Bertold Spuler, *Die Mongolen in Iran: Politik, Verwaltung, und Kultur der Ilchanzeit 1220–1350* (Berlin: Akademie Verlag, 1968), p. 238.

[46] Boyle, *Successors*, p. 220.

[47] For the Ismāʿīlī order, see Marshall G. S. Hodgson, *The Order of Assassins: The Struggle of the Early Nizârî Ismâ'îlîs against the Islamic World* ('s-Gravenhage: Mouton & Co., 1955); for a convenient summary of the reasons for the decline and fall of the ʿAbbāsids, see John A. Boyle, ed., *The Cambridge History of Iran, 5: The Saljuq and Mongol Periods* (Cambridge: Cambridge University Press, 1968), pp. 345–349.

[48] John A. Boyle, "The Death of the Last ʿAbbāsid Caliph: A Contemporary Muslim Account," *Journal of Semitic Studies*, 6:2 (Autumn, 1961), pp. 145–161.

certain Muslims with vast responsibilities at court and suspecting them of embezzlement of state funds. He needed their special skills. Khubilai differed from his predecessors: he settled in North China, not Mongolia, and the Mongols were vastly outnumbered by the Chinese in his territory. He used the Central Asian Muslims as a convenient buffer between the Mongol ruling elite and his Chinese subjects. Yet he did, during part of his reign, issue edicts aimed at restricting the practice of Islam, and he surely recognized that the Muslims in their positions as merchants and tax collectors engendered the hostility of the Chinese. His occasional repressive policies towards Islam were usually inspired by political and economic, not religious, motives. He was concerned lest the Muslims in government become too powerful. Gross misuse of such power might provoke further Chinese opposition to Mongol rule. Khubilai thus depended on the Muslims, but he remained suspicious of their political ambitions and their economic manipulation. Moreover, his Confucian, Buddhist, and Christian advisers, by their accusations and insinuations about the Muslims, contributed to his suspicion.[49]

Little is known of Khubilai's early relations with Muslims. His mother Sorkhakhtani Beki was revered by the Persian historians. Though she was herself a Nestorian, she recognized the political value of supporting (and in turn receiving the support of) all the leading religions in the Mongol territories. She provided the funds for the construction of the Khaniyya *madrasa* in Bukhara as well as other Muslim religious buildings.[50] She also offered alms to the Muslim poor. Since her son Khubilai was granted an appanage in North China, he apparently had few dealings with Muslims during her lifetime. Before he became the kha-ghan in 1260, most of his non-Mongol advisers were Chinese Confucians and Buddhists and Tibetan Buddhists. Such luminaries as Yao Shu 姚樞 (1203–1280), Liu Ping-chung 劉秉忠 (1216–1274), and Pags-pa (Pa-ssu-pa 八思八, 1235–1280) proffered advice and assistance to Khubilai in the early stages of his career.[51] He was more than willing to seek the counsel of the Chinese residing in the lands assigned to him by his brother Möngke. He went out of his way to invite talented Chinese and Tibetans

---

[49] For some of the Buddhist advisers, see Paul Ratchnevsky, "Die mongolischen Grosskhane und die buddhistische Kirche," *Asiatica: Festschrift Friedrich Weller zum 65. Geburtstag* (Leipzig: Otto Harrassowitz, 1954), pp. 491–495.

[50] Barthold (see n. 16 above), p. 473; d'Ohsson (see n. 24 above), pp. 264–267.

[51] On Liu, see Hok-lam Chan, "Liu Ping-chung 劉秉忠 (1216–74): A Buddhist-Taoist Statesman at the Court of Khubilai Khan," *T'oung Pao*, 53:1–3 (1967), pp. 98–146; on Yao, see YS 158:3711–3716; and on Pags-pa, see YS 202:4517–4519, and the essay by Herbert Franke in this volume.

to serve him, often offering lavish rewards for their help.[52] Few Muslims, however, were present in his entourage in this early stage. Since his base was in North China, he initially employed Chinese advisers.

To judge from the available evidence, Khubilai was not biased against Islam. He shared his mother's tolerant attitude toward most religions. Marco Polo quotes him as follows: "There are four prophets who are worshipped and to whom everybody does reverence. The Christians say their God was Jesus Christ; the Saracens Mahomet; the Jews Moses; and the idolaters Sagamoni Burcan, who was the first of the idols; and I do honour and reverence to all four, that is to him who is the greatest in heaven, and more true, and' him I pray to help me."[53] These beliefs were more than likely nurtured in Khubilai at an early phase of his life and career. Within a few years after he became the khaghan, he began to turn more frequently to non-Chinese advisers and administrators. Several incidents prompted him to question the loyalty of his Chinese underlings and to doubt the possibility of a peaceful accommodation with the Southern Sung dynasty, which ruled South China. The first involved his efforts to reach a settlement with the Southern Sung. In 1260, he dispatched Hao Ching 郝經 (1222–1275), one of his principal Chinese advisers and officials, as an envoy to negotiate an agreement with his Chinese neighbors to the south. Instead, the Sung court imprisoned Hao and severed its relations with Khubilai.[54] Sung officials were also involved in a second incident that caused Khubilai to suspect some of his closest Chinese advisers of disloyalty. In 1262, they encouraged Li T'an 李璮, the most powerful official in Shantung, to rebel against Mongol rule. Li, whose family had ruled most of Shantung for more than fifty years, mobilized his troops to challenge Mongol authority. Since Shantung had sizeable salt and copper deposits and was thus a key economic area in North China, Khubilai immediately sent a large force to crush the rebels.[55] Within a few months, the Mongols had routed the insurgents

---

[52] Li Chieh 黎傑, *Yüan shih* 元史 (Hong Kong: Hai-ch'iao Ch'u-pan-she 海僑出版社, 1962), pp. 178–184; according to a contemporaneous source, Khubilai sought assistance from any quarter. He is quoted as saying: "Those who present memorials to make proposals may present them with the envelopes sealed. If the proposals cannot be adopted, there will be no punishment. But if the proposals are useful, the Court will liberally promote and reward the persons who make the proposals in order to encourage the loyal and sincere ones." Quoted from Yan-shuan Lao, "The *Chung-t'ang shih-chi* of Wang Yün: An Annotated Translation with an Introduction" (Ph. D. dissertation, Harvard University, 1962), p. 24.

[53] Moule and Pelliot (see n. 5 above), p. 201.

[54] Dietlinde Schlegel, *Hao Ching (1222–1275): ein chinesischer Berater des Kaisers Kublai Khan* (Bamberg: Offsetdruckerei Kurt Urlaub, 1968), pp. 66–67.

[55] Otagi Matsuo 愛宕松男 "Ri Dan no hanran to sono seijiteki igi 李璮の叛乱と其の 政治的意義," *Tōyōshi kenkyū* 東洋史研究, 6:4 (Aug.–Sept., 1941), pp. 253–255.

and killed Li. Khubilai discovered shortly thereafter that he faced opposition not only from presumably trustworthy provincial governors but also from leading officials and advisers at court. His prime minister Wang Wen-t'ung 王文統, who happened to be Li T'an's father-in-law, was accused of abetting the rebels. Khubilai quickly detained and then executed Wang.[56]

Understandably enough, Khubilai became wary of relying solely on the Chinese for advice and assistance. After 1261, more Muslims and Uighurs were entrusted with positions of authority in government. The Mongols and the Se-mu were accorded special privileges.[57] Muslims, for example, were exempt from regular taxation.[58] A Muslim could be appointed as darughachi (or agent), a position that no Chinese could hold.[59] The court imposed other restrictions on the Chinese. Seeking to limit the opportunities for armed insurrections, the Mongols prohibited private ownership of weapons by the Chinese.[60] In short, the court discriminated against its Chinese subjects and favored the Muslims.

Small wonder, then, that the Muslims were found in all regions of China in Yüan times. Muslims had settled in northwest China as early as the T'ang dynasty. The Yüan, however, actively encouraged them to settle there and offered inducements and assistance. As a result, Kan-chou 甘州, Su-chou 肅州, and Yen-an 延安 each had separate and sizeable Muslim quarters. In 1274, the Muslims built a mosque in Kan-chou.[61] References to Muslim communities with their own religious leaders (Ta-shih-man 答失蠻 in Chinese, from Persian danishmand) abound in Chinese and Persian sources. Since northwest China borders on Muslim Central Asia, it is not surprising that Muslims reached that area. More astonishing is their presence in north and northeast China. A Muslim community apparently built a mosque in Khubilai's summer capital at Shang-tu.[62] Muslim officials and craftsmen resided in the capital at Ta-tu. In Shantung, they were involved in horse trading;[63] in Honan, a Muslim settlement of one hundred eighty-six households

---

[56] Hsiao (see n. 10 above), pp. 60–61.

[57] John W. Dardess, Conquerors and Confucians: Aspects of Political Change in Late Yüan China (New York: Columbia University Press, 1973), p. 35.

[58] Erich Haenisch, Steuergerechtsame der chinesischen Klöster unter der Mongol-enherrschaft, in Berichte über die Verhandlungen der Sächsischen Akademie der Wissen-schaften zu Leipzig (1940), p. 15.

[59] YS 82:2052.

[60] Meng (see n. 7 above), p. 56.

[61] Tazaka (see n. 2 above), p. 613.

[62] Yoshito Harada, Shang-Tu: The Summer Capital of the Yüan Dynasty in Dolon Nor, Mongolia (Tokyo: Toa-Koko Gakukwai, 1941), p. 16.

[63] Tazaka (see n. 2 above), p. 699.

farmed land given to them by the court;[64] and in Chen-ting circuit 眞定路 in modern Hopei, a group of Muslim scholars founded a school.[65] Muslim merchants travelled all the way to Korea. Korean sources report that a number of Muslim residents in Korea were killed during the 1272–1273 Rebellion of the Three Patrols (*Sam Pyŏlch'o*).[66] The Muslims who resided or travelled in North China may be divided into two groups. First were those—primarily merchants and tax collectors or financial administrators—who voluntarily came to North China from Persia and Central Asia. Second were those, primarily craftsmen, architects, or anyone with a desirable skill, whom the Mongols forced to move to China.

The same combination of voluntary colonization and forced migration produced the Muslim settlements in southwest China. Szechwan attracted Muslim merchants and craftsmen because of its strategic location on the trade routes to Burma and India and because of its commercial prosperity. Yunnan, however, became the main center for the Muslims in the region. Khubilai had conquered much of Yunnan in military campaigns conducted in 1252–1253, but it was not to have a civil administration until 1274, when he appointed a Muslim governor for the province. This Muslim governor brought numerous co-religionists with him to Yunnan. Of the Yunnanese officials mentioned in the *Yüan shih* 元史 (the *Yüan History*, which deals with the dynasty through 1368, the year of its downfall), thirty-one are Mongols, thirty-seven are Chinese, and thirty-two are *Se-mu* people.[67] The *Se-mu* generally held much more influential positions than the Chinese.

Trade was also the main attraction for the Muslims who settled in southeast China. The fine harbors of the southeast had drawn foreign traders there in the T'ang and Sung. When Khubilai's forces finally occupied South China in 1279, they neither expelled nor imposed new restrictions on Muslim merchants. Muslim defectors to the Yüan cause had, in fact, been extremely helpful. The defection of the Muslim P'u Shou-keng 蒲壽庚, the superintendent of maritime trade (*T'i-chü shih-po shih* 提舉市舶使) at Ch'üan-chou 泉州, was particularly useful because it offered a naval force to the Mongols, who had no true navy of their own and whose maritime expedition against Japan in 1274 had just ended

---

[64] YS 15:327.

[65] Tazaka (see n. 2 above), p. 702.

[66] Cited in William E. Henthorn, *Korea: The Mongol Invasions* (Leiden: E. J. Brill, 1963), p. 74.

[67] Hsia Kuang-nan 夏光南, *Yüan-tai Yün-nan shih-ti ts'ung-k'ao mu-lu* 元代雲南史地叢考目錄 (Shanghai: Chung-hua Shu-chü 中華書局, 1935), p. 75.

disastrously.[68] Late in 1276, P'u shifted his allegiance from the Southern Sung to the Yüan, bringing ships and wealth to his new allies.[69] Khubilai rewarded P'u by appointing him as supervisor of maritime trade for Kwangtung and Fukien (*Tu t'i-chü Fu-chien Kuang-tung shih-po shih* 都提舉福建廣東市舶事) and investing him-with the title of left vice-minister (*chung-shu tso-ch'eng* 中書左丞) of Fukien. Of the thirty super-intendents of trading ships in Fukien during the Yüan, one-third were Muslims. The Yüan court no doubt promoted overseas trade because "the Mongols ... were trying to gain the good will and support of the businessmen."[70] It permitted the Arab and Persian merchants to trade in Ch'üan-chou as long as they abided by its commercial regulations. A branch office of the *Wo-t'o tsung kuan-fu* 斡脫總管府 or "Central Bureau supervising the *Ortakh*" (which was later to be known as the *Ch'üan-fu-ssu* 泉府司 or "Supervising Money Bureau") was established in the city both in order to regulate the *ortakh* or Muslim merchant associations and to provide loans and encourage them.[71] The Arabs and Persians who resided in Ch'üan-chou formed virtually self-governing communities. An official known as the *Shaikh al-Islam* (in Chinese, *hui-hui t'ai-shih* 回回太師) was the leader of the community and served as an intermediary between it and the Mongol authorities. The *qāḍī* (in Chinese, *hui-chiao-t'u fa-kuan* 回教徒法官) interpreted Muslim laws and principles for the settlement. The Muslim quarter had its own bazaars, hospitals, and at least one mosque. The Yüan court did not, except for a brief but important period during Khubilai's reign, prevent the Muslims from following such dictates of Islam as circumcision and abstention from pork. Neither did it impose the Mongol or Chinese languages on the Muslims. Arabic and Persian were still spoken by many members of the community.

The Mongols adopted, with some exceptions, the same *laissez-faire* policy toward the Muslim communities in other southeastern cities. Hangchow, the former capital of the Southern Sung, was another center for Arab and Persian traders. The city, which was probably the most populous in the world at that time, was a magnet for Muslim merchants and craftsmen bent on enriching themselves.[72] Like their co-religionists

[68] Kuwabara Jitsuzo, "On P'u Shou-keng," *Memoirs of the Research Department of the Toyo Bunko*, 7 (1935), pp. 58–60.

[69] For more on P'u, see Maejima Shinji 前嶋信次, "Senshū no Perushiyajin to Ho Jukō 泉州の波斯人と蒲壽庚," *Shigaku* 史學, 25:3 (1952), pp. 256–321.

[70] Lo Jung-pang, "Maritime Commerce and Its Relation to the Sung Navy," *Journal of the Economic and Social History of the Orient*, 12:1 (1969), p. 95.

[71] Tazaka (see n. 2 above), p. 664.

[72] According to Jacques Gernet in *Daily Life in China on the Eve of the Mongol Invasion*,

in Ch'üan-chou, the Muslims in Hangchow were allowed to select their own leaders. The Shaikh al-Islam, chosen from the mullāhs (man-la 滿剌, a leader of the community who was well versed in the Islamic theology) in the region, governed the community. In 1281, a mosque was constructed in the city.[73] The Yüan court generally permitted the Muslims to fast during Ramaḍān, to circumcise male infants, to recite the Koran, and, ignoring Mongol law, to slaughter animals in their own fashion. According to the fourteenth-century traveller Ibn Baṭṭūṭa, musicians could often perform songs in Arabic and Persian as well as in Chinese. Orchestras composed of three hundred to four hundred men played Muslim music at banquets given in his honor.[74] Thus, despite restrictions imposed by Khubilai late in his reign and by several of his successors, the Hangchow Muslims were still a self-governing and prosperous community as late as the 1320s.[75]

Some Muslims in the southeastern provinces attained high office. According to the gazetteer of Chekiang province, they served as censors, darughachi, and pacification commissioners.[76] Similarly, in Canton, Foochow, and other coastal cities, the Yüan appointed Muslims to positions in government, particularly in the financial administration. Khubilai's edicts and regulations were often translated into Persian and Arabic, implying that Muslims played an influential role in government.[77] The Muslim settlements in the southeastern cities had their own leaders who were entrusted with religious and legal jurisdiction over their co-religionists.

Khubilai tolerated and, on occasion, rewarded the Muslims in these various regions of China because they were useful to him in ruling

1250–1276 (tr. by H. M. Wright, [Stanford: Stanford University Press, 1970, paperback ed.]), "The population of Hangchow had, by 1275, gone beyond the million mark" (p. 28). Shiba Yoshinobu, in "Urbanization and the Development of Markets in the Lower Yangtze Valley," in Crisis and Prosperity in Sung China, ed. by John W. Haeger (Tucson: The University of Arizona Press, 1975), p. 22, notes that "The best estimates [for the population of Hangchow] range from 1.5 to 5 million." Marco Polo extolled Hangchow as "the greatest city which may be found in the world, where so many pleasures may be found that one fancies himself to be in Paradise." (Moule and Pelliot [see n. 5 above], p. 326).

[73] Chan Po-lien 詹柏煉, "Yüan-tai Hang-chou I-ssu-lan chiao-ti yen-chiu 元代杭州伊斯蘭教的研究," Chung-hua wen-hua fu-hsing yüeh-k'an 中華文化復興月刊, 3:8 (1970), pp. 31–32.

[74] Gibb (see n. 6 above), p. 295.

[75] H. Cordier, tr., Les voyages en asie au xiv siècle du bienheureux frère Odoric de Pordenone (Paris: Ernest Leroux, 1891), p. 313.

[76] Tazaka (see n. 2 above), pp. 685–686, quoting the Che-chiang t'ung-chih 浙江通志.

[77] Henry Yule (tr. and ed.), The Book of Ser Marco Polo the Venetian Concerning the Kingdoms and Marvels of the East (3rd. ed., rev. by Henri Cordier, New York: Charles Scribner's Sons, 1903), vol. 1, p. 29.

China. They promoted trade with the rest of Asia and served as tax collectors and financial administrators. Khubilai did not need to rely solely on Chinese advisers and officials. He could employ some Muslims in government. They appeared more loyal than the Chinese because they were utterly dependent on the Yüan court for their position and power. Moreover, it was far easier to control the thousands of Muslims than the millions of Chinese. Also, by using Muslims as supervisors of trade, tax collectors, and the like, Khubilai ensured that some of the Chinese hostility against foreign rule would be directed at the Muslims, not at the Mongols.

Yet, despite their contributions, Khubilai remained suspicious of the Muslims. Like his uncle Chaghadai and his brother Hülegü, he was not totally convinced of their loyalty and trustworthiness. For example, he needed their advanced military technology but was reluctant to appoint them to the highest ranks in his army. Muslims, even those whom the Mongols considered the most reliable, rarely commanded military expeditions. Nāṣir-al-Dīn (Na-su-la-ting 納速剌丁), the son of the first Muslim governor of Yunnan Saiyid Ajall Shams al-Dīn (Sai-tien-ch'ih Shan-ssu-ting 賽典赤贍思丁), proved an exception to this rule. In 1277, the court dispatched him to lead a military campaign against Burma.[78] Khubilai and his government, however, generally excluded the Muslims from involvement in the military. Only as a last resort would the court even permit Muslims to supervise the Mongol arsenal.[79] It also repeatedly limited the number of horses that individual Muslims could own. In 1263, it confiscated two-thirds of the horses owned by Muslims.[80] Khubilai was unwilling to provide even seemingly loyal non-Mongols with weapons and horses that could be turned against his own troops.

IV. Muslim Contributions to Early Yüan

Direct leadership of the military aside, the Muslims were permitted and, in fact, encouraged to contribute to all other facets of Yüan society. The Yüan needed assistance in ruling China and in developing and using new machines and techniques. Reluctant to rely wholly on Chinese advisers and officials, Khubilai turned to the Muslims. He sought Muslim advice

---

[78] YS 125:3066; T'u Chi, *Meng-wu-erh shih-chi*, 80:3b; Paul Pelliot, *Notes on Marco Polo* (Paris: Librarie Adrien Maisonneuve, 1959–63), vol. 2, pp. 793–794.

[79] Gunther Mangold, *Das Militärwesen in China unter der Mongolen-Herrschaft* (Dissertation, Universität München, 1971), p. 202.

[80] *Ta Yüan ma-cheng chi* 大元馬政記 in *Kuang-ts'ang hsüeh-chün ts'ung-shu* 廣倉學宭叢書 (rpt. Peiping, 1937), p. 18. For more on horses and the Yüan, see "Some Notes on the Horse-Policy of the Yüan Dynasty," by S. Jagchid and C. R. Bawden, *Central Asiatic Journal*, 10:3–4 (Dec., 1965), pp. 246–268.

and assistance in three areas. First, since the Mongols knew little about the economic operations of a sedentary agricultural society, he required Muslim financial administrators as well as merchant associations. Second, Khubilai was eager to use Muslim advances in astronomy, medicine, armaments, and archiecture for China. Third, he encouraged Muslim colonization of Yunnan as a means of bringing that province within the purview of the central government. Each of these areas will be considered separately.

A. *Muslims and the Yüan Economy*

In the first years of his reign Khubilai needed income. His younger brother Arigh Böke (A-li Pu-ko 阿里不哥), representing those nomadic Mongols who resented Khubilai's apparent preference for a sedentary, Chinese-like society and court, challenged his claim to the throne in a war that lasted from 1260 to 1264; the rebellion of Li T'an, though shortlived, forced Khubilai to send a large force to Shantung; by the late 1260s, Khubilai's cousin and Ögödei's grandson Khaidu (Hai-tu 海都) posed a threat in Central Asia, prompting Khubilai to dispatch an expedition, led by his son Nomukhan (Na-mu-han 那木罕), to assert his authority over the region—a mission that it could not accomplish,[81] and Khubilai's troops met stubborn resistance in attempting to conquer the Southern Sung dynasty. These expeditions were costly. Simultaneously, Khubilai built new capitals at Shang-tu and at Ta-tu, established postal stations throughout his territory, and promoted numerous public works projects.[82] The combination of military expeditions and public works could not be sustained without additional revenue.

To obtain the needed funds, Khubilai sought help from the infamous Muslim finance minister Ahmad. Since Ahmad's exploits have been studied by several scholars, there is no need to describe his career in detail.[83] The *Yüan History* classifies him as one of the "villainous" ministers, and Chinese and Western sources alike revile him for exploiting and oppressing the Chinese.[84] Marco Polo believed that Ahmad had "bewitched" Khubilai "with his spells."[85] According to Marco Polo,

[81] John W. Dardess, "From Mongol Empire to Yüan Dynasty: Changing Forms of Imperial Rule in Mongolia and Central Asia," *Monumenta Serica*, 30 (1972–73), pp. 135–136.

[82] For more detail about the postal system, see Peter Olbricht, *Das Postwesen in China unter der Mongolenherrschaft im 13. und 14. Jahrhundert* (Wiesbaden: Otto Harrassowitz, 1954), pp. 43–50.

[83] See, in particular, Herbert Franke, "Ahmed: ein Beitrag zur Wirtschaftgeschichte Chinas unter Qubilai," *Oriens*, 1:2 (1948), p. 222.

[84] YS 205:4558–4564.

[85] Moule and Pelliot (see n. 5 above), p. 214.

Khubilai's support allowed Aḥmad to acquire a fortune and to indulge his sexual appetite. My intent here is not to excuse his excesses, but to show that Aḥmad knew that he would be judged by the amount of revenue collected for the court. The more revenue he raised, the greater his power, prestige, and income. According to the Chinese accounts, he abused his power and imposed an inordinate tax burden on the Chinese. To be sure, he profited from his postion, but it must be remembered that his accusers (i.e., those who wrote the Chinese accounts) were officials unsympathetic to his policies.

Aḥmad's main financial goals, simply stated, were to register all eligible taxpayers, to impose state monopolies on certain products, and to increase tax revenues. From 1262 until his death in 1282, he directed the state financial administration.[86] One of his first tasks was to enroll taxable households that had not been included in earlier tax lists. In 1261, some 1,418,499 households in North China were listed in tax registers; by 1274, the number had been increased to 1,967,898 households.[87] A regular system of land taxation was instituted. In addition, the revenue from the taxes on merchants grew from 4,500 ingots of silver in 1271 to 450,000 ingots by 1286.[88] (The first figure does not include revenues from merchants in South China while the second figure does.) Aḥmad also attempted to use the state monopolies for additional revenue. He established quotas for the monopolized goods which were to be turned over to the government. Chün-hsü chou 鈞徐州 in Honan, for example, had a quota of 1,037,070 catties (chin 斤) of iron, 200,000 of which would be fashioned into farm tools and sold to farmers in return for grain.[89] Revenues from the salt monopoly grew from 30,000 ting in 1271 to 180,000 ting by 1286.[90] In 1276, Aḥmad forbad private production of copper tools, reserving that for the government. Even earlier, he had instituted state monopolies on tea, liquor, vinegar, gold, and silver, all of which were profitable. Control bureaus (t'i-chü-ssu 提舉司) were founded to supervise the laborers and merchants who worked on the monopolies and to prevent private trade in these products.[91] In short, Aḥmad's policies were lucrative for the state treasury.

[86] YS 205:4558–4559. More research is needed to determine whether Aḥmad increased taxes disproportionately and whether he garnered enormous profits by virtue of his position at court.

[87] Franke (see n. 83 above), p. 232.

[88] Tamura Jitsuzō 田村実造, et al., Ajia-shi kōza アジア史講座 (Tokyo: Iwasaki Shoten 岩崎書店, 1955–57), p. 282.

[89] Ch'en Pang-chan 陳邦瞻, Yüan-shih chi-shih pen-mo 元史紀事本末 (rpt. Taipei: Commercial Press, 1968), p. 30.

[90] Tamura (see n. 88 above), p. 282.

[91] Schurmann (see n. 29 above), pp. 147–148.

Yet the Chinese sources accuse him of cronyism. Of the eleven men he chose to direct the state monopolies, four were definitely Muslims and one other may have been.[92] Muslims and other non-Chinese dominated the major financial positions in government. Some Chinese were recruited into the financial administration, but they generally received low-ranking positions. One of the most damning accusations levelled at Aḥmad was that he attempted to place his inexperienced and perhaps unqualified and incapable sons in influential posts in the bureaucracy. He succeeded in having his son Mas'ūd (Mo-su-hu 抹速忽) appointed the *darughachi* of the commercial center of Hangchow, a political plum which offered numerous opportunities for personal profit. But Aḥmad encountered opposition in naming his son Ḥusain (Hu-hsin 忽辛) as intendant in Ta-tu. The chancellor of the right, a Mongol named An-t'ung 安童, objected that Ḥusain had no training for the position.[93] This argument apparently failed to sway the court, and Ḥusain continued his climb in the bureaucracy, becoming an important official in Kiangsi by 1279.

Opposition to his policies provoked Aḥmad's resentment and vengefulness. He despised most of Khubilai's Confucian and Buddhist advisers and had sharply divergent views on government policy. Shih T'ien-tse 史天澤 (1202–1275), Lien-hsi-hsien 廉希憲 (1231–1280), and others among Khubilai's closest counselors repeatedly objected to Aḥmad's tax policies, arguing that the new levies were an intolerable burden on the Chinese populace. They accused him of profiteering and of having a "sycophantic character and treacherous designs."[94] He, in turn, accused some of them of embezzling state funds and of unbecoming personal conduct. The Chinese sources assert that Aḥmad falsely accused Ts'ui Pin 崔斌, an official in Chiang-huai 江淮 who was one of his opponents, of pilfering government grain and had the emperor order Ts'ui to be executed.[95] Whether the source on this particular case is accurate or not, it is true that many of his opponents left government service in the 1270s. Unlike Ts'ui Pin, most were neither executed nor imprisoned. Some retired of their own accord. Unable to persuade Khubilai to limit Aḥmad's power, the Confucian scholar Hsü Heng 許衡 (1209–1281) retired from active involvement in court politics to become

[92] Franke (see n. 83 above); YS 205:4560–4561.

[93] Hsiao (see n. 10 above), p. 67. For more on An-t'ung, see Igor de Rachewiltz, "Muqali, Bōl, Tas, and An-t'ung," *Papers on Far Eastern History*, 15 (March, 1977), pp. 56–58.

[94] Hok-lam Chan, "Wang O (1190–1273)," *Papers on Far Eastern History*, 12 (September, 1975), p. 53.

[95] Li (see n. 52 above), p. 64; Ch'en (see n. 89 above), p. 30.

director of the National College (*Kuo-tzu chien* 國子監). The Uighur Confucian Lien-hsi-hsien retired after Aḥmad accused him of embezzlement, adultery, and other improprieties.[96] Fortunately for Aḥmad, some of Khubilai's advisers died of natural causes in the 1270s. Liu Ping-chung died in 1274, Shih T'ien-tse in 1275, Chao Pi 趙璧 in 1276, Yao Shu in 1279, and Tou Mo 竇默 in 1280. With the death of these opponents, Aḥmad became even more powerful at court.[97]

The Persian accounts of Aḥmad's career differ somewhat from the Chinese assessments. Rashīd al-Dīn writes that "Aḥmad held the vizierate with honor for nearly 25 years."[98] He is praised for promoting Chinese trade with the Muslim world and presumably for protecting Muslims within China. The Muslim records omit mention of the charges of nepotism, exploitation, and profiteering levelled at Aḥmad in the Chinese sources. Viewed from a different perspective, however, the Chinese accusations appear less serious. Bringing relatives and likeminded associates into the government was perfectly sensible. If Aḥmad were to overcome opposition and implement his policies, he needed to place his supporters in influential positions in government. The creation of such cliques was condemned by traditional Chinese thinkers, but Aḥmad recognized that he could not succeed without sympathizers, most of whom would be Muslims, in the bureaucracy. He may, in fact, have exploited the Chinese, as their historians assert, by imposing heavy taxes and high prices on essential goods monopolized by the government. But his position at court, not to mention possible promotions and rewards, depended on his ability to satisfy the seemingly insatiable revenue requirements of the Mongols. In his defense, one might say that he was merely an agent, albeit a dedicated and effective one, of the Mongol court, which had a considerable need for income. The Chinese charge of profiteering rests partly on evidence uncovered after Aḥmad's death. About two months after his assassination, a jewel that had been given to Khubilai for his crown was found in Aḥmad's house.[99] Was the precious stone planted there by his enemies? If not, why did his wife and son not transfer the jewel to a less obvious location? Why was it so easy for

---

[96] J. Deguignes, *Histoire générale des Huns, des Turcs, des Mongols, et des autres Tartares occidentaux* (Paris: Desaint & Saillant, 1756–58), vol. 3, p. 152; de Mailla (see n. 31 above), vol. 9, pp. 313–15.

[97] For a brief summary of the influence of these advisers on Khubilai, see Yao Ts'ung-wu 姚從吾, "Hu-pi-lieh tui-yü Han-hua t'ai-tu ti fen-hsi 忽必烈對於漢化態度的分析," *Ta-lu tsa-chih* 大陸雜誌 (July 15, 1955), pp. 22–31.

[98] Boyle, *World Conqueror*, p. 291.

[99] A. C. Moule, *Quinsai with Other Notes on Marco Polo* (London: Cambridge Univ. Press, 1957), p. 80.

government officials to find it in his house? Why should Aḥmad have kept it in such a conspicuous place? The evidence against Aḥmad here is suspect. He may have stolen government and imperial goods, but it is worth remembering that his accusers were the Chinese officials who had opposed his financial policies.[100]

The other Muslim involvement in finances, which Aḥmad also encouraged, was the promotion of commerce. Muslim merchants served as intermediaries in the overland trade from China to Central Asia, Persia, and the Middle East. They imported camels, horses, carpets, and jades and other precious stones and exported Chinese textiles, ceramics, lacquerware, ginger, and cassia.[101] The postal stations located along the trade routes to Central Asia and Persia, which were maintained by the Mongols, no doubt facilitated this commerce. Muslims also took part in the overseas trade between China and India, Southeast Asia, and Persia. From Foochow, Ch'üan-chou, Hangchow, and other southern Chinese ports, they transported Chinese ceramics, silks, and copper cash westward and returned with precious stones, rhinoceros horns, medicines, incense, carpets, pepper, nutmeg, and other spices.[102] Some of the Chinese ceramics, in particular, were specially designed for export. The Chinese exhibited a "genuine willingness ... to supply wares in forms agreeable to Muslim taste." [103]

Individual merchants, as well as the *ortakh*, contributed to the Yüan economy. According to Yüan regulations, foreign merchants were required to convert their precious metals into paper currency as soon as they set foot in China.[104] This policy was extremely profitable for the court, and the merchants abided by this regulation because it granted them entry into the lucrative trade with China. The *ortakh* also performed invaluable services for the court. These merchant associations

[100] Olschki (see n. 5 above), p. 411, offers a different, harsher assessment of Aḥmad's influence on government.

[101] Li (see n. 52 above), p. 295.

[102] Kuwabara (see n. 68 above), p. 25; Grousset (see n. 41 above), pp. 381–84; on the foreign, specifically Muslim, communities in the coastal regions of the Southern Sung, see Laurence J. C. Ma, *Commercial Development and Urban Change in Sung China (960–1279)* (Ann Arbor: Department of Geography, University of Michigan, 1971), pp. 39–43.

[103] Margaret Medley, *Yüan Porcelain and Stoneware* (New York: Pitman Publishing Corporation, 1974), p. 6; the production of ceramics for Muslims in China and in foreign countries continued into the Ming. See, for example, Kamer Aga-Oglu, "Blue-and-White Porcelain Plates Made for Moslem Patrons," *Far Eastern Ceramic Bulletin*, 3:3 (September, 1951), pp. 12–16.

[104] Lien-sheng Yang, *Money and Credit in China: A Short History* (Cambridge: Harvard University Press, 1952), p. 46; for paper currency in the Yüan, the standard work is Herbert Franke, *Geld und Wirtschaft in China unter der Mongolen-Herrschaft* (Leipzig: Otto Harrassowitz, 1949).

were founded to raise capital for caravans travelling across Eurasia.[105]
In the early years of the Mongol conquests, they provided badly-needed
loans to the Mongol nobility.[106] The Mongols, in return, eventually
granted tax-farming privileges to them. In 1267, as the Yüan, under
Khubilai, established itself in China, it created the "Central Bureau
Supervising the *Ortakh*." This office began to loan funds (known as
wo-t'o-ch'ien 斡脫錢 or "ortakh money"), which it obtained from the
Mongol elite and from the government, to the *ortakh* at 0.8 percent
monthly interest, which was lower than the 3 percent monthly interest
charged to most borrowers. In 1281, the "Central Bureau Supervising
the *Ortakh*" became the "Supervising Money Bureau," and the funds it
loaned were now called *Ch'üan-fu ying-yün-ch'ien* 泉府營運錢.[107] The
ortakh used these loans either to finance trade caravans or to loan funds
at a higher rate of interest to Chinese merchants. Since the Chinese
borrowed directly from these merchant associations instead of from the
Mongols, they perceived the Muslims as the principal beneficiaries of
the tidy profits of usury. Again, the Muslims diverted Chinese hostility
from the Mongols.

Because of their services to the Yüan court, the excesses of the Muslim
merchant associations were tolerated. Some of the merchants com-
mandeered soldiers to accompany and protect them on their travels;
others illegally lodged at the official postal stations; and still others used
improper methods to force borrowers to repay their loans promptly.[108]
The Yüan sources record complaints about these abuses, but stern
warnings, rather than stiff punishments, were the main tactics used to
control the *ortakh*. Aḥmad and the financial administrators who succeeded him, as well as the government offices founded to supervise the
ortakh, did not restrict the Muslim merchants as long as they paid taxes
and carried on trade with foreign lands. The Muslim merchants, in turn,
supported Aḥmad and the financial administrators who succeeded him.

B. *Muslim Contributions to Yüan Culture*

The Mongols had, since earliest times, actively solicited technical assistance from foreigners. In the first years of their conquests, they had

---

[105] Compare with the Middle Eastern institution known as the *commenda*. See A. L.
Udovitch, "Commercial Techniques in Early Medieval Islamic Trade," in D. S. Richards,
ed., *Islam and the Trade of Asia* (Philadelphia: University of Pennsylvania Press, 1970),
pp. 37–50.

[106] Murakami (see n. 25 above), p. 164.

[107] Yang (see n. 104 above), p. 97.

[108] Weng Tu-chien 翁獨健, "Wo-t'o tsa-k'ao 斡脫雜考," *Yen-ching hsüeh-pao*
燕京學報, 29 (June, 1941), p. 207.

deported numerous craftsmen from China, Central Asia, and Persia to Karakorum and the rest of Mongolia. Khubilai, in particular, recognized the value of foreign specialists. Even before he succeeded his brother Möngke as the supreme ruler of China, he was eager to obtain the services of Muslim craftsmen and astronomers.[109] When he became the khaghan in 1260, he vigorously recruited foreign craftsmen, doctors, and bureaucrats. He sent a message, via Maffeo and Niccolo Polo, to the Pope, requesting one hundred "wise" Christians ostensibly to debate the representatives of other religions at his court, but probably also to assist in the administration of China.[110] In 1285, 1288, and 1290, he dispatched envoys to South India to seek not only precious goods but also skilled craftsmen, interpreters, and doctors.[111] Foreigners who were employed as artisans by the government were well treated. They received good pay and clothing and food allowances and were exempt from corvée labor. Unlike slaves or forced laborers, they were permitted to own land and had the same rights as other non-Mongols.[112]

The Yüan court valued Muslim medicines and architecture. Two branches of the *Kuang-hui-ssu* 廣惠司 (Imperial hospitals), composed of Muslim doctors, were established in Ta-tu and Shang-tu to treat the emperor and the court.[113] Mongol officials apparently consulted Muslim physicians, and thirty-six volumes of Muslim medicinal recipes were found at the court in Ta-tu. Starting in 1268, a drug known as *sharbat* (*she-li-pieh* 舍利別), which was used as a laxative and to counter colic, was imported from Samarkand. Muslim medicines were readily available at pharmacies.[114] Khubilai and the court were attracted not only by Muslim doctors and medicines but also by their architects. Muslims constructed mosques and minarets throughout China. Khubilai selected a Muslim architect named Yeh-hei-tieh-erh 也黑迭兒 to help in designing his capital at Ta-tu.[115] The city, which Marco Polo praised lavishly

[109] YS 90:2297.

[110] Moule and Pelliot (see n. 5 above), p. 79.

[111] W. W. Rockhill, "Notes on the Relations and Trade of China with the Eastern Archipelago and the Coast of the Indian Ocean during the Fourteenth Century," *T'oung Pao*, 15 (1914), pp. 438–440; Khubilai sought to obtain medicines from Korea. For this, see Chŏng In-ji 鄭麟趾, *Koryŏ-sa* 高麗史 (Tokyo, 1909), vol. 3, p. 519.

[112] Chü Ch'ing-yüan, "Government Artisans of the Yüan Dynasty," in E-tu Zen Sun and John de Francis, ed., *Chinese Social History: Translations of Selected Studies* (Washington: American Council of Learned Societies, 1956), pp. 237–239.

[113] Jutta Rall, *Die vier grossen Medizinschulen der Mongolenzeit* (Weisbaden: Franz Steiner Verlag, 1970), pp. 30–31.

[114] Fang Hao 方豪, *Chung-hsi chiao-t'ung shih* 中西交通史 (Taipei: Chung-hua Wen-hua Ch'u-pan-she, 1967), vol. 3, p. 149.

[115] G. N. Kates, "A New Date for the Origins of the Forbidden City," *Harvard Journal of Asiatic Studies*, 7 (1942–43), p. 197; Ch'en Yüan, *Western and Central Asians in China*

in his account of his travels in Asia,[116] was, to be sure, a Chinese city, but Muslim craftsmen undoubtedly took part in its construction.

Aspects of Muslim culture entranced the Yüan court. The Muslims were themselves attracted by Chinese culture and transmitted Chinese medical innovations, aesthetic principles (which affected Persian painters and ceramicists), playing cards, stamps and seals, and possibly printing to Persia and to the Middle East.[117] Since the principal concern of this essay, however, is the Muslim impact on China, the Chinese effect on the Islamic world cannot be considered here. The Mongols encouraged and were influenced by certain manifestations of Muslim culture. Central Asian and Persian musicians performed Muslim music at court ceremonials and introduced the Chinese to different musical instruments.[118] Muslim poets and lyricists contributed poems and songs to these performances. A-li Yao-ch'ing 阿里耀卿 and his son Li Hsi-ying 李西瑛 wrote poems in Chinese which were included in major collections of Chinese poetry.[119] In the fourteenth century, several Muslims achieved renown as poets in the Chinese language. "Muslim blue" dye was employed in the production of the renowned blue and white porcelains of this era, and Muslims occasionally supervised the government porcelain factories. The Yüan court also evinced interest in works written in Arabic and Persian. In 1289, it founded the *Hui-hui kuo-tzu hsüeh* 回回國子學 (National College for the Study of Muslim [Script]) for the study of the Arabic script.[120] Five Yüan officials enrolled immediately, and the court, for a time, had its own translators and interpreters. Yüan China was even interested in Middle Eastern cooking. Several Muslim dishes were introduced into China at this time and were listed in the

Under the Mongols, L. C. Goodrich and Ch'ien Hsing-hai, trs. (Los Angeles: Monumenta Serica Institute, 1966), pp. 218–225.

[116] Moule and Pelliot (see n. 5 above), pp. 212–213; for the recent excavations of the Yüan capital, see the articles in *K'ao-ku* 考古, 1972, No. 1, pp. 19–28; 1972, No. 4, pp. 54–56; 1972, No. 6, pp. 2–11, 25–34.

[117] On the medical influences, see Jutta Rall, "Zur persischen Übersetzung eines Mo-chüeh, eines chinesischen medizinischen Textes," *Oriens Extremus*, 7 (1960), pp. 150–157. On other influences, see L. C. Goodrich, *A Short History of the Chinese People* (New York Harper & Bros., 1969, 3rd ed.), p. 179.

[118] YS 77:1926.

[119] Liu Ming-shu 劉銘恕, "Yüan hsi-yü ch'ü-chia A-li Yao-ch'ing fu-tzu 元西域曲家阿里耀卿父子," *Bulletin of Chinese Studies*, 8 (September, 1948), pp. 105–109; Ch'en (see n. 89 above), p. 108.

[120] YS 81:2028; Otagi Matsuo 愛宕松男, "Gendai shikimokujin ni kansuru ikkōsatsu 元代色目人に関する一考察," *Mōko gakuhō* 蒙古学報, 1 (1937), p. 44; Paul Ratchnevsky, "Rašīd ad-Dīn über die Mohammedaner-Verfolgungen in China unter Qubilai," *Central Asiatic Journal*, 14:1–3 (1970), p. 180.

imperial conpendium of Yüan dietary practices. As one scholar has noted, "noodles" and "even such dishes as *chiao-tzu* [i.e., dumplings], which have become a staple and household feature in Chinese cuisine, might have come to China from the 'Western barbarians' [i.e., Middle East]"[121] during the Mongol period.

Since the Muslim contributions to Yüan science and technology are well known, they need not be described in detail here. Persia was the source of many of these innovations. The observatory at Marāgheh (Azerbaijan), erected around 1258 with imperial funds and patronage by Nāṣir al-Dīn al-Ṭūsī (d. 1294), had built new astronomical instruments and had made important discoveries.[123] In 1267, the Persian astronomer Jāmal al-Dīn (Cha-ma-lu-ting 札馬魯丁) came to China to transmit these discoveries. He brought along diagrams of an armillary sphere, sundials, an astrolabe, a terrestrial globe, and a celestial globe, as gifts for the court. He also offered a new calendar, known as the *Wan-nien-li* 萬年曆, to the Yüan.[123] With all this encouragement and assistance, Khubilai established, in 1271, the Institute of Muslim Astronomy (*Hui-hui ssu-t'ien chien* 回回司天監). The Chinese astronomer Kuo Shou-ching 郭守敬 (1231–1316) used the Persian diagrams and calculations to build his own instruments and to devise his own calendar, the *Shou-shih-li* 授時曆, which with minor revisions was employed for much of the Yüan and Ming dynasties.[124] The Muslims also contributed to geographic knowledge and map-making during this period. Arab and Persian travellers and traders transmitted information about Central Asia and the Middle East, so that "geography in China [flourished], incorporating data on the non-Chinese world taken from Arab sources."[125] A Yüan

---

[121] Herbert Franke, "Additional Notes on Non-Chinese Terms in the Yüan Imperial Dietary Compendium Yin-shan cheng-yao," *Zentralasiatische Studien*, 4 (1970), p. 16.

[122] Boyle, *Cambridge History*, pp. 668–673; Karl Jahn, "Wissenschaftliche Kontakte zwischen Iran und China in der Mongolenzeit," *Osterreichischen Akademie der Wissenschaften*, 106 (1969), pp. 199–200.

[123] Joseph Needham, *Science and Civilisation in China*, vol. 3 (Cambridge: Cambridge University Press, 1959), pp. 372–374; Chang Kuei-sheng, "The Maritime Scene in China at the Dawn of Great European Discoveries," *Journal of the American Oriental Society*, 94:3 (July-September, 1974), p. 350; Alexander Wylie, "The Mongol Astronomical Instruments in Peking," *Chinese Researches* (Shanghai, 1897), p. 16.

[124] YS 7:136; see Juliet Bredon, *Peking: A Historical and Intimate Description of its Chief Places of Interest* (Shanghai: Kelly and Walsh, Ltd., 1931, 3rd ed.), p. 30, for a twentieth-century description of the observatory. For Kuo Shou-ching, see YS 164: 3845–3852.

[125] Herbert Franke, "Sino-Western Contacts Under the Mongol Empire," *Journal of the Royal Asiatic Society: Hong Kong Branch*, 6 (1966), p. 59. For the world map, see W. Fuchs, *The Mongol Atlas of China by Chu Ssu-pen* (Peiping: Monumenta Serica Monographs, No. 8, 1946).

world map of this period, which was probably based on information derived from Muslim sources, is fairly accurate in its rendering of Asia and Europe.

The Muslims provided military assistance at a critical juncture in the struggle between the Yüan and the Southern Sung. From 1268 to 1273, the Mongol forces had besieged the towns of Fan-ch'eng 樊城 and Hsiang-yang 襄陽, which provided "access to the fertile Middle Yangtze basin."[126] The Chinese forces had stubbornly resisted the Mongol assaults and had spurned all the Mongol demands for submission. Just at this time Khubilai's nephew (his brother Hülegü's son) Abakha, the Ilkhan of Persia, sent two Muslim military specialists, Ismā'īl and 'Alā al-Dīn, to help the Mongol troops.[127] They built a mangonel and a catapult which were capable of hurling huge rocks over a considerable distance.[128] One of the rocks hit the central tower at Hsiang-yang, and, according to the Chinese accounts, the whole city shook.[129] Fear of more such explosions caused the Chinese forces in the town to surrender.

This cursory appraisal clearly demonstrates that the Yüan court relied on the Muslims for a variety of services. Yet the Muslims were not accorded sole jurisdiction in any single area. The court used Chinese doctors as well as Muslim ones.[130] Mongol and Chinese officials cooperated with Muslim craftsmen in the numerous building projects initiated during the Yüan.[131] Such Chinese astronomers as Kuo Shou-ching worked together with the Persian Jamāl al-Dīn. The Yüan court was apparently reluctant to allow the Muslims to dominate any area or institution. It balanced each appointment of a Muslim to a major official position with that of a Chinese or Mongol to avert over-reliance on any one group.

C. Muslim Colonization of Yunnan

It is all the more surprising, then, that the Yüan court selected a Central Asian Muslim, Saiyid Ajall Shams al-Dīn, to govern the newly con-

---

[126] Herbert Franke (see n. 125 above), pp. 60–61.

[127] Their biographies are found in YS 203:4544–4545. See also Pelliot (see n. 78 above), pp. 4–5.

[128] YS 203:4544.

[129] L. C. Goodrich and Feng Chia-sheng, "The Early Development of Firearms in China," Isis, 36:2 (1945–46), p. 118; Moule (see n. 99 above), pp. 75–76.

[130] For an illuminating study of the reasons for the Chinese interest in medicine during the Yüan, see Sherman E. Lee and Wai-kam Ho, Chinese Art Under the Mongols: The Yüan Dynasty (1279–1368) (Cleveland: Press of Case Western Reserve University, 1968), pp. 83–84.

[131] Ch'en (see n. 89 above), pp. 221–224.

quered territory of Yunnan. This region, now a province in southwest China, was the only land in China to be ruled by a Muslim. The motives underlying this appointment are puzzling. Perhaps the court looked upon Yunnan as an important thoroughfare in trade with Burma and India and, since the Muslims were the most important merchants in the Mongol dominions, a Muslim governor for Yunnan was logical. Or the court may have perceived of Yunnan as a fine territory in which to settle some of the Muslims whom the Mongols had moved eastward from Central Asia and Persia. Yunnan was still sparsely inhabited, and its inhabitants were primarily illiterate, non-Han-Chinese peoples. The Mongols may have decided that a policy of encouraging the Muslims, rather than the Chinese who were more hostile to Mongol rule, to colonize the region was sensible. Or the court may have delegated this power to Saiyid Ajall because it considered him trustworthy and a loyal subject.

Whatever the motives, the Yüan court chose wisely. Descended from a distinguished family in Bukhara,[132] Saiyid Ajall had led one thousand of his cavalry in surrendering to the Mongols during Chinggis Khan's campaigns in Central Asia. His Mongol captors were evidently impressed by his ability and loyalty, for shortly after his surrender they began to appoint him to increasingly responsible positions. During Ögödei's reign, he served first as a *darughachi* in Shansi and then was promoted to a position in Yen-ching (modern Peking). Little is known of his activities from the time of Ögödei's death in 1241 until Möngke's coronation in 1251. But, under Möngke, he continued his climb in the Mongol administration.[133] Möngke selected him to be the chief administrator of the circuit of Yen-ching. Then, recognizing Saiyid's talent and loyalty, Möngke ordered the Central Asian Muslim to accompany him on his military expedition against the Southern Sung in 1259. Saiyid took charge of the supplies for the campaign.[134] The expedition ended with Möngke's illness, which is identified as dysentery by some scholars, and death. But, once again, Saiyid reappeared as an official in the government of the new khaghan. In 1260, Khubilai appointed him as pacification commissioner (*hsüan-fu-shih* 宣撫使) in Yen-ching, and within a year he was offered a position in the central secretariat (*Chung-shu sheng* 中書省).[135] He was apparently competent in these positions

---

[132] For a study of his ancestors, see Omeljan Pritsak, "Āli-Burhān," *Der Islam*, 30:1 (January, 1952), pp. 81–96.

[133] Shimazaki Akira 島崎昌, "Gendai no kaikyōjin Saitenseki Tanshitei 元代の回教人賽典赤瞻思丁," *Kaikyō ken* 回教圈, (July, 1939), pp. 13–15.

[134] A. Vissière, *Études Sino-Mahométanes* (Paris: Ernest Leroux, 1911), vol. 1, pp. 6–7.

[135] YS 125:3063.

because by 1264 Khubilai had commissioned him to be the virtual governor of much of modern Shensi, Kansu, and Szechwan. Here he was credited with conducting an accurate census, which brought more households on the tax rolls, and with effectively organizing his army. In 1271, he even led his soldiers to Hsiang-yang to assist in the Mongol siege of that town. The court, recognizing his contributions, offered him many rewards, including 5,000 Chinese ounces of silver and other gifts.[136] In 1274, however, Khubilai bestowed the highest honor by appointing him governor of Yunnan.

Khubilai apparently believed that effective rule of Yunnan was essential. In 1252 and 1253, he had led the military expeditions that had brought Yunnan within the Mongol dominions. He was undoubtedly aware of the strategic location of Yunnan on the trade routes from China to Burma and India. Moreover, his troops could use Yunnan as a base from which to launch assaults against Burma and, perhaps, Sung China.[137] Control of the region was, for Khubilai, a high priority. He started to establish military colonies in each of the thirty-seven circuits of Yunnan.[138] He also began to encourage high-ranking Muslim officials to migrate to the region, offering them land, money, and other incentives. The Muslim colonists arrived in three waves. The first accompanied Khubilai in his initial conquest of Yunnan; the second reached the region in the early years of Khubilai's reign; and the third accompanied Saiyid when he became governor in 1274.

Saiyid's first objectives in Yunnan were to strengthen the military and economic control of the Yüan. Before taking up his post, he studied the topography, the economy, and the customs of Yunnan. Once he reached Yunnan, he sought to gain the confidence of the native, non-Chinese peoples. He established guards and garrisons throughout the region, but he instructed his soldiers not to provoke the "barbarians." When several of his officers deliberately attacked some native people, he executed them.[139] With such even-handed and fair policies, he quickly won over much of the non-Chinese population. He also moved rapidly to create a postal system for communication, defense, and commerce. His policies promoted the economic prosperity of Yunnan. He encouraged the growth of agriculture, ordering his men to teach farming and forestry to the local people. Before his arrival, the people of Yunnan "had no rice of

---

[136] Vissière (see n. 134 above), pp. 9–11.

[137] Tazaka (see n. 2 above), pp. 644–645.

[138] Hsia (see n. 67 above), p. 13.

[139] H. M. G. d'Ollone, *Recherches sur les Musulmans Chinois* (Paris: Ernest Leroux, 1911), p. 68.

[140] Ch'en (see n. 89 above), p. 58.

any variety, no mulberry trees, and no hemp."[140] Probably Saiyid's most significant contribution to the economy was his promotion of irrigation projects in the Kunming region, some of which were still used in the twentieth century. He built reservoirs and dams, so that floods and droughts would not impair the farming season.[141] His Muslim subjects improved conditions of trade, and he permitted the use of the traditional cowry shells as a medium of exchange in order to inspire the local people to engage in commerce. Finally, he lightened the tax and corvée burdens on the population, making it easier for them to accept Mongol rule.

Despite his own background, Saiyid did not impose Islam on Yunnan. Instead he introduced Chinese customs and culture. He promoted the use of Chinese marital and funeral ceremonies, built Confucian schools, and made available copies of the Confucian classics. Though he constructed two mosques, he also built a Confucian temple and a Buddhist monastery.[142] In short, he intended to Sinicize, not to Islamicize, Yunnan. Similarly, those of his sons who resided and became officials in Yunnan promoted Chinese culture in the region. He died in 1279 (and in 1297 was posthumously awarded the title of *Hsien-yang wang* 咸陽王 or "Prince of Hsien-yang"), and two of his sons, Nāṣir al-Dīn and Mas'ūd (*Ma-su-hu* 馬速忽) succeeded him as governors of Yunnan.[143] Both continued their father's policies in the area. Nāṣir al-Dīn, in addition, participated in military campaigns in Burma and Annam and served as an official in Shensi and at the capital.[144] In April of 1292, however, he was accused of stealing 130,000 *ting* of paper money and was executed.[145] His four brothers were not implicated. They continued to hold influential positions in Yunnan, Kwangtung, and Kiangsi and received numerous honors and lavish rewards.

Yunnan was the one area in early Yüan China in which Muslim jurisdiction was virtually unchecked. In their other institutions and in other geographic locations, the Mongols had developed restraints on Muslim power. And even in Yunnan they ensured that their objectives were shared by Muslims dispatched to govern the region. Saiyid Ajall sought to promote economic and military advances, to integrate Yunnan with the rest of China, and to foster the sinicization of the non-Chinese

---

[141] Fang Kuo-yü 方國瑜, "Kuan-yü Sai-tien-ch'ih fu-Tien kung-chi 關於賽典赤撫滇 功績," *Jen-wen k'o-hsüeh tsa-chih* 人文科學雜誌, No. 1 (1958), pp. 48–49.

[142] L. C. Goodrich, "Westerners and Central Asians in Yüan China," *Oriente Poliano* (Rome, 1957), p. 8.

[143] Louis Hambis, *Le chapitre cviii du Yüan che* (Leiden: E. J. Brill, 1954), p. 126, n. 4.

[144] Olschki (see n. 5 above), p. 333.

[145] YS 17:361; *Meng-wu-erh shih-chi*, 80:4b.

peoples. Though he was accompanied by Muslims and was presumably not averse to encouraging conversions to Islam, he did not urge the creation of a Muslim state that might seek independence from Yüan China. The Mongols would not, in any case, have employed a devout Muslim who espoused the concept of *jihād* (Holy War). They selected a Muslim who was not committed to conversion of all non-believers. Yet a large Muslim community did, in fact, develop in Yunnan, partly because most of the inhabitants were not ethnically Chinese and were thus more willing to convert to Islam (and maintain their distinctiveness from Chinese culture) than to the Buddhism and Confucianism of China. Partly, too, as Muslims, they would receive tax privileges which were not made available to the other religions.

V. Yüan Repression of Islam

With all of these Muslim contributions to the economic, political and cultural welfare of the Yüan, it may seem surprising that the court began in the late 1270s to issue regulations that were clearly anti-Muslim. Yet, from the Mongol perspective, the new policies were justifiable. The Islamic states and towns along China's border appeared hostile to the Yüan. Starting in the 1270s, Ögödei's grandson Khaidu, with the support of Muslims in Central Asia, repeatedly threatened China's northwestern frontier lands.[146] Khubilai sent several military expeditions, but Khaidu either evaded or defeated them. The court was also forced to dispatch troops across the northwestern border in 1278, 1280, and 1282 to quell disturbances in which the Muslims participated.[147] Farther to the west, Muslim states had thwarted Khubilai's Mongol allies and constantly challenged the Mongol governors of Persia. The Mamlūk dynasty (1250–1517) of Egypt, under its ruler Baybars I (r. 1260–1277), had halted the Mongol advance in the Middle East at the battle of 'Ain Jālūt in 1260. Taking advantage of the divisions within the Mongol empire, it allied itself with the Mongol Golden Horde in Russia and continued to probe the defenses of the Ilkhanate of Persia while preventing it from expanding westward.[148] Since Khubilai was in touch

---

[146] Dardess (see n. 81 above), pp. 135–143.

[147] Saguchi Tōru 佐口透, "Mongorujin shihai jidai no Uigurisutan モンゴル人支配時代のウイグリスタン," *Shigaku zasshi* 史学雑誌, 54:8 (August, 1943), pp. 819–820.

[148] On Baybars I, see Syedah Fatima Sadeque, *Baybars I of Egypt* (Dacca: Geoffrey Cumberlege, Oxford University Press, 1956); and Étienne Marc Quatremère, tr., *Histoire des Sultan Mamlouks, de l'égypte* (Paris: Oriental Translation Fund, 1837), vol. 1, pp. 104–106.

with and allied to the Ilkhans Hülegü (d. 1265) and Abakha (d. 1282), he was aware of the Muslim hostility to the Mongols in the Middle East.

Similarly, Khubilai recognized that the Muslims had generated hostility in China. His Chinese advisers had repeatedly denounced the ambitiousness and ruthlessness of the leading Muslim officials, particularly Aḥmad and his followers. Many Chinese despised the Muslim tax collectors, merchants, and financial administrators, and their hatred of the Muslims in government was certainly well known to Khubilai. Since the Buddhists at court, among whom were some of Khubilai's closest advisers, also resented the power of the Islamic financial administrators, they must have attempted to persuade Khubilai to impose limits on the Muslims in the capital. At the same time, essays and popular anecdotes satirizing Muslim avariciousness, vulgarity, and "strangeness" started to appear at this time. Khubilai himself may have been concerned about the growing power of the Muslims in government. His own grandson, Prince Ananda, had been raised in a Muslim household, and as an adult had, according to Rashīd, converted most of the 150,000 troops under his command to Islam.[149]

These feelings provoked hostility toward the Muslims. A Christian official known in the Chinese texts as Ai-hsüeh 愛薛 instigated additional anti-Muslim sentiment. Having held positions in the bureaus of astronomy and medicine, he had some influence in Yüan government.[150] Rashīd al-Dīn accused him of inciting slaves and laborers in Muslim households to bring false charges against their masters. And, according to Rashīd, Ai-hsüeh himself falsely accused Maulānā Burhān al-Dīn Bukhārī, one of the leaders of the Muslims in China, of a crime (Rashīd does not specify the crime) and had him exiled.[151]

Rashīd also asserts that Khubilai, abetted by Ai-hsüeh and by his Chinese advisers, began in 1279 to adopt a harsher policy toward the Muslims. Late in that year, Muslim merchants from Siberia and Central Asia arrived in court to offer gerfalcons and an eagle as tribute. Khubilai invited them to a banquet, but they would not eat the meat because the animals had not been slaughtered in the Muslim fashion. Incensed by this refusal, Khubilai issued an edict in January of 1280 prohibiting the

[149] One of the more interesting such satires, written in the late Yüan, is translated by Herbert Franke in "Eine Mittelalterliche chinesische Satire auf die Mohammedaner," *Der Orient in der Forschung: Festschrift für Otto Spies zum 5 April 1966*, ed. by Wilhelm Hoenerbach (Wiesbaden: Otto Harrassowitz, 1967), pp. 202–208; for more on Ananda, see Boyle, *Successor*, pp. 323–328.

[150] For more on Ai-hsüeh, see A. C. Moule, *Christians in China Before the Year 1550* (London: Society for Promoting Christian Knowledge, 1930), pp. 228–229.

[151] Boyle, *Successors*, p. 294.

Muslim method of slaughtering sheep and imposing the death penalty on transgressors.[152] The *jasagh* had already specified the death penalty for anyone using the Muslim method, but enforcement of this provision had been lax. Now Khubilai demanded strict adherence to the *jasagh* regulation of slaughtering. With encouragement from Ai-hsüeh and his followers, Khubilai also forbad the practice of circumcision. Finally, Rashīd concludes his list of accusations by noting that Ai-hsüeh and other Christians "sought to attack them [Muslims] by representing to the Qa'an that there was a verse in the Qur'ān which ran: 'Kill the polytheists, all of them!'" Obviously disturbed by this quotation from the Muslim Holy Book, Khubilai asked his Muslim advisers whether they considered him a polytheist. A Muslim sage from Samarkand finally calmed Khubilai by responding that "Thou art not a polytheist since thou writest the name of the Great God at the head of thy *yarlighs* [edicts]. Such a one is a polytheist who does not recognize God, and attributes companions to Him, and rejects the great God."[153] Khubilai was apparently satisfied with this response, but, according to Rashīd, he was not deterred from his policy of restricting the Muslims.

Whether all the specific incidents recounted by Rashīd actually took place is difficult to tell, but the Chinese sources confirm that the court issued a series of anti-Muslim edicts. On January 27, 1280, it imposed the death penalty for anyone slaughtering an animal in the Muslim way.[154] Earlier it had levied taxes and demanded corvée labor from the Muslims.[155] Khubilai and the court were apparently concerned about the growing power of the Muslims, and they were certainly aware of Chinese opposition to the Muslims in government. That Chinese hostility was directed at the Muslims suited their purposes, but they wanted to avoid two difficulties. One was an overly powerful Muslim presence in the government, and the other was a rebellion precipitated by the exactions of the Muslims. Thus Khubilai's repressive edicts were inspired more by political considerations than by hatred of Islam.

According to the Chinese and Persian accounts, Khubilai himself was not involved in the assassination of Aḥmad in 1282. Aḥmad's financial policies had aroused the opposition of leading Chinese advisers at court. Perhaps as critical, Chen-chin 眞金, Khubilai's son and the heir apparent, had joined the opposition. Chen-chin had received some of his

---

[152] YS 10:217–218; W. Heyd, *Histoire du commerce du Levant au moyen âge*, F. Raynaud, tr. (rpt. Amsterdam: Adolf M. Hakkert, 1967), vol. 2, p. 245.

[153] Boyle, *Successors*, p. 295.

[154] *Ta Yüan sheng-cheng kuo-ch'ao tien-chang* 大元聖政國朝典章 (Taipei: Wen-hai Ch'u-pan-she 文海出版社, 1963), pp. 763–764.

[155] Haenisch (see n. 14 above), p. 17; YS 134:3266, 9:183.

formal education from Chinese tutors and thus sympathized with the Chinese advisers.[156] He despised Aḥmad and objected to the prominent positions in government accorded to Aḥmad's sons and relatives. Others in the Mongol ruling elite, who feared Aḥmad, swelled the opposition to the Muslim financial administrator.[157] On the night of April 10, 1282, while Khubilai resided in Shang-tu and was conveniently out of the capital, a group of Chinese conspirators lured Aḥmad out of his house and assassinated him.[158] Shortly thereafter, Khubilai returned to the capital and executed the conspirators. Within a few months, however, Khubilai's Chinese advisers persuaded him of Aḥmad's treachery and corruption. Khubilai had Aḥmad's corpse exhumed and hung in a bazaar at the capital; then he had it placed on the ground and had carts driven over the head, and allowed his dogs to attack the corpse. Several of Aḥmad's sons were executed, his property was confiscated, and most of the officials specifically appointed by Aḥmad were dismissed. It seems unlikely that Khubilai participated in or sanctioned the assassination plot, but the removal of Aḥmad certainly benefited the court's anti-Muslim campaign.

The anti-Muslim policy persisted until 1287. In that year, Sengge (Sang-ko 桑哥), the financial administrator who eventually succeeded Aḥmad, pleaded with Khubilai to reverse his policy towards the Muslims. He argued that "All the Muslim merchants have departed from hence [i.e., China] and no merchants are coming from the Muslim countries; ... and all this because for the past seven years they have not slaughtered sheep. If it be so commanded, the merchants will come and go...."[159] If the court changed its policy, the revenues derived from Muslim merchants would increase. Rashīd asserts that several Muslim leaders bribed Sengge to champion their cause. Whatever Sengge's motivation, Khubilai relented and issued an edict permitting Central Asian merchants to slaughter sheep in the traditional Muslim way. Muslim merchants reappeared, but one incident recounted in the Chinese histories illustrates Khubilai's less than welcoming attitude towards some Muslim traders. In 1293, a Muslim merchant sought to sell pearls to Khubilai, but the khaghan declined this offer, noting that his money could be better spent to "relieve the people."[160]

Nonetheless, Muslim traders and craftsmen continued to play an

[156] Herbert Franke, "Could the Mongol Emperors Read and Write Chinese?," *Asia Major*, 3 (1952–53), pp. 29–30.

[157] Franke (see n. 83 above), p. 235.

[158] Moule (see n. 99 above), pp. 79–88.

[159] Boyle, *Successors*, p. 294.

[160] De Mailla (see n. 31 above), vol. 10, p. 456.

important role for the rest of Khubilai's reign and, in fact, for the remainder of the Yüan dynasty. But no individual Muslim at the Yüan court would be as powerful as 'Abd al-Raḥmān or Aḥmad. As the Mongol rulers became increasingly sinicized, they tended to rely on their Chinese subjects for government tasks that had earlier been performed by the Muslims. By the Ming dynasty, the Muslims were no longer employed as financial administrators or tax collectors and were thus not used as scapegoats. Though commercial disputes and minor revolts bedevilled Muslim relations with the Chinese during the Ming, there were no major Muslim rebellions until the seventeenth century.[161]

It seems clear that the student of Chinese civilization from the thirteenth century to the present must take into account the role of the non-Chinese Muslims, the Mongols, and other foreigners. China was composed not only of Han Chinese, but also of numerous, diverse, and influential ethnic groups.

---

[161] See my article "Muslim and Central Asian Revolts," cited in n. 2 above. One minor insurrection occurred in the late Yüan. For this, see Chang Hsing-lang, "The Rebellion of the Persian Garrison in Ch'üan-chou (A.D. 1357–1366)," *Monumenta Serica*, 3 (1938), pp. 611–627. But also see Maejima Shinji, "The Muslims in Ch'üan-chou at the End of the Yüan Dynasty," *Memoirs of the Research Department of the Toyo Bunko*, 31 (1973), pp. 27–51, and 32 (1974), pp. 47–71.

Tibetans in Yüan China

HERBERT FRANKE

A study of the role of Tibetans in China under Mongol rule is made difficult by several problems of definition. From the very start a student is faced with the question whether and to what degree Tibet was at all a part of the Mongol empire. The answer to this question will determine whether we should regard Tibetans in Yüan China as a national minority living in a territory subject to some sort of Sino-Mongol control, or as foreigners from a country that remained outside the sinitic world. Another source of difficulty and confusion is the inconsistency of terminology. The Chinese sources of the period use several terms to designate Tibet and the Tibetans. The most frequently used names under the Yüan were T'u-fan 土 (吐) 番, Hsi-fan 西番, and Wu-tsang 烏藏 or Wu-ssu 思 -tsang. Of these T'u-fan is derived from tib. *Bod*, the self-designation of the Tibetans. Hsi-fan, "Western Bod," is a Sino-Tibetan hybrid form, whereas Wu-tsang and Wu-ssu-tsang are Chinese orthographies for the Tibetan name dBus-gtsang, a word which referred in Yüan and Ming times to Central Tibet.[2] According to Tibetan sources, the region of dBus had Lhasa and gTsang Shigatse as its center. Other indigenous names occurring in Chinese sources of the Yüan period are To-ssu-ma 朵思麻 (or T'o-ssu-ma 脫思麻 / 馬) and To-kan-ssu 朵甘思.[3] The latter renders Tibetan mDo-k'ams, the name of the modern Amdo region with Khams, west of Szechwan province, whereas the former name seems to refer to the territory south of the lake

[1] The author is greatly indebted to Dr. Helga Uebach and J. L. Panglung, M.A., Kommission für zentralasiatische Studien, Bavarian Academy of Sciences, Munich, for their tibetological assistance.

[2] For the old names of Tibet in Chinese sources, see Otto Franke, *Geschichte des chinesischen Reiches*, vol. 3 (Berlin, 1937), pp. 22–24. On Yüan and later terminology, see Josef Kolmaš, *Tibet and Imperial China*, Occasional Paper 7, The Australian National University (Canberra, 1967), p. 27; and R. A. Stein, *Recherches sur l'Epopée et le Barde au Tibet* (Paris, 1959), pp. 283 and 313 note 125. The location of dBus-gTsang is also discussed in Turrell V. Wylie, *The Geography of Tibet according to the 'Dzam-gling-rgyas-bshad* (Roma, 1962), p. 64. The Chinese orthographies of Tibetan names in Yüan dynasty sources vary frequently. See also note 3 below.

[3] Also written T'u-kan-ssu 突甘斯, *Yüan shih* 元史 (Peking: Chung-hua Shu-chü, 1976) (hereafter abbreviated as YS), 202:4519.

Kokonor and the upper course of the Yellow River. The name To-ssu-ma might go back to Tibetan mDo-smad.[4] As long as the Chinese sources use these geographic names, the reference to Tibet or parts of Tibet offers no problems. But the Tibetan monks, which played such a great role under the Mongol emperors, are frequently called only "Western Monks," hsi-seng 西僧, a loose term which could include Tibetans, Nepalis, or even Indians and also Tangut monks coming from the territory of the former Tangut state of Hsi-Hsia, which was named Ho-hsi 河西, "West of the (Yellow) River," under the Yüan. "Western" does therefore not refer to one single nation but is a term as loose as "Muslim" (hui-hui 回回) which, under the Yüan, might designate any followers of the Islamic faith, regardless of their national or linguistic background.

Another difficulty in studying the role of Tibetans in China under Mongol domination is due to the character of the sources. Chinese history was written by Chinese intellectuals, and the majority of these were not active Buddhists. A negative bias in all official and most private sources as far as the attitude towards Buddhism is concerned must therefore be expected. The picture changes as soon as one turns to Tibetan sources. These are exclusively Buddhist-Lamaist and concerned only with the propagation of the faith. Activities of Tibetan lamas in Yüan China, which appeared to the Chinese as arrogant and insolent and at the best as foreign extravaganzas, may be viewed in Tibetan sources as selfless missionary efforts aimed at influencing Mongol rulers and propagating the doctrine of the Buddha throughout the whole empire. Privileges accorded to the lamas might have seemed excessive to the Chinese, even to Chinese monks, but they are taken for granted by the Tibetan clergy as the innate and fundamental right of the Buddhist monk in secular society. At the risk of oversimplification it could be said that the respective sources reflect the genuine antagonism between state and religion, and that the aim of the Tibetan lamas was precisely to bridge the gulf between religion and state by creating a theocratic theory of secular rule. It is evident that a fully comprehensive study of the role of the Tibetan monks cannot dispense with taking into account the Tibetan sources, above all the writings of the Sa-skya sect, something for which the author is not qualified.[5]

A last problem of a more general nature relating to our theme is the

[4] R. A. Stein, Recherches pp. 199, 229; T. V. Wylie, The Geography of Tibet, p. 112 (on mDo-smad).

[5] For a preliminary survey, see Josef Kolmaš, "Tibetan Sources," in Donald Leslie, Colin Mackerras, Wang Gungwu, editors, Essays on the Sources for Chinese History (Canberra, 1973), pp. 129–140.

question whether it is at all appropriate to speak of Tibetans in China as if their nationality would be relevant. It would perhaps make more sense to speak of Buddhist clerics who happened to be Tibetans. The influence of the lamas in China rested solely on their religious position and not on their nationality. This sets the Tibetans apart from a national minority such as the Uighurs. We find Uighurs in all walks of life, in military and civilian offices as well as in the arts and letters, and also in the Buddhist clergy. Uighur influences are apparent in many fields under the Mongol emperors, and Buddhism is only one of them. The activity of Tibetans, on the other hand, is confined to Buddhism alone. We do not know that any Tibetan layman ever reached prominence in China under the Yüan. When Tibetans are mentioned by name in the *Yüan History* (*Yüan shih* 元史), they are tribal chieftains in the border regions who were mostly, it seems, not under direct and permanent control of the Sino-Mongol authorities.

The question whether Tibet was ever conquered by the Mongols, in the sense that China was conquered, is obscured by the conflicting data preserved in later Buddhist Mongolian and Tibetan records. According to these, Chinggis Khan had marched into Tibet and been converted to Buddhism. But it can be shown that this is a pious fiction which emerged later and cannot be corroborated from contemporary sources.[6] The Chinese sources remain silent, and all concrete data for later years of Mongol rule in China show that there was little if any direct control of Tibet proper. In the thirteenth century the Tibetans had a reputation for being dangerous brigands. Khubilai Khaghan is said to have regarded them as fond of fighting.[7] Furthermore Marco Polo has nothing good to say on the subject of Tibetans: "Otherwise, the people are idolaters and thoroughly wicked, for they do not think it sinful to steal and act badly. They are the greatest criminals and thieves on earth."[8] It is true that the

---

[6] Luc Kwanten, "Chingis Khan's Conquest of Tibet: Myth or Reality?" *Journal of Asian History*, 7:1 (1974) pp. 1–23. The same author's unpublished Ph. D. dissertation, "Tibetan-Mongol Relations during the Yüan" (University of South Carolina, 1972), was not available to the writer. Recent Russian contributions to the problem of Tibetan relations with China and the Mongols are Yu. N. Rerikh, "Mongolo-tibetskie otnosheniya v XIII i XIV vv," in *Filologiya i istoriya mongol'skikh narodov* (*Pamjati akademika B. Ya. Vladimirtsova*) (Moscow, 1958), pp. 333–345; and S. Kuchera, "Mongoli i Tibet pri Chingiskhane i ego preemnikakh," in *Tataro-Mongoly v Azii i Evrope* (Moscow, 1970), pp. 255–270. Rerikh's article was translated into English by Janice Nattier and published in *Tibet Society Bulletin* (Bloomington, Indiana), 6 (1973), pp. 40–55.

[7] YS 202:4520.

[8] *Marco Polo. La Description du Monde*. Texte intégral en Français moderne avec introduction et notes par Louis Hambis (Paris, 1955), p. 164. European medieval authors also regarded the Tibetans as cannibals; see *Hystoria Tartarorum C. de Bridia Monachi*, ed.

Mongols established several offices for Tibet and the Tibetan borderlands with the purpose of stabilizing the Western border of their Chinese
dominion, but the geographic chapter of the *Yüan History* has to admit
that practically nothing was known about Wu-tsang, that is, Tibet
proper.[9] Nevertheless, Wu-tsang was regarded on paper as a Circuit (*lu*
路) along with two other territories called Na-li-su 納里速 and Ku-erh-
sun 古兒孫 (also written Ku-lu-sun ｜ 魯 ｜).[10] The chapter on officials in
the *Yüan History* contains a long enumeration of the various offices
subordinate to the *Hsüan-cheng yüan* 宣政院, the metropolitan bureau
for Buddhist and Tibetan affairs on which a few details will be given
below. Also To-ssu-ma, the Kokonor region, was organized as a Circuit
as was To-kan-ssu. It seems that the majority of these offices had a
military character. Postal stations were organized in these Tibetan
borderlands and in Central Tibet (Wu-tsang), doubtless in order to
provide a courier service for transportation and traffic,[11] a service which
was mostly used by Tibetan clerics travelling between their homelands
and China. All these offices mentioned in the *Yüan History* were

---

Alf Önnerfors (Berlin, 1967), p. 14, and the description given of Tibet which the author calls
Burithebet: "Burith dicitur lupus et bene congruit incolis terre, qui tamquam lupi seuientes
patrem mortuum parentela congregata commedere consueuerunt." Burith must be con-
nected with Old Turkic *böri*, "wolf"; see D. Sinor, "Mongol and Turkic Words in the Latin
Versions of John of Plano Carpini's Journey to the Mongols (1245–1247)," in *Mongolian
Studies*, ed. L. Ligeti (Budapest, 1970), pp. 540–541. John of Plano Carpini's *Istoria
Mongalorum* has a very similar version of the text quoted above; see the text of John's
Istoria Mongalorum in Anastasius van den Wyngaert, ed., *Sinica Franciscana*, vol. 1
(Quaracchi-Firenze, 1929), ch. 5, p. 61, where it is said that if someone's father dies,
"omnem congregant parentelam et comedunt eum, sicut nobis dicebatur pro certo." The
same is reported by William of Rubruck with respect to Tibet where, he writes "homines
solentes comedere parentes suos defunctos, ut causa pietatis non faciunt aliud sepulcrum
eius nisi viscera sua" (van den Wyngaert, *Sinica Franciscana*, p. 234). Anthropologists
would call this custom endocannibalism. William of Rubruck adds that the Tibetans make
the skullcaps of dead relatives into drinking vessels from which they drink merrily to the
memory of the departed. This might be a distant reflection of the use of human skulls in
Lamaist rituals.

[9] YS 60:1434.

[10] YS 17:367; 87:2198. Na-li-su renders perhaps Tibetan *mnga-ris*, "subjected territory."
The identification of Ku-erh-sun or Ku-lu-sun is doubtful. One could perhaps think of a
relation with the Tibetan word for tent, *gur*. In later Tibetan geography we frequently find
the name Mnga-ris skor-gsum, which refers to Southwestern Tibet. See T. V. Wylie, *The
Geography of Tibet*, pp. 55, 64. Its identification with Ku-erh-sun/Ku-lu-sun is, however,
purely conjectural. See also Han Ju-lin 韓儒林, "Yüan-ch'ao chung-yang cheng-fu shih
tsen-yang kuan-li Hsi-tsang ti-fang ti 元朝中央政府是怎樣管理西藏地方的," *Li-shih
yen-chiu* 歷史研究, 7 (1959), pp. 51–56.

[11] YS 17:369 (the year 1292). For the concern of keeping the roads open, see also YS
131:3183 (the year 1294).

established, it seems, after Khubilai's accession in 1260, that is, after the Mongol armies had crossed parts of Eastern Tibet on their campaign against the Nan-chao 南詔 kingdom of Ta-li 大理 and thus come into a lasting contact with Tibetans. This institutional infrastructure does not basically differ from Sino-Mongol offices in other regions of the empire, but the situation is complicated by the fact that all this was overlaid by feudal structures going back to the period of conquests.

The region bordering on Tibet had been first conquered by Köden, Ögödei's second son. In 1235 he had led a campaign against Szechwan and occupied Ch'eng-tu.[12] Thereafter he was entrusted with the "Western Territories" and took up residence in Lan-chou (Kan-su).[13] It is explicitly said that the territory allotted to him bordered on Tibet.[14] This is also recorded by Rashīd al-Dīn: "Möngke Qa'an gave him a *yurt* in the land of Tangqut and sent him thither with an army."[15] The allotment of the Tibetan borderlands to Köden was still remembered in 1343 when the Central Secretariat (*chung-shu sheng* 中書省) complained that in recent years the inheritance of this region had been left un-regulated.[16] In fact, the feudal investment with the Tibetan borderlands had been passed on to the line of Khubilai whose son A'urughchi "ruled" over Tibet. Here again the Persian historiographer mentions Tibet as a province which was inherited: "The Qa'an allotted him the province of Tibet"—and continues by recording that after A'urughchi, his son Temür Bukha inherited.[17] This is the way Rashīd al-Dīn expresses it. In Chinese terms, the "inheritance" is equivalent to the investment of A'urughchi as Prince of Hsi-p'ing 西平 and of Temür Bukha as Prince of Chen-hsi 鎮西 and Wu-ching 武靖.[18] But also Mangghala, the third son of Khubilai, is said by a Chinese source to have ruled over Tibet, Ho-hsi 河西, and Szechwan.[18] Mangghala's son Ananda was, according to Rashīd al-Dīn, "allotted the land of Tangqut,"[20] which would correspond roughly to Ho-hsi and the Tibetan borderland.

---

[12] YS 2:34–35.

[13] YS 123:3028.

[14] YS 92:2338. In this passage Köden has the epithet *a-ha*, corresponding to Mongolian *akha*, "elder brother." After the death of Güyüg, who ruled as khan from 1246 to 1248, Köden was indeed the eldest brother of the seven sons of Ögödei.

[15] John Andrew Boyle, tr., *The Successors of Genghis Khan. Rashīd al-Dīn Tabīb* (New York and London, 1971), pp. 20–21.

[16] YS 92:2338.

[17] J. A. Boyle, *The Successors of Genghis Khan*, p. 244.

[18] These events were in 1269 and 1297, respectively. See Louis Hambis, *Le chapitre CVIII du Yuan che* (Leiden, 1954), pp. 141–142.

[19] YS 14:302.

[20] J. A. Boyle, *The Successors of Genghis Khan*, p. 243.

In fact, Mangghala had been invested in 1272 as Prince of An-hsi 安西 and in 1273 as Prince of Ch'in 秦. His son Ananda inherited these titles in 1282 and 1287 respectively.[21]

Thus a feudal superstructure had been laid over the local military and civilian offices just as in other parts of the Sino-Mongol empire. We may therefore perhaps regard the way in which Tibetan borderlands were administered as dual; day-to-day affairs were handled by the local and regional commanders, and they in turn were loosely supervised or directed in times of crisis by members of the imperial clan. In fact, frequently the *Yüan History* records that imperial princes were entrusted with the protection of these regions. Even as late as 1349 a prince, the descendant of an imperial son-in-law, was ordered to stabilize the situation in Tibet.[22] Another prince belonging to the imperial clan was ordered in 1354 to lead a punitive expedition against Tibetan bandits in Ho-hsi.[23] But however this unstructured organization west of the Chinese provinces was intended to function, it remains a fact that the frontier area was never fully pacified. From the early reign of Khubilai on, we read over and over again in the Basic Annals (*pen-chi* 本紀) of rebellions of Tibetan tribes, of invasions against Mongol-held garrisons, and of punitive campaigns. The "greatest criminals and thieves on earth," as Marco Polo had termed the Tibetans, could never be fully mastered even by the Mongols. They even managed in 1347 to waylay the caravan transporting wine from Qara Khocho to the capital and to kill the messengers.[24] It seems to be a fact that most of Tibet proper remained outside the direct control of the Sino-Mongol bureaucracy and that even the borderlands were throughout the Yüan dynasty an unruly and troubled region.

Tibet had little to contribute to China's economy. The country produced a brand of tea with big leaves, but the exact provenance was not known,[25] and in 1311 the tea monopoly office for Tibet was abolished—which shows that it was not worth the while to bother with Tibetan tea.[26] But there must have been some trade, because in 1277

---

[21] L. Hambis, *Le chapitre CVIII*, pp. 2, 89.

[22] YS 42:887.

[23] YS 43:915.

[24] YS 41:879. The wine was stolen by the Tibetans. In YS 34:755 it is said that "Hsi-fan Ha-la-huo-chou" (the Tibetan Qara Khocho) presented a tribute of grape wine to the court. Hsi-fan in this context is surprising because Qara Khocho in Eastern Turkestan was not a part of Tibet.

[25] YS 94:2394.

[26] YS 24:547. On the tea monopoly under the Yüan, see Herbert Franz Schurmann, *Economic Structure of the Yüan Dynasty* (Cambridge, Mass., 1956), pp. 193–202. The province of Szechwan was an important center of tea production, a fact which led

licensed border markets were established in Tiao-men 碉門 and Li-chou 黎州 for trade with Tibet.[27] Li-chou corresponds to modern Han-yüan 漢源 in Szechwan province, southwest of Ch'eng-tu, and Tiao-men, which is frequently mentioned in the *Yüan History*, must also have been situated in Western Szechwan, because this place-name occurs several times along with Ya-chou 雅州 (modern Ya-an 雅安 in Szechwan). Tibetan territory also yielded gold and silver, perhaps in the region of the upper course of the "Gold Sand River" (Chin-sha chiang 金沙江). State-controlled families were charged with mining gold and silver in Tibet, T'u-lu-kan 秃魯干, and such places, but they were converted into normal free civilians in 1272 and thus released from state serfdom.[28] The fact that licensed border markets existed for trade with Tibet is a certain indication that Tibet was treated by the Sino-Mongol government as a foreign country because no such markets existed within China proper. They were established only in the border regions, where some trade and embassy traffic entered the territory of Chinese provinces. As an aside we might mention that in 1289 Tibetans presented a black panther to the throne.[29] This animal might have come from India via Tibet. We know from Marco Polo that Khubilai had a large zoo in his capital, which contained not only animals used for hunting (gepards, falcons) but also "strange animals."[30]

All this indicates that Tibet was a *terra incognita*, a foreign country for the Chinese and Mongols of which even the geographical essentials were little known. It was the country where the Yellow River originated, but the upper course and sources of this river on which so much depended in China, both good and bad, were unknown in China until Khubilai organized an exploratory expedition in 1280. A full account of this expedition, which brought about a considerable extension of China's geographical knowledge, is contained in T'ao Tsung-i's 陶宗儀 *Cho-keng lu* 輟耕錄 (*Notes Taken during Breaks from Ploughing*), *chüan* 22, from

---

Schurmann to the assumption that "Tibetan tea" was not tea from Tibet but *for* Tibet (see p. 202, note 20). But the existence of Tibetan tea is a fact. The dietary compendium *Yin-shan cheng-yao* 飲膳正要 (*SPTK* ed.), 2:10a, says: "Tibetan tea. It is produced in that country and tastes bitter and astringent. When it is brewed, butter fat (*su-yu* 酥油) is used." This is still today the way tea is made in Tibet. The *Yin-shan cheng-yao* was presented to the throne in 1330. The use of butter for making tea is thus attested in the early 14th century.

[27] YS 9:190.

[28] YS 7:141. The name T'u-lu-kan could not be identified. There was, however, a Tibetan tribe called T'u-lu-pu 秃魯卜 which surrendered in 1309 in the border region of Szechwan, according to YS 23:512. It is possible that *kan* 干 is a misprint for *pu* 卜.

[29] YS 15:323.

[30] *Marco Polo*, tr. L. Hambis, pp. 114, 129.

where it was taken over into the *Yüan History* as a separate article (Appendix on the [Yellow] River Sources) at the end of *chüan* 63.[31]

No wonder, then, that Tibet, remaining outside the Chinese oikumene, served under the Yüan occasionally as a refuge for fugitives or as a place of exile. When a certain Chang Li-tao 張立道 got into trouble in Yunnan, he fled into Tibet.[32] In 1336 a former official of the Honan provincial government was exiled to Tibet, where he had to become a monk.[33] The most famous person exiled to Tibet under the Yüan was, of course, the last ruler of the Sung, deposed in 1276. He was dispatched to Tibet "in order to study Buddhist doctrine" in 1288.[34] In 1296 he was ordained as a Buddhist monk, but he never returned from the monastery where he was exiled. In 1322 he was ordered to commit suicide. This is not recorded in the *Yüan History*, but only in the Buddhist chronicle *Fo-tsu li-tai t'ung-tsai* (*Comprehensive Chronicle of Buddhist Patriarchs*).[35] But he is referred to as dead in the *Yüan History* in 1330 when the fields that had belonged to him tax-free were ordered to be sold and given as permanent property to a Buddhist temple which emperor Wen-tsung had founded in Chien-k'ang (modern Nanking).[36]

Thus the last ruler of the Sung ended ignominiously in an unknown place in Tibet, in the country from which had come the Buddhist priests who added religious glory and dignity to the secular power of the Mongol emperors. This was not an impact that Buddhism alone, or even

[31] Édouard Chavannes, "Les deux plus anciens specimens de la cartographie chinoise," *Bulletin de l'École Française d'Extrême-Orient*, 3 (1903), pp. 230–231; Emilio Bottazzi, "Un esplorazione alle sorgenti del Fiume Giallo durante la dinastia Yüan," *Annali dell'Istituto Orientale di Napoli, Nuova Serie* 19 (1969), pp. 529–546. For a general description of the geography of the Yellow River sources, see Klaus Flessel, *Der Huang-ho und die historische Hydrotechnik in China unter besonderer Berücksichtigung der Nördlichen Sung-Zeit* (Tübingen, 1974), pp. 5, 108. The leader of the expedition sent out by Khubilai Khaghan was a Jurchen, P'u-ch'a Tu-shih (various orthographies). The upper reaches of the Yellow River was the subject of a poem by the monk Tsung-lo 宗泐 who had been travelling in Tibet under the auspices of the first Ming emperor; see Emilio Bottazzi, "Una poesia di epoca Ming sulle surgenti del Fiume Giallo," *Annali dell'Istituto Orientale di Napoli, N.S.* 20 (1970), pp. 559–564. On Tsung-lo, see H. Franke in L. C. Goodrich and Chao-ying Fang, editors, *Dictionary of Ming Biography* (New York, 1976), pp. 1319–1321.

[32] YS 167:3916. Chang died shortly after 1298.

[33] YS 39:837.

[34] The dates are uncertain, as pointed out by Paul Pelliot, *Notes on Marco Polo*, vol. 2 (Paris, 1963), pp. 657–661. The Buddhist chronicle *Fo-tsu li-tai t'ung-tsai* 佛祖歷代通載 by Nien-ch'ang 念常 (Taishō Tripitaka, vol. 49, henceforth abbreviated as *Fo-tsu*), *chüan* 21, 707/II, records that the last Sung ruler was sent to mDo-smad in 1277. According to the Tibetan chronicle *Deb-t'er sngon-po*, he was sent to Sa-skya; see George N. Roerich, *The Blue Annals*, Part 1 (Calcutta, 1949) p. 56.

[35] *Fo-tsu, chüan* 22, 734/II.

[36] YS 34:753.

the existing Chinese Buddhist sects, could have generated. It was Tibetan Buddhism or rather Lamaism, with its long tradition of theocratic religious speculation, that achieved the final sacralization of Mongol rule over China. At the same time, Lamaism and the actions of Tibetan lamas in China were antagonistic and even provoked protonationalistic, anti-foreign feelings, not only among non-Buddhist intellectuals but even among Chinese Buddhist monks. The story of the Tibetan monks' impact on China is therefore a complicated one, and the picture that we can obtain from the Chinese sources is far from unambiguous. It would be even more complicated if we were to take into account the outlook of the Tibetan sources, where the emphasis is placed on the missionary activities of the lamas and where the secular rule of the Mongols over China is mentioned only in passing.

The story of the encounter between the Tibetan clerics and the Mongol princes and emperors has been told and retold. A full bibliography of Western and Japanese secondary literature on this topic would easily fill dozens of pages. We shall, therefore, not try to retell a story the outlines of which are already well known, but instead try to give an overall interpretive view, with only occasional details to facilitate comprehension.[37]

It all started with the letter written by Köden (the Go-dan of the Tibetan sources) in 1244 to the head of the Sa-skya pa sect, the Saskya paṇḍita Kun-dga' rgyal-mts'an (1182–1251).[38] In this letter Köden, who

[37] Only a few of the existing studies in Western languages shall be mentioned here: Paul Ratchnevsky, "Die mongolischen Großkhane und die buddhistische Kirche," Johannes Schubert, Ulrich Unger, ed., *Asiatica, Festschrift Friedrich Weller zum 65. Geburtstag gewidmet* (Leipzig, 1954), pp. 489–504; Paul Demiéville, "La situation religieuse en Chine au temps de Marco Polo," *Oriente Poliano* (Roma, 1957), pp. 193–236; the articles by Rerikh and Kuchera mentioned above in note 6; Tsepon W. D. Shakabpa, *Tibet: A Political History* (New Haven and London, 1967), pp. 61–72; Giuseppe Tucci, *Tibetan Painted Scrolls* (Roma, 1949), vol. 1, pp. 7–17; Klaus Sagaster, *Die weiße Geschichte (Čayan teüke). Eine mongolische Quelle zur Lehre von den Beiden Ordnungen Religion und Staat in Tibet und der Mongolei* (Wiesbaden, 1976); Okada Hidehiro 岡田英弘, "Mōko shiryō ni mieru shoki no Mō-Zō kankei 蒙古史料に見える初期の蒙藏関係," *Tōhōgaku* 東方学, 23 (1962), pp. 95–108. See also Turrell V. Wylie, "The First Mongol Conquest of Tibet Reinterpreted," *Harvard Journal of Asiatic Studies*, 37 (June, 1977), pp. 103–133.

For another recent study of early Tibeto-Mongolian contacts, see Dieter Schuh, *Erlasse und Sendschreiben mongolischer Herrscher für tibetische Geistliche* (St. Augustin, 1977; Monumenta Tibetica Historica Abteilung III, Band I). Schuh's conclusions, based on a careful interpretation of Tibetan documents, are similar to those of Wylie's.

[38] For a translation of the letter, see T. W. D. Shakabpa, *Tibet*, pp. 61–62; for a critical discussion of the text of Köden's letter and for a translation which differs considerably from that of Shakabpa, see Schuh, *Erlasse und Sendschreiben mongolischer Herrscher für tibetische Geistliche*, pp. 31–36 and 41. Schuh shows conclusively that the extant versions of the letter have been tampered with.

had been enfeoffed with the Tibetan borderlands as we have seen above, invited the lama to visit him, ostensibly because he believed he should have someone who could teach the Mongols moral and religious behavior and who would pray for the deceased parents of Köden. In reality, however, the letter was probably not an offer of alliance but rather a thinly disguised request for Tibetan surrender. In return, Köden promised to protect the Tibetan monks. This letter also suggests that Köden was concerned for the spiritual well-being of his clan-members. In fact, such a family-oriented attitude remained a characteristic of the relations between the Tibetan clergy and the Mongol rulers. The Tibetan-Lamaist influence on the Mongols centered on the ruling family, on Chinggis Khan and his successors. One might perhaps ask why the Sa-skya lama, and not another of the many Buddhist dignitaries in thirteenth-century Tibet, was invited by Köden. One reason seems to be that the Sa-skya school specialized in magic rituals and in the spreading of Buddhist morality. The former appealed to the unsophisticated Mongols, and the latter could be seen by them as a means to rule their subjects more effectively.[39] On the other hand, a shrewd politician like Sa-skya paṇḍita might have considered it advantageous to ally himself with the political power of the Mongols who had become overlords of China, Tibet's neighbor.

The Sa-skya paṇḍita died in 1251, and soon afterwards his secular protector Köden died. They had both been instrumental in allying the Sa-skya sect and the Mongol ruling clan, an alliance which was continued after 1251 by the paṇḍita's nephew Blo-gros rgyal-mts'an, better known under his honorific name Pags-pa (in Tibetan orthography, 'P'ags-pa, "Reverend") (1235–1280) and, on the Mongol rulers' side, by Khubilai, who was still a prince at that time. An invitation to visit Khubilai was issued in 1253, at a time when the Mongol campaign against the Nan-chao kingdom in what is now Yunnan province was under preparation. Peaceful relations with the Tibetans were crucial to the military action against Nan-chao, because the Western flank of the advancing Mongol armies would be exposed to the Tibetan border. The invitation to Pags-pa may initially have been a ploy to take him hostage and to use him as a symbol for the surrender of Tibet.[40] The young lama was indeed to become a figure of greatest importance. It was he who not

[39] K. Sagaster, *Die weiße Geschichte*, pp. 26–27. In the European Middle Ages the Tibetans were reportedly known as experts in sorcery and witchcraft; see *Marco Polo*, tr. L. Hambis, pp. 96–97.

[40] For this interpretation of Köden's and Khubilai's overtures to the Tibetan religious leaders, see the works by Wylie and Schuh cited in note 37. The best account of Pags-pa in a Western language is that in Miyoko Nakano, *A Phonological Study in the 'Phags-pa Script and the Meng-ku Tzu-yün* (Canberra, 1971), pp. 24–28.

only established a firm hold for Tibetan Buddhism in China, but who also was responsible for the Buddhist legitimation of the Mongol emperors.

There exists as yet no detailed study of Pags-pa and his activities, a study which would have to take into account Chinese, Tibetan, and Mongolian source material. This is somewhat surprising because there can be no doubt that he was one of the most influential persons in the history of medieval Buddhism. He was a deep thinker, a devoted missionary, a clever politician, and, last but not least, a phonetician of genius who invented by far the best alphabet for writing preclassical Mongolian. His alphabet not only renders the sound patterns of thirteenth-century Mongolian better than any other known script, but it also, through its use in transcribing Chinese words and texts, has rendered invaluable service for the phonetic reconstruction of Old Mandarin.

In the religious sphere, the impact of Pags-pa can be seen chiefly in two achievements. He provided the Mongol emperors with a pseudo-historical theory which incorporated them into the line of succession of Buddhist universal emperors, and he developed a theory of theocratic rule for Khubilai and his successors. We shall first survey briefly the historical theories of Pags-pa.

It had been customary in Buddhist historiography to date important events by reference to the number of years that had elapsed since the Buddha attained Nirvāṇa. As a rule, only events thought to be of special importance for the salvation of the world and for the propagation of the Law were dated in this fashion. Under Pags-pa's influence, the birth of Chinggis Khan was interpreted as having been such an event. An important text reads as follows:

"At that time a king was born in the Northern Mongol state whose virtuous fortune from previous existences had reached completeness. His name was Chinggis. He first ruled from the north over the nations with many languages, like a king turning the wheel of iron.... The younger brother of the king (Möngke) was named Khubilai and followed him on the throne of emperor (*ti* 帝) and king (*wang* 王). He subjugated many countries and territories and became powerful by extending his frontiers. He adopted the teachings and the Law of the Buddha and civilized his people according to the Law. Therefore the teachings of the Buddha flourished twice as much as before." [41]

In this passage the Mongol emperors do not appear as the legitimate or factual successors of a Chinese dynasty, but of the Buddhist universal emperors, the *cakravartinrājas* of India, Central Asia, and Tibet whom

[41] *Fo-tsu, chüan* 1, 489/II–III.

the text had mentioned in a previous passage. Chinggis Khan is viewed here as a *cakravartin* king, along with Aśoka, the Tibetan holy kings, and the mythical Mahāsamadi. The text from which the above translation was made, however, was not written by Nien-ch'ang 念常, the Chinese author of the *Comprehensive Chronicle of Buddhist Patriarchs*, but comes originally from a work written by Pags-pa himself. He wrote in 1278 a brief dogmatic treatise for Chen-chin 眞金 (1243–1285), Khubilai's son and heir-apparent, in which he outlined the basic creeds of the kind of Buddhism current in his Sa-skya sect. The title of the work is *Śes-bya rab-gsal* or "What One Should Know." It was later translated into Chinese by Šar-pa (Chin. Sha-lo-pa 沙羅巴, 1259–1314) under the title *Chang-so-chih lun* 彰所知論 and incorporated into the Chinese Buddhist Tripitaka. In *chüan* 1 of the *Comprehensive Chronicle*, Nien-ch'ang has copied verbatim two long passages from Pags-pa's work, those on the "vessel world" (*ch'i-shih-chieh* 器世界, Sans. *bhajanaloka*) and on the "sentient world of living beings" (*ch'ing-shih-chieh* 情世界, Sans. *sattvaloka*). The passage translated above comes from the *sattvaloka* section. The Tibetan original marks chronologically the birth of Chinggis Khan by stating that he was born 3,250 years after Buddha's Nirvāṇa.[42] This is, of course, quite unhistorical. The Chinese version omits the dating. The *What One Should Know* also gives religious dignity to crown-prince Chen-chin by addressing him as "Bodhisattva Imperial Prince"—one of the many instances of Buddhist sacralization conferred upon the family of Chinggis Khan by the Tibetan lamas. Because of its inherent supranational character, Buddhist sacralization was acceptable to the Mongols. It provided them with a sacral kingship that legitimized their domination over China and the world.[43]

[42] The *Śes-bya* has been reprinted in the collected works of the Sa-skya school, *Sa-skya pa'i bka' hbum* (Tokyo, 1968), vol. 6, part 1. On the text see also G. Tucci, *Tibetan Painted Scrolls*, vol. 1, pp. 103 and 257. The *Chang-so-chih lun* is no. 1645 in vol. 32 of the Taishō Tripitaka. Parts of the work have been translated into English by Prabodh Chandra Bagchi, *Sino-Indian Studies*, vol. 2 (Calcutta, 1947), pp. 136–156. The translator Šar-pa has a biography in *Fo-tsu*, chüan 22, 729/III–730/II. For the Mongolian translation of the *Śes-bya*, see Walther Heissig, *Die Familien- und Kirchengeschichtsschreibung der Mongolen*, vol. 1 (Wiesbaden, 1959), pp. 26–34.

[43] On the sacralization of the Yüan emperors see H. Franke, "Zum Legitimitäts-problem der Fremddynastien in der chinesischen Historiographie," Friedrich Prinz, Franz-Josef Schmale, Ferdinand Seibt, ed., *Geschichte in der Gesellschaft. Festschrift für Karl Bosl zum 65. Geburtstag* (Stuttgart, 1974), pp. 14–27. For a more detailed study of the legitimation of the Yüan dynasty, see Herbert Franke, *From Tribal Chieftain to Universal Emperor and God: The Legitimation of the Yüan Dynasty* (Munich, 1978). It should be added that Khubilai was regarded as an incarnation of the Bodhisattva Mañjuśrī; see K. Sagaster, *Die weiße Geschichte*, pp. 262–264. This sacralization is already attested in the greater Chü-yung Kuan inscription of ca. 1345; see N. Poppe, *The Mongolian Monuments in hP'ags-pa Script* (Wiesbaden, 1957), p. 65.

All known sources, Chinese, Mongol, and Tibetan, agree that Khubilai was given a consecration (*abhiṣeka*) in 1253. It was an initiation to the rites of dGes-pa rdo-rje (Sans. Hevajra), a tutelary deity specially worshipped in the Sa-skya monasteries and whose cult is closely linked with that of Mahākāla, a protector and defender of the faith who is, like Hevajra, represented in a terrifying aspect. It seems that rites connected with Hevajra and Mahākāla became customary for every enthronment of a Yüan emperor, a fact which is also mentioned in the Chinese sources.[44] The terrible Mahākāla was invoked when the Sino-Mongol armies went into battle. Thus Tibetan deities became the protectors of the emperors, and in fact Mahākāla remained the national protector (Tib. *mGon-po*, Sans. *nātha*) of the Mongols until our century.

The second spiritual achievement of Pags-pa was the elaboration of a theory for ruling the world, a theory which can be called Lamaist caesaropapism. Our best source is a late Mongol work called *Arban buyan-tu nom-un chaghan teüke* (*White Chronicle of the Ten Meritorious Laws*). The extant version does not date from the Yüan dynasty, but it is replete with passages which must have come from Pags-pa's time. We are fortunate to have now a very detailed and profound study of this text which has influenced deeply the Lamaist world during the last three centuries and which contains the basic ideas of the Pags-pa lama on secular rule.[45] It is the theory of the "two principles" (Mong. *khoyar yosun*), religion (*shashin*) and state (*törö*). According to these ideas, secular and spiritual salvation are something that all living beings try to obtain. Spiritual salvation consists in complete deliverance from suffering, and worldly welfare is secular salvation. Both depend on a dual order, the order of religion (*nom-un yosun*) and the order of the state, or worldly rule (*törö-yin yosun*). Just as the religious order is based on the sūtras and magic formulae (*dharaṇī*), the secular order rests on peace and quietness. The order of religion is presided over by the Lama, and the state by the Ruler. The priest has to teach religion, and the Ruler has to guarantee a rule which enables everyone to live in peace. Religion and state are thus mutually dependent. The heads of religion and state are equal, although each has different functions. The Lama corresponds to the Buddha, and the Ruler to the *cakravartin*. In each era of history these highest dignitaries appear only once. In the thirteenth-century they were

---

[44] YS 202:4521. For examples of Tantric rituals performed in order to secure victory for the Mongol armies, see the biography of the lama Tan-pa in *Fo-tsu, chüan* 22, 726/I (campaign against the Sung) and 726/III (campaign against Khaidu). The initiation of Khubilai is frequently mentioned in Tibetan writings of the Sa-skya school. See, e.g., *Sa-skya pa'i bka' hbum*, vol. 7, nos. 316, 317, 321.

[45] Klaus Sagaster, *Die weiße Geschichte* (see n. 37 above).

Pags-pa and Khubilai. Phags-pa represented the highest teacher in the present *kalpa*, namely, the Buddha, just as Khubilai was the avatar of the original *cakravartin*, Chinggis Khan. "The basis of the exalted religion is the lord of religion (*nom-un ejen*) and the head of the great secular order (*yeke törö*) is the khan who has power in the world."[46]

All this is obviously a theory of government which was neither implemented fully under the Yüan dynasty nor later in Mongolia and Tibet. It indicates, however, that the Mongol emperors of the Yüan dynasty must have seen themselves as something more than just Chinese emperors (*huang-ti* 皇帝). The relation between Lama and Ruler was not only expressed in these abstract terms. The links between Pags-pa were not limited merely to theoretical speculations, for they were additionally cemented by matrimonial alliances similar to those which existed between the Mongols and the Uighur and Korean kings. Although the Chinese sources remain silent on this point, we know from Tibetan sources that the Sa-skya lama's family and Mongol imperial clan members did intermarry. A younger brother of Pags-pa married the princess Me-'ga'-lung in about 1265, and a son from that union, born in 1268, married a daughter of Jibig Temür, the third son of Köden whom we have already met as the first Mongol prince to establish relations with the Sa-skya lamas.[47] No wonder, then, that Pags-pa and other lamas,

[46] The meeting between Khubilai and Pags-pa is the subject of a Tibetan painting in Tashilhunpo. It is reproduced in *Wen-wu*, 1959, no. 7, pp. 12–13. A large photo of this fresco was seen in the Peking Historical Museum with the caption in Chinese "Close Relations between the Yüan Government and the Region of Tibet" (May, 1977). Also on tanka paintings Pags-pa and his secular counterpart are sometimes represented.

[47] Shoju Inaba, tr., "The Lineage of the Sa skya pa. A Chapter of the Red Annals," *Memoirs of the Research Department of the Toyo Bunko*, 22 (1963), pp. 109–110. Also a great-nephew of Pags-pa by the name of Slob dpon Bsod-nams btsang-po was married to a Mongol princess. Her name is given in the *Red Annals* as Mun-dha-gan (see Inaba, p. 110). The text says that Bsod-nams btsang-po was born when his father was staying in China, and that he received the Chinese title of Duke (*kung*) and later of Prince (*wang*). He "returned to secular life" under emperor Gegen (i.e., Ying-tsung, r. 1321–1324), and died in mDo-khams. This person must be identical with the So-nan tsang-pu of the YS who was made Prince of Pai-lan 白蘭 (the Kokonor region) in 1321, entered monastic life, and re-entered secular life in 1327. His name is rendered in various orthographies. See, on him, L. Hambis, *Le chapitre CVIII du Yuan-che* (Leiden, 1954), pp. 50, 137. That he was married to a princess can be corroborated in YS 30:669–670 (1326). Her name is given as Shou-ning kung-chu 壽寧公主. She must be identical with the princess Mun-dha-gan of the *Red Annals*. This princess, who was a daughter of Kammala, the father of the T'ai-ting emperor (r. 1324–1327), died in 1330 (YS 34:760; 109:2762). A son of this union, the Slob-dpon Ratna, held the office of Preceptor of the State (*kuo-shih*), according to the *Red Annals* (see Inaba, "The Lineage"). Unless there were two princesses named Mun-dha-gan, which is not very probable, the princess was married twice, because another marriage is mentioned in the *Red Annals*, this time to a member of the Sa-skya family (see Inaba). The

acting as something like court chaplains to the Yüan emperors, frequently initiated imperial princes and princesses. It is this which accounts for the many Tibetan Buddhist personal names in the imperial clan.[48] At the same time, Buddhist indoctrination took place through a constant flow of exhortations, prayers, and catechisms addressed to members of the Mongol court. In an appendix a tabulation of Pags-pa's writings dedicated to Khubilai and his family is given which shows whom he had singled out as addressees. In some cases the colophons and incipits of his treatises can even clarify obscure points in the Chinggisid genealogy and add to what we know from Chinese, Mongol, and Persian sources. It is evident that Pags-pa's patrons and pupils, in addition to Khubilai, can be found chiefly among those princes and their families who were in some way connected with the feudal rule over the Tibetan borderlands.

After his death in 1280, Pags-pa was honored by the court in many ways. An imperial edict conferred upon him a pompous title, and in 1282 a stupa for his remains was ordered to be built.[49] Many years later, in 1321, memorial halls (*tien* 殿) were built in all circuits "modelled on the temples for Confucius, only bigger," as the anonymous author of the entry in the Basic Annals of the *Yüan History* states with some rancor.[50] A memorial inscription was commissioned from a Chinese Buddhist monk and the text written by the famous calligrapher Chao Meng-fu 趙孟頫 (1254–1322); the seal script title of the stele was prepared by another Yüan writer and artist, Yüan Ming-shan 元明善 (1269–1322).[51] Moreover, in 1324 eleven painted portraits of the late Imperial Preceptor (*ti-shih* 帝師) Pags-pa were distributed to the provinces so that clay statues could be modelled after these paintings for worship in the

---

Red Annals (*Hu-lan deb-t'er*, a Mongolian title) is also known under the Tibetan title of *Deb-t'er dmar-po* and is dated 1346. On the work see also S. Bira, "Some Remarks on the Hu-lan Deb-ther of Kun-dga' rDo-rje," *Acta Orientalia Hungarica*, 17:1 (1964), pp. 69–81.

[48] For a brief survey of these Tibetan names see Luc Kwanten, "Tibetan Names in the Yüan Imperial Family," *The Mongolia Society Bulletin*, 10:1 (1971), pp. 64–66.

[49] YS 12:249.

[50] YS 27:607. The *Fo-tsu* reports the order to build memorial shrines for Pags-pa under the year 1321; *chüan* 22, 732/III. For the shrine in Wen-chou 溫州 (Chekiang) which was built at the foot of Hua-kai Mountain 華蓋山 east of of the town and which was thoroughly repaired in 1334, the famous literatus Liu Kuan 柳貫 (1270–1342) from P'u-chiang 浦江 wrote the text of a stele. According to this text, the shrine had a clay statue of Pags-pa which was decorated with gold and many colors. *Liu Tai-chih wen-chi* 柳待制文集 (SPTK ed.), 9:12b–14b. For more on Liu Kuan, see the essay by J. Langlois in the present volume.

[51] *Fo-tsu*, *chüan*. 22, 732/III–733/II.

memorial halls.[52] Thus Pags-pa enjoyed posthumous honors comparable only to those accorded to Confucius himself.

The hold that Pags-pa established at the court and his influence was inherited and maintained by succeeding Imperial Preceptors, all of whom were Tibetan lamas and mostly his close relatives. On the institutional side, the alliance between the lamas of the Sa-skya monastery was cemented by the establishment of the Bureau of Buddhist and Tibetan Affairs (*Hsüan-cheng yüan* 宣政院). This office is unique insofar as it had no precedent in Chinese bureaucratic traditions. It was originally founded in the beginning of the Chih-yüan era (1264) under the name of *Tsung-chih yüan* 總制院 (Bureau of General Regulation) in order to manage the affairs of the Buddhist religion and of Tibet. In 1288 the notorious Sengge, himself a fervent Buddhist, memorialized that the bureau should be reorganized and the name changed to *Hsüan-cheng yüan*.[53] This name is rather colorless, literally meaning "Bureau for the Proclamation of (Imperial) Government." It contains a historical allusion insofar as the name was chosen because under the T'ang the Tibetan envoys were received in the Hsüan-cheng Hall (*Hsüan-cheng tien*).[54] The functions of this office are described in the *Yüan History* as follows: "It handled Buddhists monks as well as the territory of T'u-fan (i.e., Tibet)

---

[52] YS 29:650; 202:4518. In Tibetan art we find many portraits (or rather, idealized representations) of the Sa-skya lamas. A series of at least thirty paintings representing the masters of the Sa-skya school was dispersed some years ago; some paintings have found their way into museums. See the catalog *Tibet. Kunst des Buddhismus* (Exhibition Grand Palais, Paris, 25 March to 27 June, 1977, and Haus der Kunst München, 6. Aug. to 16. Okt., 1977), p. 128, no. 114. In some cases such paintings give the name of the persons represented. Two particularly interesting paintings with dozens of inscribed portraits of Sa-skya lamas are in the J. Zimmerman collection (New York), and are nos. 114 and 122 of the catalog. They are reproduced in the present volume. The Museo Nazionale d'Arte Orientale in Rome has two paintings (nos. 232, 233), one of which shows the Sa-skya Pandita, his father, his great-nephew Btsang-po-dpal (1262–1323), who was Preceptor of the State (*kuo-shih*), and Pags-pa. The other includes the portraits of a son of Btsang-po-dpal and of the lama Sangs-rgyas dpal, who was Imperial Preceptor from 1305 until his death in 1314. On these persons see also Shoju Inaba (see n. 47 above).

[53] YS 205:4574. For a detailed history of the Buddhist and Tibetan administrative offices see Paul Ratchnevsky, *Un code des Yuan*, vol. 1 (Paris, 1937), lxviii-lxxxvi. The account of YS 87:2193 has been translated into English by F. W. Cleaves in "The Sino-Mongolian Inscription of 1346," *Harvard Journal of Asiatic Studies*, 15 (1952), p. 41 note 39. For a study in Japanese on the *Hsüan-cheng yüan* of the Yüan, see Nogami Shunjō 野上俊静, "Gen no senseiin ni tsuite 元の宣政院について," in *Haneda hakushi sōsho kinen tōyōshi ronsō* 羽田博士頌壽記念東洋史論叢 (Kyoto, 1950), pp. 779–795; rpt. in *Genshi shaku-rōden no kenkyū* 元史釈老傳の研究 (Kyoto, 1978), pp. 221–239. See also Han Ju-lin, cited in note 10 above.

[54] Paul Pelliot, *Histoire ancienne du Tibet* (Paris, 1961), p. 20.

and they were under its jurisdiction and governed by it."[55] Its functions were dual: the management of the Buddhist clergy within the empire, including China, on the one hand, and territorial jurisdiction over Tibet, on the other. The Bureau of Buddhist and Tibetan affairs was, in fact, a fourth central agency in addition to the Central Secretariat (*chung-shu sheng*), the Censorate (*yü-shih t'ai* 御史臺), and the Bureau of Military Affairs (*shu-mi yüan* 樞密院) and enjoyed considerable independence. It was allowed to report on its affairs directly without going through the Central Secretariat[56] and could, like the other three central agencies, select its own personnel.[57] The deputy director of the bureau had always to be a Buddhist monk.[58] In view of the field of activities of the bureau, it is surprising that it is not more frequently mentioned in the legal cases contained in the *Yüan tien chang* 元典章 (*Compendium of Statutes and Sub-statutes of the Yüan*), but this proves that in many ways this Buddhist-Tibetan "ministry" remained outside the traditional bureaucratic structure of Yüan China.

Equally few passages in the existing sources refer to the local departments of the office, the *hsing* 行 or *Branch Hsüan-cheng yüan*. In 1291 an office of that name was established at Hangchow, and it existed until 1326.[59] It was reestablished some years later under Emperor Shun-ti 順帝 in 1334.[60] It seems that sometimes a local branch Bureau of Buddhist and Tibetan Affairs was created in order to deal with an emergency. Thus a branch bureau was established in 1357 as a countermeasure against Tibetan brigands.[61] At first sight it might seem surprising that an office which dealt primarily with Buddhist affairs also had military functions, but this can be explained if we regard it as a special kind of provincial government by which Tibetan affairs were handled. In military affairs concerning Tibet the bureau sometimes acted jointly with the Bureau of Military Affairs. A punitive expedition against unruly Tibetans was organized by both agencies acting in concert in 1311.[62] In the same year, an imperial decree confirmed that military affairs in Tibet came under

[55] Tr. F. W. Cleaves; see n. 53 above.

[56] YS 102:2616.

[57] YS 22:486.

[58] YS 202:4520.

[59] YS 16:350; 30:672.

[60] YS 38:820. Sometimes the *Yüan shih* distinguishes "inner" (*nei* 內) and "outer" (*wai* 外) offices. The *Fo-tsu*, *chüan* 22, 734/II, gives 1328 as the date when the 16 local *Hsüancheng yüan* branches were converted into as many directorates for the propagation of religion.

[61] YS 39:840.

[62] YS 24:543.

the jurisdiction of the Bureau of Buddhist and Tibetan Affairs.[63] Also, the management of the postal stations in Tibet was a concern of the bureau, and relief actions for postal personnel in Tibet could be organized by this office.[64]

The Chinese name of the bureau, *Hsüan-cheng yüan*, is also mentioned sometimes in the Tibetan sources (transcribed as Swon-ching dben), as are other Chinese-originating titles received by Tibetan lamas from the imperial court. The chief lamas, such as the Imperial Preceptors, were also in some cases ennobled as Duke (*kung* 公) or Prince (*wang* 王), while the regents of the Sa-skya monastery (who did not necessarily come from the lineage of the Sa-skya-pa but from different families) ruled by imperial command, using seals that were given them by the Mongol emperors.[65] They were thus treated like other secular rulers or chieftains. It seems, therefore, that Tibet was a part of the Mongol empire in a very peculiar way. It was definitely not a part of China nor one of its provinces. The greater part of Tibet was ruled by indigenous lamas whose government was sanctioned by the imperial court via the Bureau of Buddhist and Tibetan Affairs, but they received little or no interference from the emperors. The Tibetan borderlands were, in name at least, appanages of Mongol imperial princes who exercised only a very loose control through offices and military commands that were established mostly on an ad hoc basis. In Tibetan sources and also in Rashīd al-Dīn, one encounters passages like "X was commanded to rule over Tibet," but in view of what we stated before this rule was, at the most, indirect. The local positions of power were inherited and imperial investiture with Chinese titles was at best a formality.

A study of the names of persons mentioned as officials of the Bureau of Buddhist and Tibetan Affairs would show that indeed Chinese played no role whatsoever. Only Tibetan or Mongolian names occur in conjunction with the bureau and its local branches. This fact underlines its alienation from other branches of government, where at least in the lower and middle hierarchy Chinese personnel were employed. The foreign character of the bureau must have been an additional element leading to opposition among the civilian bureaucracy. The few cases where activities of the bureau are recorded in the *Compendium of Statutes and Sub-statutes of the Yüan* concern conflicts with the provin-

---

[63] YS 24:546. In 1331 the *Hsüan-cheng yüan* sent out messengers to inspect the armies stationed in Tibet. See YS 35:790.

[64] YS 26:589 (1319).

[65] For many examples, see the article by Inaba, cited in n. 47 above.

cial authorities over jurisdiction in cases involving Buddhist monks, including the ever-present problem of taxation of the clergy. Typical is perhaps the strong stand taken by the provincial administrations of Honan and Chiang-che in 1309, when they opposed the bureau's tendency to grant wholesale tax exemption not only to Buddhists but also to Taoists, Nestorians, and Muslims.[66]

There existed several other officers dealing with Buddhist affairs under the Yüan, where Tibetans and other foreigners similarly played the dominant role. One of them was the Buddhist Affairs Commission (*Kung-te shih-ssu* 功德使司). It is not described in the section on officialdom of the *Yüan History*, and only scanty details can be found in the sources. It seems that in 1280 a supervisor (*tu* 都) of the Buddhist Affairs Commission was installed, and his assignment was to report on Buddhist monks and Tibetan affairs. In this respect we are justified in regarding this office as a precursor of the Bureau of Buddhist and Tibetan Affairs.[67] After the establishment of the bureau, the authority of the Buddhist Affairs Commission seems to have been limited to the supervision of Buddhist rituals. Its personnel was cut down in 1294,[68] and in 1311 an office known as the *Yen-ch'ing ssu* 延慶司 was merged with the remnants of the Buddhist Affairs Commission and renamed *Tu kung-te shih-ssu*.[69] The *Yen-ch'ing ssu* (Office of Entertainment and Celebrations), which had been established in 1284, managed Buddhist activities and rituals including those held in various princely households.[70] The Buddhist Affairs Commission was abolished in 1329 and its affairs were taken over by the Bureau of Buddhist and Tibetan Affairs.[71] For a short while in the early years of emperor Shun-ti's reign there came into being some sixteen regional Directorates-General for Religious Affairs (*Kuang-chiao tsung-kuan fu* 廣教總管府), the officials of which were all nominated by the Bureau of Buddhist and Tibetan Affairs. This was in 1331,[72] but in 1334 the Directorates-General were abolished and reorganized as branches of the bureau.[73] The duties of

[66] YS 23:512. On the taxation of the clergy in general, see P. Ratchnevsky, *Un code des Yuan*, vol. 1, pp. 208–212, and "Die mongolischen Großkhane ..." (cited in n. 37 above).

[67] YS 11:223. See also, on the *Kung-te shih-ssu* of the Yüan, Nogami Shunjō, "Gen no kudokushishi ni tsuite 元の功徳使司について," *Shina bukkyō shigaku* 支那佛教史学, 6:2 (1942), pp. 1–11, rpt. in *Genshi shakurōden no kenkyū*, pp. 129–141; and P. Ratchnevsky, *Un code des Yuan*, vol. 1, p. 152.

[68] YS 18:384.

[69] YS 24:538.

[70] YS 89:2244.

[71] YS 33:744; 87:2194.

[72] YS 35:776; see note 60 above, and the essay by D. Farquhar in this volume.

[73] YS 38:820; 92:2335.

these shortlived directorates were the management of Buddhist monks and nuns, and its director (*tsung-kuan*) had to be a monk. We can therefore see that under the Mongol Yüan dynasty a powerful and influential Buddhist administration existed under different names, and that invariably Tibetan monks occupied the most prominent positions; this can be deduced from the names recorded in the sources.

Secular and religious power were thus amalgamated on the institutional level in Yüan rule, and imperial patronage of Buddhism remained a characteristic of Mongol rule in China. Countless entries in the sources refer to the performance of Buddhist rituals—sometimes to be organized by the Bureau of Buddhist and Tibetan Affairs—which were supposed to secure divine assistance for the well-being of the imperial family and the empire. The combined secular and religious functions of both of the Imperial Preceptors (*ti-shih*) and the institutions through which they ruled resulted in a status of Buddhist monks, particularly those from Tibet, that was almost as privileged as that of the members of the civilian and military bureaucracy. Non-Buddhist sources, in particular the *Yüan History*, are, of course, influenced by the Chinese historiographers' bias against the overly powerful status enjoyed by the Tibetan monks. One of the constant complaints of the civilian bureaucracy was the excessive or unlawful use of the government courier and postal service. It seems that Tibetan monks sometimes carried arms, a custom that was forbidden in 1276.[74] A case is reported from the year 1278 where Tibetan monks on their way to a religious feast beat postal personnel in Chen-ting 眞定 half to death.[75] Repeatedly the authorities had to forbid Tibetan monks from harrassing the population, in particular the postal personnel, with their depredations.[76] It was also decreed in 1306 that monks returning from Tibet should not use the governmental postal services and that they should be given instead boats and carts. But unauthorized use of authorization plaques by traveling monks seems to have been so widespread that an imperial injunction of 1311 tried to stop this.[77] The postal relay inspectors (*t'o-t'o-ho-sun*) also had difficulty preventing Tibetan monks from using the postal service for the transportation of private goods (presumably goods brought to China for sale).[78]

---

[74] YS 9:181.

[75] YS 130:3166.

[76] YS 12:242 (1282); 22:498 (1308); 30:669 (1326). See also YS 202:4522, where a rule prohibiting common people from striking monks is recorded.

[77] YS 24:539.

[78] See, for example, the case of 1299 in the *Yüan tien chang* 元典章 (rpt. Taipei, 1964), 16:5a; and Peter Olbricht, *Das Postwesen in China unter der Mongolenherrschaft im 13. and 14. Jahrhundert* (Wiesbaden, 1954), pp. 53, 88.

Another complaint brought forward against the Tibetan monks concerns the interference with justice. Just as giving freedom to living beings (*fang-sheng* 放生) was considered by Buddhists an act of merit, so the pardoning of prisoners was equally viewed as meritorious. The *Yüan History* reports this as follows:

"When Western [i.e. Tibetan] monks perform a Buddhist ritual, they ask to let criminals be freed and to pray for fortune, and this they call *t'u-lu-ma* 禿魯麻. Powerful people who have violated a law all bribe them to ask for their release, even in cases where [a servant] has killed his master or [a wife] her husband. The Western monks ask to wear an imperial gown of the empress and, riding on a yellow ox, they leave the palace gates and release them [i.e. the guilty ones], pretending that this will bring good fortune." [79]

In 1313 the officials of the Censorate complained that Tibetan monks on the occasion of Buddhist religious services were causing prisoners to be released.[80] This practice was not limited only to Buddhist festivals, for it also extended to the Chinese festivals such as the New Year's. This is clear from a report that the officials of the Central Secretariat in 1326 made a complaint to this effect. Some Tibetan monks had used the New Year's festival as an opportunity to obtain the release of prisoners, and that was regarded by the Secretariat officials as an interference with the statutes and as something that should therefore be forbidden. It was decreed that in future such pardons should be granted only after the case had been referred to the Imperial Clan Administration (*tsung-cheng fu* 宗政府) for revision.[81]

These and other attempts on the part of the civil officials to stop excessive releases of condemned prisoners and to prevent interference with judicial procedures and punishments by Tibetan monks show that the bureaucracy as such took a "legalist" stand, adhering to the letter of the law, whereas the ecclesiastical attitude was one of lenience and forgiveness, with or without bribes. Moreover it seems certain that the imperial prerogative of granting an amnesty was regarded by civil

[79] YS 130:3171 (ca 1294). *T'u-lu-ma* is perhaps a Chinese rendering of Tibetan *gtor-ma*, a ritual term which can also mean a Tantric offering to a deity, or an oblation in general. Cf. Helmut Hoffmann, *Die Symbolik der tibetischen Religionen und des Schamanismus* (Stuttgart, 1967), p. 60. The glossary of non-Chinese names and terms in *Yüan shih* (Taipei: Kuo-fang Yen-chiu Yüan 國防研究院, 1967), gives the ridiculous construction of Mong. *turma*, "radish." See vol. 4, p. 131.

[80] YS 24:556.

[81] YS 30:674. On amnesties under Buddhist influence, see Nogami Shunjō, "Gendai butto no menshū undō 元代佛徒の免囚運動," *Ōtani gakuhō* 大谷学報, 38:4 (1959), pp. 1–12; rpt. in *Genshi shakurōden no kenkyū*, pp. 267–284. Prof. Farquhar prefers "High Court for Mongols" for this title in English. See his essay in this volume.

officials as having been encroached upon by the actions of monks. We even have a foreign account of how a high-ranking Tibetan cleric interceded on behalf of several prisoners and succeeded in obtaining their release and pardon.[82]

In contrast with the fundamental Buddhist insistence on mercy and forgiveness, we find a harsh and cruel attitude on the part of the Bureau of Buddhist and Tibetan Affairs, that is, of the Tibetan clerics, with regard to attacks on Tibetan monks. In 1309 or shortly before, this office had succeeded in obtaining a decree which stated that in cases of brawls between Tibetan monks and common people, whoever beat a monk should have his hand cut off, and whoever insulted a monk should have his tongue cut out. But this law does not seem to have been in effect for long because the crown prince (later Emperor Jen-tsung) opposed it sharply on the grounds of incompatibility with the statutes.[83] Indeed, such mutilating punishments were not a feature of traditional Chinese law under the Yüan.

No wonder then that the Tibetan monks in full knowledge of their protected and privileged status frequently behaved with arrogance. Even Chinese monks felt antagonized, and in a Chinese Buddhist chronicle we find the following passage illustrating the feelings of Chinese monks toward their foreign colleagues:

"At that time the state honored the Western monks. Their crowd was very numerous and when entering or leaving [the palace] on horseback with their retinue [following behind], they resembled kings and grandees. These men had peaked caps of red felt and they were haughty and self-conscious. Among all the famous and virtuous [Chinese monks] there were none who did not treat them with utmost politeness. Some approached them bent over like a chime-stone, touching their garments and grasping their feet, imploring them to touch their head. This was called 'receiving benediction.' But the master [that is, the Chinese monk Liao-hsing 了性] bowed slowly and that was all. Somebody therefore called the master arrogant. He said, 'Could I dare to treat other people

---

[82] J. A. Boyle, *The Successors of Genghis Khan*, pp. 329–330. The monk "Tanba Bakshi the Tibetan" can be identified as Tan-pa (1230–1303), who has a biography in *Fo-tsu*, *chüan* 22, 725/III–727/I. Some of the imprisoned grandees mentioned by Rashīd al-Dīn can also be identified from Chinese sources. Thus Shihāb al-Dīn Qunduzi is the Sha-pu-ting who is attested as a member of the Chiang-che provincial government from 1289 to 1291. Teke Finjan is the *p'ing-chang* T'ieh-k'o who held this office in the Central Secretariat from 1292 to 1299.

[83] YS 23:512; 202:4522. The cruel punishments for those who attacked or insulted a Tibetan cleric are also mentioned in an imperial edict of 1297, which has been preserved in a Tibetan source. See Dieter Schuh, *Erlasse und Sendschreiben mongolischer Herrscher für tibetische Geistliche*, p. 128.

so negligently? I have heard that a superior person (chün-tzu 君子) loves people and that he shows this by his politeness. How can one bend one's principles so as to humiliate oneself by flattering others? Moreover, what could I ask from them concerning my relation to the Way? These people think themselves great because of their power and they behave rudely. If I were to bend because of them it would be either flattery or currying their favor. How could a superior person act in such a toadying way?' Knowledgeable people regarded this attitude as courageous."[84]

Relations between Chinese and Tibetan monks were, as we can see from this passage, sometimes not without tensions. There must have existed considerable competition as to who were the better Buddhists and who more fully understood the true meaning of the scriptures, a competition which, of course, transpired between the schools—Lamaism versus one of the Chinese schools—rather than between nationalities. It could even happen that a Tibetan would grudgingly concede that a Chinese monk had superior knowledge. The Chinese Ch'an monk Fa-wen 法聞 (1260–1317), who had studied the holy books in seclusion for six years, was once asked by the Imperial Preceptor to explain the Prajñāpāramitā. His performance impressed the Preceptor so much that he said to his followers: "Who would have said that such a monk existed in the land of the Chinese!"[85] The antagonism between Tibetan and Chinese Buddhist monks was, however, not only caused by different doctrinal attitudes. There must also have been somewhat of a language barrier. In the thirteenth and fourteenth centuries Buddhists did not have a common language in which they could converse, in contrast to the European Middle Ages, when a modicum of Latin was common to all clerics regardless of their ethnic origins. Sanskrit had not been studied in China since the Sung; the Chinese did not know Tibetan, and the Tibetans had to learn Chinese or use interpreters. To give an example, when the Chinese Ch'an monk Yün-feng 雲峯 (1219–1293) was summoned by the lama Yang Lien-chen-chia 楊璉眞加 to the court for a religious discussion about Ch'an and its transmission, a Chinese monk had to serve as interpreter.[86] Under Khubilai a Uighur who, judging from his name, came from a Buddhist family was ordered to discuss the Law with the Teacher of the State (kuo-shih 國師). But "the teacher was a Tibetan and his speech could not be understood."[87]

Apart from the language difficulties there were other elements in Lamaism which could not fail to alienate the Chinese, including Buddhists. Tantric rites frequently had a strongly sexual character,

[84] Fo-tsu, chüan 22, 733/III–734/I. The monk Liao-hsing died in 1321.
[85] Fo-tsu, chüan 22, 732/III.
[86] Fo-tsu, chüan 22, 720/I–721/II, gives a summary of these discussions.
[87] YS 134:3260.

because sexual union between properly consecrated individuals was considered a way to enlightenment (*bodhi*). Such representations on the superhuman level are well known in Lamaist art and many deities are shown in sexual embrace with their female counterparts (*prajñā*). As long as these statues and paintings were kept in temples, away from the eyes of the profane, they could not offend the Chinese. But when erotic rites were practiced at the court of the last Mongol emperor Shun-ti, the Chinese historians who recorded these events professed indignation and attributed all this to debauchery and depravity, being unaware of the religious implications. Also, the religious dances and dramatic perform-ances which Shun-ti had organized at his court were not understood by Chinese observers as legitimate rituals, but were regarded instead as strange and objectionable.[88] All these activities in the imperial palaces were organized by Tibetan lamas. Another element in Lamaism which antagonized many Chinese were the bloody offerings, which seem to have included human sacrifices. Such sacrifices of human hearts and livers to Mahākāla were even admitted to have been offered, as testified by the highest Tibetan lama, the Imperial Preceptor, in Shun-ti's reign.[89]

It is therefore not surprising that Chinese officials over and over again protested against the costly rituals, not only because they were an economic burden for the public treasuries.[90] Too many features of Lamaism as practiced by the Tibetans must have seemed incompatible with traditional Chinese concepts of propriety and therefore caused resentment. We have quoted above a passage about a Chinese monk who refused to humiliate himself in front of a lama. A similar passage elsewhere describes a parallel situation in which a Confucian scholar tried to save his dignity vis-à-vis the powerful chief lama. The "hero" is Po-chu-lu Ch'ung 李朮魯翀 (1279–1338), a prominent scholar of Jurchen ancestry. The passage reads as follows:

[88] It seems that the passages in the YS referring to the extravagances of emperor Shun-ti have been partly borrowed from the *Keng-shen wai-shih* 庚申外史 by Ch'üan Heng 權衡; H. Franke "Some Remarks on the Interpretation of Chinese Dynastic Histories," *Oriens*, 3:1 (1950), pp. 118–120. For a translation of the relevant passages, see Helmut Schulte-Uffelage, *Das Keng-shen wai-shih, eine Quelle zur späten Mongolenzeit* (Berlin, 1963), pp. 76–78; and R. H. van Gulik, *Sexual Life in Ancient China* (Leiden, 1961), pp. 259–262. For the explanation of some obscure terms, see H. Franke in *Zeitschrift der Deutschen Morgenländischen Gesellschaft*, 105 (1955), p. 386. For a biography of emperor Shun-ti (Toghōn Temür), see H. Franke in Goodrich and Fang, ed., *Dictionary of Ming Biography*, vol. 2, pp. 1290–1293.

[89] Yang Yü 楊瑀, *Shan-chü hsin-hua* 山居新話 (*Chih-pu-tsu chai ts'ung-shu* ed.), la. For a trans., see H. Franke, *Beiträge zur Kulturgeschichte Chinas unter der Mongolenherrschaft* (Wiesbaden, 1956), pp. 30–31.

[90] A good survey can be found in P. Ratchnevsky, "Die mongolischen Großkhane ..." (see n. 37 above).

"When the Imperial Preceptor came to the capital it was decreed that all court officials from the first rank down should receive him at the outskirts, riding on white horses. All the great officials bowed deeply when presenting the drink of welcome, but the Imperial Preceptor did not even move. Ch'ung alone raised the goblet and presented it standing. He said: 'The Imperial Preceptor is a follower of Shakya and the teacher of Buddhist monks in the empire. I am a follower of Confucius and the teacher of Confucian scholars in the empire. I would beg that these two should not owe politeness to each other!' The Imperial Preceptor laughed, stood up, raised his goblet and finished his drink. All those present were afraid for him [Ch'ung]." [91]

They were afraid because it must have seemed risky for a Chinese layman, even an official like Po-chu-lu Ch'ung, to fail to treat the chief lama with utmost deference.

We do not have clear indications as to the attitude of Tibetan Buddhists towards Taoism. It is true that Pags-pa himself took part in the controversies with Taoist scholars that occurred under Möngke. But the records of these discussions show that most of the monks who opposed the Taoists were not Tibetans but Chinese. Indeed the refutation of the claims of the spurious *Hua-hu ching* 化胡經 (*Canonical Text on the Conversion of the Barbarians*), which is recorded in the *Chih-yüan pien-wei lu* 至元辯偽錄 (*Debates against Falsehood Held in the Chih-yüan Reign* [1264–1294]), required a familiarity with Chinese sources which certainly Tibetans did not have. We have seen above that there existed a linguistic barrier between Chinese and Tibetans, and this would apply even more to the ability to read and understand Chinese texts like the *Canonical Text on the Conversion of the Barbarians*. The *Debates against Falsehood* is therefore a purely Chinese production. It may be assumed that the Tibetan lamas did welcome the banning and burning of Taoist books decreed in 1281, but this was after Pags-pa had died, and we have no data which show that any persecution of Taoism took place while Pags-pa held the all-important post of Imperial Preceptor and head of the Buddhist clergy.[92]

[91] YS 183:4222. Another anecdote shows also Po-chu-lu's high regard for Confucianism. The emperor asked him which of the three religions was the highest. He answered: "Buddhism is like gold, Taoism like white jade and Confucianism like the five kinds of grain." When the emperor said that consequently Confucianism would rank lowest, Po-chu-lu answered that one could live without gold or jade but not for a single day without grain. T'ao Tsung-i 陶宗儀, *Cho-keng lu* 輟耕錄 (*Ts'ung-shu chi-ch'eng* ed., Shanghai, 1936), *chüan* 5, p. 78.

[92] On the controversies between Taoists and Buddhists see, for example, Josef Thiel, "Der Streit der Buddhisten und Taoisten zur Mongolenzeit," *Monumenta Serica*, 20 (1962), pp. 1–81. For a detailed study of the authenticity of the *Pien-wei lu*, see Noritada Kubo,

The great power of Tibetan lamas was naturally resented most in the former Sung territories which had been conquered by the Mongols in 1276. Here the anti-foreign feelings of clerics and laymen alike were aroused chiefly by the misdeeds of the notorious Yang Lien-chen-chia, and particularly by the role which this monk played in the desecration and spoiling of the Southern Sung imperial tombs near Shao-hsing 紹興.[93] These incidents have been repeatedly studied, but they are important enough for assessing the impact of Tibetans on China to be summarized in this essay too.

It is not quite clear whether Yang was a Tibetan or a Tangut. The family name Yang is attested for both Tibetans and Tanguts. For example, the Tangut scholar Yang To-erh-chih 楊朵兒只 (Dorji) was a man from Ning-hsia 寧夏.[94] Dorji is, of course, the Tibetan Buddhist name rDo-rje (Sans. *vajra*, "thunderbolt"), and it is probable that Lien-chen-chia also renders a Tibetan Buddhist name. It might be reconstructed as Rin-čén skyabs,[95] a name which is attested in Tibetan sources, but so far no person with this name can be identified with the Yang Lien-chen-chia of the Chinese sources. A Chinese Buddhist source calls him the Great Master Yang Lien-chen-chia of Yung-fu 永福.[96] Yung-fu could be the name of a place, and indeed a market-town (*chen* 鎮) of that name existed in the Tibetan borderlands.[97] But Yung-fu could also be the abbreviated name of a Buddhist temple in the capital, the Shang Yung-fu Ssu 上永福寺.[98] It was not uncommon for Buddhist monks, Chinese and Tibetans alike, to be designated by the temple to

---

"Prolegomena on the Study of the Controversies between Buddhists and Taoists in the Yüan Period," *Memoirs of the Research Department of the Toyo Bunko*, 26 (1968), pp. 39–61.

[93] The best study on the subject is that by Paul Demiéville, "Les tombeaux des Song Meridionaux," *Bulletin de l'École Française d'Extrême-Orient*, 25 (1925), pp. 458–567, reprinted in Paul Demiéville, *Choix d'Études Sinologiques (1921–1970)* (Leiden, 1973), pp. 17–26. On the Southern Sung tombs see also the article by Yen Chien-pi 閻簡弼, "Nan-Sung liu-ling i-shih cheng-ming chi chu ts'uan-kung fa-hui nien-tai k'ao 南宋六陵 遺事正名暨諸攢宮發毀年代考," *Yen-ching hsüeh-pao* 燕京學報, 30 (1946), pp. 27–50, which supplements some details to Demiéville's basic study. An instructive survey is also given in P. Demiéville's article "La situation religieuse ..." (see n. 37 above), pp. 212–215, repr. in *Choix d'Études Sinologiques*, pp. 185–188.

[94] YS 179:4151–4155.

[95] P. Ratchnevsky, "Die mongolischen Großkhane ..." (see n. 37 above), p. 494, note 50, reconstructs it tentatively as Rin-č'en skya.

[96] *Fo-tsu, chüan* 21, 710/II.

[97] According to YS 24:543, Yung-fu was raided by Tibetans in 1311.

[98] The Yung-fu Ssu is mentioned in *Fo-tsu, chüan* 21, 710/II, in the same passage cited in note 96. According to YS 27:598, the construction work for the Yung-fu Ssu was stopped in 1320.

which they were attached. Thus the passage would refer to Yang's temple where he originally resided.

Nothing is known of Yang's early career. With regard to court cliques under Khubilai Khaghan, we know he was a protégé of the equally notorious Sengge, whose arrogance and greed finally caused his ruin in 1291.[99] But Yang's career had in fact begun before Sengge came to power. In 1277, only one year after the fall of Hangchow, Yang was appointed Supervisor of the Buddhist Teaching South of the (Yangtze) River (*Chiang-nan tsung-she chang shih-chiao* 江南總攝掌釋教).[100] This office, with headquarters in Hangchow, gave Yang unlimited control over the Buddhist monasteries in the newly annexed former Sung territories. Yang must have regarded it as one of his duties to restore to the Buddhists those former stupas and temples which had been converted to secular or Taoist use under the Sung. Indeed, one Buddhist chronicle states with clearly laudatory intent that he restored over thirty Buddhist temples during the three years from 1285 to 1287. The same text gives as an example the Taoist monastery Ssu-sheng Kuan 四聖觀, which was formerly the Buddhist temple Ku-shan Ssu 孤山寺. Between seven and eight hundred Taoists are said to have given up their creed and become Buddhist monks.[101] The gold, silver, and other precious vessels from the Sung imperial tombs were given by Yang as a donation for the redecoration of the T'ien-i Ssu 天衣寺 in Hangchow in 1284.[102] Also, buildings which had formerly been part of the Sung tombs were destroyed and the sites used for Buddhist temples (1285). The mausoleum for emperor Ning-tsung had orginally been the site of the Buddhist temple T'ai-ning Ssu 泰寧寺. This temple in the vicinity of Shao-hsing was destroyed under the Sung and made into a temporary mausoleum for Ning-tsung; Yang restored the site to the Buddhists. The same had happened with the Lung-hua Ssu 龍華寺 in Hangchow. Here the Sung emperors had secularized the temple and converted it into the offering site for the sacrifices to heaven and earth. Also, in this case Yang requested that the Sung offering-place should be made a Buddhist temple again "so

---

[99] On Sengge see H. Franke, "Sen-ge. Das Leben eines uigurischen Staatsbeamten zur Zeit Chubilai's dargestellt nach Kapitel 205 der Yüan-Annalen," *Sinica*, 17 (1942), pp. 90–113, an article which needs many revisions.

[100] YS 9:188 gives as names of the appointees in Chiang-nan Seng K'ang-chi-hsiang Ling-chen-chia chia-wa 僧亢吉祥伶真加加瓦. It is not certain if this refers to one person only (Yang) or to several. Chi-hsiang sounds like a monk's name. Chi-hsiang normally renders Sanskrit *śrī* or Tibetan *dpal*. Is this an epitheton for Yang, or was K'ang Chi-hsiang another monk appointed at the same time? It is also not clear what Chia-wa (* *gawa*) transcribes.

[101] *Fo-tsu, chüan* 21, 710/II. The Ku-shan Temple was at the West Lake near Hangchow.

[102] YS 13:269.

that prayers for the life of the Crown Prince can be performed there." A decree endorsed Yang's proposal.[103] But Yang was not content with restoring temples. One year later (1286) he obtained a decree to the effect that all the lands and fields which had formerly belonged to destroyed Buddhist temples should be handed over to him and the proceeds used for repairing the temples.[104] In the same year Sengge ordered Yang to send as hostages to the court several clansmen of the imperial Sung family and relatives of empresses.[105] In 1288 Yang reported to the throne that of the former Sung palaces one had been made into a stupa and five into temples. The buildings had been completed and now an edict ordered that 150 ch'ing 頃 of dry and irrigated lands should provide the economic basis for the maintenance of the temples.[106] All these activities, which Yang and others may well have regarded as acts of Buddhist devotion undertaken in the interest of propagating the true religion, did not only arouse strong Sung-loyalist feeling. Even officials of the Mongol government in Hangchow opposed them. When Yang and his subordinates began constructing various buildings in the former palace grounds of Hangchow, they wanted to use as a cornerstone a stele on which the nine Confucian classics were inscribed in emperor Sung Kao-tsung's handwriting. This was prevented by an official in Hangchow who would not tolerate this misuse of a cultural relic.[107]

The year 1291 saw the disgrace not only of Sengge but also of Yang and of the others who had apparently misbehaved in Chiang-nan. In the fifth month an investigating committee was ordered to look into the unauthorized appropriation of government materials and theft of property comitted by Yang.[108] It took some time before the authorities could complete the inventory of the riches which Yang had collected during his term of office. In the third month of 1292 his illicit profits from bribes and misdeeds were estimated at 116,200 ting 錠 of paper money and 23,000 mou 畝 of rice-fields.[109] In the monograph on Buddhism and Taoism in the Yüan History, the list of spoils is more detailed. In addition to the items mentioned above, Yang and his cohorts are said to have stolen 1,700 ounces of gold, 6,800 ounces of silver, 9 jade belts, 111 jade vessels, 152 precious shells, and 50 ounces of big pearls. He had desecrated 101 tombs, and his activities had caused the death of four

---

[103] YS 13:271–272.
[104] YS 14:285.
[105] YS 14:285.
[106] YS 15:309.
[107] YS 170:3989.
[108] YS 16:346; 120:2958.
[109] YS 17:362.

innocent people.[110] Again some years later, in 1299, the Chiang-nan Supervisory Office for Buddhist Teaching was abolished altogether.[111]

It is stated that among the bribes that Yang accepted were beautiful girls. This is not surprising in view of the fact that Tibetan lamas in those days were, as a rule, not pledged to a celibate life. Yang himself had wives; they were "confiscated" in 1291 and brought to the capital.[112] He also had a son by the name of An-p'u 暗普, a commissioner of the Bureau of Buddhist and Tibetan Affairs who received in the second month of 1291 an appointment as *tso-ch'eng* (vice director) of the Chiang-che provincial government.[113] But resentment against Yang in Chiang-nan was so widespread that An-p'u was dismissed from his Hangchow office by the fifth month of the same year.[114] This official disfavor was, however, only temporary. The Basic Annals of the *Yüan History* record that in 1311 An-p'u, commissioner of the *Hui-fu yüan* 會福院 and of the Bureau of Buddhist and Tibetan Affairs, was ennobled as Duke of Ch'in 秦國公.[115] The *Hui-fu yüan* was an intendancy of the Buddhist temple Hu-kuo Jen-wang Ssu 護國仁王寺, which was built in 1274 and existed under the name of *Hui-fu yüan* between 1310 and 1316.[116] There can hardly be any doubt that the An-p'u ennobled in 1311 was indeed identical with the An-p'u who was a son of Yang.

The affair of Yang and his crimes had fiscal consequences which continued to occupy the attention of government authorities for years. Yang had apparently organized the repair and maintenance of Buddhist temples by allotting them not only fields but also tenants. As tenants they were exempt from the payment of government taxes. Very soon after Yang's fall in 1291, therefore, the people in Chiang-nan who had ceased to pay government taxes were admonished to resume payment according to the general regulations.[117] And in the third month of 1292 the fields and tenants who had come under the jurisdiction of monastic bureaus (*seng-fang* 僧坊) were required to be handed back to their previous landlords.[118] As late as 1299 the problem of tenants on temple fields had still not been entirely resolved. The Central Secretariat memorialized that in Chiang-nan over 500,000 households had originally been

[110] YS 202:4521.
[111] YS 20:427.
[112] YS 16:352.
[113] YS 17:370.
[114] YS 17:373.
[115] YS 24:548.
[116] YS 87:2208.
[117] YS 16:348.
[118] YS 17:362.

registered as normal taxpayers (*min* 民), but that Yang had had them registered under false pretences as temple tenants. The Secretariat therefore asked that this be rectified, an advice which was followed.[119] It is not by coincidence that this action took place only a few months after the final abolition of Yang's former office, the Supervisory Office for Buddhist Teaching in Chiang-nan.

The desecration of the Sung tombs and the destruction of former Sung palaces and altars would, even without the revolting treatment of the deceased emperors' remains,[120] have been sufficient to arouse hatred among the population of the former Sung state and to increase the alienation towards Tibetan lamas which must have existed anyway. Yang's conduct not only violated deeply rooted Chinese feelings which considered the destruction of tombs as acts of impiety, but also led to a flare-up of pro-Sung loyalist feelings.[121] Even Buddhist monks were outraged at Yang's behavior. The monk and painter Tzu-wen 子温 , also known as Wen Jih-kuan 温日觀, who was famous for his paintings of grapes and was very fond of wine, was once invited by Yang for a taste of a famous brand. Wen refused to drink even a single drop and shouted "Grave-robber" at him.[122]

At this point we must, however, remind ourselves that Yang might have seen himself as a missionary and a faithful follower of his creed, according to which the building of temples and stupas were acts of religious merit. But, being unfamiliar with Chinese ways and with Chinese ideas of loyalty and piety, he inevitably and inadvertently antagonized the population in Chiang-nan. We might also ask if there were many more lamas like him, whose activities were less spectacular than his and were therefore not recorded by the court historians. Yang left his marks until today because he was a patron of Buddhist architecture and sculpture. He was responsible for the carving of the esoteric (Tantric) statues at Fei-lai feng 飛來峯 near Hangchow, and his name appears as the chief donor in an inscription dated 1292. These sculptures are specimens of Lamaist iconography, although they are Chinese in style.[123] The influences of Tibetan Lamaist art on Yüan China are obviously an important part of the impact of Tibet on Chinese culture.

[119] YS 20:428.

[120] See on this P. Demiéville, "Les tombeaux des Song Méridionaux" (see n. 93 above).

[121] The most comprehensive early source on the reactions of the Chinese to the desecration of the Sung tombs is in *chüan* 4 of the *Cho-keng lu*. The current editions of the *Cho-keng lu* all have an appendix by P'eng Wei 彭瑋 dated 1469, which voices more indignation at the crimes committed by Yang.

[122] Cheng Yüan-yu 鄭元祐 , *Sui-ch'ang tsa-lu* 遂昌雜錄 (*Shuo-k'u* ed.), vol. 28, 2b. From there the anecdote has passed into the *Cho-keng lu, chüan* 5, p. 87.

[123] Heather Karmay, *Early Sino-Tibetan Art* (Warminster, 1975), p. 24, with illustration.

In Chinese intellectual life outside Buddhism no Tibetan ever became prominent.[124] Whereas many Uighurs, and not a few other Turks, Persians, and Syrians, became writers of Chinese poems and essays, painted in Chinese style, and distinguished themselves as calligraphers, we find no Tibetan under the Yüan who achieved similar prominence. This is in sharp contrast with the role that Tanguts played in Yüan China. One of the first propagandists for Confucianism was a Tangut, Kao Chih-yao 高智耀, who was for sometime affiliated with Köden. According to Ch'en Yüan the Tanguts produced more poets in Chinese than any other of the "national minorities" in the thirteenth and fourteenth centuries.[125] The Tanguts were racially and linguistically closely related with the Tibetans and they were also mostly Buddhists. But the Tangut state of Hsi-Hsia had borrowed many cultural elements from China and thus the Tanguts had little difficulty in adapting themselves fully to Chinese culture. Contrary to a current popular belief, the Tanguts were not exterminated after the fall of their state in 1227, for Tangut culture remained an important element in China until the end of the Yüan. The Tangut Tripitaka was printed in China (Hangchow) in 1302,[126] and as late as the 1340s the Tangut language was considered important enough to have it included in the multilingual inscription of the Chü-yung Kuan 居庸關 pass-gate along with Sanskrit, Mongolian, Uighur, Chinese, and Tibetan. When the three dynastic histories of the Sung, Liao, and Chin were compiled, two Tanguts took part in the compilation of the official *Sung History* (*Sung shih* 宋史).[127] Thus Tanguts were broadly active both within Buddhism and Chinese literature, whereas the Tibetans' activities were confined to Buddhism.

If we try to assess the impact of the Tibetans on Yüan China, we are

---

[124] In contrast, Chinese historical traditions were known to Tibetans under the Yüan. The *Red Annals* contains a list of Chinese rulers from the Chou on and refers expressly to the account on Tibet in the *T'ang shu* 唐書 (*t'ang zhu t'u-hven*); see *Deb-t'er dmar-po* (Gangtok, Sikkim, 1961), fol. 12a, pp. 6–7; and Sh. Bira, "Some Remarks on the Hu-lan Deb-ther," *Acta Orientalia Hungarica*, 17:1 (1964), p. 71 note 8. Chinese historical sources were translated into Tibetan (see Bira, in the work just cited). The genealogy of Chinese rulers in the *Red Annals* was in the 15th century copied into the *Blue Annals* (George N. Roe-rich, *The Blue Annals Part One* [Calcutta, 1949], pp. 47–60). Both Annals also include a genealogy of the Mongol rulers which seems to be based directly on Mongolian sources.

[125] Ch'en Yüan 陳垣 (tr. Ch'ien Hsing-hai and L. C. Goodrich), *Western and Central Asians in China under the Mongols* (Los Angeles, 1966), p. 129. On p. 285 eight prominent Tangut writers and artists are listed.

[126] On the illustrations of the Tangut Tripitaka, see Heather Karmay, *Early Sino-Tibetan Art*, pp. 35–45.

[127] H. Franke, "Chinese Historiography under Mongol Rule: The Role of History in Acculturation," *Mongolian Studies. Journal of the Mongolia Society*, 1 (1974), pp. 16–17. See Hok-lam Chan's essay in this volume for a detailed study of the compilation.

first confronted with the almost universal bias of Chinese historians against Buddhism as such and against Lamaism in particular. The introduction to the chapter on Buddhism and Taoism in the *Yüan History* states that after the rise of the Yüan, Buddhism was held in such high esteem and the Imperial Preceptors flourished so mightily that there was simply no comparison with former times.[128] The *Yüan-shih chi-shih pen-mo* 元史紀事本末 (*The Topical Yüan History*), by the late Ming authors Ch'en Pang-chan 陳邦瞻 and Tsang Mou-hsün 臧懋循, devotes the whole of *chüan* 18 to the topic "Reverence for the Buddhist Teaching."[129] In a postscript to this chapter Chang P'u 張溥 condemns the Yüan attitude towards Buddhism as excessive and finally leading to the ruin of the state.[130] What offended these critics was the high prestige accorded the Tibetan lamas, who are blamed with having seduced the unsuspecting Mongol emperors into wasteful and corrupting practices. A similar stand was taken by the Ch'ing scholar Chao I 趙翼. He too attributed the decay of Yüan rule to pro-Buddhist excesses.[131] These examples could be easily multiplied. Furthermore, Western historians have shared this negative evaluation, as the following statement shows: "The Buddhist clergy contributed to the impoverishment of the country and to financial crisis through tax evasion, hoarding and export of precious metals and valuables, and also to increased exploitation and distress of the agricultural masses who had to feed the numerous monks and priests; through arbitrariness and unlawful acts the clergy increased discontent among the population and thus accelerated the fall of the Yüan dynasty."[132]

It is certainly correct to say that a considerable part of the blame for the accelerated fall of the Yüan must be borne by the Tibetans, but we may question whether the economic consequences of the Buddhist cult ever reached a degree which was ruinous to the national economy of China. Certainly discontent existed among the masses, but apart from the obvious illegalities committed by monks like Yang Lien-chen-chia which provoked literati contempt in Chiang-nan, we do not find in China under the Mongols popular movements directed against the

[128] YS 202:4517.

[129] On Ch'en Pang-chan (d. 1623), see L. C. Goodrich and C. N. Tay in *Dictionary of Ming Biography*, vol. 1, pp. 176–178.

[130] On Chang P'u (1602–1641), see Tu Lien-che in A. W. Hummel, ed., *Eminent Chinese of the Ch'ing Period* (Washington, D.C., 1943), vol. 1, pp. 52–53.

[131] Chao I (1727–1814), *Kai-yü ts'ung-k'ao* 陔餘叢考 (Shanghai, 1957), *chüan* 18, pp. 351–355, esp. p. 354.

[132] Translation after P. Ratchnevsky, "Die mongolischen Großkhane ..." (See n. 37 above), p. 504.

Tibetan monks or against the Buddhist clergy in general. On the contrary, Chinese Buddhist monks with sectarian backgrounds played a prominent role in some rebellions during the reign of the last Mongol emperor Shun-ti. After the founding of the Ming dynasty, Chinese emperors, chiefly the Hung-wu 洪武 and Yung-lo 永樂 rulers, continued to shower imperial favors upon the Lamaist clergy in Tibet and tried to establish good relations between the Chinese court and the Tibetan dignitaries of the Karma-pa sect. In the later Yüan this sect had supplanted the Sa-skya-pa in importance.[133] It is true that Tibetan lamas were extremely powerful and frequently behaved arrogantly. Their power was noticed by the Persian historiographer Rashīd al-Dīn, who stated that "great authority is attached to their word."[134] It might even be possible to regard clericalism as a political element in Yüan China. But again we would have to ask if the impact of the Tibetan lamas on China was really stronger or more nefarious than the Buddhist impact under other dynasties in China which practised and patronized Buddhism. It seems that the combination of foreignness and Buddhism was a mixture which inspired more acute criticism among the educated Chinese than one of these elements alone would have. For the Mongols, on the other hand, the Tibetan lamas of the Yüan period remained venerable figures and shared a place in their politico-religious history. For the Tibetans, what was foreign and unacceptable to the Chinese ruling elite became a glorious past and part of a national heritage which was at the same time believed to have been a decisive step on the road to salvation for all mankind.

[133] For a survey of early Ming-Tibetan relations see H. Karmay, *Early Sino-Tibetan Art*, pp. 55–83.

[134] J. A. Boyle, *The Successors of Genghis Khan*, pp. 302–303. The text by Rashīd al-Dīn mentions expressly Tanba (on whom see above note 82) and Kanba. It was not possible to identify Kanba.

V. ART AND LITERATURE

The Role of Wu-hsing in
Early Yüan Artistic Development
Under Mongol Rule

CHU-TSING LI

Although there has been no agreement among scholars as to the nature of the response to Mongol rule by Chinese culture during the Yüan Dynasty, the existence of a strong impact by the former on the latter is generally conceded. In order to assess the nature of the Chinese response, I have chosen to make a detailed study of a prefecture in the heart of Chiang-nan 江南 where the native sentiment of the southern Chinese was very strong. Wu-hsing 吳興, also known as Hu-chou 湖州, is located on the southern shore of Lake T'ai, about fifty miles north of Hangchow. A scenic, wealthy, and cultured prefecture, it played a vital role in Chinese history for centuries, attaining its greatest significance during the early Yüan. It is my intention here to look more closely at the cultural and artistic development of Wu-hsing in order to gain a more comprehensive understanding of the Chinese cultural response to Mongol rule.[1]

I. Wu-hsing's Geographical Importance and Cultural Tradition

The origin of the term Wu-hsing dates to the period of the Three Kingdoms, when the *chün* 郡 (commandery) of Wu-hsing was first established. This area came under the administrative control of Yangchow, Hangchow, or K'uai-chi at different times in early China. During the Sung period, it came under the administrative unit of Che-hsi 浙西 circuit. The Yüan government incorporated it within Chiang-che

---

[1] The present subject has been explored to some extent in three of my previous publications: *The Autumn Colors on the Ch'iao and Hua Mountains: A Landscape by Chao Meng-fu* (Ascona: Artibus Asiae, 1965); "The Development of Painting in Soochow during the Yüan Dynasty," in *Proceedings of the International Symposium on Chinese Painting* (National Palace Museum: Taipei, 1972); and "The Uses of the Past in Yüan Landscape Painting," in *Artists and Traditions: Uses of the Past in Chinese Culture*, ed. by Christian F. Murck (Princeton: The Art Museum, Princeton University, 1977), pp. 73–88. The present paper is a full development of this subject in connection with Mongol rule.

江浙 Branch Secretariat (*hsing-sheng* 行省), while in the Ming and Ch'ing periods, as at present, it constituted the northernmost part of Chekiang Province. The terms Wu-hsing and Hu-chou were sometimes used interchangeably, but at other times were quite distinct, depending on the administrative system of the period. During the Yüan, Wu-hsing, or more precisely Hu-chou Prefecture, comprised six districts.[2] Occasionally the term Wu-hsing was used to refer to the capital city of the prefecture, Wu-ch'eng 烏程.

Throughout Chinese history, Wu-hsing, situated between the two most famous cities in the Chiang-nan area, Hangchow and Soochow, has been known for its exceptional cultural brilliance and extraordinary natural beauty. Writing in the middle Ming, the scholar Hsü Hsien-chung 徐獻忠 (1483–1559) observed in his introduction to a collection of materials pertaining to Wu-hsing:

"Wu-hsing is located in the upper reaches of the lake region. Its people are known for their frugality and simplicity, without any habits of trickery or luxury. Since the time of the Han, many a gentleman has come to take up residence here, and many others who crossed the river after the fall of the Northern Sung have done the same. There is reason for that. With its frugality and its gentlemanly tradition, this area has been known for its adherence to right decorum and propriety."[3]

On a stele dedicated to P'an Yüan-ming 潘元明 (d. 1382), who served as Chief Administrative Officer of Chekiang under Chang Shih-ch'eng 張士誠 (1321–1367) when the latter was in control of this area toward the end of the Yüan, one finds another interesting reference to Wu-hsing:

"From T'ang and the Five Dynasties to the southward retreat of the Sung court [in 1127], Wu-hsing was closest to [the city that became] the temporary capital of the Sung [Hangchow]. The Rivers T'iao 苕 and Cha 霅 run through the city. Many dukes and princes of the Sung found it convenient to settle here, with their mansions overlooking one another, their boats and carriages coming and going, smoke from their stoves intermingling. Thus the prefectural city of Wu-hsing rose above the river banks and marshy lands. Its buildings were well-constructed, strong and refined. This is something that neighboring prefectures are unable to match."[4]

Among the most famous descriptions of Wu-hsing is that written by Chou Mi 周密 (1232–1298), a resident of the city for many years prior to the fall of the Sung:

[2] A more detailed account of the administrative changes in Hu-chou throughout Chinese history can be found in the 1874 HCFC, 3.

[3] See WHCKC, introduction by Hsü Hsien-chung. This work was first published in 1560.

[4] See WHCSC 16:7b.

"The scenery of Wu-hsing is elegant and elevating. In times of peace and prosperity, many scholar-officials lived there. Among the leading houses of the city was the mansion of the Prince of Hsiu 秀, [posthumously named] An-hsi 安僖 [Chao Tzu-ch'eng 趙子偁 (d. 1144), the father of Emperor Hsiao-tsung (r. 1163–1189) and brother of Emperor Kao-tsung, who took up residence in Wu-hsing when serving as a judge in Hu-chou]. It was a great sight. The fact that two rivers run through the city is something unique in the world. It is natural that many prominent people built their gardens and ponds here."[5]

The geographical importance of Wu-hsing had also been observed by the famous poet-painter Su Shih 蘇軾 (1036–1101), who served as a prefect there late in the eleventh century:

"Since the Eastern Chin Dynasty Wu-hsing has been known as a good land, noted for its elegant and elevating scenery. This is because Wu-hsing excels in its geographical location, as seen in the praises by the people in the past. It has Chia-ho 嘉禾 as its neighbor in the east, Yü-hang 餘杭 in the south, Mt. T'ien-mu 天目 guarding the west and Chen-tse 震澤 [i.e., Lake T'ai] eddying in the north. At the rear crouches Pien Peak 卞峯, and the River T'iao flows in front. Its people live together on the flat stretches of fertile soil. All these indicate that it is an outstanding place in the southeast."[6]

Wu-hsing's economic position is reflected in a succinct statement current during the Sung Dynasty: "When there is a good harvest in Soochow and Hu-chou, the whole world will enjoy plenty" (*Su Hu shu, t'ien-hsia tsu* 蘇湖熟天下足).[7] Clearly, Wu-hsing has several basic factors that make it important geographically: fertile soil, lavish natural beauty, and proximity to both Hangchow and Soochow.

In addition to its geographical importance, Wu-hsing had a great cultural heritage. Perhaps because of its beauty and prosperity, many outstanding men of culture became associated with Wu-hsing even before the Yüan. In the field of arts and letters, Wu-hsing is especially rich in great names.[8] For our purposes here, the most important figures were Wang Hsi-chih 王羲之 (321–379) and his son Hsien-chih 獻之 (344–388), both known as great calligraphers; Yen Chen-ch'ing 顏眞卿 (709–785), a great T'ang calligrapher; and Su Shih, the Sung poet and painter

[5] See Chou Mi, *Kuei-hsin tsa-chih* 癸辛雜識 (rpt. *Chung-hua ku-chi ts'ung-k'an* 中華古籍叢刊, Taipei, 1968), *ch'ien*: 5a–b.

[6] 1475 HCFC, 2:4a.

[7] See Tung Ssu-chang 董斯張 (1586–1628), comp., *Wu-hsing pei-chih* 吳興備志 (*Ssu-k'u-chüan-shu chen-pen* 四庫全書珍本 ed., series 9), 27:4b.

[8] Lists of the prefects of Wu-hsing can be found in all editions of the gazetteers of Hu-chou. The present discussion is based on the list found in the 1542 HCFC, 3:1b.

mentioned above. Their related styles established the long tradition of great calligraphy associated with this area. In addition to these Hu-chou prefects, there were other important scholars who made contributions to the cultural heritage of Wu-hsing. One of the most famous was Lu Yü 陸羽 (d. 804), whose well-known *Ch'a-ching* 茶經 (*The Classic of Tea*)[9] helped to inspire a great love for tea. Wu-hsing became a producer of teas which were regarded as among the best in China. Another was the T'ang poet Chang Chih-ho 張志和 (ca.742–ca.782), a close friend of Lu Yü, who was so attracted by the beauty of Wu-hsing that he came to live there as a hermit, calling himself "Fisherman of Mist and Waves" (*yen-p'o-tiao-t'u* 烟波釣徒). Chang originated the tradition of the "Fisherman's Song" (*Yü-fu tz'u* 漁父詞), a landmark in the history of Chinese literature which exerted a strong influence in later periods, especially the Yüan.[10] A third was Chiang K'uei 姜夔 (ca.1155–ca.1221), a great poet and musician, who settled in this area.[11] No doubt, all these people were a source of great inspiration to later residents of Wu-hsing.

Artistically, we can mention, in addition to the calligraphers named above, a number of important painters who were natives of Wu-hsing. In the Sung period, one of the great early landscape painters, Yen Wen-kuei 燕文貴, was a native of Wu-hsing. Later, in the Southern Sung, there were a number of interesting painters active in this area. They will be discussed in the next section.[12]

During the Southern Sung period, Wu-hsing was also noted for its gardens, which, according to Chou Mi, numbered more than thirty in his own time near the end of the Southern Sung. Distinctive also was the existence of a number of great libraries, notes on which are preserved in the *Wu-hsing ts'ang-shu lu* 吳興藏書錄 (*Record of the Libraries of Wu-hsing*). A passage by Chou Mi describes the vicissitudes of book collections there:

"In the old families of my district, ... there were extensive collections with about 100,000 folios (*chüan* 卷) each. Later, ... there were libraries with tens of thousands of volumes. All of them have been completely dispersed.... In my family, we have been collecting books for three generations. The taste of my late father for books was especially great,

[9] See Francis Ross Carpenter, tr., *The Classic of Tea* (Boston: Little Brown, 1974).

[10] References to these people can be found in the 1874 HCFC, Vol. 90. On Chang Chih-ho see Hellmut Wilhelm, "The Fisherman Without Bait," *Asiatische Studien*, 18–19 (1965), pp. 90–104.

[11] References to Chiang K'uei can also be found in 1874 HCFC, vol. 90. See also Shuen-fu Lin, *The Transformation of a Chinese Lyrical Tradition: Chiang K'uei and Southern Sung Tz'u Poetry* (Princeton, 1978).

[12] References to some of these painters can be found in 1874 HCFC, Vol. 80.

2. Kun-dga' sñiṅ-po (1092-1158), spiritual ancestor of the Tibetan Sa-skya lamas, ringed by important Sa-skya deities and historical persons.

1. Gayadhara, the Bengali saint who visited Tibet in the eleventh century, ringed by important Sa-skya deities and historical persons.

1. Chao Meng-fu. The autumn colors on the Ch'iao and Hua Mountains.

2. Ch'en Lin. Hoary cliffs and old trees.

3. Wang Meng. Scenic dwelling
at Chü-ch'ü.

4. Chao Meng-fu. Rivers and mountains.

5. T'ang Ti. Landscape after
Wang Wei's poetry.

6. Chu Te-jun. Playing the Ch'in
under the trees.

7. Yao Yen-ch'ing. Fishing boats in a snowy river.

1. Hsien-yü Shu. Transcription of poem
by Ma Chiu-ch'ou, "Song of the Diaphanous
Mirror'' (*T'ou-kuang ku-ching ko*).
Undated, details from the album.

2. Hsien-yü Shu. Colophon to the
Lan-t'ing, formerly in Yüan Hao-wen's
collection, dated 1297.

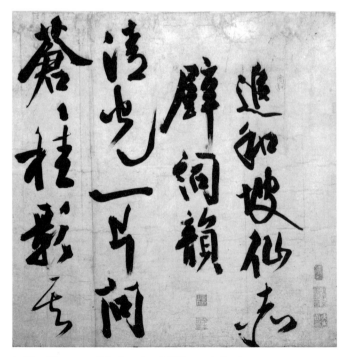

4. Chao Ping-wen. Colophon dated 1228 to painting by
Wu Yüan-chih, ''Red Cliff'' (*Ch'ih-pi fu*).
Detail from hand-scroll.

石御史

篯大德

三年七月

十七日書

伯幾書筆法少有古法之為可寶王煟跋

3. Hsien-yü Shu. ''Admonitions to the Imperial Censors'' (*Yü-shih-chen*),
dated 1299. Detail of last four lines of hand-scroll,
followed by Chao Meng-fu's colophon in one line.

千民樓塔

逡獨雨

廢丰通

雲宣黎

5. Yeh-lü Ch'u-ts'ai. Poem and inscription praising
Liu Man, dated 1240. Detail from hand-scroll.

6. Jen Hsün. "Old Cypress." Dated 1160, detail from rubbing; signature in cursive script, "Lung-yen."

7. Hsien-yü Shu. Transcription of poem by Han Yü, "Song of Stone Drums" (*Shih-ku ko*). Dated 1301; detail in cursive script from hand-scroll.

8. Hsien-yü Pi-jen. Colophon dated 1309 to his father's transcription of a poem by Tu Fu (scroll dated 1298).

for he went even so far as selling off his land and property in order to carry on his literary pursuits, searching for and buying books without any regard for costs. He built up a collection of more than 42,000 folios and more than 1,500 rubbings of stone inscriptions [dating] from the Three Dynasties down to the present day. These were stored in two halls, named Shu-chung 書種 and Chih-ya 志雅, respectively. Every day he spent his time collating texts, feeling as if he were a man of great wealth...." [13]

It is against this kind of geographical, historical and cultural setting that we can examine the impact of Mongol rule in the Wu-hsing area, particularly on the intellectuals and artists.

II. WU-HSING AND ITS ARTISTIC TRADITION IN THE SOUTHERN SUNG

Wu-hsing began to play a more important role as a cultural center during the Southern Sung period, when the capital was established at Lin-an 臨安 (Hangchow). After the fall of K'ai-feng in 1126, many people from the north settled in Hangchow and in the surrounding areas. Naturally, because of the characteristics mentioned above, Wu-hsing attracted many types of people. While Hangchow became a city of official activities, Wu-hsing, because of its beauty, good food, and culture, remained a place for relaxation. Poets, artists, and scholars were especially interested in its scenic beauty. Since the court was established in Hangchow, many members of the imperial clan took up residence in nearby areas, including Chia-ho, Ch'ien-t'ang, K'uai-chi, and Wu-hsing. Thus, the ancestors of the painter Chao Meng-chien 趙孟堅 became established in Hai-yen[14] and those of Chao Meng-fu 趙孟頫 in Wu-hsing,[15] during the twelfth century. Many officials loyal to the Northern Sung, such as the ancestors of Chou Mi, who were natives of the Tsinan area in Shantung,[16] moved south and resettled in this area during the same period. Although the original population of Wu-hsing consisted predominantly of members of five major clans,[17] the early Southern Sung immigration brought many additions.

[13] See Cheng Yüan-ch'ing 鄭元慶, *Wu-hsing ts'ang-shu lu* (Shanghai: Ku-tien Wen-hsüeh Ch'u-pan-she, 1957), pp. 10–11.

[14] See Hsü Shuo 徐碩, *Chih-yüan Chia-ho chih* 至元嘉禾志 (1288; rpt. *Ssu-k'u ch'üan-shu chen-pen*, 8th series), 13:23a, for a note on Chao Meng-chien. See also my contribution in SB, Painters, pp. 2–7.

[15] For a biography of Chao Meng-fu, see YS 172:4018–4023; and Li, *Autumn Colors*, pp. 81–84.

[16] For a biography of Chou Mi, see *Hsin Yüan shih* (Taipei, I-wen ed.), 237:4a; Li, *Autumn Colors*, pp. 17–23; and my contribution in SB, Vol. I, pp. 261–268.

[17] This is mentioned in WHC 16:4a.

During the Southern Sung period, Hangchow was the undisputed center of Chinese art, with the painting academy in the court as the dominant force. As a result of imperial patronage and its high academic standards, the court attracted many talented people from various parts of the country, and set the tone and style for nearly all of Southern Sung art.[18] Many other cities—such as Soochow, Nanking, Ningpo, K'uai-chi, all in the Chiang-nan area, and others in Kiangsi and Anhwei—became small satellite centers, each with traditions of its own. Among these, Wu-hsing, though not extensively recorded, is perhaps the most interesting.

In the books that have survived, only a few names can definitely be associated with Wu-hsing during the Southern Sung. One important example from the early period is Chiang Shen 江參, who seems to have held a unique position in his attempt to take as models two Five Dynasties painters, Chü-jan 巨然 and Tung Yüan 董源. The joint tradition of these two artists was characterized by wet brushwork, big dots, and hemp-fiber texture-strokes used to describe the moist lushness of the Chiang-nan landscape.[19] In the same period Chao Po-su 趙伯驌, a seventh-generation direct descendant of the first emperor of the Sung and a prefect of Hu-chou, was, together with his more famous brother Chao Po-chü 伯駒, known for blue-and-green landscapes based on T'ang models.[20] A third interesting Wu-hsing painter, the monk Fan-lung 梵隆, was noted for pai-miao 白描 (ink outline) figure paintings in the manner of the Northern Sung painter Li Kung-lin 李公麟 (ca.1040–1106).[21] Interestingly, these three very original artists were not at all connected with the Hangchow Academy. Indeed, their art is indicative of the great stylistic diversity which existed outside the academy in the early part of the Southern Sung.

Toward the end of the twelfth century, academic tastes completely dominated the court; attention was directed primarily at the rather sterile minutiae and naturalism of flower-and-bird painting and the more creative misty and romantic landscapes of the Ma-Hsia School. Even within this conventional and somewhat stagnant atmosphere, however,

---

[18] There are few studies of Southern Sung art in general. In the Chinese language, in addition to *chüan* four of THPC, there is only Li O 厲鶚, *Nan-Sung yüan hua lu* 南宋院畫錄 (rpt. Taipei: Shih-chieh Shu-chü, 1968), written in the eighteenth century. In Western languages, besides Siren's CP, there is also only James Cahill's *The Art of Southern Sung China* (N.Y.: Asia House, 1962).

[19] Chiang Shen is mentioned in THPC 4:71, and is the subject of an article by Fu Shen, "Notes on Chiang Shen," in the *National Palace Museum Bulletin*, 1:3 (July 1966).

[20] Chao Po-su is mentioned in THPC 4:69 and in the 1874 HCFC, 5:16a. For a biography see Ellen Laing's contribution in SB, Painters, pp. 8–15.

[21] Monk Fan-lung is mentioned in THPC 4:74.

which characterized the second phase of the Southern Sung, there was one painter who tended to be different. This was Yü Ch'eng 俞澂, a native of Wu-hsing who became active in the last quarter of the twelfth century. By exploring the bamboo and old rock themes originated by the Northern Sung literati Wen T'ung 文同 and Su Shih, Yü Ch'eng mounted a challenge to the established coventions of the Hangchow Academy.[22]

In the final phase of Southern Sung art—the period comprising the last fifty years before the fall of Hangchow—the situation took a new turn. Although the academy was still the dominant force, no important and creative figures emerged. As a result, various artistic directions and approaches outside the academy began to take shape. Monk painters such as Mu-ch'i 牧谿 and Jih-kuan 日觀 became quite active in developing their specialties. Among the creative painters of that period was Chao Meng-chien, who, as a renowned painter of ink narcissi, epidendrums, and plum blossoms, was an important figure in the literati tradition.[23] Although a native of Hai-yen, he served as an official in Wu-hsing in the middle of the thirteenth century. Another interesting painter of this era was Chao Meng-k'uei 趙孟奎, a cousin of Chao Meng-fu and a native of Wu-hsing, who was known for his bamboos, rocks, and orchids.[24]

The main factor distinguishing the Southern Sung artists connected with Wu-hsing from their contemporary counterparts in the imperial academy is that they seem to have taken some Northern Sung or earlier masters as their models. Further, rejecting the naturalism and romanticism of the academy, they embraced various aspects of literary theory, and thus tended to intellectualize their art. Taken individually, these cases might not appear to be significant. Viewed as a group, however, they seem to reflect a trend away from the prevailing court tastes and toward a more sophisticated approach to art. Thus, in spite of their geographical proximity, the intellectual atmospheres in Wu-hsing and Hangchow appear to have been quite different, radically so, in late Southern Sung times.

It has been generally—and correctly—assumed that the Southern

[22] Yü Ch'eng is mentioned in THPC 4:71. He lived in the period when the academy was dominated by some of the most famous painters of the Southern Sung, such as Liu Sung-nien 劉松年, Li Sung 李嵩, Hsia Kuei 夏珪 and Ma Yüan 馬遠.

[23] Chao Meng-chien is mentioned in THPC 4:69. Colophons on some of his more important scrolls are recorded in Pien Yung-yü 卞永譽, *Shih-ku-t'ang shu-hua hui-k'ao* 式古堂書畫彙考 (1682; Taipei: Cheng-chung Shu-chü, 1958), Vol. 15; and Wu Sheng 吳升, *Ta-kuan lu* 大觀錄 (1713; Taipei: National Central Library, 1970), vol. 15.

[24] Chao Meng-k'uei is mentioned in THPC 4:70.

Sung academy was so strong in its domination of art that other currents were blocked by it. From literary records and a few surviving original works, however, we can reconstruct a more accurate picture of that period. Doubtless the academy was in a position to dictate the predominant tastes of the period. But at the same time, many other currents seem to have flourished outside Hangchow. The various painters of Wu-hsing mentioned above, whose works differed significantly from those of artists at the court, are typical of these currents. Beyond those already mentioned, painters of ink bamboos, ink plum blossoms, and various other subjects were recorded in Hai-yen, Lin-hai, and Ch'u-chou, all in Chekiang. Other artists were active in Kiangsi and Anhwei.[25] When the imperial academy was obliterated after the fall of Hangchow to the Mongols in 1276, these other trends began to grow stronger, reflecting a feeling of dissatisfaction with the academic control of the Southern Sung period and an interest in moving in other directions. In these new developments, Wu-hsing seems to have played a leading role.

III. Wu-hsing in the Early Yüan

After capturing Hsiang-yang and Fan-ch'eng in Hupei, the Mongols decided to mount a major offensive against Chiang-nan in order to take Hangchow. In 1274, General Bayan's army moved fast along the southern bank of the Yangtze River to capture Chien-k'ang (Nanking). From this important base, Bayan separated his army into three forces and proceeded toward Hangchow. While the left flank took to the sea and landed in Hai-yen and the central force captured Ch'ang-chou and P'ing-chiang (Soochow), the right flank followed the west shore of Lake T'ai and turned directly toward the capital. Wu-hsing was located between the central and right flanks of Bayan's attack. At Tu-sung-kuan 獨松關 (Lone Pine Pass), on the western approach to this prefecture, a big battle was fought between the Sung garrisons and Bayan's right-flank force during the eleventh month of 1275. In spite of the natural advantage which this mountain pass gave the Sung forces, the Mongols overran the defenders and moved quickly toward Wu-hsing.[26] In the city the prefect Chao Liang-ch'un 趙良淳 tried to lead a resistance in spite of a famine. When efforts proved fruitless, however, he and his wife became martyrs for the Sung cause by hanging themselves.[27]

---

[25] See *chüan* 4 of THPC for many references to the geographical background of Southern Sung artists.

[26] For this aspect of its history, see 1475 HCFC 1:3a; and Chang Wen-tien 張文甸, "Tu-sung-kuan tsai Nan-sung chih shih-chi 獨松關在南宋之史蹟," *Yüeh-feng* 越風, 15 (1936), pp. 4–6.

[27] See 1573 HCFC 9:9a.

In the first month of 1276, when the fall of Hangchow was imminent, Bayan moved his headquarters from Chien-k'ang to Wu-hsing to conduct negotiations with the Sung court. Finally, in the second month they entered Hangchow, taking the young emperor and the two empress dowagers as hostages.[28] When the captives were sent north to Ta-tu 大都 (Peking), they passed through Wu-hsing, accompanied by a few court officials.[29]

That Wu-hsing suffered a considerable amount of damage as a result of this turmoil is evidenced by the experience of Chou Mi, whose family home was burned down in 1276. Having lost everything including, certainly, the collection of books and rubbings mentioned above, he was forced to move to Hangchow, where he lived for the rest of his life.[30] Many of the great libraries mentioned by him must have suffered a fate similar to that of Chou's. It is not difficult to imagine other immediate damage that might have been inflicted on the cultural life of the city.

After the Mongol conquest, Hu-chou became a new administrative unit termed a lu 路 (circuit). The imperial agent's office of darughachi was located in Wu-hsing, and it oversaw the six districts under it. Thereafter the area was governed by officials from the north, sometimes Mongols, sometimes other non-Han people, and sometimes northern Chinese, in accordance with the Mongol policy of discriminating against the southern Chinese.[31] It is interesting to note that, according to a fiscal survey taken in 1290, the circuit comprised 236,577 households, while the district of Wu-ch'eng, where the circuit government was located, had a total of 68,437 households, including 68,341 households of southerners and 96 households of northerners.[32] Throughout the Yüan Dynasty, all but one of the twenty recorded darughachi were either Mongols or other foreigners.[33]

The ravages of war and the change in administration did not destroy the culture of Wu-hsing entirely. In fact, in some ways these events may have served to strengthen the native Han Chinese scholars' interest in their own cultural tradition. As a result of the collapse of the Sung, many

[28] See the biography of Bayan in HYS 159:7–9. For poems written by one of the accompanying officials when they reached Hu-chou, see Wang Yüan-liang's 汪元量 poems in Sung shih i-pai shou 宋詩一百首 (Shanghai: Chung-hua Shu-chü, 1959 [3rd printing, 1965], pp. 116–117.

[30] See Hsia Ch'eng-t'ao 夏承燾, T'ang Sung tz'u-jen nien-p'u 唐宋詞人年譜 (Shanghai, 1961), p. 348.

[31] See Meng Ssu-ming 蒙思明, Yüan-tai she-hui chieh-chi chih-tu 元代社會階級制度 (Peiping, 1938).

[32] See 1475 HCFC 8:9a, on population.

[33] See 1874 HCFC 5:11b–14a. It is possible that some of the nineteen were se-mu-jen 色目人 rather than Mongols and that the only Chinese name on that list may have been a northerner.

of the area's native intellectuals were forced to return there after the termination of their official careers. This was how, in fact, Ch'ien Hsüan 錢選 and Chao Meng-fu came to return to Wu-hsing to live a life of retirement, bringing to the region ideas they had gathered from other parts of South China. Many other late Sung men of culture chose to live there.[34]

It is well known that during this period, shortly after the fall of the Sung, a group of scholars and poets there came to be known as "The Eight Talents of Wu-hsing." Among this distinguished group were the painters Ch'ien Hsüan and Chao Meng-fu.[35] All of them may have been pupils of the Wu-hsing scholar Ao Chi-kung 敖繼公.[36] Ao was by all indications the most famous Confucian scholar in Wu-hsing at the end of the thirteenth century, attracting pupils not only from the immediate locale but also from throughout China. Ch'ien Hsüan is mentioned in a colophon as having studied with Ao,[37] and Chao Meng-fu himself mentioned that Ao was his teacher in a letter to Wu Ch'eng 吳澄 (1249–1333), the great Confucian scholar of early Yüan discussed in the essays by Lao and Gedalecia in this volume.[38] Although records concerning the others are scanty, it is quite possible that they all were Ao's pupils. Elsewhere it is noted that while Ao was a native of Ch'ang-lo 長樂 in Fukien, he lived a simple life in Wu-hsing. Although in Sung times he had passed the *chin-shih* examination, Ao did not choose to serve as an official, but instead devoted his time to the study of the classics. It was said that during the middle of the reign of Ch'eng-tsung 成宗 (1297–1307), Ao was recommended for an appointment as instructor in Hsin-chou 信州 in Kiangsi. He died, however, before he could assume this position.[39]

---

[34] The poets Hsiao Te-tsao, Wen Ch'i-weng, and Mou Tzu-ts'ai, for example, are mentioned in WHCKC 3:5, 3:6a–b, and 3:10b. The scholar Yü-wen Kung-liang 宇文公諒, who moved to Wu-hsing at this time, has a biography in T'an Cheng-pi 譚正璧, ed., *Chung-kuo wen-hsüeh-chia ta-tz'u-tien* 中國文學家大辭典 (Taipei, 1967), p. 3052.

[35] The first mention of the "Eight Talents" (*pa-chün* 八俊) was made by Chang Yü 張羽 (1333–1385), in his *Ching-chü chi* 靜居集 (SPTK ed.), 3:8a. In Western languages, a discussion of this group can be found in James Cahill, "Ch'ien Hsüan and His Figure Paintings," *Archives of the Chinese Art Society of America*, 12 (1958), p. 13.

[36] Short biographies of Ao can be found in 1542 HCFC 4:3b, WHCKC 3:11b, and 1874 HCFC 90:23.

[37] This colophon by Huang Kung-wang 黃公望 (1269–1354) can be found in the photograph of the *Floating Jade Mountain Dwelling* scroll of the Shanghai Museum available through the Freer Gallery of Art. It is also recorded in Pien Yung-yü, *Shih-ku-t'ang shu-hua hui-k'ao*, 17:2a–b.

[38] See *Sung-hsüeh chai wen-chi* 松雪齋文集 (SPTK ed.), 6:6b.

[39] *Sung Yüan hsüeh-an* 宋元學案 (Taipei: Shih-chieh Shu-chü, 1961), 52:964.

The importance of Wu-hsing as a center of Confucian learning continued through the early Yüan, until at least the time of Ao Chi-kung. The Hu-chou Prefectural Gazetteer of 1542 notes that "most of the famous literati of Hu-chou were his pupils" and that he had compiled a collection of his own literary works in twenty folios.[40] Later in the *Wu-hsing chang-ku chi* (*Historical Records of Wu-hsing*), printed in 1615, it is said that "numerous famous literati of Wu studied under him."[41] This is an indication of his great influence. Unfortunately, at present only one of Ao's works, an annotation of the *I-li*, a Confucian book on the rites datable to the Han Dynasty, remains, so we have no way of judging the breadth of his scholarship.[42] Moreover, it seems that most of his pupils' works shared the fate of his own. Among the writings of those who definitely studied under him, only Chao Meng-fu's collected works are still extant.[43] None of the literary works by the other "Eight Talents" have survived, although their titles are still known.[44] As a result, we know very little about their Confucian learning or their literary activities. Yet the material cited above nevertheless indicates the importance of Wu-hsing as a center of Confucian studies during the early Yüan.

Perhaps the best indication of Wu-hsing's political importance in the early Yüan is its apparent role as a source of talent for the governmental posts of the new dynasty. Ch'eng Chü-fu 程鉅夫 (1249–1318), one of the first southerners to earn the trust of Khubilai Khaghan (r. 1260–1294), entered into service under the Mongol emperor in 1276. In 1286, under special instructions from Khubilai, he travelled to Chiang-nan to enlist the support of the leading literati and he invited more than twenty scholars to go to Ta-tu for official appointments.[45] While most of those invited were from Hangchow, it is clear from various sources that he attempted to enlist a number of men from Wu-hsing as well. Chao Meng-fu, one of the "Eight Talents of Wu-hsing," was perhaps the most important member of Ch'eng's first contingent of recruits. Unfortunately, of the nine others whose names are still known, only a few can be identified in terms of geographical origin. Among these, Chang Po-ch'un 張伯淳, from Chia-hsing, which adjoined Wu-hsing, was Chao Meng-

[40] 1542 HCFC 4:3b.

[41] WHCKC 3:11b.

[42] See 1874 HCFC 57:40a–b.

[43] Many editions of this work are available. The one in the SPTK is a facsimile of a Yüan edition.

[44] See 1874 HCFC 57:36b–37a.

[45] Ch'eng's biographies are found in YS 172:4015–4018 and HYS 189:1a.

fu's brother-in-law.[46] Others from Wu-hsing who were invited, some of whom declined, included:

Wen Chi-weng 文及翁, a *chin-shih* of the late Sung, who lived in Wu-hsing and, though approached many times, declined to serve the Yüan government.[47]

Chang Te-mao 張德茂, who also declined the invitation of Ch'eng Chü-fu.[48]

P'ang P'u 龐樸, who at first declined Ch'eng's offer, but later accepted a position. He became a compiler of the histories of Sung, Liao and Chin within the Hanlin Academy.[49]

Mou Ying-lung 牟應龍 (1247–1324), another of the "Eight Talents," was probably not among the first to be asked, but was eventually offered a post and served as a teacher in Li-yang 溧陽 (Kiangsu).[50]

It is impossible to determine exactly how many Wu-hsing scholars were recruited by Ch'eng Chü-fu, for he made several trips to complete his mission, and the records are incomplete.[51] That he must have had contact with many scholars in Wu-hsing is evidenced in a statement concerning the life of Ch'ien Hsüan:

"In Wu-hsing in the early Yüan there were the so-called 'Eight Talents,' with Tzu-ang [Chao Meng-fu] as their head, and Shun-chü [Ch'ien Hsüan] as one of them. During the Chih-yüan reign (1264–95), when Tzu-ang entered the imperial court through recommendation, all the others made use of his connections to secure official positions. Only

---

[46] The other nine known southerners invited by Ch'eng are all mentioned in the biographies of Ch'eng referred to in n. 45. See the papers by Lao and Gedalecia in this volume on this subject. Chang (1242–1302) had his first appointment as instructor of Confucian studies in Hangchow circuit. Later he was in the court in Ta-tu as a member of the revitalized Hanlin Academy.

[47] This is mentioned in his short biography in WHCKC 3:6b.

[48] His biography is in 1573 HCFC 8:4b.

[49] His biography is in 1874 HCFC 90:22a.

[50] His biography is in YS 190:4337–4338, and HYS 234:8a.

[51] In addition to the short list mentioned in the biographies of Ch'eng Chü-fu cited in n. 45 above, much of the information concerning southerners invited to serve in the Yüan government can only be found in individual biographies. A number of articles have been written about this subject: Chou Tsu-mo 周祖謨, "Sung wang hou shih Yüan chih ju-hsüeh chiao-shou 宋亡後仕元之儒學教授," *Fu-jen hsüeh-chih* 輔仁學誌, 14:1–2 (1946), pp. 191–214; Yao Ts'ung-wu 姚從吾, "Hu-pi-lieh tui-yü Han-hua t'ai-tu ti fen-hsi 忽必列對於漢化態度的分析," *Ta-lu tsa-chih* 大陸雜誌, 11:1 (1955), pp. 22–32; Yao Ts'ung-wu, "Ch'eng Chü-fu yü Hu-pi-lieh p'ing Sung i-hou ti an-ting nan-jen wen-t'i 程鉅夫與忽必列平宋以後的安定南人問題," *Wen-shih-che hsüeh-pao* 文史哲學報, 17 (1968), pp. 353–379; and Sun K'o-k'uan 孫克寬, *Yüan-tai Han wen-hua chih huo-tung* 元代漢文化之活動 (Taipei, 1968), pp. 345–363.

Shun-chü showed disagreement and spent his time in poetry and painting to the end of his life...." [52]

Of the "Eight Talents," seven assumed Yüan appointments by one means or another, and this fact, when combined with our knowledge of Ch'eng's recruiting policies, indicates that Wu-hsing served as a kind of talent pool in the early Yüan.

It is easy to see the effect of Wu-hsing's cultural role in early Yüan times. While in the Southern Sung it had been an important prefecture because of its proximity to the capital, although the capital was in distant Ta-tu, Wu-hsing continued to play an important role because of its new ties with the Yüan court. As the most outstanding figure among the southern scholars who took up positions in Ta-tu, Chao Meng-fu created possibilities for southern intellectuals. While he and many others spent years in the north, their experiences there broadened them, opening up new horizons, and when they returned to the south they were able to draw on these experiences. At the same time many northerners—among them Kao K'o-kung 高克恭 (1248–1310), Li K'an 李衎 (1245–1320), and Hsien-yü Shu 鮮于樞 (1257–1302)—came to the south. The resultant interaction between north and south created a vital cultural, intellectual, and artistic atmosphere, as Marilyn Fu's study of Hsien-yü Shu in this volume has shown. A new era also began in Wu-hsing.

IV. WU-HSING AS THE LEADING ARTISTIC CENTER IN EARLY YÜAN

As we have seen, the Southern Sung Academy, which had been dominated by a series of strong personalities and creative minds from its inception in 1127, was without an innovative leader in the last decades of the dynasty. The most creative period in the history of the academy ended with Ma Yüan 馬遠 and Hsia Kuei 夏珪. Although we have no precise dates for these artists, they seem to have been most active in the first quarter of the thirteenth century. By the middle of the century there were no longer any great leaders or innovative talents among the artists active at court. When the Mongols vanquished the Southern Sung in 1276, they established their capital in the north, and Hangchow lost its political influence. While the latter remained, for a period, an important cultural and artistic center, a number of other centers emerged and began to challenge its dominance. Among them the most important was Wu-hsing, where the circumstances of existing artistic talent and intellectual

---

[52] See Chang Yü, Ch'ing-chü chi, 3:8a–b. This statement is quoted by many gazetteers as well as by Cahill in his article cited in n. 35 above.

fervor created an environment favorable for the development of new possibilities.

The leading painters in Wu-hsing at the beginning of the Yüan were Ch'ien Hsüan and Chao Meng-fu, who, although separated in age by nearly a generation, were close friends. At that time, Ch'ien was probably in his early forties, while Chao was only in his early twenties.[53]

Perhaps what made Wu-hsing most interesting was the combination of Ch'ien Hsüan and Chao Meng-fu. Ch'ien Hsüan's status as an *i-min* 遺民 (lit., "leftover subject") or Sung loyalist earned for him the respect of many intellectuals of that time who, having grown up and served under the Southern Sung, had no opportunity or desire to serve the foreign dynasty. Ch'ien thus became a symbol of their loyalty to the Sung and of their frustration under the new regime. Chao Meng-fu, on the other hand, having become the leading southerner among Yüan officials, was admired by those who aspired to serve in the Yüan government. Thus between them, there was something for all Yüan intellectuals to look to for inspiration and guidance. Interestingly, in spite of their differences in politics, the two men seem to have remained good friends until the end of their lives and to have shared similar artistic and cultural ideals. They were together in Wu-hsing during the decade from 1276 to 1286. Afterwards, Ch'ien remained in Wu-hsing and Chao travelled to Ta-tu and to other places; but they must have exchanged ideas occasionally and both certainly continued to develop their artistic theories.[54]

Together with the remaining "Eight Talents," both Ch'ien and Chao seem to have crystallized a number of ideas that were already current at that time. Although both had served under the Sung, they do not seem to have been entirely satisfied with the state of the fine arts of that period.

Indeed, a general feeling of dissatisfaction with the Southern Sung became quite apparent in the early Yüan period. Although not all of this discontent originated in Wu-hsing, some of the people from that area seem to have been behind it. In one of the most important books of art criticism written during that period, T'ang Hou's 湯垕 *Hua-lun* 畫論, this attitude is reflected most explicitly.[55]

Although T'ang Hou did not live in Wu-hsing, he was frequently in contact with Chao. He regarded Chao as one of the two most important

---

[53] For the biographical materials on Ch'ien Hsüan, see Cahill's article mentioned in n. 35 above. For those on Chao Meng-fu, see n. 15 above.

[54] Although there are indications of disagreements in their views of serving under the Mongols, these do not seem to have affected their friendship.

[55] See HL, p. 52.

painters that China had produced since the beginning of the Southern Sung. Hence, his views must have been strongly influenced by those of Chao.[56] Hsia Wen-yen 夏文彥, a native of Wu-hsing who later settled in Yün-chien 雲間 (modern Sung-chiang, Kiangsu), expressed similar opinions in his *T'u-hui pao-chien* 圖繪寶鑑 (*Precious Mirror of Painting*).[57]

Feelings of dissatisfaction with the Southern Sung were directed not solely toward painting but also toward literature. In a preface to a book of poetry by the Wu-hsing native Wang Fang-shu 王方叔, Chao Meng-fu wrote:

"During the last years of the Sung, literary style was very bad. Scholars of the classics did not consider it wrong to depart from the principles of the classics and devoted instead their efforts to establishing their own strange and sensational theories. Composers of prose-poems (*fu* 賦) did not consider it incorrect to employ minutiae and trivia [in their writings], and considered weaving together the novel and the clever as their achievement."[58]

Similar views also found expression in the writings of a number of people who, though not residents of Wu-hsing, were either Chao Meng-fu's friends or relatives. In the biography of Tai Piao-yüan 戴表元, a good friend of Chao's, the *Yüan shih* 元史 (*Standard History of the Yuan*) makes the following statement:

"Originally he had lamented the fact that toward the end of the Sung the *ch'i* 氣 [vital force] of literature had withered and its style had grown twisted. When the distortion became intense he gallantly took as his own responsibility the task of revitalizing the culture (*ssu-wen* 斯文)."[59]

In the biography of Yang Tsai 楊載, one of the best-known poets of the early Yüan and a close friend of Chao Meng-fu, it is also stated: "He once told his students: 'In poetry one should draw his materials from the Han and Wei Dynasties, and his sounds and rhythms from the T'ang.' After the appearance of his poetry, the weaknesses of the late Sung were all swept away."[60] A late Yüan statement concerning Ch'ien Hsüan's calligraphy by T'ao Tsung-i 陶宗儀, a distant relative of Chao Meng-fu, reflects a similar attitude: "Ch'ien Hsüan's ... small *k'ai* 楷 (formal) calligraphy has method (*fa* 法), but he was never able to shed the decadent and stagnant style of the late Sung (*Sung chi shuai-chien chih*

---

[56] This point is discussed in Li, *Autumn Colors*, pp. 70–80.

[57] The THPC, with preface dated 1365, is a standard source for Yüan painting.

[58] See Chao's "Ti-i shan-jen wen-chi hsü 第一山人文集敍," in *Sung-hsüeh chai wen-chi*, 6:11a. Cf. the translation in my "The Uses of the Past," p. 80.

[59] YS 190:4336.

[60] YS 190:4341.

ch'i 宋季衰寒之氣).''[61] These statements all express a general dissatisfaction with literary culture at the end of the Southern Sung and seem to represent attitudes that were particularly prevalent in Wu-hsing.

Whether or not this feeling against the Southern Sung extended to political matters is not an easy question to answer. There is no doubt that many early Yüan scholars were unhappy with the state of affairs that had prevailed toward the end of the Southern Sung. Chao Meng-fu's acceptance of Khubilai Khaghan's invitation to serve, for example, in spite of his own family tie with the Sung imperial clan, would seem to suggest that he lacked a strong attachment to the Southern Sung. Even though he revealed certain misgivings about his career under the Yüan, he did not seem to be entirely unhappy about his actions.[62]

What distinguished Wu-hsing as the leading artistic center in early Yüan times was the direction it took and the theories it formed, for these became the basic framework for Yüan painting in general. Since this has been dealt with in detail elsewhere, only a brief summary needs to be repeated here.[63] Criticizing Southern Sung painting as superficial and vulgar, both Ch'ien Hsüan and Chao Meng-fu went back to earlier Chinese painting to establish the idea of "antique spirit" (*ku-i* 古意) as one of the most important elements in art.[64] This interest in the distant past brought them to a new understanding of the achievements of past masters. Artists thus went back, for sources of new inspiration, not only to the Northern Sung, but also to the Five Dynasties, the T'ang, and the Six Dynasties. This breadth of interest greatly expanded the artistic horizon of the early Yüan, bringing about a release of creative energy. Moreover, a new attempt to emphasize the close relationship between painting and calligraphy led to experiments in brushwork that made it possible to achieve new forms of expression. All of these became the foundation stones of Yüan painting style.

One of the outstanding characteristics of the Wu-hsing artists in the

---

[61] See his short biography in T'ao's *Shu-shih hui-yao* 書史會要 , quoted in Chang Ch'ou 張丑, *Ch'ing-ho shu-hua fang* 清河書畫舫 (1876 ed.), *ts'e* 6, p. 71b.

[62] This has been discussed by Frederick Mote, "Confucian Eremitism in the Yüan Period," in *The Confucian Persuasion*, ed. by Arthur Wright (Stanford: Stanford University Press, 1960), pp. 202–240; Li, *Autumn Colors*, pp. 81–84; and Chu-tsing Li, "The Freer Sheep and Goat and Chao Meng-fu's Horse Paintings," *Artibus Asiae*, 30 (1968), pp. 311–322.

[63] See this author's two works on Chao Meng-fu cited in the last note, and also "The Uses of the Past in Yüan Landscape Painting," in *Artists and Traditions: The Uses of the Past in Chinese Culture*, ed. by Christian Murck.

[64] This is discussed in Li, *Autumn Colors*, pp. 70–80; in the article in *Artists and Traditions* cited in n. 1; and in Susan Bush, *The Chinese Literati on Painting* (Cambridge, 1971), chapter 4.

early Yüan was the range and breadth of their art. All through the Southern Sung, painters, restricted by the conventions of the academy, had been more or less individually confined to one or two specialties, such as birds-and-flowers, figures, or landscapes. But the Yüan painters Ch'ien Hsüan and Chao Meng-fu were interested in studying a wide range of genres and in painting all kinds of subjects. According to the *T'u-hui pao-chien*, Ch'ien was noted for "figures, landscapes, flowers and plants, feathers (birds) ... and blue and green landscapes."[65] Chao, in the words of T'ao Tsung-i, excelled in "horses, landscapes, figures, flowers and bamboos, and birds."[66] This is definitely one aspect of the experimental spirit of the Wu-hsing artists. In addition to Ch'ien and Chao, some of the latter's descendants, such as Chao Yung 趙雍 and Chao Lin 趙麟, were also noted for this breadth of interest.[67]

There is no doubt that one important factor which promoted this artistic breadth in Wu-hsing during the early Yüan was the strong impact of Mongol rule. Although some Chinese intellectuals at that time were interested in continuing Southern Sung culture as an expression of their loyalty, this was not true of Wu-hsing. The artists there instead launched a retrospective search of the antique past for models that could serve to revitalize the commitment to the Chinese tradition. This approach was best represented by Ch'ien Hsüan. Although his art had first come out of the Southern Sung bird-and-flower tradition connected with the academy, he gradually moved away from the pure naturalism of that tradition to various types of archaic styles. At the same time, Chao Meng-fu's trip to Ta-tu in 1287 opened up new contacts and artistic possibilities. In some respects, both men found a way to liberate themselves from the restrictions of the academic tastes of Hangchow and to cope creatively with Mongol rule.

One direct result of Chao Meng-fu's presence in Ta-tu was probably the new interest in horse painting.[68] Paintings of horses had been popular during the T'ang period, when tribute bearers brought the emperors handsome steeds from Central Asia. As court painters, leading artists such as Han Kan 韓幹 had had to paint "portraits" of these horses. In the Sung period, however, when the Central Asian connection was broken, there was no longer any demand for this kind of painting. The only exception was Li Kung-lin, who turned horse painting into a different kind of expression. But in the Yüan period, with the Mongol

---

[65] See THPC 5:97.

[66] See T'ao Tsung-i, *Cho-keng lu* 輟耕錄 (rpt. Taipei: Shih-chieh Shu-chü, 1963), p. 105.

[67] See THPC 5:96–97.

[68] See Li, "The Freer *Sheep and Goat* and Chao Meng-fu's Horse Paintings," *Artibus Asiae*, 30 (1968).

interest in horses, horse painting was once again in demand, especially in the court. Although the Yüan does not seem to have had an academy in Ta-tu, a number of painters there performed official works. One example is Liu Kuan-tao 劉貫道, who depicted Khubilai Khaghan hunting.[69] Liu and others like him were official or semi-official painters in Ta-tu. Some of the painters from the south, such as Jen Jen-fa 任仁發 and Wang Yüan 王淵, can be considered in the same category.[70] Even though there was no formal academy, the artistic interests of the few Mongol patrons seem to have been similar to those who had served in the Hangchow Sung government: bird-and-flowers, figures, and other more decorative types, including horses.

Ultimately, the greatest manifestation of the artistic response to Mongol rule can be found in the inward quality of Yüan painting. This is especially true for the works of Ch'ien Hsüan and Chao Meng-fu and their close associates. The period right after 1276 was one of introspection forced upon these artists by the sudden political changes and by the establishment of Mongol rule. It was during this period that they had the time to reflect and to develop their own ideas. With the power of the academy broken, a new sense of freedom was felt. Some of the elements that had lain dormant during the Southern Sung began to surface. One of these was the literati tradition, which seems to have been retained in Wu-hsing as well as in some other areas around Hangchow. Another was the custom of literary gatherings, resulting in part from the increased amount of free time enjoyed by the intellectuals. A third was an intense interest in the classical tradition of Chinese culture, which led to a review of the traditional values that were then facing the challenge of Mongol domination. Out of this era of soul searching came the new elements in the art of the Yüan Dynasty.

V. WU-HSING AND THE BLUE-AND-GREEN LANDSCAPE

Perhaps the best measurement of the Chinese response to Mongol rule in the realm of painting lies not in the subject matters that may have appealed to the Mongols, but in the changes in style, iconography, and theory in the first several decades of Yüan rule. It is easy to regard the new interest in horse paintings, narrative scrolls, official portraits, and decorative bird-and-flower works as in part the product of an effort to

[69] See *Select Chinese Painting in the National Palace Museum* (Taipei, 1966), Vol. 5, Nos. 17 (Liu Kuan-tao), 15 (Chao Yung) and 16 (Chao Lin).

[70] Jen Jen-fa is the subject of a dissertation now in progress by Marc Wilson; and of an article, "Three Horses and Four Grooms," by Sherman E. Lee and Wai-kam Ho, in the *Cleveland Museum of Art Bulletin*, 47 (April 1961), pp. 66–71.

please the new rulers. However, in a more subtle way, the artistic response can best be seen in three types of landscape painting which were revitalized by the painters in Wu-hsing. These were the landscapes in the blue-and-green manner, those in the Tung Yüan manner, and those in the Li Ch'eng 李成 and Kuo Hsi 郭熙 manner.

Blue-and-green landscape had a long history in China, although apparently the term *ch'ing-lü shan-shui* 青綠山水, as a designation for this genre of painting, did not come into general use until the Yüan period. The use of colors by early Chinese painters was quite common, and this was especially true for blues and greens in mountains and rocks. Many examples can be found in the wall paintings of the Tun-huang Caves dating from T'ang times.[71] But the term *ch'ing-lü shan-shui* does not appear in early painting texts. The early survey of painting history entitled *Li-tai ming-hua chi* 歷代名畫記, by Chang Yen-yüan 張彥遠 (fl. ca. 845), makes no mention of the term. But it does note that "in ancient paintings [the artists] did not use *t'ou-lü* 頭綠 (crude green) and *ta-ch'ing* 大青 (crude blue)."[72] Similarly, the Northern Sung scholar Kuo Jo-hsü 郭若虛 (fl. ca.1070), in his catalogue of paintings entitled *T'u-hua chien-wen chih* 圖畫見聞志, makes no use of this term. Yet he uses an analogous term, *cho-se shan-shui* 著色山水, or "colored landscape," in reference to works by Tung Yüan and others.[73] "Colored landscape" is also used in the *Hsüan-ho hua-p'u* 宣和畫譜, the famous catalogue of paintings compiled in the Hsüan-ho era (1119–1125). In this work the T'ang artist Li Ssu-hsün 李思訓 (early eighth century) is credited with originating this style: "The colored landscapes by contemporaries are often based on his [i.e., Li Ssu-hsün's], but they seldom attain his excellence."[74] The catalogue also links Tung Yüan with Li by noting:

"But painters only praised his [i.e. Tung Yüan's] colored landscapes, saying that the scenes and objects are gorgeous and sumptuous, in the manner of Li Ssu-hsün. Now, studying the paintings of Tung Yüan, I have come to realize this point. For there were not many colored landscapes in that period, and few were able to imitate Ssu-hsün's. Thus he was especially noted for this."[75]

---

[71] For some of the landscape paintings in the Tun-huang Caves, see Basil Gray, *Buddhist Cave Paintings at Tun-huang* (London, 1959), and Anil de Silva, *The Art of Chinese Landscape Painting* (New York, 1964). See also some of the recently discovered T'ang wall-paintings in tombs, such as *T'ang Li Ch'ung-jun mu pi-hua* 唐李重潤墓壁畫 and *T'ang Li Hsien mu pi-hua* 唐李賢墓壁畫 (both Peking: Wen-wu Ch'u-pan-she, 1974).

[72] Chang Yen-yüan, *Li-tai ming-hua chi* (*Hsüeh-chin t'ao-yüan* 學津討原 ed.), 2:7a.

[73] Kuo Jo-hsü, *T'u-hua chien-wen chih* (*Hsüeh-chin t'ao-yüan* ed.), 10:2b.

[74] *Hsüan-ho hua-p'u*, 10:3a.

[75] *Hsüan-ho hua-p'u*, 11:1b.

These discussions in the *Hsüan-ho hua-p'u* are important because they link together the northern and southern schools of landscape painting, schools which in later times, especially during the late Ming, were incorrectly viewed as representatives of opposing artistic trends. In late Sung times, and, as we shall see below, in early Yüan times, these schools were seen as closely connected. The tradition of colored landscape bound them together.

It was in the Southern Sung and early Yüan that the term *ch'ing-lü shan-shui* came to be used as a designation for the kind of colored landscape that today is associated with the term. Interestingly, the earliest documented usage occurs in reference to landscapes painted on Korean fans. In the *Hua-chi* 畫繼 (preface dated 1167), by the Sung scholar Teng Ch'un 鄧椿, we read: "The blue and green that they put [on the fans] is very unusual, different from that used in China. They used copper-blue (*k'ung-ch'ing* 空青) and sea-green (*hai-lü* 海綠) to do them." [76]

The term "blue-green" should be examined in the context of similar terms which were in common use in Sung times. Perhaps the most important of these was the term *chin-pi* 金碧 or "gold and jade-blue." This term was introduced in the *Hsüan-ho hua-p'u* in reference to some Japanese paintings. [77] Later on, the Sung scholar Chao Hsi-ku 趙希鵠, in his *Tung-t'ien ch'ing-lu chi* 洞天清祿集 (ca.1190), used the term to designate colored landscapes. His words are important:

"The gold and jade-blue landscape was started by the lesser General Li [Chao-tao 李昭道, a son of Li Ssu-hsün] of the T'ang, and was later continued by Wang Chin-ch'ing [i.e. Wang Shen 王詵], Chao Ta-nien 趙大年, and recently by Chao Ch'ien-li [i.e. Chao Po-chü]. In general, there was at the beginning no separation between gold and jade-blue landscapes and ink landscapes, for what mattered was how they were conceived and composed. If more gold and jade-blue are used, as such colors are used nowadays in painting, without capturing the consonance of expression, what is the virtue in that? Although different from ink [landscapes], they will be subject to the same weaknesses as those." [78]

In this passage the expression "gold and jade-blue" is used in reference to colored landscapes, just as the term *cho-se shan-shui* was used earlier. In the Southern Sung texts, the two terms are used interchangeably. The aforementioned Teng Ch'un uses the term to describe the works of Wang Shen: "His landscape paintings followed those of Li Ch'eng, with the

[76] *Hua-chi* (Peking, 1963), 10:126.
[77] *Hsüan-ho hua-p'u*, 12:13a.
[78] *Tung-t'ien ch'ing-lu chi* (*Mei-shu ts'ung-shu* 美術叢書 ed.), 28b.

texture method (*ts'un* 皴) in gold-blue that appears to have an antique feeling." [79]

It was only in Yüan times, however, that the term *ch'ing-lü* came to be generally used in a way that was interchangeable with *cho-se* and *chin-pi*. The earliest passage we have is in the *Hua-chi pu-i* 畫繼補遺 (preface dated 1298), a supplement to *Hua-chi* by Chuang Su 莊肅. In this work Chuang noted that Chao Po-chü, who accompanied the Sung emperor to the south when the court retreated in 1127, was "skillful in blue-and-green landscapes." [80] Later, in T'ang Hou's important *Hua-chien* (ca.1330), the works of Chao Po-chü are placed in the tradition of "colored landscapes" and "gold and jade-blue" paintings which began with Li Ssu-hsün: "In Li Ssu-hsün's colored landscapes, there are brilliant contrasts between the gold and jade-blue, forming the method of a school of its own. ... A member of the Sung imperial clan, Chao Po-chü, whose cognomen was Ch'ien-li, later imitated him. His works are very attractive, but without the spirit of antiquity." [81]

Still later, Hsia Wen-yen, in his *T'u-hui pao-chien* (preface dated 1365), used the same wording in a discussion of Li Ssu-hsün's legacy: "Li Ssu-hsün ... used the brilliant contrasts between the gold and jade-blue, forming the method of a school of his own. Most of the colored landscapes done by later painters followed him." [82] Although the biography of Chao Po-chü in this work does not touch on this point, it is raised in the biography of Ch'ien Hsüan: "His blue-and-green landscapes followed those of Chao Ch'ien-li [i.e. Chao Po-chü]." [83] From that time on the term "blue-and-green" was in general use.

Having outlined the development of blue-and-green landscape paintings by reference to the technical terms used to describe them, we can now draw a number of conclusions. First, since in the pre-T'ang and T'ang landscapes colors were generally used, there was no need to refer to them with a special term. Then, in the Sung period, when a distinction was made between those done in colors and those done mainly in ink, the more specific term "colored landscape" came to be used. In the Yüan period, when the opposition between ink landscape and the decorative colored landscape began to emerge in art criticism, the term "gold and jade-blue" became identified with the painting tradition that had come down from Li Ssu-hsün. Chao Po-chü was then linked to Li in

[79] *Hua-chi*, 2:14.

[80] This book, published in Peking in 1963 with *Hua-chi*, was written in 1298, according to Chuang's preface. The quotation comes from 1:3.

[81] *Hua-chien*, 9.

[82] See THPC 2:14.

[83] See THPC 5:97.

this context. This is probably where Ch'ien Hsüan derived his ideas of "blue-and-green" landscape.

There seems to be no question but that Ch'ien Hsüan and Chao Meng-fu got some of their models of blue-and-green landscape directly from the Southern Sung, since the blue-and-green tradition never died out in the Sung period. According to the *T'u-hui pao-chien* of 1365, throughout the Southern Sung the "blue-and-green" or "colored land-scape" went on without interruption. At the beginning of the Southern Sung, Chao Shih-tsun 趙士遵, an uncle of Emperor Kao-tsung (r. 1127–1162), painted in the manner of Li Chao-tao of the T'ang period. Later, the brothers Chao Po-chü and Po-su, in the middle of the twelfth century, became the best-known painters of this genre. Indeed, many other blue-and-green landscape painters could be cited as possible sources of Ch'ien Hsüan's painting in this genre, but the most important source was Chao Po-chü.

Unfortunately, it is difficult for us now to identify definitely the type of blue-and-green landscape done by Chao Po-chü, for among the existing attributions to him there is a considerable variety. One painting, how-ever, demands our special attention. This is the long handscroll *Chiang-shan ch'iu-se* 江山秋色 (*Autumn Colors on Rivers and Mountains*), now in the Palace Museum in Peking.[84] It is a grand and broad Sung landscape, but with the mountains all painted in strong blue and green. The main problem is that this painting, although painted with marvellous tech-niques and elaborate details, shows little relationship with Ch'ien Hsüan's works.

Turning directly to the works of Ch'ien Hsüan, we find that there are some seven landscape handscrolls which have been attributed to Ch'ien, all but one of which are executed in bright colors. Although serious problems of authenticity are involved (two of them are identical in composition), they do present enough stylistic relationships to enable us to form a coherent view of Ch'ien's style. Unfortunately, in spite of the fact that Ch'ien Hsüan's signatures and poems appear on most of these scrolls, none of them is dated. But to judge from the colophons on his paintings, in his later years he tended to paint landscapes rather frequently. This is indicated by the following colophon by Chao Meng-yü 趙孟籲, brother of Chao Meng-fu, on the *Shan-chü t'u* 山居圖 (*Mountain Dwelling*): "In his youth, Shun-chü [Ch'ien Hsüan] loved to paint. When depicting flowers and plants, he brought them almost

---

[84] One section of this scroll is reproduced in Sirén, CP, Vol. 3, Pl. 271. The whole painting is reproduced in *Chung-kuo hua* 中國畫 (Peking, 1959).

totally alive. People competed to acquire them. In his later years his art tended to be bland and simple; he painted mostly landscapes." [85]

Also, in one of the frequently recorded works, *Hsüeh-chi Pien-shan t'u* 雪霽弁山圖 (*Mt. Pien after Snow*), Ch'ien himself wrote: "In the twenty-ninth year of Chih-yüan (1292), I stayed on the shore of Lake T'ai. After a snowfall, I was on a boat sailing on the river. Looking west toward Mt. Pien, I painted this and wrote the following poem for it. [The poem is omitted here.]" [86]

Both of these statements suggest that his landscapes were done in the latter part of his life.

Without actual dates to go by, we can only arrange them in terms of style. The earliest one, in terms of the style of both the painting and the calligraphy, is probably the *Kuei-ch'ü-lai t'u* 歸去來圖 (*Returning Home*), now in the Metropolitan Museum.[87] The composition is divided roughly into two halves. The right half depicts the poet T'ao Yüan-ming 陶淵明 (365–427) standing on a boat in the foreground, against some distant mountains in the back. The left half shows large willows along a riverbank, leading to the gate of a country house, in front of which the poet's wife and two boys await his arrival. It is a typical Southern Sung composition, and the treatment is not unlike that in some of the round fans mentioned above, combining a number of realistic details, such as the gate, the willows, the figures and the boat, with relatively stylized ones, such as the rocks, the riverbanks, distant mountains, and the reeds by the riverbanks. It is a very pleasant, decorative painting.

Next are the two versions of the *Lan-t'ing kuan o t'u* 蘭亭觀鵝圖 (*Wang Hsi-chih Watching the Geese*), one of which is in the Metropolitan Museum and the other in the Palace Museum, Taipei.[88] The compositions are entirely identical, but the Metropolitan Museum version has Ch'ien's own inscription, while the Taipei one does not. In this painting (both versions) some of the features are similar to those in the *Returning Home*, such as the Southern Sung composition, the stylized mountains and rocks, the decorative colors and patterns. But it is also more stylized, more detached, and more artificial than the *Returning*

---

[85] See Wu Sheng, *Ta-kuan lu*, 15:50b.

[86] Wu Sheng, *Ta-kuan lu*, 15:49a.

[87] This painting has been published in Sherman E. Lee and Wai-kam Ho, *Chinese Art under the Mongols* (Cleveland, 1968), Cat. No. 184.

[88] The Metropolitan Museum version has been published in Lee and Ho, *Chinese Art under the Mongols*, Cat. No. 185; and Wen Fong and Marilyn Fu, *Sung and Yüan Painting* (New York, 1973), Cat. No. 13. The Palace Museum version has been published in the KKSHL 4:73.

Home. Moving away from the realistic approach, it has become archaic.

This archaism becomes more evident in *Yen-chiang tai-tu t'u* 烟江待渡圖 (*Waiting for the Ferry by the Misty River*),[89] in the Palace Museum, Taipei. In this work the stylization of trees and rocks is more complete, and the composition, although still retaining the misty effect of the Southern Sung, is nevertheless moving away from it. The figures are smaller and the feeling is more detached. In the *Mountain Dwelling* in the Palace Museum, Peking, the stylization of the details becomes more intensified, and the decorative effect even stronger.[90]

Some interesting changes can be seen in another painting of the same title, *Mountain Dwelling*, also held by the Palace Museum, Peking.[91] Although some degree of misty effect is retained, the Southern Sung style of composition is absent, and instead one observes a mountain group in the center. All the objects, including the mountains, trees, houses, bridges, and boats, have been pushed back to create a greater sense of detachment. This work seems to be based on models that preceded the Southern Sung, such as those of Mi Fu 米帝 (1052–1107) and others of the late Northern Sung period.

The seventh scroll is unique. *Fu-yü shan chü t'u* 浮玉山居圖 (*Dwelling on the Floating Jade Mountain*), now in the Shanghai Museum, is mostly in ink, with only slight use of colors.[92] It is well documented in a considerable number of Ming and Ch'ing catalogues and has many Yüan colophons.[93] Although there is still the same stylization of rocks and mountains, trees and foliage, and reeds, the treatment is different, more natural and free. Most startling is the composition. All the objects seem to be lined up near the picture plane, forming a screen across the picture rather like those in works of the Six Dynasties and early T'ang. Most interesting is the attempt of the artist to handle the elements as pure visual shapes rather than as natural objects. Thus there is a strong contrast between the two halves of the picture, with the right side dominated by trees and the left side by mountain formations, both silhouetted against the plain background. Also interesting are the small rocks in the lower section of the painting, which can be found in works

[89] This is published in the KKSHL 4:69–73.

[90] This is published in Sirén, CP, Vol. 6, Pl. 34.

[91] This is published in *Chung-kuo li-tai hui-hua hsüan-chi* 中國歷代繪畫選集 (Peking, 1963), Pl. 68.

[92] This painting has been published several times, including Max Loehr, *Chinese Painting after the Sung* (New Haven, 1967), Fig. 2; and Richard Barnhart, *Marriage of the Lord of the River* (Ascona: Artibus Asiae, 1970), Fig. 23.

[93] See Pien Yung-yü, *Shih-ku t'ang shu-hua hui-k'ao*, 17:159–165. Colophons by Huang Kung-wang, Ku Ying, Cheng Yüan-yu, Ch'iu Yüan, Ni Tsan, and Chang Yü.

of the Six Dynasties. It is certainly a work based on a model much more archaic than those used in the other six paintings, but, at the same time, it is also based on an actual mountain near Wu-hsing.

If this arrangement of the seven scrolls in terms of a developmental sequence is acceptable, Ch'ien Hsüan would then seem to have started with the basic elements of Southern Sung blue-and-green landscape, probably related to some of Chao Po-chü's works, and to have moved gradually back through the T'ang and eventually to the Six Dynasties. This evolution is a reflection of his own spiritual development.

In contrast to Ch'ien, Chao Meng-fu seems to have followed rather a different course in his blue-and-green landscape painting. Unlike the works of Ch'ien, Chao's are mostly dated and are thus capable of giving us a more definite idea of his development.

Two short handscrolls on silk can be identified as works of Chao Meng-fu's early years, and were probably executed before his first trip to Ta-tu. The first, *Weng-yu t'u* 罋牖圖 (*Tzu-kung Visiting Yüan Hsien at His Humble Hut*), in the Palace Museum, Taipei, is unsigned and undated, but has Chao's seals.[94] The painting is somewhat related to Ch'ien's *Returning Home* in its combination of realistic figures and stylized rocks. One detail, the gate to the hut, is very close to the gate in Ch'ien's work. In composition and general treatment, Chao's painting places more emphasis on the picture plane and the surface patterns. Thus he seems to have used an early work as his model, probably one of the Six Dynasties.

The second handscroll is *Yu-yü ch'iu-ho t'u* 幼輿邱壑圖 (*The Mind Landscape of Hsieh Yu-yü*), now in the Princeton Art Museum. It is neither signed nor dated, but Chao's son, Chao Yung, who wrote one of the many Yüan colophons on the scroll, considered it to have been an earlier work.[95] Based on the life of a Six Dynasties poet, the painting is also most appropriately derived from models of that period. The mountain forms are reminiscent of those in Ku K'ai-chih's 顧愷之 works; the screen-like arrangement of the mountains, the patternized placing of trees and rocks, the opening of a vista on the left end, and the additive method of composition, all point to the Six Dynasties as their source.

The next step in Chao's development is reflected in his *Ch'iao Hua ch'iu-se* 鵲華秋色 (*Autumn Colors on the Ch'iao and Hua Mountains*),

---

[94] Reproduced in *Ku-kung ming-hua* 故宮名畫, Vol. 5, No. 3; and KKSHL 4:110–113.

[95] Reproduced in Chu-tsing Li, "Stages of Development in Yüan Landscape Painting," Part 1, *National Palace Museum Bulletin*, 4:2 (1969), Fig. 1; Barnhart, *Marriage of the Lord of the River*, Fig. 24; and James Cahill, *Hills Beyond a River* (New York, 1976), Fig. 10.

dated 1296, in the Palace Museum, Taipei (Fig. 1).[96] Since this has been discussed extensively elsewhere, there is no need for details here. In spirit, this painting is somewhat akin to Ch'ien Hsüan's *Floating Jade Mountain*, especially in the treatment of the mountains and trees as visual elements and in the handling of the brushwork. In contrast to the last two paintings, this work, as is indicated by some of the colophons, was based on Wang Wei 王維 of the T'ang and Tung Yüan of the Five Dynasties. But, in addition, the painting depicts an actual site north of the city of Tsinan in Shantung. This blending of the past and present and of the imaginary and the real is an indication of Chao Meng-fu's approach. It is somewhat close to Ch'ien's *Floating Jade Mountain*, which depicts a mountain near Wu-hsing.

In terms of the blue-and-green landscape, both Chao Meng-fu and Ch'ien Hsüan seem to have reached their most exciting stage toward the end of the thirteenth century. From the early use of this type of painting for essentially decorative purposes, to its use in the second stage of development as expressions of archaism, blue-and-green landscape evolved into creative works embracing both scholarly learning and direct experience. Thus, in its third stage, blue-and-green landscape painting is a reflection of the mind of the literati. Blue-and-green landscapes in the *oeuvres* of Ch'ien and Chao established a new foundation for art, totally different from those of the past, and set the Yüan apart as a major era of artistic creation.

The blue-and-green landscape thus symbolized a number of the basic ideas in the mind of the literati in early Yüan. First, it was an expression of their longing for the past—a beautiful, colorful, and dreamy portrayal of the past in Chinese history—and of their attachment to the great Chinese tradition in a period of radical and unpleasant change. Second, it was a reflection of their desire to follow the examples of hermits of the past, especially those of the Six Dynasties such as T'ao Yüan-ming and Hsieh Yu-yü, as an escape from the present. Third, it was an indication of the new aesthetic values they were searching for, again as an expression of their high and noble ideals in a time of adversity. These new values found their correlatives in the move away from strict form-likeness, the increase in the importance placed on brushwork, and the deepening of the relationship between painting and calligraphy.

It is interesting to observe that during the early Yüan both Ch'ien Hsüan and Chao Meng-fu began turning away from the more colorful and decorative aspects of blue-and-green. In the *Floating Jade Mountain*, Ch'ien almost discarded colors entirely, while Chao was most interested

---

[96] See Li, *Autumn Colors*, in which this painting is thoroughly discussed.

in brushwork in his *Autumn Colors*. Both painters set the direction that landscape painting eventually took in the Yüan. With the new emphasis on brushwork, the deepened relationship between painting and calligraphy, and the heightened freedom of expression, strict realism was not stressed. In this new type of landscape, they achieved a new sense of expression—simple but subtle, personal but universal, embodying the aesthetic principles as well as the noble character of the literati. It is, in a way, a demonstration of their spiritual independence from Mongol rule.

With the new emphasis on pure ink painting, the blue-and-green style gradually went into a decline, even though it continued to receive attention throughout the Yüan period. A few examples will suffice to illustrate the later development, which still centered in Wu-hsing. Chao Meng-fu's *Tung-t'ing tung-shan t'u* 洞庭東山圖 (*The East Tung-t'ing Mountain*), now in the Shanghai Museum, is one of an original pair of paintings depicting the two major islands in Lake T'ai.[97] Although undated, it seems to be a work of the late 1290s, since in terms of the style of his calligraphy it appears to postdate the *Autumn Colors*. Here, perhaps Chao was more interested in direct depiction rather than in the experimental spirit typified by the *Autumn Colors*.

It was probably natural for painters among Chao Meng-fu's family members to continue exploiting some of the ideas of the blue-and-green. His son's painting, Chao Yung's *Horses and Groom* of 1352, is a large painting on silk depicting a group of beautiful horses and one groom under three large trees against an open landscape.[98] The horses are beautifully drawn, and the landscape is done in bright colors, especially the mountains in the background, in the standard blue-and-green manner. It suggests a compromise between Chao Yung's family tradition and the Mongol taste. The painting is beautiful, pleasant, and decorative. Done in the 1350s, when rebellions were beginning to spread throughout the land, the painting indicates that Chao Yung, who at that time was serving as a high official in Chiang-nan under the Mongols, may have been eager to please the ruling group. Thus it is a far cry from Chao's *Autumn Colors*.

The blue-and-green tradition persisted into the late Yüan in Wu-hsing. Ch'en Lin 陳琳, a pupil of Chao Meng-fu, showed a close relationship to his teacher in the *Hoary Cliffs and Old Trees*, now in the Palace Museum, Taipei (Fig. 2). Two other artists, Meng Yü-chien 孟玉澗 and Wu T'ing-hui 吳庭暉, are mentioned in the *T'u-hui pao-chien* as having been

---

[97] Published in *Shang-hai po-wu-kuan ts'ang-hua* 上海博物館藏畫 (Shanghai, 1959), Pl. 10.

[98] In the Palace Museum, Taipei, and published in *Ku-kung ming-hua*, Vol. 5, No. 15.

painters of this genre.[99] Among the extant works which are attributed to them, however, none can attest to this aspect of their art. We are more fortunate with respect to the greatest of the late Yüan Wu-hsing painters, Wang Meng 王蒙, a grandson of Chao Meng-fu. His *Ch'iu-shan ts'ao-t'ang* 秋山草堂 (*Cottage on an Autumn Hill*), in the Palace Museum, Taipei,[100] most likely an early work, shows some links to Chao Meng-fu's *Autumn Colors*, although it is more pleasant and even sentimental, less archaic and provocative. In contrast, his *Chü-ch'ü lin-wu* 具區林屋 (*Scenic Dwellings at Chü-ch'ü*), also in the Palace Museum, Taipei (Fig. 3),[101] is a product of Wang Meng's full maturity. It shows his exploration into the potentials of the colored landscape as a means of expressing his fascination and bewilderment. Its contents are some fantastic sites around Lake T'ai, filled with strange rock formations, secret passages, swirling movements, bright colors, and nervous energy. Again, like the *Autumn Colors*, it is a painting based on actual scenes, but, by blending natural objects with archaic elements, it transforms them into something unworldly. In this, it is Wang Meng's own vision.

Wang Meng has never been known as a painter of the blue-and-green landscape, and its transformation in his hands marks a creative departure from the traditional and standard treatment of this genre. Like his grandfather Chao Meng-fu, Wang Meng in his later years found in ink painting the best vehicle for expression. In this way the whole stream of Wu-hsing artists in their experiments on the potentials of the blue-and-green or colored landscape came to an end. From Ch'ien Hsüan to Wang Meng, a series of ideas, from bright colors, decorative quality, patterning, space denial, archaism, and primitivism, to an integration between the real and the imaginary, marked their search for a new means of expression in a world of rapidly changing values. Eventually, a solution was found in pure ink painting, and the blue-and-green was left behind.

But one type of blue-and-green landscape persisted into the Ming period. Because of its archaic quality, it was particularly well suited for imaginary scenes, especially the lands of the immortals. The richness of the blue, green, and gold, the various bright colors, and the dreamlike quality, seem to have been all that were needed for those kinds of subjects. Ch'en Ju-yen's 陳汝言 *Hsien-shan t'u* 仙山圖 (*Land of the Immortals*), the paintings of Shih Jui 石銳 of the early Ming, and the many paintings of Ch'iu Ying 仇英 in the early sixteenth century, are

---

[99] A short reference to both of them can be found in THPC 5:103.

[100] Published in *Ku-kung ming-hua*, Vol. 6, No. 19; and FGMY, Fig. 408.

[101] Published in *Ku-kung ming-hua*, Vol. 6, No. 20; FGMY, Fig. 411.

part of this tradition.[102] They gave the blue-and-green tradition a new life, but a more decorative and conventional one, a far cry from the great experiments of the Yüan period which had resulted from the artistic and intellectual search by the painters of Wu-hsing in a time of stress and tension.

VI. WU-HSING AND THE TUNG YÜAN AND KUO HSI TRADITIONS

Though Wu-hsing is identified with the blue-and-green tradition in the Yüan, as has been shown above, it is generally much better known in the history of Chinese art for having revived an interest in the Five Dynasties painter Tung Yüan. This new importance of Tung Yüan came as a result of Ch'ien Hsüan and Chao Meng-fu's interest in the blue-and-green landscape, for Tung himself was known in Sung and Yüan sources as a painter of both colored and ink landscapes.[103] Writers of colophons on Ch'ien's *Floating Jade Mountain* and Chao's *Autumn Colors* clearly pointed to Tung Yüan as the source of both paintings.[104] Strangely, in later Chinese art criticism, Tung came to be regarded as the great master of ink landscape, but his colored landscape was seldom mentioned. In any event, the Yüan revival of interest in Tung Yüan, and the development from the blue-and-green to ink landscape, were both major achievements of the Wu-hsing school.

[102] Ch'en's painting has been published in Lee and Ho, *Chinese Painting under the Mongols*, Cat. No. 264. It is held by the Dean Perry Collection, Cleveland. Shih Jui's two works are reproduced in *Hashimoto Collection of Ming and Ch'ing Painting* (Takatsuki, 1973), No. 2; and *Bulletin of the Cleveland Museum of Art* (October, 1975), Figs. 2–6. Many of Ch'iu Ying's scrolls of this type can be found in American collections, especially the one at the Nelson Gallery of Art in Kansas City.

[103] In both the *T'u-hua chien-wen chih* and the *Hsüan-ho hua-p'u*, Tung Yüan is described as a painter of both types of landscapes. It was late in Northern Sung, after the literati painters had praised Tung for his free use of ink, that the new image began to take shape. During the Yüan the process seems to have been repeated. By late Yüan he became known primarily as an ink landscape painter. See Li, *Autumn Colors*, pp. 60–69; and Barnhart, *Marriage of the Lord of the River*, pp. 22–49.

[104] In the *Floating Jade Mountain* scroll, none of the extant colophons by Yüan and Ming literati actually mentions Tung Yüan, but many of them refer to Wang Wei as Ch'ien's source. However, in one of the colophons originally written by Chao Meng-fu for this scroll but apparently cut away later, Chao said that the painting was thoroughly based on Tung Yüan. See Sun Yüeh-pan 孫岳頌, *P'ei-wen chai shu-hua p'u* 佩文齋書畫譜 (Taipei: Hsin-hsing Shu-chü, 1969), 85:6a. This is also mentioned in Barnhart, *Marriage of the Lord of the River*, p. 45. In the *Autumn Colors* scroll, again many colophons refer to Wang Wei as Chao Meng-fu's source, but Tung Ch'i-ch'ang 董其昌 brings out the Tung Yüan idea in several of his colophons on this scroll.

The T'ang artist Wang Wei has also been associated with Tung Yüan as a source of both the paintings mentioned above. Some of the colophons on Chao's *Autumn Colors*, for example, refer to Wang Wei and Tung Yüan in this context. Later art critics often considered Wang and Tung the originators of the poetic landscape, which was usually executed in ink.[105] Ch'ien Hsüan's *Floating Jade Mountain* is mainly in ink, and as such the colophon writers linked it directly with the Tung Yüan tradition. As mentioned above, both of these paintings treat mountains and trees as visual elements rather than as natural objects to be literally represented. Hence they employ arbitrary shapes and spaces, and exploit free handling of brushwork. As noted, both Wang Wei and Tung Yüan were generally regarded as artists of this approach, although Ch'ien and Chao brought about important developments which led to a new aesthetic. Yet it should be noted that, by Yüan times, Wang Wei was already rather remote. Few of his works survived to serve as models. Tung Yüan, however, was not nearly as remote a figure, and many of his works were still available. Thus both the *Floating Jade Mountain* and the *Autumn Colors* show primarily the influence of Tung Yüan.

A crucial change in Yüan painting took place early in the fourteenth century when Chao Meng-fu painted the *Shui-ts'un t'u* 水村圖 (*Water Village*) in 1302 (Fig. 4). The scroll, now in the Palace Museum, Peking, again has been thoroughly discussed elsewhere.[106] Here only a few relevant comments need be made. Done entirely in ink, *Water Village* retains an emphasis on visual forms but gives up the earlier stylizations, so much so that some friends of Chao in their colophons commented on its authentic quality in relation to real landscape. As I have indicated before, Chao was moving toward Tung Yüan and the Northern Sung landscape. *Water Village* was a real breakthrough in his attempt to integrate the past and the present, the Tung Yüan tradition and his own style, and representation and expression into a new synthesis.

The Tung Yüan tradition, now combined with the new ideas of Chao Meng-fu, began to take root in the Yüan. Gradually, as the colored landscape of Tung Yüan was forgotten, Tung Yüan became entirely identified with the ink landscape tradition done by free brushwork and wet ink. It was a new kind of landscape. Instead of the very obvious archaic elements, such as the compressed space, arbitrary shapes, patternization, and decorative quality, the new landscape is done entirely in

[105] The change in taste for Wang Wei and Tung Yüan is the topic of discussion in both the books by this author and Barnhart mentioned in n. 103 above. A new appreciation for their works coincided with the upsurge of literati painting in late Northern Sung times and in the Yüan.

[106] See Li, *Autumn Colors*, pp. 53–59.

ink, with more convincing space and natural shapes. What distinguishes this new landscape is the very free and spontaneous brushwork. No object, whether mountain, tree, or rock, is depicted with the elaborate detail of T'ang or Sung painting. Without colors, the painting is less decorative or patternized, thus less ostentatious. But it is more subtle, in agreement with the very pure taste of the literati. Furthermore, the brushwork, while showing versatility in the handling of ink, is also the prefect reflection of the literati ideal—informal, free, spontaneous, pure, subtle, and noble.

This new solution, so well worked out by Chao Meng-fu in the beginning years of the fourteenth century, gradually became the standard landscape style of the Yüan. Starting from Wu-hsing, it spread all over Chiang-nan, and eventually became very influential even in Ta-tu. Chao himself did a series of paintings, including the *Ch'iu hsing shi i* 秋興詩意 (*Poetic Feeling in Autumn*) and a number of album-sized works, along this line.[107] Some of his family members in Wu-hsing, especially Chao Yung, continued in this direction. But the influence of this new interpretation of the Tung Yüan style was especially strong in Wu-hsing's neighboring districts of Soochow, Sung-chiang, and Chia-hsing. From these areas came many of the late Yüan masters of ink landscape.[108]

Yet, in working out this new development, Chao did not stay unchanged but continued to absorb new ideas and to break new ground. Some three months after he had painted the *Water Village*, he executed a longer scroll, *Ch'ung-chiang tieh-chang* 重江疊嶂 (*Rivers and Mountains*), also in ink on paper (Fig. 5).[109] Although both paintings are based on a river view and although their general aspects display some common similarities, their details are far apart. The composition and mountain and tree forms are all very different, pointing to quite different models. Indeed, while the *Water Village* is based on Tung Yüan, *Rivers and Mountains* is derived from Kuo Hsi.

The Kuo Hsi tradition, often linked with the early artist, Li Ch'eng,[110] had undergone very peculiar development in the Sung period. Not long after Li's own time, court tastes were said to have changed so much that

[107] *Poetic Feeling in Autumn* is reproduced in *Chung-kuo ming-hua chi* 中國名畫集 (Shanghai: Yu-cheng Book Co., 1909), Vol. 1, p. 98; the album leaves were published in *T'ang Sung Yüan Ming Ch'ing hua-hsüan* 唐宋元明清畫選 (Shanghai, 1960), Pls. 15–17.

[108] Concerning the Four Masters of Late Yüan, see FGYM.

[109] This painting, in the Palace Museum (Taipei), has been published in *Three Hundred Masterpieces in the National Palace Museum* (Taichung, 1959), No. 145; and also in Li, "Stages of Development in Yüan Landscape Painting," Part 1, Fig. 5.

[110] Li Ch'eng is the subject of a special study by Wai-kam Ho: "Li Ch'eng and the Mainstreams of Northern Sung Landscape Painting," in *Proceedings of the International Symposium on Chinese Painting* (Taipei: National Palace Museum, 1972), pp. 251–283.

his works were discarded in the palace. But he seems to have inspired many followers within the Northern Sung painting academy. It is not surprising, then, that, in the early years of the Southern Sung in Hangchow, there were many artists working in his manner. According to the *T'u-hui pao-chien*, a number of the court painters in Emperor Hui-tsung's academy in the Northern Sung went south after the collapse of K'ai-feng. They resettled in Hangchow as members of the new painting academy.[111] Strangely, however, after this generation of painters, who were active until the middle of the twelfth century, no more painters are recorded as Kuo Hsi's followers. This was probably due to the growing dominance of Li T'ang 李唐, who was active in the Southern Sung academy of painting. Taking as his model the style of the Northern Sung master Fan K'uan 范寬, Li transformed it into a new style of his own, emphasizing the sharp-cut, big-axe texture of rocks and mountains, misty effects, and asymmetrical composition. These then became the foundation stones of the Ma-Hsia School toward the end of the twelfth century. Thus, for over a century, from the middle of the twelfth century to the fall of the Southern Sung, Kuo Hsi was not an influential force in the academy. In North China, however, Kuo Hsi, together with Li Ch'eng, continued to exercise great influence. This was true during the Chin Dynasty as well as into the early Yüan period. It is not surprising, therefore, that by the end of the thirteenth century a number of northern painters working in the Li-Kuo tradition were active in the capital city.[112] Quite possibly, Chao Meng-fu, during his long sojourns in Ta-tu, came into contact with the Kuo Hsi tradition. Fascinated by it, he may have introduced it to his close associates in both Ta-tu and Wu-hsing.[113]

Although a few of Kuo Hsi's works were available in some of the major collections of the Chiang-nan area, there seems to have been no interest in them before Chao Meng-fu. In Ta-tu and Tsinan and in the many other cities Chao passed through on his trips between the north and south, he must have seen a considerable number of Kuo's works as well as those of his imitators. Among his own extant paintings, the recently published fan, *Chiang-ts'un yü-lo t'u* 江村漁樂圖 (*River Village—*

---

[111] See THPC 4:74, 76, 77. They include Yang Shih-hsien, Chang Chia, Ku Liang, Hu Shun-ch'en, and the monk Ch'ao-jan.

[112] See THPC 5:97, 98, 99. They include Shang Ch'i, Liu Jung, Ch'iao Ta, and Liu Kuan-tao.

[113] Some of his close associates, such as Chu Te-jun 朱德潤, could have absorbed Chao's ideas when they served with Chao in Ta-tu. Of course, not all of the followers of the Li-Kuo tradition in the Yüan were necessarily associated with Chao. For example, Lo Chih-ch'uan 羅稚川, a painter of this tradition from Kiangsi, is not known to have had any connection with Chao.

The Pleasures of Fishing), now in the Cleveland Museum, may date to the early years of Chao's life. If so, it marks the beginning of his interest in Kuo Hsi.[114] In *Rivers and Mountains* (1303), this interest was already fully developed.

This new direction can be seen in another painting, *Shuang-sung p'ing-yüan* 雙松平遠 (*Twin Pines in a Flat Vista*).[115] This painting represents Chao Meng-fu's ultimate solution of the Kuo Hsi manner. Turning away from the strictly centralized composition which he had used in the *Mind Landscape of Hsieh Yu-yü*, the *Autumn Colors* and the *Rivers and Mountains*, he seems to have taken a step beyond the *Water Village*. In *Twin Pines* we find asymmetrical composition, prominent foreground with the focus on one or two objects, empty middle ground, and distant mountains, all based on the Kuo Hsi models but without their extensive use of mist, great detail, and the wash technique. Here the Kuo Hsi manner is simplified to the point that the brushwork is the most prominent element in the painting. In fact, the brushwork and the calligraphy of the inscription are totally unified. This became a model for many of the late Yüan painters.

By comparing the developments of Ch'ien Hsüan and Chao Meng-fu, we can draw some interesting conclusions. Starting from a Southern Sung foundation, Ch'ien gradually moved backward in time in his search for inspiration from the past. This would seem to be a natural course for someone who was loyal to an ideal—the Chinese tradition. As a Sung "leftover subject" (*i-min*), whose life was confined more or less to the area between Wu-hsing and Hangchow, Ch'ien Hsüan was interested in tracing his way back to the roots of the great tradition. In contrast, despite his indebtedness to Ch'ien in his early years, Chao Meng-fu seems to have acquired a different outlook as a result of his travels in North China after accepting Khubilai Khaghan's invitation. Perhaps benefitting from Ch'ien's experience in painting, he seems to have worked from the Six Dynasties down to his own time and to have introduced both the Tung Yüan and Kuo Hsi traditions to Chiang-nan

---

[114] This fan painting, formerly in the C. C. Wang collection, has recently been extensively published. See James Cahill, *Hills Beyond a River: Chinese Painting of the Yüan Dynasty* (New York and Tokyo, 1976), p. 44; Richard Vinograd, "*River Village—The Pleasures of Fishing* and Chao Meng-fu's Li-Kuo Style Landscape," *Artibus Asiae*, 15:2–3 (1978), pp. 124–134; and Sherman E. Lee, "River Village—Fisherman's Joy," *Bulletin of the Cleveland Museum of Art*, 66:7 (October 1979), pp. 271–288.

[115] In the Metropolitan Museum, N.Y., and published in Wen Fong and Marilyn Fu, *Sung and Yüan Paintings*, Cat. No. 14. A second version of this painting is in the Cincinnati Art Museum. Although the Metropolitan Museum version is not unanimously accepted, it seems sensible to see in that painting an image of Chao's last phase of development in landscape.

as new, revitalized forces in painting. This is perhaps an indirect consequence of Chao's acceptance of Mongol rule.

In a larger context, both Ch'ien and Chao, by going back to the Chinese tradition to re-experience the past, were able to develop a new literati style that seems to have served as a counterweight to the devastating effect of the Mongol conquest. Paradoxically, through both the sense of loyalty on the part of Ch'ien Hsüan and the prestige and influence exercised by Chao Meng-fu, the new literati style was widely accepted in the Chiang-nan area, forming the foundation for the brilliant late Yüan developments in art. Wu-hsing was thus the most important center of art in the early Yüan period.

After the death of Chao Meng-fu in 1322, Wu-hsing continued to be an important art center, although its great age was more or less over. There were many artists active in Wu-hsing, but most of them were only followers rather than innovators. Still Wu-hsing retained its own special character. While the blue-and-green landscape and the Tung Yüan tradition went on, it was the Kuo Hsi tradition which tended to dominate the post-Chao tastes of Wu-hsing. Since this was also Chao Meng-fu's latest development, it was only natural that his descendants and followers should continue the interest. Mention has already been made of the painting in blue-and-green by Chao Yung, *Horses and Groom*, dated 1352. While the horses in this painting are derived from T'ang models, and the landscape from the blue-and-green of the T'ang, the several large trees in the foreground are unmistakably based on Kuo Hsi. Among Chao Meng-fu's followers, two were well known as painters in the Kuo Hsi manner. T'ang Ti 唐棣, a native of Wu-hsing, was typical, as seen in his *Fang Wang Wei shih i* 仿王維詩意 (*Landscape after Wang Wei's Poetry*), in the Ernest Erickson Collection, New York (Fig. 6). A protégé of Chao Meng-fu in his younger years, Chu Te-jun, who, although originally from the Soochow-K'un-shan area, served as the prefect of Ch'ang-hsing 長興 district in Hu-chou circuit, was also deeply influenced by Chao's interest in the Kuo Hsi tradition, as seen in the *Lin-hsia ming ch'in* 林下鳴琴 (*Playing the Ch'in under the Trees*), in the Palace Museum, Taipei (Fig. 7). A third artist, Yao Yen-ch'ing 姚彥卿, who flourished in the 1360s, attempted to blend elements of both the Kuo Hsi and Tung Yüan traditions, as reflected in his *Yu yü hsien* 有餘閒 (*Leisure Enough to Spare*) in the Cleveland Museum and the *Hsüeh-chiang yü-t'ing* 雪江漁艇 (*Fishing Boats on a Snowy River*) in the Palace Museum, Peking (Fig. 8).[116] As has already been noted, during

---

[116] For T'ang Ti see Kao Mu-sen 高木森, "The Life and Art of T'ang Ti," *National Palace Museum Quarterly*, 8:2 (Winter 1973), pp. 43–56. For Chu Te-jun, see the

the middle Yüan, from about 1320 to 1340, the influence of the Kuo Hsi tradition in Chiang-nan was quite extensive. In the early works of Wu Chen 吳鎮, Ts'ao Chih-po 曹知白, and Wang Yüan, Kuo Hsi's influence may be seen in their use of the theme of the two pines.[117] But the strongest influence of Kuo Hsi remained in Wu-hsing.

VII. THE DECLINE OF WU-HSING'S ARTISTIC DEVELOPMENT IN EARLY MING

Late in the Yüan period, a new situation emerged to signal the decline in the importance of Wu-hsing. Hangchow, which had brought Wu-hsing to prominence in the Southern Sung, gradually lost its position as a political and cultural center. Ta-tu in the north became the political center, although it was not the cultural one. Culture remained centered in the Chiang-nan area, but within Chiang-nan there was a new shift. Soochow now became the new focus, by virtue of its central location in Chiang-nan and of its control of the commercial and manufacturing activities of the area. Most important of all, it attracted scholars, poets, artists, and other intellectuals from all over China. In short, it took over the position previously enjoyed by Hangchow and Wu-hsing.

The change in the importance of both Wu-hsing and Soochow had a great deal to do with the Mongols. As mentioned before, in the early Yüan Wu-hsing played a major role either as the administrative head-quarters of the Western part of Chekiang, or as a place for some of the intellectuals to develop new ideas, or even as a source from which the Mongols drew support for their rule. After the death of Chao Meng-fu, even though his sons and grandsons served either in Ta-tu or in the Hu-chou area, the Wu-hsing influence became quite limited. As their works show, none of the artists of Wu-hsing in the later Yüan was able to equal Chao Meng-fu in either aesthetic quality or artistic innovation. Some-how, all the major ideas of Ch'ien Hsüan and Chao Meng-fu, including the blue-and-green landscape, the Tung Yüan tradition, and the Kuo Hsi manner, persisted longer in Wu-hsing than in other areas.

In contrast, Soochow in the course of the Yüan became a much more vital city. By attracting many artists from various parts of the country,

biography in Feng Kuei-fen 馮桂芬, comp., *Su-chou fu-chih* 蘇州府志, (1883 ed., rpt. Taipei: Ch'eng-wen Shu-tien, 1970), 91:17a–b. Yao, recently identified as Yao T'ing-mei 姚廷美, and his three extant works and one attribution are discussed in Richard Barnhart, "Yao Yen-ch'ing, T'ing-mei, of Wu-hsing," *Artibus Asiae*, 39:2 (1977), pp. 105–123.

[117] See Li, "Stages of Development in Yüan Landscape Painting," Part 2, *National Palace Museum Bulletin*, 4:3 (July–August 1969), pp. 1–9.

some for patronage, others for intellectual atmosphere, and still others for its more independent thinking, the city began to take a leading role in late Yüan artistic developments. By the Chih-cheng period (1341–1368), Soochow was undoubtedly the most interesting place in Yüan art. It was here that the Tung Yüan tradition finally and fully blossomed.[118]

Perhaps the major factor in the uneven importance of Wu-hsing and Soochow during the late Yüan was their relationship with the Mongol government in Ta-tu. Because of Chao Meng-fu's service in Ta-tu, and the continuation of this association by some of his descendants and protégés, Wu-hsing became thoroughly identified with the idea of accommodation with the Mongols. Both Chao Yung, his son, and Chao Lin, his grandson, served as high officials in the Hu-chou area at one time, and both T'ang Ti and Chu Te-jun also served as Yüan prefects.[119] This strong identification with the Mongols in the declining years of the Yüan became an artistic liability. Not only did the Wu-hsing people become conservative in politics, but they also became less creative in artistic expression. In contrast, Soochow attracted the more independent intellectuals, including some of the Sung "leftover subjects" (*i-min*) in the early years of the Yüan. Later, some of the literati who had left the court in Ta-tu retired to Soochow. K'o Chiu-ssu 柯九思 is the leading example. Still later, Soochow became the city of the rebellious leader Chang Shih-ch'eng, who made it his capital in a tenuous relationship with the Yüan government. Toward the end of the Yüan, during the 1350s and 1360s, Soochow attracted some of empire's most creative scholars, painters, and poets. The political and cultural atmosphere in that period must have been most exciting for the leading minds who were searching for a way out for themselves as well as for the whole country. They made Soochow a great city.

In spite of its close tie with Ta-tu, Wu-hsing in the last years of the Yüan also saw a considerable amount of troubles. During the 1350s the Mongol regime developed many internal problems in Ta-tu and their rule began to break apart, with many rebel groups in open defiance. From the T'ai-chou 泰州 area north of Yangchow, Chang Shih-ch'eng

---

[118] See Chu-tsing Li, "The Development of Painting in Soochow during the Yüan Dynasty," *Proceedings of the International Symposium on Chinese Painting* (Taipei: National Palace Museum, 1972), pp. 483–528. For a vivid picture of Soochow in the late Yüan and early Ming, see F. W. Mote, *The Poet Kao Ch'i* (Princeton: Princeton University Press, 1962). The painters Lu Kuang 陸廣, Chao Yüan 趙原, Ch'en Ju-yen, Chou Chih 周砥, and Ni Tsan 倪瓚, who were among the important Soochow artists at this time, all have biographies in DMB.

[119] All of them enjoyed long official careers, serving under the Mongols. Their prominence was partly due to the help of Chao Meng-fu.

started looking south toward the lower Yangtze Valley. Based in northern Anhwei, Chu Yüan-chang 朱元璋 attempted to capture Nanking and to make it his fortress for conquering the whole country. Ch'en Yu-liang 陳友諒, starting from Hupei, was moving eastward toward the lower Yangtze delta. In southern Chekiang, Fang Kuo-chen 方國珍 tried to go north toward the same area. The rich area of Hangchow, Wu-hsing, and Soochow became the center of contention among these rival groups. It was defended by scattered troops under the Yüan government, especially a group of aborigines organized as the Miao 苗 army.[120]

Many violent incidents occurred around Wu-hsing. In 1352, the Red Turbans under the rebel leader Hsü Shou-hui 徐壽輝 overran the I-feng Bridge 儀鳳橋 area of Wu-hsing, defeating the Miao army, with burnings and killings spreading in all four directions.[121] In 1356, the forces of Chang Shih-ch'eng, after their conquest of Soochow, moved southward into Hu-chou and took four of the six districts there. According to detailed reports, these forces, led by Chang's minister, P'an Yüan-ming, began to attack Wu-hsing in the third month of that year. Wu-hsing, still under the Yüan, was again defended by the fierce Miao army. It was said that, "There was great violence in the areas where the Miao army was, especially Wu-hsing. The people fled for their lives. Those who were lucky enough to survive under the sharp arrows and javelins often had their noses and ears cut off. Seldom did one see anyone still intact."[122]

Late in 1356, the forces of Chu Yüan-chang, moving south from Nanking, captured Hu-chou's An-chi 安吉 district. In the following year they took Ch'ang-hsing. Thus Chu's forces stood virtually side by side with the forces of Chang Shih-ch'eng and the Miao army.[123] During 1357, in a strange gesture, Chang negotiated a peace with the Yüan government and accepted an appointment in this area. For five years, from 1357 to 1362, Wu-hsing was under Chang's control. But, in 1362, Chang declared his independence from the Yüan and proclaimed himself the Prince of Wu, retaining control of this area. Finally, Chu Yüan-chang in 1366, in his final push to gain control of the entire region, defeated Chang Shih-ch'eng's forces and occupied Wu-hsing.[124] The ordeal suffered by Wu-hsing through these years of incessant warfare can be imagined.

[120] In addition to the accounts in Mote's *The Poet Kao Ch'i*, some of the most interesting episodes concerning the fighting among the rebel groups in late Yüan can be found in 1542 HCFC 1:8a, and in WHCSC 16:8a.

[121] See WHCSC 16:17a–b.

[122] See WHCSC 16:8a.

[123] See 1542 HCFC 1:8a.

[124] See 1542 HCFC 1:8a.

All these disruptions must certainly have hastened the end of Wu-hsing as a viable cultural center. Although records are scattered, we can reconstruct some of the developments. Until the late Yüan, various descendants of Chao Meng-fu were still serving as government officials. But after 1368 nearly nothing is recorded about them. The main line of the Chao family, so prominent in the Yüan, seems to have come to an end, although some collateral relatives were still known.[125] In other aspects, the ravages of war probably took a heavy toll in Wu-hsing. In addition to a few scattered instances of atrocities, great libraries and art collections must have been burned down and famous mansions and gardens destroyed. As mentioned before, among the "Eight Talents of Wu-hsing" in the early Yüan, only Chao Meng-fu's literary works have come down to us, while those of the other seven members have disappeared; quite possibly they were lost during the late Yüan.[126] Wu-hsing's days as an intellectual and artistic center were over. Throughout the Ming period, it was Soochow which, having managed to survive the fighting of the late Yüan, was to play the leading role, not only in the Yangtze delta, but in all of China.

Yet the last days of Wu-hsing had their bright side as well. Several of the great late Yüan painters were active here. Chang Yü 張羽 and Hsü Pen 徐賁, for example, who became known as two of the "Four Master-poets of early Ming," came to live in Wu-hsing during the late Yüan.[127] Although Chang Yü was a native of Kiangsi, he moved to Wu-hsing to take over the directorship of the An-ting 安定 Academy there. He in turn invited his friend Hsü Pen to leave Soochow, probably in the days after Chang Shih-ch'eng had declared independence from the Yüan regime. Hsü then went to Wu-hsing to dwell at Mt. Shu 蜀山 as a recluse painter. In addition to these figures, there was also Wang Meng, known in early Ming times as one of the "Eight Masters of Wu-hsing," undoubtedly as an echo of the "Eight Talents" of the early Yüan.[128] Although we cannot document his presence in Wu-hsing, we do know that he occasionally visited nearby Soochow and K'un-shan 崑山. Thus, in view

[125] No record is available on what happened to the Chao family after the collapse of the Yüan, although several prominent people were among their relatives. These included Wang Meng, T'ao Tsung-i, and Shen Meng-lin 沈夢麟.

[126] The destruction of the Wu-hsing area in the late Yüan, judging from the limited materials available, must have been extremely severe. It is still a puzzle why so few of the literary writings of people from this era have survived.

[127] See the biographies of Chang Yü and Hsü Pen in 1573 HCFC 8:13b.

[128] See my biography of Wang Meng in DMB, pp. 1392–1395. The Eight Masters of Wu-hsing are mentioned in the biography of Chang T'ung 章同 in the 1874 HCFC 75:2b–3a.

of the fact that many Chinese associated him with Wu-hsing, it is very likely that he spent some time there.

In any event, Wang Meng and Hsü Pen seem to have been responsible for the development of a new style of landscape in the late Yüan. This was a style in which mountains are depicted at close range, with crowded details of trees, rocks, waterfalls, and cottages spreading all over the picture. The brushwork was relatively free and stemmed from the Tung Yüan and Chü-jan tradition.

The "Eight Masters of Wu-hsing" were also known by the name of their poetry society, the "Lien-yin she" 聯吟社 or "Composing Together Society." Four of the eight are known primarily as poets.[129] The other four, including Wang Meng, were all both poets and painters. Although little is known about their paintings, to judge from their subject matter they seem to have been largely extensions of Chao Meng-fu's art. Of this group, Wang Meng was undoubtedly the most important painter, with his own innovations.[130]

Yet, even with this group of poets and painters, Wu-hsing could never recapture the glorious days of the early Yüan. Their activities were more or less faint echoes of those of Ch'ien Hsüan and Chao Meng-fu. Only Wang Meng and Hsü Pen seem to measure up to the standards set by the earlier painters. While both Wang and Hsü seem to have regarded Wu-hsing as a place in which to retire as hermits in time of war, they viewed Soochow as the venue for their more active expressions. As a result, they too became chiefly a part of the scene in Soochow, sharing its outlook and its artistic development. Wang Meng's later works, especially those from the 1360s on, were products of Soochow, with its interest in the Tung Yüan tradition, in free brushwork, and in intimate quality. They were quite different from those of the Wu-hsing painters who tried to continue Chao Meng-fu's late interest in the Kuo Hsi tradition.

At the same time Wang Meng is also the great painter who closes the last chapter of the artistic development of Wu-hsing. Throughout the Ming period, while Soochow saw generations of great painters, Wu-hsing fell completely silent after Wang Meng, with almost no name

---

[129] I refer to Shen Meng-lin (a descendant of Chao Meng-fu), Ts'ao K'ung-chang 曹孔章 (who served for a time as an instructor in Hu-chou), Hu Yüan-su 胡元素, and Shen Shih-ch'eng 沈士誠. Shen Meng-lin was probably the best known. His literary collection, the *Hua-hsi chi* 花谿集, is extant. (The Gest Library at Princeton University holds a microfilm copy of a Ch'ien-lung period edition.)

[130] The other three were Chang T'ung, a painter of orchids; Hsin Shu-keng 辛叔耕, known for his wintry forests; and Meng Yü-chien, a blue-and-green landscape painter. See 1874 HCFC 75:2b (for Chang T'ung), 75:4b (for Hsin Shu-keng), and 80:33b (for Meng Yü-chien).

worth mentioning. Perhaps one slight exception is the early-fifteenth-century painter Shen Hsün 沈巽. Only one painting by this man is known to be extant.[131] This work, in ink on paper, shows that, even after a whole century, Chao's influence was still strongly felt in his prefecture. Indeed, it is a perfect testimony to the way in which Chao's achievements dominated the scene in Wu-hsing long after his death.

Chao Meng-fu lived during the time when the Mongols consolidated their rule in China. The country enjoyed a period of peace and stability and attempts were made by some of the rulers to achieve a cultural unity that would join the Mongols and the Chinese. Because of his complex background and his ability to adjust to the changing moral standards and cultural needs, Chao was able to synthesize the Mongol desires and the traditional Chinese requirements. This was his great creative achievement. Of course, he had many inner conflicts and unresolved ideas. But, on the whole, just as in politics he was able to resolve some of the contradictions between the Mongols and the Chinese, in the cultural sphere he was mainly responsible for promoting the formation of a cultural unity.[132] After his death in 1322, Mongol rule began its gradual decline. Contradictions between the Mongols and the Chinese grew more severe, and the opposition between Ta-tu and the Chiang-nan area more pronounced. During the days when Chao Meng-fu enjoyed his leadership of the southerners, Wu-hsing became a symbol for the accommodation between the Mongols and the Chinese. With the collapse of the Yüan, its synthesis was shattered and its achievement became a thing of the past.

[131] Shen's biography appears in 1874 HCFC 80:34a. There are two identical versions of this painting. Besides the one at the Princeton Art Museum, a second is in the Avery Brundage Collection of the Center of Asian Art and Culture, San Francisco.

[132] See the discussion of this idea in my *Autumn Colors*.

The Impact of the Re-unification:
Northern Elements in the Life and Art of
Hsien-yü Shu (1257?–1302)
and Their Relation to
Early Yüan Literati Culture

MARILYN WONG FU

INTRODUCTION*

When Chao Meng-fu 趙孟頫 (t. Tzu-ang 子昂, 1254–1322; Wu-hsing 吳興, Chekiang) returned south in the spring of 1295 on his way home to Wu-hsing, Chekiang, after a period of almost ten years in the capital, it marked a turning point in his career from the standpoint of the history of art. He brought back with him a group of paintings and calligraphy as substantial evidence of an experience and changing esthetic view which, as demonstrated in his own calligraphy and painting, would significantly redirect the course of later art from the Yüan onward.[1] His northern experience would form the basis for an approach founded on a return to ancient models which would differentiate his work to an ever-increasing degree from that of his older contemporaries, such as Ch'ien Hsüan 錢選

---

*In this essay, the archaic spelling Tsin is adopted for the native Chin 晉 dynasty (265–420) in order to avoid confusing it with the Jurchen Chin 金 dynasty (1115–1234).

This paper has benefitted from criticism on several points by Chu-tsing Li, Hok-lam Chan, Yan-shuan Lao, John D. Langlois, Stephen West, and Paul Buell. I owe them my sincere thanks. I am otherwise grateful to my husband Shen C. Y. Fu, and my teachers Wen Fong and Shujiro Shimada for their encouragement and aid on problems regarding Hsien-yü Shu's life and art.

[1] Chao brought back some twenty-three paintings ascribed to the Tsin, T'ang and Sung periods, four examples of T'ang calligraphy, twelve assorted antiquities, and some books and rubbings. This list is recorded in YYKYL, pp. 87–93; see also Li, pp. 20–21.

For Chao's activities, see YS 172:4018–4023; Yang Tsai 楊載, "Chao-kung hsing-chuang 趙公行狀," in SHCWC, *hsing-chuang*, 1a–2b; Ou-yang Hsüan 歐陽玄, "Chao Wen-min kung shen-tao-pei 趙文敏公神道碑" in *Kuei-chai wen-chi* 圭齋文集 (SPTK ed.), 9:9b–19b; the chronology by Toyama Gunji 外山軍治 in SZ 17, pp. 16–18; and the bibliography given in Li, *Autumn Colors*, p. 1, n. 1.

(ca.1235–after 1300, Wu-hsing, Chekiang),[2] who had also retired to Wu-hsing along with Chao following the fall of Hangchow to the Mongols in 1276.

The importance of his northern trip to Chao's experience as a painter is summed up by Chu-tsing Li in his study, *Autumn Colors on the Ch'iao and Hua Mountains*: "For Chao Meng-fu, then, who might have known some pre-Southern Sung paintings in his early years in south China, *his ten-year sojourn in the north must have been a revelation*, liberating him from the restrictions of the Southern Sung tradition and turning T'ang and Northern Sung into a new and living force in him" [my italics].[3] If the northern experience was crucial to Chao Meng-fu's career, it could have happened only as a result of the re-unification under the Mongols: for the first time in more than a century southerners could travel freely to the north, and, equally important, northerners also came south to serve in office. Recent studies have focused with good reason on Chao Meng-fu's outstanding contribution to Yüan painting.[4] It is now appropriate to look into the activities of some of the northerners who came south in the early years following the re-unification and to consider the extent of their contributions to early Yüan literary culture, particularly to the visual arts.

The effects on the arts of southerners travelling north, and of north-erners travelling south were of course not precisely the same, as the situations preceding the re-unification differed greatly. There is no doubt that a north-south polarization occurred with the sack of Pien-liang 汴梁 (Kaifeng) in 1127, anticipated by the founding of the Jurchen-Chin state in North China in 1115, and the corresponding flight of the Sung court south to Hangchow.

It is known that the Jurchens made purposeful efforts in the sack of Pien-liang to preserve and to seize a good deal of Sung material culture.

---

[2] For Ch'ien Hsüan and his art, see James Cahill, "Ch'ien Hsüan and His Figure Paintings," *Archives of Asian Art*, 12 (1958), esp. pp. 15–17; Wen Fong, "The Problem of Ch'ien Hsüan," *Art Bulletin*, 52 (1960), esp. pp. 175, 182–84; and Lee and Ho, pp. 27–30, 92–93.

[3] Li, *Autumn Colors*, p. 21.

[4] Studies pre-dating 1964 are given by Li in *Autumn Colors*, p. 1, n. 1; see also Li, "The Freer *Sheep and Goat* and Chao Meng-fu's Horse Paintings," *Artibus Asiae*, 30 (1968), pp. 279–326; "Stages of Development in Yüan Landscape Painting," *National Palace Museum Bulletin*, 4, nos. 2, 3 (1969); "The Development of Painting in Soochow during the Yüan Dynasty," *Proceedings of the International Symposium on Chinese Painting* (Taipei, 1972); and "The Uses of the Past in Yüan Landscape Painting," *Artists and Traditions*, C. Murck, ed. (Princeton, 1976), pp. 73–88; Richard Barnhart, *Marriage of the Lord of the River* (Ascona, 1970); and Lee and Ho (1968).

In addition to the classics and the *Tzu-chih t'ung-chien* 資治通鑑, the works of Su Shih 蘇軾 (1036–1101) and Huang T'ing-chien 黃庭堅 (1045–1105) were specifically designated. A conspicuous sign of their cultural voraciousness was the removal of the Ten Stone Drums from Pien-liang to Yen-ching 燕京.[5] Chinese scholars under Jurchen rule not only carried on traditions of Sung literary culture, but also considered themselves guardians of the tradition in a way which their southern counterparts did not.[6] In the realm of the arts, and particularly in calligraphy, for example, Chin artists carried on the styles practiced by the scholar-amateurs of the Northern Sung, Su Shih, Wen T'ung 文同 (1019–1079), and Mi Fu 米芾 (1052–1107). Emperor Chang-tsung 章宗 (r. 1189–1208) openly imitated Sung Hui-tsung's 宋徽宗 "slender-gold" script style (*shou-chin t'i* 瘦金體) and also sought to create an art collection of distinction.[7] By the fifth generation of Jurchen rulers, the degree of sinicization and devotion to arts and to letters was quite clear: Chang-tsung became the Chin counterpart of the artist-connoisseur-emperor Hui-tsung (r. 1100–1125) of the Northern Sung and of Hui-tsung's son Kao-tsung 高宗 (r. 1127–1162) in the Southern Sung.[8] This

---

[5] Hsü Meng-hsin 徐夢莘, *San-ch'ao pei-meng hui-pien* 三朝北盟會編, 73, 77, as quoted in Hsü Ping-ch'ang 徐炳昶, "Chin Wan-yen Hsi-yin shen-tao pei shu-hou 金完顏希尹神道碑書後," *Shih-hsüeh chi-k'an* 史學季刊 (Peking, 1936), 1/12–13; and Toyama Gunji, "Kinjin to sho 金人と書," SZ 16, p. 29.

Su Shih and Huang T'ing-chien were members of the "conservative" faction (in opposition to Wang An-shih's reforms) which the Chin meant to re-instate. See Liu Ch'i 劉祁, *Kuei-ch'ien chih* 歸潛志 (*Chih-pu-tsu chai ts'ung-shu* 知不足齋叢書 ed.), 12:6a, as quoted in H. L. Chan, *Historiography of the Chin: Three Studies* (Wiesbaden, 1970), p. 158.

[6] On this subject see especially H. L. Chan, *Historiography* (cited above); also Toyama Gunji, *Kinchōshi kenkyū* 金朝史研究 (Kyoto, 1964); Jing-shen Tao, *The Jurchen in Twelfth-Century China: A Study of Sinicization* (Seattle, 1976); for the arts, Susan Bush, "Clearing after Snow in the Min Mountains," *Oriental Art*, 11 (1965), pp. 163–172; "Literati Culture under the Chin," *Oriental Art*, 15 (1969), pp. 103–112; and *The Chinese Literati on Painting* (Cambridge, Mass., 1971), esp. pp. 87–117; K. T. Wu, "Chinese Printing under Four Alien Dynasties," *Harvard Journal of Asiatic Studies*, 13 (1950), pp. 447–523; and of particular relevance, a lecture delivered by Professor Herbert Franke, "The Chin Dynasty as Precursors of the Mongols in China," Princeton University, September 25, 1974.

[7] See Toyama's study of Chang-tsung, which includes a list of thirty-six works, in *Kinchōshi kenkyū*, pp. 660–675. For Hui-tsung's artistic activities, see SZ 15, pp. 37–44, pls. 115–116; and Betty Tseng Yu-ho Ecke, "Emperor Hui Tsung, the Artist: 1082–1136" (Ph. D. diss., New York University, 1972).

Several sources indicate that Chang-tsung was the grandson of Hui-tsung. See Ecke (cited above), pp. 32 and 214–216, who provides a biography of Chang-tsung from *Ta Chin kuo-chih* 大金國志; also Yüan Chüeh 袁桷, *Ch'ing-jung chü-shih chi* 清容居士集 (SPTK ed.), 45:9b; and Chou Mi, *Kuei-hsin tsa-chih* 癸辛雜識 (*Chin-tai pi-shu* 津逮秘書 ed.), hsia 下, 41b. I am indebted to Hok-lam Chan for the latter two references.

attitude toward arts and letters, extending from the emperor on down, made Chin scholars and artists suitable carriers of the literati legacy.[9]

In the writings on calligraphy and painting of early Yüan masters in the scholarly tradition, frequent mention is made of certain Chin figures, particularly Wang T'ing-yün 王庭筠 (1151–1202; Pohai 渤海, Liao-ning).[10] Like Yüan Hao-wen 元好問 (1190–1257; T'ai-yüan 太原, Shan-si) in literature, Wang T'ing-yün become a key figure in the picture of early Yüan literati culture drawn by scholars. Wang was ranked as the heir to the ink bamboo tradition begun in the Northern Sung by Su Shih and Wen T'ung, and he was considered by T'ang Hou 湯垕, the leading painting critic of the mid-Yüan, as the equal of Chao Meng-fu in being the best painter and calligrapher of the last two hundred years.[11] Li K'an 李衎 (1245–1320, Chi-ch'iu 薊邱, Hopei), the leading early Yüan painter

[8] Chang-tsung's identification with Hui-tsung was enhanced by the fact that he declared the Chin the successors to the Northern Sung as the legitimate dynasty. This occurred in a series of discussions on the "legitimate line of succession" held between 1194 and 1202. Hsüan-tsung initiated the same discussions and re-affirmed Chang-tsung's verdict in 1214. By implication the Southern Sung was dismissed as an illegitimate regime. For a full exposition, see H. L. Chan, *Theories of Legitimacy in Imperial China: Discussions on "Legitimate Succession" under the Jurchen-Chin Dynasty (1115–1234)* (University of Washington Press, in press).

[9] Kao-tsung was also determined to continue the artistic activity established by his father, including the amassing of collections of art. Painting and calligraphy were dominated by the influence of his enthusiastic patronage. The styles of his court painters, notably Ma Yüan and Hsia Kuei, and his personal style of calligraphy extended in radiating circles of influence to the whole of Hangchow and the Southern Sung at large. In calligraphy other styles continued the spirit of individualism established by the Northern Sung masters, but they were practiced with an increasing abandon and disregard for ancient models (cf. SZ 16, pp. 1–24, pls. 1–45). Landscape painting of the Academy reflected the southern geography, and in concept, was strikingly modern in emotional overtones and stress on technical facility. It was a truly new and current style of painting recognizable immediately as "Southern Sung."

Academy-sponsored art nevertheless effectively represented an "anti-literati" force, for its perfection of technique and outward uniformity undermined the individuality and independence of the scholar. Not that the literati tradition died in the Southern Sung, but that the few adherents of literati ideals and styles were not sufficient to offset the dominance of the Academic ideals. (For a recent analysis of these points, see A. C. Soper, "The Relationship of Early Chinese Painting to its Own Past," *Artists and Traditions*, pp. 21–47.) The literati tradition in the Southern Sung went "underground," and was carried on with enthusiasm by, among others, the circles of Ch'an 禪 monks acquainted with Su Shih and Huang T'ing-chien. The literati undercurrent merged with the Ch'an monks' tradition, especially in calligraphy, lending strength to both "movements."

[10] See CS 126:2730–2732, and his biography and epitaph by Yüan Hao-wen 元好問 in *Chung-chou chi* 中州集 (SPTK ed.), 3:22ab, and in *I-shan hsien-sheng wen-chi* 遺山先生文集 (SPTK ed.), 6:8b–14a (see also n. 83, 84 below).

[11] T'ang Hou 湯垕, *Hua-lun* 畫論 (ISTP 11), p. 9. (See also n. 89 below.)

of ink bamboo, traced the source of his art to Wang and his son, Wan-ch'ing 萬慶 (fl. 1200–after 1262?).[12]

Through the eyes of early Yüan scholars and artists, the Chin period and its literati were not merely receptors of the older culture, but, more importantly, *preservers* and *transmitters* of essential elements of the cultural legacy left by the Northern Sung at a time when the makeup of that culture was to be fundamentally altered. From this point of view the preservation of literati values by the Chin takes on added significance in view of the role which northerners travelling south in the early Yüan were to play in the transmission of these values to southern artists.[13]

H. L. Chan's studies of Yüan Hao-wen and Liu Ch'i 劉祁 have shown how a conscious effort was made by northerners, or *nan-kuan* 南冠 (emigrants to the south), in the early Yüan to preserve aspects of their literary and historical culture for future generations. From the stand-point of the succeeding generations, such northerners did not "fall short" of Sung standards. Scholars who came south were faced not only with the preservation and continuation of traditional values, but with its restoration as well; they had not only to heal the wounds of a bifurcated culture, but one whose survival was now threatened by total alien rule.

---

[12] In the preface to his treatise on bamboo painting (see below, n. 80), Li K'an says that he first learned through Wang Wan-ch'ing's works, and then was led to the study of his father's and ultimately to Wen T'ung's 文同 art. Wan-ch'ing, whose name is sometimes written as Man-ch'ing 曼慶 (I follow the *Chung-chou chi*, cited above), was T'ing-yün's adopted son; see Bush, "Clearing" (cited in n. 6), p. 9, n. 27, for details. Wan-ch'ing's dates are not known; I have estimated them on the basis of two dated colophons.

[13] In the history of art, the literati, or scholar-amateur, phenomenon was one of the major intellectual and esthetic contributions of Chinese arts and letters to world culture. Its chief tenets exemplify the flowering of Chinese culture and represent a distinctive esthetic. Poetry, calligraphy, and painting were regarded as primary forms of expression of the learned; moral integrity and personal cultivation reflected themselves in the quality of literary and artistic expression, and an amateur status in the pursuit of these arts was stressed. In calligraphy and painting, the literati movement reached a height in the Northern Sung as part of a total efflorescence of Sung culture. The Yüan was a key turning point in its development. The late-thirteenth to early-fourteenth centuries witnessed both a revival and a consolidation of ideas and ideals of the scholar-amateurs of the eleventh and twelveth centuries. Two aspects were noteworthy: the *fu-ku* 復古 mentality, which in essence was a reassertion of the validity of past models as a basis for present change and innovation; and the continuation and intensification of Northern Sung scholar-amateur interests in calligraphy and painting and their ultimate merger as expressions of the total cultivated man. If one asks how the *fu-ku* movement can be distinguished in the Yüan from the "normal Chinese instinct to look backward" for models, the probable answer would be that in the Yüan this interest was much more systematic and ultimately more far-reaching in its effect on later generations than before. For recent discussions, see Bush, *Chinese Literati* (cited above, n. 6), and Wen Fong, "Archaism as a 'Primitive' Style," *Artists and Traditions*, pp. 89–112.

From this point of view, these northerners—i.e., those whose ancestors had served the Chin—made important contributions to Yüan culture. First, many were in a position to inherit and to transmit the literary values of their immediate predecessors. They themselves were not witnesses to brutal political defeat by the Mongols, but were far enough removed by generation to look upon their ancestors as progenitors of a distinct literary and artistic tradition. Early Yüan literati painters and calligraphers were able actively to practice and to reinforce in a continuing fashion the tenets which their fathers, grandfathers, and great-grandfathers inherited from Northern Sung literati. Second, because of this continuity, when cultivated northerners came south, the southern literati immediately recognized the differences and value of their accomplishments.

The young Liu Kuan 柳貫 (1270–1342, P'u-chiang 浦江, Chekiang), who by the mid-Yüan was to become a prominent scholar and Hanlin academician, witnessed this situation and was struck by it. In a colophon appended to a letter which Hsien-yü Shu wrote to a friend, Liu recalls the time when he met many of these northerners:

"Colophon by Liu Kuan to Hsien-yü Shu's letter to Ch'iu O"

"It has been noted before that during the Chih-yüan 至元 era (1264–1294), the prominent persons from the Central Plain (Chung-chou 中州) were extremely numerous. It was a period of time which was not too distant from the fall of the Chin, and old loyalists from the Sung were still living. Roads and communications had just undergone massive unification, and the weapons and banners [of the Mongol army] were spread out in the four directions covering the Yangtze and Huai Rivers. There were no longer any restrictions in travel between north and south. Literary activity flowed freely, and northerners and southerners admired and respected each other. Both were anxious to see each others' works, which had previously been inaccessible to them.

"Among those who journeyed south to serve in the government and who best loved the mountains and waters of Ch'ien-t'ang 錢塘, were five whom I knew: Li Chung-fang [Li Yu 李有, died ca. 1300?, from Yen-ching, Hopei], Kao Yen-ching [K'o-kung 高克恭, 1248–1310, a Westerner born in Ta-t'ung, Shansi], Liang Kung-fu [Tseng 梁曾, 1242–1322, from Yen-ching, Hopei], Hsien-yü Po-chi [Shu, 1257?–1302, from Yü-yang, Hopei] and Kuo Yu-chih [T'ien-hsi 郭天錫, ca. 1248–1302?, from Ta-t'ung, Shansi].

"When Chung-fang [Li Yu] and Yen-ching [Kao K'o-kung] were exhilarated, they would paint bamboo and rocks, groves and valleys. Po-chi's writing in running and cursive scripts attained a capable standard. Kung-fu [Liang Tseng] and Yu-chih [Kuo T'ien-hsi] and the three other gentlemen liked to compose poetry together and to examine and authenticate specimens of calligraphy and famous paintings, old vessels and antiquities. Thus the scholars of the Wu-Yüeh 吳越 area [Kiangsu and Chekiang] were led to prominence by these several gentlemen [from the north].

"When Yen-chung the Surveillance Commissioner (*lien-fang* 廉訪) [Ch'iu O 仇諤, 1250–1300, from Ta-tu] came back from the south in Fukien, he was invited by Po-chi [to stay in Hangchow with him] for several consecutive weeks and months. At the time, Chao Tzu-ang [Meng-fu] had just left his post in Ch'i-chou [Shantung, i.e., he had asked for leave in the spring of 1295] to return home to Wu-hsing; he also came to join the gentlemen at those gatherings. I did not have a chance to meet the honorable Surveillance Commissioner, but I heard about his strumming the *ch'in* 琴, playing his own compositions, and oftentimes transposing the key to an old melody. [He played so well that] everyone present was aroused to fill their winecups repeatedly and empty them forthwith. Ah, he was another extraordinary product from the north!

"After several years, Chung-fang passed away first in his post in the Records Office of the Branch Censorate (*Hsing yü-shih-t'ai chao-mo-kuan* 行御史臺照磨官). Po-chi had just been appointed as Registrar in the Court of Imperial Sacrifices (*T'ai-ch'ang-ssu tien-pu* 太常寺典簿) when he, too, died. The Surveillance Commissioner was serving in Kao-yu [Kiangsu], when he became ill; he went to Yangchow to be treated and died there. Yen-ching was called to court late in life; he took up the post of Minister of Punishments (*Hsing-pu shang-shu* 刑部尚書) and Custodian of Ta-ming [Hopei]. Kung-fu entered the Academy of Worthies (Chi-hsien [yüan] 集賢院) as an Academician (*hsüeh-shih* 學士) and Tzu-ang retired [to Wu-hsing] as Hanlin Academician for the Transmission of Directives (*Han-lin hsüeh-shih ch'eng-chih* 翰林學士承旨). These latter gentlemen lived to a reasonable age before they died.

"Parting and coming together, living and dying—no one can predict these events. But even today the people of Ch'ien-t'ang still remember with pride those gentlemen [from the north]: they think that Fate must have planned this meeting for them on our soil prior to their coming. Be that as it may, those joyous gatherings between literary men are given out with exceeding parsimony by the Creator (*tsao-wu-che* 造物者). Even though we would prefer more of such occasions, they are simply not to be gotten.

"When I served in the capital I was a good friend of his Excellency's [Ch'iu O] son, the Investigating Censor (*Chien-ch'a yü-shih* 監察御史). He brought out this calligraphy of Po-chi's [for me to see]. It even had Tzu-ang's inscription at the end.

"Now this is all very distant, and poetry meetings are very quiet. I have written something about the flourishing past to show my sadness about the present decline. It is like the sound of the neighbor's flute—it recalls in me such deep feelings that I want to cover my ears and hide."[14]

It is clear from this account by a slightly younger southern contemporary that the activities of the early Yüan scholars were exciting and deeply enriched by the presence of these northerners. It is particularly significant in the phrase "The scholars of the Wu-Yüeh area were led to prominence through these several gentlemen." Several things can be inferred from his statement. One is that both northerners and southerners were in a very receptive frame of mind during those early Chih-yüan years from 1264–1294, which began in north China, overlap the fall of Hangchow, and extend to the death of Khubilai. Both northerners and southerners were anxious to exchange points of view and felt an urgent need to absorb new ideas. This expansive spirit is often felt at the beginning of a dynasty. But in late-thirteenth-century China, the re-unification contained a blessing in disguise: it allowed a free flow of new blood and interests such as had not occurred in quite the same way in any other dynasty. The political bifurcation had fostered a cultural regionalism which proved a healthy interval. In the visual arts, there was an opening up of cultural channels. The regionalism was not merely linked to conservative or progressive trends, but actually involved differences of substance and style. The interval of cultural separatism had given birth to a gap in traditions offering a perspective in the arts whereby subsequent generations could focus on issues particularly sensitive to change. If Chao Meng-fu had had a chance all along to see examples of Tsin, T'ang, and Sung works, for example, and if Southern Sung and Chin painting styles had not been so distinct, the course of Yüan art might have been very different, and the changes Chao helped to institute would have appeared far less revolutionary.

Thus, Liu Kuan's statements underline the positive contribution which northerners were making to the southern culture. His observations also reflect mid-fourteenth-century Yüan society which had by then settled into different patterns of stability. The later generation of mid-to-late-Yüan southerners, in looking back to the early Yüan, did not see the northerners as being heir to a declining tradition, which would be the case if they were viewed from the heights of the Northern Sung accomplishments. The measurements were being made with a different ruler. The northerners had in their favor the Mongol social codes, the

---

[14] *Liu Tai-chih wen-chi* 柳待制文集 (SPTK ed.), 18:12a–b, "Pa Hsien-yü Po-chi yü Ch'iu Yen-chung hsiao-t'ieh 跋鮮于伯幾與仇彥中小帖."

earlier transition to the Yüan political institutions, and the continuous literary and artistic traditions from the Northern Sung. These factors fostered cultural stability and self-confidence which, when combined with other intrinsically northern traits (such as moral severity and physical vigor), put them on a different footing when compared with the southerners in the realm of the visual arts.

It would be idle speculation to ask what Northern Sung culture would have been like if it had continued for another century without regional separatism and all its implications. Toward the end of the Chin period, Sung culture in the south had taken on its own distinctive expression. For along with the shift of the capital were all the attendant factors of change—an ultra-refined and luxurious way of life for the upper classes which, reaching a modal peak in the Northern Sung, was continued and intensified in the Southern Sung. This mode of vision, expressed in all its languor and seductive charm in the paintings of Southern Sung court life, contrasted sharply with the severe, almost harsh, styles and subjects of northern artists. The Jurchens seem to have embraced a stern morality which made them suitable perpetuators of Northern Sung culture as an *ideal*. Thus in the arts the formal vehicle for these ideals continued in an almost pure form.[15] By contrast, Southern Sung artists introduced changes so new and modern that they ostensibly rejected the modes set forth by the Northern Sung amateurs.

It is beyond the scope of this essay to enter into a more detailed description of literati culture in the north preceding 1234, or of Southern Sung Academy and literary activity preceding 1279 and the Mongol conquest. The picture presented here in broad strokes is meant to provide a background to what happened in the early Yüan and to my discussion of the early Yüan master Hsien-yü Shu, whose activities come to bear on some of these cultural issues.

HSIEN-YÜ SHU'S BACKGROUND

Hsien-yü Shu (t. Po-chi 伯幾, h. K'un-hsüeh-min 困學民, 1257?–1302; Yü-yang 漁陽, Hopei)[16] was an exact contemporary of Chao Meng-fu,

---

[15] That the Chin artists were so effective in their perpetuation and "conservation" of Northern Sung styles is proved in part by the confusion with Northern Sung styles in the traditional attributions of the past. Only recently have art historians attempted to isolate and give definition to "what is Chin" stylistically. (See studies by Bush, cited n. 6, above.)

[16] Other *hao* 號 of Hsien-yü Shu are: Hu-lin yin-li 虎林隱吏, Shui-lien tao-shih 水簾道士, Chi-tzu chih i 箕子之裔, Chung-shan hou-jen 中山后人, Chih-chi tao-jen 直寄道人, Wei-shun-an 委順菴 and Hsi-ch'i hsien-sheng 西溪先生.

For brief biographies, see HYS 237:86; *Yüan shih lei-pien* 元史類編 (Sao-yeh shan-fang

but died some twenty years before him. A relatively obscure name today, he was known in his time as a calligrapher, poet, connoisseur, and collector and counted as one of the more colorful and talked-about personalities in the art circles of Hangchow in the early years of the Yüan dynasty.

Hsien-yü Shu was a member of a literary circle whose activities centered around Hangchow, or Lin-an 臨安, the former Southern Sung capital. Chao Meng-fu was its most prominent member. Several were northerners who, like Hsien-yü Shu, had emigrated to the south. A Uighur and a Central Asian were in the group. Some were born in the south and declared themselves Sung loyalists; others, like Chao Meng-fu, held high office and lent their prestige to the circle. Among the gentlemen in this coterie, in addition to Hsien-yü Shu and Chao Meng-fu, were Teng Wen-yüan 鄧文原 (1258–1328, Mien-chou 綿州 [Pa-hsi 巴西], Szechwan), Chou Mi 周密 (1232-after 1308, Ch'i-chou, Shantung; later Ch'ien-t'ang), Tai Piao-yüan 戴表原 (1244–1310, Feng-hua 奉化, Chekiang), Ch'iu Yüan 仇遠 (1247–after 1327, Nan-yang 南陽, Honan;

掃葉山房 ed.), 36:27a; *Yüan shih hsin-pien* 元史新編 (Shen-wei t'ang 慎微堂 ed.), 47:66; *Yüan shih hsüan* 元詩選 (Hsiu-yeh ts'ao-t'ang 秀野草堂 ed.), 29 *erh-ping* 二丙; *Yüan shih chi-shih* 元詩紀事 (rpt. Taipei, 1968), 8:128–130; these sources consist mainly of extracts taken from material found in Liu Kuan, *Liu Tai-chih wen-chi*; Chao Meng-fu, SHCWC; Hsien-yü Shu's own poems, in *K'un-hsüeh-chai chi* (*Yüan shih hsüan, erh-ping*); and SSHY. This material will be quoted in the following discussion. The SSHY entry is the earliest purely biographical source.

Recent studies on Hsien-yü Shu include the following: Fushimi Chūkei 伏見冲敬, *Shohin* 書品, 181 (1967); P'an Po-ying 潘伯鷹, *Wen wu* 文物, 1961, No. 10, pp. 55–60; Fukumoto Gaichi 福本雅一, *Shoron* 書論, 6 (1975), pp. 90–92; and entries by Nakada Yūjirō, SZ 17, pp. 160–163, 184–185.

There are three theories concerning his birthdate: a) 1256/1257, as given in such secondary sources as Wu Hsiu 吳修 (1765–1827), *Hsü i-nien-lu* 續疑年錄 (1812, *Yüeh-ya t'ang ts'ung-shu* 粤雅堂叢書 ed., *ts'e* 159), 1:11a; Chiang Liang-fu 姜亮夫, *Li-tai ming-jen nien-li-pei-chuan tsung-piao* 歷代名人年里碑傳總表 (1937), p. 369; T'an Chia-ting 譚嘉定, *Chung-kuo wen-hsüeh-chia ta-tz'u-tien* 中國文學家大辭典 (1934), no. 3238. b) 1246 as given in Lu Hsin-yüan 陸心源, *I-ku t'ang t'i-pa* 儀顧堂題跋 (1890), 13:17a (I am indebted to Chiang I-han for this latter reference). Unfortunately, Lu does not give any source for his 1246 birthdate, and it still remains to be uncovered in the course of my own research. c) 1228/29 as suggested by Kung Ch'iu-nung 龔秋穫 in *Shu-hsüeh tsa-chih* 書學雜志 (Ch'eng-tu, 1943), 2, pp. 17–24. I deal with these theories in more detail in my dissertation on Hsien-yü Shu.

Hsien-yü Shu's death date in late 1301 or early 1302 is fortunately confirmed by several contemporary sources and by a dated colophon by his son, Hsien-yü Pi-jen, as well as by his own late works. The uncertainty about his birthdate and his death at 75 *sui* (if born in 1228), 57 *sui* (if born in 1246), or 47/48 *sui* (if born in 1256/1257), causes grave problems in defining his over-all artistic development. Until further evidence is uncovered, however, the question of his birthdate remains inconclusive.

later Ch'ien-t'ang), Pai T'ing 白珽 (1248–1328, Ch'ien-t'ang), Chang Po-ch'un 張伯淳 (1242–1302, Chia-hsing 嘉興, Chekiang), Li K'an (1245–1320, Chi-ch'iu, Hopei), Kuo T'ien-hsi (ca.1248–ca.1302?, Ta-t'ung 大同, Shansi), Kao K'o-kung (1248–1310, Central Asia; born Ta-t'ung, Shansi), Ch'iao K'uei-ch'eng 喬簣成 (fl. 1270–1313?, Yen-ching, Hopei), Wang Chih 王芝 (fl. ca.1285–1300?, Ch'ien-t'ang), Kung K'ai 龔開 (1222–1307, Huai-yin 淮陰, Kiangsu), Lien Hsi-kung 廉希貢 (ca.1240–1300, Uighur, Khotan), Huang Chin 黃溍 (1277–1357, Chin-hua, Chekiang), Liu Kuan (1270–1342, P'u-chiang, Chekiang), Yü Chi 虞集 (1272–1348, Lin-ch'uan 臨川, Kiangsi), and others. The literary activities of these gentlemen spanned other areas of Yüan culture, so that various strata of late-thirteenth- and early-fourteenth-century cultural history can be glimpsed through their interpenetrating relationships.

Hsien-yü Shu was considered by Yü Chi as one of the three great calligraphers of the early Yüan, the other two being Chao Meng-fu and Teng Wen-yüan.[17] In recent times Chao's fame has eclipsed that of both Hsien-yü Shu and Teng Wen-yüan, but in their own day they were equally well known and regarded as calligraphers. Hsien-yü Shu was a third-generation descendant of a scholarly family who had lived under the "golden years" of the Chin dynasty during the reigns of Shih-tsung 世宗 (1161–89) and Chang-tsung (1189–1208). His great-grandfather (active ca. 1150–1180?) and grandfather (ca. 1185–1215) were natives of Te-hsing fu 德興府 (modern Cho-lu hsien 涿鹿縣, Hopei).[18] The great-grandfather was known for his wide learning and literary skills, although he did not place high in the official examinations, and he held an official position under the Chin regime for only a brief time. The family was wealthy and became known in the area for a number of philanthropic deeds. The grandfather also had a love for learning, but he concerned himself with a general education and did not seek an official position.

In the opening years of the Chen-yu 貞祐 reign of the Chin period (1213–1216), when the Mongol forces were descending southward into Chin territory, Hsien-yü Shu's grandfather, then about thirty *sui* 歲, was slain while fleeing the Chü-yung pass 居庸關. He left a widow and

[17] *Tao-yüan hsüeh-ku lu* 道園學古錄 (SPTK ed.), 10:8a, "Pa Hsien-yü Po-chi yü Yen ch'u-shih han-mo 跋鮮于伯幾與嚴處士翰墨."

[18] Biographical details concerning Hsien-yü Shu's forebears are derived from *Hsien-yü fu-chun mu-chih-ming* 鮮于府君墓志銘, composed by Chou Ti 周砥 (ca. 1230–90?; see below, n. 30) and transcribed by Chao Meng-fu; see *San-hsi t'ang hsü fa-t'ieh* 三希堂續法帖, Liang Shih-cheng 梁詩正 (1697–1763), ed. (rpt. T'ai-nan 臺南, 1971), *ch.* 5. As primary material on Hsien-yü Shu's life is scanty, this epitaph offers valuable information on the family history.

Hsien-yü Shu was the eldest son of his father's first wife, a native of Loyang. Unfortunately, Hsien-yü Shu's birthdate or age was not mentioned in the epitaph.

several young children, including Hsien-yü Shu's father, Kuang-tsu 光祖 (1205–1281), who was ten at the time. After eighteen years of wandering as far south as Pien-liang and Hsü-chou 許州 (modern Hsü-ch'ang 許昌, Honan), the family finally settled in Fan-yang 范陽, Hopei (modern Cho-hsien), close to Cho-lu, the ancestral home.

The father, Hsien-yü Kuang-tsu, is pictured in his youth as a strong-willed but generous person who threw himself into his studies and who was willing to risk his life for a friend. In his later career, he was occupied in the transport of grain, living for fifteen years in Pien-liang. He died at seventy-seven *sui* in Huai-an, on his way to Yangchow, where he was to retire under the care of his son, Hsien-yü Shu. He was buried years later in Hangchow, where Hsien-yü Shu was to find his adopted home.

Hsien-yü Shu's northern origins and his ancestors' affiliations were very much a part of his personal identity, long after he had moved south and settled in Hangchow. He consistently signed his name, "Hsien-yü Shu of Yü-yang," which is the old name for Chi-chou 薊州, or the ancient Yu 幽 region in Hopei, which formed a part of the modern day Cho-lu hsien of his ancestors. His personal seals *Chi-tzu chih i* 箕子之裔 and *Chung-shan hou-jen* 中山后人 also reflect these northern roots.[19]

Traditionally, the climate and geographical terrain of North and South China have been sufficiently different over the several-thousand-year development of Chinese civilization to produce significant differences of temperament and of physical build, as well as to foster a difference in general behavior patterns in individuals and in social customs and manners. Such generalizations may strike an outsider as vague and perhaps even superstitious, but the differences were noticed during Hsien-yü Shu's time and were commented on by his contemporaries. His northern heritage formed a major underlying force in his art, and the members of his circle, particularly the southerners, found it important in their view of him and would invariably mention it.

[19] The double surname Hsien-yü is rare, but contrary to appearances, it is not a foreign or Turkic name, but Han-Chinese. Its origin is said to trace back to the Chou dynasty when Wu Wang 武王 (r. 1122–1115 B.C.) enfeoffed Chi-tzu 箕子, the Viscount of Chi, at Ch'ao-hsien (modern Korea). Chi-tzu's descendants took the place name Hsien-yü as surname. A seal of Hsien-yü Shu's with the legend *Chi-tzu chih i* 箕子之裔 ("Descended from Chi-tzu") acknowledges this pedigree. Another seal reads *Chung-shan hou-jen* 中山后人 ("Descendant of Chung-shan"), which refers both to the range of mountains found in the Central Plain of China, the Chung-yüan, and to a Chou state in north China occupied during the Spring and Autumn period by a northern tribe called the Pai-ti 白狄. This region is associated with present-day Cheng-ting hsien 正定縣 in modern Hopei. By assuming the byname "Chung-shan hou-jen," Hsien-yü Shu was also acknowledging his northern tribal ancestry.

Hsien-yü Shu served the Mongols in several posts, all in some capacity as clerk or registrar. Sources remain silent as to the character of his youth previous to the later 1270s. He appears to have held no fewer than five official posts, the highest being Recorder in the Court of Sacrificial Worship.[20] It is by this title, *t'ai-ch'ang*, that he is most frequently referred to by later writers. Hsien-yü Shu's sister married a Uighur prince, Dor-digin 朵兒的斤 from Kao-ch'ang 高昌, whose antecedents had inter-married with members of Chinggis' clan. Later Hsien-yü Shu's nephew Bayan-bukha-digin 伯顏不化的斤 (d. 1359) was a *darughachi* of the Ch'ü-chou circuit 衢州路 (Chekiang) during the first half of the Chih-cheng 至正 era (1341–68).[21] The familiar relation may have been helpful in securing Hsien-yü Shu's early official positions, since Dor-digin was so highly placed. This has several other implications. It has been suggested that Hsien-yü Shu's northern and Uighur connections may have contributed a protective role to his associations with southerners, and to some of the offices he held may have been sinecure positions.[22] Be that as it may, the fact that Hsien-yü Shu did hold office was important for his career as a calligrapher and as a man of letters, for it was through office that he made his most important friendships and was able to travel south to Yangchow and Hangchow, thereby gaining exposure to life in the leading cultural centers. We may therefore speak of his "Hangchow

[20] The following five posts are those for which I have found specific references and dates:
1278 Clerk in the provincial censorate (*Hsing-t'ai chieh-shih-t'ai yüan* 行台節史台掾). Hsien-yü Shu was probably in Yangchow at the time. See *Shuo-fu* 52: *K'un-tsa*, 19b.
1286 Clerk in the Finance Commission (*San-ssu shih-yüan* 三司史掾). Hsien-yü Shu was resident in Hangchow at the time. See SYTWC 2:1b–12b.
1287 Registrar in the Che-tung Regional Pacification Office (*Che-tung hsüan-wei-ssu ching-li* 浙東宣慰司經歷). See Lu Hsin-yüan, *I-ku t'ang t'i-pa* (1890), 13:17a.
1295 Head clerk in the Eastern route of the Regional Pacification Office (*Tung-tao hsüan-wei-ssu tu-shih* 東道宣慰司都事). See "Chang Yen-heng hsing-chuang kao chüan 張彥亨行狀稿卷" in the Lin Po-shou collection, National Palace Museum, Taipei.
1301/2 Registrar in the Court of Imperial Sacrifices (*T'ai-ch'ang tien-pu* 太常典簿). See colophon by Wu Na 吳訥 dated 1438 to a scroll by Yüan I 袁易, "Ch'ien-t'ang tsa-chi 錢塘雜記," in *Shang-hai po-wu-kuan ts'ang li-tai fa-shu hsüan-chi* 上海博館藏歷代法書選集 (Peking, 1964), vol. 12.

[21] YS 195:4411 and HYS 116 identify Po-yen Pu-hua's mother as the daughter of Hsien-yü Shu, whereas SSHY (7:19a) states he is the nephew. This latter information is repeated in Ch'en/Goodrich, p. 191, and also in Chuang Shen 莊申, "Yüan-tai wai-chi hua-chia ti yen-chiu 元代外籍畫家的研究," in *Chung-kuo hua-shih yen-chiu* 中國畫史研究 (Taipei, 1969), pp. 196–206. Chuang's study quotes all relevant information but does not note or resolve the inconsistency. Further research is needed.

[22] Comments offered by Professors John Langlois and K. K. Sun at the Yüan workshop, Princeton, 1975.

years" in that it was life in this southern city, with its mild climate, scenic beauty, and its social and artistic amenities, which helped to create a career of distinction for him. Thus, while the northern trip was the catalyst in Chao Meng-fu's career as an artist, the southern period of Hsien-yü Shu's life counts as the chief transforming factor in his life. That the paths of these two gentlemen would cross in a manner beneficial to them both and to the future of Yüan calligraphy and painting was a function of the re-unification under the Mongols, as we shall soon see.

Hsien-Yü Shu's Career and Artistic Activities

The year 1278 (the fourteenth year of the Chih-yüan period) is the earliest firm date surrounding Hsien-yü Shu's life. As a clerk in the provincial censorate, he was presumably in Yangchow.[23] Before long he would travel to Hangchow and meet Chao Meng-fu. Chao would rise much higher in the ranks of Yüan officialdom than would Hsien-yü Shu, but he would remain a lifelong friend. The exact year of their meeting is not certain, but it is of interest to look for a moment at the differences in their historical situations.

By the years 1276–1278 the Mongol armies had finally succeeded in overtaking the Chiang-nan region and the Southern Sung capital, Lin-an (Hangchow). Northern China, or the area north of the Huai River, had experienced the protracted period of Mongol take-over some decades earlier in 1234, when Jurchen-Chin territory was seized. Thus a youth such as Hsien-yü Shu brought up in the north would have had a close, but not entirely similar, response to the political and social upheaval of the dynastic change that a southern youth such as Chao Meng-fu would have had. A descendant of the Sung royal family, Chao grew up in Wu-hsing in the heart of Chiang-nan. He was in his mid-twenties when China was conquered by the Mongols. Later, Chao would be faced with the serious decision of whether or not to serve the new alien government: in 1286 he answered the call from Khubilai, summoning talented scholars from the south to the capital.[24] Politically, the course of Chao Meng-fu's life would be quite different from that of Hsien-yü Shu's. Yet, in the arts, they found a profound mutual understanding and interest, and their talents would bring them together as if there had been no difference in their backgrounds and political ranks. Their close association causes us

[23] *Shuo-fu* 52; *K'un-tsa*, 19b; and Hu Yü-chin 胡玉縉, *Ssu-k'u ch'üan-shu tsung-mu t'i-yao pu-cheng* 四庫全書總目提要補證 (Peking, 1964), p. 984. See also below, n. 38.

[24] For a recent study of this topic, see Sun K'o-k'uan 孫克寬, "Chiang-nan fang-hsien yü Yen-yu ju-chih 江南訪賢與延祐儒治," in *Yüan-tai Han wen-hua chih huo-tung* 元代漢文化之活動 (Taipei, 1968), pp. 345–363.

to consider the role which a northerner like Hsien-yü Shu played in the formation of Chao Meng-fu's views on the arts and in the development of the literati movement as it was to be further defined in the Yüan.

In a poem written in 1307, Chao Meng-fu looks back over their thirty-year friendship. By then Chao was recognized as one of the most brilliant men of the period, who, personally favored by the emperor Ayurbarwada (Jen-tsung 仁宗), would be repeatedly raised to higher positions of authority and prestige. The poem is pertinent here because it reveals much about what life was like under the Mongols for two gentlemen of refinement and superior artistic talent who also got along well. It contains the most salient aspects of their friendship and tells us what Chao remembered best about Hsien-yü Shu after his death:[25]

In life parting may still hold future meetings.
But in death one is separated forever.
You, Po-chi, have been dead for five years,
But the pain of thinking about you makes it feel like yesterday.
I was born south of the Yangtze River,
And you grew up north of the Huai River.
I recollect how I heard of your eminent reputation,
And it was in office that we were able to meet.
I was well past twenty years of age,
And your black hair was as glossy as lacquer.
We became fast friends with nothing between us:
As soon as I saw you, it was as if from a familiar past.
In the spring we would go out boating together,
And in the evening we would sit together talking.
You had the spirit of a hero about you, and your voice was as
    resonant as a gong.
When excited by some subject, your whiskers would bristle like
    spears;
In debate on some point, your voice would be raised to a pitch,
And your discussion would always be essential and precise.
We would talk about the manufacture of tripods of the magni-
    ficent Shang kings,
Or the style of the handsome Han steeds.
Together we would appreciate an unusual essay
Or analyze some point of mutual doubt.
In brocaded bags you kept scrolls with jade rollers—
Specimens of Tsin and T'ang calligraphy incredibly wonderful.

[25] "Ai Hsien-yü Po-chi 哀鮮于伯幾," SHCWC 3:2a–b. On the probable date of their meeting, 1284, see below, n. 52.

They were so dazzling in their brilliance
That anyone who saw them could not but feel intimidated.
No one but you, Po-chi, with your superb discrimination
Could have gathered together these treasures from the past.
Recently you acquired a jade buckle
That was marvelously worked with coiling dragons.
You lovingly took it in your hands and then passed it around
    for others to appreciate,
And the joy could be seen plainly in your face.
With deep concentration you would study old calligraphy
Until the pond beside your studio where you washed your
    brushes would be black with ink.
In our exchange of letters and essays,
We would always learn from each other.
At the time, I was studying Chung Yu's 鍾繇 (A.D. 151–230)
    writing,
And I transcribed your father's epitaph on stone.
Chiang-nan was a place which you loved,
But the climate and humidity made you suffer.
We did not expect that you would pass away while you were in
    office as *feng-ch'ang* 奉常,
And till now whenever I see your writing,
I cannot bear to look at it.
Now the Fang-ching 方井 road where you lived is lonely and
    desolate,
And pine and bamboo cover over your cottage.
There is little pure *ch'i* 氣 on heaven and earth:
Someone like you is so rare to come upon!
In your portrait, you look dignified in your dark red robe,
When I face it, tears fall to my chest.
How remote is time and space—
Will there be an end to the sorrow I feel!

From the preceding, several important points may be noted. One was
Chao Meng-fu's awareness of their different regional backgrounds. He
says specifically: "I was born south of the Yangtze, / And you grew up
north of the Huai" (我生大江南，君長淮水北). During the Southern Sung
period, the Huai River constituted the natural boundary demarcating
North China, conquered in 1126 by Jurchens, from the Chiang-nan
region of the Southern Sung where Chao grew up. In saying that Hsien-
yü Shu *grew up* north of the Huai, Chao himself was recognizing that his
friend's youth and formative years were spent in the north. Even the
parallel form of the couplet intensifies the complementary aspect of their

friendship, which no doubt contributed to its depth and long-lasting quality. We can imagine how Chao Meng-fu must have been struck by the physical appearance of this northerner with the "spirit of a hero," whose hair was "glossy as lacquer" and with a voice as "resonant as a gong." While the latter two traits are often mentioned in favorable descriptions, the "spirit of a hero" (ch'i-hao 氣豪) was a quality which invariably would be mentioned by other contemporaries in their poems about Hsien-yü Shu. Later on in the poem, Chao speaks of how Hsien-yü Shu loved Chiang-nan, but that he could not bear the climate. This was another feature of their contrasting backgrounds. Hsien-yü Shu's family would also suffer from the southern transplantation,[26] and this difference in climatic conditions may have been a factor which contributed to Hsien-yü Shu's premature death.

Another point of importance is their mutual enjoyment of antiquities and the range and quality of Hsien-yü Shu's personal collection of antique vessels, jade buckles, and Han horses. Each item would be the potential subject of discussion and debate between them. When Chao mentions the dazzling quality of the Tsin and T'ang calligraphy he collected, we can be certain that Chao was not exuding flattery. By 1307 Chao had travelled back and forth from the capital to the south several times and would have been able to see and compare the best of what he saw in the north with the southern collections.[27] These collections and the key objects in them were the rallying point of several important literary gatherings which enlivened Hangchow life for both northerners and southerners. This is an important aspect of early Yüan cultural life to which we shall return later. Further, Chao's admiration of Hsien-yü Shu's *study* of old calligraphy is also worthy of note: Hsien-yü Shu did not merely collect old calligraphy, but made it the object of research, investigating it with the intensity and motivation of a true scholar. The prominent calligrapher and high official Teng Wen-yüan was also to remark on Hsien-yü Shu's industrious study of the old masters.[28]

Chao also says that they exchanged letters and essays. Several of these are extant but unrecorded in either Chao's or Hsien-yü Shu's collected works.[29] They include discussions on the subject of ancient paintings and

[26] Hsien-yü Shu's wife and two sons suffered from various internal ailments for which he consulted Taoist herbalists. See the five extant letters in SMS 122, pls. 1–9.

[27] Chao had returned from the capital to the south on several informal leaves in 1287, 1289, 1292, 1295, 1297 and 1299.

[28] See Teng Wen-yüan's colophon dated 1312, to Hsien-yü Shu's "Yu Kao-t'ing shan Kuang-yüan chi 游高亭山廣院記," in Chu Ts'un-li 朱存理, T'ieh-wang shan-hu 鐵網珊瑚 (1728) (shu-p'in 書品), 5:28a.

[29] "Tzu-ang Po-chi ho-ts'e 子昂伯幾合冊," extant in the Palace Museum, Taipei; see KKSHL 3:227–228, and as reproduced KKFS, vols. 16 and 17.

calligraphy which provide insight into the critical attitudes toward the past which they held. Such exchanges were part of a lively ongoing interest which reveals ideas in the process of formation; such exchanges provided the basis in the early Yüan for the movement later called *fu ku* 復古—"restoration of antiquity." Indeed, the frequency and casualness with which such interest in calligraphy and antiquities are noted indicates the inordinate amount of leisure time that was spent in antiquarian pursuits during the Chih-yüan years of the early Yüan, all of which would have a profound impact on the art of subsequent generations.

Chao Meng-fu also mentions that he had transcribed Hsien-yü Shu's father's epitaph. The epitaph, composed by another contemporary, Chou Ti 周砥 (ca.1230–1290?),[30] forms the basis for what little we know of Hsien-yü Shu's early background and immediate ancestry. Its transcription took place relatively early in Chao Meng-fu's career, ca.1290, before he was recognized as the most eminent calligrapher of the day. Yet Hsien-yü Shu's choice of Chao reveals the friendship at hand, the former's early critical insight, as well as Chao Meng-fu's esteem of Hsien-yü Shu.

Finally, Chao mentions that Hsien-yü Shu passed away while in office. This is important because later historians have mistakenly believed that Hsien-yü Shu gave up his office and retired to Hangchow. He may have done so for a brief time (hence his *hao*, Hu-lin yin-li 虎林隱吏, "Hermit-clerk of Hu-lin, i.e., Hangchow"), but we do have evidence that he held at least three positions subsequent to his settling in the south. We can see that Chao Meng-fu was genuinely moved by his past friendship with Hsien-yü Shu and his remembrance of it. In the course of their lifetime, they exchanged several poems and letters which enable us to reconstruct the quality of this fruitful relationship. In one poem, for example, Chao thanks Hsien-yü for a zither (*ku-ch'in* 古琴) which he had specially made for him, and describes his friend like this:

"... Po-chi, the descendant of the Viscount of Chi, is a gentleman of abundant beard. / His talent and intellect are startling and stride beyond the ordinary. / He brought home an old log of *wu-t'ung* 梧桐 wood and sought out a champion craftsman to carve it ... / I had just gotten back from the north and was overjoyed to see him. / He handed me the zither

[30] Chou Ti was Chancellor of the National College at the time: (He is not to be confused with the poet-painter of the early Ming [*Ming shih* 明史, *chüan* 285], whose name is sometimes pronounced Chou Chih.) Chou Ti's dates are not known. According to the epitaph, Chou was twenty when he first met Hsien-yü Shu's father; then thirty years later, he met Hsien-yü Shu in Yangchow where the latter was mourning his father's death (i.e., ca. 1281); Chou was then asked by Hsien-yü Shu to compose the epitaph. I have computed Chou Ti's approximate dates on the basis of this relationship.

for me to keep,/And ever since I received it, I have been unable to sleep...." [31]

This is one of six recorded poems which Chao wrote to Hsien-yü Shu during their lifetime. [32] It records also their mutual attachment to the ancient Chinese zither, the *ku-ch'in*. Both Chao and Hsien-yü Shu were not only accomplished musicians, but connoisseurs of the instrument. [33]

Another expression of Chao's friendship with Hsien-yü was the portrait that Chao painted of him which he mentions in his poem of 1307. It is no longer extant, but Yü Chi, the prominent scholar-official of the next generation, knew them both in their prime and left a memorable poem on the portrait which allows us to complete our descriptive picture of Hsien-yü Shu. Here is Yü Chi's "Eulogy on a small portrait of Hsien-yü Po-chi painted by Chao Meng-fu":

> He [Po-chi] restrained the heroism of [northern] wind, sand, furs, and the sword,
> To take up the joys of [southern] lakes, mountains, maps, and the histories.
> In calligraphy he was equal to Mi [Fu] and Hsüeh [Shao-p'eng] 薛紹彭, and still had something more to offer.
> His total spontaneity (*feng-liu* 風流) could be compared to the Tsin and [Liu-] Sung masters without immodesty.
> This is why his excellency Wu-hsing [Chao Meng-fu] drew this portrait with the method of "an iron rod writing in the sand"—
> To be carved for posterity as rare jade.
> In a thousand years, those of great vision will still understand the wonderful art of these two gentlemen [Chao Meng-fu and Hsien-yü Shu], from a time long past. [34]

A phrase such as "the heroism of [northern] wind, sand, furs, and the sword" (風沙裘劍之豪) conjures up a distinct picture, which Yü Chi contrasts nicely with the second line, "the joys of [southern] lakes,

---

[31] "Hsieh Hsien-yü Po-chi hui-chen-yü ch'in ... 謝鮮于伯幾惠震餘琴 ...," SHCWC 3:13a–b.

[32] The five other poems are found in *ibid.*, 2:11a–b, 3:10b, 3:11a–b, 3:13a–b, 4:17b.

[33] A substantial portion of Hsien-yü Shu's *K'un-hsüeh chai tsa-lu* is taken up by lists of famous zithers owned by contemporaries. He notably begins the list with the *ku-ch'in* named "Spring Thunder" belonging to the Minister Yeh-lü Ch'u-ts'ai, which had formerly been in the Chin imperial collection and was housed in the Ch'eng-hua-tien. See *K'un-tsa* 20a–21b.

[34] "T'i Hsien-yü Po-chi hsiao-hsiang 題鮮于伯幾小象," *Tao-yüan hsüeh-ku lu*, 10:8b. Yeh Sheng 葉盛 (1420–74) claims to have seen the portrait. See his *Shui-tung jih-chi* 水東日記 (rpt. Taipei, 1965), 4:9b. I am grateful to Shen Fu for this reference.

mountains, maps and the histories" (湖山圖史之樂). Not only does this juxtaposition pinpoint the differences of physical terrain, climate, and dress, but also the occupations and state of culture with which the northern and southern regions had been commonly identified by the Yüan period. Yü Chi says explicitly that not only were there differences combined in the person of Hsien-yü Shu, but also that he had had to "restrain" (lien 斂) his northern traits, presumably because they were so strongly evident in him. Yü Chi also pays him the great compliment of saying he was equal in calligraphic stature to Mi Fu (1052–1107) and Hsüeh Shao-p'eng (fl. about 1050–1100?). Mi and Hsüeh were two of the most esteemed scholar-calligraphers of the Northern Sung; to be comparable was sufficient, yet Hsien-yü Shu still had qualities they did not possess. Indeed, Yü Chi says, his personality could be compared to the Tsin and Liu-Sung masters. Is this mere flattery?

Although the poem is undated, it was presumably written close to the end of Hsien-yü Shu's life, when there was little reason for Yü Chi to seek any favors of him. Yü already figured quite prominently in Yüan government and literary circles by that time and had established his own reputation. What Yü Chi was aiming at in the poem was a characterization of Hsien-yü Shu's *personality*. In doing so, he uses the device of historical precedent. Albeit customary, the importance lies in *which* precedents Yü Chi chose for comparison. Yü Chi sees Hsien-yü Shu (and Chao Meng-fu by implication) in the artistic tradition established by the Tsin and Liu-Sung masters, and he specifies the two aspects which are worthy of comparison: Hsien-yü Shu's calligraphy and his personality. The concept of the relationship between a man's art and his personality is fundamental in Chinese literary and esthetic theory, and it is a key to the understanding of the development and high achievement of the fine arts in general. The parallel form of Yü Chi's lines emphasizes this intimate relationship and reveals to us that he is not making a simple comparison, but is actually offering a historical judgment on the lines of tradition. In the second line, his mention of Hsien-yü Shu's personality as being comparable to the Tsin and Liu-Sung masters gives us an equation of "calligraphy = personality," and, in addition, supplies us with the historical anchor. He also uses the highly pregnant phrase *feng-liu* (lit. "wind-flow"). While the ideal of personality as given in a phrase such as *feng-liu* has had complex historical and literary associations, its meaning could also relate to specific personalities. Such cultural heroes of the Wei-Tsin period as T'ao Ch'ien 陶潛, Wang Hsi-chih 王羲之, Wang Hsien-chih 王獻之 and Chi K'ang 嵇康, and later of the Sung as Su Shih, Huang T'ing-chien, Mi Fu, and Hsüeh Shao-p'eng, all gave definition to the phrase by virtue of the distinction of their personal character and artistic genius. Thus Yü Chi's praise of Hsien-yü Shu in this context takes on added meaning.

It becomes clear from the numerous descriptions by his contemporaries that Hsien-yü Shu was highly admired in his lifetime. To win the admiration of Chao Meng-fu also implied a deep mutual exchange between them. Hsien-yü Shu played a strong supportive role in the formation of Chao's view of the arts, and in some cases he may even have initiated an idea, the potential of which was brought to fruition by Chao, who lived twenty years beyond him.

The period of the early 1280s was eventful for Hsien-yü Shu and Chao Meng-fu in terms of the artistic activity in which both took part and in the formation of their esthetic views. This activity also reveals several significant ways in which northerners and southerners could come in contact with each other to exchange ideas. Visits to collections to view specific works of art were among the most important. Often lists were made of things seen, and comments on the quality of objects were made by those present. Literary gatherings were another. These were held not only to compose poetry, but also to view objects newly acquired. They differed from the visits to collections in that they were slightly more formal, often having a guest list, and such gatherings often centered on the personalities present, rather than on the art being shown.

The visits to collections were important because they tell us the kinds of objects being held in collections, what was in circulation, and the opinions on the relative quality and quantity of holdings. In addition, they represent an opportunity for artistic contact between the artist—a potential producer of art—with art of the past, and inform us of the chief ingredients for an eventual "mix." The literary gatherings were important for the human contact of personality with personality. They give us an idea of who knew whom, and possible sources of influence. They represent an intermingling of different outlooks and generations which are major factors in the transmission and continuity of intellectual and artistic traditions in any period.

The chief sources of information for these two types of gatherings are the notebooks kept by interested persons, such as Chou Mi and Hsien-yü Shu, and colophons attached to works of art. These colophons may be extant, but the majority are recorded and found only in collected works or records of painting and calligraphy. Colophons have an advantage over notes in that they can often take us into the mind of the writer. They represent, for the most part, considered opinions resulting from a direct communion of the writer with an object of art which he held in his hand and had an opportunity to examine at close view. The colophon is a literary record of that experience. It gives the historian specific insight, and it registers attitudes held at that moment or recalled in tranquillity. Moreover, they are often dated, whereas, notes frequently are not. If the colophon is extant in its original form on a work of art, it provides the historian with both visual and documentary material, for the actual handwritten specimen can be used in the reconstruction of the master's calligraphic corpus, in ways which a purely literary record cannot. In the case of a prolific master like Chao Meng-fu, for example, there are abundant examples of extant colophons (not all of which are genuine, however), whereas only a handful of colophons by Chou Mi are extant. Fortunately, a good number by Hsien-yü Shu exist to enrich the printed record.

For example, in 1284 Hsien-yü Shu remounted an important scroll which he had acquired two years earlier by an exchange of old books and calligraphy. The scroll was the "Draft memorial on the martyrdom of his nephew Chi-ming" (*Chi chih [Chi-ming] wen kao* 祭姪 [季明] 文稿) in "running" and "cursive" scripts by the T'ang calligrapher and statesman Yen Chen-ch'ing 顏真卿 (709–785).[35] The manuscript by Yen had been in the illustrious collection of the last Northern Sung emperor Hui-tsung and was recorded in his catalogue of calligraphy, the *Hsüan-ho shu-p'u* 宣和書譜.[36] It was then, and is still now, one of the most admired and celebrated works from the hand of the T'ang master for whom the majority of works existed only in the form of rubbings from carved steles. Having obtained the scroll, Hsien-yü Shu excitedly inscribed the work twice, once in 1286 and again in 1288. He also impressed his personal seals on the borders of the work.[37] He tells us that, according to the imperial catalogue, Hui-tsung had twenty-six examples of Yen Chen-ch'ing's calligraphy, of which this was one; he then describes the imperial seals, which are still found on the work, and how he acquired the scroll by exchange. The acquisition of such an important scroll lent enormous prestige to Hsien-yü Shu's collection; moreover, it was to constitute a major source of influence on his own calligraphic style. The colophon also represents the earliest dated example of Hsien-yü Shu's writing. Stylistically the work of this great T'ang master of the northern tradition embodied the hidden strength and ultimately classical discipline which, in strict "regular" script, served as a chief stylistic source of influence to the Northern Sung and Chin masters. That Yen Chen-ch'ing's style as

[35] The scroll, dated 758, is in the collection of Wang Shih-chieh at the Palace Museum, Taipei; see KKSHL 1:20, and KKFS, vol. 5.

[36] *Hsüan-ho shu-p'u* 宣和書譜, preface dated 1120 (ISTP ed), 4:89–94. For an examination of the authorship and date of compilation, see Ecke, "Emperor Hui-Tsung" (cited above, n. 7), pp. 14–17, 20–22.

[37] Colophons reproduced in KKFS 5:7a–8a.

shown in the "Draft Memorial" would reveal itself in Hsien-yü Shu's freehand writing later, testifies to the influence of his personal collection on his art, to the continuity of traditions, and to his dedicated study of the old masters. This scroll was probably not Hsien-yü Shu's first acquisition of old calligraphy, but it can be considered one of his most significant and relatively "early" in an account for which we have so little material predating the 1280s.

In 1285 Hsien-yü Shu made a brief trip to the capital and was able to acquire another scroll of calligraphy, possibly of less artistic importance than the preceding, but certainly of historical and literary significance for him. It was a work containing the handwritten letters of famous poets and essayists from North China (*Chung-chou ming-kung han-mo* 中州名公翰墨). Hsien-yü Shu's acquisition of this work reveals his continued interest in the literary tradition of the north, for over the years he kept biographical records of Chin literati. These are found in Hsien-yü Shu's *K'un-hsüeh chai tsa-lu* 困學齋雜錄, a collection of miscellaneous notes in six categories named after his studio, the *K'un-hsüeh chai*.[38] (On this title, see below.) One entire section, titled "Chung-yüan shih-fu ch'u-ch'u 中原士夫出處," consists of biographical comments on northern poets and scholars from the Chung-yüan (Central Plain, or China heartland) who retired from service or served the Chin at some time in their careers. The entries total twenty-two persons, many active in the generation of Hsien-yü Shu's father and grandfather. Hsien-yü Shu concludes that in 1285 he had obtained the ink manuscripts of letters and poems of the persons named and that he had had them remounted as a scroll in 1290.[39]

---

[38] The *K'un-hsüeh chai tsa-lu* is extant in two main editions, the aforementioned *Shuo-fu* edition, which consists of 45 consecutive entries, and the *Chih-pu-tsu chai* edition (*chüan* 29, *ts'e* 232), which is divided into six sections on the following topics: 1) biographical notes on recent and contemporary poets, 2) old forms of "heavenly branches and earthly stems," 3) biographical notes on emigré scholars from central (north) China, 4) names and owners of antique zithers, 5) a list of antiquities and their owners, and 6) calligraphy and painting he had seen.

The *Shuo-fu* edition appears to be an abridgement of the *Chih-pu-tsu chai* edition, but the former contains several entries which the latter does not, notably the early office he held in 1278. For a concise summary of these textual differences and an exhaustive study of the *Shuo-fu* and its various editions, see Ch'ang Pi-te 昌彼德, "Shuo-fu k'ao 説郛考," *Chung-kuo tung-ya hsüeh-shu yen-chiu chi-hua wei-yüan-hui nien-pao* 中國東亞學術研究計劃委員會年報, vol. 1 (1962), esp. pp. 204–205. I am indebted to John Langlois for this reference.

[39] The scroll is not extant. The title appears as cited in *Shuo-fu* 52: *K'un-tsa*, p. 20, but as "Chung-yüan ming-kung han-mo 中原名公翰墨" in the *Chih-pu-tsu chai* edition of *K'un-tsa*, p. 20a. On the two editions, see Ch'ang Pi-te, "Shuo-fu k'ao," pp. 204–205 (n. 38 above).

The importance of these entries lies in several counts. Little information is found elsewhere.[40] While Hsien-yü Shu's notes are not as exhaustive or systematic as those of Yüan Hao-wen or of Liu Ch'i, they still are evidence of his long-standing interest in the northern poets and their place in the literary and calligraphic tradition. For example, Hsien-yü Shu mentions that there is an order and ranking to their works. Although the ranking is unknown to us today, we nevertheless make note of his interest as a critic more than as a historian. He evidently sought to distinguish levels of artistic quality rather than to provide historical facts.

In addition, it is significant that Hsien-yü Shu sought to collect the handwritten manuscripts of these poets' works and presumably printed editions as well. To any other man of letters, it would have been enough to obtain a printed edition of their poetry, but for Hsien-yü Shu as connoisseur and critic, equal importance lay in their being *mo-chi* 墨跡, "ink traces" or "originals," from the hand of the poets. In mounting them together as he did in 1290, he imbued in them a new and important stature as both historical documents and art objects. One historian has pointed out that Hsien-yü Shu also recopied the poems and presented them to another prominent northerner, the censor Kuo T'ien-hsi,[41] who would have been particularly appreciative of Hsien-yü Shu's effort. This would have been a further sign of these northerners' mutual interest in their own traditions.

Hsien-yü Shu's interest in his northern heritage was not short-lived. It formed a distinctive part of his personality recognized by his contemporaries, and it also provided the rich counterpoint to his trans-

---

The variant character in the title of the scroll is of some interest: "Chung-chou 中州" versus "Chung-yüan." The latter would mean Central China and a more general designation for the large area fed by the Yellow River and its tributaries. On the other hand, "Chung-chou," meaning "middle territories," is more specific, indicating the ancient name for Honan and referring to the region of North China conquered by the Chin, traditionally considered to be the center of Chinese civilization. Yüan Hao-wen titled his important collection of the works of Chin poets *Chung-chou chi* 中州集. H. L. Chan has suggested that in doing so, Yüan Hao-wen may have been challenging the idea that the Southern Sung played the leading role in the perpetuation of culture during that period. See H. L. Chan, *Historiography*, pp. 71 and 107, n. 9.

[40] As H. L. Chan has shown, biographical material on Chin literary figures is preserved primarily in private writings, such as those of Yüan Hao-wen and Liu Ch'i, and it is their writings that provided the main sources for the biographies in the Chin history (*ibid.*, chs. 2 and 3, esp. pp. 134 ff.). Several poets, such as Yang Hung-tao, Ts'ao Chü-i and Ch'en Shih-k'o, mentioned by Hsien-yü Shu in *K'un-tsa*, were friends of Liu Ch'i, but were not included in the Chin history.

[41] Tsung Tien 宗典, "Pien Kuo Pi fei Kuo Yu-chih chi ch'i wei-hua 辨郭畀非郭祐之及其偈畫," *Wen wu*, 1965, No. 8, p. 36.

planted Hangchow life. He often turned to the writings of these northern scholars and poets as the basis for important calligraphic works, as we shall see below.

Sometime in 1293, Hsien-yü Shu acquired an object of the sort which commanded a special enthusiasm among Hangchow collectors.[42] It was a bronze mirror which exhibited the special property of "translucency": when held against the light, the decoration on its back could be seen on its smooth polished surface. The phenomenon of this "light penetrating" or diaphanous mirror (*t'ou-kuang ching* 透光鏡) was admired and sought after by several collectors in Chou Mi's circle.[43] Earlier the Chin dynasty poet Ma Chiu-ch'ou 麻九疇 (1174–1232)[44] wrote an ode to such mirrors which helped to further their fame in the north. Chou Mi himself wrote a eulogy, and several collectors in Hangchow continued to prize these special "magic mirrors." Hsien-yü Shu liked the poem by Ma Ch'iu-ch'ou so much that he transcribed the text, "Song of the Diaphanous Mirror" (*T'ou-kuang ku-ching ko* 透光古鏡歌),[45] in large characters of "regular script" (*k'ai-shu* 楷書) (Fig. 1). This masterpiece is one of two works extant in that script style, the other being the "Admonitions to the Imperial Censors" (*Yü-shih chen* 御史箴), a work in a similar format which he was to execute later in 1299, to which we will turn shortly. The "Song" is a scroll of exceptional quality and exhibits an immense vigor typical of his large-sized writing. Hsien-yü Shu's transcription, originally a handscroll now mounted as an album of separate leaves, is not dated, but it represents his mature style and must have been executed sometime after 1293, when he acquired the object and felt moved to transcribe Ma's eulogy to it.

By the summer of the next year, 1286, Hsien-yü Shu was back in

[42] Chou Mi, *Chih-ya t'ang tsa-ch'ao* 志雅堂雜抄 (pref. 1332; *Pi-chi hsü-pien* 筆記續編 ed., rpt. Taipei, 1969), *shang* 上, 24b–25a; and YYKYL, p. 29.

It should be noted that the *Chih-ya t'ang* appears in several editions. The edition cited above contains no preface, but the contents are complete in nine sections (*shang, hsia*), with entries dating from within the ten-year period 1274–1294. There are two entries containing the date *i-ch'ou* 乙丑 (1265), which is a misprint for *chi-ch'ou* 己丑 (1289). The *Mei-shu ts'ung-shu* 美術叢書 (ISTP ed.) is incomplete, containing only the sections on the arts, but it does contain a preface dated 1332 by Shih Yen 石巖 (t. Min-chan 民瞻, fl. 1300–35?).

[43] *Chih-ya t'ang, shang* 上, 24b–25a, and *hsia* 下, 25b.

[44] CS 126; *Chung-chou chi*, 6:6b–7b; *Kuei-ch'ien chih*, 2:3b–4a; *K'un-tsa*, 19b; and SSHY 8:3b. T'ao and Yüan report that Ma was a calligraphy prodigy, that he excelled in cursive script and that he could execute large writing several feet in height. Unfortunately, I have been unable to locate any examples of Ma's calligraphy. It is possible that Hsien-yü Shu saw an example of his handwriting and that the large size served as a precedent for his transcription of Ma's poem.

[45] The album is extant in the Palace Museum, Taipei; see KKSHL 3:51 and reproduced in KKFS 17:20–34.

Hangchow, where he inscribed his scroll by Yen Chen-ch'ing after it had been newly remounted. In that year he was also shifted to the post of clerk in the Finance Commission (*San-ssu shih-yüan* 三司史掾).[46] In the meantime he acquired another example of T'ang calligraphy, a scroll attributed to the T'ang master Hsü Hao (703–782) transcribing the text of the *Kao-shen* ("Patent") by Chu Chü-ch'uan (*Hsü Hao shu Chu Chü-ch'uan Kao-shen chüan* 徐浩書朱巨川告身卷).[47] This scroll, extant today, had also been in the collection of the Sung emperor Hui-tsung, and it, too, was recorded in his imperial catalogue of calligraphy.[48] This fact, and the presence of the four early seals of the emperor found on the scroll, were all carefully and proudly recorded by Hsien-yü Shu in his colophon.

One of the chief events of the year 1287 was the occasion at which several leading poets and officials gathered at the invitation of the collector and connoisseur Chou Mi[49] to inscribe a famous scroll recently acquired by him. Chou Mi, whose original ancestors were from Ch'i-chou, Shantung, had settled in Hangchow in 1277 from Wu-hsing, Chekiang, where his estate had been sacked the previous year by the invading Mongols. Some ten years later, when Hsien-yü Shu met him, Chou had become a well known figure in literary circles and had formed his own group of poets and art lovers. It is of considerable interest that among the gentlemen who came to admire Chou's new acquisition were Chao Meng-fu, Teng Wen-yüan, Hsien-yü Shu, Ch'iu Yüan, Pai T'ing, and others. The scroll acquired by Chou Mi was a rubbing of the *Pao-mu chih* 保母誌, ascribed to the Tsin master Wang Hsien-chih (344–388). The *Pao-mu chih*, dated 365, was the epitaph of Wang Hsien-chih's governess, Li I-ju 李意如.[50] Consisting of a brief text in ten lines, it had attracted considerable attention among connoisseurs of the day, because

---

[46] SYTWC 2:11b–12b.

[47] The scroll is extant in the Palace Museum, Taipei; see KKSHL 1:24–27, and KKFS, vol. 6.

[48] *Hsüan-ho shu-p'u*, 3:94–96.

[49] HYS 237; Hsia Ch'eng-t'ao 夏承燾, "Chou Ts'ao-ch'uang nien-p'u 周草窗年譜," in *T'ang-Sung tz'u-jen nien-p'u* 唐宋詞人年譜 (Shanghai, 1961), pp. 315–370; Li, *Autumn Colors*, pp. 21–22 and n. 30; and the biography by C. T. Li in Herbert Franke, ed., *Sung Biographies* (Wiesbaden, 1976), pp. 261–268.

Biographical references on Chou are limited, but much material can be found in his own writings as he was a prolific author and observer of the times. Besides his *Yün-yen kuo-yen-lu* and *Chih-ya t'ang tsa-ch'ao* cited above, the *Kuei-hsin tsa-chih* and *Ch'i-tung yeh-yü* 齊東野語 are of value.

[50] See the *fu-lu* 附錄 (supplement section) to Yeh Shao-weng 葉紹翁 (fl. 1220–25?), *Ssu-ch'ao wen-chien-lu* 四朝聞見錄 (*Chih-pu-tsu chai* ed.), 1a–28b, where the colophons are recorded in their entirety.

the stele from which the rubbing was taken had been discovered as recently as 1202. Uncovered along with the stele was an inkstone engraved on its reverse side with the three characters, "Tsin [dynasty] Hsien-chih," and, on the edge of the inkstone, the Tsin reign era, "Yung-ho 永和." This find and the content of the stele inscription convinced many scholars of the absolute authenticity of the work, which some even believed to have been carved by Wang Hsien-chih himself. According to Chao Meng-fu's colophon, three members of their circle were each in possession of a rubbing of the Pao-mu text. Chao says, "In the winter of *ping-hsü* (1286), Po-chi (Hsien-yü Shu) acquired one version. Later Kung-chin (Chou Mi) acquired this version ... and in the 8th month of *ting-hai* (1287), I acquired another on my way back from the capital."[51] Thus we know that in addition to inscribing Chou Mi's version with a colophon, both Chao Meng-fu and Hsien-yü Shu had acquired rubbings of this monument. The confluence of interests between Chao, Hsien-yü, and those in Chou Mi's circle was to continue to an even greater degree in the next two decades. This scroll, for example, circulated among their group for the next thirty years. The colophon by Chao also constitutes the earliest dated reference of his relationship with Hsien-yü Shu, one which probably commenced some two or three years earlier through the introduction of Chou Mi.[52]

Sometime toward the end of this year 1287, Hsien-yü Shu assumed the post of Registrar in the Pacification Office (*Hsüan-wei-ssu ching-li* 宣慰司經歷).[53] His activities among the Hangchow collectors took on an accelerated pace, and it was probably his entry into Chou Mi's circle which led to the increased opportunities to view other Hangchow collections. According to Chou Mi's notes, he and his friends made the rounds of the most outstanding Hangchow collections, such as those of Wang Chih (fl. ca.1285–1300?) and Ch'iao K'uei-ch'eng (fl. ca.1270–after 1313?).[54] As could be expected, there were frequent visits to

[51] *Ibid.*, 16a–b.

[52] Hsien-yü Shu probably met Chao Meng-fu in 1284 when the two were in Hangchow, the former to remount his newly acquired work, the *Chi chih kao* 祭姪稿 (see above, no. 36), and the latter to study with Tai Piao-yüan (see Tai's preface dated 1298 in SHCWC).

[53] Lu Hsin-yüan, *I-ku t'ang t'i-pa*, 13 : 17a.

[54] For Wang Chih, see "Ts'ao-ch'uang nien-p'u," p. 356; *Chih-ya t'ang*, shang 上, 1a, 3a, 6a–b, 29a, and *hsia* 下, 25a–b, 26a, 27a, 28a; YYKYL, pp. 25, 30, 34, 38; and *K'un-tsa*, pp. 5b, 22a, and 28a–b, where Hsien-yü Shu lists the works known to be in Wang's collection.

Ch'iao K'uei-ch'eng 喬簣成 appears to be the same person as Ch'iao Ta 達, also known as Ch'iao Ta-chih 達之, who is listed in Wu Chen 吳鎮, *Wen Hu-chou chu-p'ai* 文湖州竹派 (ISTP ed., 12), as a Hanlin Academician, a painter of landscapes in the Li Ch'eng manner and of ink bamboo after Wang T'ing-yün and Wen T'ung; Hsia: THPC, p.

each other's residences whenever anything of quality or interest came their way. For example, following Hsien-yü Shu's colophon of 1286 on the "Draft Memorial" of Yen Chen-ch'ing, there appears a brief colophon by Chou Mi,[55] and in Hsien-yü Shu's colophon of 1288 to the *Kao-shen* scroll attributed to Hsü Hao, he notes that because Ch'iao was about to set off westward on a new appointment, he brought the calligraphy over to Ch'iao's house for him to enjoy before leaving.[56] From offhand remarks such as these, we may judge the intensity of interest in antique works which these collectors shared among them. Indeed, although Hsien-yü Shu did become the owner of several significant works of calligraphy, he and others need not even have "owned" them in order to have possessed them in an empirical sense.

Another masterpiece of calligraphy extant today which was renowned in the Hangchow area at the time was the "Preface to an Essay on Calligraphy" (*Shu-p'u hsü* 書譜序) dated 687 by Sun Kuo-t'ing 孫過庭 (648?–703?). This work was famous both for its content—the exposition in elegant prose of the principles and subtle art of calligraphy—and its calligraphy style, a restrained, classically balanced cursive script.[57] In the Northern Sung period the work had been in the imperial collection of the emperor Hui-tsung,[58] and, by Hsien-yü Shu's time, had fallen into private hands. The collector Chiao Ta-ch'ing 焦達卿 (fl. ca.1275–1290?),[59] discerning by any standards, had "three treasures" (*san-pao* 三寶): Sun's *Shu-p'u,* Wang Hsi-chih's "Letter of the 17th" (*Shih-ch'i t'ieh* 十七帖), and an antique zither (*ku-ch'in*). The latter, said to rival those in the Sung imperial collection, was "never borrowed or lent."

84, also includes an entry under the name Ch'iao Ta and containing the same information. Hsien-yü Shu refers to him as *mi-shu-lang* 秘書郎, active during the Chih-yüan 至元 era. Cf. *K'un-tsa,* pp. 11a, 21a, 22a, 25a–b, and 26a; *Chih-ya t'ang, shang,* 4a, 7a, 9a; *hsia,* 18a, 23a and 25b.

Wang Chih and Ch'iao K'uei-ch'eng were but two of the forty-one collectors listed by Chou Mi in the YYKYL, certainly an impressive number. We can judge the quality of their collections by the number of works still extant today. This is a rich subject which awaits future study.

[55] See KKSHL 1:20 and KKFS 5:7b for illustrations.

[56] KKSHL 1:21.

[57] Its position in calligraphy theory is equivalent to that of Liu Hsieh's 劉勰 *Wen-hsin tiao-lung* 文心調龍 (*The Literary Mind and the Carving of Dragons*) in poetics. In the Sung the work consisted of two scrolls; the first scroll is extant in the Palace Museum, Taipei; see KKSHL 1:15–16 and KKFS, vol. 2. Roger Goepper has recently completed a translation and extensive study of this important work; see his *Shu-p'u: Der Traktat zur Schriftkunst des Sun Kuo-t'ing* (Wiesbaden, 1974); also Fujiwara Sōsui 藤原楚水. *Shofu-zoku: Shofu no kenkyū* 書譜続：書譜の研究 (Tokyo, 1973).

[58] *Hsüan-ho shu-p'u,* 18:403–404.

[59] For his collection, see YYKYL, pp. 25–26; and *Chih-ya t'ang, shang,* 24b, and *hsia,* 24a.

Chiao did lend his *Shu-p'u* to Hsien-yü Shu, however, for Chou Mi says
he saw it while at Hsien-yü's house.[60] This fact not only testifies to
Chiao's esteem of Hsien-yü Shu, probably a mutual one, but also to the
certainty that the famous works of the day had an avid audience, an
inner circle among which circulated the finest works in private hands. It
was the taste and interest of such collectors as these that were forming
the artistic milieu of the time.

Such personable exchanges of treasures meant that Hsien-yü Shu had
an opportunity to study great works such as the *Shu-p'u*. Moreover,
these great monuments played an important role in the development of
his own calligraphic style. The admiration shown by the collectors for
Sun Kuo-t'ing was part of a prevailing interest in the Tsin masters, for
Sun was considered in the direct line of transmission of the classic
tradition of the two Wangs, Wang Hsi-chih and his son Wang Hsien-
chih.[61] Hsien-yü Shu showed equally intense interest for both the Tsin
and T'ang masters, and in the next year this interest would be reinforced
by another work of singular importance.

In the first lunar month of 1289 Hsien-yü Shu made a short trip and
passed through the San-ch'ü 三衢 district of Chekiang. In doing so he
was able to view and to inscribe comments on a rubbing of the so-called
Ting-wu version of the legendary masterpiece of Wang Hsi-chih, the
"Preface to the Orchid Pavilion Gathering" (*Lan-t'ing chi hsü* 蘭亭集序),
a work which has become the most celebrated in the whole history of
calligraphy. Like Chou Mi's rubbing of the *Pao-mu chih*, this rubbing of
the *Ting-wu Lan-t'ing* 定武蘭亭 was enhanced by an impressive pedigree
of colophons from the Sung and Yüan periods, still extant today in
fragmentary condition.[62] This rubbing had the distinction of having
come from the collection of the prominent Northern Sung scholar,

---

[60] *Chih-ya t'ang*, *hsia*, 24a.

[61] See entry and brief biography of Sun Kuo-t'ing in *Hsüan-ho shu-p'u*, 18:403–404,
where it is noted that Sun's *hsiao-k'ai* was often confused with that of the two Wangs.

[62] Reproduced with colophons in SMS., vol. 56. The so-called "Ting-wu" Lan-t'ing is the
version of the *Lan-t'ing hsü* originally written in A.D. 353 by Wang Hsi-chih and said to
have been copied during the reign of T'ang T'ai-tsung by the leading calligrapher Ou-yang
Hsün 歐陽詢 (557–641). The stele upon which the copy was carved was said to have
remained in the imperial precincts until the Five Dynasties, when the capital was sacked; it
then fell into the hands of the Liao-Khitan royal family who brought it north and installed
it at Chen-ting, Hopei. During the Sung dynasty, this area became known as Ting-wu, and
since that time, the place-name became attached to the stele and the rubbings taken from it.
During the 11th century, the stele became the property of Hsüeh Hsiang 薛向 and his son
Shao-p'eng 紹彭 (see n. 63).

For the history of this complex problem, see Sang Shih-ch'ang 桑世昌, *Lan-t'ing k'ao*
蘭亭考 (preface dated 1209; ISTP ed.), esp. *ch.* 3 and 6, and SZ 4, p. 163; and Lothar
Ledderose, *Mi Fu and the Classical Tradition of Chinese Calligraphy* (Princeton, 1979), esp,
chs. 1 and 3.

collector, and calligrapher Hsüeh Shao-p'eng,[63] with whom, we re-member, Yü Chi compared Hsien-yü Shu. The Hsüeh family at one time owned the original stone stele on which the celebrated *Ting-wu Lan-t'ing* was carved. Hsüeh Shao-p'eng is known to have made several precious rubbings from it. Then he defaced five characters on the stone in order to mark the rarity of the complete rubbings. Hsüeh subsequently also took rubbings from the stone after defacement and had a second version recarved.[64] The rubbing Hsien-yü Shu acquired and inscribed was one of the latter. Preceding Hsien-yü Shu's colophon was an undated one by the painter Ch'ien Hsüan (ca.1235–1300). Ch'ien said that he had seen only one other in Wang Chih's collection and had thought that it was superior until he saw this one, which far surpassed it. Hsien-yü Shu's colophon follows: "Among the myriad ink rubbings of the *Lan-t'ing*, the Ting-wu version best preserves the brush concepts of Wang Hsi-chih. This particular specimen was made by Hsüeh Shao-p'eng's family, so there is no room for argument—one knows that it is the genuine thing! Written in 1289 aboard a boat on the way [from] San-ch'ü (Chekiang), passing through An-jen chen."

The quality of the calligraphy found in Hsien-yü Shu's colophon shows the degree to which such a work inspired him, for it is one of the finest examples from his hand. Sometime after his colophon of 1289, the scroll entered the hands of the Buddhist monk Tu-ku 獨孤 of the T'ien-t'ai sect (it has since also become known by that name, the "Tu-ku-pen 獨孤本"). Chao Meng-fu managed to obtain the scroll later in 1310, and was so enamored of it that, taking it along on a boat trip north to the capital, he wrote a total of thirteen enthusiastic colophons over a period of over a month. The rubbing with its valuable colophons has since become known as the "Lan-t'ing of the Thirteen colophons" (蘭亭十三跋).

From extant material such as this, it is evident that an increasing number of major works whose artistic stature we can still judge today passed through Hsien-yü Shu's and his contemporaries' hands. It is also possible to trace the degree of the influence which these works exerted on his own artistic development and on that of his contemporaries. These

[63] SS 328:10588, under his father, Hsüeh Hsiang; also SZ 15, pp. 11, 17, 184–185. Hsüeh's dates are not known; I use the *circa* 1050–1100 on the basis of his being a contemporary of Mi Fu 米芾 (1052–1107). Hsüeh's calligraphy is relatively rare, but there are several works in the Palace Museum, Taipei; see KKFS, vol. 12.

[64] Rubbings from the undamaged stele were known as *wei-sun wu-tzu pen* 未損五字本, while those from the re-carved stele were known as *wu-tzu sun pen* 五字損本. Cf. Sang Shih-ch'ang, *Lan-t'ing k'ao*, 3:21–22, 6:54–55; SMS, vol. 56, explanatory text pp. 64–65, and the complete text to the colophons, esp. Chao Meng-fu's first colophon, p. 66.

scrolls enjoyed a high degree of mobility among the literati in and around Hangchow: when something of importance reached one scholar's hands, it was bound to have been viewed by others as well. If we accept the hypothesis that ancient works exert significant influence on the artistic movements of any generation in the form of a renascence, then this influence was particularly acute in the early Yüan. Traditionally cherished and valuable objects like antiquities, calligraphy, and paintings have continuous lifetimes. They exist forever in the present. Except in the case of recently excavated works, there are actually few "new" works of antiquity to be "discovered." It is rather the susceptibility of a viewer to a work of art and the potential of his sensibility to induce change which make any work of art of potentially creative importance to any one generation.

The several scrolls mentioned above as from the Northern Sung imperial collection are also an indication of the vicissitudes which imperial treasures, in particular, often undergo during a change of dynasty. Many works from Hui-tsung's collection passed into the consecutive collections of Kao-tsung and then found their way back north into Chin Chang-tsung's collection, or into the private collections of northerners like Hsien-yü Shu at the fall of the Chin.[65] In other words, political unification of north and south was actually part of a pattern which influenced the fate of imperial collections, leading often to their breakup and passage into private hands. At the beginning of the Yüan, this was particularly noticeable. The availability of hitherto inaccessible works of art from imperial collections to scholars with the successive changes of dynasties in the north and south released hundreds of antiquities, calligraphies, and paintings onto the market and provided tremendous possibilities and stimulus for artistic change. It is important to remember that many of the "acquisitors" were also *producers* of art, not mere collectors, and that they were in a position to influence and to alter prevailing artistic trends. In this way the new artistic milieu of the Yüan was gradually formed. We note specifically that the collectors named by Chou Mi and Hsien-yü Shu were relatively little-known figures whose biographies were not recorded in the official annals. There were, of course, a considerable number of high-ranking officials among the major collectors, and these, too, formed part of the milieu as time went on. This new mixture of collectors seems to be an entirely new pheno-

[65] For example in 1289, Chou Mi records a visit in which he and Hsien-yü Shu saw some thirteen paintings and calligraphy belonging to Ch'iao K'uei-ch'eng, all of which had originally come from Hui-tsung's collection, and then subsequently passed into Chin Chang-tsung's hands. See *Chih-ya t'ang*, *hsia*, 23a–b; the date *i-ch'ou* 乙丑 (1265) is a misprint for *chi-ch'ou* 己丑 (1289).

menon which took place in the early Yüan as a result of the Mongol conquest. This is an important subject which deserves study.

Toward the end of 1293 and early in 1294, Hsien-yü Shu composed a series of forty quatrains on the occasion of his returning to Yangchow on his way to Chiang-che.[66] The poems give a brief history of the region—the wealth of natural resources, the urban growth, and the Mongol invasion of the city. During his earlier stay, the poet "humbly received a salary and dared to forget" about the shame of being employed by the invaders. For five years, he says, he drafted memorials and letters, but still had enough leisure to accumulate fond memories of Yangchow; he composed new poems in the presence of friends, went horseback riding, visited scenic spots, and climbed mountains.[67] Returning to the same place, he feels disquieted and restless, and the past seems remote: how different Yangchow is now—new houses fill the small streets and alleys, and half his friends are in their graves; customs have changed to suit those of the barbarians and even common speech has also been affected. He is suddenly happy to find the road to his home, but, finally, he can only be sad at the departing boat and be pained at having to leave the city of such happy memories.

The Yangchow poems are notable not only for their autobiographical content and for the material they offer on a hitherto undocumented part of Hsien-yü Shu's career, but because they also tell of the reactions of a returnee to a place occupied by the Mongols. In this case, his northern background and his southern emigration complicate his thoughts, but certainly his observations touch on some basic aspects of daily life. Changes of place and the character of a neighborhood, of friends, of everyday customs and speech—all show the extent to which Mongol rule had altered lives during the approximately ten-year period from the very fall of the south, or ca.1278, when Hsien-yü Shu first arrived in Yangchow, to ca.1293, when he returned. It is difficult to say on a more objective level whether much of the sense of loss and nostalgia which permeates these poems could be found in any poem by any poet on returning to a familiar and much-loved place. There is no doubt that Hsien-yü Shu felt a truly deep affection for his life in the south, regardless of the importance the north and its traditions had for him. In terms of the character of the man, it would be most just to say that Hsien-yü Shu was as proud of his northern background as he was happy

---

[66] "Yang-chou wu-yen ssu-shih-yün 揚州五言四十韻," in Fang Chün-i 方濬頤, *Meng-yüan shu-hua-lu* 夢園書畫錄 (1877), 5:14–18.

[67] The exact year of Hsien-yü Shu's earlier arrival in Yangchow is not clear, but it was probably in 1278; this would agree with Chou Ti's account in the father Kuang-tsu's epitaph. See n. 30 above.

to be living in the south, and that both were equally important to him for different reasons. It was really the quality of southern life which offered so much to him and to which he himself contributed to such a lively degree.

The best description of Hsien-yü Shu's life in the south is given by the poet Tai Piao-yüan (1244–1310, Feng-hua, Chekiang) in his "Record of the K'un-hsüeh Studio." In this essay, which we render in full below, Tai describes the quality of the life Hsien-yü Shu had found in the south, the joys of his vast collection of antiques, the warm friendships made, and the establishment of his famous studio, the K'un-hsüeh chai. We see what Hsien-yü Shu would be leaving behind whenever he went north on an appointment and the reasons the south meant so much to him:[68]

"In the spring of the year *ting-hai* [1287], I met Hsien-yü Po-chi in Hangchow. At that time Po-chi had been chosen because of his talent to assume the post of *San-ssu shih-yüan* [clerk in the Finance Commission (to which he was appointed in 1286)]. His personality and bearing had a manly heroism about it (*i-ch'i hsiung-hao* 意氣雄豪). In the morning he would set out to work with his brushes and papers and would debate with his superiors over right and wrong. If one word did not agree with his idea of the right, he would sail off, happy to give up his seal of office and be out fishing and hunting in the mountains.

"When he went out riding, all the people would gather round and the oldsters would fix their eyes on him and point him out to the [youngsters], saying: 'That is His Excellency, our venerated Hsien-yü!' When his duties were over and he went home, he would burn incense and do some writing. Then he would take out [his collection] of bronze tripods and ceremonial vessels which had some several hundred decades of antiquity, and arrange them in rows outside on his steps in the daylight. He would seek out breaks and losses of characters in the inscriptions with the intensity and excitement of someone who had to have it done in a moment for the next day.

"There were no lowly guests at his door, and those who came would be found chanting, quoting, and composing among pine and bamboo. Wine cups would be raised till drunkenness was in order, and when exceedingly drunk, Po-chi would just let himself go with singing and strange writing, and all of this would please him immensely. Even though I am a simple person, upon seeing Po-chi like this, I truly felt he was a most marvelous and quite uncommon person, beyond the pale of this world.

"Now five years have passed, and his name is suddenly nowhere to be

[68] "K'un-hsüeh chai chi," SYTWC, 2:11b–12b.

heard. When asking why, this reply came: 'Po-chi has gotten tired and impatient with daily affairs; he closed his door and refused all guests, and built himself a small studio, calling it K'un-hsüeh chih chai ("The Studio of Learning acquired after a painful feeling of Ignorance"). He wants to restrain his excesses, to discipline and find his lost mind, and try to minimize his faults.'[68a] When I heard this, I sighed to myself and said: 'Is it true that in this world there are those with Po-chi's talent who must achieve learning by such self-imposed discipline?' In so asking, I felt that he was all the more extraordinary for doing so. Chu-ko K'ung-ming [Liang 諸葛亮, 181–234, the brilliant strategist and patriot of the Three Kingdoms period] was a man of lofty principles who refused to serve, but once he came out of retirement, he enabled [Liu Pei 劉備, who later became ruler] to establish the rival state of Shu like the third leg of the tripod. And yet Chu-ko's original ambition was to take hoe in hand and to plow the fields and become a farmer of Nanyang. So, too, Chi K'ang 嵇康 [or Hsi K'ang, 223–262, poet, philosopher, musician and one of the "Seven Sages of the Bamboo Grove"] as a dragon among men, did not let the Three Dukes interrupt his pleasure at working with hammer and anvil (probably a reference to the story in which Chi K'ang ignores his rival Chung Hui 鍾會 [225–264] while forging iron[68b]). They had the capacities to adapt and to conciliate, to advance and retreat. How can this be done by someone of inferior learning?

"Now I have compared Po-chi with Chu-ko and Chi K'ang as compatriots, and he is certainly not inferior to them. [Po-chi] must have had many complex reasons to do this, but I suspect that he is probably distressed by what is going on in this world. There are certainly many ways to be distressed. Po-chi is not distressed by wants or desires, nor by the fruits of success or shame, achievement or loss. He is superior to the common person by leaps of millions. As to his likes, even a sage cannot avoid burdens, and [Po-chi] is even more capable of making light of them. His situation makes me think of the perfect fighting cock raised by

(a) The reference to Hsien-yü Shu's "lost mind" comes from Mencius (*Meng-tzu*, VI.1.II; Legge, p. 414), in which he says that men know how to seek for fowl and dogs when they are lost, but do not know to look for their minds when they have lost it: "The great end of learning is nothing else but to seek for the lost mind." I am grateful to John Langlois for identifying the reference to Mencius.

(b) For Chi K'ang's biography, see *San-kuo chih* (*Wei*) 三國志 (魏) (Peking, 1973), 21:605, and *Chin shu* 晉書 Peking, 1974, 49:1369–1379; also R. H. van Gulik, *Hsi K'ang and His Poetical Essay on the Lute* (Tokyo, 1941).

The reference to the "Three Dukes" (*san kung* 三公) may be as symbols of Confucian rank and power, all of which Chi K'ang was repudiating. For an analysis of the intellectual and social history of the period under discussion, see E. Balazs, "Nihilist Revolt or Mystical Escapism," *Chinese Civilization and Bureaucracy*, H. M. Wright, trans. (New Haven, 1964), esp. pp. 238–242.

Chi-hsing-tzu 紀渚子, who stood woodlike, undisturbed by the cockcrow of his opponent, or the story of the sage Keng-sang Ch'u 庚桑楚 living in the Wei-lei 畏壘 mountains, whose presence there brought prosperity to the villagers, but who himself remained dissatisfied with his own imperfections.[68c] How could Po-chi not achieve gradual perfection in his learning!

"Thereupon those who know Po-chi said to me, 'Your words describe Po-chi quite aptly. Why don't you compose something for his studio?' As this was originally a 'record of learning acquired after a painful feeling of ignorance,' I record it here."

Tai Piao-yüan was clearly a gifted writer, for the "Record" contains not only vivid descriptive detail and personal characterization, but also a reflective and philosophical admonishment to Hsien-yü Shu and his attempt to perfect himself by enforced study. Indeed, Hsien-yü Shu's efforts were met with similarly mixed responses by other members of his circle. A second "Record of the K'un-hsüeh Studio" was written by an older contemporary, Yü Te-lin 俞德鄰 (chin-shih 1273), which contains Yü's thoughts on the matter.[69] When Yü confronted Hsien-yü Shu with his decision not to seek further office but to devote himself to study, Hsien-yü Shu replied: "When I was young, I did not really apply myself to my studies. Now that I am in office, I feel nothing but a hollow emptiness. How can I put up with myself like that?" With that in mind, Yü continued, Hsien-yü built his studio and named it with a plaque reading "K'un-hsüeh."[70]

Several significant references to the phrase "K'un-hsüeh" may be found in the Confucian classics which may help to explain Hsien-yü's philosophical position. I refer to the *Analects* of Confucius[71] and the *Chung-yung* 中庸 (*Doctrine of the Mean*).[72] Hsien-yü Shu's philosophical

(c) The references are to the *Chuang-tzu*, ch. 19, "Ta sheng 達生"; and ch. 23, "Keng-sang Ch'u 庚桑楚"; see the translation by James Legge, *Tao-te-ching and the Writings of Chuang Tzu*, pp. 460 ff., and pp. 514 ff.

[69] Yü Te-lin, *P'ei-wei chai wen-chi* 佩韋齋文集 (*Ssu-k'u ch'üan-shu chen-pen* 四庫全書珍本 ed.), 9:6a–8a. I am indebted to Shen Fu for this reference.

[70] Hsien-yü Shu was not the first to use the phrase "k'un-hsüeh" as a studio name. The prominent Sung scholar Wang Ying-lin 王應麟 (1223–96) titled his collected works *K'un-hsüeh chi-wen* 困學紀聞.

[71] The first is found in the "Analects of Confucius" (*Lun-yü*), XVI/9: "Those who are born with the possession of knowledge are the highest class of men. Next are those who become wise by learning. After them come those who have to toil painfully in order to acquire learning. Finally, to the lowest class are those who toil painfully without ever managing to learn." (Trans. Legge, *The Chinese Classics* [rpt. Hong Kong, 1963], Vol. 1, pp. 313–314.)

[72] *Chung-yung* 中庸, XX/9: "Some are born with knowledge [of duties of universal obligation]; some know them by study, and some acquire the knowledge after a painful feeling of their ignorance (*k'un erh chih-chih* 困而知之). But the knowledge being

bent and sense of inadequacy were not solely Confucian, however. Tai
Piao-yüan was correct in pointing to the two stories from the *Chuang
Tzu* 莊子, because here were precedents which showed the subjective
nature of learning and the awareness of one's gifts. The solution to a
subjective problem was met subjectively, or at least by a form of
intellectual withdrawal and self-imposed discipline which led to the
establishment of his studio.

The exact date of the establishment of the studio is not clear, but the
earliest reference from Hsien-yü Shu's own hand is a colophon dated
mid-year 1290, which he signs with the epithet, "written by the Hermit-
Clerk of Hu-lin at the temporary residence of the K'un-hsüeh Studio."[73]
Thus the turn of the year in the period of 1289–1290 seems quite
plausible as the earliest date for the studio. Within the next ten years
before Hsien-yü Shu's death in 1302, this studio would be the scene of
many pleasant artistic diversions, and one of the important bases from
which the interest in the restoration of antiquity (*fu-ku*) would assume
increasing importance.

Hsien-yü Shu's self-imposed seclusion was interrupted by a northern
appointment which occasioned the important autobiographical poem,
"Leaving Home" (戊子十二月十二日別家).[74] Before the year was up,
however, Hsien-yü Shu was back in the south, for there are three
instances in which he and Chou Mi visited the collections of other
Hangchow friends: by the sixth month (July 9, 1289), he managed to be
back to see Ch'iao K'uei-ch'eng's new acquisitions; then in the seventh
month (August 12, 1289), and the intercalary tenth month (December 5,
1289), they once more visited Wang Chih's extensive holdings.[75]

---

possessed, it comes to the same thing." (Trans. Legge, *The Chinese Classics*, vol. 1, p. 407.)

Hsien-yü Shu probably had both meanings in mind when he named his studio. But it is
important to note, as Yü Te-lin does in his "Record," that regardless of the different classes
of intellectual endowment, in the end to possess the learning is what matters. Legge aptly
renders *k'un erh chih-chih* as "knowledge acquired after a painful feeling of ignorance."
This seems to best describe Hsien-yü Shu's condition. It was not so much a question of
whether he did or did not possess knowledge, and did or did not toil away at the
attainment of what he lacked, but rather, that he *felt he lacked it* and had to correct this
condition. This is what Tai Piao-yüan refers to as finding his "lost mind."

[73] Colophon to Mi Yu-jen 米友仁 (1074–1153), "Cloudy Mountains" (*Yün-shan t'u*
雲山圖), handscroll now in the Metropolitan Museum of Art, New York; see *Shih-ch'ü
pao-chi san-pien* 石渠寶笈三編 (1793–1817) (Taipei, 1968 rpt.), 3:1452–54. The painting
has been recently published in Fong and Fu, cat. no. 6, pp. 74–75, 141–142.

[74] "Wu-tzu shih-erh-yüeh shih-erh-jih pieh-chia" (Leaving home: on the 12th day of the
12th moon of the year *wu-tzu* [January 5, 1289]), in *K'un-hsüeh chai chi*, 1b–2a. I follow Lu
Hsin-yüan's correction of the date *wu-wu* 戊午 (1259) as a misprint for *wu-tzu* 戊子
(1288/89); see his *I-ku t'ang t'i-pa*, 13:17a.

[75] *Chih-ya-t'ang, hsia*, 23a–b, 25a, and 27a; see also "Ts'ao-ch'uang nien-p'u," p. 357.

In spring of 1297, Hsien-yü Shu had the opportunity to examine another fine specimen of the Lan-t'ing preface. It had passed through the hands of several prominent literati, among them the Chin poet and scholar Yüan Hao-wen.[76] In his colophon (Fig. 2) Hsien-yü Shu observes that it was carved of high quality stone and that it was the finest of its kind he had seen "in his lifetime"; moreover, it carried the collector's seals of the illustrious poet Yüan Hao-wen, thus making it doubly valuable. Hsien-yü Shu thereupon closes with the date and the fact that he "respectfully inscribed it with folded hands and bowed head." Chao Meng-fu would inscribe the scroll some fourteen years later in 1309.

Hsien-yü Shu's colophon on this work is important for two reasons. First, it gives evidence of continued contact, by him and others in his circle, with Tsin-T'ang works, especially Wang Hsi-chih and the Lan-t'ing group. Three examples of important colophons by Hsien-yü Shu have been mentioned which testify to his close study of this one masterpiece. Second, this last colophon mentions the Chin literatus Yüan Hao-wen and provides further evidence of Hsien-yü Shu's links with northern traditions. There were many other aspects of the rubbing on which he could have commented, but Hsien-yü Shu chose the fact that it bore Yüan Hao-wen's seals (and was therefore presumably also in his collection). Hence, the value of the work was further enhanced for him. In addition, to judge from the criticism of the Lan-t'ing given in his ca. 1293 colophon to the Shen-lung version in Kuo T'ien-hsi's collection, Hsien-yü Shu did not easily praise the existing Lan-t'ing examples. Each had its own merits, and he admitted to being overjoyed to own but one specimen. The criticism here, that this Ting-wu version is "the finest I have seen in my life," is not a contradiction; it is his highest praise.

In late spring of the next year 1298, an important gathering took place at Hsien-yü Shu's garden studio. Several of the prominent literati from Chou Mi's circle were present. The highlight of the event was another scroll of Wang Hsi-chih, one in cursive script belonging to the censor Kuo T'ien-hsi. Chao Meng-fu recorded his impressions and the roster of guests, leaving it for posterity in a colophon at the end of Kuo's scroll:

"On the 23rd day of the 2nd moon of the 2nd year of the Ta-te era [April 5, 1298], the following persons gathered at Hsien-yü Po-chi's garden pond

---

[76] The rubbing is extant in the Palace Museum, Taipei, and is referred to as "Sung-t'a wu-tzu sun-pen Lan-t'ing 宋搨五字損本蘭亭" (Sung rubbing of the Lan-t'ing with the five defaced characters); it is uncatalogued, but included in the Palace Museum Photographic Archives, nos. 5070–75. The rubbing was recently published with brief comments by Chang Kuang-pin 張光賓, "Ku-kung po-wu-yüan shou-ts'ang fa-shu yü pei-t'ieh 故宮博物院收藏法書與碑帖," *National Palace Museum Quarterly*, 9:3 (1975), p. 13 and pl. 2. He notes that there are three seals of Yüan I-shan 元遺山.

[twelve persons are named]. . . . [Kuo] Yu-chih brought out a genuine work of Yu-chün's [Wang Hsi-chih] called *Ssu-hsiang t'ieh* 思想帖 ('Deep thoughts'). It had the force of dragons leaping at the gate of heaven and tigers crouching at the phoenix pavilion. Everyone who looked at it could not but sigh and lament at how impossible it was to come across a work of such divine presence. Meng-fu signed." [77]

This apparently modest colophon to a letter of five lines represents a remarkable gathering of talents. First, the list contains important persons, many of whom were holding or were to hold high office during and after this period. Chang Po-ch'un (1242–1302, Chia-hsing, Chekiang) was a Ju-hsüeh 儒學 professor in the Hangchow circuit and an auxiliary academician in the Hanlin Academy;[78] Chao Meng-fu was just embarking on a rising career, and by that year he had just refused the dual posts of prefectural administrator in the Shansi circuit and agricultural intendent in Hopei. Teng Wen-yüan (Mien-chou, Szechwan) was an instructor in the Ch'ung-te 崇德 prefectural government, but later would reach the peak of his career as an auxiliary academician in the Academy of Worthies and become Chancellor of the National College.[79] Li K'an (Chi-ch'iu, Hopei) held office as a co-administrator of the directorate general of the Chia-hsing Circuit and as prefectural administrator of Wu-yüan chou and later would gain favor with Emperor Jen-tsung and reach the post of Minister of Personnel.[80]

These gentlemen were prominent enough during their lifetimes and after to have their biographies included in the official Yüan history. There were two other northerners, or *nan-kuan*, other than Hsien-yü Shu: Li K'an and Kuo T'ien-hsi. As indicated by this gathering of notables, Kuo's collection of painting and calligraphy was worthy of attention. Li K'an gained fame as a painter of bamboo and was author of a systematic treatise on bamboo painting. Lien Hsi-kung 廉希貢 (ca.1240–1300?) was a Uighur and a good

[77] "Wang Yu-chün Ssu-hsiang t'ieh 王右軍思想帖," as recorded in Pien: SKT, vol. 1, 6:187–188. For an illustration of the work, see SZ 4, pl. 77.

[78] YS 178:4147, and *Yüan shih hsüan* (erh-ping). Chang was one of the southerners whom Khubilai summoned to serve the court in 1287.

[79] YS 172:4023–4025, *Yüan shih hsüan* (erh-ping), and SSHY 7:2b; examples of Teng's calligraphy, which are extant primarily in the form of colophons, may be found in KKFS 18:1–7.

[80] HYS 188. *Yüan shih hsüan, kuei-chi* 癸集 (ping 丙), 1b, and his treatise on bamboo painting, *Chu-p'u hsiang-lu* 竹譜詳錄 (ISTP 11). He was known for both ink bamboo and colored bamboo in "blue-green style"; see his handscroll in ink on paper in the Nelson Gallery, Kansas City (Lee and Ho, cat. no. 242), with two excellent colophons by Chao Meng-fu and Yüan Ming-shan, dated 1308 and 1309; and his pair of hanging scrolls in the Metropolitan Museum of Art (*ibid.*, cat. no. 241), and Fong and Fu, cat. no. 24, pp. 128–134, 151.

friend of Hsien-yü Shu's. He served as an academician in the Chao-wen
Institute 昭文館 and was one of the several northerners mentioned by Liu
Kuan in his important colophon to Hsien-yü Shu's letter.[81] As to the
others, their importance lay in their personal collections and interest in
antiquities: Hao Su 郝肅 (fl. ca.1295–1300?), Ma Chü 馬昫 (fl.
ca. 1295–1300?), Ch'iao K'uei-ch'eng and Wang Chih were all mentioned by either Chou Mi or Hsien-yü Shu in their various writings.[82]

In this discussion of Hsien-yü Shu's artistic activities, we have touched
on several northern elements which reveal his continuing interest in his
heritage and its influence on his art, but so far we have not mentioned Wang
T'ing-yün. Hsien-yü Shu seems to have come across an actual example of
Wang's work quite late in his career. The lateness, however, only
contributed to an increased intensity and excitement in his understanding
and reaction to it.

In the spring of 1300 Hsien-yü Shu had the opportunity to study a
remarkable work of an artistic stature which we can judge today: Wang
T'ing-yün's scroll of painting and calligraphy, "Secluded Bamboo among
Withered Branches" (Yu-chu k'u-ch'a 幽竹枯槎). Wang T'ing-yün
(1151–1202)[83] was a poet and high-ranking scholar-official from the Pohai region (modern Liao-ning). He was considered the leading painter and
calligrapher in the Chin both by his contemporaries, and later by Yüan
critics. He was judged, in fact, to be the equal of Mi Fu and Chao Meng-fu.
Yüan Hao-wen's high estimation of him is seen in several eulogies and in
his composition of Wang's epitaph.

The colophons by his admirers found on this scroll provide a fitting
conclusion to our discussion of Hsien-yü Shu and his relation to the
northern tradition and also provide more material to support the assertion
that the Chin scholar-painters acted as successful transmitters of the literati
tradition into the early Yüan. Fourteen colophons by early Yüan and Ming
scholars are appended to the scroll, of which Hsien-yü Shu's is the first and
earliest:

"On the right is Mr. Huang-hua's [i.e. Wang T'ing-yün's] painting of
secluded bamboo among withered branches which is followed by his
genuine self-inscription. I have often thought that the ancients who excelled

[81] See above, n. 14. Hsien-yü Shu says Lien served in the Salt Distribution Commission
of Liang-Che; see his K'un-tsa, 6b–7b, 14b, 21a. See also YYKYL, p. 66, and SSHY 7:17a
(translated in Chen/Goodrich, p. 187). Lien's dates are not known; I have estimated them
on the basis of his friendship with Hsien-yü Shu.
[82] For Hao Su, see YYKYL, p. 70, K'un-tsa, 24b; for Ma Chü, see K'un-tsa, 8a and 21b.
[83] See above, n. 10. In SSHY 8:2b, Wang is listed after Chao Ping-wen (and Chao
himself after Chang-tsung and four Jurchen aristocrats), indicating the position he held
according to traditional Yüan critics. He also heads the Chin listings in Hsia: THPC, p. 79.

in calligraphy ought to excell in painting, too: that is because calligraphy and painting possess the same basic principles. There has seldom been a case when someone who could do one could not do the other. Few can become famous for both, however, because the superior achievement invariably overshadows the less superior one. For example, the two Wangs [Hsi-chih (307–365) and his son Hsien-chih (344–388)] of the Tsin dynasty, or Hsüeh Chi 薛稷 (649–713) of the T'ang, or more recently, the Su 蘇 family of father and sons [Hsün 詢 (1009–1066), Shih 軾 (1036–1101) and Ch'e 轍 (1039–1112)]: in these cases their calligraphy overshadowed their painting. On the other hand, in the case of Cheng Ch'ien 鄭虔 (fl. ca.740–760), Kuo Chung-shu 郭忠恕 (fl. ca.950–960), Li Kung-lin 李公麟 (1049–1106) or Wen T'ung 文同 (1018–1079) and others, their [accomplishment in] painting overshadowed their [accomplishment in] calligraphy. Only with Mi Yüan-chang [Fu (1052–1107)] were calligraphy and painting so excellent that both became equally famous [and are also extant] today. After Mi Yüan-chang, there was only one person like that—Mr. Huang-hua.

"If you study this scroll carefully, you will see that there is painting in the calligraphy, and calligraphy in the painting. It is resplendent with a natural truth and overflows with a primal spirit. When I saw it I was speechless and couldn't believe that it was painted with just an ordinary brush. In the past two hundred years, there has been nothing like it.

"Now there is no lack of famous paintings by the ancients. But as to those which can purify human bones and marrow, refresh man's heart and eyes, and lift him out of filth and foulness beyond the wind and dust to make him as free and bouyant as an immortal—one could hardly talk about [paintings of such transcendent quality like that] at the same time as ordinary paintings!

"Hsien-yü Shu of Yü-yang respectfully inscribes and submits on the 3rd day after shang-ssu 上巳 [3rd day of 3rd moon] of the 4th year of the Ta-te 大德 era [March 27, 1300]." [84]

After more than six hundred years, the scroll has lost none of the primal vigor and adherence to the principles of nature which so moved Hsien-yü

[84] Published in its entirety in *Shohin*, 30 (July 1962), pp. 2–37, and recorded in *Shih-ch'ü pao-chi hsü-pien* (1791–93) (Ch'ung-hua-kung), 124 ff.; for other records of this work, see J. C. Ferguson, *Li-tai chu-lu hua-mu* 歷代著錄畫目 (Peking, 1934), 40a. The colophon writers are: 1) Hsien-yü Shu, dated 1300; 2) Chao Meng-fu, undated; 3) Yüan Chüeh, undated; 4) T'ang Hou, undated; 5) Ma K'o-fu 馬克復, dated 1304; 6) Shih Chung-wei 史仲微, undated; 7) Kung Su 龔璛, undated; 8) K'ang-li Nao-nao 康里巎巎, undated; 9) not signed or dated; 10) Pan Wei-chih 班惟志, undated; 11) Chin Ying-kuei 金應桂, dated 1305; 12) Yüan Ming-shan 元明善, undated; 13) Chang Ning 張寧, dated 1476; 14) Li Shih-shih 李士實, 1477 (?). I have seen this work only in reproduction.

Shu. His enthusiasm was not guarded: he attributed life-giving and spiritually renewing qualities to the painting and the calligraphy, and his description conveys a genuine sense of spiritual communion.

On a more prosaic level, several ideas of critical importance to the literati movement are contained in Hsien-yü Shu's colophon. In the context of this discussion, only the most important will be discussed: the concept of the similar origin and function of calligraphy and painting. Voiced as early as the eighth century, when painting gained independence as an expressive art, the idea had become especially important by the tenth century during the Northern Sung period. Only then did the amateur ethic and efforts of literati like Su Shih, Wen T'ung and others lend to painting a respectability which made it, alongside the sister arts of poetry and calligraphy, an acceptable pursuit for the cultivated gentleman. The emphasis which Hsien-yü Shu gives calligraphy as an equal to painting reveals the extent to which early Yüan literati saw a renewed importance in calligraphy, seeking precedents for it and for painting as *dual vehicles* of expression. It is through such intuitive insight, articulated with a critical emphasis, that the merger between calligraphy and painting was taking place in the early Yüan. The precedents themselves are notably from the Tsin, T'ang, and Sung periods. The importance of the Northern Sung is given by example—the Su family, father and two sons, Kuo Chung-shu, Li Kung-lin, Wen T'ung and Mi Fu. Incidentally, no *Southern* Sung precedents are mentioned. Furthermore, in the two hundred years since the last of the great Northern Sung masters, only Wang T'ing-yün rightfully gained fame in both painting and calligraphy. An extremely high tribute paid him.

The merger of painting and calligraphy is then succinctly stated in the following phrase: "[In looking at Wang T'ing-yün's work] there is calligraphy in the painting and painting in the calligraphy" (詳觀此卷，畫中有書，書中有畫). In this statement, at this early date, 1300, Hsien-yü Shu reveals his stature as a critic and his importance not only to the Yüan literati movement, but to its whole history. Before him, Su Shih had made the famous comment about the T'ang poet-painter Wang Wei 王維 (699–759), that "When savoring Mo-chieh's [i.e. Wang Wei's] poems, the poems contain paintings, / When looking at Mo-chieh's paintings, the paintings contain poems"[85] (味摩詰之詩，詩中有畫，觀摩詰之畫，畫中有詩). In terms of the development of the literati esthetic from the T'ang through Sung, Hsien-yü Shu has completed another critical step in

[85] Recorded in Chao Ling-chih 趙令畤, *Hou-ch'ing lu* 侯鯖錄 (*Chih-pu-tsu chai* ed.), 8:9a. Cf. Bush, *Chinese Literati*, p. 25; Su Shih also made a similar statement about Tu Fu's poetry and Han Kan's paintings; see Bush, *ibid.*, pp. 22–28, where she cites several key quotations from the works of Northern Sung literati illustrating this idea.

the recognition of the close alliance between painting and calligraphy. This is the clearest and possibly the earliest statement by a Yüan artist of this vital concept. Later Chao Meng-fu would be quoted as saying: "Rocks as in *fei-pai* 飛白 [script], branches as in *chou* 籀 [i.e., 'seal' script]; when painting bamboo, one ought to have mastered thoroughly the Eight Methods [in calligraphy]. Those who understand these principles realize that the roots of calligraphy and painting have always been one."[86]

Chao's statement is a more explicit directive than Hsien-yü Shu's, revealing the development of the actual technique of painting as well. Around 1300, however, Chao's thoughts on this matter were still unformulated. Following Hsien-yü Shu's colophon of 1300, there appears Chao's undated colophon to Wang T'ing-yün's painting: "Whenever I see the painting and calligraphy of Huang-hua, it makes my spirit feel truly refreshed. This scroll is especially outstanding in its perfection. Meng-fu." From this sequence of colophons it may be inferred that Hsien-yü Shu had an earlier perception of the alliance of calligraphy and painting; it is quite clearly formulated in his mind, even though briefly stated without elaboration.[87]

The importance of Wen T'ing-yün's position in the eyes of Yüan scholars is underlined in the several colophons following Chao Meng-fu's, in particular the five by Yüan Chüeh 袁桷 (1266–1327), T'ang Hou (fl. 1290–1300-after 1322), Ma K'o-fu 馬克復 (fl. ca.1300), Kung Su 龔璛 (1266–1321), Nao-nao 嶩嶩 (1295–1345), and Yüan Ming-shan 元明善 (1269–1322). These scholars represent an impressive mixture of northerners, southerners, and foreigners: Yüan Chüeh was from Ch'ing-yüan 慶元, Chekiang; T'ang Hou from Kiangsu; Ma K'o-fu active in Ching-k'ou 京口, Kiangsu; Kung Su from Kao-yu 高郵, Kiangsu; Nao-nao, a sinicized Central Asian of Turkish ancestry; and Yüan Ming-shan from Ch'ing-ho 清河, Hopei.

Yüan Chüeh's comments are brief, but he makes the significant point that Wang T'ing-yün's style is descended from Mi Fu (1052–1107), and, agreeing with critical opinion, that Wang is not inferior to him. Proceeding a step further, Yüan agrees with the judgment that Wang is not even inferior to Wen T'ung. Now it is known from Su Shih's

---

[86] As recorded in Ts'ao Chao 曹昭, *Ko-ku yao-lun* 格古要論 (1387), 1:9b. I have not had access to a copy of this work, but used the facsimile printed in P. David, *Chinese Connoisseurship: The Ko-ku yao-lun* (London, 1971), which purports to reprint the Shu Min edition published in 1388–97; cf. the translation on p. 15. Other editions apparently contain the variant phrase that "bamboo leaves ought to be painted as in *pa-fen* script."

[87] The inception and chronology of this critical concept need further study. I present it here only on the basis of my limited findings.

perceptive insight and unrestrained praise that Wen T'ung had reached truly immeasurable heights of expression in both his calligraphy and painting. For Su, Wen represented the quintessential amateur painter whose poetry, essays, calligraphy, and painting were but the "leftover elements of his virtue (*te* 德)."[88] It is the measure of Yüan Chüeh's esteem that he ultimately compares Wang T'ing-yün to Wen T'ung.

This unrelenting praise of the Chin master is repeated in T'ang Hou's long colophon, which is also worth quoting in its entirety:

"Whenever scholars amuse themselves by painting, the form of the object invariably follows the brush and is transformed [by the brush]. When a scene comes forth from inspiration, it is made new [by the inspiration]. [No longer is it necessary] to lick the brush or spit on the ink, to take five days to paint the water and ten for a rock. Former painters who were extremely careful about composition and the placing of elements are like the calligraphers who excelled in clerical or seal scripts. [Nowadays] when scholars lodge their ideas in brush and ink, they are like calligraphers who write 'mad' cursive: if they did not have the wealth of learning of ten thousand books in their breast, or did not command the eight principles [of calligraphy] at their brushtip, they could not create the subtle principles [of this art].

"In addition to his literary works and calligraphy, Mr. Wang Huang-hua of the Chin has also paid some attention to playing with ink and, during the Ta-ting 大定 (1161–90) and Ming-ch'ang 明昌 (1190–96) eras, has gained fame for it. This painting of secluded bamboo and withered branches is abbreviated in execution, yet at the same time has an antique feeling. The poetry is vigorous and the calligraphy untrammeled. It can compare with the ancient masters in its excellence. What he has entrusted in this work in a moment of pure inspiration and intense feeling can be passed on for a hundred generations and still be seen by us through the broken silk to earn our admiration and fondness. This was the extent of his achievement!

"T'ang Hou of Tung-ch'u (Kiangsu). My hands cannot bear to put down this painting, so I leave a eulogy of praise. [The eulogy is not translated here.]"

In the history of art, T'ang Hou is best remembered for his theoretical treatises, "Discussion of Painting" (*Hua-lun* 畫論) and "Critical Notes

---

[88] "Wen Yü-k'o hua mo-chu p'ing-feng tsan 文與可畫墨竹屏風贊," in *Su Tung-p'o ch'üan-chi ch'i-chung* 蘇東坡全集七種 (Taipei: Shih-chieh Shu-chü, 1964), vol. 1, 20:277 (cf. Bush's translation, *Chinese Literati*, p. 12); "Mo-chün t'ang chi 墨君堂記," 31:381; and "Wen Yü-k'o hua sun-tang ku-yen-chu chi 文與可畫篔簹谷偃竹記," 33:394–395 (cf. Bush's translation, p. 37) present some of Su's key ideas.

on Painters Past and Present" (*Ku-chin hua-chien* 古今畫鑑).[89] These treatises consist of a critical exposition of the faults and merits of "ancient" and "modern" painters in chronological order with brief biographies. They represent the most complete record extant of Yüan scholar-painters' views distilled through the eyes of a critic who held Mi Fu, Wang T'ing-yün, and Chao Meng-fu in highest esteem. His admiration for Mi is shown in the numerous direct quotes he makes from Mi's writings, and for Wang and Chao in the fact that he believed the two masters to be the greatest painters of the past two hundred years.[90]

Despite the importance of T'ang's works, exceedingly little is known about him. T'ang Hou's father was T'ang Ping-lung 湯炳龍 (1241– ca.1319) (see below), better-known than his son as a poet and connoisseur. The father was in fact active in Chou Mi's and Hsien-yü Shu's Hangchow circle. He also attended the poetry gatherings and painting-viewing sessions where he inscribed his observations. There is evidence, therefore, that the level of discrimination and taste of the young T'ang Hou was very much influenced by his father's eye and by the company of his father's friends. Thus it is no accident that T'ang Hou accords such high praise to this work and that his ideas are so close to Hsien-yü Shu's, presenting several of the same issues in more developed form. It took a second-generation connoisseur to record in a more systematic manner the taste and esthetic preferences being formulated by the older generation.

Although T'ang's formulation of these concepts shows the significant advance and consolidation of literati values over that of earlier Yüan observers like Hsien-yü Shu, many of these same issues were also noted earlier by Chin poets, usually, however, only as part of a poem, or as a thought imbedded among others.[91] Hsien-yü Shu's colophon is devoted solely to the exposition of the idea of painting and calligraphic values and represents an advance in formulation over theirs. And while more advanced, T'ang's colophon is more prosaic, or academic. It is significant that T'ang speaks of painting as an amusement, for by the Yüan this approach had not only become widespread among scholars, but also was practiced as a true class of *amateurs*. T'ang underlines this amateur aspect when he notes that the "form of the object follows the brush and is transformed by it" ([士大夫遊戲迻畫] 往往象隨筆化). He contrasts the painters of the past—who took pains and painted as part of their

---

[89] ISTP edition, vol. 11. The text of the *Hua-chien* is believed to have been compiled about 1328; see Yü Shao-sung 余紹宋, *Shu-hua shu-lu chieh-t'i* 書畫書錄解題 (Peking, 1932), 6:26a–b, where the *Ssu-k'u ch'üan-shu tsung-mu* editors are quoted. See also Bush, *Chinese Literati*, pp. 124–130.

[90] *Hua-lun*, p. 9.

[91] Cf. Bush, "Literati Culture," pp. 103–112, and *Chinese Literati*, pp. 87–111.

leisure—with the new kind of painting, the "mad cursive" script in calligraphy. In this freest of cursive writing, the forms are but vehicles for the expression of the brushwork, the character and learning of the man. Reflecting this artistic liberty, painting was done not on commission, but on inspiration (*hsing* 興). In this lies the heart of the literati values championed by the later Yüan masters.

The importance of Wang T'ing-yün's work to northerners themselves, even before the appreciation lavished in the Yüan, is seen in the fifth colophon on the scroll by a certain Ma K'o-fu whose identity is thus far obscure. Ma says that until recently this scroll was in the collection of Hao Chi-hsien, a high-placed *se-mu-jen* 色目人 (Central Asian), who obtained the scroll when he was Minister of Personnel and was serving in T'ai-yüan, Shansi. Hao Chi-hsien is better known as Hao T'ien-t'ing 郝天挺 (1247–1313) of the Yüan dynasty, who later became a chief councilor of state; he was born into the To-lu-pieh tribe and had adopted a Chinese name.[92] Tutored by Yüan Hao-wen, Hao T'ien-t'ing undoubtedly gained the proper esteem for Wang's work from his teacher. Ma K'o-fu's colophon says that even though Hao was busy with official duties, he carried the scroll on all his travels between north and south, when one day a friend saw it and coveted it. Hao preferred to avoid hard feelings, so he finally let him have the scroll. The friend was Shih Yen 石巖 (fl. 1300–1335?).[93] Shih was active in Ching-k'ou, across the river from Yangchow, so that, as Ma K'o-fu points out, "everytime he passed through, he had to go and see it."

The connection of the former owner of this scroll, Hao T'ien-t'ing, with Yüan Hao-wen should not go unappreciated. It was through an important and vital upholder of traditional and literary values such as Yüan Hao-wen, and as further transmitted through a Central Asian like Hao T'ien-t'ing, that such literary ideals were continued into the Yüan.

This point is further verified by the eighth colophon writer, Nao-nao (1295–1345).[94] Nao-nao, who once held office as Hanlin academician for the transmission of directives, was no mean calligrapher. Critics have

---

[92] YS 174:4065–4066, and Ch'en/Goodrich, p. 135. Hao T'ien-t'ing of the Yüan should not be confused with Hao T'ien-t'ing (t. Chin-ch'ing) of the Chin, and the teacher of Yüan Hao-wen; see *Chung-chou chi*, 9:5b.

[93] See *Yüan shih hsüan, kuei-chi* (*i* 乙), 69b; Shih wrote the preface dated 1332 to Chou Mi's *Chih-ya t'ang*; I have estimated his dates on that basis.

[94] YS 143; SSHY 7:17b–18a; Ch'en/Goodrich, pp. 23, n. 32, 24 ff., 188, 193–197; and F. Cleaves, "K'uei-k'uei or Nao-nao?" HJAS, 10 (1947), pp. 1–12. For examples of his calligraphy, see SZ, pls. 44–47. A famous handscroll by Nao-nao in cursive script transcribing Liu Tsung-yüan's 柳宗元 "Tzu-jen chuan 梓人傳" is in The Art Museum, Princeton University; see Shen C. Y. Fu, *Traces of the Brush: Studies in Chinese Calligraphy* (New Haven, 1977), pp. 86–87, 103.

paired him with Chao Meng-fu as "Nao-nao in the north and Tzu-ang in the south." An anecdote told by his contemporary Yang Yü 楊瑀 (1285–1361) relates that upon hearing that Chao could write 10,000 characters per day, Nao-nao replied that he habitually wrote 30,000 per day before putting down his brush.[95] Much can be said of such total assimilation and mastery of the traditional culture by a Central Asian that he would gain independent fame as a calligrapher. Here is Nao-nao's estimation of Wang T'ing-yün: "The personal integrity, the calligraphy and the painting of Mr. Huang-hua are all so excellent and wonderful that high-placed scholars and officials all treasure and want to collect his work. When I look at this scroll, it gives me a free and easy feeling. It makes me want to meet him in a dream and discuss calligraphy with him. The Khangli, Nao-nao inscribed."

In summary, the colophons to this scroll by Wang T'ing-yün offer an excellent illustration of the kind of inter-mingling of northern and southern interests witnessed and described by Liu Kuan. The scroll itself became a focal point for the concentration and development of key literary and artistic ideals, notably as seen in the comments of Hsien-yü Shu and T'ang Hou. Moreover, as each colophon was added, there was in actual fact a continuity and thread linking like minds which reached from past masters to the Yüan writers. The scroll itself, as given life by Wang T'ing-yün, acted as a vehicle for the preservation and transmission of literati values.

THE "ADMONITIONS" SCROLL AND THE NORTHERN TRADITION

The specific importance of the northern literary and calligraphic traditions to Hsien-yü Shu's art can best be seen through an important work which he executed in 1299, "Admonitions to the Imperial Censors" (*Yü-shih chen* 御史箴).[96] It transcribes moral cautionaries to that institution

---

[95] As recorded in *Shan-chü hsin-hua* 山居新話 (1360) (*Chih-pu-tsu chai* ed.), 46a; cf. the same anecdote as recorded in T'ao Tsung-i, *Cho-keng-lu* 輟耕錄 (1366) (rpt. Taipei: Shih-chieh Shu-chü, 1971), 15:223–224. See also the annotated translation of Yang Yü's work by H. Franke, "Beiträge zur Kulturgeschichte Chinas unter der Mongolenherrschaft: Das Shan-kü sin-hua des Yang Yü," *DMG: Abhandlungen für die Kunde des Morgenlandes* 32.2 (Wiesbaden, 1956), p. 117.

[96] The scroll is in The Art Museum, Princeton University; it is partially illustrated in Tseng Yu-ho Ecke, *Chinese Calligraphy* (Philadelphia, 1971), cat. no. 34; and Shen C. Y. Fu, *Traces of the Brush*, pp. 15–17, 32–33, 140–141. The work was originally fifty-four lines long in 204 characters, but the first twenty-six lines were lost in 1945 when the Russians looted the imperial precincts. The opening inscription by its former owner, Chang Ta-ch'ien 張大千 (born 1899), relates the incident.

The work is recorded in *Shih-ch'ü pao-chi ch'u-pien* (1744–45), 31:6–7. I am grateful to Shen Fu for locating this reference.

of advisors to the throne, the Censorate (Fig. 3). Each brush-written character of the scroll measures 4–5 inches in height. Like his transcription of Ma Chiu-ch'ou's "Song of the Diaphanous Mirror," Hsien-yü Shu wrote this in a bold and direct manner with a slightly worn-out brush. His personal characteristics in this script type can be seen in the balanced, stable structure of the characters, and in the rounded, even thickness of the brush strokes. For the most part he held the brush upright, and, working with a controlled and steady pressure, Hsien-yü Shu produced strokes with a plump rounded quality which were not overly fleshy. An immense vigor is sustained throughout the scroll, and the total impression conveyed is monumental and immediate in its impact.

The importance of the scroll lies not only in its esthetic quality, but in its text and author. The author of the "Admonitions," who was not identified by Hsien-yü Shu in the scroll itself, was the prominent Chin poet and official Chao Ping-wen 趙秉文 (1159–1232, h. Hsien-hsien lao-jen 閑閑老人, Fu-yang 滏陽, Hopei).[97] The fact that the author of the "Admonitions" essay was a scholar under the Jurchen-Chin relates again directly to Hsien-yü Shu's heritage. As noted above, Hsien-yü Shu's great-grandfather served the Chin government for a time; daring and heroic qualities were attributed to him, the grandmother and the father, and these very qualities were also cited by Hsien-yü Shu's contemporaries as descriptive of him. These affiliations with his past and with Chin literary culture are reflected foremost in the fact that the author, Chao Ping-wen, was the leading Chin literary figure and the sponsor of Yüan Hao-wen. Moreover, the text itself was important to Hsien-yü Shu because he transcribed it at least three times: this scroll, a version on silk, and one to be carved in stele form.[98]

Veneration for its author and the high seriousness of the essay must have dictated the choice of the script type—the large formal k'ai 楷 style ("regular" or "block" standard script).[99] The selection of Chao's text

---

[97] CS 110:2426–2429; *Chung-chou chi*, 3:25a–b; SSHY, 8:2b. Chao was recommended by Wang T'ing-yün to the Hanlin Academy in 1195 during the Ming-ch'ang era. The text of the *Yü-shih chen* is recorded in *Hsien-hsien lao-jen fu-shui wen-chi* 閑閑老人滏水文集, (SPTK ed.), 17:182. I am again indebted to Shen Fu for this reference.

One of the reasons Chao wrote the "Admonitions" may have been the low state of moral conscience and ineffectiveness of the office toward the end of the Chin. Other scholars such as Liu Ch'i were disturbed by this; see Chan, *Historiography*, p. 139; and Tao, *The Jurchen*, pp. 45–46.

[98] The other two are not extant. See Li Tso-hsien 李左賢, *Shu-hua chien-ying* 書畫鑑影 (1891), 13:9; Fang Chün-i, *Meng-yüan shu-hua lu* (1877), 5:17, respectively.

[99] In Hsien-yü Shu's total oeuvre (some 50 works), this formal script is rare. He wrote in three major script types: "cursive" (large and small), "semi-cursive" or "running" script

leads one to reflect on Hsien-yü Shu's historical situation: here was an essay composed by a Han-Chinese for censors serving an alien Jurchen emperor, and subsequently transcribed by another Han-Chinese serving a second alien regime, the "barbarian" Mongols. One can be assured that the complex social and political implications of his choice were part of the consciousness of the transcriber, and indeed of the intellectuals for whom the scroll was intended as a work of calligraphic art.

Existing brush examples of Liao, Chin, or "predynastic" Yüan calligraphy are rare. The most important examples happen to come from the hands of two major cultural figures from the north, Chao Ping-wen and Yeh-lü Ch'u-ts'ai 耶律楚材. One element distinguishes the writing of both and relates them to Hsien-yü Shu's "Admonitions" scroll—their size and monumentality.

Chao Ping-wen's work is a colophon to a painting depicting the famous "Prose-poem on the Red Cliff" (Ch'ih-pi fu 赤壁賦) by Su Shih (Fig. 4).[100] The writing, totaling thirty-two lines, was executed in 1228. The general impression is bold and direct, even harsh, in comparison to the stable, balanced forms of Hsien-yü Shu's "Admonitions." Chao's work reflects the strong influence of Northern Sung predecessors, Su Shih, Huang T'ing-chien, and especially Mi Fu. This is evidenced in the free composition of the characters in a column, in the extreme contrasts of thick and thin, flat and elongated brush strokes, as well as in the uninhibited spirit of the whole. Chao Ping-wen's personal use of the brush differs from the Northern Sung, however, in the directness of his attack. There are exaggerated contrasts in the strokes and an unfinished coarseness which go far beyond what Mi Fu, or other Northern Sung masters, would have considered fitting. Most of all, Chao displays a raw energy which would have been foreign to his Northern Sung predecessors.

This same kind of "rawness" is seen in the exceptional scroll written in 1240 by Yeh-lü Ch'u-ts'ai (1189–1243) (Fig. 5).[101] Written in twenty-

---

(large and small), and "regular." In this last category, only two works in large regular script survive.

[100] The scroll, the only known example of Chao's writing, is extant in the Palace Museum, Taipei; see *Three Hundred Masterpieces in the Palace Museum* (Taipei, 1959), 3 : 132; Chao's colophon is titled "Chui-ho P'o-hsien Ch'ih-pi tz'u-yün" and is not recorded in his collected works. The painter, Wu Yüan-chih was identified in a colophon by Yüan Hao-wen, no longer attached to the scroll. See KKSHL 4 : 99–101, and *I-shan hsien-sheng wen-chi*, 40 : 16b; and Bush, "Literati Culture," fig. 1, pp. 104–105.

[101] The scroll, also the only known example of Yeh-lü's writing, is extant in the John M. Crawford, Jr., collection, and published by Achilles Fang in *Chinese Calligraphy and Painting in the Collection of John M. Crawford, Jr.* (New York, 1962), cat. no. 37, pp. 93–94. According to Professor Fang, the text is not reprinted in any of Yeh-lü's collected works. There are a number of important colophons attached: 1) Sung Lien 宋濂,

one lines in a formal *k'ai* style, it praises the good government of an official who presided over a region in northwest Shansi. Each column contains but three to four characters. Yeh-lü was not known as a calligrapher, and indeed were this scroll not to exist, his calligraphic abilities would be lost to us, for he is not mentioned in any of the contemporary or later accounts of calligraphy. It is evident that he had practiced assiduously the strict regular script of Yen Chen-ch'ing, and that this commemorative style suited his temperament, to the degree that it could accurately reflect and express the largeness of his personality. The brush is wielded with such forthright vigor and uncompromising resoluteness that, even more than in Chao Ping-wen's work, one feels the energy, the disciplined power, and the strength of mind of this eminent Khitan nobleman.

The visual elements in the calligraphy of these two prominent scholar-statesmen are introduced here to underline the bold creative forces which formed the immediate tradition out of which Hsien-yü Shu, his father and grandfather grew; Chao and Yeh-lü would have been their contemporaries. Hsien-yü Shu spent his formative years in the north—this is known from Chao Meng-fu's poem—and he would have been well into his maturity when he assumed his southern posts in Yangchow and Hangchow. Thus the dominance of the northern cultural tradition and subsequent admiration of these figures and their accomplishments must have long been planted in his consciousness, if not by direct contact with their works of calligraphy, then through their writings.

A northern lineage in calligraphy was described by the early Ming scholar Hsieh Chin 解縉 (1369–1415, Chi-shui, Kiangsi), who served in the Wen-yüan ko 文淵閣 and who acted as a censor under the first Ming emperor. In his essay *Shu-hsüeh ch'uan-shou p'u* 書學傳授譜 he traced Hsien-yü Shu's calligraphic ancestry from Mi Fu in the Northern Sung to Wang T'ing-yün, then to Wang's son, Wang Wan-ch'ing (fl. 1200-after 1262), to Chang T'ien-hsi 張天錫, and finally to Hsien-yü Shu.[102] According to Hsieh, Mi Fu's tradition branched into a northern and a southern line. The southern consisted of Mi's son, Mi Yu-jen 米友仁 (1074–1153), Chang Chi-chih 張即之 (1186–1266), and finally Chao Meng-fu. While Hsieh does not stress the development of these two branches, it is significant that he saw a distinct *northern* line that was linked to regional traditions.

According to this lineage, the important predecessor to Hsien-yü Shu

---

undated; 2) Li Shih-cho 李世倬, dated 1743; 3) Tai Liang 戴良, dated 1349; 4) Li Shih-cho; 5) Ku Cheng T'ao 顧鄭濤, dated 1352; 6) Kung Su 龔璛, dated 1321.

It is partially illustrated in Ecke, *Chinese Calligraphy*, cat. no. 27.

[102] Pien: SKT 3:127.

was Chang T'ien-hsi. Very little is known about him. T'ao Tsung-i
陶宗儀 includes him in his *Shu-shih hui-yao* 書史會要, saying he was a
native of Ho-chung 河中, Shansi, and active under Chin Chang-tsung's
reign (1189–1208); his "regular" script followed Liu Kung-ch'üan
柳公權, and his cursive was derived from the Tsin and Sung masters.[103]
Chang seems to have excelled in large writing, so that he was under
constant order from Chang-tsung to execute the signs and plaques for
the various imperial halls; in addition, he wrote a treatise on cursive
script, *Ts'ao-shu yün-hui* 草書韻會. Unfortunately, nothing from Chang's
hand survives today. Therefore, the works of other Chin writers must
serve to fill this gap.

Large writing is important in the lineage to Hsien-yü Shu, and Chao
Ping-wen also was remembered for his large script. Actually Chao not
only composed the text of the "Admonitions," but he also transcribed a
version of the essay for a friend in large characters. In 1278 the
prominent scholar Wang Yün 王惲 (1227–1304, Wei-chou 衛州, Honan)
saw Chao's scroll in the collection of a friend, Chang Lin-yeh 張隣野.
Wang took a great liking to it, and a copy was made and given to him in
1282, when he was in the capital serving as a censor.[104] Wang Yün's
colophon to the scroll records this; furthermore, it was written after he
had had the opportunity to see the collection of some 147 calligraphy
pieces and 81 paintings which had entered the Mongol court in 1276.[105]

As a direct student of Yüan Hao-wen and a learned and enthusiastic
connoisseur of the arts, Wang Yün would have viewed Chao's scroll with
special respect for the links it bore with his immediate past. He writes:

"... His excellency [Chao Ping-wen's] calligraphy is not too rare, but if
one were to speak of large writing with characters the size of a fist, so
bold and vigorous, monumental and extraordinary, combining the styles
of Yen [Chen-ch'ing] and Su [Shih], while at the same time exhibiting its
own individuality, then this must be considered the best of all his works.

"By nature I have always had a fondness for antiquity, and have never
tired of studying calligraphy. So whatever I have had the opportunity to
see has satisfied my intentions. It is as Ou-yang [Hsiu] said, that
objects gather around those persons who have a feeling for them...."[106]

Whether Hsien-yü Shu ever saw the scroll by Chao Ping-wen or knew

---

[103] SSHY 8:5a.

[104] Wang Yün 王惲, *Ch'iu-chien hsien-sheng wen-chi* 秋澗先生文集 (SPTK ed.), 38:3a.

[105] Wang Yün lists these works by title in his *Shu-hua mu-lu* 書畫目錄, written in 1276;
see *ibid.*, 41:11b–12b and 94:11a–14b. See also, Hin-cheung Lovell, *An Annotated Bibliography of Chinese Painting Catalogues and Related Texts* (Michigan, 1973), pp. 104–105.

[106] "Yü-shih-chen hou-chi 御史箴後記," *Ch'iu-chien wen-chi*, 38:2b–3a. Thanks go to
Shen Fu for this reference.

of Wang Yün's colophon is not known. It is conceivable that if he had
been in the capital in the late 1270s and early 1280s, Hsien-yü Shu might
have heard of the scroll and chanced to see it. In that case, the size of the
characters and the associations with the literary figures would have
provided an important precedent for him. Wang Yün's colophon is
otherwise important for the observation that Chao Ping-wen's calligraphy combined the styles of Yen Chen-ch'ing and Su Shih.

Another master of the northern tradition who would have provided
the background for Hsien-yü Shu's early development is Jen Hsün 壬詢
(ca.1110–ca.1188, I-chou 易州, Hopei).[107] Yüan Hao-wen considered
Jen the foremost calligrapher of his day, admired his poetry, and wrote
colophons to several of his works. Jen's family was renown for its
collection of scrolls, which were said to number in the hundreds. His
father Jen Kuei 壬貴 practiced calligraphy and the martial arts.

Jen's style also combined the art of the masters Yen and Su. Two
works by Jen survive, both in rubbing form. One is an epitaph of Wan-
yen Hsi-yin 完顏希尹, the sinified Jurchen general and shaman active
under Chin Hsi-tsung 熙宗 (1135–1149).[108] Written in strict *k'ai-shu*, the
epitaph is significant for its close adherence to the style of Yen Chen-
ch'ing. Yen was the major influence in *k'ai-shu* in the Northern Sung—
especially for the Four Great Masters, Ts'ai Hsiang 蔡襄, Su Shih,
Huang T'ing-chien, and Mi Fu, all of whom based their early training
and *k'ai* style on Yen's script. While Yen's style went out of fashion in
the Southern Sung, however, it was carried on with vigor in the north.
This influence, seen in the work of Jen Hsün, Chao Ping-wen, and Yeh-
lü Ch'u-ts'ai, represents a continuation and—indeed, judging from the
quality of the writing—a revitalization of the T'ang master's script. It is
important too, that Yen Chen-ch'ing was a northerner (Lang-yeh 瑯琊,
Shantung) and also a remote descendant of that paragon of Confucian
virtue Yen Chih-t'ui 顏之推 (531-after 591). Yen Chen-ch'ing's writings
were in great demand during his lifetime, and a sizable proportion was
written to be carved in stele form. Thus it is understandable that his
influence would remain dominant in the north where a larger number of
steles had survived.

The second extant work by Jen Hsün is a poem on an old cypress, *Ku-*

---

[107] *Chung-chou chi*, 2:17b; *I-shan wen-chi*, 40:8b–9b; and SSHY 8:3a. Jen's dates are
not recorded; I have computed them on the basis of a dated poem (1188) and Yüan's
comment that he died in his seventies. Jen is also known as a painter; see T'ang Hou, *Hua-
chien*, p. 44; but nothing is extant.

[108] The epitaph is published and illustrated in Hsü Ping-ch'ang (n. 5 above), pp. 3–18.
An enlarged detail and an *in situ* snapshot of the stele in Chi-lin are found in Toyama,
Kinchōshi, pl. 1 and figs. 3, 4, pp. 427 and 442.

po hsing 古柏行, dated 1160 (Fig. 6).[109] The calligraphy is a forthright combination of Yen Chen-ch'ing and Su Shih styles, a spontaneous mix of "regular" and "cursive" elements. The T'ang master's bluntness is especially evident in the rounded brushlines and short horizontal strokes. Jen's signature shows a linear strength which is close to the "wild cursive" (*k'uang-ts'ao* 狂草) of Chang Hsü 張旭, another T'ang master-calligrapher.

The importance of the works by Chin writers to Hsien-yü Shu is a matter of style in its largest sense. It is less one of strict formal correspondence, although that could be found in a detailed analysis, and more a matter of a regional spirit. It also has to do with a concept of the function of writing and of calligraphy as a monumental form capable of expressing a total freedom. The common factor in the works of these calligraphers preceding Hsien-yü Shu is a direct brush attack followed by bold simple brush movements and propelled by a raw vigor. There is little concern for the perfection of individual strokes as linear entities or for the balance and structure of individual characters. These distinctions are necessary on a formal level, because these very differences would distinguish the twelfth and early thirteenth-century northern masters' works from those of the late thirteenth- and early-fourteenth-century works of Yüan dynasty masters some two generations later.

When Hsien-yü Shu wrote the "Admonitions" scroll he did so as a work of calligraphy, not merely as a historical document. Thus the multilayered literary, political, and even stylistic implications were intended to be understood by his circle of friends. And, indeed, the scroll was seen by many. Upon completion, it circulated among several members of the Hangchow circle who enhanced its historical value by appending comments. The colophons of fourteen prominent Yüan dynasty poets, scholars, and officials are now found attached to it.

These are the writers whose colophons are appended to Hsien-yü Shu's "Admonitions" scroll:

1. Chao Meng-fu, no date.
2. Teng Wen-yüan, no date.
3. Chang Ying 張楧 (1260–1325, Hsi-ch'in 西秦, Kansu), no date.
4. Chou Ch'ih 周馳 (ca.1260–1325?, Tung-ch'ang 東昌, Shantung), colophon dated 1304.
5. T'ang Ping-lung 湯炳龍 (1241-after 1319, Shan-yang 山陽, Kiangsu), no date.

[109] Two rubbings are extant: in the Fujii-yurinkan, Kyoto; and the Freer Gallery of Art, Washington, D.C.; reproduced partially in SZ 16, fig. 42, p. 28; see also his *hao* "Lung-yen" in a cursive style, p. 173. I am grateful to Hin-cheung Lovell of the Freer, for locating the rubbings and providing me with photographs.

6. a. Ch'iu Yüan 仇遠 (1247-after 1327, Nan-yang 南陽, Honan)
   b. Ku Wen-ch'en 顧文琛 (fl. ca.1295–1305?, Chia-hsing 嘉興, Chekiang)
   c. Pai T'ing 白珽 (1248–1328, Ch'ien-t'ang 錢塘, Chekiang)
   d. Han Yu-chih 韓友直 (fl. ca.1295–1305?, Chi-shan 稽山, Honan)
   e. Han Yu-wen 韓友聞 (fl. ca.1295–1305?, Chi-shan, Honan)
   (A joint colophon signed by the five gentlemen, no date)
11. Yüeh Yüan-chang 樂元璋 (fl. ca.1285–1305?, Tung-p'ing 東平, Shantung), colophon dated 1304.
12. Kuo Ta-chung 郭大中 (fl. ca.1300–1320?, An-yang 安陽, Honan), no date.
13. T'ai Pu-hua 泰不華 (Bukha) (1304–1352, Pai-yeh [Baya'ud], Southern Russia), no date.
14. Mo Ch'ang 莫昌 (fl. 1300-after 1352, Wu-hsing, Chekiang), colophon dated 1352.

Among the fourteen, eight are particularly worthy of comment in this context: those by Chao Meng-fu, Teng Wen-yüan, Chang Ying, Chou Ch'ih, Ch'iu Yüan, Pai T'ing, T'ang Ping-lung, and T'ai Pu-hua. Chang and Chou were northern poets who had emigrated to Hangchow and with whom Tai Piao-yüan exchanged several poems.[110] Ch'iu Yüan later adopted Ch'ien-t'ang as his residence; he and Pai T'ing had achieved literary fame in the late Southern Sung and were known as "Ch'iu and Pai."[111] T'ang Ping-lung was a poet and connoisseur whose son, T'ang Hou, would later become the art theorist and leading Yüan spokesman for literati ideals.[112] T'ai Pu-hua (or T'ai Bukha, 1304–1352), the prominent scholar-warrior from the Mongol Baya'ud tribe, rose to high ranks in the Yüan bureaucracy as Minister of Rites and died a martyr in the Fang Kuo-chen 方國珍 rebellion.[113]

In many respects this scroll with its important colophons contains typical aspects of Hsien-yü Shu's life. It was dated 1299, three years before he died at the height of his career.

The colophons appear to have been written after Shu's death in 1302; the earliest is dated 1304. Chao Meng-fu's colophon appears first,

---

[110] For Chang Ying, see *Yüan shih hsüan, kuei-chi* (*chia* 甲), 8a, and YYTWC 20:4b. For Chou Ch'ih, see HYS 237; YSLP 36; *Yüan shih hsüan* (*san-ping* 三丙); SSHY 7:4a.

[111] For Ch'iu Yüan, see HYS 237; YSLP 36; *Yüan-shih chi-shih*, 7:9b; *Yüan shih hsüan* (*erh-chia* 二甲); SSHY 7:6a. For Pai T'ing, see HYS 237; YSLP 36, *Yüan shih hsüan* (*erh-chia* 二甲); SSHY 7:6a.

[112] For T'ang Ping-lung, see *Yüan shih hsüan* (*san-chia* 三甲); his dates are not recorded, but I have computed them on the basis of a colophon dated 1319 to the *Pao-mu-chih* (see above, n. 50), which says he was 79 *sui*.

[113] YS 143:3423–3426; HYS 217; SSHY; see Ch'en/Goodrich for extensive quotes and translations of the above, pp. 28–33, 120–121, 197–199.

directly after Hsien-yü Shu's inscription, but according to the final colophon by Mo Ch'ang, Chao was invited to inscribe the scroll later when it was in Mo's collection.. Mo's colophon is dated 1352 and refers to the time he had shown the scroll to Chao:

"... Formerly when I lived in Hangchow, I was a neighbor of Chao Wen-min [Meng-fu], whom I asked to inscribe this scroll. His excellency unrolled it and looked at it thoughtfully several times, then said to me: 'Everyone knows the wonders of Po-chi's calligraphy, but no one knows why it is so wonderful. Only I know why.' He enjoyed it appreciatively for a long time, and then took brush in hand and inscribed the colophon at the end...."

Chao's colophon, which is inserted after the final line of Hsien-yü Shu's signature and before Teng Wen-yüan's colophon, is but a single line in length:

"Each brushstroke of Po-chi's calligraphy contains antique method (ku-fa 古法). It qualifies as a supreme treasure. Meng-fu inscribed."

Here Chao brings out the important notion of ku-fa—"antique method." It is a point mentioned in slightly different ways in other of the colophons. Teng Wen-yüan, for example, names a specific sixth-century work as being the source of Hsien-yü Shu's ku-fa:

"Po-chi was profoundly diligent in his practice of calligraphy. Few contemporary persons know this fact. This calligraphy is based on the principles of the I-ho ming 瘞鶴銘 ('Inscription on the Burial of a Crane'). Looking at it one is moved to sighing endlessly. Wen-yüan."

Teng Wen-yüan noticed Hsien-yü Shu's diligence in the practise of calligraphy on more than one occasion in his colophons, and this aspect is repeated in the succeeding colophon by T'ang Ping-lung on the "Admonitions" scroll:

"Even since Po-chi came south, he has been conscientious in the practise of calligraphy for twenty years. In his late years he surpassed himself, and was truly qualified to gain fame in this world. Moreover, this is one of his finest works.... Inscribed by T'ang Ping-lung of Shan-yang [Kiangsu]."

Following this is a joint colophon by five persons. It is brief, but brings out two points mentioned earlier by the other writers:

"This writing looks exactly like the Li-tui chi 離堆記 and is comparable not only to the I-ho ming. Connoisseurs will see and appreciate this. Ch'iu Yüan of Nan-yang [Honan], Ku Wen-shen of Hsieh-li [Chekiang], Pai T'ing of Ch'ien-t'ang, and Han Yu-chih and Han Yu-wen of Chi-shan seen together at the Te-ch'ing-t'ang."

The Li-tui chi refers to an essay by a certain T'ang personage named

Hsien-yü Chung-t'ung 鮮于忠通. It was transcribed on the side of a cliff in Pao-ning fu 保寧府, Szechwan, by the famous calligrapher Yen Chen-ch'ing in 762 at the invitation of the Hsien-yü family.[114] By Sung times the cliff had suffered much damage; its cliff-high position plus its relatively inaccessible location caused it to be neglected so that, among Yen Chen-ch'ing's works, it is not well known nor well preserved. Today only some 58 characters are distinguishable.

As far as is known, Hsien-yü Shu never mentioned the *Li-tui chi*; therefore, there is no proof that he saw this particular work of Yen Chen-ch'ing's. That Hsien-yü Shu was a profound admirer of Yen, however, is known, for Yen's finest surviving manuscript entered Hsien-yü Shu's collection as early as 1282. The importance of the *Li-tui chi*, other than the coincidence of the author's surname, is that it may well have been an antique source which Hsien-yü Shu had studied; its mention by contemporaries is a clue not to be ignored. The *Li-tui chi* as we know it today is written in enormous *k'ai-shu*, and it displays a freer concept of style than is usually seen in Yen's stele inscriptions. The structure of the characters is broader, and there is a fuller, rounder use of the brush. The impression of fullness in the brushwork is accentuated by the worn condition of the cliff surface from which the rubbing was taken. Generally its formal style and physical condition bear comparison to the *I-ho ming*.

The *I-ho ming* ("Inscription on the Burial of a Crane") was an epitaph dated to 514, composed and erected for a pet crane. It had been famous since the Sung and rubbings taken from it had been greatly prized.[115] Hsien-yü Shu owned two versions, testifying to his more than casual interest in it. There were actually several aspects of the *I-ho ming* which were important for Hsien-yü Shu. He himself kept a pet crane, partly because he was fond of animals (he also raised a giant turtle), and partly because of the Taoist philosophic connotations associated with cranes. The crane was somewhat of a celebrity among Hsien-yü Shu's friends. When it died, it was buried near West Lake and its funerary rites were attended by poets who composed elegies in its honor.[116] Thus, as an essay, the content of the *I-ho ming* had a sentimental value for Hsien-yü Shu. But it bore an antiquarian and esthetic value as well. The epitaph

[114] This account is taken from Kanda Kiichirō 神田喜一郎, SZ 10, pp. 157–158; see pls. 32–33 for illustration.

[115] This account is taken from Toyama Gunji, SZ 5, pp. 19–23; see pls. 22–33.

[116] As recorded in T'ien Ju-ch'eng 田汝成, *Hsi-hu yu-lan chih-yü* 西湖遊覽志餘 (rpt. Peking, 1965), 11:192. Yü Chi, Liang Tseng and Chang Yü were among the poets who eulogized the deceased crane.

had been carved into the face of a cliff on one of the islands near West Lake in the Ch'ien-t'ang River.[117] Sometime before the Sung period, lightning struck the cliff and dislodged the carved boulder, whereupon it sank to the bottom of the river. Rubbings made from the cliff inscription were in demand and scarce in the Sung, but could be taken only at certain times in the fall or winter when the level of the river sank to reveal the submerged rock. Even then, complete impressions were seldom achieved, and the scarce rubbings taken from the battered rock surface took on a ghostlike appearance.

The adventure surrounding the *I-ho ming* only added to its mystique. The calligraphy itself was unusual. As a cliff inscription, it was written in large-sized script. Its chief stylistic characteristics lay in the even thickness of the brushwork, which gave an impression of roundness in the strokes, and in its assymetrical relationship and balance of the characters. The weathered condition of the stone also enhanced its mystery. During the Sung it was considered a model of ancient writing, and its actual date and authorship were a subject of debate. Some attributed the calligraphy to Wang Hsi-chih, and others credited it to Yen Chen-ch'ing.[118] The Sung calligrapher Huang T'ing-chien (1045–1105) was deeply influenced by it and considered it the "ancestor of large sized writing," and the *Lan-t'ing hsü* the "ancestor of small sized writing." [119]

By the Yüan period, the *I-ho ming* had attracted a scholarly following and had acquired its own tradition of critical literature and a superstructure of later re-carvings, much like that of the *Lan-t'ing hsü*. The artistic ramifications of these two examples of antique calligraphy were enormous. They represented ideals of esthetic perfection. By the early Yüan they were still the subject of much attention and had already entered the artistic life of Hsien-yü Shu in fundamental ways, as part of his collection and as a stylistic factor in his calligraphy, as noted here by the colophons. By the first generation of Yüan literati, this intense antiquarianism shown by Hsien-yü Shu, Chou Mi, and others, particularly with respect to works which had interested Northern Sung scholars, was instrumental in helping to promote the revival of the past—i.e., the

---

[117] Toyama, SZ 5, pp. 19–23.

[118] *Ibid.*, p. 20.

[119] "Shu Wang Chou-yen 'Tung-p'o t'ieh' 書王周彥東坡帖," *Shan-ku t'i-pa* 山谷題跋 (ISTP 22), 9:92. For a complete exposition of the significance of the *I-ho ming* as an artistic monument and its relation to Huang's calligraphy style, see Shen C. Y. Fu, "Huang T'ing-chien's Calligraphy and His *Scroll for Chang Ta-t'ung*: A Masterpiece Written in Exile" (Ph.D. diss., Princeton, 1976), pp. 224–233.

fu-ku movement—before such interest reached its full development later in the second and third generations of Yüan artists and calligraphers.

By way of example, let us return to the colophon on the "Admonitions" scroll and examine the comments by T'ai Pu-hua. It is to these very two works which he refers:

"On the right is the scroll by Hsien-yü Po-chi transcribing the *Yü-shih chen*. In the handling of the brush, he has grasped the ideas handed down by the *Lan-t'ing*; in the structure he is immense and direct, and imitates the *I-ho ming*. 'Seal,' 'clerical,' 'flying-white' and other methods occasionally appear [in the brushwork]. It is truly a work done in harmony [with Heaven] in our time. The venerable Sung-hsüeh [Chao Meng-fu] said that 'in every stroke there is antique method.' This statement describes it completely! It ought to be collected as a treasure. T'ai Pu-hua of Pai-yeh inscribed."

T'ai Pu-hua's comments on the scroll are significant on several counts. For one, he was a non-Han Chinese who reached the highest ranks of officialdom and was thoroughly sinicized with regard to traditional aspects of Chinese learning. He was one of the few non-Han Chinese compilers of the Sung dynastic history. As a cultivated gentleman and master of a distinctive hand of calligraphy, he was known to write in at least four script types: "regular," as shown in this colophon, "running," "seal," and "clerical." [120]

Like Yeh-lü Ch'u-ts'ai and other distinguished non-Han persons in the Yüan whose writings are still extant, these gentlemen reveal the degree to which the traditional Han culture could be assimilated. Their works show that calligraphy and the Han literati culture could serve as expressive extensions of their personality and native culture (even while they likewise represented a submergence or rejection of their ethnic traits). [121]

T'ai Pu-hua was in the second-generation "line of transmission" of the artistic values which Hsien-yü Shu and other early Yüan persons were cultivating. Without them there would be few links to these values for

---

[120] Ch'en/Goodrich (pp. 199–200) quotes Su T'ien-chüeh's comments on T'ai Pu-hua and lists a group of ten recorded works of inscriptions from steles. I have not been able to locate any extant examples of these rubbings. Other colophons by T'ai Pu-hua do exist in "running" script, however.

[121] Ch'en Yüan's study has produced abundant evidence in this regard. See also the excellent articles by Herbert Franke, "Sino-Western Contacts under the Mongol Empire," *Journal of the Royal Asiatic Society, Hong Kong Branch*, 5 (1966), pp. 49–72, and especially "Chinese Historiography under Mongol Rule: the Role of History in Acculturation," *Mongolian Studies*, 1 (1974), pp. 15–26; also, Tao, *The Jurchen*, pp. 68–117.

the subsequent generation. As T'ai Pu-hua's colophon to the "Admonitions" scroll makes quite clear, he understood the significance and subtlety of these antique representations of culture as models of emulation. Moreover, the quality of his calligraphy as seen in extant examples such as this corroborates the depth of his understanding, and validates his judgment as more than mere lip service.

THE "SONG OF THE STONE DRUMS" AND HSIEN-YÜ SHU'S PERSONALITY

The full power and sweep of Hsien-yü Shu's calligraphy style is seen to even more striking advantage in his cursive writing. An exemplary work, the "Song of the Stone Drums" (*Shih-ku ko* 石鼓歌), was written in 1301, a year before his death (Fig. 7). The scroll is a transcription of Han Yü's 韓愈 (768–824) poem in praise of the Ten Stone Drums and beseeching their preservation from random destruction.[122] Even though it was written a year before his death, Hsien-yü Shu was in fine form. The scroll demonstrates sixty-three lines of unmitigated vigor and high spirits. In accounts by Yüan contemporaries, it was the spirit of his performance that was striking. In this regard, Hsien-yü Shu's calligraphy contrasts and complements Chao Meng-fu's, each a distinguished contribution to Yüan calligraphy. Chao Meng-fu sought a polish and perfection in his writing which was expressed to greatest advantage in strict *k'ai-shu*. His most memorable writings are commemorative inscriptions or records which were intended to be carved into stone and which could absorb his perfectionist temperament.

Hsien-yü Shu's formal writing attained a standard which qualifies him as a great master, but it was in the freer "cursive" and "running" scripts that the breadth of his personality was most fully expressed. His contemporaries recognized this, so that to watch him perform with the brush was considered a memorable event. Here is a description by Liu Kuan, one of several colophons written to calligraphy and poetry by Hsien-yü Shu. Liu caught the spirit of Hsien-yü Shu's personality in a few phrases which have been quoted often in the official histories and private journals:

Liu Kuan's "Colophon to Po-chi's own 'Poems Written While Drunk' in Ch'en Ch'ing-fu's collection":

"His Excellency Hsien-yü has a magnificent air of the vast northern regions about him. Whenever he is drunk, he recklessly abandons himself

[122] The scroll is extant in the John M. Crawford, Jr. collection and was published by Achilles Fang in the Crawford catalogue (see above, n. 101), cat. no. 40, pp. 98–99, and in Ecke, *Chinese Calligraphy*, cat. no. 38.

to chanting poetry and to writing calligraphy, creating an endless variety of extraordinary and marvelous forms. These drinking poems of his are outstanding and are among his special favorites. Whenever he feels happy, he can be found reciting them for other people...." [123]

Those who saw Hsien-yü Shu perform, especially when intoxicated, never failed to remark on the impressive sight which he made with brush in hand. There was something about his personality—which contemporaries described, as Liu does here—that harked "of the vast northern regions," or, as Tai Piao-yüan did, "of a manly heroism" (*i-ch'i hsiunghao*)—that invariably captured their attention. Hsien-yü Shu carried his northern heritage about him, and it was a quality of which his southern compatriots were instantly aware.

Hsien-yü Shu understood the concept of abandon, *i* 逸, or "untrammeledness." He threw himself into his art in a way which would not have befitted the more dignified Chao Meng-fu. Therefore, even though Chao Meng-fu did write an excellent cursive hand, it was not his most accommodating script. In a colophon dated 1310, written to a work of cursive calligraphy brought to him by Hsien-yü Shu's son, Chao recalls their mutual study of calligraphy and concedes that Hsien-yü Shu's achievement in cursive was superior to his:

"I studied calligraphy together with Po-chi. Po-chi soon exceeded me by far. I tried with all my might to catch up, but couldn't. Now Po-chi is gone. The world now recognizes that I am good at calligraphy. That is what is known as calling someone Buddha, when the real Buddha is not there! ..." [124]

If we compare Hsien-yü Shu's cursive with that of his northern predecessors, we would have to acknowledge the boldness and vigor that they have in common. But we would also have to acknowledge distinct changes which have occurred. Hsien-yü Shu's writing commands the same breadth, sweep, and drive which recommends the writing of Chao Ping-wen, Jen Hsün, and Wang T'ing-yün. This is a judgment of the brush energy and formal disposition of the characters over the total length of the scrolls in question. To focus on the brushwork methods and individual structures would reveal the aspects of Hsien-yü Shu's writing that differ most significantly. The Chin writers, like the Southern Sung masters, were working very much in the shadow of the Northern Sung masters, especially Mi Fu and Su Shih. What they developed beyond those masters was an even greater emphasis on the extremes of

---

[123] "Pa Ch'en Ch'ing-fu so-ts'ang Hsien-yü Po-chi shu tzu-tso yin-chiu shih 跋陳慶甫所藏鮮于伯幾書自作飲酒詩," *Liu Tai-chih wen-chi*, 18:13a.

[124] "Chao Sung-hsüeh chu-t'ieh 趙松雪諸帖," Chu Ts'un-li, *T'ieh-wang shan-hu* (1600), 5:23b.

brushwork—exaggerated contrasts of thick and thin, flat and round brushstrokes, and wet and dry ink. These contrasts were combined with a certain disregard for the principles and methods of brushwork which had formed the basis for the early training of the Northern Sung masters themselves, i.e., the methods of Yen Chen-ch'ing and other T'ang calligraphers. While in some cases a certain formal resemblance to the Northern Sung styles could be seen, the actual resemblance was spiritual, with the brushwork and forms being stretched to the outer boundaries of orthodoxy. Whereas individualism and freedom of the Northern Sung masters were founded on the methods and discipline of the ancient past, the Southern Sung and Chin masters built their accomplishments on the art of the recent past. In a positive sense they developed the individuality and spirit of individualism which were the essence of the Northern Sung legacy.[125] But in a negative sense, they developed the crown without the root.

This is not to say that the Chin calligraphers did not study ancient masters. Their colophons were also found on many of the same works. But theirs was an appreciation of a different kind, without the same intensity or sense of directed purpose, or with the enormous breadth of the early Yüan masters. The reasons for this have been hinted at in the course of this essay. For one, the ancient masterpieces which Hsien-yü Shu, Chao Meng-fu, and others saw in the early Yüan were far greater in number. An inordinate number came from the imperial collections, either of Chang-tsung or of Kao-tsung. That means that the previous generation of scholars were quite likely deprived of the privilege of viewing these works, let alone having them in their homes for prolonged study. When Wang Yün was in the capital in 1276, he had an opportunity through his connections to see the masterpieces that had come from the Sung collections. It made a great impression on him. With the breakup of the imperial Sung and Chin collections after the re-unification, and the initial lack of interest on the part of the Mongols to maintain or to build collections on a large scale, these works entered the hands of eager and devoted art lovers like Hsien-yü Shu. The rounds of visits to local collections which he and Chou Mi made document a tremendous upsurge of antiquarianism on the part of private scholars. In the history of collecting, a major subject that deserves separate study, the early Yüan stands out as quite unusual in this regard. Private collecting seems to have come of age. It was a popular and current thing to do.

The re-unification offered the enormous prospect of mobility of persons and art. This mobility cannot be underestimated, and it accounts

[125] On this important subject, see the dissertation by Shen Fu (cited above, n. 119), ch. 6.

in part for the rise in popularity of collecting. But the re-unification also offered other possibilities. From one point of view, it could be said that Chinese culture was threatened with near annihilation, to the extent that the traditional avenues of employment and official recognition were limited. The changes of rule which led to changes in the imperial institution and social structure in essence left a situation which was not comparable in any other dynasty to the same extent: it left scholars by themselves with a limited degree of court censorship. In the arts the independence led to a desire to preserve the past through a dogged spirit of self-cultivation. It was actually a selfish thing in terms of artists' personal goals. Nowhere are there colophons stating that "art" was to be produced for later generations. It was an introspective, inner-directed form of self-improvement: assiduous practice of calligraphy and study of old masters, literary gatherings where everyone enjoyed themselves with wine and poetry. There was really little thought of the impression it would leave on posterity or the "preservation of the culture" in an altruistic way, at least among the artistic elite. In this sense, then, there is little trace in calligraphy materials of the cultural threat of the Mongols. Scholars were glad to be left alone. They were getting a privacy which in the past had been meted out to them only with long periods of exile (Su Shih and Huang T'ing-chien did their best calligraphy while in exile).

This is not to draw the picture in overly rosy and optimistic tones. But a threat need not always be met by a negative response. The Chih-yüan era in particular, as described by Liu Kuan and others, reveals a surprising ferment, when far-reaching assessments of the "state of the culture" were made in the arts. Burying themselves in the glories of the past, and absorbing what nourishment suitable to their needs and temperaments, artists came forth with forms and styles which previous generations could not produce or conceive of producing. This is the essence of the periodicity which lies beneath art historians' attempts at describing change.

CONCLUSION

That Hsien-yü Shu's influence made its mark on a very important group of intellectuals in the south can be seen through two additional colophons. The following comments by Huang Chin, a leading member of the Chin-hua school, are appended to an example of Hsien-yü Shu's calligraphy:

"In my youth, I had the privilege of being in Hsien-yü Shu's company and often heard His Excellency talk about the methods of learning [i.e., improving one's] calligraphy. My friend Hsü Wen-wei 徐文蔚 (unidentified) studied with him, but I did not. Nowadays when people catch only a glimpse of some fragments of [Hsien-yü Shu's] calligraphy, they are able in most cases to gain some fame among the common people [by virtue of their imitation of his style]. Sadly, I have become old and weak. Even so, I would like to devote more time to my calligraphy again, so that I can be placed at the end of the list of gentlemen superior in this art. But I do not know whether I am able or not. Now as I have the opportunity to view His Excellency's transcription of Su Shih's poems, it is as if I can see him before me wielding the brush and working the ink just as before. Recollecting the past this way only makes me feel ashamed and regretful." [126]

Friendship with Hsien-yü Shu did not fundamentally alter the life of an intellectual like Huang Chin, but it touched the edge of his existence enough so that, upon seeing an example of his writing, Huang Chin had regrets about not having worked harder on his handwriting. If this was the case with someone whose primary mode of expression was not calligraphy, then one might expect that for those who were inclined toward the arts, Hsien-yü Shu might have made a greater impression in his encouragement of them. Huang Chin implies this, when he says that ordinary people were inspired to betterment as a result of seeing some of Hsien-yü Shu's writing. One need not overemphasize this influence. Hsien-yü Shu's certainly cannot be measured against the almost universal impact of Chao Meng-fu in the fourteenth century and centuries thereafter. But just as it was important to differentiate the influence of the Four Great Sung masters into two branches—one of formal resemblance and the other of spiritual resemblance—the same could be done here. Hsien-yü Shu's personality and love of the arts left its mark on people's memories; he influenced them through this avenue.

Shortly after Hsien-yü Shu's death, his son Hsien-yü Pi-jen 鮮于必仁 (t. Ch'ü-chin 去矜, ca.1285–ca.1325?) travelled to Chin-hua, Chekiang, and appears to have taken up residence there.[127] He wrote the following colophon to a work of his father's which he saw in a friend's collection (Fig. 8):

---

[126] "Pa Hsien-yü kung shu 跋鮮于公書," *Chin-hua Huang hsien-sheng wen-chi* 金華黃先生文集 (SPTK ed.), 22:6b–7a.

[127] YS *Hsin-pien* (47) and SSHY (7:11b) record that Pi-jen became famous for his *san-ch'ü* 散曲 lyrics, and that his calligraphy continued the art of his father. This latter observation is verifiable in the single published work of his (SZ 17, p. 161), a colophon dated 1309 attached to Hsien-yü Shu's transcription of Tu Fu's 杜甫 poem, "Mao-wu wei ch'iu-feng so-p'o ko 茅屋爲秋風所破歌," dated 1298, in the Fujii-yurinkan collection, Kyoto.

Pi-jen's dates are not known; I have estimated them on the basis of this colophon and several early references by Hsien-yü Shu to his baby sons.

"My late father's calligraphy is most abundant in the Chin-hua area [of Chekiang], but this scroll is slightly different from the others. It documents his warm friendship with Mr. Yü-ch'eng 玉成 [Wang Ch'eng 王城 (1247–1324)] which attained the depth seen in this scroll. Since the *kuei-mao* year [1303] when I came here [to Chin-hua], I have been searching for old records [of my father's circle of friends]. Fortunately, the grandson of the gentleman Yü-ch'eng's brother, Tzu-yüeh 子約, is here, and I have planned to meet with him about these matters.

"Whenever I see this scroll, I never tire of looking at it and cannot put it down. Tzu-yüeh ought to treasure it.

"The second son, Hsien-yü Ch'ü-chin, bows a hundred times and respectfully writes this on the second day of early autumn of the *chi-yu* year [August 7, 1309]."

Thus it is no accident that prominent Chin-hua intellectuals like Liu Kuan, Huang Chin, and others knew of Hsien-yü Shu and could regard his work with the admiration they did. It seems fitting that a northerner who came south, who derived so much from southern culture, and who in turn contributed so much to it in terms of his own northern heritage, should leave the most abundant works and possibly the strongest spiritual influence in a thoroughly "southern" stronghold such as Chin-hua.

The purpose of this essay has been to point out, through the artistic activities and the calligraphy of the northern master Hsien-yü Shu, some of the aspects of traditional literati culture and art which were preserved in the north shortly preceding the Mongol conquest and to show how such elements were transmitted by northerners such as Hsien-yü Shu to the south after the re-unification. This process of transmission contributed essential aspects of continuity to the traditional culture during the early Yüan and enabled the firm establishment of literati values among the scholarly elite during the difficult time of transition after the Mongol conquest. The enthusiasm and studiousness with which literary and artistic activities were conducted by early Yüan scholars, northern and southern, Western and Central Asian, contributed in large part to the continuity of culture and to the high artistic achievements of the later Yüan artists.

Mongol Influence on
the Development
of Northern Drama

STEPHEN H. WEST

THE WEDGE

An Apology

The question of Mongol influence on drama might seem to be a cut-and-dried topic. After all, Yoshikawa Kōjirō 吉川幸次郎 and Aoki Masaru 青木正兒 have spilled much ink on exactly that subject, seemingly confirming once and for all the conviction of Wang Kuo-wei 王國維 (1877–1927) and his Ming sources that the Mongols caused the development of drama, and that it was the literati who had nurtured the etiolated sprouts of a folk art to full-blown radiance in the Yüan.

But as new archaeological finds of the past decade have been gradually revealed to the world in the pages of China's archaeological and cultural journals, they have worn away at this fundamental belief until the whole organism, from its roots to its branches, must be reassessed and reevaluated. The reassessment is important, not only for the intellectual and cultural historian, but for the literary historian and critic, because it will influence the analysis of the dramatic form itself. All art is sustained on the creative tension between convention and originality and exists under the tyranny of tradition. So to define its source is to take a first step toward defining the ritual conventions of the form, a preliminary stage to a discussion of such purely literary elements as structure, theme, character, or the symbolic language of the playwright.

This essay attempts that basic reevaluation. It is a discussion of the classical theories of the rise of drama in China, an analysis of them in light of literary evidence and archaeological finds, and an attempt to redefine the role that the Mongols played in both the development and growth of drama. Inevitably, the essay raises more questions than it answers, for drama does not live in a vacuum, and to examine its roots is to leave the soil around them unsettled.

Act I

Rationalization

Historically there have been two distinct theoretical outlooks on the
development of drama in the Yüan. Naturally enough for a performing
art, these two generalized points of view deal either with authorship and
play production or with audience and play appreciation. But these are
merely internal polarities of a unified perspective that has persisted from
the fourteenth century until the present day. This perspective is a
classical one, representing a literary or intellectual point of view that is
traditionally authoritative and standard. I refer, of course, to the traditional authority of the literati. It is reflected to an uncommon degree in
the early theories of the rise and development of drama. The reason for
this is simply that drama was a folk art in which the elite class of China
developed a strong interest. Hence, the classical theories for the development of Yüan drama are a rationalization of this interest. One approach
constitutes an attempt to answer the implied but unasked question,
"Why did men of the high tradition stoop to writing plays?" The central
issue of their statements, therefore, is a definition of the relationship of
the literatus-as-playwright to his social and political world, and ultimately to the Mongol court.

The parallel to this approach is the attempt to define the audience of
drama. This is potentially a valuable method for understanding the
development of performing literature. But, again, the center of interest is
the Yüan court. Almost all discussions of the role of the audience have at
their core the belief that the support of the Mongols and their patronage
of acting troupes somehow sustained the dramatic tradition. Significantly, the role of the urban and rural audience figures only slightly in
these theories. It is true that the critics were operating on the same
assumption that we all do, namely that audience is a significant force in
determining the authorship of any literature, whether performed or
written. But because of the great traditional authority of the literati, the
critics' attention to the dramatic audience has been narrow and exclusive.

Among those who speculate on authorship, there are two major
schools: those who state that drama was an expression of frustration and
discontent, and those who state that it came about because of the
abolition of the examination system. The first group emerges earlier.
Being closer to the age, and perhaps feeling more need to justify both
drama, as a literary form, and its authorship as a proper endeavor, they
sought to define the social and political role of the writer, and found for him
a proper niche in the conventional forms of protest. Chu Ching 朱經,

writing in 1364, felt impelled to class the first dramatists as *i-lao* 遺老, surviving elders of the previous dynasty of Chin. His argument must be seen in the greater framework of justifying the work of his friend Hsia Po-ho 夏伯合, author of the *Green Bower Collection* (*Ch'ing-lou chi* 青樓集), a miscellany of anecdotes on actresses and performers.[1] But it is, nevertheless, the kind of statement that one might expect to find preserved, for it attributes to the early writers of drama the role of "compulsory eremite," one who withdraws rather than serve a usurping (or alien) dynasty.[2] Chu wrote,

"A gentleman in regard to his own age: who does not wish his talent to surpass that of others? Who does not wish his actions to be sufficient [reflection] of the self? Will [a gentleman] be satisfied with throwing himself away? Now there are times of adversity and of felicity and there are fated lots of failure and success. Therefore, talent, perhaps, cannot be under [one's] control nor can actions, perhaps, be concealed. When it is an age of felicity and success, then the music of bell and drum in garden and grove is not yet finished and the gentleman enjoys it properly; when it is an age of adversity and failure, then he abandons himself along river and lake in poetry and wine and does not return. The gentleman [in this case] is not one that has control over his own [fate]. When our resplendent Yüan first brought the world together, the *i-lao* of Chin, like Tu San-jen [Tu Shan-fu 杜善夫], Pai Lan-ku [Pai P'u 白樸], and Kuan I-chai [Kuan Han-ch'ing 關漢卿] did not deign to serve and be advanced. So they dallied in the wind and sported with the moonlight; and thus enchanted, they passed their years."[3]

---

[1] Portions of this work are translated and discussed by Arthur Waley, in "The Green Bower Collection," included in his *The Secret History of the Mongols* (London, 1963), pp. 89–107. We might conjecture here that Chu Ching is reacting to the pressure of Neo-Confucianism, the values of which were ascendant at the time. In the past two years, much additional material on the role of literati in the development of drama has come to light. The bulk of this evidence supports the conclusions reached in the third part of this essay. The evidence is too voluminous to be listed here in its entirety. The reader is referred to W. L. Idema and Stephen H. West, *Chinese Drama from 1100 to 1450: A Source Book* (forthcoming). Chapters 2 ("The Institutional and Professional Affiliation of Actors and Entertainers") and 3 ("Some Literati Views of the Social Role of Entertainers and Theater") contain extensive discussions of literati influence on and participation in drama, theater, and writing clubs, with translations of pertinent texts. The article by Ting Ming-i, cited in n. 47 below, has been translated by this writer in *Journal of Chinese Archeology*, 1 (1979).

[2] I have borrowed this term from F. W. Mote, "Confucian Eremitism in the Yüan Period," in Arthur F. Wright, ed., *Confucianism and Chinese Civilization* (New York, 1964), pp. 258, 279–290.

[3] Chu Ching, preface, in Hsia T'ing-chih 夏庭芝, *Ch'ing-lou chi* (CKK ed.), vol. 2, p. 15.

This early explanation may be seen in two ways. First, it may be viewed as a classical attempt to grant to these writers some traditional sanction as exemplars of conduct. The second is to see it as an assertion that the authors of early Yüan drama were, for the most part, men of civilian status or exceptionally low bureaucratic position. By imputing to these writers the morally imperative, but still self-imposed action of political withdrawal, one can claim for them a moral legitimacy normally reserved for men of higher political success or of literary merit earned in the traditional forms. These playwrights were doubly blessed in the eyes of Chu Ching, not only because they acted in accordance with Neo-Confucian values by not serving two rulers, but because they could claim the full support of the entire Confucian tradition by refusing to serve a non-Chinese, hence non-civilized, ruler.

With the passing of the Yüan, this latter theme came to be emphasized. The motive for action was no longer viewed as self-generated but was seen instead as a direct outcome of Mongol resistance to sinicization and the Mongols' utter disregard for traditional cultural values and expressions. That is, the Mongols gradually emerged as cultural villains who actively frustrated the ambitions and desires of the literati, denying them access to orthodox political, literary, and hence historical respectability. This is a subtle change, but an important one, because it attributes to the Mongols the responsibility for driving literati into the unusual literary pursuit of drama.

This was the prevalent opinion during the Ming and Ch'ing, and was often repeated by historians of and apologists for drama. Hu Shih 胡侍 in Ming times first spoke of it in his *Chen-chu ch'uan* 眞珠船 (*A Boat of Pearls*, preface d. 1548), and the statement was later echoed in the writings of Li K'ai-hsien 李開先:

"At that time, the censorial and secretarial officials, the prime ministers, the main officials of commanderies and districts, and all important posts were filled by men of their [Mongol] nation. Men of the Central Plain were kept down in the lower ranks of the bureaucracy where they could not unfold their ambitions. Kuan Han-ch'ing, for instance, was an official in the Imperial Academy of Medicine, Ma Chih-yüan 馬致遠 was an officer of the Chiang-che Branch Secretariat, Cheng Te-hui 鄭德輝 was a clerk of the Hangchow circuit.... The rest who were forced into clerical jobs or who finished their years as civilians were even more numerous. So, they took their talents that could [otherwise] have been [better] utilized and in every case entrusted them to the 'branch tips' [i.e., frivolous pursuits] of sound and song in order to unroll their fellings of depression, discontent, aroused sentiment, and forbearance.

Theirs is what is called 'crying out over not attaining fair [treatment].'"[4]

This statement was countered by Wang Chi-te 王冀德, who stated that such writers as Kuan Yün-shih 貫雲石 and Hu Chih-yü 胡祗遹 were all men of eminent official rank.[5] His defense falters, however, because he has failed to discriminate writers of *san-ch'ü* 散曲, the lyric form, from those who wrote dramatic verse. I doubt that Wang was blind to the distinction. What seems more likely is that he wanted to substantiate the position of playwrights by making them stars in a constellation that included both poets and playwrights. Dramatists thereby shared the luster of their comrades.

One can sense in the above statements a reluctance to grapple with a central issue: why did the dramatic form become so popular when elite writers had at their disposal an orthodox poetic tradition of "righteous resentment and remonstrance" that included the "Great Preface" to the *Book of Songs* and the poet of Ch'u, Ch'ü Yüan 屈原 (ca.340–290 B.C.)? After all, one was faced with the contrast of the Southern Sung, whose writers, shunning a thriving theatrical tradition, still turned to "poetry and wine" to dispel their sorrow and give vent to their grievances.[6]

Those Ming critics who tried to grapple with this problem did so only at the expense of historical accuracy. Both Tsang Chin-shu 臧晉叔, editor of *Yüan ch'ü hsüan* 元曲選 (*Selected Yüan Lyrics*), and Shen Te-fu 沈德符, in *Wan-li yeh-huo pien* 萬曆野獲編 (*Literary Acquisitions of a Rustic Scholar of the Wan-li Era*), despite the complete lack of historical evidence, held that the Yüan had selected and promoted its officials on the basis of the ability to write dramatic lyrics. This, too, may be seen as an attempt to rationalize literati interest: if one cannot explain the actions of a writer satisfactorily, then one can elevate the form itself to a position of equality with the more traditionally accepted modes of expression. Tsang wrote,

"The Yüan selected its officials on the basis of the *ch'ü* 曲, establishing twelve categories; and men like Kuan Han-ch'ing matched their skills and abilities to make their names known. As for their personal participation on the stage, their covering of their faces with powder and ink to live

---

[4] Hu Shih, *Chen-chu ch'uan* (TSCC ed.), 4:35; repeated with variations in Li K'ai-hsien 李開先, "Chang Hsiao-shan hsiao-ling hsü 張小山小令序," *Li K'ai-hsien chi* 李開先集 (Peking, 1959), vol. 1, p. 298, and in Wang Chi-te 王冀德, *Ch'ü-lü* 曲律 (CKK ed.), vol. 4, p. 147.

[5] Wang Chi-te, *Ch'ü-lü*, p. 147.

[6] Yoshikawa Kōjirō, Cheng Ch'ing-mao 鄭清茂, tr. *Yüan tsa-chü yen-chiu* 元雜劇研究 (Taipei, 1954), p. 118.

the life of an actor, or their consorting without cease with actors and singing girls—perhaps theirs is the [same] as the sentiment of the Sages of the Bamboo Grove of Western Chin who abandoned themselves and cast their feelings in wine—I dare not say." [7]

This statement from Tsang's "Preface" to the second part of *Selected Yüan Lyrics* is no more than wishful thinking.[8] Yet it stood along with other interpretations of historical factors in the rise of drama until early in the present century. It was Wang Kuo-wei who, in his pioneering work *Sung Yüan hsi-ch'ü k'ao* 宋元戲曲考 (*Researches on Sung and Yüan Drama*), brought a more objective methodology to the study of drama and its antecedents.

Wang regarded the elite interest in drama as a product of converging historical circumstances. He pointed first to the corruption of *chin-shih* 進士 ("presented scholar") degree status in the Chin, when the expanding influence and power of clerks in government seriously undermined the traditional authority of degree holders. This phenomenon is well-documented in a thirteenth-century private history, the *Kuei-ch'ien chih* 歸潛志 (*Records Written on Returning to Retirement*), which gives a contemporary eye-witness account of the decline of the scholar-bureaucrats at the court of the penultimate Jurchen emperor, Hsüan-tsung 宣宗.[9] According to Wang, the lessening of the traditional authority of literati officials, along with the abrogation of the examination system by the Mongols for some eighty years, created a social environment which in turn produced the great Yüan playwrights. Wang wrote as follows:

"When the Mongols destroyed the Chin, the examination system was abolished for some eighty years, an occurrence unprecedented in its history. So, unless they were clerks, there was no method of advancement for [literati] writers. Therefore, it is no cause for wonder that most drama writers were clerks. The statement by Shen Te-fu ... and Tsang Chin-shu ... that officials were selected on the basis of their *tz'u* 詞 and *ch'ü* [lyric] compositions is totally groundless." [10]

Wang went on, however, to equate the corruption of the *chin-shih*

---

[7] *Yüan ch'ü hsüan* (Peking: Chung-hua Shu-chü, 1958), vol. I, pp. iii–iv.
[8] Shen Te-fu, in *Wan-li yeh-huo pien*, said essentially the same thing. The original is unavailable to me, but see the quotation in Wang Kuo-wei 王國維, *Sung Yüan hsi-ch'ü shih* 宋元戲曲史 (Hong Kong, 1964), p. 84.
[9] Liu Ch'i 劉祁, *Kuei-ch'ien chih* 歸潛志 (*Chih-pu-tsu chai ts'ung-shu* 知不足齋叢書 ed.), *chüan* 7–9; and Hok-lam Chan, *The Historiography of the Chin Dynasty: Three Studies* (Wiesbaden, 1970), pp. 147–157.
[10] Wang Kuo-wei, *Sung Yüan hsi-ch'ü shih*, pp. 84–85.

examination and degree with a low level of literary training. The Chin writers, he said, were unfit to "pursue scholarly affairs":

"Moreover, the lofty writing of canons and regulations was something that they were not used to doing. The new form of drama had just emerged at that time, and they engaged in it. Among them there were one or two heaven-sent talents who were able to fulfill their strength and talent; thus Yüan drama became an imperishable form."[11]

Wang has attempted here to answer the questions that his predecessors had shied away from for so many years. The rise of literati interest in drama could, for Wang Kuo-wei, be traced to two stimuli: (1) the intensified influence of yamen clerks in the bureaucracy and the subsequent diminution of literati status, and (2) the corrupt examination system of the Chin that left scholars and writers untrained in literary-bureaucratic forms.

Historically, the first hypothesis can be verified. The Chin had venerated Confucian learning throughout their history, except for a brief period of resurgent nativism in the mid-twelfth century,[12] and had sought to emulate the traditional methods of selection and promotion of officials. As was especially true in the reign of Chang-tsung 章宗 (1189–1208), most of the Chin officials were also scholars who had passed the *chin-shih* examinations. During this high point of Chinese participation in the government, all officials, as Wang Yün 王惲 noted, "from prime minister to court clerk were *chin-shih* degree holders," and "all institutions and principles were made at court by learned scholars."[13]

But this golden age of the dynasty and the scholar-bureaucrat was soon closed by the reign of Hsüan-tsung (1213–1223), which saw the nadir of literati participation in Chin government. Not only did Hsüan-tsung regularly promote his personal attendants to influential advisory positions at the expense of *chin-shih* degree holders, but his prime minister Chu-hu Kao-ch'i 朮虎高琪 promoted yamen clerks to high position to solidify his personal support in the administration.[14]

This decline in normal bureaucratic mobility for the scholar was paralleled by the growth of an examination curriculum that offered little

---

[11] *Sung Yüan hsi-ch'ü shih*, pp. 84–85.

[12] For a discussion of this and related matters, see Jing-shen Tao, *The Jurchen in Twelfth-Century China: A Study of Sinicization* (Seattle: University of Washington Press, 1976). See also Yao Ts'ung-wu 姚從吾, "Chin Shih-tsung tui-yü chung-yüan Han-hua yü Nü-chen chiu-su ti t'ai-tu 金世宗對於中原漢化與女真舊俗的態度," in *Tung-pei shih lun-ts'ung* 東北史論叢 (Taipei, 1959), pp. 118–179.

[13] *Ch'iu-chien hsien-sheng ta ch'üan wen-chi* 秋澗先生大全文集 (SPTK ed.), 32:11a.

[14] Chan, *Historiography of the Chin Dynasty*, p. 149.

training in statecraft or policy-making. The examination system in the later years favored the *lü-fu* 律賦 or regulated rhyme-prose form. Liu Ch'i 劉祁, the author of the private history mentioned above, could scarcely conceal his contempt for the examination process. He sharply criticized those who were in charge:

"I can remember my father saying that during the T'ai-ho reign period (1201–1208) those who were in charge [of the examinations] would test for poetry and rhyme-prose, having already determined [that these would be the criteria] for rejecting or selecting [candidates]. When they reached the policy (*ts'e* 策) and discourse (*lun* 論) sections, they would do no more than use their pens to mark temple-name taboo violations or imperial title violations and they would simply count the number of characters in [these essays] and the frequency of markovers and strikeouts." [15]

While there were sporadic attempts to halt this practice and to restore a balance between practical and belletristic writings in the examinations, the procedure changed but little down to the end of the dynasty. [16]

Wang Kuo-wei's unfavorable view of Chin scholarship seems to be drawn from these criticisms by Liu Ch'i, and from the generally recognized lack of a sound tradition of classical learning in the Chin. [17] Wang makes the mistake, however, of assuming that bureaucratic prose is a standard by which to measure literary accomplishment. I do not think we can, in light of Liu Ch'i's own statement that the examinations emphasized poetic forms, accept this deduction. Skill in belletristic forms is by no means dependent on one's social or official station, nor on one's skill in administrative prose.

This is precisely the point that Yoshikawa Kōjirō challenges in his own discussion of the rise of drama. Yoshikawa accepts the idea that the abolition of the examination system and the expansion of the power of clerks were in large part responsible for the sudden upsurge of literati interest in drama in the early Yüan, but he refutes, with an impressive array of evidence, Wang's statement on the low level of Chin writing. He demonstrates, for instance, that writers continued to apply their literary skills long after there was any possibility of using them to obtain political position. He implies, in fact, that the promotion of clerks and the decline in bureaucratic mobility may have intensified writers' interest in and practice of non-administrative forms. [18]

Yoshikawa asserts that Wang Kuo-wei and his predecessors have

---

[15] *Kuei-ch'ien chih*, 8: 1a–1b.

[16] *Kuei-ch'ien chih*, 8: 1a–1b.

[17] This was recognized from a very early period. See, for example, the preface to the *Wen-i chuan* 文藝傳 in CS 125: 2713–2714.

[18] Yoshikawa, *Yüan tsa-chü yen-chiu*, p. 118.

failed to answer the central question of why writers did not use traditional forms to express their feelings. His own answer to the question is that several factors converged at this time to alter drastically the worldview of the writer, changing for all time the relationship between literary production and the social and political world.[19]

He points out that the trend in early Yüan was to use men of practical experience in administrative affairs—bureaucratic experts instead of scholars. This practice, which has its roots in the rising importance of administrative, non-scholarly skills in the Chin, was supported not only by the Mongol rulers, but by the Mongols' Chinese advisers as well. This resulted in the denial of official bureaucratic status to writers, as well as in the lessening of the peer respect that was normally due the writer in the Chinese social world. Therefore, Yoshikawa asserts, as the goals of writing changed—that is, as belles-lettres were no longer directed toward the acquisition of either political or social status—the social orientation of writers changed. Due to this fundamental shift in attitudes, writers gained the freedom to explore non-traditional forms of literature. This freedom was strengthened by the laissez-faire attitude of the early Yüan rulers and by the lack of a strong official sanction against non-orthodox behavior. Thus, according to Yoshikawa, the new developments in writing were only part of a general social and intellectual reorientation that witnessed new developments in calendrical systems, mathematics, and Confucianism.[20] While the abolition of the examination system was the direct cause of literati interest in drama, the determining factor was a total reorientation of the writer-scholar in a non-traditional social and intellectual order.

Two basic concerns run like continuous threads through these historical statements on authorship. One is a concern for the low social status of the writer, the other for his choice of drama as a suitable mode of literary expression. The unwritten assumption behind these statements, indeed behind their very conception, is that the literati were responsible for, at the very most, the rise of drama, or at the very least for bringing it to its zenith in early Yüan. The Mongols, therefore, are seen as the direct stimulus behind this interest: first as cultural villains who either forced scholars into political withdrawal or thwarted literati interests by abolishing the examination system, and then as practical rulers who promoted expertise at the expense of traditional generalist knowledge. The one flaw in these collective historical arguments is that the Chinese literati had at their disposal a tradition of emotional expression in the

[19] *Yüan tsa-chü yen-chiu*, pp. 118–120.
[20] *Yüan tsa-chü yen-chiu*, pp. 118–120.

standard poetic forms that dated back to the earliest periods of written literature. The only successful attempt to resolve this paradox has been to ascribe to the elite writer a complete reorientation of goals in the social and political world, a solution that also comes at the expense of the Mongols.

The parallel interest in the audience of drama is, in most ways, complementary to theories of authorship. The basic premise of the "audience critic" is that drama was written in the vernacular tongue because the Mongols, who constituted the primary audience, were "crude, militaristic, and brutal" nomads who did not care for and were unable to penetrate Chinese learning. There is a great deal to support this argument. We know that many of the steles and edicts of that period were written in vernacular Chinese. But this theory is, in some ways, like looking through the wrong end of a telescope. It still assumes that the literati bent their talents and used a vulgar form precisely so they could reach their new overlords.[21]

Aoki Masaru has offered an amplification of this basic premise, and has suggested that the Mongols, lacking a high material culture, found pleasure only in the four cardinal vices of "wine, sex, pleasure, and music," and that they therefore promoted drama and music because of the intense pleasure that they obtained from it. During the Chin period there had been an independently developing interest in music and proto-drama among the elite writers. Following the Mongol conquest those writers and their successors expanded upon old proto-dramatic forms to serve Mongol interest, striving to raise the literary excellence of farce plays, but keeping the final product simple enough for the Mongols to understand.[22]

I have stated the general premises of the audience critics here because it seems to me that they are, by and large, merely extensions of the basic concerns over authorship. The audience critics' approach may still be seen as an attempt to explain away literati interest and participation in drama. None of the critics, with the exception of Yoshikawa, expresses any concern for the role that the theatrical tradition, the convention, played in the development of *pei-ch'ü* 北曲 (northern drama). And Yoshikawa himself explains away this influence with a wave of the hand:

"Of course, as for the composition of drama, I have no intention of

---

[21] This subject needs study. There is some evidence that, for instance, *p'ing-hua* 評話 tales may have been written expressly to educate Mongol emperors in Chinese history. See W. L. Idema, *Chinese Vernacular Fiction: The Formative Period* (Leiden, 1974), pp. 89–97.

[22] Aoki Masaru, Wang Ku-lu 王古魯, tr., *Chung-kuo chin-shih hsi-ch'ü shih* 中國近世戲曲史 (Shanghai, 1936), pp. 65–68.

deprecating the participation of actors and the illiterate class. The spirit of 'the everyday world of market places' that fills dramatic works and the strength and vitality of a literary form that can portray this world can be imagined to have been brought to dramatic works by writers and an audience that comes from the people. I am not negating this view. But, according to everything that I know, the popular literature of China before this time, when it was simply in the hands of the people, never attained any level of maturity; it was necessary to wait for literati participation before it crystallized into the beautiful gem that it is. I do not think that drama is any different." [23]

We confront here a bias that is both sanctioned by tradition and determined by the nature of historical evidence. If one looks carefully at the evidence that Yoshikawa has culled in his discussions of the authors and audience of Yüan drama, we find that it comes almost exclusively from the standard dynastic histories or from the collected writings of literati. One would indeed be surprised if it did not reflect the biases of the elite writer.

Yoshikawa derives part of his evidence from the style of Yüan drama, committing a serious anachronistic error. He states that the reason that Yüan drama is so difficult to read today is that it is an admixture of dead slang and high refinement. He reasons that the only way that playwrights could write such language was because of their thorough knowledge of the classical literature of China.[24] He then produces some evidence that demonstrates this skill with classical letters: the *ting-ch'ang tz'u* 定場詞 or "declamatory verse" of the play *Han-kung ch'iu* 漢宮秋 (*Autumn in the Han Palace*), which he rightly points to as a poem of great skill; the *hsien-yün* 險韻 or "daring rhymes" of Kao Wen-hsiu 高文秀; and other typical literary sleights of hand. But his argument is not strong, simply because of the textual history of the plays. We know that, with the exception of the *Yüan-k'an tsa-chü san-shih chung* 元刊雜劇三十種 (*Thirty Yüan Editions of Dramatic Works*), all extant copies of plays have passed through the hands of an editor or an actor who was part of the elite world, either a Ming litterateur who was practicing a legitimate interest in the theater, or an actor of the court.[25] Yoshikawa's argument cannot be supported on the basis of the arias preserved in the *Thirty*

[23] Yoshikawa, *Yüan tsa-chü yen-chiu*, p. 109.

[24] *Yüan tsa-chü yen-chiu*, pp. 107–108. We might also note that this same mixture would make it very difficult for the Mongol audience to understand.

[25] The full title of this text is *Chiao-ting Yüan-k'an tsa-chü san-shih chung* 校訂元刊雜劇 三十種 (*Collated and Corrected Yüan Editions of Thirty Dramas*). It was compiled by Cheng Ch'ien 鄭騫, and represents a collation against four editions of Yüan texts of *tsa-chü*. It was published in Taipei by Shih-chieh Shu-chü in 1962.

Yüan Editions of Dramatic Works. Beyond that, we must realize that we are, in most cases, dealing with Ming creations, rewrites, or recensions of older texts, done in a salon atmosphere.

ACT II

Rebuttal

Most of the arguments of authorship and audience that impute to the Mongols the primary role of stimulus to the development of drama can be countered with evidence that shows a long and sustained theatrical development before the Mongol invasions.

We have assumed until the last decade that all theatrical activity before the Yüan, that is before the advent of full-fledged literati involvement, was proto-drama: farce skits, jokes and japes, musical interludes, and kinetic performances. But during the past fifteen years, archaeological work in the People's Republic of China has brought to light new visual evidence that bears directly on the history of the theater. It has become clearer, in the light of this evidence, that the roots of northern drama actually go back to the playlets, skits, and monologues of the variety show of the Sung called *tsa-chü* 雜劇, and to their Chin dynasty counterparts, the *yüan-pen* 院本. Our analysis of these variety shows has been hampered by the fragmentary nature of the literary testimony. We have, for instance, no actual description of the *tsa-chü* variety show of Northern Sung, although there are numerous mentions of their perform-ance.[26] Our earliest descriptive analysis of the *tsa-chü* is found in the memoirs of the Southern Sung capital Lin-an 臨安 (modern Hangchow). These memoirs, *Meng-liang lu* 夢梁錄 (*Records of a Millet Dream*), *Tu-ch'eng chi-sheng* 都城紀勝 (*A Record of the Splendors of the Capital*), and *Wu-lin chiu-shih* 武林舊事 (*Old Affairs of Wu-lin*), provide both brief narrative descriptions of the *tsa-chü* and a catalogue of some 280 titles of entertainments now lost.[27] For the Chin dynasty *yüan-pen*, we have only the secondhand account of T'ao Tsung-i 陶宗儀. In his *Cho-keng lu*

---

[26] There are numerous mentions of *tsa-chü* in *Tung-ching meng-hua lu* 東京夢華錄 in its many descriptions of festivities and entertainments put on for the emperor's pleasure. There are, however, no analytical descriptions of a variety show.

[27] The four major sources of information on the variety show of the Southern Sung are: 1) Anon., *Hsi-hu lao-jen fan-sheng lu* 西湖老人繁勝錄 (ca.1250); 2) Wu Tzu-mu 吳自牧, *Meng-liang lu* 夢梁錄 (ca.1274); 3) Anon., *Tu-ch'eng chi-sheng* 都城紀勝 (ca.1235); and 4) Chou Mi 周密, *Wu-lin chiu-shih* 武林舊事 (ca.1260). All may be found in *Tung-ching meng-hua lu (wai ssu-chung)* 東京夢華錄 (外四種) (Shanghai, 1956). The 280 titles are found in *Wu-lin chiu-shih*. This section of the present essay has been abstracted from the author's *Vaudeville and Narrative: Aspects of Chin Theater* (Wiesbaden, 1977), pp. 1–24.

輟耕錄 (*Notes Taken during Breaks from Ploughing*, preface dated 1366),
he provides a similar description and a list of some 690 *yüan-pen* script
titles.[28] From these two sources, separated by more than a century, we
have been in the uncomfortable position of collating the lists and
descriptions to extrapolate a common ancestor, the Northern Sung
variety show.

Archaeological evidence has, in the main, substantiated conclusions
wrung from these literary remains and has, in addition, provided important new dimensions to our understanding and interpretation of them.
Above all, the finds have confirmed a direct link between the variety
shows and northern music-drama and have opened the door for speculation that the form we know as *pei-ch'ü* may have developed prior to the
Mongol invasions.

The earliest description of a variety show performance is found in *A
Record of the Splendors of the Capital*, a memoir of Hangchow written in
about 1235. The description is repeated with minor changes in *Records of
a Millet Dream*, written circa 1334. Below is a composite description
translated from these two sources:

"It is said that the *mo-ni* 末泥 is the leader of the *tsa-chü*, a
performance given by four or five people. First, a common, familiar
story is done for one section, which is called the *yen-tuan* 艷段. Next is
performed the *cheng tsa-chü* 正雜劇, a name applied to two sections. The
mo-ni leads the action, the *yin-hsi* 引戲 issues orders, the *fu-ching* 副淨
pretends doltishness, and the *fu-mo* 副末 makes jokes on the *fu-ching*.
Sometimes another person is added who is called the *chuang-ku* 裝孤
('dissembling as an official'). The one who first plays the *ch'ü-p'o* 曲破
and then the *tuan-sung* 斷送 is called the *pa-se* 巴色. Generally, the
whole thing is a story, with the emphasis on comedy. Singing, recitation
and dialogue are common to all [the actors].

"Since it is basically [performed] to warn by example and is obscure in
its reproof, therefore [the actors] who reveal [such admonitions] at the
first opportunity are called faultless insects. Even when done in front of
the emperor it brings no chastisement or punishment, for in an instant
they bring a smile to the Sage's [i.e., to the emperor's] face. Generally, if
there is any criticism or if a censor [desires] to state a case openly but the
emperor will not permit it, then the actors cloak the case in a story to
criticize with import hidden; thus no displeasure shadows the emperor's
face.

"There is also a *tsa-pan* 雜班(扮) called a *niu-yüan-tzu* 紐元子 or *pa-
ho* 拔禾, which was the final portion, the *san-tuan* 散段, of the perform-

---

[28] T'ao Tsung-i, *Cho-keng lu* (rpt. Taipei, 1963), pp. 366–386.

ance. During the time the [Sung capital] was at Pien-ching [Kaifeng], village yokels and country bumpkins would rarely venture into the city, so [actors] would compose this skit. Most of them would dress up as old villagers of Hopei or Shantung to provide laughs." [29]

This passage suggests that the *tsa-chü* variety show of Southern Sung times was a four-act performance framed by a musical prelude and postlude. The following chart summarizes the various parts:

Prelude	*"ch'ü-p'o"*	*Begin dancing*
Introduction	*yen-tuan*	Opening section
Main body in two sections	*cheng tsa-chü*	Actual variety performance
Trailer	*san-tuan*	Dispersal section
Postlude	*tuan-sung*	Musical send-off

It is clear from the context of the composite passage from the two texts that this description is of a court performance. We can postulate, however, on the basis of other passages and other sources, that this basic form of variety show also characterized market-place performances, and that farce was still a major feature of the presentation—although undoubtedly it was the country bumpkin and not the subtle intrigues of court politics that provided grist for the urban mill of parody.

While we have no way of knowing for sure, it was probably a market-place performance of *yüan-pen* that is described in T'ao's *Notes Taken during Breaks from Ploughing*. T'ao's catalogue of script titles is prefaced by a brief discussion of the *yüan-pen* troupe, portions of which read:

"T'ang had its *ch'uan-ch'i* 傳奇; Sung had its *hsi-ch'ü* 戲曲, *ch'ang-hun* 唱諢, *tz'u-shuo* 詞說; Chin had its *yüan-pen*, *tsa-chü*, and *chu-kung-tiao* 諸宮調. *Yüan-pen* and *tsa-chü* were, in fact, one. In this dynasty they first separated to become two. In *yüan-pen* there are five people [i.e., five role types]. One is called the *fu-ching*, whom the ancients called the *ts'an-chün* 參軍, and one is called the *fu-mo*, whom the ancients called the *ts'ang-ku* 蒼鶻 (hawk). A hawk can strike birds and fowl, and the *fu-mo* can strike the *fu-ching*—thus their names. One is called the *yin-hsi*, one the *mo-ni*, and one the *ku-chuang*. There is also a *yen-tuan*, which means *yüan-pen*, but is simpler. In it the *fu-ching* has some random words. There is recitation, acrobatics, and mime." [30]

As we can see from this passage, the dominant role types in *yüan-pen* and *tsa-chü* were the straight-man/comic team of the *fu-ching* and the *fu-*

---

[29] *Tu-ch'eng chi-sheng*, pp. 96–97; *Meng-liang lu*, pp. 308–309.
[30] *Cho-keng lu*, p. 366.

mo. Furthermore, their repertoire, according to the Sung capital memoirs and the short notice of T'ao Tsung-i, seems to have been limited to a farce skit that culminated in a fracas in which the *fu-mo* strikes the *fu-ching*. If, however, we look at the catalogues of titles in *Old Affairs of Wu-lin*, and especially in T'ao's *Notes*, it immediately becomes clear that the range of performances is far broader than mere farce.

A possible explanation of the seeming conflict between the description of the performances and the obviously larger format suggested in the catalogues lies in understanding the two terms, *tsa-chü* and *yüan-pen*.

The earliest mention of the *tsa-chü* is found in *Tung-ching meng-hua lu* 東京夢華錄 (*A Record of Dreams of the Florescence of the Eastern Capital*, preface dated 1147). This notice and its subsequent notices in the Southern Sung memoirs indicate that the term had both a broad and a narrow meaning. In its broad sense it referred to the entire variety performance, and in its narrow sense it referred only to the discrete middle segment of the variety performance, the *cheng tsa-chü*. If we take into consideration the generally accepted etymology of the term *yüan-pen*, that it is a contraction of the phrase *hang-yüan chih pen* 行院之本 (scripts from the actors guilds),[31] then we can posit a similar range of meanings for *yüan-pen*: that is, both as a general term in North China for "variety show," and as a specific term referring to the farce skits of the discrete *yüan-pen* segment. This assumption is corroborated by an investigation of the fourteen categories of T'ao's list, in which one major section, "The various and sundry *yüan-pen* large and small" (*chu-tsa ta-hsiao yüan-pen* 諸雜大小院本), contains approximately thirty percent of all the titles.[32] Moreover, a significant number of the titles in this particular section are of scripts that parody scholars (*suan* 酸), courtesans and females (*tan* 旦), and venal officials (*ku* 孤). It is this group of *yüan-pen* farces that occur most often in later Northern dramas and provide in them delightful moments of comic relief.[33]

But there were other elements in the entire variety show, and the role they played in the development of music-drama was as important as that played by these miniature farce plays. We are fortunate in that we have a third piece of literary evidence that fills some of the gaps in our

[31] This is the commonly accepted etymology, first postulated by Chu Ch'üan 朱權 in *T'ai-ho cheng-yin p'u* 太和正音譜. See Hu Chi 胡忌, *Sung Chin tsa-chü k'ao* 宋金雜劇考 (Shanghai, 1958), pp. 8–12, 19–20.

[32] T'ao Tsung-i, *Cho-keng lu*, p. 369.

[33] The farce interludes in Yüan and Ming drama were well studied by Tanaka Kenji 田中謙二 in "Genbon kō 院本考," *Nippon Chūgoku gakkai hō* 日本中国学会報, 20 (1969), pp. 169–191.

knowledge about the other constituents in the variety performance. It is the famous *san-ch'ü* suite, "The Country Bumpkin Knows Nothing of the Theater" (*Chuang-chia pu-shih kou-lan* 莊家不識构闌). This light-hearted look at the theater was written by Tu Shan-fu 杜善夫, a poet-dramatist who was active in Honan and Hopei between 1224 and 1231, and who died in the last part of the thirteenth century. Although this suite has recently been rendered into literate and elegant English by Professors James I. Crump and David Hawkes, below is a less elegant, but more literal translation that attempts to identify the technical elements.[34]

The Country Bumpkin Knows Nothing of the Theater

(tune: *shua-hai-erh* 耍孩兒)

When winds are fair, rain seasonal, all people are peaceful and
     happy,
But none have joy like us farming folk;
The mulberry silkworms and five grains have all yielded full,
And the government offices relented on taxes.
Since our village had blessings to repay,
I came to town to buy paper [cash] and [incense] fire.
I'd just passed the head of the street,
When I saw a speckled-green paper banner hanging down
And under it a crowd of clamorous, noisy people.

(coda: six)

Saw a man whose hands were propped on a fat-pillared door,
In a loud voice calling, "Please, please,"
Saying, "For latecomers it'll be filled, no place to sit."
Yelling, "The first half's a *yüan-pen* called *T'iao-feng-yüeh*
     調風月,
"The back half a *yao-mo* 么末, *The Actor Liu Shua-ho* 劉耍和."
In a louder voice he cried, "So good it's over before you know
     it, worth a hard-won cheer" (tentative translation).

(coda: five)

He got 200 cash before he let me pass,
Just as I entered the door, up rose a wooden slope.

---

[34] J. I. Crump, "Yüan-pen, Yüan Drama's Rowdy Ancestor," *Literature East and West*, 14:4 (1970), pp. 481–483; David Hawkes, "Reflections on Yüan Tsa-chü," *Asia Major*, 16 (1970), pp. 75–76.

I saw them piled layer on layer, sitting round in a circle,
Raising my head, saw it looked just like a bell-tower,
But gazin' down, it was a whirlpool of people.
Saw some "ladies" sittin' on a platform—
It wasn't a festival for "welcoming idols,"
But they banged the drum and rang the gong, never stopping.

(coda: four)

A lone girl did several turns,
Before long leading out her band.
Among them was a good-for-nothing
Wrapped in a black turban, the top stuck through with a brush.
Full-face limed, streaked with black,
I knew how he got along.
Head to toe, his whole body
Was covered by a cotton-flowered robe.

(coda: three)

He intoned a *shih* 詩, then a tz'u 詞,
Spoke a *fu* 賦 and sang;
Not too bad, either.
All things he talked of, all the same (tentative translation);
Lots of flowery words and clever phrases to remember.
But when it approached the end,
He spoke, lowered his head and slapped his feet.
The *ts'uan* 爨 was finished, the second half about to be
    played.[35]

(coda: two)

One was Squire Chang,
The other changed to Brother Two.
Walking, walking, they said they were on their way to town.
Seeing a young girl standing under a shade,
The old man bent his mind to strategies, scheming to have her
    to wife,
Sending Brother Two off to arrange the union.
All she wanted was beans or grain, wheat and rice—
Did she ask for gauze or silk, satin or cotton?

---

[35] The term *yao-po* 么撥 has been interpreted in two ways: as "the *yao*-[*mo*] was about to
be played," and as "the second half [i.e. the *yao*] was about to be played." That *yao* means
"second half" is well attested in Yüan and Ming texts. I am following Hu Chi's
interpretation. See *Sung Chin tsa-chü k'ao*, p. 72.

(coda: one)

Making the Squire go forward, daring not go back,
Causing him to raise his left foot, daring not raise the right,
Back and forth, up and down—all because of *that* one!
Now his heart is fuming and burning,
And he strikes with his flesh bat, breaking it in half.
I say this will give rise to depositions and claims,
And I have to laugh again.

(coda: tail)

But a bladder of piss is bursting so
There's nothing I can do,
But struggle to hold it, to see some more
And to let this jackass make me laugh.[36]

This piece, written sometime before 1250, is surely the most detailed description of a *yüan-pen* performance left to us. The important elements of this suite for understanding the sequences of performance in the variety show are those that describe the first three parts: a musical prelude, played by the female troupe; the *ching* monologue, here described as a *ts'uan*; and the comic-dramatic performance, *T'iao-feng-yüeh*, described by our full-bladdered country cousin.

Both technical terms used in the suite—*ts'uan* and *yao-mo*—appear as headings of categories in T'ao Tsung-i's catalogue of titles. The *ts'uan* comprises one of eleven major sections, and under its heading are listed 107 titles.[37] It was highly specialized type of performance that was suited to the *yen-tuan* and consisted mainly of song and dance routines or, as in this case, of monologues.[38] The *yao-mo* is thought to have comprised a portion of the catalogue entitled *yüan-yao* 院么, which Hu Chi 胡忌 takes to be a contraction of *hang-yüan chih yao-mo* 行院之么末, "*yao-mo* from the entertainers' guilds."[39] There is sufficient evidence to indicate that the *yao-mo* was either a fledgling northern drama, or that it

---

[36] This translation follows the text and notes of Ogawa Yōichi 小川陽一, "Tō Zanfu saku sankyoku 'Sōka fu shiki kōran' yakuchū 杜善夫作散曲 '莊家不識构闌' 訳注," *Shūkan tōyōgaku* 集刊東洋学, 18 (1967), pp. 78–86.

[37] T'ao Tsung-i, *Cho-keng lu*, pp. 366–386.

[38] The term *ts'uan* has been the subject of much debate. Feng Yüan-chün 馮沅君, *Ku-chü shuo-hui* 古劇說彙 (Peking, 1956), thinks that it is a phonetic variant of *yen* in the term *yen-tuan*, and that it therefore meant "opening segment." Hu Chi, however, provides substantial evidence that the *ts'uan* was an independent performance that was incorporated into the variety show. See *Sung Chin tsa-chü k'ao*, pp. 193–199.

[39] Hu Chi, *Sung Chin tsa-chü k'ao*, pp. 221–225.

was a transitional form in the developmental stage from simple to complex music drama. Feng Yüan-chün 馮沅君, for instance, considered it to be the source of northern drama:

"In recent years many scholars of the history of drama believed that the ancient theater underwent great innovation between the Chin and Yüan. In our view, the important point of the innovation was the expansion or fleshing out of the *yao-mo* sections of *yüan-pen* and the *cheng tsa-chü* sections of the Sung variety show to the exclusion of sections that were purely comic or slapstick."[40]

Hu Chi, on the other hand, is more cautious with his statements, but still suggests that the *yao-mo* was the transitional performance that witnessed the first adaptation of *ch'ü* style music to spoken drama.[41]

I suspect, however, that our country cousin did not describe to us the *yao-mo*, which was entitled *The Actor Liu Shua-ho*, but rather the *yüan-pen, T'iao-feng-yüeh*. It is apparent that the *yüan-pen* (constituent element) usually preceded a second dramatic performance. This can be corroborated by comparing Tu Shan-fu's suite with another *san-ch'ü* suite on the theater written by Kao An-tao 高安道 in the early fourteenth century, when Yüan drama was at the height of its popularity. This suite is troublesome because of the highly colloquial nature of its language, and annotators have as yet been unable to agree on what some of the lines mean. But enough can be gleaned to give the following outline.

Growing weary of the responsibility of high position, an official decides to retire with his companions of the wine cup for a day in the brothel district. "Wearied of wandering along willow-lined paths/And of longing over misty blossoms," however, they change their minds and visit the theater. Making their way through the hustle and bustle, they are admitted by an oaf of a doorkeeper, "a real ox," and arrive just in time for the performance to begin:

> The flute-playing *pa-se* crooks his pursed lips,
> The drum-striking *ch'ui-ting* balls his left hand
> And beats out a soft roll.
> Those on the music benches hump their backs like toads,
> And mint vendors swell their throats to shout.

Finding a good seat, our official spies the actresses sitting on the music benches. Ugly as gargoyles up close, from a distance they entrance the audience. But, he tells us, they are miserable performers: they sing the

---

[40] Feng Yüan-chün, *Ku-chü shuo-hui*, p. 72.
[41] Hu Chi, *Sung Chin tsa-chü k'ao*, p. 72.

p'o-tzu out of tune, and the few graceful movements of their "four-part" dance are spoiled by the sight of lice running down their arms.

When they are finished, a series of individual performances comes on. These include "waving the red flag," "the old man in rabbit fur," "sled shoes," "the judge," and the "pimple-faced ghost." These ineptitudes are then followed by the *yüan-pen* troupe. The *mo-ni* stumbles through a poem; the *fu-mo* and *fu-ching* have an altercation; then the troupe "destroys a script on officials, courtesans, or scholars." After going off with a series of tumbles, the *yüan-pen* troupe is followed by what is clearly a serious dramatic performance. It is complete with a male lead playing an emperor, and a female lead who, our official tells us, "Has a body as gross as a water buffalo/And sings like a hoarse deserted dog." There is also another female lead (*wai-tan* 外旦) who smells "rank and fetid," and a limed and painted character, "crazy with insults," clearly the *ching*.[42]

The performance described in this suite, which includes a full Yüan drama, is similar to the earlier variety shows in structure. If we compare the entries from *Records of A Millet Dream*, Tu Shan-fu's suite, and Kao An-tao's cycle of poems, we find the following similarities:

Millet Dream	*"Tu Shan-fu"*	*"Kao An-tao"*
Prelude/*ch'ü-p'o*	Prelude/instrumental by female troupe	Prelude/*p'o-tzu*
Introduction/*yen-tuan*	Introduction/*ts'uan*	Troupe dance/skits
Main body: sec. 1	1. *yüan-pen*	1. *yüan-pen*
sec. 2	2. *yao-mo*	2. dramatic performance
Trailer/*san-tuan*	(suite finished)	Troupe dance
Postlude/*tuan-sung*		(suite finished)

The comparison of these three sources, between them spanning a hundred years, suggests a great continuity in the actual format of the variety performance. Any change in performance, then, on the basis of this continuity, would have to come from one of the constituent elements. Here, we might return to T'ao Tsung-i's earlier statement that *yüan-pen* and *tsa-chü* were originally the same thing and that they split into two separate forms at the beginning of the Yüan. This suggests a radical change in the nature of the middle segment of the variety performance.

---

[42] This summary and translation follow Hu Chi's annotations; *Sung Chin tsa-chü k'ao*, pp. 311–325.

Archeological finds have provided invaluable evidence. During the past twenty years, there have been four major finds that bear directly on the history of the theater. Three have brought to light tomb tiles or frescoes that have pictorial representations of *yüan-pen* or *pei-ch'ü* acting troupes, and one has produced a miniature stage and five dolls that are replicas of a *yüan-pen* troupe. The earliest dated find is a group of three tiles from a Northern Sung tomb, unearthed in Honan in 1958.[43] They show the role types of a Northern Sung *tsa-chü* engaged in performance (Fig. 1).

(Fig. 1) Line Drawings of Yen-shih *hsien* 偃師縣 Tomb Tiles
A. from *Wen-wu* 5 (1960), p. 41; B, from *Wen-wu* 5 (1960), p. 42.

This find has been particularly significant because the costumed characters show that a relatively complex drama was thriving some one-hundred years before the development of either *hsi-wen* 戲文 (Southern Sung drama) or *pei-ch'ü*.[44] When these finds are compared to another set of engravings of an acting troupe found in a tomb dated 1260, well into the flourishing period of *tsa-chü*, we find no distinct differences in either costuming or posturing (Fig. 2).[45]

[43] See Hsü P'ing-fang 徐苹芳, "Sung-tai ti tsa-chü tiao-chuan 宋代的雜劇雕磚," *Wen wu* 文物, 1960, No. 5, pp. 40–42; and Chao Ching-shen 趙景深, "Pei-Sung ti tsa-chü tiao-chuan 北宋的雜劇雕磚," in *Hsi-ch'ü pi-t'an* 戲曲筆談 (Peking, 1962), pp. 230–238.
[44] Chao Ching-shen, "Pei-Sung ti tsa-chü tiao-chuan," in *Hsi-ch'ü pi-t'an*, pp. 231–238.
[45] *Hsi-ch'ü pi-t'an*, p. 234.

(Fig. 2) Line Drawings of Carving on Wall Facing
Sarcophagus of Sung Te-fang

The similarities between the characters of the engravings and the tomb tiles suggest a continuity in the impersonation of characters on stage, and provide strong evidence that drama, in the basic meaning of that word, existed long before the Yüan.[46]

A second point about these unearthed finds is that they have all, with the exception of the Honan excavation, been unearthed in the P'ing-yang area of Shansi. In addition to these frescoes, figurines, and a tomb engraving, there have come to light steles and records of stage construction and refurbishing that show an unbroken theater tradition from sometime in the early eleventh century (1005) to the late fourteenth century. These stages were constructed of durable material, usually brick and tile. They were built on the premises of temples to local agricultural or cultural deities, either as integral parts of the temples themselves or as immediately adjacent structures. This has vast implications for theories

[46] *Hsi-ch'ü pi-t'an*, p. 234.

of the rise of drama. For it demonstrates quite clearly that the development of a theatrical tradition was limited neither to the Sung court nor to an urbanized environment.[47] And it suggests that religious activities may have played an important role in fostering these developments.

We have, then, ample evidence that drama existed before the rise of either *hsi-wen* or *pei-ch'ü*. But what of T'ao Tsung-i's statement? What did he mean when he said that *yüan-pen* and *tsa-chü* split to become two forms? The answer to that question lies in the ambiguity of the term *tsa-chü*. As we know, *tsa-chü* meant variety show, but it also was the common term for northern music-drama performed on the stage.[48] It appears that T'ao was suggesting that drama grew gradually from the middle section of the *yüan-pen* variety show to become an independently recognizable form.

But how did *tsa-chü*, constituent element, evolve into *tsa-chü*, music drama? Here we must rely on our knowledge of the development of music between the twelfth and thirteenth centuries. One of the most popular vernacular forms of entertainment of that period was the *chu-kung-tiao* (medley), a long narrative poetic form that represents, musically, a transitional stage between the *tz'u* and *ch'ü* forms. If we can accept the traditional dates ascribed to the extant works of *chu-kung-tiao* (i.e., ca. 1000–1200), then we can place the development of *ch'ü*-style music—that is, lengthy suites of single stanza tunes written to one mode—in the late twelfth or early thirteenth centuries. Its incorporation into drama probably happened very shortly after that—perhaps in the last years of the Chin, or in the interregnum between that dynasty's fall and the establishment of the Yüan.

This would provide an explanation for the sudden leap that seems to occur between *spoken* and *musical* drama. The archaeological finds have shown that a complex dramatic performance existed as far back as Northern Sung, and literary evidence has produced clues that the variety show of Sung and Chin produced not only farce skits, but also serious dramatic productions, many with the same titles as those of later northern drama. The same evidence, however, also indicates that dialogue, not song, was the major feature of their performance. But it was only a short and logical step, once *ch'ü* style music had been brought to

[47] Ting Ming-i 丁明夷, "Shan-hsi chung-nan-pu ti Sung Yüan wu-t'ai 山西中南部的宋元舞臺," *Wen-wu*, 1972, No. 4, pp. 47–56; and Liu Nien-tz'u 劉念茲, "Ts'ung chien-kuo hou fa-hsien ti i-hsieh wen-wu k'an Chin Yüan tsa-chü tsai P'ing-yang ti-ch'ü ti fa-chan 從建國後發現的一些文物看金元雜劇在平陽地區的發展," *Wen-shih lun-ts'ung* 文史論叢 (Hong Kong, 1974), pp. 388–404.

[48] Hu Chi, *Sung Chin tsa-chü k'ao*, pp. 1–6.

maturity, to combine it with dramas that already had a strong story line, and produce the form we know as *pei-ch'ü*.

The conclusions that I have suggested here are tentative, and will remain so as long as archaeological finds of significance are made. But our present state of knowledge seems to suggest that northern drama was the product of a long evolution of dramatic and musical forms that coalesced during the critical period in the early thirteenth century.

ACT III

Reevaluation

In light of this new archaeological evidence that shows a long and sustained period of theatrical development, we must refute earlier statements on Mongol influences on the rise of drama. We must reconsider the relationship of the literati to drama, taking into account the parallel phenomena of the theatrical convention itself and the new social and intellectual outlook of the age. Such a reconsideration will help to define more precisely the parameters of Mongol influence, both direct and indirect.

Three major areas of Mongol influence can be seen as determinants in the rise or development of drama. The first is Mongol patronage, whether direct, such as by the court, or indirect through the medium of Chinese myriarchs (*wan-hu* 萬戶) in the north. The second is the abolition of the examination system and the promotion of practical administrators at the expense of the degree holder; while this had, I believe, little effect on the *rise* of drama, its long-range influences were both important and substantive. The third is in the area of language, especially in the importation and usage of Mongolian words and terms in drama.

The question of patronage can be divided into two distinct stages that roughly correspond to the periods of conquest and rule. During the first period, the Mongols made heavy use of Chinese defectors as civil and military rulers of North China.[49] During the second, they directly patronized actors, performers, and troupes at court in Ta-tu. When the Mongols conquered North China, they established several semi-independent areas that were controlled by Chinese or Khitan overlords

---

[49] Igor de Rachewiltz, "Personnel and Personalities in North China during the Early Mongol Period," *Journal of the Economic and Social History of the Orient*, 9:2 (1966), pp. 102–107. This theory of actor-literatus interaction was first suggested to me by Professor J. I. Crump.

who held high rank in the Mongol military hierarchy. These overlords functioned as both civil and military rulers and held special discretionary powers over the people under their control, ruling over their special areas of influence with little effective central coordination.[50] Their powers stemmed from the support given them by Chinggis Khan's generals, Mukhali and Bo'ol, the two leaders of the North China campaign. Both of these men, and later Ögödei, at the suggestion of Yeh-lü Ch'u-ts'ai 耶律楚材, either recommended or directly promoted Chinese officials to high positions in the Mongol hierarchy, bestowing on them the status and privileges due Mongols in the same positions. These overlords were responsible in many areas for the perpetuation of Chinese cultural forms and values, and many of them staffed their organizations with dispossessed Chin scholars. Some even sought to continue the bureaucratic and ritual practices of the Chin, establishing schools to promote traditional education and Confucianism.[51]

The most influential of these myriarchs were Chang Jou 張柔, in Pao-chou (Hopei), Shih T'ien-ni 史天倪 and his brother T'ien-tse 史天澤 in Chen-ting (Hopei), Liu I 劉愐 in Ta-t'ung (Shansi) and Yen Shih 嚴實 in Tung-p'ing (Shantung). Under their protection and patronage, large groups of scholars and writers gathered in a secure and comfortable atmosphere where they were encouraged to continue their intellectual lives. Such eminent and diverse writers as Yüan Hao-wen 元好問 and Pai P'u were given encouragement and respect under the aegis of the likes of Yen Shih and Shih T'ien-tse. We might also note that in his reconstruction of Pao-ting, Chang Jou had two theaters constructed.

Eminent writers and scholars were usually spared by the Mongols, who otherwise pursued a policy of plunder and occasional slaughter. They formed part of a larger group of people who were of use to the Mongols and who were either taken to Karakorum or confined to the headquarters of one of the myriarchs. This group was usually comprised of artisans, craftsmen, men of the Three Teachings (Buddhism, Confucianism, and Taoism), and actors. Liu Ch'i noted in his eyewitness account of the fall of the Chin capital Pien-liang to the Mongols that "physicians, men of the Three Teachings, and craftsmen" were sent out of the city before the Mongols looted it.[52] Sung Tzu-chen 宋子貞, in his memorial inscription for Yeh-lü Ch'u-ts'ai, wrote:

[50] Rachewiltz, "Personnel and Personalities in North China," pp. 125–127.

[51] See Yüan Kuo-fan 袁國藩, "Tung-p'ing Yen Shih mu-fu jen-wu yü hsing-hsüeh ch'u-k'ao 東平嚴實幕府人物與興學初考," Ta-lu tsa-chih 大陸雜誌, 23 (1962), pp. 383–386; and Rachewiltz, "Personnel and Personalities in North China," pp. 125–127.

[52] Kuei-ch'ien chih, 11:11b.

"At that time there were 1,470,000 households avoiding the [Mongol] troops in Pien. As before, [Yeh-lü] memorialized that the classes of artisan, craftsman, Confucian, Buddhist, Taoist, physician, and diviner be picked out to be scattered and reside in the area north of the river, to be provided for by government office. After this time, in attacking and taking the various walled cities of [the region of] the Huai and Han [rivers], this suggestion was relied on as a definitive precedent."[53]

This practice is also noted in the biography of Mukhali, where it is remarked, "Liu Yen 劉琰 of Kuang-ning 廣寧 and T'ien Ho-shang 田禾尚 of I-chou 懿州 surrendered, whereupon Mukhali said, 'If we let these rebellious bandits live, there will be nothing with which to admonish later [generations].' With the exception of the artisans, craftsmen, and actors, he slaughtered them all."[54]

We know that actors who were captured performed for Chinggis Khan,[55] and we presume that they also came under the patronage of the northern myriarchs. This suggests that there was a long period of concentrated and close interaction between elite writers and members of the acting profession. This fact, coupled with the knowledge that many late Chin writers had an interest in the theater,[56] suggests that the era immediately following the Mongols' defeat of the Chin may have been the seminal period of elite interest in drama. This is borne out partly by the history of Pai P'u, who in his youth was raised by the classical writer Yüan Hao-wen, but who became a playwright after his receipt of patronage from Shih T'ien-tse. Close relationships between elite writers, actors, and wealthy patrons may also be one of the major factors in the formation of writers' guilds, to whom many of the anonymous plays of the Yüan are attributed.[57]

As for court patronage, we are forced to rely on written testimony of literati who witnessed such affairs. The two most famous reporters of the early period are Hu Chih-yü and Wang Yün. Both of these men were intimate with members of the court theatrical groups, and exchanged several poems with actresses and other performers. It is interesting to note that few of their poems specifically mention drama. References to

[53] Sung Tzu-chen 宋子貞, "Chung-shu ling Yeh-lü kung shen-tao pei 中書令耶律公神道碑," *Kuo-ch'ao wen-lei* 國朝文類 (SPTK ed.), 57:15a.

[54] YS 119:2932.

[55] Yoshikawa, *Yüan tsa-chü yen-chiu*, p. 53.

[56] *Yüan tsa-chü yen-chiu*, pp. 51–52.

[57] On writers' guilds, see Feng Yüan-chün, *Ku-chü shuo-hui*, pp. 17–18, 57–58; Sun K'ai-ti 孫楷第, *Yeh-shih yüan ku-chin tsa-chü k'ao* 也是園古今雜劇考 (Shanghai, 1953), pp. 388–393; and Ogawa Tamaki 小川環樹, *Chūgoku shōsetsu shi no kenkyū* 中国小説史の研究 (Tokyo, 1968), pp. 54–56.

strictly musical or kinetic performances are far more common. Hu Chih-yü, for instance, wrote a cycle of poems that was presented to Khubilai at his "Long Life Ceremony" in 1264. The titles of the seven poems in this cycle are "Wielding the Club," "The Welcoming Drum," "Wrestling," "Children Climbing a Pole," "Various Modes," "The T'ai-p'ing Drum and Clappers," and "Fighting Toads."[58] None of these performances was a northern drama, and it is uncertain whether, in fact, true *tsa-chü* dramas were performed at court before the fourteenth century, although evidence of their performance after this time is strong.

Our speculations about the literacy of the Mongol emperors in Chinese may be brought to bear here.[59] We know, for instance, that the early Mongol emperors, Khubilai included, had little more than rudimentary knowledge of Chinese (and were illiterate in the language).[60] We would suspect, therefore, that drama, the arias and dialogue of which were probably difficult to understand, would be somewhat tedious alongside other performances that had more visual or aural appeal. One is reminded of the performances in Western countries by Peking Opera troupes, where the emphasis is placed on mime, military arts, acrobatics, and other visual elements.

Nevertheless, Khubilai was responsible for establishing two court bureaus, the *I-feng ssu* 儀鳳司 and *Chiao-fang ssu* 教坊司, which were responsible for music and acting, and which performed both court rituals and popular performances.[61] We may conclude on the basis of this interest that drama, if it was produced at court, was no more than a small part of a larger variety performance.

It is toward the end of the Yüan that court poetry begins to be explicit about drama—a time that also sees the stirrings of literati interest in it as a literary form. We have, for instance, two poems, one by Yang Wei-chen 楊維楨 and one by Chu Yu-tun 朱有燉, that describe the presentation of a drama to the court by a playwright. Yang's poem attributes the two dramas that were presented to an "actor-remonstrator" of the

[58] These seven poems are scattered throughout *chüan* seven of *Tzu-shan ta ch'üan-chi* 紫山大全集 (*Ssu-k'u ch'üan-shu chen-pen* ed.), but are collected together in Yoshikawa Kōjirō, "Shokyuchō sadan 諸宮調瑣談," in *Yoshikawa Kōjirō zenshū* 吉川幸次郎全集 (Tokyo, 1970), vol. 14, pp. 569–572. They were originally of one cycle, but were later scattered when the Ssu-k'u compilers restored the collection from the *Yung-lo ta-tien* 永樂大典.

[59] See Herbert Franke, "Could the Mongol Emperors Read and Write Chinese?" *Asia Major*, N.S. 3 (1958); and Yoshikawa Kōjirō, "Gen no shotei no bungaku 元の諸帝の文学," *Yoshikawa Kōjirō zenshū*, vol. 15, pp. 232–303.

[60] See the works cited in n. 59.

[61] Yoshikawa, *Yüan tsa-chü yen-chiu*, pp. 54–56.

"Great Chin," Kuan Ch'ing 關卿.[62] Chu Yu-tun, writing sometime later, speaks of the delight that these new dramas brought to the court:

> The first to harmonize sound and music was Kuan Ch'ing,
> The *tsa-chü* "I-yin fu T'ang 伊尹扶湯" was submitted;
> It was transmitted into the Forbidden Garden; the palaces were delighted—
> That whole time you could listen everywhere to the singing of these new sounds.[63]

There is some speculation that the two dramas mentioned were presented to the court by none other than Kuan Han-ch'ing.[64] However, the fact that neither play is attributed in any bibliography to Kuan makes the attribution unlikely. It is the strongest evidence we have of early dramatic performances in the Yüan court, but it is interesting to note that both of these poems were written well after the fact—in very late Yüan and early Ming—and one is suspicious of whether it was fact, or merely hearsay.

We do know that a play by the late Yüan playwright Pao T'ien-yu 鮑天祐 was a particular favorite of the court. Chu Yu-tun, the grandson of Ming T'ai-tsu, founder of the Ming dynasty, wrote about this performance in his "One Hundred Court Poems," a cycle that sings of life in the Yüan court and which is based upon stories the author heard from an old court nurse. One of the poems reads this way:

> "A Corpse Impeaches Duke Ling" ("Shih chien Ling kung 屍諫靈公")—they performed this play;
> One morning it was sent on for [him within] the nine-fold gates to know.
> An edict was received to give it to the Secretariat,
> And on every circuit all were instructed to sing this play.[65]

Other useful information can be derived from Chu's cycle of poems, including the frequent production of theatricals and the Mongol preference for northern music:

> A renowned actress from Chiang-nan, named "Piercing Needle,"

[62] Yang Wei-chen, "Kung-tz'u 宮詞," *T'ieh-yai hsien-sheng ku yüeh-fu* 鐵崖先生古樂府 (SPTK ed.), 14:1b.

[63] The original is unavailable to me; I am following Yoshikawa, *Yüan tsa-chü yen-chiu*, pp. 55–56.

[64] The attribution of this drama to Kuan Han-ch'ing is probably to stress the fact that only morally uplifting pieces by the finest playwrights were performed at court.

[65] Yoshikawa, *Yüan tsa-chü yen-chiu*, pp. 54–56.

> Presented into the Emperor's household, worth a myriad gold;
> Don't sing southern tunes in front of others,
> For within the Inner [Chambers, i.e. in the palace] all is
>   northern music.[66]

Thus it is apparent that as the years passed the Mongols increasingly patronized the theater at court, and were probably responsible for sustaining at least one mode of its development from a theater of the people to a theater (or a closet drama) of an elite class who were centered at court.

The only substantiated performances of *tsa-chü* drama were late in the reign, when the interests and abilities of the Yüan emperors in traditional Chinese learning were at their highest level. This correlates with the emergence of special treatises that deal either with drama, or with *ch'ü*, the musical form that gives drama its unique structure. For instance, the "Ten Rules on Writing *Tz'u* [i.e. *ch'ü*]" (*Tso tz'u shih fa* 作詞十法) in Chou Te-ch'ing's 周德清 *Chung-yüan yin-yün* 中原音韻 (*Rhymes of the Central Plain*) was written in 1324; Chung Ssu-ch'eng's 鍾嗣成 *Lu kuei pu* 錄鬼簿 (*Register of Ghosts*), a bibliographical and biographical study of Yüan playwrights, has a preface dated 1330; and the *Ch'ing lou chi* (*The Green Bower Collection*) was written within the same period as that of the previous two items. *The Green Bower Collection* provides the best evidence of literati interest in drama, recounting with zest the patronage that men of letters lavished on singing girls and actresses. Altogether the work lists some twenty such scholars, from elder survivors of the Chin to contemporary Yüan officials, who associated with these females.

This sustaining patronage by the Mongol emperors and the sudden burst of interest in the dramatic form, when viewed against the general decline in popularity of the *tsa-chü* in the marketplace, suggest that two theatrical traditions were beginning to emerge: one that was maintained in the rural and urban popular environment, and another that developed in the court or in the studies of the elite. The eventual decline in *tsa-chü* as a popular entertainment form is associated with its shift southward and the subsequent rise of southern drama (*k'un-ch'ü* 崑曲). And while the dramatists of *tsa-chü* faded away into obscurity, there can be little doubt of the rise of an amateur dramatic tradition among the literati, who began the conscientious collection of materials that resulted in the anthologies of plays in the Ming.

This phenomenon is probably tied to the second area of Mongol influence: the abolition of the examination system and the rise of bureaucratic professionalism. As we noted above, these two events had

---

[66] *Yüan tsa-chü yen-chiu*, pp. 54–56.

little direct influence on the early development of drama. At first, in the years between 1230 and 1270, there was only sporadic interest in drama on the part of elite writers, represented by the likes of Tu Shan-fu or Pai P'u, and it is difficult to ascertain whether the immediate political situation caused this interest, or whether it was an outgrowth of a previous interest among Chin scholars. There is some evidence that literati interest in drama, or in performing arts, goes far back into the Sung. There are the examples of Ou-yang Hsiu 歐陽修 and Chao Ling-chih 趙令畤 (Su Shih's close friend), eminent men of letters who wrote lyrics for court performances.[67] Moreover, while we have no data on Tung Chieh-yüan 董解元, author of the only complete extant medley, "Medley on the Western Chamber,"[68] the high literary quality of his medley testifies to the level of attainment of some writers of performing literature. Moreover, the number of plays written on corrupted youth, or on youths of good families who turned to the dissolute life of acting, bespeak a growing (and to elite eyes, unhealthy) interest in the theater on the part of members of the elite. But, while we have some evidence that the theater (not necessarily drama) attracted Chin writers, the very paucity of that evidence still suggests that their interest was not extensive.

We can only speculate that, as the dynasty fell and the frustrations of the scholar-writer increased, his orientations also changed. And, as part of this change in goals, those elite writers under myriarch patronage in North China collaborated with actors to produce dramatic texts for performance. This implies not only the existence of elite participation in a popular literary-performing form, but also the interaction of folk literature with the elite world of letters. We can see, as the years pass, an intensification of literati interest in drama as a legitimate literary tradition. Literati participation, then, moved from association with the general theater (either as individual writers or as members of *shu-hui* 書會 [writers guilds]) to participation in a tradition that was an accepted part of the elite way of life.

Thus the long-term effect of the abolition of the examination system and the early rejection of Chinese traditional literary values, while not immediately significant in the development of the theatrical tradition, were important. For they are the beginning of a reorientation of the writer. It is this long-term influence that has heretofore been relatively neglected in scholarship. W. L. Idema's recent book on the origins of

[67] See Liu Yung-chi 劉永濟, *Sung-tai ko-wu chü-ch'ü lu-yao* 宋代歌舞劇曲錄要 (Shanghai, 1957), *passim*.

[68] This work has recently been translated: Li-li Ch'en, tr., *Master Tung's Western Chamber Romance* (Cambridge, England, 1977).

Chinese vernacular fiction[69] has offered some speculations on both the relationship of drama and fiction, and the relationship between the literati and vernacular narrative. His conclusion that it was the literati of China, not the folk, who produced the *hua-pen* 話本 and the short story has a direct bearing on understanding Mongol influence in drama. For it indicates that the trend among the elite writers to produce vernacular literature probably began in that crucial period in early Yüan, when classical literature had lost a degree of its social and political value. This association is strengthened by his well-documented evidence that *hua-pen* are closely linked to drama, and probably derivative of dramatic scripts—as narrative retellings of the story.

A crucial distinction remains to be made in terms of literati interest and its relationship to drama: the distinction between oral and written literature. Determining what role literati played in the production of working scripts, if indeed any were ever written down, and what role they played in the creation of dramatic literature, remains a difficult task. Such a discussion, while pressingly relevant to an understanding of the role of the elite writer in the popular tradition, and hence to an understanding of Mongol influence in that tradition, is not possible here. But it will remain a central issue in this whole constellation of issues. For we are, in essence, assessing Mongol influence only in terms of the literati; perhaps this is our only choice, given the nature and extent of the material left to us. But that naturally biases the case in favor of *written* literature and may, in truth, have little to do with a dramatic tradition that developed in the marketplaces and temple grounds of major urban centers and peripheral areas in China. Extant texts, of course, have little value for this inquiry since, except for *Thirty Yüan Editions of Dramatic Works*, they are all scripts that have passed through the hands of both court actors and elite editors and that were preserved and tidied up to be *read*, not performed. Indeed, they were meant to be read by an elite audience for whom printed drama had become a legitimate interest.

As for the third area of Mongol influence, language, there is little that can be said. It is true that Mongolian words occur occasionally in drama, but they are not used frequently, and then only for novelty's sake. One has the feeling that, along with Jurchen, Khitan, Persian, and Uighur, they were part of the patois of the era, and that their appearance in drama indicates no more than that they were used in the street slang of the North at that time.[70]

---

[69] *Chinese Vernacular Fiction: The Formative Period.*

[70] See Shih Chung-wen, *The Golden Age of Chinese Drama, Yüan Tsa-chü* (Princeton, 1975), p. 176.

ACT IV

Retrospection

There has been, in the past two decades, enough archaeological evidence unearthed to show that a long popular dramatic tradition has existed in China since at least the eleventh century. This evidence refutes the earlier statements that the Mongols were responsible for the rise of drama through their dispossession of the literati. It also refutes the assumption that it was the literati who brought the dramatic form to its height. What seems more plausible is that drama, as a self-sustaining and self-developing tradition, had by the thirteenth century simply matured to the point that it offered a suitable and attractive vehicle for literary expression. Under the Mongols, the elite writer of the north found himself adrift in an unfamiliar world, cut off from social and political success and denied the peer respect that the traditional forms of litera-ture would normally have provided. Given the time and the opportunity to consort with actors on an intensive and prolonged basis, he began to participate in dramatic activities, writing scripts and perhaps even performing. Thus, the elite writer from this transitional period onward played a major part in developing drama from a purely performing art to a written literature. This general interest in vernacular writing continued into the Ming, with the elite writer cultivating not only drama, but also the short story, as modes of literary expression.

A major question that remains is the extent to which the written tradition relates to the performing tradition. While we have evidence for Mongol patronage of writers and of court performances, we have in the final analysis very little information about their influence on popular convention. The archaeological evidence argues strongly for a native development of the theater in both rural and urban environs, completely independent of any Mongol influence. We can at most speculate that the lack of a strong sanction against the public theater in the early years perhaps stimulated its growth. But Mongol influence, as far as our evidence shows, was mainly felt by the elite writer. In the end, we must conclude that the rise and development of northern drama was a native phenomenon, but that the Mongols were influential in making that popular tradition a part of the elite world. Popular art was always within easy reach of the educated, and one can imagine that Chinese literati inevitably maintained a peripheral interest in performing literature. But the convergence of social and literary forces in the Yüan, some of which were products of Mongol policies, intensified that peripheral interest and made drama a legitimate (though not central) amateur pastime.

APPENDIX 1

(For the Chapter by H. L. Chan)

Orthodox Chronology	*Wang's New Chronology*
	(Post-Sung, pre-Ming Chinese rulers represented by Chu Yüan-chang's ancestors)
1279 Last year of the Southern Sung dynasty Yüan emperor Shih-tsu (Khubilai)	Te-tsu (Emperor Hsüan) 1279–1299 great great grandfather of Chu Yüan-chang
1280 Chih-yüan 17 Chih-yüan (1264–1295)	
1295 Ch'eng-tsung (Temür) Yüan-chen (1295–1297) Ta-te (1297–1308)	
1299 (Ta-te 3)	I-tsu (Emperor Heng) 1299–1318
1308 Wu-tsung (Khaishan) Chih-ta (1308–1312)	great grandfather
1312 Jen-tsung (Ayurbarwada) Huang-ch'ing (1312–1314) Yen-yu (1314–1321)	
1318 (Yen-yu 5)	Hsi-tsu (Emperor Yü) 1318–1339
1321 Ying-tsung (Shidebala) Chih-chih (1321–1324)	grandfather
1324 T'ai-ting ti (Yesün Temür) T'ai-ting (1324–1328) Chih-ho (1328)	
1328 Ming-tsung (Aragibag) T'ien-shun (1328)	Birth of T'ai-tsu, i.e. Chu Yüan-chang
1328 Wen-tsung (Tugh Temur) T'ien-li (1328–1330) Chih-shun (1330–1333)	
1332 Ning-tsung (Irinjibal)	
1333 Shun-ti (Toghōn Temür) Yüan-t'ung (1333–1335) Chih-yüan (1335–1341)	

1339 (Chih-yüan)   Jen-tsu (Emperor Ch'un, d. 1344)
                                              1339–1351 (?)
        Chih-cheng (1341–1368)   father

1352 (Chih-cheng 12)   T'ai-tsu (Emperor Kao)
                                            (Chu Yüan-chang)
                                            Founding of the Ming dynasty

        Ming emperor
        T'ai-tsu

1368 Hung-wu 1   Hung-wu 1
        (Hung-wu, 1368–1398)

APPENDIX 2

(For the Chapter by Herbert Franke)

WRITINGS OF PAGS-PA LAMA SUBMITTED TO THE MONGOL COURT

(PRELIMINARY LIST OF RECIPIENTS)

The number in the last column refers to the number of texts in vol. 6 and 7 of the *Sa-skya pa'i bka' hbum*, reprinted Tokyo, 1968.

1. Khubilai Khaghan (r. 1260–1294)

Date	Occasion	Text
1255–80	Gratulatory verses for the New Year's (with the exception of 1259 and 1260)	320
1271	Buddhist teachings written on Khubilai's request	210
1271	Commentary to above	154
1262 or 1274	Prayer for Khubilai because of donations for monks	250
1275	Prayer for Khubilai because of donation of a Prajñāpāramitā written with gold	301
no date	Prayer for Khubilai because of donation of a stupa	311

2. Chen-chin (Jingim), second son and crown-prince of Khubilai, nominated heir-apparent in 1273, d. 1286

Date	Occasion	Text
1275 and 1277	Letters to Chen-chin	223
1276	Prayer for Chen-chin because of donation of a Prajñāpāramitā written with gold	296
1277	Buddha's life according to the Vinaya	293
1277	Prayer for Chen-chin because of donation of texts written with gold	297
1278	Prayer for Chen-chin because he had Buddhist scriptures translated	295
1270	*Šes-bya* written for Chen-chin	1

9. Temür Bukha, perhaps the eldest son of A'urughchi and grandson of Khubilai Khaghan, attested for 1286 and 1297

1276	Buddhist treatise written on request of Temür Bukha	220

10. Tegüs Bukha (tib. De-gus bho-ga). Unidentified.

1276	Buddhist treatise written on request of Tegüs Bukha	219

11. Alkhui (Tib. 'Al-ge), great-grandson of Köchü, who was a son of Ögödei Khan. Attested 1285–1307

1275	Letter to Alkhui expressing joy that Alkhui lives in harmony with Khubilai. Written in Čoṅ-to (Chung-tu = Peking)	258
1275	Letter to monk Rin-č'en in the service of Alkhui. Written in Čoṅ-to (Peking)	259

12. Lady Tügel Turmïsh (Tib. Du-gal dur-mis). Unidentified, perhaps a princess

no dates	Two prayers for Lady (*dpen-mo*) Tügel Turmïsh	273, 274

13. Unidentified grandson of Khubilai Khaghan

1259 (?) or 1268	Prayer for the boy Dharmapāla Rakṣita, a name given to the boy by Pags-pa. He was son of "Prince Bodhisattva" K'yu-mč'og-skyoṅ who was, according to text no. 311, a son of Khubilai Khaghan	318

An investigation of the historical circumstances in which the works listed above were written must be reserved for further study. The names of the addressees give, in any case, an indication to which members of the imperial family Pags-pa entertained the closest relations.

INDEX

A-li Yao-ch'ing (Muslim poet) 285
Abākhā (1234–82, second ruler of Ilhkhanate, r. 1265–82) 287, 292
'Abbāsid Caliphate 270
'Abd al-Rahmān (Muslim official, d. 1246) 263, 265–66, 268, 270, 295
academies 111; deteriorating quality 119; guidelines for study 115–16; *shan-chang* (headmaster) 115, 117–18, 122–24, 131–23; in Sung times 116; foundings 117
Academy of Calendrical Studies (T'ai-shih yüan) 29
Academy of Imperial Sacrifices and Rituals (T'ai-ch'ang li-i yüan) 29
Academy of Scholars in the K'uei-chang Pavilion (K'uei-chang ko hsüeh-shih yüan) 29
Academy of Worthies (Chi-hsien yüan) 29, 223, 224, 233, 408
"Admonitions to the Imperial Censors": see *Yü-shih chen*
agents (*ta-lu-hua-ch'ih*, M. *darughachi*) 43; see also main entry *darughachi*
agricultural colonies (*t'un-t'ien*) 50
Aḥmad (Muslim official, d. 1282) 263, 278–83, 292–93, 295
Ai-hsüeh (Christian official) 292–93
alchemy 215, 229, esoteric 229; *see also* elixir school
An-p'u (son of Yang Lien-chen-chia) 324
An-t'ung (Mongol official, 1245–93) 280
Analects 177
Ananda (Mongol prince, d. 1307, Muslim rebel) 292, 300–01
"antique spirit" 346
Ao Chi-kung (Yüan scholar) 340–41
Aoki Masaru (modern scholar) 434, 443
Arigh Böke (Mongol prince, d. 1266) 269, 278
Armaments Court (Wu-pei ssu) 31, 50
Arban buyan-tu nom-un chaghan teüke 308
Arughtu (*fl.* 1313–37) 79
A'urughchi (son of Khubilai) 300
Autumn Colors on the Ch'iao and Hua Mountains: see *Ch'iao-hua ch'iu-se*
Autumn Colors on Rivers and Mountains:

see *Chiang-shan ch'iu-se*
Ayurbarwada (Jen-tsung, 1285–1320, r. 1311–20) 8, 243, 385; *see also* Jen-tsung

Baghdad 270
Baiju (d. 1323) 67
Baljuna covenant 261
Batu Khan (1207–55, first khan of Khipchak khanate, r. 1227–55) 269
Bayan (1236–94, Mongol general) 241–42, 338–39
Berke Bukha (*fl.* 1340s) 79
blue-and-green landscape 336, 347, 348–59*ff.*; symbol of Yüan painting 356; terminology of 349–51; and Wang Meng 358
Book of Changes (*I ching*) 4, 5, 219, 227 235, 247
"branch" agencies 52
"branch" censorates and Central Secretariats 52; *see also* Hsing chung-shu sheng
'branch"Ministries of Works 40–41
"branch" Ministry of Revenue 40
Buddhism 297; *see also* lamaism
Buddhist historiography 306
Bukhara 270, 271, 288
Bureau of Military Affairs (Shu-mi yüan) 30, 35, 40, 49
Bureau of Tibetan and Buddhist Affairs (Hsüan-cheng yüan) 33, 35, 47, 48; see also main entry
bureaucratic professionalsim 462; *see also* clerks
Burma 288, 289

calligraphy and painting 410–11
"Celestial Master" (*t'ien-shih*) 212, 231
Censorate (Yü-shih t'ai) 30, 34, 35, 41, 53, 54, 312, 316
Central Asians 165; see also *se-mu-jen*
Central Secretariat (Chung-shu sheng) 30, 33, 35, 43, 265, 288, 300, 312, 316, 324–25; branch offices 53
Ch'a-ching 334
ch'a-yüan (censorial office) 54
Chaghadai (second son of Chinggis Khan, d. 1242) 270, 277; and Muslims 267

LIST OF CONTRIBUTORS

HOK-LAM CHAN Professor of Chinese History, School of International Studies and Department of History, University of Washington, author of many articles on Chinese historiography, and of *Li Chih in Contemporary Chinese Historiography* (1980) and *Theories of Legitimation in Imperial China* (forthcoming); Ph.D. Princeton University.

DAVID M. FARQUHAR Associate Professor of History, UCLA, Ph.D. Harvard, author of many articles on Mongol, Manchu, and Yüan history, now working on political and social institutions of the Yüan period and a handbook of Yüan government.

HERBERT FRANKE Professor, University of Munich, Germany, Ph.D. Universität Köln, author of *Chinese Texts on the Jurchen* (2 vols., 1975 and 1978), *From Tribal Chieftain to Universal Emperor and God: The Legitimation of the Yüan Dynasty* (1978), and many articles and books, now doing research on the history and institutions of the Chinese dynasties of conquest, 10th–14th centuries.

MARILYN WONG FU Visiting Lecturer, School of Architecture, University of Virginia, Ph.D. Princeton University (expected Fall 1980), formerly lecturer at Yale University and Assistant Curator of Far Eastern Art, Metropolitan Museum of Art, New York; author (with Shen C. Y. Fu) of *Studies in Connoisseurship: Chinese Paintings from the Arthur Sackler Collection* (2nd ed. 1976) and *Traces of the Brush: Studies in Chinese Calligraphy* (2nd ed. 1980); current research interests: all aspects of calligraphy (Chinese and otherwise) and the role of writing as a form of literary expression; the creative process in the Chinese cultural setting.

DAVID GEDALECIA Associate Professor of History, College of Wooster, has published articles on Neo-Confucianism in *Philosophy East and West* and *Journal of Chinese Philosophy*, Ph.D. Harvard University; now working on the life and philosophy of Wu Ch'eng and on the evolution in the thought of Chu Hsi.

JOHN D. LANGLOIS, JR. Associate Professor of History, Bowdoin College, has published articles in *Journal of Asian Studies* and *Harvard Journal of Asiatic Studies* on Yüan intellectual history, Ch'ing views of the Yüan period, and Sung and Yüan law, Ph.D. Princeton University; now doing research on Ming dynasty legal system.

YAN-SHUAN LAO Associate Professor of East Asian Languages & Literatures, Ohio State University, author of "Southern Literati in Early Yüan: Some Aspects as Reflected in Poetry" (1979) and "Poetry as Commentary during the Yüan-Ming Interval" (1980) (both in Chinese); now doing research on the roles played by Yüan intellectuals and on the institution of *li* (ritual) under Mongol rule; Ph.D. Harvard University.

CHU-TSING LI Judith Harris Murphy Professor of Art History, University of Kansas, author of *A Thousand Peaks and Myriad Ravines: The Charles Drenowatz Collection of Chinese Paintings* (1974) and *Trends in Modern Chinese Painting (The C. A. Drenowitz Collection)* (1979); now preparing "Biographies of Yüan Painters" and "Studies in Yüan Painting"; Ph.D. University of Iowa.

MORRIS ROSSABI Associate Professor of History, Case Western Reserve University, author of *China and Inner Asia* (1975), "Muslim and Central Asian Revolts" (1979), and "Two Ming Envoys to Inner Asia" (1976); now writing a biography of Khubilai Khaghan; Ph.D. Columbia University.

K'O-K'UAN SUN Professor of Chinese Literature, Emeritus, Tunghai University, Taiwan; author of numerous articles and books on T'ang poetry, Yüan history, Ch'ing poetry, and other subjects, plus *The Development of Taoism in Sung and Yüan Times* (1972) and *Han Chinese Cultural Activities in the Yüan Period* (1968), both in Chinese.

STEPHEN H. WEST Associate Professor of Oriental Studies, University of Arizona, author of *Vaudeville and Narrative: Aspects of Chin (1115–1234) Theater* (1977) and, with Wilt Idema, *Chinese Drama (1100–1450): A Source Book* (forthcoming); now doing research on Chinese drama and preparing a translation of *Tung-ching meng-hua lu* 東京夢華錄; Ph.D. University of Michigan.

Library of Congress Cataloging in Publication Data
Main entry under title:

China under Mongol rule.

   Includes index.
   CONTENTS: Farquhar, D. M. Structure and function in the Yüan Imperial Govern-
ment.—Hok-lam Chan. Chinese official historiography at the Yüan Court.—Yan-shuan
Lao. Southern Chinese scholars and educational institutions in early Yüan.—[etc.]
   1. China—History—Yüan dynasty, 1260–1368—Addresses, essays, lectures. I. Lan-
glois, John D., 1942 –
DS752.C48   951'.025   80–8559
ISBN 0-691-03127-4
ISBN -691-10110-8 (pbk.)